THE GOLDEN HORIZON

THE GOLDEN HORIZON

EDITED TOGETHER WITH

AN INTRODUCTION

BY

CYRIL CONNOLLY

LONDON
WEIDENFELD & NICOLSON
LIMITED

First published 1953

To SONIA BROWNELL

PRINTED IN ENGLAND AT THE CURWEN PRESS

CONTENTS

CONTENTS

CONTENTS

GLIMPSES OF GREATNESS

PERSONAL ANTHOLOGY

CONTENTS

INTRODUCTION

BETWEEN Christmas 1939 and New Year 1950, *Horizon* ran to some ten thousand pages: the purpose of this anthology has been to select six hundred. This could have been made possible only by inventing certain rules and keeping strictly to them. Since the plates which illustrated our Art articles no longer exist, it was decided that Art must go; and Art included painting, sculpture, the cinema and architecture—and music too. The first rule, then, was 'Literature only'. Now no magazine can rise superior to the judgement of its editor, and, looking back, I felt that I could not always trust myself where articles on philosophy and psychology were concerned, or politics and economics; they might not be the best of their kind; they might be obsolete, and, in any case, they are difficult to mix. So are reports on places, which are apt to date; and in the end, therefore, I was left with stories, poems, reportage and literary essays from which to make a selection. One more rule: to avoid essays and stories which have become well known through being reprinted, like the work of Arturo Barea, Elizabeth Bowen, E. M. Forster, Anna Kavan, Arthur Koestler, George Orwell, Sir Osbert Sitwell, Martin Turnell, Lionel Trilling and Evelyn Waugh. And one final rule: to avoid contributions which have been translated from other magazines, or long critical essays which are in reality glorified book reviews—and not to include articles on living writers whose subsequent work may have belied them.

This made a large dent in ten thousand pages and the question of arrangement then arose. It seemed in retrospect that *Horizon* had enjoyed three moments of historical importance. The first was at the beginning of the last war when it served as a rallying point where writers might clear their minds and pool their experiences. From 1939–41 Stephen Spender was a co-editor and it was due largely to him that we printed such good war poetry and such intelligent articles about war aims; on the other hand *Horizon* at that time manifested a tendency to become a Left-wing 'school magazine' with a rather naïve attitude to other writers. This complacency was dispelled by Orwell: 'In the last twenty years,' he wrote, 'Western civilization has given the Intellectual security without responsibility and in England, in particular, it has educated him in scepticism while anchoring him almost immovably in the privileged class. He has been in the position of a young man living on an allowance from a father whom he hates. The result is a deep feeling of guilt and resentment, not combined with any genuine desire to escape.'

In the next phase we undertook a stock-taking of Western culture under pressure in the two long series, 'Novelist-Philosophers' and 'Studies in Genius', and the magazine came genuinely to represent Western Literature, past and present, and so was able to carry abroad an international humanist warmth and curiosity in the wake of the invading armies. This was the second historical moment. Thus, Occupied France had always been something of an obsession, the stricken Paris of Pierre Jean Jouve's wonderful poem:

Ville atroce, O capitale de mes journées
O ville infortunée, livrée aux âmes basses!

We obtained some of the first accounts of the underground movements and, when the city was liberated, we were fortunate to receive a first impression of its literary activities which came with the force of a discovery. 'In the literature of these four years', wrote Philip Toynbee (September 1944), 'France has been incomparable and undeniably superior.' Articles about Italian literature, new German writing, and recent Greek poetry followed, even as *Horizon* was bringing news of English culture to these countries. (A special edition in French on English literature during the war sold 10,000 copies.) The last historical moment was one not of advance but of retreat, retreat into an aesthetic puritanism which refused to be misled by optimistic estimates of the benefits which would accrue to art from a welfare State or a divided Europe, or even from the comings and goings of air-minded culture diffusionists. This phase of consolidation has naturally less to show for itself than the two others, although the association with our fellow dissidents in America from 1946 onwards was highly rewarding.

In this anthology, '*Horizon's* History of the War' illustrates those historical moments when literature seemed to follow life like a barge on a quiet canal towed by a madman on a motor-cycle. The 'History of the War' is impressionistic and is intended to re-create a chain of moods by an interlocking arrangement of poems and reportage. Thus Spender's 'September Journal' recalls not only the first innocent days of the war, but the innocent Germany of the Weimar Republic as evoked by the youthful poet in the image of his friend Curtius—the father lost. At the end of the war section we see an older Spender, a veteran war artist in words, revisiting 'C.' in this same Germany—a 'father found' who has altered almost as unrecognizably as his disciple. The two extracts are intended to mark the passage of time, even as Bertrand Russell's article is, alas, a realistic post-war answer to H. G. Wells's pre-war optimism and the almost affectionate 'Message from Moscow'; or as Sartre's 'Case for Responsible Literature' is put into true perspective by being shown in its 'Resistance' context.

The 'Entertainments' that follow are animated by the straightforward desire to please without which any magazine must founder; we begin with the serene atmosphere of two writers of the pre-1914 generation, and continue with a brilliant parody of science fiction and Soviet dog experiments, followed by a run of disturbing stories about Schizoids whose heroes seem to fulfil Rudolph Friedman's description, 'The intellectual type of today can most often be represented by a tall, slightly stooping figure, with the skin drawn tightly across the cheek bones, the pale sadistic lips desiring to cut to pieces even as they utter, the eyes attempting to reproduce the severe and compelling gaze of the father and yet at the same time strangely powerless and watering with the pathos of the son slowly moving out of life.'

The excitable narrator of 'The Moment of Truth' would seem their feminine counterpart, and so I have included Arthur Waley's masterpiece, 'Mrs. White', to prove that *Horizon* could always publish a story about normal people—before Hermann Hesse (who since has won the Nobel Prize) magically closes the Schizoid Cycle.

'Glimpses of Greatness' is a section which was all the time forming without our being aware of it, a carillon of memories covering a recurring situation, the Maestro in all his simplicity and wisdom garrulously confronting his treacherous dumb disciple. The Princess Edmond de Polignac was blown to our shores (as in 1870 and 1914) by the gale of the world, like some splendid sun-fish, and her reminiscences—the only literary utterance of this great lady of the nineteenth century who was also a patron of the most advanced music of the twentieth—were put in order by Raymond Mortimer and now take their place in this gallery of living portraits on which the dust of contemporary indifference is already settling.

'Personal Anthology' contain the two dozen poems that I like the best and the choice is quite irrational. Thus I enjoy Brian Reed's 'Girl Dozing' because it reminds me of an early Passmore, Rexroth because I admire Chinese poetry, 'The Half of Life' because (like Hoelderlin) I was thirty-five when I read it, and there is also some American poetry included for its streamlined formal perfection.

A 'Prospect of Literature' is the section which has been most amputated by reprintings. I would have liked to have made a whole volume of these long essays which were the core of the magazine and which cover most of the outstanding writers of England and France, but I have had to confine myself to the best which have not been reprinted. The first four are humanist appreciations, while the 'Notes for an Estimate of Peacock' is a good example of Marxist criticism, the Beddoes almost Existentialist, and the Svevo alive with awareness of Freud. Indeed Lionel Trilling's 'Freud and Literature' (*Horizon*, 92) can be imagined as terminating the series which should have included Graham Hough's 'George Eliot' and Martin Turnell's 'Baudelaire'.

I hope that all these sections can be read straight through like so many short books and will give pleasure to readers who have never heard of the magazine, though I cannot myself contemplate the selection without a pang for so much that has been omitted. Another volume for the Arts and Sciences, the 'Places' and the Politics, would still not suffice—for how can we recapture, between the covers of a book, the tempo of a monthly review? Editing a magazine is a form of the good life; it is creating when the world is destroying, helping where it is hindering; being given once a month the opportunity to produce a perfect number and every month failing, and just when despair sets in, being presented with one more chance. Plop! The afternoon post falls on the carpet, the letter-box becomes a periscope on the outside world, encouragement arrives and fat subscriptions, notices in other magazines, letters from California and Brazil, contributions from all over the world, one of which may have been long awaited and another be totally unexpected and yet just as good. And when each number appears, it carries a faint fragrance of the month when it bloomed, the aroma of transience; of bean flowers or laburnum; of days shortening and the muffin man; of broken hearts or broken armies; the cup Hemingway brewed the night before D-Day, or the Doodlebug in Bedford Square. In a young fighter-pilot's diary a whole page was found printed in capitals with the words: 'My Story accepted by *Horizon*!' It was his first story and his last, for a few months later 'the Pupil' was killed in the Battle of Tunisia. How can an anthology perpetuate his excitement or convey the depression of the black-out hanging over so many other stories and poems or darkening the animated discussions of the editors?

For the essential feature of *Horizon* was dual control. 'Favourite Daydream' I wrote in 1933, 'to edit a monthly magazine entirely subsidized by self. No advertisements. Harmless title. Deleterious contents.' In 1939 I found my friend Peter Watson was prepared to launch it. At first he wanted to produce an art review in Paris that would replace the *Minotaure*. I thought England's need was greater, and Hitler cast his vote in my favour. Peter Watson's main interests were modern painting and music, mine were literature and psychology, Spender's poetry and politics. We were friends, and so able to forgive each other discrepancies of temperament and even the comments which were repeated by so many other friends; and the key to *Horizon* lies in the Bouvard-Pécuchet relationship between Peter Watson and myself. As Hardy, I emulated his despair, as Laurel, he financed my optimism. He likes art to be slightly incomprehensible, while I fall an easy victim to political quacks and neurotic journalists; he is impressed by straw in the hair, I am taken in by a fire in the belly: we were made to compromise. And so his anthology still remains ungathered, although there are few young painters, composers, or sculptors of whom the world now buzzes whose work was not encouraged in *Horizon's* art pages.

A magazine is greater than those who produce it, and both transcends and transforms them. For many months before *Horizon* appeared we could talk of nothing else: in the warm June sunshine of the Rue du Bac or through crazy summer afternoons in London. I remember holding forth about it to Robert Byron on the August evening at Glenarm when news of the Hitler-Soviet pact came through on the wireless, and a few miles away, at Cushendun, in mutual unawareness, Louis MacNeice was marinating the poems which were later to become the first contributions to our opening number.

C.C.

ACKNOWLEDGEMENTS

Acknowledgement is gratefully made for the use of the following material originally published in *Horizon*

MESSRS. ALLEN & UNWIN for 'Mrs. White' from Arthur Waley's *The Real Tripitaka.*

MESSRS. B. T. BATSFORD for 'From Libyan Diary' from Cecil Beaton's *Near East.*

MESSRS. JONATHAN CAPE for 'Dedicatory Stanzas' (To Stephen Spender) from *Georgics of Virgil* by C. Day Lewis and the article 'Wilde and Conder' from *Chiaroscuro* by Augustus John.

MESSRS. CHATTO AND WINDUS for 'Success' a poem by William Empson.

MESSRS. COLLINS, SONS & CO. for 'The Romantic Catastrophe' from Peter Quennell's *Byron in Italy.*

MESSRS. DENT & SONS for three poems by Dylan Thomas.

MESSRS. FABER & FABER for 'The Rider Victory', a poem by Edwin Muir; 'Sceptre-Struck, Spellbound, Beloved', a poem by George Barker from *News of the World*; 'A Face', a poem by Marianne Moore from *Collected Poems*; two poems by W. H. Auden from *The Age of Anxiety* and *Nones*; two poems by Louis MacNeice, 'Cushendun' and 'The Libertine', and two poems by Stephen Spender, 'O Night O Trembling Night' from *The Edge of Being*, and 'Air Raid'.

MESSRS. HAMISH HAMILTON for 'Belsen' from *Eclipse* by Alan Moorehead.

THE HOGARTH PRESS for William Sansom's story 'Building Alive' and Laurie Lee's poem 'Equinox'.

MESSRS. JOHN LEHMANN for Roy Fuller's poem 'The Divided Life' from *Epitaphs and Occasions* and Laurie Lee's poem 'Day of these Days' from *Bloom of Candles.*

MESSRS. MACMILLAN for two poems by Edith Sitwell, 'Eurydice' and 'A Simpleton'.

MESSRS. JOHN MURRAY for two poems by John Betjeman, 'A Subaltern's Love-Song' from his *Selected Poems* and 'The Old Liberals' from a forthcoming volume.

MESSRS. ROUTLEDGE & KEGAN PAUL for 'An Early Death', a poem by Sidney Keyes from his *Collected Poems.*

MESSRS. SECKER & WARBURG for the poem 'Escape' by W. R. Rodgers and Alberto Moravia's short story 'Back from The Sea'.

THE SOCIETY OF AUTHORS and MRS. CICELY BINYON for Laurence Binyon's poem 'The Ruins'.

Grateful thanks are also accorded to:

MESSRS. HARCOURT, BRACE (New York) and PARTISAN REVIEW (New York) for Randall Jarrell's 'The Death of the Ball Turret Gunner' and two poems by W. H. Auden, 'Lament for a Lawgiver' and 'Song'.

THE VANGUARD PRESS (New York) for Paul Goodman's 'Iddings Clark'.

NEW DIRECTIONS (New York) for three poems by Dylan Thomas.

LIBRAIRIE GALLIMARD (Paris) for 'Zone Libre' by Louis Aragon, 'Three Poems' by Paul Eluard, 'The Case for Responsible Literature' by J. P. Sartre, and 'La Pomme de Terre' by Francis Ponge.

THE OXFORD UNIVERSITY PRESS, INC. for permission to use Poem from *XAIPE* by E. E. Cummings. Copyright 1944, 1945, 1946, 1947, 1948, 1949, 1950, by E. E. Cummings.

THE GOLDEN HORIZON

I

HORIZON'S
HISTORY OF THE WAR

1939

LOUIS MACNEICE

CUSHENDUN

Fuchsia and ragweed and the distant hills
Made as it were out of clouds and sea:
All night the bay is plashing and the moon
    Marks the break of the waves.

Limestone and basalt and a whitewashed house
With passages of great stone flags
And a walled garden with plums on the wall
    And a bird piping in the night.

Forgetfulness: brass lamps and copper jugs
And home-made bread and the smell of turf or flax
And the air a glove and the water lathering easy
    And convolvulus in the hedge.

Only in the dark green room beside the fire
With the curtains drawn against the winds and waves
There is a little box with a well-bred voice;
    What a place to talk of War.

August 1939

STEPHEN SPENDER

FROM SEPTEMBER JOURNAL

I MUST put out my hands and grasp the handfuls of facts. How extraordinary they are! The aluminium balloons seem nailed into the sky like those bolts which hold together the irradiating struts of a biplane between the wings. The streets become more and more deserted and the West End is full of shops to let. Sand-bags are laid above the glass pavements over basements along the side-walk. Last night during the black-out there was a tremendous thunderstorm. We stood at the bottom of Regent Street in the pouring rain, the pitch darkness broken intermittently by flashes of sheet lightning which lit up Piccadilly Circus like broad daylight.

SEPTEMBER 4TH

Greenwood and Sinclair were on the wireless last night. They talked about gallant Poland, our liberties, democracy, etc., in a way which raised very grave doubts in my mind. Greenwood even talked about fighting the last war to end war. Personally, I prefer Chamberlain's line to all this sanctimoniousness, which is that he has done his best to give Hitler everything but now feels that he can give nothing more. I dislike all the talk about God defending the right. God has always defended the right, and after such a long experience, he of all people should realize the utter futility of it. Personally, if I were a close adviser of God, I'd press him to decide the issue one way or the other once and for all and not go on playing this cat and mouse game between right and wrong.

Doubtless my own contempt for my father's recruiting speeches during the War is what undermines my faith in political arguments. When I start a train of argument it is like one of those trains on the Berlin underground which strut confidently above the street on their raised viaducts, surrounded below by the tenements which seem to ask whether after all everything is going quite so well as the passengers, flashing through the slums, seem to think.

I shall try to recollect Germany as it was in 1929–32 when I lived there for several months of each year. The people I knew there were not like the present rulers of Germany, not like the S.S. men, not like the army, though I think I understand the army. Germans have a greater capacity, I should say, than any other people, of evoking the idea of peace—Ruhe. To us and to the French, peace is a negative state when we are getting on with our business and private lives and are not at war. But to the Germans a state of peace is something positive and breathing and constructive, as opposed to a state of war. The positive idea of peace permeates a great deal of German romantic literature and music. Works like the slow movements of Beethoven's Second and Fourth Symphonies are hymns to peace. They summon up a vision of a landscape exhaling peace. Daemmerung is a peaceful word, and words like Heim, Heimat, Friede, Ruhe, are loaded with a greater weight of emotion than the corresponding words in other languages. Other peace-music is Schubert's songs, Beethoven's early piano and piano-and-violin sonatas.

Perhaps it is that the German landscape is particularly peaceful. I think of the Rhine at evening, the Harz mountains, the shores of the Alster at Hamburg with the heavy scent of lime blossom on a summer evening.

I have a German relative who is the wife of a U-Boat Commander. They live in Kiel, which has just been bombed. She plays the piano very well. Recently she came to London and she played an early Beethoven sonata to us at my grandmother's flat. After she had played the slow movement her face was streaming with tears. 'Excuse me,' she said, 'but this music is so full of peace.'

Ten years after the War, Germany was full of peace, it dripped with peace, we swam in peace, no one knew what to do with all the German peace. They built houses with flat roofs, they sunbathed, they walked with linked hands under the lime trees, they lay together in the pine forest, they talked about French art. Above all, everything was new, and everyone was young. They liked the English very much and they were sorry about the War. They talked about the terrible time they had during the inflation.

This was in Hamburg. I used to bathe, and I went to parties of young people. I had never enjoyed parties before and I never have since, but these were like living in the atmosphere of a Blue Period Picasso. Everyone was beautiful, and gentle, everyone was poor, no one was smart. On summer evenings they danced in the half light, and when they were tired of dancing they lay down in the forest, on the beach, on mattresses, on the bare floor. They laughed a great deal, smiling with their innocent eyes and showing well-shaped, but not very strong, teeth. Sometimes they let one down, sometimes the poorer ones stole, for example, but there was no Sin. I am not being ironic. There really was no sin, like there is in this kind of life in Paris or London.

Of course, it was all very superficial, it has been blown away now. I could not dance. I could not speak German. I stood rather outside it. I think now of the sad refugees who were the exquisite, confident students of the Weimar Republican days. Perhaps it was all fictitious, but now in letting the mirage fade from the mind, I got very near to the truth, because everything in Germany is inclined to be fictitious. The German tends to think of his life as an operatic cycle emerging from a series of myths. There was the War, then there was the Inflation, then there was the period of Youth and the Weimar Republic, then there was the Crisis, then there was Hitler. Every German can readily explain him or herself in terms of What We Have Been Through.

SEPTEMBER 9TH

Yesterday morning while I was waiting for a bus, some soldiers passed down the road singing 'It's a long way to Tipperary'. An unshaved and very ragged old tramp wearing the ribbons of several medals so loosely attached to his coat that they were almost falling off, said to me: 'They're singing now, but they won't be singing when they come back. Hearing 'em sing reminds me of when I went out to fight in them trenches. We went out singing, but we didn't sing for long.'

In the afternoon I got a taxi to Waterloo before going into the country. We were stopped near Southampton Row by five Frenchmen carrying a flag and singing the Marseillaise. The taximan said to me: 'They won't be doing that for long'.

SEPTEMBER 12TH

Today I applied for a job as a translator at the War Office. Yesterday I received a printed slip from the Ministry of Information saying that my name was on a list of writers who may be used later. But I don't think I have a chance, as I'm told that they are very over-crowded with applicants. Nor do I think that the War Office will want me, as there must be many translators far better qualified. But as long as I can write and read a good deal each day,

I am not really bothering. What I would like most is to complete three books, this Journal, a novel and a book of poems, before I am called up.

I want to remember all I can about Ernst Robert Curtius.

For some reason, E—— became very excited at the idea of our meeting. He therefore arranged that I should go specially to Baden-Baden in order to meet Ernst Robert. What I find difficult to explain is my own willingness to fall in with this proposal. It may have been that I had in any case later to meet my grandmother at Hamburg, so that it was quite convenient; or it may have been due to a certain trustfulness and credulity in my nature which I still pay dearly for, and which, in those days, led me to fall in with every suggestion that was made to me. I might have been less willing had I reflected that Curtius might not want to see me.

This thought did not trouble me. I simply got out of the train, booked a room in a hotel and, as soon as I had washed, walked straight to the house where Ernst Robert was staying. I do not remember the details, I only remember the feeling of that first meeting. As far as I can recall the house was outside the town and I had to walk some way along a road past various hotels and then along a path through the edge of woods before I came to it. I think that I was shown into a room on the first floor, and perhaps there was a cold meal with fruit and wine laid on a table with a white cloth spread over it. There were bay windows opening out on to a balcony, and a pleasant freshness of the forest at evening filled the room. Everything, I think, gave me an impression of coolness, and for some reason I thought that the host and hostess were ill. The host, whose name I never knew, was dressed in a white suit, and both he and his wife seemed pale.

I did not stay long enough to get to know them for Curtius immediately stepped forward, grasped my hand firmly and told his friends that he would go to a Bierhalle in Baden with me.

Railway journeys have a disconcerting effect on me. They stimulate me so much that all my usual impressions seem to flow much faster, with the train, like a film that is shown very quickly. I cannot check this. In spite of myself every sort of sensation pours through my mind during a train journey, and when I was younger and played at 'thinking books' a project for some unwritten novel or play would force all its images on to me during a journey. This excess of stimulation leaves me afterwards in a state of drugged tiredness in which I appear stupid to myself and either am able to talk revealingly, or else get confused in every word I say. I was in this mood that first evening, and I talked very freely and indiscreetly to Ernst Robert about my life at Hamburg.

He listened to me with an amusement which slightly yet affectionately was laughing at as well as with me. It forgave a lot. In my deepest friendships, with Auden, with Christopher Isherwood and with Curtius, I have been conscious of being thus 'taken with a pinch of salt'. Sometimes it is disconcerting to be laughed at when one is serious, but as long as it is done affectionately, one is grateful to people who enable one to see oneself a little from the outside. From the first, Ernst Robert's attitude to me was one of gentle raillery; and I think that because he saw so far beyond me and at the same time loved me, I owe more to him than to any other older person.

Being anxious to impress him, I talked about literature, and especially about Dostoievsky, whom I was reading then. I was interested in madness, partly because at school and Oxford I had been taught to regard myself as mad, and because Auden, who, when he was an undergraduate, was anxious to maintain a certain superiority over his contemporaries, always treated me as a lunatic! Experiences like my cerebral excitement during train journeys, my excessive credulity, my lack of a complete understanding with even my best friends, so that I always felt they stood to some extent *outside* me—bore out the theory of madness. Above all, I was, like everyone, in search of that ecstasy which is so lacking in our civilization that even war and violence are to some people a secret consolation in a world of routine governed by material values; that ecstasy which justifies every kind of unscrupulousness and adventurousness in private life. In Hamburg E——, with his collector's zeal, had discovered an expressionist artist, a woman with a real talent for drawing, recently released from a lunatic asylum where she had done some really terrifying portraits of the lunatics. In Hamburg, she had done a portrait of me making me look wild and mad. I was proud of this, and took Ernst Robert to my hotel bedroom to see it. But, so far from being impressed or interested, he would scarcely even look at it. He said that it was mad and that I did not need to be mad.

During the next few days I walked much with him in the Black Forest, we went swimming together, we drank beer every evening. He criticized Dostoievsky, he told me to read other books than the Russians, particularly the French. I showed him poems I had written, and, to my surprise, instead of reading them with the superiority which I might have expected from a scholar immersed in the world's greatest literature, he read them with evident delight, and made some translations of them, which were afterwards published in the *Neue Schweizer Rundschau*. He listened to my accounts of my life at Hamburg, and scandalized me by treating this life, which I thought of so seriously, simply as pornography in which he was unashamedly interested. But to him it was pornography, it was not, as it then appeared to me, ecstasy.

SEPTEMBER 19TH

With Curtius I was in contact with the Germany of Goethe, Hoelderlin and Schiller. That is an Apollonian Germany, a Germany of the sun, not the Dionysian Germany of Hitler who rouses himself from a torpid dullness into a frenzy of words and actions. After the war and the blockade, perhaps even the Germans who lay with no clothes on, crucified by the sun, expressed the need for a Germany of 'Light, more Light'.

It was not the madness of Hoelderlin that Curtius liked but the peaceful development of a poem such as *Brot und Wein* in which the sun-steeped and vine-bearing German landscape is lifted at the end of the poem into a unity with the German conception of Greece. We read Hoelderlin together, and later on the poems of the Greek Anthology, particularly the erotic ones, because he had a taste for such poetry.

Curtius was an egoist, an egoist of the liberal, Goethe tradition. His life was organized with an enlightened selfishness: he did not take more than he could take, nor give more than he could give. He would not put himself out even for his best friends, if he thought that his own resilience was going to be depressed by their needs. One could say, perhaps, that he was a fair-weather friend. Once, when I was hard up, I wrote asking him if he could introduce me to people in Berlin to whom I could give English lessons. He wrote back about other things, ending his letter with the curt 'leider kann ich keiner Verbindungen für Ihnen im Berlin schaffen'. I asked a friend of his about this, and he told me how at a period of crisis and confusion in his life, Ernst Robert had cut himself off from him completely. I myself have a tendency in my relationships with people never to refuse anything, and often to promise far more than I can undertake. I know how this leads to a feeling of resentment which affects one's relationships with people and to a fear of making new acquaintances who may plunge one into new commitments. Ernst Robert remained happy and broad and objective. He would not lose this by identifying himself with others in their predicaments.

I do not mean that he was unsympathetic, but that he was unself-sacrificing because what he had was of too great an objective value to himself and to others to sacrifice. He did not enter into their lives because his generosity lay in the freedom with which they could enter into his.

If one accepted this, he gave a great deal.

Once when I was staying at Bonn, I went into Cologne for a night and got into an extremely nasty scrape. I liked going to very squalid places and I went to a hotel near the railway station, in the lowest part of the town. When I got into bed I didn't notice that the lock of the door was on the outside instead of the inside, so that the guests in this hotel were like prisoners locked into their rooms, instead of guests who could lock out intruders. In the middle of the night the door was flung open and a man came who put his hands to my throat and threatened to throttle me unless I gave him my money. He was much stronger than I, and I was undressed, so I asked him to pass me my clothes. He did this, and I gave him my money. It amounted to about 60 or 70 marks, which he did not seem to think enough, so he said he would take my coat as well. I protested, but it did not seem much use, so I asked him to leave me a mark at least, to pay my fare back to Bonn. He flung a mark down on the marble-topped table beside my bed, and ran out of the room. I lay in bed staring into the darkness and listening to the noises from outside of whores talking and screaming, and a continuous sound like water running away into the darkness. I felt as though I had reached the goal of something horrible and mysterious in my life, as though it were unfolded from my own flesh and a part of myself. I did not resent the theft, because I thought of it as something I had let myself in for. I did not blame the thief at all, for what had happened seemed an automatic consequence of my choosing this way of life, and, in short, I felt passive, as though a whole process which I had called into being by my own actions were now happening to me, and I knew that I would never escape from this. Because I knew this, it was very difficult for me to resist, but at last I realized that I must do something, so I sat up in bed and shouted for the landlord. A few minutes later, he and two or three other men came into the room, switching on the light, and standing round my bed as though I were an invalid, seriously ill, and they were the specialists whom I had summoned. 'Why are you making such a noise in my respectable hotel?' asked the landlord, in injured tones. 'Until you came here I always had the highest reputation. I shall call the police.' 'For heaven's sake, do call them,' I answered, feeling that I was now prepared for any kind of disgrace, 'I would like to speak to them very much.' This seemed to make him hesitate, and he said quite kindly, 'Why, what do you want then?' 'Someone in your hotel has just stolen all my money,' I said. 'This is a disgrace,' said the landlord, 'I won't have things like this going on in my hotel. Why do you come here and bring this disgrace on me?' 'It isn't my fault,' I answered, 'I am very sorry. I don't mind my money being stolen, but I must have my coat and also an assurance that my trousers won't be stolen, else I won't be able to get home.' 'Nothing else will be stolen,' said the landlord honourably, 'I can assure you of that.' 'Well, might I at least have my coat back?' I asked. He nodded to one of the other men who left the room and returned a few seconds later with my coat on his arm. Then he said 'Good night,' reassuringly, and they left the room.

I felt that nothing else was likely to happen, but I could not sleep, and continued to lie with eyes open in a waking nightmare. At last it was dawn. Then for the first time it occurred to me that when I arrived on the previous night, I had been made to pay my bill before taking a room. Therefore there was not the slightest reason why I should stay any longer. It surprised me to realize that I was free and that nothing final had happened. I quickly put on my clothes and ran downstairs and out of the hotel, without anyone stopping me. I ran until I came to the river. Outside it was cold and raw. In the grey light the cathedral and the bridges and the modern Exhibition Building had a photographic quality. Suddenly I started laughing. I had a gay sensation of release.

After an hour or so of waiting, I went back to Bonn. When I had rested and changed, I called on Ernst Robert, partly to borrow some money from him. When he saw that I was upset he took me for a walk by the Rhine. Full of shame, I told him my story. But to my surprise, instead of being shocked, disappointed or upset, he started laughing, and, putting his arm round me, patted my shoulder.

While I have been writing this last page and a half, I have had the wireless on, performing Hitler's latest speech. His voice varies from a cavernous rumbling to the peaks of an exalted hysteria from which he shrieks like a raucous beast of prey, until the whole chorus of his followers breaks into a stormy night's thunder of triumphant hatred. Undoubtedly there is something disintegrating about that voice, that applause, and everything they stand for. The cities of one's mind seem to be bombarded, as though a threat could make them fall to pieces. He speaks of a new, terrible, secret weapon, which, if the English oppose him, he will use. When he does this, I feel as though the world could be destroyed by pressing a button, and he were a madman who had access to this button and was about to press it.

The black-out time gets a few minutes earlier each evening, so one notices more than ever the drawing in of the autumn evenings. Actually, the weather has been particularly fine lately, the streets glitter a biscuit yellow all day, the crowds waiting at the bus stops for the few buses give the town an air of festivity, the sand-bags on the side-walks, the strips of paper on the windows, the balloons in the sky, are all sufficiently new in the bright sunlight to be interesting and almost gay.

The moon shines above the London streets during the black-outs like an island in the sky. The streets become rivers of light. The houses become feathery, soft, undefined, aspiring, so that any part of this town might be the most beautiful city in the world, sleeping amongst silk and water. And the moon takes a farewell look at our civilization everywhere. I have seen it as an omen in Valencia, Barcelona, and Madrid, also. Only the houses were not plumed, feathery, soft, there: the moon was brighter, and they seemed made of white bone.

September 11th

I had lunch with Tom Eliot a few days ago at his club. The stupid thing is that I can hardly remember anything of what he said. I remember that we had cheese, which he chose. We each had a half of draught beer. He smoked his French cigarettes. He was gentle and courteous as he always is, and he talked freely. He asked me what I was doing, and I said, I think, writing my posthumous works, and that I wasn't taking any official job. He said, 'I think it's very important that as many writers as possible should remain detached, and not have any official position'. I mentioned that I had sent my name to the Ministry of Information and the War Office, but had had no reply. He had done ditto to the F.O. and had also had no reply.

He said it was very important that one should, at all costs, go on writing now. 'It doesn't seem to me to matter very much whether, at the moment, it is or isn't very good. The important thing is to keep going. Probably it's impossible to do excellent work while things are so disturbed.'

I mentioned that I hadn't been able to work, so had started this journal. He said: 'Yes, that's an excellent idea. Just writing every day is a way of keeping the engine running, and then something good may come out of it.'

We talked a little about Joyce. 'If he wrote anything now, it would have to be so entirely different from *Finnegans Wake*, that one can easily imagine that the reorganization of his whole way of thinking would be too much for him.' I said that perhaps he might write something very simple, and added that one could imagine his thought being clear and simple, as, indeed, it is in parts of *Finnegan*, but that it would be difficult to imagine his using a simpler vocabulary, and still more so abandoning his linguistic inventions.

Eliot said that he did not care to listen to Beethoven so much as formerly just now. We both agreed on Bach and Gluck for the War.

I said how necessary I felt it to be lucid in poetry when the world was so chaotic. Eliot said he thought the poetic drama might be a way of attaining to lucidity, because, I suppose, it puts one outside oneself, whereas the poem tends today to be an introspective monologue. I said I was at once attracted by, and sick of, public events being dealt with in a public manner in poetic plays. He agreed that the problem was to write about a smaller theme—perhaps family life—which had all the implications of what is going on in the world outside. A play which to some members of the audience would be taken at its face value, and which would mean much more to others.

OCTOBER 26TH

Advantages of living alone

Increase of energy and creativeness because I can indulge without remorse in the brutal selfishness of being a writer.

When I was living with someone, I was always reproaching myself for not paying her sufficient attention. This meant that all the time I felt under a certain restraint. It also derives from my attaching far too much importance to people's whims and moods, which always make me feel that I have *done something wrong to them*. I feel that pleasures which people might, in fact, easily sacrifice, are mysteriously important, and this makes any decision very difficult. I always feel that anyone else can be more satisfactory than I am. In fact, altogether, there is a lack of confidence in my behaviour within a possessive relationship. The effect of this is not to lessen but rather to increase egotism.

It is really rather disturbing to write this. I do not even entirely understand what I am trying to explain yet. But what it comes to is that when someone I am with, whom I am accustomed to think of as happy, is unhappy, I experience a feeling of deep apprehension, a sense that nothing is ever going to be better now, because I have discovered the final truth that *everything is wrong*. At the same time, a corresponding distress of my own is revealed by my companion's unhappiness, and I soon feel that it is this which is making her unhappy, so that I am responsible for all the defects in both our characters.

But it is not only unhappiness that distresses me in people, but also tiredness, laziness and other weaknesses. When I was sixteen and we used to go home in the Tube from my grandmother's house on Sunday evenings, a thing that irritated me almost beyond bearing was if my sister or her companion, who were with me, yawned. The fact is that I was very tired myself, but it was impossible for me to relax, even so far as to yawn, and the fact that there were people who yawned unthinkingly, not accepting the necessity I saw of never revealing when one was tired, maddened me.

I know quite well that I am now giving myself away far more than if I confessed, for example, that I had committed a murder. The real crimes in contemporary bourgeois intellectual society are puritan traits of character.

However, there is no reason after all why I should not be frank. It is as though a special set of rules applies to my own life which does

Crowds, across all Europe, are beginning to feel they've been left in
the lurch.
But it's worse than that. It's something they couldn't tell anyone,
ever.

He's abandoned his post because he was the greatest of all informers,
And now he's gone to report. He never had a moment's leisure.
He was paid by so many powers that one shakes with shame
To think of them. Time, the Army and Navy, Pain and Blame,
The Police, the Family, and Death. No one will escape. He got every
name.
And he wasn't at all what he said he was. Mr. Pleasure.

BRIAN HOWARD

THE FALL OF FRANCE

IT HAD been at the end of May when I went to tea with a not unintelligent Russian woman and the Baronne de V. The latter was quite a friend of mine; she genuinely liked music, and painted slight, but fresh, little landscapes. The Nazis were near Paris, at Vernon, and the suspense was severe. At tea, the conversation so shocked me that I protested, but I am sure it was the *bien-pensant* conversation of all France at that moment:

They: 'Ce salaud! on doit le fusiller!'

I: 'Qui?'

They: 'Blum, cher ami. *Blum*, naturellement. Thorez aussi. J'en suis sûre que c'est lui qui donne les discours sur le radio allemand.'

I: 'Fusiller Blum?'

They: 'Mais sur le champ! C'est épouvan*table*. Il a volé tout l'argent que nous avons donné pour la ligne Maginot. Voilà pourquoi les Boches, etc., etc.'

Shaking with anger, their extremely distinguished faces pinched into masks like newts, they expatiated; and my vigorous protests were simply ignored. Then, suddenly, a French doctor in uniform ran up the steps of the terrace; a devoted, charming young man who was giving up his short leave to his patients. He described the German advance:

'Three million men are advancing shoulder to shoulder with their Chicago-guns at the hip. It is indescribable.'

Next: 'Some parachutists are dressed from head to foot in pale blue, with transparent pale blue parachutes, and each one has a bomb in his hand, painted flesh-colour.'

The women: 'No!'

The officer: 'Yes, they look like something by Schiaparelli.'

More talk and tea. Then the officer left. He said, with a tender kind of dignity, kissing the women's hands: 'I never expect to see you again, of course.'

There was no more anger that day.

W. R. RODGERS

ESCAPE

The roads of Europe are running away from the war,
Running fast over the mined bridges and past the men
Waiting there, with watch, ready to maim and arrest them,
And strong overhead the long snorings of the planes' tracks
Are stretching like rafters from end to end of their power.
Turn back, you who want to escape or want to forget
The ruin of all your regards. You will be more free
At the thoughtless centre of slaughter than you would be
Standing chained to the telephone-end while the world cracks.

TOM DRIBERG

PARTY LINE

Reassembling on the border
We realize in reassembly.

Coming out of the dream, it is clear now
Clear to us again
Clear that there is a border.

See the dotted line. On the Ordnance Survey
It turns to and fro. A loop of it,
Red for the next county, misled us.

No dotted line to sign, but clean continuous
And, to convince, bending to be
A hair-spring, tautening to needle.

The ranks reassemble on the borderline.

C. DAY LEWIS

DEDICATORY STANZAS

FOR A TRANSLATION OF THE GEORGICS

(To Stephen Spender)

Poets are not in much demand these days—
We're red, it seems, or cracked, or bribed, or hearty
And, if invited, apt to spoil the party
With the oblique reproach of emigrés:
We cut no ice, although we're fancy skaters:
Aiming at art, we only strike the arty.
Poetry now, the kinder tell us, caters
For an élite: still, it gives us the hump
To think that we're the unacknowledged rump
Of a long parliament of legislators.

Where are the war poets? the fools inquire.
We were the prophets of a changeable morning
Who hoped for much but saw the clouds forewarning:
We were at war, while they still played with fire
And rigged the market for the ruin of man:
Spain was a death to us, Munich a mourning.
No wonder then if, like the pelican,
We have turned inward for our iron ration,
Tapping the vein and sole reserve of passion,
Drawing from poetry's capital what we can.

Yes, we shall fight, but—let them not mistake it—
Not for the ones who grudged to peace their pence
And gave war a blank cheque in self-defence,
Nor those who take self-interest and fake it
Into a code of honour—the distorting
Mirror those magnates hold to experience.
It's for dear life alone we shall be fighting,
The poet's living-space, the love of men,
And poets must speak for common suffering men
While history in sheets of fire is writing.

Meanwhile, what touches the heart at all, engrosses.
Through the flushed springtime and the fading year
I lived on country matters. Now June was here
Again, and brought the smell of flowering grasses
To me and death to many overseas:
They lie in the flowering sunshine, flesh once dear
To some, now parchment for the heart's release.
Soon enough each is called into the quarrel.
Till then, taking a leaf from Virgil's laurel,
I sang in time of war the arts of peace.

Virgil—a tall man, dark and countrified
In looks, they say: retiring: no rhetorician:
Of humble birth: a Celt, whose first ambition
Was to be a philosopher: Dante's guide.
But chiefly dear for his gift to understand
Earth's intricate, ordered heart, and for a vision
That saw beyond an imperial day the hand

Of man no longer armed against his fellow,
But all for vine and cattle, fruit and fallow,
Subduing with love's positive force the land.

Different from his our age and myths, our toil
The same. Our exile and extravagances,
Revolt, retreat, fine faiths, disordered fancies
Are but the poet's search for a right soil
Where words may settle, marry, and conceive an
Imagined truth, for a regimen that enhances
Their natural grace. Now, as to one whom even
Our age's drought and spate have not deterred
From cherishing, like a bud of flame, the word,
I dedicate this book to you, dear Stephen.

Now, when war's long midwinter seems to freeze us
And numb our living sources once for all,
That veteran of Virgil's I recall
Who made a kitchen-garden by the Galaesus
On derelict land, and got the first of spring
From airs and buds, the first fruits in the fall.
And lived at peace there, happy as a king.
Naming him for good luck, I see man's native
Stock is perennial, and our creative
Winged seed can strike a root in anything.

ARTHUR WALEY

CENSORSHIP

A poem in the Chinese style

TO HSIAO CH'IEN

I have been a censor for fifteen months;
The building where I work has four times been bombed.
Glass, boards and paper, each in turn,
Have been blasted from the windows—where windows
are left at all.

It is not easy to wash, keep warm and eat;
At times we lack gas, water or light.
The rules for censors are difficult to keep;
In six months there were over a thousand 'stops'.
The Air Raid Bible alters from day to day;
Official orders are not clearly expressed.
One may mention Harrods, but not Derry and Toms;
One may write of mist, but may not write of rain.
Japanese, scribbled on thin paper
In faint scrawl tires the eyes to read.
In a small room with ten telephones
And a tape-machine concentration is hard.
Yet the Blue Pencil is a mere toy to wield,
There are worse knots than the tangles of Red Tape.
It is not difficult to censor foreign news,
What is hard today is to censor one's own thoughts,—
To sit by and see the blind man
On the sightless horse, riding into the bottomless abyss.

GAVIN EWART

SONNET

The point where beauty and intelligence meet,
Where intersecting lines cross and divide,—
Happy were I to lie between those feet
Or by that rare and warm and lovely side—
You are the centre of my moving world,
The cold Ideal to which I daily move
Although iron flags of battle are unfurled,—
You are not yet, though might still be, my love.
And I, before the happy, tough battalions
Engulf me or the frozen seas of Norway,
Have still my dreams of cities and of dalliance
But most of you as standing in a doorway,
Who might, though I so dissipate my life,
Be mistress or, fear of the young, a wife.

1941

ALUN LEWIS

ALL DAY IT HAS RAINED....

All day it has rained, and we on the edge of the moors
Have sprawled in our bell-tents, moody and dull as boors,
Groundsheets and blankets spread on the muddy ground.
And from the first grey wakening we have found
No refuge from the skirmishing fine rain
And the wind that made the canvas heave and flap
And the taut wet guy ropes ravel out and snap.
All day the rain has glided, wave and mist and dream,
Drenching the gorse and heather, a gossamer stream
Too light to move the acorns that suddenly
Snatched from their cups by the wild southwesterly
Pattered against the tent and our upturned dreaming faces.
And we stretched out, unbuttoning our braces,
Smoking a Woodbine, darning dirty socks,
Reading the Sunday papers—I saw a fox
And mentioned it in the note I scribbled home;
And we talked of girls and dropping bombs on Rome
And thought of the quiet dead and the loud celebrities
Exhorting us to slaughter and the herded refugees;
Yet thought softly, morosely of them, and as indifferently
As of ourselves and those whom we for years
Have loved and will again
Tomorrow maybe love; but now it is the rain
Possesses us entirely, the twilight and the rain.

And I can remember nothing dearer or more to my heart
Than the children I watched in the woods on Saturday
Shaking down burning chestnuts for the school-yard's
    merry play,
Or the shaggy patient dog who followed me
Through Sheet and Steep and up the wooded scree
To the Shoulder o' Mutton where Edward Thomas
    brooded long
On death and beauty—till a bullet stopped his song.

LOUIS ARAGON

ZONE LIBRE

Fading de la tristesse oubli
Le bruit du cœur brisé faiblit
Et la cendre blanchit la braise
J'ai bu l'été comme un vin doux
J'ai rêvé pendant ce mois d'août
Dans un château rose en Corrèze

Qu'était-ce qui faisait soudain
Un sanglot lourd dans le jardin
Un sourd reproche dans la brise
Ah ne m'éveillez pas trop tôt
Rien qu'un instant de bel canto
Le désespoir démobilise

Il m'avait un instant semblé
Entendre au milieu des blés
Confusément le bruit des armes
D'où me venait ce grand chagrin
Ni l'œillet ni le romarin
N'ont gardé le perfum des larmes

J'ai perdu je ne sais comment
Le noir secret de mon tourment
A son tour l'ombre se démembre
Je cherchais à n'en plus finir
Cette douleur sans souvenir
Quand parut l'aube de septembre

Mon amour j'étais dans tes bras
Au dehors quelqu'un murmura
Une vieille chanson de France
Mon mal enfin s'est reconnu
Et son refrain comme un pied nu
Troubla l'eau verte du silence

A. TOLSTOY

A MESSAGE FROM MOSCOW

CYRIL CONNOLLY, STEPHEN SPENDER, *Horizon*

THANK you for friendly greetings to Soviet writers. We are happy to establish with English and American intellectuals deep mutual understanding and mutual aim laying principles of justice, goodwill —indispensable grounds for future growth humanitarian culture in world.

We Soviet writers, as our Red Army and all united fraternal consolidated peoples Soviet Union, are full of optimism. Fight is stubborn, difficult, and enemy like wounded monster exerting all its strength, but power and resistance of our Army grows each day, while strength Hitler's Army each day wanes. Especially difficult for Germans last week's battle. On important directions front we destroyed five divisions—separate columns of three hundred tanks completely destroyed to last machine—also several separate large infantry and tank formations. Offensive violence enemy diminishing. Among German war prisoners more and more often we come across youths or elderly soldiers badly dressed and exhausted who are unfamiliar with automatic guns. Our guerrilla fighters paralyse transport of German munitions and petrol, more and more frequently Germans bury their tanks in the earth, using them as forts. German infantry trained only to carry out lightning war, compelled change methods to war manœuvres, which it poorly understands, and is quickly falling into a state of panic. Frequently our troops discover Germans chained to machine-gun or tankists whom German officers have locked in buried tanks.

Such facts bring serious reflections. For example, advancing German infantry drives before it on our line of fire captured women children refugees. German army hides behind women's skirts and children's bodies—only an army struck with deadly inner disintegration could stoop to such ignominy.

In name of Soviet literature please give friendly and fraternal greetings to writers of England and America—to all who dedicate their lives to the annihilation of bloody and vicious fascism on our beautiful earth. On us all depends that this black night more quickly passes.

ALEXEI TOLSTOY

DYLAN THOMAS

DEATHS AND ENTRANCES

On almost the incendiary eve
    Of several near deaths,
When one at the least of your best loved
    And always known must leave
Lions and fires of his flying breath,
    Of your immortal friends
Who'd raised the organs of the counted dust
    To shoot and sing your praise,
One who called deepest down shall hold his peace
    That cannot sink or cease
    Endlessly to his wound
In many married London's estranging grief.

On almost the incendiary eve
    When at your lips and keys,
Locking, unlocking, the murdered strangers weave,
    One who is most unknown,
Your polestar neighbour, sun of another street,
    Will dive up to his tears.
He'll bathe his raining blood in the male sea
    Who strode for your own dead
And wind his globe out of your water thread
    And loud the throats of shells
    With every cry since light
Flashed first across his thunderclapping eyes.

On almost the incendiary eve
    Of deaths and entrances,
When near and strange wounded on London's waves
    Have sought your single grave,
One enemy, of many, who knows well
    Your heart is luminous
In the watched dark, quivering through locks and caves,
    Will pull the thunderbolts
To shut the sun, plunge, mount your darkened keys

And sear just riders back,
Until that one loved least
Looms the last Samson of your zodiac.

STEPHEN SPENDER

AIR RAID

In this room like a bowl of flowers filled with light
The family eyes look down on the white
Pages of a book, and the mild white ceiling,
Like a starched nurse, reflects a calm feeling.

The daughter with hands outstretched to the fire
Transmits through her veins the peaceful desire
Of the family tree from which she was born
To push tendrils through nights to a promiseful dawn.

In the grey stone house and the glass-and-steel flat
The vertical descendants of the bones that
Have sprung from the past, are supported on floors
And protected by walls from the wind outdoors.

In their complex surroundings, they act out the part
Of the flesh home of the human heart,
With limbs extending to chairs, tables, cups,
All the necessities and props.

They wear the right clothes and acquire the safe ways,
Hear the news, discuss golf, and fill out their days
With work, and meals brought from the kitchen range.
And no one sees anything empty or strange

In all this. And perhaps that is right. Nothing is
Until an unreasoning fury impinges
From a different vision of life, on their hearth.
It explodes; and tears the place down to earth.

Then the inside made outside faces the street.
Rubble decently buries the human meat.
Piled above it, a bath, cupboards, books, telephone,
Though all who could answer its ringing have gone.

Standing untouched is a solitary wall,
Half a floor attached, which failed to fall.
Involved pink patterns and light blues line
That rectangle high up where they used to dine.

Distressed passers by are bound to observe
The painted paper, like the polished curve
Salivaed with mother-o'-pearl, in a shell
Where a living sensitive snail did once dwell.

But the home has been cracked by metallic claws,
Years of loving care ground to rubble in jaws,
And the delicate squirming life thrown away
By the high-flying purpose of a foreign day.

E. J. SCOVELL

DAYS DRAWING IN

The days fail: night broods over afternoon:
And at my child's first drink beyond the night
Her skin is silver in the early light.
Sweet the grey morning and the raiders gone.

H. G. WELLS

FUNDAMENTAL REALITIES

IT IS impossible to discuss the outcome of the present war at all hopefully or usefully unless certain fundamental realities are continually borne in mind. The first of these is the complete change in the conditions of human life that has occurred since the beginning of the century. There has been an abolition of distance, so that events are now practically present and simultaneous throughout the planet, and such a release of material and human energy as to make the pre-existing control of human affairs by a patchwork of independent sovereign governments increasingly ineffective and dangerous in the face of large-scale profiteering private enterprise and terroristic gangsterism. Three broad necessities face man. He has to secure himself against a new sort of warfare that is rapidly destroying the moral and material fabric of his civilization, he has to protect world resources from exhaustion by short-sighted exploitation for private profit, and he has to extend the protection of a common basic law to all mankind. The first necessity can be met only by the establishment of a federal world control of the air and its associated services and supplies; the second by a federal conservation of world resources, and the third by accepting such a statement as the Sankey Declaration of Human Rights as the fundamental law of the world. None of these things was even practicable fifty years ago. They are now imperative, if the present collapse of human affairs into disorder and degeneration without limit is to be arrested. No schemes and constructive forecasts can be taken seriously which do not fall within the requirements of this threefold programme. The world has become one—and this is no metaphor, but a primary political fact. We can no longer parcel out human affairs and talk about the Future of *our* Empire or the Future of Britain except as a contributory part of the whole problem of mankind. We have to be continually on our guard against lapsing back into historical traditional ways of thinking in this respect. All existing political and administrative authority throughout the world is provisional, pending the development of world federal organizations. Their common future is a merger. Britain is for mankind and not mankind for Britain. If these essentials can be presented forcibly and clearly to men's minds, if they can be sustained and spread by a lucid and vigorous educational propaganda, so that they become the directive creative form of politics everywhere, there is hope for mankind. But there is no hope if intelligent English-speaking people, of whom the readers of *Horizon* are a sample, muddle up the issues by shifting their standpoints to and fro between the general and the particular, if they hide these broad ruling conceptions beneath a tangle of secondary suggestions of all sorts and sizes. The world at large wants a clear lead, and it is from the artists, writers and teachers, to whom *Horizon* appeals, that plain directives must come, if they are to come at all. People do not want a collection of odd parts and makeshifts from us. They do not want—how can I put it?—something like a rummage sale from the mental content of a humane, liberal minded but patriotic and sentimental vicar, with one son in the Civil Service, one in India and one in the Air Force. In the present crisis of human affairs, a well-meaning programme of quasi-progressive shreds and patches can easily be more mischievous, by distracting and dispersing energy and goodwill, than deliberate opposition. The threefold way as I have stated it is the plain way for rational mankind in common, and we cannot make it too clear.

GEORGE ORWELL

WELLS, HITLER AND THE WORLD STATE

WHAT has Wells to set against the 'screaming little defective in Berlin'? The usual rigmarole about a World State, plus the Sankey Declaration, which is an attempted definition of fundamental human rights, of anti-totalitarian tendency. Except that he is now especially concerned with federal world control of airpower, it is the same gospel as he has been preaching almost without interruption for the past forty years, always with an air of angry surprise at the human beings who can fail to grasp anything so obvious.

What is the use of saying that we need federal world control of the air? The whole question is how we are to get it. What is the use of pointing out that a World State is desirable? What matters is that not one of the five great military powers would think of submitting to such a thing. All sensible men for decades past have been substantially in agreement with what Mr. Wells says; but then sensible men have no power and, in too many cases, no disposition to sacrifice themselves. Hitler is a criminal lunatic, and Hitler has an army of millions of men, aeroplanes in thousands, tanks in tens of thousands. For his sake a great nation has been willing to overwork itself for six years and then to fight for two years more, whereas for the commonsense, essentially hedonistic world-view that Mr. Wells puts forward hardly a human creature is willing to shed a pint of blood. Before you can even talk of world reconstruction, or even of peace, you have got to eliminate Hitler, which means bringing into being a dynamic not necessarily the same as that of the Nazis, but probably quite as unacceptable to 'enlightened' and hedonistic people. What has kept England on its feet during the past year? Partly, no doubt, some vague idea about a better future, but chiefly the atavistic emotion of patriotism, the ingrained feeling of the English-speaking peoples that they are superior to foreigners. For the last twenty years the main object of English left-wing intellectuals has been to break this feeling down, and if they had succeeded we might be watching the SS-men patrolling the London streets at this moment. Similarly, why are the Russians fighting like tigers against the German invasion? In part, perhaps, for some half-remembered ideal of Utopian Socialism, but chiefly in defence of the Holy Russia (the 'sacred soil of the Fatherland', etc., etc.), which Stalin has revived in an only slightly altered form. The energy that actually shapes the world springs from emotions—racial pride, leader-worship, religious belief, love of war—which liberal intellectuals mechanically write off as anachronisms, and which they have usually destroyed so completely in themselves as to have lost all power of action.

The people who say that Hitler is Antichrist or, alternatively, the Holy Ghost are nearer an understanding of the truth than the left-wing intellectuals who for ten dreadful years have kept it up that he is merely a figure out of comic opera, not worth taking seriously. All that this idea really reflects is the sheltered conditions of English life. The Left Book Club was at bottom a product of Scotland Yard, just as the Peace Pledge Union is a product of the navy. One development of the last ten years has been the appearance of the 'political book', a sort of enlarged pamphlet combining history with political criticism, as an important literary form. But the best writers in this line—Trotsky, Rauschning, Rosenberg, Silone, Borkenau, Koestler and others—have none of them been Englishmen, and nearly all of them have been renegades from one or other extremist party, who have seen totalitarianism at close quarters and known the meaning of exile and persecution. Only in the English-speaking countries was it fashionable to believe, right up to the outbreak of war, that Hitler was an unimportant lunatic and the German tanks made of cardboard. Mr. Wells, it will be seen from the quotations I have given above, believes something of the kind still. I do not suppose that either the bombs or the German campaign in Greece have altered his opinion. A life-long habit of thought stands between him and an understanding of Hitler's power.

Mr. Wells, like Dickens, belongs to the non-military middle class. The thunder of guns, the jingle of spurs, the catch in the throat when the old flag goes by, leave him manifestly cold. He has an invincible hatred of the fighting, hunting, swashbuckling side of life, symbolized in all his early books by a violent propaganda against horses. The principal villain of his *Outline of History* is the romantic military adventurer, Napoleon. If one looks through nearly any book that he has written in the last forty years one finds the same idea constantly recurring: the supposed antithesis between the man of science who is working towards a planned World State and the reactionary who is trying to restore a disorderly past. In novels, Utopias, essays, films, pamphlets the antithesis crops up, always more or less the same. On the one side science, order, progress, internationalism, aeroplanes, steel, concrete, hygiene: on the other side war, nationalism, religion, monarchy, peasants, Greek professors, poets, horses. History as he sees it is a series of victories won by the scientific man over the romantic man. Now, he is probably right in assuming that a 'reasonable', planned form of society, with scientists rather than witch-doctors in control, will prevail sooner or later, but that is a different matter from assuming that it is just round the corner. There survives somewhere or other an interesting controversy which took place between Wells and Churchill at the time of the Russian Revolution. Wells accuses Churchill of not really believing his own propaganda about the Bolsheviks being monsters dripping with blood, etc., but of merely fearing that they were going to introduce an era of common sense and scientific control, in which flag-wavers like Churchill himself would have no place. Churchill's estimate of Bolsheviks, however, was nearer the mark than Wells's. The early Bolsheviks may have been angels or demons, according as one chooses to regard them, but at any rate they were not sensible men. They were not introducing a Wellsian Utopia but a Rule of the Saints, which, like the English Rule of the Saints, was a military despotism enlivened by witchcraft trials. The same misconception reappears in an inverted form in Wells's attitude to the Nazis. Hitler is all the war-lords and witch-doctors in history rolled into one. Therefore, argues Wells, he is an absurdity, a ghost from the past, a creature doomed to disappear almost immediately. But unfortunately the equation of science with common sense does not really hold good. The aeroplane, which was looked forward to as a civilizing influence but in practice has hardly been used except for dropping bombs, is the symbol of that fact. Modern Germany is far more scientific than England, and far more barbarous. Much of what Wells has imagined and worked for is physically there in Nazi Germany. The order, the planning, the State encouragement of science, the steel, the concrete, the aeroplanes, are all there, but all in the service of ideas appropriate to the Stone Age. Science is fighting on the side of superstition. But obviously it is impossible for Wells to accept this. It would contradict the world-view on which his own works are based. The war-lords and the witch-doctors *must* fail, the commonsense World State, as seen by a nineteenth-century liberal whose heart does not leap at the sound of bugles, *must* triumph. Treachery and defeatism apart, Hitler *cannot* be a real danger. That he should finally win would be an impossible reversal of history, like a Jacobite restoration.

But is it not a sort of parricide for a person of my age (38) to find fault with H. G. Wells? Thinking people who were born about the beginning of this century are in some sense Wells's own creation. How much influence any mere writer has, and especially a 'popular' writer whose work takes effect quickly, is questionable, but I doubt whether anyone who was writing books between 1900 and 1920, at any rate in the English language, influenced the young so much. The minds of all of us, and therefore the physical world, would be perceptibly different if Wells had never existed. Only, just the singleness of mind, the one-sided imagination that made him seem like an inspired prophet in the Edwardian age, make him a shallow inadequate thinker now. When Wells was young the antithesis between science and reaction was not false. Society was ruled by narrow-minded, profoundly incurious people, predatory business-men, dull squires, bishops, politicians who could quote Horace but had never heard of algebra. Science was faintly disreputable and religious belief obligatory. Traditionalism, stupidity, snobbishness, patriotism, superstition and love of war seemed to be all on the same side; there was need of someone who could state the opposite point of view. Back in the nineteen-hundreds it was a wonderful experience for a boy to discover H. G. Wells. There you were, in a world of pedants, clergyman and golfers, with your future employers exhorting you to 'get on or get out', your parents systematically warping your sexual life, and your dull-witted schoolmasters sniggering over their Latin tags; and here was this wonderful man who could tell you about the inhabitants of the planets and the bottom of the sea, and who *knew* that the future was not going to be what respectable people imagined. A decade or so before aero-planes were technically feasible, Wells knew that within a little while men would be able to fly. He knew that because he himself *wanted* to be able to fly, and therefore felt sure that research in that direction would continue. On the other hand, even when I was a little boy, at a time when the Wright brothers had actually lifted their machine off the ground for fifty-nine seconds, the generally-accepted opinion was that if God had meant us to fly He would have given us wings. Up to 1914 Wells was in the main a true prophet. In physical details his vision of the new world has been fulfilled to a surprising extent.

But because he belonged to the nineteenth century and to a non-military nation and class, he could not grasp the tremendous strength of the old world which was symbolized in his mind by ignorant fox-hunting Tories. He was and still is quite incapable of understanding that nationalism, religious bigotry and feudal loyalty are far more powerful forces than what he himself would describe as sanity. Creatures out of the Dark Ages have come marching into the present, and if they are ghosts they are at any rate ghosts which need a strong magic to lay them. The people who have shown the best understanding of Fascism are either those who have suffered under it, or those who have a Fascist streak in themselves. A crude book like *The Iron Heel*, written nearly thirty years ago, is a truer prophecy of the future than either *Brave New World* or *The Shape of Things to Come*. If one had to choose among Wells's own contemporaries a writer who could stand towards him as a corrective, one might choose Kipling, who was not deaf to the evil voices of power and military 'glory'. Kipling would have understood the appeal of Hitler or for that matter of Stalin, whatever his attitude towards them might be. Wells is too sane to understand the modern world. The succession of lower-middle-class novels which are his greatest achievement stopped short at the other war and never really began again, and since 1920 he has squandered his talents in slaying paper dragons. But how much it is, after all, to have any talents to squander.

1942

J. MACLAREN-ROSS

THIS MORTAL COIL

I WAS on picquet that night, I'd just come off the door. It was about ten o'clock and when I came in the guard-room I expected to find them all dossed down for the night. But instead they were up, firewatchers and all, some standing about, some sitting on benches by the table, and Corporal Weemes, the Picquet Commander, sat on the table itself. All looked so expectant that I said: 'What's up? Scheme on or something?'

'No, no,' they said. 'It's Kelly.'

'Kelly?'

They pointed to a corner of the room, by the telephone table. What I had taken for a heap of blankets lay there. But these evidently concealed a man of some sort, because as I looked at them they began to heave and writhe about: at the same time a series of grunts came from underneath them. The fellows bounced up and down on the bench, some clapped their hands in glee.

'He's starting,' they said. 'He's got started.'

Corporal Weemes looked at his watch. 'Ten o'clock,' he said. 'On the dot. He always starts off at ten.'

The grunts were succeeded by an awful, unearthly sound, like a wolf howling. At first it was muffled by the blankets, but as these fell off and a head emerged, it positively filled the room with its volume.

'What's wrong with him?' I said. 'Is he sick?'

'Ssh!' they said. 'Just wait till he gets properly going.'

'Reg'lar circus,' Corporal Weemes said.

The howl died down and became split up into words. These, unintelligible at first, clarified suddenly into a shout: 'The rotten bastards!'

'He's off,' they said, shaking with laughter.

'Rotten bastards!' came the shout. 'I'll learn you, you rotten sods!'

'That's right, Kelly,' someone shouted from the bench. 'Brass the buggers up.'

'Company, shun!' came from under the blanket. 'Or-der—HUP! As you were!' He'd a good word of command, anyhow. 'Company will advance. Right-turn!'

'But is he asleep?' I said.

'Sure he's asleep,' Corporal Weemes said. 'He's dreaming, see?'

'Ab-out TURN!' Kelly shouted in his sleep. 'Pick up that step, you sods!'

'Proper sarmajor, ain't he?' they said in admiration.

'Look out, Kelly!' somebody shouted. 'Here comes the R.S.M.'

'B—— the R.S.M.' came back from Kelly. The fellows rocked with laughter, one nearly fell off the bench. 'That's right, Kelly boy,' they shouted. 'You size him up!'

'Where's Joan?' they asked him next. 'She's looking for you, Kelly. Joan! Wake up! Joan's his girl,' they explained to me.

'Joan?' Kelly mumbled. He was puzzled. The transition from parade ground to girl was too much for him to accomplish at a moment's notice.

'Yes, Joan!' they shouted, hopping about from foot to foot. 'She wants you, Kelly boy!'

Kelly kicked off all his blankets. One got entangled with his boots, but he got rid of it at last, muttering 'Rotten bastard'. But the idea of Joan was evidently uppermost in his mind, and he murmured at the same time 'Darling'.

Sitting up, still asleep, with all his equipment on, he was revealed to be a small, dark lad about twenty. 'Joan,' he murmured, 'my sweet darling,' and kissed his haversack. The fellows were delighted. 'Go it, Kelly!' they screamed. 'Give her the works!'

Thus encouraged, Kelly became passionate. He embraced the haversack and, holding it tightly, climbed on top of it. He fell off and rolled over, hitting his head a whack on the door. But the blow did not fetch him to; he lay on his back murmuring 'Dearest love', and feeling for the haversack.

L/C Staines, N.C.O. i/c firewatching, came dashing in. 'Have I missed anything?' he asked. 'How long's he been started?'

'You're in time, Corp. Only got to Joan so far.'

'That's all right, then.' L/C Staines sat down by the telephone table, quite close to Kelly. He had a ringside seat. The boxing metaphor is justified because the haversack, formerly representing his girl, now apparently became identified in Kelly's dream with some mortal enemy. He clinched with it and delivered a short-arm jab to the straps.

'Go it, Kelly!' the chaps shouted. 'You got him groggy. You got him on the ropes. Go in and K.O. him, Kelly boy!'

Kelly did his best. He abandoned boxing for all-in wrestling and took a large bite of Blanco from the flap of the haversack. But the haversack in his mind had evidently hit back: he rocked sideways and slipped down by the wall, shaking his head. One of the blokes began slowly to count him out. 'One—two—three—four—.'

'Can't get up,' Kelly mumbled in a bemused voice, punch-drunk. He took a swing at the air and missed. He hit the door instead and laid his hand open.

'Surely that'll wake him?' I said.

'Don't you believe it,' one of the blokes said. 'Hammond hit him on the nut with an entrenching tool once and *that* didn't wake him. Nothing'll wake him once he starts on this stunt. He don't feel nothing, see?'

'What does he do when he's not asleep? Is he a boxer?'

'Not likely. Look at him daytime you wouldn't think butter'd melt in his mouth. Don't swear neither not unless he's dreaming.'

A stream of obscenity began to pour from Kelly as though released by these words. He'd been counted out and was now standing on his head in a kneeling position, as if about to perform a somersault. In this posture he appeared so funny that everybody again burst out laughing. But Kelly himself continued to swear, with his face close to the floorboards. It soon became apparent that his epithets were addressed not to anyone in particular but to the army in general.

'Doesn't he like the army?' I said.

'Dunno,' Corporal Weemes said. 'We have to chase him about sometimes. Bit of a dodger in his way. Lazy. Ain't a bad lad, not really, though.'

'Done any defaulters?'

'He done plenty of *them*. Just come off, matter of fact. Come off last night.'

'B—— the army!' Kelly was shouting in his sleep. 'S—— the jankers! S—— 'em all! Give me my civvy clothes,' he began to sing in a horrible toneless voice. 'Give me my civvy . . . clothes,' and the fellows slapped their knees and danced around him in delight. Then he went back to saying, 'B—— the army!' in a tone of such stridency that L/C Staines leaped up off his chair. Either his sense of discipline was outraged or else he was afraid the duty officer would overhear.

'Come on, Kelly,' he said in a voice of command. 'That's enough, lad. Come on, wake up!'

He grasped Kelly by the braces and swung him upright. With his other hand he administered a smart cuff on the ear. While delivered smartly it was still heavy enough to rock Kelly's head on his shoulders. But Kelly's eyes remained obstinately closed, and as if it were a reflex action his boot shot out at Staines's kneecap. Staines, an expert on unarmed combat, dodged nimbly back, releasing Kelly, but at the same time jerking his bayonet from its scabbard and tossing it on the telephone table. Kelly fell on his face and lay there, with blood dripping on the blankets from his cut hand.

'That's got it,' Staines said.

'The bayonet?'

'Yeh. He can be awkward sometimes. Remember that time, Williams, when he walked in his sleep? In Don Company?'

'Cor, don't I!' Williams said. 'I won't forget that not in a hurry. Fixed bayonet, all in his sleep, and come charging down the hut. We was all scared stiff. Then he come charging back again.'

'What'd you do?' I asked.

'We all got out right sharp and shut the door. After 'bout a quarter hour we looks in again and there he was sleeping sound, bayonet back in scabbard and all. Bloody rum bloke Kelly is, no error.'

'He's getting married next week,' another man said. 'Joan. His tart. Cor,' he chortled, 'I reckon she won't half get a surprise the first night, eh?'

'Getting married?' I said.

'Ah. Put in for leave today. Pass signed and all. He seen the Padre.'

'But damn it all he oughtn't to get married when he gets these fits. He ought to see the M.O. Or the psychiatrist.'

'Psychiatrist? Ain't that the bloke what they took Wiggs to, that they said was loopy?'

'Ah. Got his ticket and all, Wiggs did.'

'Reckon old Kelly'd get his ticket?'

'Nah, he ain't loopy. He's all right. Won't remember nothing about it when he wakes up.'

'Why don't you send him sick?' I asked Corporal Weemes.

'Wouldn't do no good,' Weemes said. 'He don't believe he does it, see? Thinks we're kidding when we tell him.'

Meanwhile one of the fellows had got hold of a broom and was dancing round Kelly jabbing him in the ribs with it, while Kelly, flat on the floor, made feeble efforts to snatch the broom away. But this comic relief roused a storm of protest from the others.

'Nah, let him be! Put the broom down!'

'It ain't fair poking him like that. Not with the broom.'

So the broom was abandoned. But Kelly now began to cry. 'They got me again,' he sobbed. 'They got me on another charge and I ain't done nothing! I ain't done nothing to nobody!' His body shook with sobs.

Immediately the fellows gathered round him. 'It's all right, Kelly boy. You ain't on no charge, mate. You don't have to take on,' and gradually Kelly was convinced. His sobs subsided and briefly he went through his whole repertoire, 'Sweet darling, rotten bastards, Company shun,' finishing up with a decisive 'B—— the army!'

Then his head fell peacefully back, and he at once began to snore. Two fellows came forward and covered him with his blankets again. The performance was evidently at an end.

'Will he be all right now?' I asked.

'Right as rain. Won't wake till réveillé. Unless the alarm goes.'

Corporal Weemes looked at his watch. 'Okay, lads. Ten forty-five. Pack it in now. Kip down.'

L/C Staines stood up and said in his parade ground voice: 'Come on. Next man on firewatching. Quick march!'

A steel helmet was clapped on, rifle snatched up, the door banged behind them. We all moved towards the beds and fairly soon we were sound asleep: even Kelly, dreamless now, huddled in his blankets with the blood drying on his cut hand, snoring quite happily to himself.

Only Corporal Weemes stayed awake, sitting up on the bench with a sixpenny thriller, because a Picquet Commander must not sleep on duty.

TWENTY QUESTIONS

1. Do you believe that every human being is either a knave or a fool?
2. Have you noticed how it is always the people with more money than you who invariably try to cheat you?
3. Do you agree that what this country needs is a Cromwell?
4. Do you think it is right to lie to the masses for their own good?
5. Do you think people will swallow anything?
6. Do you think the Fall of France was due to neglect of the family?
7. Do you think we overvalue human life?
8. Do you think (1) Progress, (2) Culture, and (3) Civilization are a lot of bunk?
9. Do you agree that Black Marketeers should be shot?
10. Do you think we need a Youth Movement in England?
11. Do you think women are unhappier since they have had more freedom?
12. Do you think the Art and Literature of a country can only be appreciated by the inhabitants of that country?
13. Do you agree that no Jew has ever been a great creative artist?

14. Do you think the seventeenth century was morally greater than the eighteenth or nineteenth?
15. Do you think the Art and Literature of our country at some time in the past has been vitiated by foreign influences and has never quite recovered?
16. Do you feel that an artist should not travel or live in cities, but be part of a rural community with a strong regional life?
17. Do you think we all should be made to work very much harder after the war, and to do without a great many things?
18. Have the Intellectuals let you down?
19. Should those who lived abroad before the war, or who led irregular lives, have things made a bit hot for them?
20. Do you agree that the existence of the individual can only be justified through the dynamism of the race?

If you can say 'Yes' to more than half these questions you are definitely Fascist-minded; if you can say 'Yes' to fifteen you are lucky not to be in Brixton prison; if you can say 'Yes' to twenty you should stand at once for Parliament as an Independant.

ROLLO WOOLLEY

THE PUPIL

THERE was no wind. The windsock was an empty sleeve hanging limp and lifeless from its post. Smoke from the two factory chimneys rose in slender columns into the great basin of hazy sky. It was one of those summer afternoons when one has to climb up through a few thousand feet of sultry haze before reaching the clear sky, and then the haze turns into a black circle of horizon round a dome of lucid blue. Below, the haze clouds look like watery ghosts, blurred pre-natal shapes, but above it they curve and curl into clear white lines, forming miniature ranges of white sky mountains.

On the edge of the aerodrome the pupil lay on his back shielding his eyes from the sun. He watched the little training aeroplanes flying overhead as they made their approach into wind, some floating down so gently and gracefully that they ended just skimming the top of the grass, while others foundered with sudden indignant bursts of engine as if they were afraid to land. Occasionally the pupil looked up to anticipate a doubtful landing; sometimes he sat up to scan the field for any sign of his flying instructor, only to fall back again on to his couch of parachute and sandbags. Planes kept drawing up and new pupils clambered in and out of the back cockpit. Slowly the old men reached up to swing the propellers, stepping warily aside to avoid the sudden flashing whirl of blades. Again and again their hoarse voices repeated the familiar ritual: petrol on, switches off, throttle closed. Contact, Contact! The afternoon crept on to the usual sequence of planes arriving and waiting and taxying away. The petrol wagon shuffled along for refuelling; the Naafi car came, bringing cups of murky tea and little round cakes. The sun moved slowly round over the camouflaged hangar roofs and every now and then breaths of cooler air disturbed the slender stems of smoke. Aeroplanes continued to follow each other round and round like noisy scurrying insects.

The pupil was asleep when his instructor came; he opened his eyes to see a helmet swung mockingly over his face and the instructor in his black flying suit towering over him like a black shadow.

'Get up,' he said, 'you've got to fly.'

The instructor threw off his parachute and sat down on the sandbags; he began fumbling in a pocket, chucking out maps and matches and old letters and bits of paper; then he lit a cigarette and smoothed out a piece of paper.

'Got a pencil?' he said. 'You've got about an hour. But get her filled up first.'

The pupil stood rubbing his eyes, a little dizzy with heat and sleep.

'Yes, sir,' he said.

The instructor was writing something on the slip of paper. He glanced casually up at the sky.

'Still all right for a spot of aerobatics I should think. Anyhow you can climb up and see. Try and get in number ten and twenty-two will you?'

'Okay, sir,' said the pupil.

He bent down to sign the paper.

'Bring her back and put her on pickets, sir?'

The instructor nodded.

The pupil smiled and walked over to his plane. It had just been refuelled and one of the old swinger men was shoving chocks in front of the wheels. Switches off. Contact. 'Contact!' he shouted back. It started up easily, sending a cool gush of air playing round the pupil's head, ruffling the grass behind. He felt refreshed and eager to fly up through this heaviness of yellow haze, like a swimmer waiting to dive into the clear water of a pool.

It was soon after six o'clock when the pupil left the ground. The plane climbed with a comfortable humming sound, and he touched back on the stick with small jerks of the fingers to feel its power of lift, seeing the nose of the plane leap up and down responsively. From the rear cockpit the wings seemed to him separate entities which could roll and twist as if by some mysterious understanding. Still climbing he raised each wing gently in turn to convince himself of their obedience, rather as one calls or beckons to some perfectly trained animal. He kicked viciously at the rudder to enjoy the gusts of wind tearing at his face. He was the master, the supreme commander, alone: this, he thought, is the real thrill of flying solo, this huge power contained like magic in the palm of one's hand. . . .

Already he had escaped the tiresome ring of planes circuiting the aerodrome, and setting the throttle he trimmed her to climb steadily up; he could take his hands off the controls and let the plane lift him with a rich throb of engine higher and higher into the haze. The haze caught the light like the dust swimming in shafts of sunlight that slant through closed shutters. Only things yellow and orange coloured stood out in it; here and there he could recognize a new house being built or shining yellow fields of corn. The pupil climbed on confidently, knowing that he was flying over familiar country.

At three thousand feet he was emerging into clearer sky and the ground sank away uncertainly in colourless depth below. A layer of cumulus cloud floated above the sea of haze, presenting rows of white beads strung out from horizon to horizon. He searched for gaps between those white clouds, and climbed on higher and higher, circling round the cloud bases. The sun shone dazzlingly bright in an emerald ceiling of sky; just a tip, a tiny segment, was cut by the dark edge of haze, and where this tip touched it began to turn into a long streak of gold.

The pupil sang as he climbed. He felt himself the only thing moving in this empty bowl of sky, the only being living in its blue clarity. This sense of freedom is so exhilarating that the pilot feels he must turn and dive and spin to accompany his singing and so assert his presence in this vast loneliness: he has to boast to the earth that he is above it, for all who love flying seek to achieve freedom from its shapes and shadows, escaping the rigidity and the permanence of the land. The music of the sky has the freedom of all space and the relentless rhythm of all time. So locking the slots the pupil braced himself in his straps and dived. At seven thousand feet he had plenty of height to spare. He looped, he turned on the stall, reaching into the depths of sky and rushing down in effortless sweeping circles. . . . He tried rolling the plane: again and again he poised the nose delicately on the cloud horizon and eased her slowly, deliberately round. He imagined the instructor commenting, correcting, shouting down the speaking tube. But there was only the blurred droning of engine in his ears, and he whispered to himself, 'Lovely . . . Christ, how lovely!'

As he glided down, the pupil leant over the side scanning the country below him, hoping to find some familiar landmark. He could pick out the blue smoke of a village on the edge of some woods, and imagining he had drifted a bit to the north while doing aerobatics, he turned south. He opened a map and looked on it for the woods, but he thought that they were perhaps too small to show up. It was impossible to see far to the right now because the sun was a rose red glow in the haze. A pink ribbon of canal caught the light and he followed it gratefully, turning from side to side uncertainly in search of a town. He was flying over flat fields in which cattle grazed peacefully. Late harvesters were finishing work, he could see their black coats bicycling in twos and threes down the lanes. He was flying lower to see more clearly; some children waved to him from a haystack and he waved back, refusing to admit to himself that he was beginning to feel lost and afraid. He tried to calculate how far away he could have flown in an hour, for already he was due down at the aerodrome. Presently he came across a fair-sized landing ground where some bombers were revving up in preparation for night flying; a cheerful blaze of light flooded from the open hangar doors, and men were carrying red lamps across the field. He circled round half wanting to land, hesitating: seeing the lights had somehow given him confidence, and at the same time a sense of foolishness made him reluctant to give up so soon. He turned away, altering his compass to south-east.

Soon the first darkness of night was creeping over the horizon, slurring lines and shapes, but he reckoned there was light enough to see for another half-hour yet. He found himself flying parallel to a railway; it was hard to read the map in this half light, so he stuck it in a pocket. The railway lines seemed to go on maddeningly straight for ever, disappearing into the darkness, and gradually he surrendered to the hopeless feeling of being lost and wanting only to land, but it seemed too late now to try finding a way back to the field with lights. The country was changing; it became more wooded and small hills rose all round him. Long white fingers of mist were reaching out from the valleys; the land darkened with new shadows; the evening seemed to menace him with its beautiful tranquillity. He wiped the windscreen with his fingers and peered ahead. Suddenly he was flying in the middle of the white mist. It had taken him unawares, wrapping itself treacherously round him in chill moist folds. He felt an icy fear seize him that he was flying into the hills; for a moment it paralysed his body. The instruments showed uncertain flickering needles; helplessly he watched the air-speed rising as the nose went down, then he opened the throttle and pulled back on the stick with the tenseness of the inexperienced pilot. The needles seemed to settle down and he climbed up, not caring in which direction. He only wanted to get higher, higher . . .

When at last he came out of the mist the altimeter was reading two thousand feet and he was flying over an unbroken sea of silken white; waves of gloom lay in its hollows. It was mysterious and very beautiful. The pupil shivered a little; he tried to wind his scarf tighter round his neck, but his fingers were numb with cold and fear. Flying was difficult because it was so hard to distinguish the instruments and he could only guess the position of the horizon. An ugly mask of fog sprawled across the sky and smothered the last flickering red of the sun; little grey wisps of it came to meet him. Looking over the side he could see flames tearing out of the exhaust, and it gave him the impression that he was burning a path into the night.

The pupil shouted down the speaking tube to an imaginary pilot in front. Then he put the end of his ear phones to his mouth and shouted down that, so that this time his voice struck back loud and harsh in his ears, and in the engulfing blackness it cheered him because it was so real. The plane slid now through empty tenebrous gaps of cloud and still he climbed up. The engine made a far-away sound which hummed itself in a comforting drone into his mind. His body relaxed and succumbed to a feeling of unutterable drowsiness. He imagined he was in a country train which crawled along a familiar line, very slowly, stopping at lots of small halts and stations; they were beginning to light the lamps at each station and guards shouted and swung lanterns in the mist; he watched the red sparks from the engine fly past the carriage window and vanish in the darkness; he was a small boy on his way back from school.

Again he shouted to hear his own voice. It was much colder and he reckoned he must be some six thousand feet up, but it was impossible to read the altimeter. He felt braver now because there was no longer any alternative: he could only climb on into the ever deepening chasm of cloud: he was alone, challenging the night. He had the feeling that he dreamed and yet was awake in his dream. . . .

Suddenly the night lay over and under the plane. It floated in a sparkling ocean of stars, free again in a land of frozen beauty. He switched off and turned off the petrol, but for ages the engine continued to fire and splutter. Then the movement of the propeller became slower and slower; it swung itself jerkily, painfully round until it stopped, hanging there like a dead thing, and there was no sound. Only the rushing, whistling air singing in the rigging wires. This was how he wanted it. This was how it should have been in his dream. The pupil unfastened the straps of the safety harness which secures the pilot in the cockpit. Then very slowly, very carefully, he rolled the plane over on to its back until he no longer felt anything firm or solid beneath him, and he was falling, falling, into an icy space, like a sleeper into the deepest of sleep.

LAURENCE BINYON

THE RUINS:

FIVE POEMS

I

Now is the time for the burning of the leaves.
They go to the fire; the nostril pricks with smoke
Slowly wandering into the weeping mist.
Brittle and blotched, ragged and rotten sheaves!
A flame seizes the smouldering ruin, and bites
On stubborn stalks that crackle as they resist.

The last hollyhock's fallen tower is dust:
All the spices of June are a bitter reek,
All the extravagant riches spent and mean.
All burns! the reddest rose is a ghost.
Sparks whirl up to expire in the mist, and wild
Fingers of fire are making corruption clean.

Now is the time for stripping the spirit bare,
Time for the burning of days ended and done,
Idle solace of things that have gone before.
Rootless hope and fruitless desire lie there:
Let them go to the fire with never a look behind.
The world that was ours is a world that is ours no more.

They will come again, the leaf and the flower, to arise
From squalor of rottenness into the old splendour,
And magical scents to a wondering memory bring,
The same glory, to shine upon different eyes.
Earth cares for her own ruins, naught for ours.
Nothing is certain, only the certain spring.

II

Never was anything so deserted
As this dim theatre,
Now that, in passive greyness, the remote
Morning is here,
Taming the ghostly sparkle of the half-lit
Pale chandelier.

Never was anything disenchanted
As this silence!—
Gleams of soiled gilding on curved balconies,
Empty! immense
Dead crimson curtain, tasselled with its old
And staled pretence!

Nothing is heard but a shuffling, a knocking
Of pail and mop:
Two women there, inconsequently chatting,
Straighten or stoop,
And the ancient dust into the shadowy air
Floats wandering up.

The living voices are gone, the voices
That laughed and cried.
It is as if the whole marvel of the world
Had blankly died,
Inert as a drowned body, abandoned
By the ebbing tide.

Beautiful as water, beautiful as fire,
The voices came;
They made the eyes to open and the ears to hear,
The hand to lie intently motionless,
The heart to flame.
The radiance of reality was there,
Splendour and shame.

Slowly an arm dropt, and an empire fell.
We saw, we knew.

A head was lifted, and a soul set free.
Abysses opened into heaven and hell.
We heard, we drew
Into our own veins courage of the truth
That searched us through.
But the voices are all departed,
The vision dull.
Daylight disconsolately enters
Only to annul.
The vast space is hollow and empty
As a skull.

III

Cold springs among black ruins! Who shall say
Whither or whence they stream?
If it could be that such translated light
As comes about a dreamer in his dream—
And he believes with a belief intense
What morning will deride—if such a light
Of neither night nor day
Nor moon nor sun
Shone here, it would accord with what it broods upon,—
Disjected fragments of magnificence!
A loneliness of light without a sound
It shattered on wreckt tower and purpled wall,
(Fire has been here!)
On arch and pillar and entablature
As if arrested in the act to fall.
Where a home was, is a mis-shapen mound
Beneath nude rafters. Still,
Fluent and fresh and pure,
At their own will
Amid this lunar desolation glide
Those living springs, with interrupted gleam,
As if nothing had died:
But who will drink of them?

Stooping and feeble, leaning on a stick,
An old man with his vague feet stirs the dust,
Searching a strange world for he knows not what
Among haphazard blocks and crumbled brick.
He cannot adjust
What his eyes see to memory's golden land,
Shut off by the iron curtain of Today:
The past is all the present he has got.
Now as he bends to peer
Into the rubble, he picks up in his hand
(Death has been here!)
Something, defaced, naked and bruised; a doll,
A child's doll, blankly smiling with wide eyes
And O how human in its helplessness!
Pondered in weak fingers,
He holds it, puzzled; wondering, where is she,
The small mother,
Whose pleasure was to clothe it and caress,
Who hugged it with a motherhood foreknown,
Who ran to comfort its imagined cries,
And gave it pretty sorrows for its own?
No one replies.

IV

Beautiful, wearied head,
Bent back against the up-thrown arm behind,
Why are your eyes closed? Is it that they fear
Sight of these vast horizons shuddering red
And coming near, and near?
Godlike shape, would you be blind
Rather than see the young leaves falling dead
On blasts of a foul wind
All round you, as if, O disinherited!
The world that you had willed
Since upon earth laughter and grief began
Should only in final mockery rebuild
A palace for the proudest ruin, Man?

Or are those eyes closed for the inward eye
To see, beyond the tortures of today
The hills of hope serene in liquid light
Of reappearing sky—
This black fume and miasma rolled away?
Yet O how far thought spurs the onward sight!
The unforeshortened vision opens vast,
Hill beyond hill, year upon year amassed,
Age beyond age, and still the hills ascend,
Height over farthest height,
Though each has seemed (but only seemed) the last,
And still appears no end,
No end, but all an upward path to climb,
To conquer, at what cost!
Labouring on, to be lost
On the mountains of Time.

What are they burning, what are they burning,
Heaping and burning in the thunder-gloom?
Rubbish of the old world, dead things, merely names,
Truth, justice, love, beauty, the human smile,—
All flung to the flames!
They are raging to destroy, but first defile,
Maddened because no furnace will consume
What lives, still lives, impassioned to create.
Ah, your eyes open; open and dilate.
Transfigured, you behold
The Python that had coiled about your feet,
Muscle on muscle, in slow malignant fold,
Tower now and tauten, impending opposite—
A fury of greed, an ecstasy of hate
Concentrated in the small and angry eye.
Your hand leaps out in the action to defy,
And grips the unclean throat, to strangle it.

V

From shadow to shadow the waters are gliding, are gone.
They mirror the ruins a moment, the wounds and the void;
But theirs is the sweetness of silence in places apart;
They retain not a stain, in a moment they shine as they shone,
They stay not for bound or for bar; they have found out a way
Far from the gnawing of greed, from the envious heart.

The freshness of leaves is from them, and the springing of grass.
The juice of the apple, the rustle of ripening corn.
They know not the lust of destruction, the frenzies of spite.
They give and pervade, nor possess, but silently pass.
They perish not, though they be broken; continuing streams,
The same in the cloud and the glory, the night and the light.

KATHLEEN RAINE

NEW YEAR 1943

Stairways into space, and windows into sky,
And the tear-wet streets, with cloud-torn moonlight shining,
Ways underground are open, and the trains are running
Oh to what end, in this dream-entangled city?

The streets were full tonight
With the dense human darkness—noisier
With the talking of feet, and laughter,
Night-cries of 'Taxi', and the flagging light

Of men and women walking in their thought
Like ghosts in overcoats and uniforms,
Their bodies, grown invisible, scarcely felt,
Alone, or mated, in the London night.

You meet them everywhere—their touching hands,
Fingers made intricate with bones and nerves,
Playing like birds; or hanging still in sleep
Though eyes are open, while men's thoughts run deep.

Oh where, into the night, into the underground
Into the sky, into dark seas, do they go,
The young boys who flash torches in the dark
For their sweethearts in mimic dress, the counterpart
Of war, the service-girl, the glamour-girl, the tart?

Girls' hair, like florists' flower, and coloured lips and eyes
In farewell greet the RAF's young heroes,
Gauche in the close-up of love, and close-up death—
Never in meagre childhood taught how to die, and kiss.

They stray, enchanted, in this crumbling city,
Where the safe homes of childhood house the winds,
Through whose uncertain present lies our way
To love, to death, our certainty, our strangeness.

CECIL BEATON

FROM 'LIBYAN DIARY'

I

ONCE you have shown your passes, and are admitted into the fraternity inside the barriers of the desert—yes there is a barbed wire entrance to the desert—you will find a spirit comparable to that on a great ship many miles out at sea. Everyone isolated here is working together selflessly towards the same goal, each person is making his particular piece of effort towards the common cause, with no thought as to promotion or award. The result is most stimulating. In fact, in spite of everything, there is much to feel glad about in the desert.

To whichever service or allied nation he belongs, the stranger will find a welcome that is unimaginable elsewhere. He will be received, without question, not only as an honoured guest, but as a long-lost friend. Everyone is a potential host; everyone seems jovial.

A new code of manners springs up: friendliness reaches such heights that unwritten laws have to be made so that the hospitality that is readily offered must, on occasions, be tactfully refused. No matter to what strain the cook-house has already been put by the difficulties of communications, invitations to share what rations remain will always be pressed, even if an acceptance means your host 'tightening his belt' or 'going dry'. Drivers on the desert road are so generous that hitch-hiking is one of the surest means of transport.

Certain conventions prevail. Not only for hygienic reasons must you bury the débris of your picnic meal, but the regulation reads: 'You must leave the desert as you would hope to find it'.

The soldiers enjoy making their criticisms: they resent the poverty of the B.B.C. programmes in comparison to the richness of the German light music; they grumble about the irregularity of the mails, the shortage of reading matter, and the lack of news in the local papers that trickles through from Cairo. Yet, though it could be said that in all the world there can be no more wasteful, heartless and purposeless theatre of war, a more unsuitable habitation for human beings, still the desert possesses its advantages. There can be no more healthy battle ground. Most men are physically fitter than ever before. Life here is primeval. It is simple with the simplicity of the animals: yet it seems that from this simplicity springs a new contentment. In the desert the men are contented, they become 'sand happy'.

In the desert the mess secretaries, like housewives out on shopping expeditions, are always on the look-out for the means of 'coming by' fresh additions to their stores. They will swap sugar and tea for small eggs from the Senussi tribes. Some of them are conscientious enough to keep a dozen hens, and to travel with them in the back of their trucks when they move their camping sites. Although under battle conditions the hens may not produce enough eggs for breakfast, they supply the wherewithal for an occasional omelette. When on leave, the men spend much time buying up innovations that, when brought to the front lines, become almost literally worth their weight in gold. The trouble spent in these small ways repays every effort, for it is by such trifles that an extra fillip can be given to morale.

Some of the dining-tables in the mess tent are adorned with wild flowers picked from the desert scrub. A certain rivalry stimulates the various messes. I heard one squadron leader, in charge of the camp's messing, after seeing the glass display at the mess at which he had just lunched, telephone back two hundred miles to his orderly telling him that last night's Chianti bottle must be saved and used in future on the table as a water jug.

In the desert one becomes so hungry that each meal is devoured voraciously. Perhaps it is the salt in the air that creates in most men in the desert a craving for sweets and chocolates. Like schoolchildren, soldiers beg their friends to bring them back some toffee from leave. Most Generals manage to preserve a bottle of lollipops on the desk in their caravan.

Life is sometimes baffling for the new arrival in the desert. A great importance is given to numbers that have no apparent significance. There is no explanation as to why 000 Squadron, a few miles away, is at Landing-Ground 42, but, eventually, these figures may acquire a familiar ring in the ear.

Notices put up warning you against particular forms of violent death are sometimes just as casual as if the park authorities had erected a one-foot railing for you to 'keep off the grass'. A cryptic notice reads: 'Mines, keep out'. What particular form of horrors the skull and cross-bones signify I do not know, but, bewildered by these signs, when I saw 'Kill that fly!' posted up, I asked what it meant. 'Kill that fly!' was the reply.

The poverty of the desert has its paradoxes. Whisky is perhaps less rare than ginger beer or soda water; petrol is less scarce than water. Our soldiers have surprised German prisoners by the extravagance of washing out their shirts in petrol. Often a man prefers his water ration to be used for tea than for cooking.

Here, men, who have given up their worldly possessions, live with little other impedimenta than a razor, sleeping-bag, roll of lavatory paper and a packet of cigarettes. Perhaps it may be comforting to know that, thus far, the life of a soldier in this desert has been preferable to the life in the trenches of 1916.

It is reassuring to learn that it is possible, when life has been reduced to its essentials, to find that there is, after all, more in it.

Although fully conscious that it is a literary crime to publish a diary, I shall now make considerable use of the notes I wrote in the desert.

Monday, 27 April. Travelled to the 'Canal zones'. After four weeks from home, I am at last in the desert, my destination from the first. The landscape is eventless and ugly: unvarying scrub-sand-dunes, mottled with rubble, hummocks of biscuit colour, square miles of desolation.

The course of the road is marked by old tar barrels. When the track itself is buried (as it often is) after a sandstorm, the barrels stand out, clear and immobile, to guide the lorries on their way to Suez.

Wednesday. Went to visit Randolph Churchill, who has rejoined the Commandos, who are doing a preliminary training before the real course starts in three weeks' time. We watched some of the men falling from heights of eighteen feet in various ways: on one foot, on both feet, sideways, backwards: they jumped through a hole in a high rostrum in quick succession, just as if in a troop-carrying aircraft they were given the word to take to the sky. From a complicated structure of iron girders, on trapeze ropes they swung high in the air, while unfastening their parachute harness in a given number of seconds before somersaulting on to the mattress below that represents the sea. They are made to jump from a truck travelling at a speed of thirty-five miles an hour. 'The faster it goes the less you are likely to damage yourself,' I was told. The men are considered 'cissies' if they get hurt by doing things the wrong way—the training is pretty tough.

On the way to an air station, where they have the Liberators, we passed many large Prisoners of War camps, guarded by sentries perched high on lookout platforms. But these prisoners are mostly Italians and without urge to escape. Their fate is to be kept penned up in this waste-land behind barbed wire, with little to pass away the days but the interest of three meals a day and a turn at the washing tap.

Another R.A.F. Mess: I talked to several of the men here. They each have interesting stories to tell, if you can get them into the right mood and give them a feeling of friendliness. They enjoy an opportunity to talk to a newcomer. One of them confided: 'It's pretty foul, sometimes, when a bloke you have been with a lot doesn't come back. There was a chap named Jock that everyone liked especially. The day he "had it" the Commanding Officer was absolutely white in the face: "Jock didn't get back," was all he said, and he went off by himself. We felt particularly badly about it as Jock would have got a Bar to his D.F.C. if he'd lived. And there was a fellow named Mac, a swell guy. I had a bad time of it when Mac "had it". He was a grand little chap, only about five feet tall but as brave as a lion—absolutely first class he was. I was the Flight Commander at the time, and we'd had a series of big "do's" over Benghazi. Mac had been out on the previous show, a terrific one, but he begged me to let him go again this time. He was a wizard pilot, had just been made a Pilot Officer, and his enthusiasm was terrific. Well, I let him go. That night the ack-ack was brutal. Buckets of it everywhere. The aircraft were lurching about in a regular fifth of November firework display. It's not funny having to "deliver the groceries" in those circumstances. With shells bursting near the side of the plane, any moment, I thought I would have "had it". Suddenly I saw someone alongside me "had it". There was a terrific explosion which knocked me end over tip and then I saw that one of our bombers had been hit. It looked like a blazing waterfall, bits falling everywhere. It was terrific. When we got back I found out it was Mac who had got that shell. I've never felt so badly about anything before. But the funny thing about it was that some months later we were in the mess, when there, at the other end of the tent, in a Captain's uniform, was the very living image of Mac—I could hardly believe my eyes. I really thought I was seeing things. It made me feel quite ropy. The C.O. came over quietly and said he wanted me to talk to this chap. He was the exact replica of Mac, only wearing glasses and a bit greyer, perhaps even thinner and smaller. We had a drink together, he said he was a Captain in the last war, and talked about nothing in particular, when suddenly he asked if we couldn't go somewhere where it was quiet and he could talk to me alone. "Mac often mentioned you in his letters: Mac was my only son," he said, "Mac was all I cared about in the world, all I had to live for, in fact. My wife had died, my daughter was killed in the bombing at Birmingham and, as you know, Mac has gone. Now I want you to tell me exactly how he met his death. I don't want to be spared anything. I don't want you to think of my feelings, but I'm haunted by the idea of not knowing what happened to him. You must tell me everything."

'"But, Sir, I can't do that, we never do."

'"But I insist, I want you to tell me exactly what happened, I must know."

'"But, Sir, in the Service that's one thing we never talk about, it's just one of those unwritten rules that aren't broken."

'"I insist!" the little man said emphatically, beating his fist on his knee. "I told the Commanding Officer that was my intention in wanting to speak to you."

'Well, you can imagine how embarrassed I felt. I called for a double whisky each, and then another and yet another. After a time we were both well "under way", but I could "take" it better than he could and I gave him more than I took. I started to tell him some stories and he told me some. We roared with laughter, and we had quite a jolly evening until eventually he passed out completely. Two of our fellows had to carry him off and we gave him a bed for the night.

'Poor little chap, it was not at all a "good show" really, and I felt rather badly about what I had done. But what else could I do? I mean it wasn't any good getting morbid, he would only have cried or done something stupid like that.'

We listen to the German radio for the quality of their music, which, relayed by the hour, is so much better than ours. We all listen to 'Lili Marleen', a tango sung by a woman named Anderson with a seductive voice. This tune has become to Germany what 'Tipperary' was to us in the last war. The story of its success is surprising. When the Germans first took control of the radio in Belgrade they had a spare fifteen minutes to fill up their programme —what to do? A soldier, near by, said, 'How about playing this, it's my favourite gramophone record. It's old and rather scratched but it's good.' It was the record of 'Lili Marleen' that had been made by Anderson in Berlin several years ago. It had not been a success. Anderson became impecunious. But that night when the record was played in Belgrade again many thousands wrote in to ask who was the singer, what was the song?—a big success. Each time the record was played its reception was more rapturous. Now, whenever the song is sung in Germany, in night clubs, in restaurants, the whole assembly stands and joins in singing. Anderson has been brought from obscurity to remake the record, has become a national heroine, and spends all her time singing this song. Three times a night it is released over the air to the troops. It is because we are unable to produce any song to compare with it, that night after night, our men in the desert listen to 'Lili Marleen'. I lay pondering on the incongruities of war, and it struck me as ironical that at the same time hearing the reverberation of the bombs at Mersa Matruh, I, in common with so many of our troops, should be listening to the musical programmes of the enemy radio.

JOSEPH KESSEL

PHILIPPE GERBIER'S NOTEBOOK

FRANCE is a prison. One feels threats, misery, anguish, misfortune there like a heavy ceiling which every day is lowered closer to our heads. France is a prison, but illegality provides an extraordinary means of escape. Papers? we get them made. Ration-cards? we steal them from the Mayor. Cars and petrol? we take them from the Germans. Obstructionists? they are suppressed. Laws and rules exist no longer. Illegality is a shadow which glides through their network.

Nothing is too difficult because we have begun by what is most difficult of all, the neglect of our essential instinct of self-preservation.

* * *

Travel Scene.

My train stops at Toulouse station longer than it should. Gestapo men go through our identity cards. They are in my coach. They enter my third-class compartment. Nothing happens. Their footsteps recede. But another policeman comes along and makes a sign to one of the travellers to follow him. The traveller turns his back on the German, stoops as if to pick up the newspaper he has dropped. And we all see him take a revolver from under his armpit, take off the safety catch, and put it back in his coat pocket. All that quite naturally and very fast, with absolute calm. The traveller takes his suitcase and goes out. The train remains at a standstill. In our compartment we all sit in silence. The train moves off. The traveller reappears. 'They have made a mistake,' he says as he takes his place. He cuts a cigarette in two and smokes half of it. Conversation is resumed in the carriage.

In the corridor of a third-class carriage where everyone is wedged up against each other, a young girl keeps casting a quick glance at a fairly large parcel, wrapped up in cheap paper and lying a few yards from her. The travellers shuffle their feet, they come and go and jostle it as they get in and out at stations. The parcel tears and bursts open. The young girl moves away. The contents burst out. Piles of clandestine newspapers. Passengers pick them up. The girl has disappeared. Result of the shortage of suitcases, of brown paper and good string.

A resistance-group, as night was falling, removed many of the sewer gratings in Marseilles. The Germans and their friends alone have the right to go out after curfew. There is no one to regret among those who have broken bones at the bottom of the sewers.

The Gestapo, and the French police under them, put at every big railway station men gifted with a special visual memory, who have carefully studied the photographs of the patriots they are looking for. They are 'physiognomists' like the employees in the gambling rooms of the big casinos, who had to remember all the players.

The Gestapo likes to employ elderly men, with a debonair appearance and a ribbon in their buttonhole, for shadowing. People are less suspicious of these greying gentlemen. When one is shadowed by them the danger is not yet really close. They place you, localize you and pass on the information. But if afterwards you see younger and stronger men in your wake, expect the worst.

* * *

Felix, Lemasque and Jean François are working all out to organize some mountain shelters where those who won't be deported are in hiding.

Visited Lemasque's sector.

I am not emotional, but I do not think I shall ever forget what I have seen. Hundreds and hundreds of young people returning to savagery. They can't wash. They can't shave. Their long hair hangs over cheeks burnt by the sun and the rain. They sleep in holes, in caves, in the mud. Their food is a terrible daily problem. The peasants do what they can, but that can't last indefinitely. Their clothes fall off in tatters, their shoes are torn to shreds. I've seen boys wearing old bits of tyre for shoes, or even bits of bark tied round their feet with laces. I've seen others whose only costume was an old potato sack split in two and tied round the loins like a negro's pants. One can't tell any longer where these boys come from. Are they peasants, workmen, employees, students? They all wear the same hunger, the same misery, the same anger and the same bitterness on their faces. The ones I visited were well disciplined under Lemasque and his helpers. We get them as much food and as much money as we can. But there are thousands of fugitives in the various maquis. No secret organization can look after even their most primitive needs. Either they must die of hunger then, or take to looting, or give themselves up. And winter hasn't come yet. Cursed be those who put such a choice before our young men.

* * *

Lemasque has improved wonderfully. The affairs he was in charge of while I was in London and his present job have taught him decision and authority. His nerves are under control. His spirit is disciplined, but shines out with a slow fire. He has a powerful action on the feelings of those who live by instinct such as he commands.

I had no time to see the territories of Jean François and Felix. I have to make an urgent report to London on this inspection by the next mail.

* * *

Felix has sent me a liaison agent with a whole list of things needed in his maquis. At the bottom of the list the following note:

'Vichy has sent a company of *gardes mobiles* to the region to track us down. I have got into touch with the captain. We have talked and we understand one another. He said to me, "Don't be afraid, I was an officer of the Republican Guard. I took my oath to defend the Republic. Today the Republic is in the maquis. I shall defend it there."'

* * *

Mathilde has made a discovery which confirms some information about which we weren't quite sure.

The dressmaker where Mathilde has taken an attic has a son of about twelve. Like all town children of our time he has a grey skin, flabby muscles and a famished look in his eyes. He is very gentle and has great delicacy of feeling. Mathilde is very fond of him. This little boy works as a page at the Hotel T. The job is a good one, not so much for his salary as for the scraps from the restaurant that he is sometimes given. Mathilde was asked to share one of these feasts. She said nothing was more pathetic than to see the little boy pretending that he wasn't hungry so as to give more to his mother, and the mother enacting the same comedy, when neither could take their eyes off the food.

Well, lately the child has been sleeping terribly. He moans, cries, screams in his sleep, and seems to suffocate. The shivering fits which seize him are almost convulsions. He seems delirious and calls out 'Stop hurting. Don't kill her. I implore you not to cry like that.'

In desperation his mother has consulted Mathilde, whom she still takes for a nurse. Mathilde spent part of the night listening to the little boy's nightmares. Then she woke him up gently. A woman who has had as many children as Mathilde, and loved them so much, knows how to speak to boys. The dressmaker's son has told her everything. For about a week he has been put under the orders of the guests who occupy the third floor of the hotel. He has to wait on the landing and answer the bell. The whole floor, he says, is occupied by ladies and gentlemen who speak French well but are all Germans. They entertain a great deal. There are men and women who always come between two German soldiers. And these French people's eyes always look unnatural, as if they are afraid and do not wish to show it. And they are always taken to the same room,

No. 87. Almost always cries, and peculiar noises and moans are heard. The noises stop and then go on again. And again. 'Till it makes you ill, I assure you, Madam,' said the child to Mathilde. 'The screams of the women they are hurting, they are worse than anything. And if you could see in what a state they leave. Often they are taken into another room and then they bring them back. And it begins again. I didn't want to speak to anyone about it because I was afraid to think about it.'

That was how we discovered the whereabouts of the Torture Chamber for this town.

* * *

Next day Mathilde asked me what advice I would have given the dressmaker about her son.

'But to take him away from the hotel at once,' I said. 'Well, I persuaded her to let him stay on,' said Mathilde. 'It is so valuable to have a spy in such a place. Above all an innocent one.' Her mouth narrowed, and she looked at me inquiringly with a very sad expression. I had to force myself to tell her she was right.

* * *

A SEVERE BLOW FOR OUR NEWSPAPER

It was set up at several different printers, a portion in each. Thus the typesetters who worked for us could do it quickly and weren't noticed. Then the leads were carried the same day to a letter-box among ten others, arranged along a corridor. The comrade who had the house and used the letter-box took out the leads and brought them to another printer's where the newspaper was printed. Yesterday the bottom of the letter-box, too old doubtless, fell out, and the leads tumbled out in the corridor. A fool of a tenant who was passing thought that they were explosives (nearly every day there is a bomb outrage in the town). The tenant warned the police. Our friend is already in his cell. The Gestapo have asked for him.

I think he will resist in room 87. But at all costs we must change all our printers. At present, with the German tortures, our rule is absolutely strict. As soon as a comrade who knows anything is arrested we assume *a priori* that everything which he knows the Gestapo knows too. I have changed my name and address.

* * *

The captain of the Gardes Mobiles has kept the promise he made Felix. He hasn't found a single deserter from deportation in the Maquis. Every day he does a round of the woods and the valleys, but is careful to send ahead a motor cyclist scout who makes an infernal din. In this way everyone is warned. But the Captain has just let Felix know that two officers of the S.S. have arrived to direct and superintend the manhunt.

* * *

A brothel-owner said to one of his friends who has a bar, 'My house has been taken over by the Boches. It's never worked so hard. But I didn't want this money, it burns my fingers. I would like to use it against the Boches.' The bar-keeper spoke of this wish to the Bison. He confided it to Mathilde. She saw the brothel-owner. 'How shall I know that it is really being used against the Boches?' he asked her. 'We will put out an agreed phrase on the wireless,' she answered. We sent the phrase on. It was repeated on the wireless. We have received 500,000 francs. What's more, the brothel-keeper has put a wonderful estate at our disposal. An old general who has helped us a lot through his connections with the army and whom the police are looking for has taken refuge there already.

* * *

AN ADVENTURE OF FELIX

The Captain of the Gardes Mobiles has warned him that the two S.S. officers have begun to suspect his manœuvre, and that he couldn't resist their pressure much longer. Felix set himself to study the habits and country of the two Germans. The company of Gardes Mobiles is billeted in a big village. The two Germans have taken a chalet on the mountain side. Getting up very early they always go to breakfast in a little inn between their chalet and the village. The path to the inn is between high banks and makes a sharp bend at one place. It was a perfect site for an ambush.

Felix has a tommy-gun in his armoury. He could finish the Germans off alone. But in the village there are two stout fellows who say everywhere that they are ready for anything against the Germans. One is a postman, the other the harness-maker. Felix decides that this is their testing-time. If they are just boasters, it's better to be warned. If they are really capable of action they must be roped in. Felix suggests the job to the postman and the harness-maker. They accept.

At dawn the three men were at the bend in the path. Felix has his tommy-gun, the postman and the harness-maker their revolvers. The sun is beginning to rise. The Germans draw near. They hear them talking in their language and laughing loudly. They have no anxiety. They are the masters in a conquered country. Felix appears and turns the tommy-gun on them. The two officers look for a second at this short bearded man with his round red face. They hold their hands up.

'They understood at once,' said Felix. 'Their faces didn't even move.' Felix had only to press the trigger to finish them. But he wanted the postman and the harness-maker to pass their test. He ordered each of them to kill a man. They came up and fired several shots, closing their eyes a little, it appears. Without dropping their eyes the Germans fell with great simplicity. Their grave was prepared in advance. Felix and his accomplices threw the bodies in and arranged squares of earth covered with grass over them. Except for these three men no one would ever be able to find the graves of these two officers of the S.S.

'It was a nice bit of work,' said Felix, 'but to speak frankly my heart wasn't quite in it. These swine had really got some courage. And that look when they understood me nearly turned my stomach. We hid our arms and those of the S.S. and went to have a coffee in the bistro where the Boches were going. I wondered how my postman and harness-maker would react, because I still feel sick myself, though I've seen some bad businesses. Well, as for them, they took their coffee quietly and began to snore on the banquette. In the afternoon the postman took his letters and the other sold his rubbish as if nothing had happened.' Felix scratched his head and added, 'The French certainly have changed'.

* * *

The boss will be delighted by the postman and the harness-maker. This man with exceptional culture and intelligence only likes stories of children and simple people.

* * *

I am lodging with a young couple of very modest means. He is a clerk in a silk merchant's and spends his nights travelling as our liaison officer. His wife waits in queues, does the cooking, looks after the house, and acts as my secretary, which forces her to pass chaste nights. She has frequent fainting fits. I mention them to the husband. He finds that quite natural. All the same he loves his wife. But our business comes first.

*   *   *

I think that among those in the underground movement something is evolving in inverse ratio to their temperaments. Those who were soft, sensitive and peace-loving are getting tough. Those who were as hard as I was, as I am still, become more open to sentiment. The reason? Perhaps people who see life under smiling colours defend themselves through a kind of inner armour from the contact of the often terrible realities which the Resistance brings into the open. And perhaps people like myself, who take a fairly pessimistic view of mankind, realize from the Resistance that men are worth more than we give them credit for.

There's only the boss who remains always equal to himself. I think he must long ago have assessed the possibilities of good and evil which each human being possesses without knowing.

*   *   *

A long talk with Louis H., chief of a group with which we often co-operate. We discussed first of all a very urgent question. Louis H. has three men in a concentration camp to whom he is particularly attached. The Gestapo has claimed these three men. They are going to be handed over to it by train in four days. Louis H.'s organization has been terribly tried in the last month, and he has not got enough men to rescue his comrades. He has come to ask me if we would undertake the operation. I shall give the necessary orders.

Then, without wishing it, and as old schoolmates, regimental or war comrades do, we let ourselves drift into reminiscences. Both of us are among the veterans of Resistance. We have seen a lot of water and blood flow under the bridges. Louis H. worked out that of four hundred who formed his group at the beginning only five were left now with their life and liberty. If we have a greater proportion of survivors (a matter of luck, perhaps of organization) the work is all the same, tremendous. And the Gestapo strikes without stopping, always harder and closer. But the enemy cannot succeed in suppressing the Resistance. It's over, it's too late. We decided with

Louis H. that a year ago the Germans could, if they had shot or arrested a thousand picked men, have beheaded all our groups and disorganized the Resistance for a long time, perhaps till the war was over. Today that's impossible. There are too many resisters, and substitute resisters, helpers and accomplices. If all the men were deported the women would remain. And there are some surprising ones. Resistance has taken the shape of the Hydra. Cut off one head and ten grow again.

* * *

Louis H. having left, I had a fit of depression. It's not good to count the missing. And then I haven't been sleeping all these days. I think of the Mont Valérien, where not a day passes without executions, of that park of Chaville where every day a lorry brings the condemned before an execution squad, of the rifle-range of Z., where not a day goes by without our comrades being machine-gunned.

I have thought about the cells of Fresne, the cellars of Vichy, about room 87 in the hotel T. where every day, every night, they burn women's breasts and break their toes, and stick pins under their nails, and send electric currents through the sexual organs. I have thought of the prisons and the concentration camps where people die of hunger, of consumption, of cold, of vermin. I have thought of the team of our underground newspaper, completely renewed three times over, of the sectors where not a man, not a woman remains of those who saw the work begin.

And I asked myself as a practical thinker, as an engineer who designs a blue-print, do the results we obtain justify these massacres? Is our newspaper worth the death of its editors, its printers, its distributors? Are our little sabotages, our individual assassinations, our modest little secret army which will perhaps never go into action, are they worth our terrible losses? Are leaders like us who enflame and train and sacrifice so many stout fellows and brave men, so many simpletons, impatient people roused up for a suffocating struggle, for a war in secret, of famine and torture—are such leaders, in short, really necessary for victory?

As a practical thinker, as an honest mathematician, I have to admit that I have no idea. And even that I don't believe we are. In numbers, for all useful purposes, we work at a loss. Then I have thought, that we should in all honesty give it up. But the moment the thought of giving up has come to me I have known it was impossible. Impossible to leave to others the whole weight and care of protecting us, of rescuing us. Impossible to leave the Germans with the memory of a country without a come-back, without dignity, without hatred. I have felt that an enemy killed by us who have neither uniform nor flag nor land, that such an enemy was heavier and more efficacious in the scales which weigh a country's destiny than a whole holocaust on the field of battle. I know that we have waged the French people's most glorious war. A war of little material use, since victory is already assured us, even without our help. A war which no one compels us to wage, a war with no glory, a war of executions and assassinations, in fact, a free war. But this war is an act of love and an act of hate. In short an act of living.

'For a people to be so generous with its blood,' said the boss one day, with his quiet smile, 'that proves at least that its corpuscles are red.'

A Communist girl said to me: 'My girl friend, a little woman of no importance, was so tortured at the Santé that ever since she has escaped she has always carried poison with her. You understand, she couldn't go through that again. She would rather die. So she asked the Party for poison in case she should be taken prisoner again. Because to give up working against the Boche, you understand, is out of the question. One might as well die right away.'

* * *

I have a new name and once more I have shaved off my moustache. My hair is very long and I wear an old cape. I am bookkeeper with an industrialist who employs about a hundred workers. I sleep at the factory. The most regular identity card is not good enough any more for the police. During my retreat, the control machine, the machine to choke us, has been terribly tightened up. On account of the deportations and the deserters they demand a worker's card, a censor's certificate and a certificate of domicile. The round-ups and the dragnets go on without stopping. Trams and restaurants, cafés and cinemas, are all searched. Apartment by apartment, whole quarters are purged. It is impossible to travel a hundred kilometres in a train without being questioned by policemen. The whole business becomes impossibly difficult and the women are going to have more and more work to do.

* * *

Took a studio for our contacts. In this house I pass for a painter who likes to paint when he chooses and to entertain his friends. This morning I had a rendezvous at the studio with Jean François, Lemasque and Felix. It was months since I had seen them and we had a lot of things to arrange for their maquis. When I came up to the house the *concierge* was on the door-step gently beating an old carpet. Seeing me across the street she suddenly began to beat it with a kind of frenzy. This *concierge* has never been one of us and knows nothing of my activities. All the same, I did not go in.

* * *

This woman has deliberately saved my life. An extremely simple chain of circumstances has led to a catastrophe. In leaving his region Jean François delegated his command to an ex-officer who has plenty of authority but too much optimism and no sense of conspiracy. It was necessary for him to send a message to Jean François and to provide a liaison agent. He chose a young boy without any experience and, instead of sending him to a relay, he gave him the street address and the number of the studio. The lad, while waiting between changing trains, went to sleep. He was woken up by a comb-out. They found my address on him and he was not able to invent a plausible explanation. A trap was laid and Lemasque, Felix and Jean François were caught. It was then that the *concierge* thought of her alarm signal.

* * *

News of Jean François. The police questioned him in the studio, having before him all the papers found on Jean François, Lemasque and Felix. Jean François answered somehow or other. Suddenly he bit the commissioner in the hand and so violently that he took a piece of his palm off. He took up the papers, piled the two inspectors on top of each other and went down the staircase like a hurricane. He got the reports safely to me and has gone back to the maquis with my instructions.

* * *

News of Felix. On a scrap of India paper Felix had the address of a safety apartment taken in the name of a young girl and where I went from time to time in the guise of her protector. This address Felix had rewritten according to a code of his. When questioned, he managed to interpret the signs as a rendezvous taken on a certain day and a certain hour in a public square with an important leader of the Resistance. He confessed this with the hesitations, the reticencies and the evasions which were necessary for him to be believed, and in the same way he agreed to lead two policeman to this false rendezvous. He arrived in the middle of the square, going a few steps in front of the policemen. A tram passed. Felix jumped in, ran across and out the other side and disappeared among the passers-by. Then he wished to warn me and came back to the safety address. But in the meantime the young girl who had rented it had come to my studio, where the police had made her talk. Felix was recaptured. He was imprisoned like Lemasque at Vichy in the cellars of the Hotel Bellevue, which had been requisitioned by the Gestapo.

I saw in the factory a little workman who had passed eight months without any cause in the German quarter of the prison of Fresne. He has two ribs broken and he limps for life. What is most insupportable according to him is the heavy smell of pus which has spurted out over the walls of the cells. 'The smell of my mates who have been tortured,' he said. I think of Lemasque. I think of my old friend Felix.

* * *

News of Lemasque. He was shut up in the same cellar as Felix with handcuffs and irons on his feet. Felix was considered the most dangerous, they had it in for him for having fooled the Gestapo. They questioned him on the first day. He never came back from his interrogation, but that night, by the light of the bulbs in the ceiling, Lemasque saw the corpse of Felix being dragged down the corridor by a rope tied round the neck. Felix's body had no eyes left and no lower jaw. Lemasque felt so much fear at undergoing the same torture that quite suddenly he *knew* that he would escape. He succeeded (he will never be able to say how) in undoing the padlock which fastened the irons to his ankles. With his handcuffed arms he loosened the badly-fixed bars of the air-shaft of the cellar and, feet first, he wriggled out. There he was in the streets of Vichy with handcuffs still on his hands. The only person he knew in Vichy was an employee of the Ministry who lived in a commandeered hotel. Lemasque went to see him once to obtain a false safe-conduct. In the streets, overrun by patrols of *gardes mobiles* and the Gestapo on their beat, Lemasque, in his handcuffs, started off to look for the hotel. It was necessary that he should find it before the dawn or he would be lost. The hours go by. Lemasque wanders round Vichy. At last he thinks he has found the place. He gets into the sleeping hotel. One last effort, a desperate effort of memory, to recall the floor and the exact position of the room. At last Lemasque thinks he has remembered it. He knocks at the door, which is opened. It is indeed the comrade who is on our side. That evening a friendly workman came with a saw for metals and freed Lemasque from his handcuffs. I have had the story confirmed by the employee at the Ministry and by the workman. Without that I would always have wondered if Lemasque had not weakened and that his escape had been made easy by the Gestapo.

* * *

The Resistance Movement commits sabotage, it attacks and kills with abundance and with obstinacy and now with spontaneity. All the organizations have their combat groups. The *franc-tireurs* (mostly Communists) make up quite an army. The density of German corpses has become such that the enemy has had to give up the hostage system. They cannot any longer line up one hundred dead Frenchmen for one dead German, unless they were prepared to assassinate the whole of France. The enemy has thus almost publicly recognized that the country is above torture. But the Gestapo goes on with its terrible work. It aims at replacing all the hostages by better chosen suspects.

[*Translated by* C. C.]

PAUL ELUARD

THREE POEMS

SUR LES PENTES INFÉRIEURES

Aussi bas que le silence
D'un mort planté dans la terre
Rien que ténèbres en tête

Aussi monotone et sourd
Que l'automne dans la mare
Couverte de honte mate

Le poison veuf de sa fleur
Et de ses bêtes dorées
Crache sa nuit sur les hommes.

DOUTER DU CRIME

Une seule corde une seule torche un seul homme
Etrangla dix hommes
Brûla un village
Avilit un peuple

La douce chatte installée dans la vie
Comme une perle dans sa coquille
La douce chatte a mangé ses petits.

COUVRE-FEU

Que voulez-vous la porte était gardée
Que voulez-vous nous étions enfermés
Que voulez-vous la rue était barrée
Que voulez-vous la ville était matée
Que voulez-vous elle était affamée
Que voulez-vous nous étions désarmés
Que voulez-vous la nuit était tombée
Que voulez-vous nous nous sommes aimés.

ARTHUR KOESTLER

LETTER

Dear Sir,

In your letter of . . . October you asked me the idiotic question whether the events described in 'The Mixed Transport'—viz., the massacre of Jews—are 'based on fact' or 'artistic fiction'.

Had I published a chapter on Proust and mentioned his homosexuality, you would never have dared to ask whether my information was based on fact, because you consider it your duty 'to know'; in spite of the fact that the evidence of this particular knowledge is much less accessible than that of the massacre of three million humans. You would blush if you were found out not to have heard the name of any second-rate contemporary writer, painter or composer; you would blush if found out to have ascribed a play by Sophocles to Euripides; but you don't blush and you have the brazenness to ask whether it is true that you are the contemporary of the greatest massacre in recorded history.

If you tell me that you don't read newspapers, white-books, documentary pamphlets obtainable at W. H. Smith bookstalls—why on earth do you read HORIZON and call yourself a member of the intelligentsia? I can't even say that I am sorry to be rude. There is no excuse for you—for it is your duty to know and to be haunted by your knowledge. As long as you don't feel, against reason and independently of reason, ashamed to be alive while others are put to death and guilty, sick, humiliated, because you were spared, you will remain what you are: an accomplice by omission.

Yours truly,

ARTHUR KOESTLER

1944

ROBIN CAMPBELL

PRISONER OF WAR

ONE OF the odd things about being taken prisoner of war is that nobody to whom it happens ever seems to have imagined the possibility. When I was wounded in a raid behind the enemy lines in Cyrenaica in November 1941, it suddenly became obvious to me that I should have to be left behind when the others withdrew and that I must fall into the hands of the Germans. My first thought was, 'but this can't be happening to *me*'. After this first wild recoil I was able to examine my situation more calmly. I had quite expected to be killed and I was only wounded in the leg. I was flooded by a sense of relief. There was nothing more I could do and I began to feel almost serene (perhaps the morphia I had taken helped) and only slightly apprehensive about what the Germans would do to me.

After three months of illness and the amputation of my damaged leg, the relief at being alive was reinforced by the joy of convalescence and, even now, after two years, I still feel it sometimes.

I spent a year in various hospitals and then was sent to a prison camp for British officers in Thuringia, central Germany. Looking back, I discover that I soon adopted a double perspective for living in captivity; looking at my life from a vantage point in the future outside prison and dealing with every actual problem of avoiding discomfort in prison only as and when it arose. For a prisoner wounded in such a way that he knows he cannot escape this way of living from day to day and hour to hour, avoids fret and worry about the immediate future. He knows—or rather trusts—that one day he will emerge again into freedom, but there is nothing he can do to bring that day any nearer. He need have no anxieties except about such questions as the amount of straw in his mattress and how to make one tin of condensed milk last a week. Once inside the barbed wire perimeter of a prison camp, most of the anxieties and responsibilities of ordinary life are left on the outside. For one thing there is no money. The Germans issue special paper currency for prisoners of war, but since there is nothing to buy it represents nothing. Some prisoners used it to bet with, but I could never find any satisfaction in winning a sheaf of paper. This simplifies life enormously. It is just like being so rich that you never have to consider the cost of anything with, I suspect, the added advantage that you need suffer no anxiety about competing claims for your spending. Once you have lost the habit of possessiveness or acquisitiveness, or had it broken by circumstances, it is surprising how little you need. Though with some people acquisitiveness must be something more than a habit, for there are prisoners of war who never lose it. They exercise their miserly propensities by hoarding such rarities as razor blades, lavatory paper and matches. Numerous cardboard boxes full of more or less useful possessions accrete round these people. Every now and again they do produce with the air of a conjuror the very thing that is needed. The improvident avoid the strain of packing and unpacking numerous cardboard boxes (the usual form of prisoners' luggage) when moving camp. And since your baggage is searched for contraband both on departure and arrival, you usually have to pack three times for one journey.

Another great simplification of existence is that food and clothes are free. No amount of effort will secure a man more than his share of either—at least no ordinary effort and success is not admired. Supplies of both food and clothes are supplemented by rare parcels from home, but the Red Cross rules that no prisoner may have more than a certain number. The food supplied in the Red Cross parcels is wholesome though monotonous and so not particularly appetizing; not that this matters, because the quantity is such that the appetite never needs stimulating. It is seldom that you finish a meal without the sensation that you could easily begin all over again. This, I have always been told, is the sign of a healthy diet and I certainly found it so. Sometimes after a breakfast at 9 o'clock of two slices of German black bread with margarine and jam and a large mug of English tea with sugar and condensed milk, I became so hungry by one o'clock that I found it difficult to concentrate on whatever I was doing, but usually there would be a hunk of bread to gnaw. Prisoners from the campaign in France told me that in the first months before the Red Cross food began to arrive, they were so weak from hunger that it cost them a real effort and several rests to climb two flights of stairs. I am unusually greedy and before being captured I had been in the habit of giving a great deal of attention to food, but after about four months I could eat almost anything and I became much more interested in quantity than quality. I was only occasionally tortured by daydreams of oysters and lobster Newburg.

As to clothes, most of us, whatever our previous habits, came to regard them as only necessary coverings. There were a few persistent dandies who regularly appeared in uniforms with glittering buttons and lustrous shoes and who wore hats. They were regarded as harmless eccentrics. Not that the rest of us were very squalid, for there was an unexpressed feeling that it would be a very bad show not to shave punctually every day in spite of the fact that razor blades were extremely scarce (one blade had to do for six weeks or two months) and we had hot water only once a fortnight. Most prisoners just continued to wear a suit of battledress until it wore out and then applied to the English camp store for a new one, which they were given after a sort of means test.

By far the most unpleasant discomfort of a prison camp is the total lack of privacy. I shared a bed-sitting room about 20 feet square with fifteen other prisoners. We slept in double-decker beds which were ranged round the walls to leave space for two tables and some twelve kitchen chairs. I never grew accustomed to the gravelly hardness of these beds, which had loose wooden boards where springs should have been and on top a palliasse meagrely stuffed with straw. The longest period I was alone in this room was eighteen minutes. There was a small room used as a library where I used to go and read in the mornings; if you did not get there early enough there was no room to sit down. Even here the silence was broken by people coming to change their books at midday. To become adapted to this lack of solitude it was necessary to develop a kind of reptilian insensitiveness—like crocodiles in their tank at the Zoo, which walk over each other without either appearing to notice the other. When sixteen people live in the same room together for a year or more the evasions and other polite subterfuges of ordinary life naturally become impossible. Every word you speak to one of the fifteen is probably in the hearing of the other fourteen or some of them, so you cannot assume different personalities with different people. Nor can you hope to dissemble with success your opinion on any subject. The only hope for comfortable relationships in these circumstances is candour softened by imaginative understanding. Although every person in the room more or less knows the opinion of every other person on any subject there is plenty of discussion which, however, rather easily becomes abusive argument. Prisoners are thrown together more by the random play of chance than by any stringently selective principle, and so their views are extremely diverse. I was surprised that so many of them were agreed that politics were a dirty racket and all politicians hypocrites on the make. Apart from occasional acrimony, good temper in argument is usual because it is necessary in that sort of existence.

Living permanently surrounded by so many people with whom they are on terms of schoolboy superficial intimacy, I imagine that all prisoners at times feel intensely lonely and sick for home. Even the most insensitive have their days of black depression. It is the result perhaps, of the sterility of an existence entirely deprived of the company of women and children (though I once heard an unashamed lecher declare that he missed dogs more than women). An exclusively male community seems to me to lack emotional drive and spontaneity. Many prisoners do become very firm friends, more usually because of shared experience than common tastes, but this kind of relationship seems more comforting than stimulating. It is accurately described by the phrase 'it is so nice to be with someone you don't have to talk to unless you feel like it'.

In a tightly confined society which is compacted by the common aim of presenting a united front to the Germans, the derelictions of the individual are all on the social plane. Prisoners have found that the best, indeed only way to treat the Germans is by an uncompromising insistence upon their rights under the Geneva Convention and by instant and persistent complaint to the Protecting Power (the Swiss who periodically visit the camp) if these rights are infringed. In my experience most Germans are constantly trying to put the relationship on another footing. The attitude and conduct of one type implies: 'You are the prisoners of the Herrenvolk and we shall treat you as we think proper without any of this nonsense about international agreements. We are knightly and magnanimous, not Bolsheviks, so we will not shoot you unless you do something to annoy us.' Another type is constantly trying to insinuate a transaction into the relationship. He will say, in effect: 'Look here, you and I are sensible fellows and we neither of us want trouble and unpleasantness. I will let you do or have whatever it may be if you will just give me your word as an officer that you will not try to escape.' The concessions offered are commonly far short of the prisoners' rights laid down in the Geneva Convention. Every form of insidious tactic is used in the attempt to supplant the Convention as the basis of the relationship between prisoners and German camp authorities. The commandant of a hospital where I was for a time, one day declared that one Red Cross parcel of food a fortnight per prisoner was quite enough and that he did not propose to adhere to the rule of one parcel a week per prisoner laid down by the International Red Cross. He refused to allow the food store to be opened. The senior English doctor pointed out that the German commandant could not decide such things. His reply was: 'On the contrary; I command this hospital and I intend to see that English prisoners are not better fed than German civilians.' After a good deal of argument he proposed compromise. The English doctor remained inflexible and filed a complaint. After about a month, during which the prisoners were on short rations, he must have received orders from the German War Office, at the instances of the Swiss, to adhere to the agreed rate, for he announced with a great show of magnanimity that he had decided to issue one parcel a week to every prisoner. This arrogance has its useful side; commandants cannot abide the thought of their subordinates stooping to swindle the English. Two German quartermasters caught stealing rations meant for British prisoners received the dreaded punishment of being sent to the Eastern front.

It is easy to see that compromise with the German authorities is fatal and inflexibility essential. The lowest thing a prisoner can do in the opinion of his fellows is to betray the united front of inflexibility for his own comfort and advantage. All forms of selfishness are instantly detected and loudly denounced. Prisoners develop a hawk eye for 'rackets', but appeasement is the deadliest crime. The British have one enormous advantage over prisoners of other nationalities. They expect to be well treated. In spite of wartime propaganda about devilish Huns they are genuinely astonished and indignant if they are not cared for as honoured guests. This applies particularly to private soldiers. Their standards of food, sanitation and comfort are so high and their astonishment and disgust when expected to put up with lower standards so unfeigned and unrancorous that the Germans, unwilling to admit that their own standards are lower, are shamed into making improvements. It is quite impossible for the Germans to put across any Herrenvolk stuff in the face of the innocent arrogance of British soldiers, who are impenetrable to the idea of German superiority and simply think it uproariously funny. This baffles the Germans. In spite of persistent efforts to propagand British troops through the medium of a weekly newspaper called *The Camp*, I do not believe they have made any impression at all. *The Camp* has the usual three main lines of attack. First, the Germans are winning the war (the weekly summary of the war news is so flagrantly absurd that it defeats its end): the British should get together with the Germans, because, if the Allied Powers win, Russia will be supreme in Europe and the United States will appropriate the Empire (variations on this theme are plugged weekly in an article 'the German Point of View' which is very 'sane and moderate' in tone): the honest English working man is being exploited by capitalist Jews. These views are sandwiched between articles on such subjects as German motor-bicycle engines and German football; English football and racing results and chronicles of camp sports and concerts and other contributions written by the prisoners themselves. I suspect that hardly anybody who reads the paper reads 'the German Point of View'. If propaganda exerts its influence on the subconscious level of the mind, I suppose *The Camp* must have some influence though I have never seen the slightest sign that it has.

I believe almost every prisoner would agree that the attitude of the Germans towards the war and towards us has altered considerably since 1940. I am told by those who were captured in that year that after the fall of France the Germans were boasting that the war would be decided in their favour in a few months and that they treated English prisoners atrociously. When I was captured in November 1941 they were still full of confidence. Indeed they had grounds for confidence then. During the time I was in hospital in Athens we failed to destroy Rommel's forces in North Africa; we lost Singapore and the Russians were retreating. I had an exasperating conversation with a Stuka pilot who had broken his arm. He was full of bounce and rather condescending. He thought it foolish of us to have made war on Germany, and it was a pity they were going to have to hurt us. My argument about violated agreements failed to convince him because he would have it that the occupation of Prague had preceded the Munich Agreement. I was exasperated, too, by the German women who visited the wards and brought cigarettes and picture papers to the German troops in the Athens hospital.

They fussed about mournfully in their shabby, ill-fitting black clothes. After sympathizing over my amputated leg, one of these crows gloomily said to me one day: 'I am sure you did not want this war any more than we did, but what can people like you and I do? It's the governments that decide these things, isn't it?' No amount of talk could have shown her her mistake. It is sad to reflect that so many good, kind old and middle-aged women will have to suffer for their cow-like submission to German men. But I have no doubt that they would have thought Hitler perfectly splendid if he had won the war and that they would have been the first to applaud in foolish wonder. In Athens where these women were living, some 500 Greeks were at that time dying of starvation daily.

The ebbing of German confidence in the result of the war was quite obvious after Stalingrad (for which they had a day of national mourning) and Tunisia and was often reflected in their attitude towards prisoners. Guards become more accommodating and some even frankly conciliatory. I heard one guard say to a prisoner: 'You won't forget how good I've always been to you English?' If they had an unpopular task to perform such as making all prisoners get up in the middle of the night for a search, they would often excuse themselves by saying: 'We are sorry, but we are only doing our duty by carrying out orders'. Since obliteration-bombing began, the civilians whom prisoners meet travelling in trains from one prison camp to another are perhaps a shade less ready to start conversations. It was while travelling that I had the unforgettable experience of seeing a man literally foaming at the mouth with rage. He was a railway guard who had to hold up a train for a party of prisoners and their luggage. He shouted, he bellowed and flecks of froth flew from his lips; he was pale and shaking. He must have been boiling up against his life for a long time. When he began to shout, the blank incomprehension and mild concern on the faces of the prisoners infuriated him still more. I do not believe I have ever seen a man so angry. To pretend not to understand is the most effective answer to a shouting German unless they are in a shooting mood.

Prisoners of other nationalities (except Americans) probably have a harder time than the British. For one thing they get far less food. The Russians, for example, are underfed and many are worked to death. They are generally treated as a commodity much less valuable than cattle. I saw many who were doing hard manual labour up till a fortnight before their death from tuberculosis of the lungs. Where-ever it is possible, British prisoners give them extra food and some cigarettes. Most of those I saw seemed bewildered and childlike; at the first sign of friendliness they broke into happy smiles. In 1942, most of the French prisoners I saw seemed depressed, sloppy and surly and they displayed numerous photographs of Pétain in their sleeping quarters. But in the last year their spirits have risen and now they usually wave and shout friendly greetings to passing British prisoners. I met a French major, aged fifty-three and the father of twelve children, who had broken his arm trying to escape from his guards by jumping out of a train travelling at about twenty-five miles an hour.

German women do not always take advantage of the legal protection afforded by the Reich (which by the way, is often referred to by British soldiers as 'the Third and Last') against the amorous advances of working prisoners. In spite of notices prominently displayed in working camps warning prisoners that they are liable to ten years' imprisonment for speaking to a German woman without special permission. I met a Frenchman who had faked an illness to get into hospital to escape the attentions of a mother and her daughter at the farm where he worked. He explained that he had had an instant success with the daughter, but her mother had discovered the affair and, anxious to supplant her daughter, was blackmailing him by threatening to denounce him to the police. An English soldier told me that he had seen a woman being led through the main street of her village with a placard round her neck announcing: 'I have been the whore of a prisoner while my husband was fighting at the Eastern front'. I cannot vouch for the exact wording, but that was certainly the sense of it.

Conditions in an officer's prison camp form the perfect background for reading and writing. Being deprived of many outlets for action and freed from the mental and sensual distractions of normal life, the mind seems to need some load to grapple with if it is not to race like an engine with a slipping clutch. Particular books are hard to get and I found I could easily read and enjoy such formidably unreadable works as the life of Herbert Spencer in two volumes with a score of appendices. I found my mind worked more clearly and connectedly than ever before. For people whose only form of expression is action, the narrow confinement and monotony is a torment. We calculated that one unquiet spirit had walked at least 10,000 miles and worn out six pairs of boots since his capture simply by pacing round and round the compound—a gravel space some fifty yards square. Many prisoners learnt to play some musical instrument; one man constructed a model galleon out of toothbrush handles; quite a few played bridge or poker every evening of their lives; theatricals occupied quite a lot of the time of others; many learnt languages and worked for examinations.

On the whole I would say that captivity had a beneficial effect upon all but the most unteachable. Nobody has a job which occupies his whole energy; nobody can say: 'I've finished my work and now I will go to the cinema, pay 2s. 4d. and be entertained, or I will put on my slippers and read a detective story or turn on the radio'. Prison life is not divided into thought-tight compartments of work and play. If prisoners want entertainment they must work for it themselves. Most of them therefore find some activity which is neither completely one thing nor the other, but both at once. Their mental energy thus becomes spread over their whole waking life and it is virtually impossible in prison surroundings not to be led by this shift of perspective to some consideration of the bases on which your life and the lives of others rest. They learn to question these bases and to overhaul and sometimes to revise the values by which they have lived their lives. Those who do this seem to become more aware and more understanding. The trouble is that imprisonment goes on too long. I fancy that many people would benefit by a year of enforced inactivity and freedom from small anxieties and distractions to examine the pre-suppositions and aims of their conduct and that of others. But unless these people are practised mystics, the lack of novelty in time breeds a dreadful staleness. There are some unfortunate men who were captured in the first weeks of the war and many who have been in prison camps since the summer of 1940, who are still there.

Returning to England is an overwhelming experience for one who has been a prisoner of war. It is a distinct shock to find that the world outside is no longer hostile but anxious to be kind and helpful. Solitude and freedom to go and come and see whom you will are intoxicating. It is a form of convalescence in which all impressions are more vivid and the exercise of every faculty and appetite more deeply enjoyable. Returned prisoners are not the best people to ask about the changes in life at home, for they are concerned to recognize and greet all that has remained unchanged and familiar. The great contrast for prisoners is between England and Germany, where every civilian looks gloomy and hag-ridden. Even before the war they looked a bit like this, but I believe they have now lost confidence in the future and, though all that I was able to see of Germany convinced me that they are far from collapse, their morale is noticeably lower than at the end of 1941 when I was captured.

I think that perhaps the best way in which it is possible to help prisoners of war is for their relatives to write to them regularly. It is most depressing to feel that your absence makes no difference. It is encouraging to be told occasionally that you are being missed. To receive a letter always lessens the feeling of being a forgotten, useless exile; it strengthens the ties with the life you would like to be sharing. I found that it was not so much the big events that I was glad to hear about as details about personalities. Many prisoners are, however, passionately curious about post-war planning, and a copy of the Beveridge Report was a best-seller in the Camp. The best sort of books to send to a prisoner are books on his special subject, books of permanent serious interest and a sprinkling of contemporary novels.

Captain Campbell was taken prisoner on the Commando raid which tried to capture Rommel's Headquarters. The Commanding Officer, Colonel Keyes, V.C., was killed; Captain Campbell was severely wounded and taken prisoner.

EDWIN MUIR

THE RIDER VICTORY

The rider victory reins his horse
Midway across the empty bridge
As if head-tall he had met a wall.
Yet there was nothing there at all,
No bodiless barrier, ghostly ridge
To check the charger in his course
So suddenly, you'd think he'd fall.

Suspended, steed and rider stare,
Leaping on air and legendary.
In front the waiting kingdom lies,
The bridge and all the roads are free.
But halted in implacable air
Rider and horse with stony eyes
Uprear their motionless statuary.

WOODROW WYATT

LETTER FROM FRANCE

DEAR B.—Forgive me if I answer your letter publicly, but I've had several letters asking the same sort of questions and I haven't time to answer them all—and yours asks them the most bluntly.

'It does excite me your being in the front line,' you say. 'I want to know—what do you feel when you see people dead and above all what feelings do you have when you actually kill someone. . . . Tell me about the Germans, the expression on their faces. . . . I can't wait to hear some hundred per cent news on what is really happening, and who to believe: the reporters who say the French are sniping away like mad and resenting and hating your arrival and that the Germans have behaved very well *or* the ones who say that the

French are in ecstasies over you boys at being liberated, but why having their homes blasted to hell should make them this way I can't follow. . . .'

You will think I'm rather a fraud because I'm not in the front line and never have been. Up till now I've been a staff officer with a vehicle made up as an office to work in and almost as comfortable as in England. I've always fed in a mess and had a shower when I wanted one and only for the first four or five weeks did I have to sleep in a slit trench—ever since I've had a tent. I've done no marching, no crawling in the fields. I didn't even land on D-Day but on D+6. All the same I suppose I know a little about the unpleasant side of war although I've never killed a German—only a very small number of people in this impersonal war can say they have. I think I've met two. In the front line you hardly ever see the Germans unless they have surrendered and there's no cold steel. If a party of Germans do show themselves you may see some fall when you fire at them but whose bullet killed them no one ever knows. No it is a different process. Suppose there are a group of Germans in a wood. It is bombed and it is shelled. Then the infantry with or without tanks go forward. If all goes well the Germans withdraw and the only ones left are ready to give themselves up. If it goes badly the German automatic and small arms fire kills and wounds so many infantry that they have to stop. Maybe they go back to where they started or perhaps they try to get round behind the Germans. If they are lucky the Germans leave the wood or surrender. If they are unlucky the Germans make it too hot for them to advance any farther. Sometimes it happens that our infantry take the wood, and the Germans make a sudden counter-attack using the same methods, and the machinery is reversed. The only reason why either side ever leave a place is because they will be killed if they stay there and that is also the only reason why the other side don't go into it. It's got nothing to do with bayonet charges or man-to-man fighting. If you don't believe me go and look at Lebissey Wood just north of Caen after the war and see the shell and bomb holes every yard or so and then consider whether you would have stayed there waiting for someone to arrive with a bayonet.

I was surprised to find war both less and more frightening than I expected. It was less frightening because the shells and bombs didn't come directly at you very often and there were long periods when we were probably safer than London was with the flying bombs. It was more frightening because when they did fall near it was absolute terror. I crouched in a slit trench plotting the course of each whine and thinking this time it's a direct hit. The deadliest things are the anti-personnel bombs. They fall in clusters spattering shrapnel at all heights from nought to ten feet and the only protection is to be below ground.

Another frightening thing is driving along a road that is being shelled. I did this a lot in the early period of our advance. It was amazing how the traffic blocks that the staffs had been moaning about for days disappeared whenever the shelling started. Then the only vehicles to be seen were single ones going very fast and one or two burning out on the side of the road. On a road like that there are always recognized shelling centres and it is unnerving to go through a village and see a wall suddenly collapse across the street a hundred yards ahead; to pass craters in the road still smoking from newly fallen shells and to hear them landing on either side just behind you.

But that kind of war is probably over for the staffs now. It was a freak period for the headquarters of Divisions and Corps to be three to four miles from the front line and within easy shelling range—caused by the lack of room in the tiny bridgehead. Now they are spaced out again and administrative units and rear echelons no longer jostle the forward troops like a crowd on the way to a football match.

What impresses me most about the front line is not violence but the absence of it. When the battle was stationary for a while I often drove down to visit the forward units. The approach was always the same. The quick change from the hubbub and noise of the jumbled convoys in the back areas to roads deserted save for an occasional civilian walking very slowly. A few cattle in the fields grazing among the dead and swollen bodies of their fellows, but no farm workers. A complete silence—not even the sound of birds, a sense of being in an unreal world with no life, so that even the people in the villages timidly looking out of their shell-damaged houses don't seem alive. There is no reality because no one is doing his normal job. Even the war does not exist—until you see a notice 'You are in sight of the enemy now' and a little further on 'Drive slowly—dust causes shells' and then a few steel-helmeted soldiers cautiously poking their heads out of slit trenches to see who is going by. At my destination the same slightly eerie atmosphere would persist. I would park my car very carefully out of sight behind some bushes or a wall and walk across to the Headquarters. There I would find the people I was looking for in a dugout or an armoured vehicle, oppressed by the same feelings as my own and talking quietly as though afraid the enemy across the fields or on the other slope of the hill opposite might overhear. The opening exchange of courtesies wasn't the weather but 'How many times have you been shot up today?' followed by a visit to the latest shell or mortar holes, much as one might go and see how the sweet peas were coming on in a country garden. Sometimes, before I left, the stillness would be broken by the enemy's 'Moaning Minnies' (multi-barrelled mortars) and we would scatter for the slit trenches, becoming aware of life again through the attempt to destroy it.

'What do you feel when you see people dead?'

Just an urgent desire to get by quickly and a feeling of revulsion which is greater or less according to the length of time the body has been dead. Rotting corpses, cattle or soldiers, distend and putrefy and their faces become liquescent flesh covered with crawling flies and maggots. There is no difference in appearance between decomposing men and decomposing animals and the same stench comes from both of them.

I feel worse when I see someone not physically but morally dead. In the last war it was called 'shell-shock'; now it is 'exhaustion case' or colloquially 'bomb happy'. It happens when a man can no longer stand the shells and bombs and the nearness of death. He loses control of his limbs, he surrenders everything to the torture of fear and his mind abdicates his body. I once gave one of them a lift. He was a tall man and I saw him being dragged along by two stretcher-bearers, his feet shuffling about while they held him up by his arms slung round their shoulders. They humped him into the front of the jeep where he lay twitching, gangling and pitiful, his head hanging loosely over the back of the seat. Every time a shell exploded in the distance the whole of his body contorted sharply, became almost rigid and upright, then went loose again. His face was blotched and unshaven, without characteristics, and his long arms and legs hung expressionlessly from his body. As we drove he groaned continuously and earthy non-human sounds came out of his dropped mouth.

When we reached a first-aid post we pushed him out of the jeep and tried to lay him on the ground but he resisted, his legs and arms waved violently and he tried to sit up, groaning louder in panic. He was conscious of nothing—like a decapitated chicken which runs convulsively in the farmyard for a few minutes before it falls. Until he had slept and rested for a fortnight he would remain a whimpering heap and perhaps he will always start and jump at noise.

You ask me what the Germans look like. I don't know what they look like when they're fighting or sitting behind their lines, but I do know what they look like when they've been taken prisoner. You must remember that a large part of the German Army is made up of impressed men from occupied territory—Poles, Jugoslavs, Russians, Czechs. Sometimes there are as many as 30 per cent of these in the formations facing us. Naturally they tend to give themselves up soonest, and when they do they sit about the prisoner-of-war cage dazed and apprehensive. When they've been given something to eat and they realize they're not going to be treated unkindly they brighten considerably and laugh and chatter like children, jumping up eagerly whenever one of the guards gives them a job to do.

The Germans proper are in two categories—the ordinary conscript and the S.S. The former look similar to their alien comrades although a little cleaner and more intelligent. They don't talk much and seem apathetic and relieved to be out of the war after five years of it. They go on obeying orders and fighting, not from malice or perverseness, but because it is outside their comprehension and will to do otherwise.

The S.S. are very different. They are usually young, not out of their teens. In appearance they are pale and thin with long hair brushed back from their foreheads. They are very dirty and smell—presumably because many of them have a code never to wash and they live up to it. While they don't look like Nietzsche's 'jubilant monsters' it is quite probable that they really have 'come from a ghastly bout of murder, arson, rape and torture'. Before they leave a town, if there is time, they ransack it. The details have been published often so I will only tell you a few of the things I have come across. At Messei they ran through the streets firing into the windows and pulling out the women—one woman there told me how she had lain under the table as they fired shots in the wall behind her and followed it by throwing in incendiary grenades. At Caen in the houses they had taken over they left their excreta smeared on the floors and sometimes on the linen and just before we went in they drove the people into the caves and went through the houses senselessly smashing the furniture and destroying anything of value. At Flers after the air raid on D-Day they set fire to any of the houses in the centre of the town that hadn't been hit. In one village, because somebody annoyed them they drove the thousand inhabitants into one building and burnt it down. When the S.S. are fighting they keep firing their weapons until they are surrounded—then they suddenly surrender before they can be killed. Once prisoners they try to look unconcerned and to demonstrate, with a half sneer, that they are still the Herrenvolk. They don't mix with the other prisoners, but stand apart despising everything. They are the deliberately created 'Dead End Kids' who have had their vices encouraged and praised as virtues by the authorities, and it will be a remarkable reformatory that will ever persuade them of anything else.

About the French. For the first six weeks at least we were definitely unpopular in many parts of the newly liberated areas and in the regions immediately behind them. Understandably so. During the occupation the Germans *did* behave very well—especially in the coastal districts where they were anxious to avoid trouble from the civil population during invasion. They stayed in their camps and barracks, and didn't obtrude into the life of the community. In all their contacts they were extremely polite and took great pains not to offend against local customs and pride. M. le Maire was respected. German soldiers didn't get drunk, didn't loot, didn't rape and demanded nothing. So long as the French didn't interfere with the activities of the Army they were secure and unmolested—it was only the members of the Resistance Movement who were caught who suffered. More than that—the Germans bought farm produce in large quantities and paid very well for it, and there was plenty of work to be had in the factories and with contractors working for the Germans. In the country there was prosperity and the prospect of it continuing—particularly as Germany deported little forced labour from among the farm workers. The country people, being materialistic, weren't discontented and it didn't matter who was in control while there was a good return for their work. Government for such people is a distant thing, a matter of names. They are concerned with the effects on them personally and these were good.

With our arrival this vanished. They were plunged into some of the greatest destruction of the war. Their villages and little towns were obliterated by air, sea and land. Their homes were destroyed, hundreds of them were killed, their cattle were slaughtered in the fields, their crops devastated, their orchards ruined, their roads torn up. They were driven away from their farms and their livelihood. Neither the big towns like Caen nor the Germans could buy what they had to sell even in those rare instances where they could go on producing it. Every big attack meant more huge bombardments with more mutilation of the property and land of a people highly endowed with the sense of property—and all day and night the noise of explosions was in their ears. At the beginning, too, there was some looting by soldiers and the digging up of potatoes and vegetable crops was common. It didn't compare favourably with the Germans and liberation was hardly preferable to occupation. As the mass of soldiers, equipment, vehicles, tanks, poured into a very small area the civilians felt enmeshed in a fearful military machine and they remembered the Anzio beach-head and other Allied invasions which had clung to the coast for several months before any general advance took place. The Germans had anticipated that feeling by sticking up posters just before the invasion showing a snail crawling up the map of Italy with a Union Jack in one nostril and a Star-Spangled Banner in the other and underneath the words: 'The speed of a snail is 0.9 km. a day'. They remembered, too, that before the Germans left they had been confident that the bridge-head couldn't be held and that in a very short time they would be back again.

The bombing of the towns was hard for them to understand. When a town with only twenty-five Germans in it has been flattened and many French people killed it is difficult to explain that the object was not in fact to kill them, but to stop the Germans bringing reinforcements through it for a vital forty-eight hours. An English woman living inland told me that after some of the raids people would say, 'When they come we won't welcome them—we'll spit in their faces'. And the German poster displayed everywhere, showing Joan of Arc, her hands manacled, burning at the stake with blazing Rouen Cathedral in the background and the caption 'The Assassins always return to the scene of their crime' may have had some effect. If bitterness is not to continue after the war and be a hindrance to Anglo-French relations it should be explained clearly and frequently, as it can be, why it was necessary 'for their homes to be blasted to hell', as you say in your letter, and why it was an inevitable part of Allied strategy that they should be.

Not everyone felt this way, probably not the majority, and from the first there was much friendliness and pleasure that we had landed. And when it became clear that we weren't going to be driven into the sea, that the great break-through was succeeding, the whole atmosphere altered. Men and women stood on the sides of the road laughing and waving and making the 'V' sign at passing columns. At every newly captured village there was tremendous enthusiasm. The people came out on the street, smothered the soldiers with kisses and embraces, gave them wine, shouted 'Bravo', cheered and clapped, threw flowers and sometimes almost impeded the advance in their excitement. Even in Caen the inhabitants were wild with happiness for several days after we went in and I didn't see a single house that hadn't been damaged in some way. For the most part the streets and houses were brick-dust and rubble. At the moment of success the fear that the whole of France was destined to be a battleground, over which the machinery of war would slowly tear its way for months, disappeared. Now, the emotions you would expect from a people just freed from an invader were displayed without reservation and with all the appearances of being genuine—the farther inland, the greater the display. This doesn't mean that the French changed overnight—it is natural to applaud success and I have no doubt that ill will still exists in many places, particularly in the country. I have never found any corroboration for stories about French snipers.

LIBERATION I

JEAN-PAUL SARTRE

THE CASE FOR RESPONSIBLE LITERATURE

SINCE the writer has no possible means of escape, we wish him to cover his epoch exclusively; it is his only chance; his time is made for him, and he is made for it. Balzac's indifference in the days of '48 and Flaubert's frightened incomprehension of the Commune are to be regretted; regretted *for the writers' own sakes*: for there lies something which they have missed for ever. We want to miss nothing in our time: there may be other epochs more beautiful, but this is ours; we have only *this* life to live, in the midst of *this* war, perhaps, of *this* revolution. It must not be concluded from this that we are preaching a kind of populism: quite the contrary. Populism is a child of old parents, the wretched offspring of the last realists: it is yet another attempt to sneak away from the mess. We are convinced, on the contrary, that one *cannot* sneak away. Were we dumb and immobile as stones, our very passivity would be an action. The abstention of one who devotes his life to writing novels about the Hittites entails taking up some kind of attitude. The writer is situated in his time: each word has its reverberations, each silence too. I hold Flaubert and Goncourt responsible for the repressions which followed the Commune, because they wrote not a single line to prevent them. It may be said that it was none of their business: but was the case of Calas the business of Voltaire? the sentence on Dreyfus the business of Zola? the administration of the Congo the business of Gide? Each one of these writers, in some particular circumstance of his life, weighed up his responsibility as a writer. The occupation has taught us ours. Since by our very existence we influence our time, we must decide that this influence shall be deliberate. Again we must specify: it is not unusual for a writer to concern himself, in his own small way, with shaping the future. But that is a vague, conceptual future, embracing the whole of humanity and on which no definite light can be cast: will history come to an end? will the sun be extinguished? what will be the condition of man under the socialist regime of the year 3000? We leave these dreams to the anticipatory novelists: it is the future of *our* epoch which should be the object of our concern: a limited future, which can hardly be distinguished from the present—for an epoch, like a man, is primarily a future. It is formed by its current toils, by its undertakings, by its more or less long-term projects, by its rebellions, by its struggles, by its hopes: when will the war end? how will the country be re-equipped? how will international relations be planned? what will be the social reforms? will the forces of reaction triumph? will there be a revolution, and what form will it take? This is the future we choose for ourselves, and we desire no other. It is not by chasing after immortality that we will make ourselves eternal: we will not make ourselves absolute by reflecting in our works desiccated principles which are sufficiently empty and negative to pass from one century to another, but by fighting passionately in our time, by loving it passionately, and by consenting to perish entirely with it.

[*Translated by* NATALIA GALITZINE]

LIBERATION II

PAUL VALÉRY

MY FAUST

THE CRYSTAL GIRL

Act II. Scene V.

JOY. FAUST. (*He comes from the garden holding a rose*)

FAUST (*to himself*): Is this perhaps the culmination of my art? I am living. And only living. There lies the achievement . . . Now at last I that was have ended by making me what I am. This is now my sole significance. Here and now I am the present itself. A true marriage of self and presence, a perfect interchange with no matter what may come. No remainder. No longer any mystery. Now the infinite is definite. The non-existent has ceased to exist. If consciousness is what the mind must produce in order that what IS may BE—then

I, FAUST, am now pure and perfect consciousness. Fullness. Fulfilment. I am what I am. This is the culmination of my art, the classic age of the art of existence. This is my achievement: To be living. Is this not everything? Yet there must be awareness of the fact . . . There is no question of reaching this high upland of existence without such awareness. How many adventures, arguments, dreams and errors there needs must be in order to gain the freedom to be what one is—and nothing but what one is! What is perfection but the suppression of what we lack? Deficiency is always superfluous . . . But, at present, it is clear to me that the slightest glance, the slightest sensation, the least of life's acts and functions, have become the equivalents of the propositions and inner promptings of my mind . . . This is the supreme condition in which everything is summed up in living, wherein, at a smile from me, all questions and answers are rejected . . . TO LIVE . . . My masterpiece is to breathe and feel. I am born each moment for each moment. TO LIVE . . . I BREATHE. What else is there? I BREATHE . . . And every breath I take is always the first, each one expands anew those inner wings which beat true time. They bear the one that is from the one that was to the one that is to be . . . I AM. An extraordinary thing, surely! To be suspended above death as a stone might hang in space. It is incredible . . . I BREATHE, nothing more. The heavy scent of my flowers impels me to breathe, and I feel the smell of the fresh earth, increasingly desired, increasingly desirable, affecting my powers of breathing. I BREATHE, no more, for there is nothing more. I BREATHE and I SEE. It is sweet to look upon this place . . . Yet what does this place matter? What does it matter what one sees? It is enough to SEE, and to know that one sees . . . It is a whole science in itself. I see that pine tree. What does the pine itself matter? It might just as well be an oak tree. I should see it. And that roof of shining slate could as well be a mirror of still water. I should see it. And as for the irregular line of those distant hills which enclose the landscape, I feel in my hands the power to redraw as I please its long, flexible contour . . . TO SEE, then, is to see as well one thing as another; to see what is is to see what may be . . .

JOY (*aside, and approaching him cautiously from behind as if moved by an irresistible force*): I cannot stand so far away. It would be like standing away from myself . . . What would he say if I were to kiss his hand? What would he do?

FAUST (*to himself*): I BREATHE and I SEE . . . Yet what is perhaps more present in presence is this: I TOUCH . . . (*he strikes the arm of the bench on which he is sitting*). And at one stroke I discover and create what is real . . . My hand, though, in touching feels itself touched. That is what real means. Nothing more.

JOY (*behind him, under her breath*): He is talking and I am talking to myself; but we are not exchanging words at all. And yet it is impossible that there should not be in what he is feeling and in what I myself feel a . . . a living likeness. The present moment is too pregnant, too heavy with the ripe fruit of a wonderful day, for two people, even as different as we are, not to feel themselves similarly at the end of their resistance to the pressure of events . . . Similarly overladen and satiated as we both are, and as it were charged with an almost intolerable force of happiness that cannot release itself, or find its natural outlet, expression or end . . . A kind of death. . .

FAUST (*aside*): Yes. What is there more real? I touch. I am touched. An old author said: To touch and to be touched is the property of bodies alone . . . (*A silence. Joy has placed her hand gently on his shoulder.*) Someone is touching me . . . Who? (*With emotion*) Dear Joy, is it you? . . . I thought you'd gone . . .

JOY: Yes, it's me . . . Why do you call me *dear* in that way?

FAUST: Because you touched me . . . Ah! my dear, why did you touch me?

JOY: I was afraid you might fall asleep while dreaming . . . It's unwise, you know . . .

FAUST: I have nothing to fear from one more sunset . . . Leave your hand there.

JOY: No. Why should I leave it?

FAUST: Because there's no longer any reason. Take it away.

JOY: No.

FAUST: Why?

JOY: Since it found its way there of its own accord . . . In point of fact, I don't know why it did, or why it should stay there on your shoulder, or why it should remove itself. Why? It's easy to say that. Do you yourself know, for all your learning, why you called me DEAR a moment ago? These things just happen of their own accord, like everything very important. (*She takes her hand away.*)

[*Translated by* JOHN HAYWARD]

LIBERATION III

FRANCIS PONGE

LA POMME DE TERRE

PELER une pomme de terre bouillie de bonne qualité est un plaisir de choix.

Entre le gras du pouce et la pointe du couteau tenue par les autres doigts de la même main, l'on saisit—après l'avoir incisé—par l'une de ses lèvres ce rêche et fin papier que l'on tire à soi pour le détacher de la chair appétissante du tubercule.

L'opération facile laisse, quand on a réussi à la parfaire sans s'y reprendre à trop de fois, une impression de satisfaction indicible.

Le léger bruit que font les tissus en se décollant est doux à l'oreille, et la découverte de la pulpe comestible réjouissante.

Il semble, à reconnaître la perfection du fruit nu, sa différence, sa ressemblance, sa surprise—et la facilité de l'opération—que l'on ait accompli là quelque chose de juste, dès longtemps prévu et souhaité par la nature, que l'on a eu toutefois le mérite d'exaucer.

C'est pourquoi je n'en dirai pas plus, au risque de sembler me satisfaire d'un ouvrage trop simple. Il ne me fallait—en quelques phrases sans effort—que déshabiller mon sujet, en en contournant strictement la forme: la laissant intacte mais seulement plus polie, brillante et toute prête à subir comme à procurer les délices de sa consommation.

* * *

. . . Cet apprivoisement de la pomme de terre par son traitement à l'eau bouillante durant vingt minutes, c'est assez curieux (mais justement tandis que j'écris des pommes de terre cuisent—il est une heure du matin—sur le fourneau devant moi).

Il vaut mieux, m'a-t-on dit, que l'eau soit salée, sévère: pas obligatoire mais c'est mieux.

Une sorte de vacarme se fait entendre, celui des bouillons de l'eau. Elle est en colère, au moins au comble de l'inquiétude. Elle se déperd furieusement en vapeurs, verse, grille aussitôt, bave, pfutte, tsitte: enfin, très agitée sur ces charbons ardents.

Mes pommes de terre, plongées là-dedans, sont secouées de soubresauts, bousculées, injuriées, imprégnées jusqu'à la moelle.

Sans doute la colère de l'eau n'est-elle pas à leur propos, mais elles en supportent l'effet—et ne pouvant s'échapper de ce milieu, s'en trouvent profondément modifiées (j'allais écrire s'entrouvrent . . .).

Finalement, elles y sont laissées pour mortes, ou du moins très fatiguées. Si leur forme en réchappe (ce qui n'est pas toujours), elles sont devenues molles, dociles. Toute acidité a disparu de leur pulpe: on leur trouve bon goût.

Leur épiderme s'est aussi rapidement différencié: il faut l'ôter (il n'est plus bon à rien), et le jeter aux ordures. . . .

Reste ce bloc friable et savoureux—qui prête moins qu'à d'abord vivre ensuite à philosopher.

WILLIAM SANSOM

BUILDING ALIVE

As on a fleet and smooth naval pinnace, intricate with grey cocks and rope and white-painted enumeration—we six on the Heavy Fire Unit drove swiftly through the quiet Sunday streets. Sometimes at odd corners or through a breach in the skyline of tall buildings the huge buff plume showed itself, calm and clean as sand against a pale bluish sky. We as well felt clean, in our blue flaired tunics and silver buttons, too clean for what was coming, conscious of this and awkward at a time when smudged khaki and camouflage net are the equipment of action. The streets were too clean; there were no people, the people were all hidden away cooking their Sunday dinners; one church bell pealed ceaselessly to an empty town caught in the Sunday pause.

Then, gradually, the immaculate polish showed a ruffling, stray scraps of paper suggested the passing of a crowd, a weed of splintered glass sprung up here and there on the pavements, another and invisible weed seemed to be thrusting the window frames from their sockets and ahead, as this tangle grew denser, the street hung fogged with yellow dust.

Our destination lay within the dust. Once inside it was easy to see, only the outer air had painted it opaque. But it was like driving from the streets of a town into sudden country; nothing metropolitan remained to these torn pavements, to the earthen mortar dust and the shattered brick returning to the clay. The flying-bomb had blasted a pause within the pause of Sunday morning.

Ambulances already. Two or three people stood about, handkerchiefs to their red-splashed faces. In the silence a loudspeaker called for silence. The rich living voice appealed to the dead rubble, coaxing it to make tapping noises. And men with long detecting poles weaved to and fro through the mist like slow shrimpers. We were ordered round the débris to search the broken buildings on either side.

At the top of the first flight of stairs, dark and rickety, a light shone through a crack in the unhinged door. The door came off easily. A single shadeless electric bulb hung over a tailor's table, shone weakly and yellow against the large daylit window beyond. On the table lay a pair of trousers, an iron, slivers of glass and splashes of red blood, comet-shaped, like flickings from a pen. Every lightly fixed furnishing of the room had shifted—bales of cloth, doors, chairs, plaster mouldings, a tall cupboard—all these had moved closer and now leant huddled at strange, intimate angles. Plaster dust covered everything. There was no space left in the room, there was nobody in the room. The blood led in wide round drops to the door, the tailor must have been 'walking wounded'. Had he been one of those outside, fingering blindly for the ambulance doors? The yellow bulb on its single string burned on, the only life in this lonely Sunday workroom, the only relic of the tailor's shattered patience.

Then, under the steady burning of this bulb, against its silent continuing effort, other sounds began to whisper. My number two, Barnes, looked at me quickly—the building was alive. Our boots had thudded on the stairs. Now for a moment, no more, they were quiet. They were silent, the light was silent, but falsely—for beneath these obvious silences other sounds, faint, intractable, began to be heard. Creakings, a groan of wood, a light spatter of moving plaster, from somewhere the trickle of water from a broken pipe. The whole house rustled. A legion of invisible plastermice seemed to be pattering up and down the walls. Little, light sounds, but massing a portentous strength. The house, suddenly stretched by blast, was settling itself. It might settle down on to new and firm purchases, it might be racking itself further, slowly, slowly grinding apart before a sudden collapse. I saw Barnes glance at the ceiling; he was thinking of the four floors still hanging above us; he was thinking perhaps, as I was, that the raid was still on and that any other explosion within miles might rock through the earth and shake the whole lot down. Walking in such houses, the walls and floors are forgotten; the mind pictures only the vivid inner framework of beams and supports, where they might run and how, under stress, they might behave; the house is perceived as a skeleton.

Then through the stripped window came further sounds—a distant explosion from the south, and above this the purposeful drone of a second bomb flying louder every moment. The gallows that would mark its course! To each dreadful roof gallows along the bomb's course a black sock would rise to swing like a sentence rather than a warning of death. The sound approached like a straight line. It approached thus for many people . . . everyone on the half-circle of its sound fanning forwards would attach the bomb to themselves. It could drop anywhere. It was absolutely reasonless. It was the first purely fatal agent that had come to man for centuries, bringing people to cross their fingers again, bringing a rebirth of superstition.

Down in the courtyard they were carrying a man out from the opposite block. We caught a glance of him through the twisted framework of an iron footbridge. They had laid him on a blanketed stretcher on the grey rubble. He lay still, bloodless, only his face showing, and that plastered with the same sick grey dust. It lay evenly on him, like a poisonous mask—he looked gassed with dust. Once he struggled, his head turned from side to side. He seemed to be trying to speak. It was as if his real face, clean and agonized, tried to be free and show its pain.

Now, in the long moment it takes these bombs to fly their swift distances—now the drone was already changing its note. The first remote aerial wavering, like a plane engine far up and away, had strengthened and bolted its direction upon our area. It was coming all right. We waited, though there was no time to wait, no real time but only the expansion of a moment so alert, and listened then for the drone to sharpen itself into the spluttering drum-beat of a jet-engine. But beneath this sound, separated from us by widths of sky, the little murmurs of secret life, fearful in their intimacy, could still be heard. And still fixed in a second's glance at the wounded man below, our eyes absorbed the whole courtyard, the waste of rubble between tall, torn office buildings. The iron bridge hung darkly between. Across it a new nest of broken pipes splayed up, a hydra head of snaky lead, but halted, paused like the rest of it. Only the oncoming sound moved deliberately, but this too was fixed, mounted on a straight, straight line that in its regular, unvarying crescendo provided only an emphasis to the stillness of the courtyard. A whole architecture, all that had ever been built, all the laborious metropolitan history had been returned to its waste beginning. The virgin scrap, the grey mortar earth, the courtyard walls torn and stripped into the texture of ancient moon-burnt rock—all these paused, taking breath. Only the little sounds sucking themselves in hinted at a new life, the life of leaden snakes, hesitating and choosing in whispers the way to blossom.

The drone was diving into a roar. We crouched down beneath the window. My eyes now near the floor found themselves facing a gap some three inches wide where the outer wall had loosened itself from the floorboards. The wall was leaning outwards. I saw my hand steady itself on a book of cloth patterns; the fingers were bleeding, the hand removed itself instinctively from the cleanish cloth, cut itself again on more glass on the floor. The bomb was above. We held our breaths, not in all that sound daring to breathe for fear we might miss the cut-out. It seemed much darker near the floor . . . the floor grew as dark as childhood. Only the amazing crack in the wall remained clear, gaping its draughty mouth. The noise grew deafening, a noise now as heavy as the shadow of a wing. Then, in a burst of anger, it seemed to double up on itself, its splutter roared double, it was diving, at four hundred miles an hour, without ever cutting out, heading like all mad anger unrestrained on to the fragile roofs . . .

The wall, like a rubber wall in a Disney cartoon, sprang out at my eyes, bulging round, then snapped back into its flat self. That happened, distinctly. Whether despite the crack it had actually expanded into so round and resilient a curve, or whether the noise and the windclap of the explosion jarred this round illusion within my own round eyes—I do not know. But that happened . . . just as the silence fell again, just as the glass rain spat again, just as an iron tank went tumbling down outside, and—it seemed a long time after the explosion, we were already up at the window—the wall of the building opposite across the courtyard wobbled and then heaved its concrete down on the wounded man and his rescuers below, burying them finally. It seemed, even at that time, extra hard for the man on the stretcher.

Swiftly the life of the house blossomed. The trickling from the pipes gushed free, cascading noisily into the courtyard. Tiles, plaster, gutter fragments and more glass lurched off the roof. A new growth was sprouting everywhere, sprouting like the naked plumbing, as if these leaden entrails were the worm at the core of a birth, struggling to emerge, thrusting everything else aside. But the house held. It must have blossomed, opened, subsided upon itself. We raced down the stairs to the concrete mass below.

As we picked, hopelessly, at the great fragments, it was impossible to forget how hard it was on the man on the stretcher. It seemed, stupidly, that he alone had had no chance.

SIDNEY KEYES

AN EARLY DEATH

This is the day his death will be remembered
By all who weep:
This is the day his grief will be remembered
By all who grieve.
The winds run down the icebegotten valleys
Bringing the scent of spring, the healing rain.
But the healing hands lie folded like dead birds;
Their stillness is our comfort who have known him.

But for the mother what shall I find of comfort?
She who wrought glory out of bone and planted
The delicate tree of nerves whose foliage
Responded freely to the loving wind?
Her grief is walking through a harried country
Whose trees, all fanged with savage thorns, are bearing
Her boy's pale body worried on the thorns.

RANDALL JARRELL

THE DEATH OF THE BALL TURRET GUNNER

From my mother's sleep I fell into the State
And I hunched in its belly till my wet fur froze.
Six miles from earth, loosed from its dream of life,
I woke to black flak and the nightmare fighters.
When I died they washed me out of the turret with a hose.

[Reprinted from *Partisan Review*]

1945

IVAN MOFFAT

ARRIVAL IN GERMANY

Germany, *7 April 1945*

SITTING in the empty lounge of a huge luxury hotel on the Rhine. It is seven in the evening. Around me there are empty rooms where there had once been balls and huge dinners. Crystal chandeliers just visible hanging in the semi-darkness. A French boy in American uniform is playing on the piano in the deserted dark ball-room. There are five people in the whole place. The swing-doors of the main entrance open and a colonel walks through looking for something. He takes off his helmet and lays it on the reception desk where no one is serving. Vaguely he looks around, peers into the dining-room. He sees a British captain having a dark and silent meal, served by a Russian girl from Kharkov. I know, because I spoke to her. The major gets up and the colonel stops him in the hall. 'Who's in charge here?' The British major is sorry, he's just moving through himself. The colonel shrugs and walks up the wide golden staircase and is seen no more. In the kitchen there is a Belgian cook talking German to the waiter, who is German. A different girl with long hair is singing in Russian. Two muddy American drivers from an armoured outfit walk through the hall. They wonder if they can have rooms. Someone says 'Take them', and they walk upstairs to a suite. A Russian youth with an apron, called Kolya, from Taganrog, hurries between side-doors with two bottles of hock. The cellar is full of it, to be had for the taking. There is an atmosphere of finding things. Two soldiers pass through the hall to the writing-room carrying a case of wine. In the damp evening, guns are firing unsteadily. The German manager of the hotel takes a look in, wearing green sports hat with stag's brush. He has heavy tortoiseshell glasses and a big face. All sense of order has gone, and he is past caring. Vainly he clicks his heels to an indifferent officer, ignores a sergeant carrying a bottle of hock upstairs. The outfit that was here has gone, and the one that is going to move in hasn't yet arrived. I have a two-bedded room. Tomorrow I shall be sleeping somewhere else. The Rhine looks peaceful, it is spring, and white blossoms are blurred in the distant mist. This hotel was the one in which Hitler met Chamberlain during the 1938 crisis. I have decided to write in the main hall because the other rooms are deserted and somehow terribly lonely. There is the feeling of suspended destiny, of the war laying itself down to die—but not where one is, somewhere else. We have passed through about ten utterly ruined rich Rhineland towns. Deserted, and the possessions spewed into the street. Heavy broken buildings. Nothing alive. An occasional church looks superficially whole, but is really a shell. The gunners and bombardiers have been most respectable in the midst of their business, and the churches are ugly as the hell round them. The Germans in the inhabited towns are calm, a little fascinated by the quantity and variety of our transport. They never look at us, we never catch an accidental smile. It is unostentatious but complete. We don't look at them much, and never speak. It is the end of a world, and one feels it intensely. Bad Godesberg. Tourist brochures. Broken bottles. Blank menu cards. Bottled cherries arrayed on dusty shelves. Heavy reams of unused paper such as this I'm using. No ribbon on the typewriter, so I'm using a carbon. 'Our Distinguished guests are reminded that each is personally responsible that the black-out regulations are strictly observed. The Direktion.' Avenues of rich middle-class villas dripping in the quiet spring rain. An old man with a black peaked cap wheeling a bicycle through his wire gateway. A bomb lies on the pavement, rusting, obscene in its isolated roundness, merd-like.

Two negroes with carbines slung over their wet open shirts are leaning in the stucco porch of a square house in a clean garden. The piano was playing all day. The hotel is empty of guests who wouldn't have to pay anyway. Somewhere in the distance Patton's columns are in Bavaria. Back in Paris my girl is sitting in the Café Flore. Here there is the quiet of the centre of the vortex that has ruined the pin-point and is destroying in a widening circle around. Colonel Stevens just came in. He sat in a plush chair and I confided my restlessness. 'It's like the end of the day in a studio after they have been shooting an important scene,' he said. 'Everyone has gone home. The props that are movable have been put away for further use. And three men who haven't gone home are sitting in the replica of the hotel where Hitler met Chamberlain.' As I was writing this, the colonel who I said disappeared, not to be seen any more, reappeared. He wore a raincoat with eagle insignia on the shoulders. His underclothes showed through where the coat was unbuttoned, and he was in bare stockinged legs. He went over rather gloomily to the reception desk and lifted the receiver of a military telephone. He waited two minutes and realized it had been disconnected by the departed outfit that had installed it. He turned and went back to bed. By now the artillery in the distance has died away completely, and all that we hear is the occasional plop of a rifle shooting at floating objects that might be mines against our bridges.

Earlier in the day they raised the American flag over the fortress of Ehrenbreitstein at Coblenz, last occupied by U.S. troops in 1923. It was cold and there were a lot of Generals. It was an isolated ceremony, high up and curiously un-American in its conception, since no one was watching except the military itself; they raised the flag and there were speeches and military music. Below, the city of Coblenz with a broken statue of the Kaiser lay before a wide green hilly landscape that seemed suspended without animation in the mist. Lifeless, embalmed. Someone remarked that it had cost us a lot of men to take that flag down for twenty-two years. We drove back in the rain past the Rhine bridges lying broken-backed and still half submerged and with the wake of the river running white around the steel trellises, as if it had always been like that. In one place a dead German lay at the edge of the river, and the water flowed over the bleached featureless whiteness of where his face had been. His uniform was still the same green that it was meant to be. Just now the colonel found the telephone operator's guest-list for September 1938. The only clue was the blankness of two pages for the twenty-first and twentieth—but I have forgotten the date of Godesberg.

Now I am alone, and a little cold. Everyone seems to have gone to bed. No clock ticks, nothing moves.

It's a very strange adventure, unforgettable of course. The war going to bed after its busy day. The fever of Germany abating after a letting of blood. No feeling of working up to a sudden hysterical armistice.

8 April

Now very deep in Germany. The people look at us more. But what can they think—they who have military things so close to their hearts? Do they think it fantastic that we have come so far over 3,000 miles of sea, or do they think us amateurs? My guess is they are very impressed. A man cried behind his window as a convoy of huge vehicles bumper-to-bumper crawled by for hours in the dust. 'Non-fraternization' is a good thing for the moment.

ALAN MOOREHEAD

BELSEN

JUST before you get to the main entrance of Belsen concentration camp—or rather the place where the camp used to be before the British burned it down—you come on a farmhouse. I suggested to the others in my party that we should turn in there and eat lunch before—rather than after—we visited the camp.

While the table was being set for us in the dining-room we were interested to know from the farmer what he thought of Belsen. 'I don't know very much about it,' he said. 'Each morning I had to drive up there with a cart full of vegetables—swedes and turnips mostly—and one of the S.S. guards took the horse and cart from me at the gate. After a bit the cart and horse were returned to me and I drove away. I was never allowed inside, and I didn't want to go in anyway. I knew something horrible was going on but I didn't ask about it lest I should find myself inside.'

We finished the meal and drove up to the gate with a special pass which General Dempsey had given the correspondents: from the first Dempsey was very keen that we should see Belsen and write about it. Although the British had only captured the place from the Germans a few days before they seemed to have things well organized. Hungarian guards were still spaced along the barbed wire fence, good-looking men who jumped eagerly to attention when an army vehicle came by. At the gate British soldiers were on guard. There were notices in English: 'Danger Typhus', 'Car Park', 'Powder Room', 'Inquiries' and so on.

A young army doctor and a captain from the Pioneers were in charge. The Captain's job was supervising the counting and burial of bodies. Possibly as a form of immunization from the grisly work he appeared to be in particularly jovial spirits.

'I love doing this,' he said, picking up the metal syringe filled with anti-louse powder. 'Come on.'

A squirt up each sleeve. One down the trousers. Two more squirts down the back and front of the shirt and a final shot on the hair. It was rather pleasant.

'We collected the local burgomeisters from the surrounding villages this morning and took them round the camp,' the doctor said.

'How did they take it?'

'One of them was sick and another one wouldn't look. They all said they had never dreamed that this was going on.'

We were now walking down the main driveway towards the first of the huts and administrative buildings. There were large crowds of civilian prisoners about, both those who strolled about in groups talking many different languages and those who sat silent on the ground. In addition there were many forms lying on the earth partly covered in rags, but it was not possible to say whether they were alive or dead or simply in the process of dying. It would be a day or two before the doctors got around to them for a diagnosis.

'There's quite a different air about the place in the last two days,' the doctor said. 'They seem much more cheerful now.'

'And the burial rate has gone down considerably,' the captain added. 'I'm handling just under three hundred a day now. It was five hundred to start with. And we are evacuating five hundred every day to the Panzer training school. It has been made into a hospital. Would you like to see the S.S. boys?'

We saw the women guards first. A British sergeant threw open the cell door and some twenty women wearing dirty grey skirts and tunics were sitting and lying on the floor.

'Get up,' the sergeant roared in English.

They got up and stood to attention in a semi-circle round the room, and we looked at them. Thin ones, fat ones, scraggy ones and muscular ones; all of them ugly, and one or two of them distinctly cretinous. I pointed out one, a big woman with bright golden hair and a bright pink complexion.

'She was Kramer's girl friend,' the sergeant growled. 'Nice lot, aren't they?'

There was another woman in a second room with almost delicate features, but she had the same set staring look in her eyes. The atmosphere of the reformatory school and the prison was inescapable.

Outside in the passageway there was a large blackboard ruled off in squares with white lines. Down the left-hand side of the board was a list of nationalities—'Poles, Dutch, Russians' and so on. Spaced along the top of the board was a list of religions and political faiths—'Communist, Jew, Atheist'. From the board one might have seen at a glance just how many prisoners were in the camp from each nation, and how they were subdivided politically and religiously. However, most of the numbers appeared to have been rubbed off, and it was difficult to make out the totals exactly. Germans seemed to make up the majority of the prisoners. After them Russians and Poles. A great many were Jews. As far as one could decipher there had been half a dozen British here, one or two Americans. There had been something like fifty thousand prisoners altogether.

As we approached the cells of the S.S. guards the sergeant's language became ferocious.

'We have had an interrogation this morning,' the captain said. 'I'm afraid they are not a pretty sight.'

'Who does the interrogation?'

'A Frenchman. I believe he was sent up here specially from the French underground to do the job.'

The sergeant unbolted the first door and flung it back with a crack like thunder. He strode into the cell, jabbing a metal spike in front of him.

'Get up,' he shouted. 'Get up. Get up, you dirty bastards.' There were half a dozen men lying or half lying on the floor. One or two were able to pull themselves erect at once. The man nearest me, his shirt and face spattered with blood, made two attempts before he got on to his knees and then gradually on to his feet. He stood with his arms half stretched out in front of him, trembling violently.

'Get up,' shouted the sergeant. They were all on their feet now, but supporting themselves against the wall.

'Get away from that wall.'

They pushed themselves out into space and stood there swaying. Unlike the women they looked not at us, but vacantly in front, staring at nothing.

Same thing in the next cell and the next where the men who were bleeding and were dirty were moaning something in German.

'You had better see the doctor,' the Captain said. 'He's a nice specimen. He invented some of the tortures here. He had one trick of injecting creosote and petrol into the prisoner's veins. He used to go around the huts and say "Too many people in here. Far too many." Then he used to loose off the barrel of his revolver round the hut. The doctor has just finished his interrogation.'

The doctor had a cell to himself.

'Come on. Get up,' the sergeant shouted. The man was lying in his blood on the floor, a massive figure with a heavy head and bedraggled beard. He placed his two arms on to the seat of a wooden chair, gave himself a heave and got half upright. One more heave and he was on his feet. He flung wide his arms towards us.

'Why don't you kill me?' he whispered. 'Why don't you kill me? I can't stand any more.'

The same phrases dribbled out of his lips over and over again.

'He's been saying that all morning, the dirty bastard,' the sergeant said. We went out into the sunshine. A number of other British soldiers were standing about, all with the same hard, rigid expressions on their faces, just ordinary English soldiers, but changed by this expression of genuine and permanent anger.

The crowds of men and women thickened as we went further into the camp. The litter of paper and rags and human offal grew thicker, the smell less and less bearable. At the entrance soldiers were unloading trucks filled with wooden latrines but these had not yet been placed about the camp, so many hundreds of half-naked men and women were squatting together in the open, a scene such as you sometimes see in India—except that here it was not always possible to distinguish men from women and indeed to determine whether or not they were human at all.

We drove through the filth in cars and presently emerging on to an open space of yellow clayey soil we came on a group of German guards flinging bodies into a pit about a hundred feet square. They brought the bodies up in handcarts and as they were flung into the grave a British soldier kept a tally of the numbers. When the total reached five hundred a bulldozer driven by another soldier came up and started nudging the earth into the grave. There was a curious pearly colour about the piled up bodies and they were small like the bodies of children. The withered skin was sagging over the bones and all the normal features by which you know a human being had practically disappeared. Having no stomach for this sort of thing I was only able to look for a second or two, but the S.S. guards and even the British soldiers there appeared to have grown used to the presence of death and able to work in its presence without being sick.

'The doctors are doing a wonderful job,' the Captain said: 'They are in the huts all day sorting out the living bodies from the dead, and it's not easy sometimes to tell the difference. Of course there are a lot who are just hopeless and they are simply left. But they are saving a lot now. We have got in all the food we want—two meals a day at 10 and 6. Come on and have a look at one of the huts. We will go to the women first.'

It was a single storey rectangular building, I suppose about a hundred feet long. Wooden bunks ran in tiers up to the ceiling and there was a narrow passage just wide enough to allow you to pass through. Since the majority of the women there were too weak to move and had no attention whatever, the stench was nauseating. Hurrying through, handkerchief to nose, one saw nothing but livid straining faces and emaciated arms and legs under the filthy bed-clothes on either side. Many were using their last strength to moan feebly for help. These animals were piled one on top of the other to the ceiling, sometimes two to a bunk.

An old hag, somewhat stronger than the others, was standing at the further door. 'I'm twenty-one,' she whispered. 'No, I don't know why they put me in here. My husband is a doctor at the front —I'm German but not Jewish. I said that I did not want to enlist in the women's organization and they put me in here. That was eighteen months ago.'

'I've had enough of this,' I said to the Captain.

'Come on,' he said. 'You've got to go through one of the men's huts yet. That's what you're here for.'

It was, if anything, more rancid than the one I had seen, but this time I was too sick with the stench to notice much except the sound of the voices: 'Doctor, Doctor'.

As we returned towards the entrance the people around us were noticeably better in health than those at the pits and the huts. As they were able to walk some instinct drew the people away from the charnel houses and up and out towards the entrance and the ordinary sane normal world outside. It was all like a journey down to some Dantesque pit, unreal, leprous and frightening. And now that one emerged into the light again, one's first coherent reactions were not of disgust or anger or even, I think, of pity. Something else filled the mind, a frantic desire to ask: 'Why? Why? Why? Why had it happened?' With all one's soul one felt: 'This is not war. Nor is it anything to do with here and now, with this one place at this one moment. This is timeless and the whole world and all mankind is involved in it. This touches me and I am responsible. Why has it happened. How did we let it happen?'

We stood there in a group, a major from the commandos, a padre, three or four correspondents, having at first nothing to say and then gradually and quietly asking one another the unspoken question.

Was it sadism? No, on the whole, not. Or, if it was sadism, then it was sadism of a very indirect and unusual kind. Relatively little torture was carried out at this camp. The sadist presumably likes to make some direct immediate act which inflicts pain on other people. He could not obtain much satisfaction from the slow long process of seeing people starve.

Then again the Germans were an efficient people. They needed manpower. Can one imagine anything more inefficient than letting all this valuable labour go to rot? The prisoners in Belsen were not even obliged to work. They were simply dumped in here and left to make what shift they could with a twice daily diet of turnip stew. Incidentally this lack of work probably led to the break-up of the prisoners' morale as much as anything.

The Germans, too, had a normal fear of disease spreading among themselves. And yet they let these thousands of bodies lie on the ground. It's true that there was not a great deal of typhus in the camp, but it had already broken out when the German commanders approached the British and offered to cede the camp under the terms of a truce.

It was not torture which had killed the prisoners. It was neglect. The sheer indifference of the Nazis. One began to see that the most terrible thing on earth is not positive destruction nor the perverse desire to hurt and destroy. The worst thing that can happen to you is for the master to say: 'I do not care about you any more. I am indifferent.' Whether you washed or ate or laughed or died—none of this was of any consequence any more because you as a person had no value. You were a slug on the ground, to be crushed or not to be crushed, it made no difference.

And having become attuned and accustomed to this indifference the guards were increasingly less affected by the suffering of the people around them. It was accepted that they should die. They were Russians. Russians die. Jews die. They were not even enemies. They were disease. Could you mourn or sympathize with the death throes of a germ?

Now here is where the evidence of Kramer, the camp commandant, comes in. To consider Kramer calmly I think we have first got to rid ourselves temporarily of our memory of that published picture of him shuffling across the yard in shackles. And we have to forget for a moment the title he was given through the world, 'The Monster of Belsen'. A friend of mine, a trained intelligence officer and interrogator in the British army, went into the whole question very carefully with Kramer and this was Kramer's statement:

'I was swamped. The camp was not really inefficient before you crossed the Rhine. There was running water, regular meals of a kind —I had to accept what food I was given for the camp and distribute it the best way I could. But then they suddenly began to send me trainloads of new prisoners from all over Germany. It was impossible to cope with them. I appealed for more staff, more food. I was told this was impossible; I had to carry on with what I had. Then as a last straw the Allies bombed the electric plant which pumped our water. Cartloads of food were unable to reach the camp because of the Allied fighters. Then things really got out of hand. In the last six weeks I have been helpless. I did not even have sufficient staff to bury the dead, let alone segregate the sick.'

Thus Kramer.

'But how did you come to accept a job like this?' he was asked. The reply: 'There was no question of my accepting it. I was ordered. I am an officer in the S.S. and I obey orders. These people were criminals and I was serving my Führer in a crisis by commanding this camp. I tried to get medicines and food for the prisoners and I failed. I was swamped. I may have been hated, but I was doing my duty.'

There was some truth in this last. Not only were the prisoners fond of hurling missiles at Kramer since we arrived, but his own guards turned on him as well. Kramer asked the British authorities that he should be segregated. He was told that in this event he would have to be shackled and to this he agreed.

Who then was responsible for Belsen and, for that matter, all the other camps? The S.S. guards? They say they were ordered. They hated the work but disobedience to Kramer meant death. Kramer says he was in precisely the same position. And so presumably do all the other Kramers above him until you reach Himmler. What does Himmler say? Himmler says he is serving his Führer. The Führer, of course, was innocent and knew nothing about the vulgar details (quite a number of Germans assured us of that). But—we can imagine Himmler saying—it was vital to protect the Führer from his enemies inside the Reich—the Jewish Bolsheviks who would have cheerfully murdered him. At this dire crisis for Germany and the Party one could not be too nice about the details—possibly some people were treated a little too harshly. But one could not afford to take chances. The Nazis were perfectly prepared to treat these prisoners with humanity, but the enemies of Germany made this impossible. They destroyed communications, they blocked the food supply. Naturally the camps suffered.

But the people of Germany? Why had they allowed this thing to be? Why had they not protested? The average German answers: in the first place we did not know these camps existed. Secondly, how could we have protested? What possibly could we have done? The Nazis were too strong.

Very well then, why did you not protest when the Nazis were rising to power?

They answer: How could we foretell that the Nazis would end with this horror? When they first came to power they embarked on a programme that was excellent for Germany: new roads, modern buildings and machines. It seemed rational and good at the beginning. When we realized that Hitler was turning to war it was already too late. By then the Nazis had claimed our children. They were Nazified in the schools. A parent would be denounced by his own child if he spoke against the Nazis. Little by little we were overwhelmed and in the end it was too late. There was no point at which we could have effectively protested. Why did not foreign countries which had the power check the Nazis soon enough? If only you had attacked us before the Nazis became too strong.

And so the blame is thrown back upon the world. No one anywhere is willing to take responsibility. Not the guard or the torturer. Not Kramer. Not Herr Woolf.[1] They were all ordered. Not Himmler or Hitler (the end justified the means); they were fighting to rid the world of the terrible menace of Jewish Bolshevism—they were ordered by their high sense of duty. Not the German people. They too had to obey. And finally not the world. Is England Germany's keeper?

That is the line of argument which we have heard as observers of this final eclipse of Germany. I write it here not because I accept or reject it, but because we are still too close to the scene to do much more than report personally and directly; and it seems a pity to give way to the downright childishness of saying that all Germans are natural black-hearted fiends capable of murdering and torturing and starving people at the drop of the hat.

If I were compelled to make some sort of direct line at this moment I would say—Yes, all mankind *is* in some way responsible for Belsen but in varying degrees. Herr Woolf, for example, is a cultured European. Surely he could have seen a little more clearly than, say, the average German workman, what the Nazi party was going to mean and have made some protest in time. Clearly, too, the Germans generally and the leading Nazis most particularly are far more embroiled in this monstrosity than anyone else. The Junkers and the Wehrmacht power-through-war class—they too are utterly compromised. But the degree of guilt varies enormously both inside and outside of the Nazi Party, inside and outside of Germany. Probably the least of all to blame is the unpolitical boy who was put into uniform and forced to come here into the German battlefield to support the tardy conscience of the world. And die for it.

[1] The German arms manufacturer whose opinions are paraphrased above.

There is only one thing possible that one can do for him now—be vigilant to snap the long chains that lead to the future Belsens before they grow too strong. A shudder of horror went round the world when the news of these concentration camps was published, but only, I think, because of the special interest and the special moment in the war. We were engrossed with Germany and it is perhaps not too subtle to say that since Germany was manifestly beaten, people wanted to have a justification for their fight, a proof that they were engaged against evil. From the German point of view Belsen was perfectly mistimed. Worse camps like Ausschwitz existed in Poland and we took no notice. Dachau was described in the late thirties and we did not want to hear. In the midst of the war three quarters of a million Indians starved in Bengal because shipping was wanted in other parts and we were bored.

The last living patient has been evacuated from Belsen. The hateful buildings have been burned down. The physical evidence of all those horrible places will soon have been wiped out. Only the mental danger remains. The danger of indifference.

FRANÇOIS LACHEVAL

LAST DAYS OF BERLIN

ON ARRIVING in Berlin, it was the indifference of the masses in the presence of catastrophe which struck you. They went about their business, did their shopping amidst mountains of ruins, made their way along pavements obstructed with bricks and mud, as if nothing had happened. In a building with a gaping façade you might find, on the fourth floor, but facing on to the back yard, a flat where gas, telephone and electricity were intact. This was quite a common occurrence. I have spent some of the most comfortable hours of my life in the one remaining room where lived, ate and slept the owners of one of the most beautiful houses in the Kurfurstrasse. Wooden arrows guided you from the street through the débris which littered the square. Most of the pictures were stored, under State protection, somewhere in a disused Silesian mine, but an interest in Matisse and Picasso remained alive, and a taste for English literature as well. Every day, between 1 and 2 p.m., diplomats from the Wilhelmstrasse, several industrialists, and friends passing through Berlin, sat down together at the one round table. There was always enough to eat, and food coupons were always refused. The host cycled eight miles to break his fifteen or sixteen hour working day at the General Staff Headquarters. We spoke freely—that is to say, all the guests knew the code of *sous-entendus* and the latest B.B.C. news without any direct allusion being made. I learned later that the lady of the house committed suicide four days after her husband was taken away to prison by the Russians . . .

The shops were empty. The windows (small apertures cut in enormous wooden panels) certainly exhibited some articles, but in practice one could buy nothing, except with the help of an '*Ausgebombtenschein*', or at the smart shops of the Unter den Linden in exchange for cigarettes. Coffee (collected stocks of which the Germans were selling in occupied countries against foreign competition) was kept for special occasions, such as receipt of compensation for one's flat or one's car, and the purchase of a suit or a bottle of brandy. I had an overcoat of pure English cloth made for me by a tailor in the Friedrichstrasse with a Polish-Jewish name. It cost me 3,500 marks, a pound of coffee and twenty cigars. Yet the best meal at the Eden cost not more than eight or ten marks. Rents and prices had been stabilized, and life cost us nothing.

At the end of January, I was present at one of the last concerts of the Symphony Orchestra conducted by Furtwangler in the Admiralspalast. Two-thirds of the seats had been given to soldiers on leave and to shock-workers. And yet, except for the blinding sheets of light which interrupted the Mozart symphony for an hour, the atmosphere was one of total *dépaysement*. It was at the time when the first convoys of refugees were arriving at the eastern stations. Exhausted women and children dead with cold were being lifted from cattle-wagons. At night, the neighbouring streets were blocked with a mass of misery sleeping on the bare pavements. (The journalists who have recently returned from Berlin with the same pitiful accounts in their notebooks—and with an anti-Soviet bias—were not there on 3 February, when Allied bombers attacked these same stations and the trains besieged by thousands who could not get into the shelters. Nor were the journalists in Poland and Czechoslovakia where these same refugees led a grand life exploiting the *Untermenschen*, who, when liberated, drove them from their countries. For the Chancelleries and the armies in the field, war can cease from one day to another: but in the East it will only cease with the end of the occupation, or with the annihilation of the Germans. This is not an opinion: it is a fact.)

* * *

The whole edifice was held together by terror alone. I will indicate later the reasons which seem to me to explain the Germans' extraordinary resistance. Its backbone was obviously constituted by Himmler's machinery (his S.S., his S.D., *Sicherheitsdienst*, and his Gestapo). I had met with it in the occupied countries, but I would never have thought that in Germany itself I could have felt so brutally its subterranean and penetrating ubiquity. In France, in Belgium, on all occasions and everywhere, one encountered pockets of free air—with some friends, in some café, in the Métro, even. Nothing like that in Germany. The possibility of treason clung to the very soles of your feet. (I was indeed surprised when, for the first time, *Germans* confided to me their dread of the unexpected double visit at six o'clock in the morning!) The law wisely neglected petty civil crimes; 'ordinary' thieves and murderers risked only being sent to the front, where even the *Himmelfahrtskommando* left them a chance to live. If, on the other hand, the accused had committed his theft under cover of the black-out, for example, or had robbed a dignitary of the Party or the State, he appeared before the *Volksgericht* for 'sabotage of the resistance forces' (*Schwachung der Wehrkraft*), and was condemned to death. A critical reflection on the regime or on the conduct of the war reported to the police involved imprisonment at least; if you had insidiously given it the appearance of eulogy (*Heimtücke*), the punishment might be capital. The Gestapo had thousands of spies at their command, who, in turn, had informers in all walks of life. It was considered heroic to listen to a foreign radio alone in one's room. It was a criminal offence not to denounce a delinquent, even if he were a member of your family. It was considered suspect to know nothing. (This terror, which did not prevent thousands of Germans from effective resistance and active post-war preparations, but which sent quite as many to concentration camps, exploited to the full the Germans' natural respect for the military hierarchy. Gedye, in his

Fallen Bastions, tells the story, which I remember well, of how the Socialists in Vienna, attacked by Dollfuss's troops, decided against occupying an important railway station, because only passengers had the right of access to the platforms. Similarly, on 20 July, General Haase, who had come to arrest Goebbels 'because Hitler was dead', caused himself to be arrested without resistance when Goebbels communicated with the Führer by telephone in his presence.)

Furthermore, it would be inaccurate to interpret 20 July as the first attempt to overthrow the Nazi yoke: it was, rather, the last victory of the S.S., resulting in the alignment of the nobility, which had hitherto succeeded in maintaining a certain aloofness (and which had, till then, suffered least from the regime). In fact, Himmler's reprisals were so swift and effective that one could not help suspecting that he knew of the plot, that he perhaps even encouraged it, as something which would inevitably give him an opportunity for action, and that only the attempted assassination, which Hitler seemed to have escaped by a miracle, had not been foreseen, or had not been foreseen in its actual form. This alignment of the nobility and that of the industrialists is an excellent illustration of the situation of the ruling classes under the Third Reich. Nazism deprived neither class of its essential prerogatives: on the contrary, it consolidated the large ancestral estates, and codified, in its Labour Charter, the right of 'leaders of enterprise' summarily to regulate their dealings with the workers. Hitlerism 'aligned' individuals in the state and within their respective classes; it did not interfere with their traditional hierarchies. It even tolerated some exceptions: Gottfried von Bismarck, though seriously compromised in the 20 July affair, was acquitted by the *Volksgericht*. Thyssen, the industrialist, whom the Germans recaptured in Paris in 1940, after he had fled from Germany through Switzerland, publicly repudiating his Nazism, yet was allowed to live peacefully at his home until the liberation by the Allies. (Where is he now, by the way?)

* * *

It cannot be denied that the 'machine' continued to revolve. Despite the bombardments and despite the limitless efforts exacted from everyone, decrease in production did not make itself felt unduly, and the distribution of food—not abundant, but two or three times superior to that allocated by the occupying armies at present—functioned without bottlenecks. As late as February, the State seemed to be in such complete control of the situation, that the black market, in butter, for example, was regulated by a coupon system: one knew that the coupons would be honoured. Trains ran with remarkable punctuality: the non-stop Berlin–Hamburg Pullman service was not interrupted until March. Even in Berlin, the S.Bahn ran all night.

Of course, deaths at the front increased in number. But their very frequency made them less noticeable; besides, it was forbidden, except in the *Schwarze Korps*, to publish them in the Press or in printed announcements, and the wearing of mourning was considered unpatriotic. People only wanted it all to end as soon as possible. How was it to end? They had a government to worry about that. I have preserved two documents which show the point to which fanaticism had become a national habit. The first is a Press cutting in which a pastor announces '*in stolzer Trauer*' the death of his eighth son; the second is a card on which a young woman informs her acquaintances '*in stille Trauer aber zugleich voll dankbarer Freude*' at the same time of the birth of her son, of the death of his father, who was killed at the front eight months before, and of her posthumous marriage with him.

The raids were terrifying, but the shelters were excellent. Enormous cellars fitted with bunks (the one under the Zoo had the cubic space of Selfridge's, and could accommodate 10,000 people) were equally distributed over the whole city. The Wilhelmstrasse shelter, fifty metres below the Adlon, provided welcome opportunities for many diplomatic conversations and social rendezvous. During the alert, a special radio station installed at Flack headquarters broadcast a communiqué on the progress of the battle. Moreover, the enemy planes did not arrive unheralded. Every German listened in to the hourly *Luftlage* broadcast by all stations, and as soon as a formation penetrated into German territory, a special transmitter for the benefit of night fighters gave its exact situation, its strength, altitude and direction. The country was divided into alphabetically designated regions, with corresponding Christian names, and although the map was secret, each household had charted a copy for itself, so as to be able to make plans in advance, or to pass the time playing the family game of 'Bertha, Bertha'. There was a red formation, a blue one, and a green one, red 2, blue 2 and so on, and bets were made as to the town over which 'they' would make their swoop ... At 'Gustav-Friedrich', you packed up your bag and joined in the nocturnal tide flowing to the shelters: Berlin would be sounding the alert in ten minutes.

The Germans seemed able to take everything in their stride: and yet the war was terrible. There was Hamburg, with its inhabitants transformed into living torches, precipitated into the middle of the city by an ascending whirlwind of fire. There was Dresden, attacked for three nights in succession; three to four thousand refugees from the East thought themselves safe there 'because there were no industries' and 'because an aunt of Churchill lives in Dresden'; the warning system was destroyed; aeroplanes, 'hedge-hopping' over the parks, machine-gunned men, women and children lying flat on the ground; at a conservative estimate, the death-roll was 120,000; the bodies were burnt on pyres erected in public squares. (Why should we ignore this? These are facts, and the Germans had accepted the risk. But how can we hope to impress those who have seen such things with photographs of corpses found in the horror camps? That was 'only' a matter of Jews, of Poles ...)

* * *

The defence against death was to live as well as possible.

The wedding of my friend F. was a great success. From Austria and from the Rhine, on leave from the Eastern front, his friends had come to Berlin, for the last time, perhaps, who knows? The evening before, a *Luftmine* had smashed all the windows of the hotel —and five hundred in the Wilhelmstrasse. But the damage had been repaired that very morning. Round the impressive buffet crowded wedding guests in full evening dress, and the remainder of 'all Berlin' ... Dörnberg, President of the Council—of that *Auswärtiges Amt* where they claimed to be able to do nothing, except to give reasons for the decisions of the S.S.—dominated the crowd with his blond six feet six. There were disputes as to who was the more beautiful, the daughter-in-law of the late Reich Ambassador to Paris, or the Hungarian wife of Mussolini's last Ambassador, Anfuso (who has been condemned to death, yet lives peacefully in Spain). Austrian princes recounted their woes: their castles invaded by refugees, their possessions sent away as far west as possible, the pictures to Salzburg, the silver to the Swiss frontier. 'It is terrible,' the Countess F. confided to me, '*die Portiere sint an der Oder . . .*'

In the evening, we met again at the Princess W.'s, of whom it was rumoured that she belonged to the S.D. She received us in the cellars of her blasted and gutted house; there was a salon-boudoir, and a 'ball-room' with a rather uneven floor. A Croatian Count (a former tennis ball-boy turned diplomat, who had ennobled himself in order to be more worthy of sharing the bed of a Ruhr magnate's wife) had lent his Cuban servants to form the orchestra. Among the guests were some convalescent officers, one with a silver shoulder, another with a wooden leg. These were the most pleasant of the lot. That night, twelve formations of Fortresses were announced over Germany; the sirens howled, but the shelter was too deep, the cold was too biting, and, with the help of the champagne, we continued to dance. A Swiss friend told me how a *Luftmine* had blasted his Legation; at two o'clock in the morning, two high officials of the Wilhelmstrasse had come to inquire into the damage, and on the following day half a company of soldiers were already at work clearing the débris . . . We went home at about four o'clock in the morning. The houses were silhouetted against a sky still red from several fires.

* * *

Then there were the foreigners. Sometimes it seemed that there were more of them than of the Germans.

In the streets, first of all: small groups, under strict guard, in the striped clothes of convicts, or in tattered, motley uniforms; Poles with a large 'P' on their backs, the Russians most wretched of all; the permanent presence of shame. Even more than the bombs, perhaps, these funereal processions evoked the vague presentiment of inexorable doom. One day other men, their compatriots, but better armed than they, would come after them, and, as Goebbels himself predicted, would take Germans away in their turn. It was hoped that regular armies would be on the spot to prevent their free vengeance. The Russians were in Silesia. I remember the conductor Karayan parting from me at the Brandenburgertor with the furtive remark that they must have reached the eastern camps where Jews were gassed . . .

The Adlon was the headquarters of prosperous foreigners: of the cunning and resourceful Déat, '*l'Allemand*' as he was nicknamed while still at the *Ecole Normale*; of General Bridoux, faithful to Pétain through stupidity, a natural reactionary, and disgusted with the Germans (he had replaced Scapini—who, in August 1944, had at last seen the light, but was being harried from one antechamber to another). It was there, too, that I met Degrelle, heavy rather than handsome, in the uniform of an S.S. officer. He was returning to the Eastern Front, and was complaining of the Germans' lack of drive; his wife and children—with a certain amount of money and some jewellery, of course—he was hoping to send off to Switzerland (he himself, at the time of writing, is still at San Sebastian).

The Adlon maintained the traditional surroundings as far as possible. To obtain a table, it was necessary to slip several cigars into the hand of a *maître d'hôtel* seemingly disdainful, yet grateful withal, and the waiters frequently bickered across the tables over cigarettes which had been left. But even so, this was better than the Esplanade, where the waiters served in their winter coats, because of the lack of heating . . .

* * *

Perhaps it is in this tenacious and completely universal will to keep up the appearances of normal life that we should look for the secret of the resistance of the German people, and this normal life, in its turn, gave them the confidence which they so desperately needed. For, when all is said and done, they knew well that the war was lost, and that this massacre of populations 'was no longer a war'. On the other hand, defeat 'would be worse than anything else'. Therefore, it was rumoured that the alliance between the British and the Russians could not last; Himmler, according to the S.S., was planning a separate peace with Stalin; the Russians would stop at the Vistula, or at the Oder, then; or, at the last moment, the British would be allowed to walk in (that is what Kesselring was trying to do when he transferred more than sixty divisions from the West to the East in March and April).

And all this time the country was sliding ever faster towards the abyss. Each month the German people bound their fate more closely to that of Nazism, and, in the hope of a final miracle, shrank before the increasing risks of a revolution. The same reflex had determined the attitude of the democracies to Hitler, who, from one crisis to another, had increasingly powerful means to oppose their eventual intervention, which was deferred each time by the hope of an improbable appeasement. To support a rising, the German resistance had at their disposal neither a parachutists' service, nor, above all, an assurance of the arrival of a liberating army. On the contrary, whether it was acclaimed or not, the Allied occupation could not fail radically to disorganize production and distribution in Germany. In the occupied countries, anti-fascism could appeal to nationalism: in Germany, it had the most murderous bombardments to justify. And finally, how could they believe that the gigantic efforts and the privations of so many years had all been vain, and that Germany, whose early aspirations had been universally recognized as legitimate, could disappear after having dominated nearly all Europe?

And yet that is what has happened, with consequences more terrible than any which one dared to imagine.

[*Translated by* NATALIA GALITZINE]

STEPHEN SPENDER

FROM 'RHINELAND JOURNAL'

COLOGNE

AT HAGEN I had seen a good deal of damage, and again at Hamm, where most of the centre of the town was destroyed. Also all along the route from Oenhausen there were bridges destroyed, detours, temporary wooden bridges touchingly named after some member of the Royal Engineers—McMahon's Bridge, Piper's Bridge, Smith's Bridge, etc.; but it was in Cologne that I realized what total destruction meant.

My first impression on passing through was of there not being a single house left. There are plenty of walls, but these are a thin mask in front of the damp, hollow, stinking emptiness of gutted interiors. Whole streets with nothing but the walls left standing are worse than streets flattened. They are more sinister and oppressive.

Actually, there are a few habitable buildings left in Cologne: three hundred in all, I am told. One passes through street after street of houses whose windows look hollow and blackened—like the opened mouth of a charred corpse; behind these windows there is nothing except floors, furniture, bits of rag, books, all dropped to the bottom of the building to form there a sodden mass.

Through the streets of Cologne thousands of people trudge all day long. These are crowds who a few years ago were shop-gazing in their city, or waiting to go to the cinema or to the opera, or stopping taxis. They are the same people who once were the ordinary inhabitants of a great city when by what now seems an unbelievable magical feat of reconstruction in time, this putrescent corpse-city was the hub of the Rhineland, with a great shopping centre, acres of plate glass, restaurants, a massive business street containing the head offices of many banks and firms, an excellent opera, theatres, cinema, lights in the streets at night.

Now it requires a real effort of the imagination to think back to that Cologne which I knew well ten years ago. Everything has gone. In this the destruction in Germany is quite different from even the worst that has happened in England (though not different from Poland and from parts of Russia). In England there are holes, gaps and wounds, but the surrounding life of the people themselves has filled them up, creating a scar which will heal. In towns such as Cologne and those of the Ruhr, something quite different has happened. The external destruction is so great that it cannot be healed and the surrounding life of the rest of the country cannot flow into and resuscitate the city, which is not only battered but also dismembered and cut off from the rest of Germany and from Europe. The ruin of the city is reflected in the internal ruin of its inhabitants; instead of being able to form a scar over the city's wounds, they are parasites sucking at a dead carcass, digging among the ruins for hidden food, doing business at their Black Market near the cathedral, which is the commerce of destruction instead of production.

The people who live there seem quite dissociated from Cologne. They resemble rather a tribe of wanderers who have discovered a ruined city in a desert and who are camping there, living in the cellars and hunting amongst the ruins for the booty, relics of a dead civilization.

The great city looks like a corpse and stinks like one also, with all the garbage which has not been cleared away, all the bodies still buried under heaps of stones and iron. Although the streets have been partly cleared, they still have many holes in them, and some of the side streets are impassable. The general impression is that very little has been cleared away. There are landscapes of untouched ruin still left.

The Rhine with the destroyed bridges over it had a frightening grandeur on the day when I crossed over the Engineers' bridge. There were black clouds broken by glass-clear fragments of sky. Gleams of light fell on the cathedral which, being slightly damaged looks like a worn Gothic tapestry of itself with bare patches in the roof through which one sees the canvas structure. But it is the comparatively undamaged cathedral which gives Cologne what it still retains of character. One sees that this is and was a great city, it is uplifted by the spire of the cathedral from being a mere heap of rubble and a collection of walls, like the towns of the Ruhr. Large buildings round the cathedral have been scratched and torn, and, forming a kind of cliff, they have a certain dignity like the cliffs and rocks under a church close to the sea.

The girders of the Rhine bridges plunged diagonally into black waters of the Rhine frothing into swirling white around them. They looked like machines of speed diving into the river, their beautiful lines emphasizing the sense of movement. Or where they do not swoop like javelins or speedboats into the river, broken girders hang from piers in ribbons, splinters and shreds, a dance of arrested movement. In the destroyed German towns one often feels haunted by the ghost of a tremendous noise. It is impossible not to imagine the rocking explosions, the hammering of the sky upon the earth, which must have caused all this.

The effect of these corpse-towns is a grave discouragement which influences everyone living and working in Germany, the Occupying Forces as much as the Germans. The destruction is *serious* in more senses than one. It is a climax of deliberate effort, an achievement of our civilization, the most striking result of co-operation between nations in the twentieth century. It is the shape created by our century as much as the Gothic cathedrals are the shape created by the Middle Ages. Everything has stopped here, that fusion of the past within the present, integrated into architecture, which forms the organic life of a city, a life quite distinct from that of the inhabitants who are after all only using a city as a waiting room on their journey through time: that long, gigantic life of a city has been killed. The city is dead and the inhabitants only haunt the cellars and basements. Without their city they are rats in the cellars, or bats wheeling around the towers of the cathedral. The citizens go on existing with a base mechanical kind of life like that of insects in the crannies of walls who are too creepy and ignoble to be destroyed when the wall is torn down. The destruction of the city itself with all its past as well as its present, is like a reproach to the people who go on living there. The sermons in the stones of Germany preach nihilism.

PROFESSOR C——

As soon as I had arrived in Bonn, I called on Professor C——. Although half of Bonn is destroyed, his ground-floor flat was in an almost untouched part of the city, and he and his wife were still living there.

I had known C—— very well before 1933. He lectured in modern languages at Heidelberg and then at Bonn. He was one of the foremost exponents of French literature in Germany under the Weimar Republic and had written books on Balzac, the French Symbolists and Proust.[1]

In the summer of 1931 a friend had given me an introduction to C—— in Baden-Baden. At this time he was a man of forty-five. We went for many walks together in the Black Forest, during which he talked much of literature. He was the only teacher I had (for he was, in effect, my teacher) who never lost sight of the direct connection between literature and living. It is difficult to define this, except to say that he talked about every subject concretely, which made one feel that one could grasp hold of and use it to enable one to live better one's own life. Another of his characteristics as a teacher was his clear grasp of what I could and could not learn. He never gave me the feeling that I ought to be good at things of which I had no understanding. He gave me instead a sense of both my limitations and my potentialities.

Shortly after I had first met him, C—— married. His wife had formerly been his student. After this I used to go every year or so to visit them, here at Bonn. He had an excellent library and many interesting things. He lived well, liking good company, good food and good wine. He and Frau C—— travelled much, particularly in France, Italy and Spain. He had connections with the outstanding writers and scholars of these countries and he was generally respected.

[1] See my *September Journal*, HORIZON, 1940.

After Hitler's seizure of power it would have been easy for him to to leave Germany and go to Paris, Madrid, Rome, Oxford or Cambridge. His position in Germany was made no easier by the fact that he had, in 1932, published a book in which he violently and even hysterically denounced the activities of the Nazis in the German Universities. This book nevertheless was a defence of the German tradition, written in a nationalist spirit. Besides attacking the Nazis, it attacked the proletarianization of literature and it criticized the influence of Jewish ideas.

Since 1933, I have often wondered why C—— didn't leave Germany. I think really the reason was a passion for continuity, a rootedness in his environment which made him almost immovable. He had modelled his life on the idea of that Goethe who boasted that during the Napoleonic struggle he had been like a mighty cliff towering above and indifferent to the waters raging hundreds of feet beneath him. If he always detested the Nazis he also had little sympathy for the Left, and the movement to leave Germany was for the most part a Leftwards one. Above all, he may have felt that it was his duty, as a non-political figure, to stay in Germany, in order to be an example before the young people of the continuity of a wiser and greater German tradition. In spite of everything, he was very German.

From 1933 to 1939 I saw little of him because I was scarcely ever in Germany, but I remember staying with him for a few days in 1934. At that time he did not concern himself with politics, but his flat had become a centre where every visitor came and upbraided the regime, usually from a Catholic point of view. It so happened that I told him there were a few people in England who thought that although the Nazis stood for many things of which the English should disapprove, nevertheless there was an idealist side to the movement, and that Hitler himself was an idealist unaware of the evil of some of the men around him.

C—— got up from the chair in his study where he was sitting, when I said this, and said: 'If you think that, come for a walk with me'. We went along the shore of the Rhine. When we had got almost as far as Godesberg, he stopped and pointing with his stick, said: 'Do you see that hotel? Well, that's the hotel where those rascals, Hitler with them, stayed a few weeks ago, and deliberately plotted the murders which took place on June 30th.' (Incidentally, it was the hotel where Chamberlain later visited Hitler.) He looked at me with an expression of finality. Then, surprisingly, he burst out laughing. We walked back to the house.

During the next years I heard from friends that his life became increasingly difficult. At first he seemed indifferent to the Nazis and went on teaching, while refusing to do any of the things which the Nazis required of him. I suppose that later on he must have compromised to some extent, or he would have been imprisoned. Apparently he became more and more unhappy and was driven into greater isolation. Sylvia Beach, who saw him in Paris in 1936 or 1937, told me that then, before he would talk to her, he insisted on taking a taxi to a café in a suburb, and even then he kept on looking round to see if he was observed. He had to stop teaching French and took to medieval Latin. Then, finally, he gave up teaching almost entirely. He and his wife saw almost no one. His reputation became gradually smothered until he was scarcely known amongst the younger Germans. Ten years ago he was well known inside as well as outside Germany. Today, in Germany, he is only known to scholars.

The rooms which had once been well lit, pleasantly furnished, were now bare and dingy. As I came in through the front door, I saw another door on my right with a notice on it: NO ADMITTANCE. FOR OFFICERS ONLY. This had been put up by the Americans who had requisitioned part of the flat when they were in Bonn. It was being kept up as a memento.

C—— was moved to see me. He took me into his library, now just a bare empty room with no carpets, very few books on the shelves, and just enough furniture for an alcove to be used as a dining-room whilst the other end of the room was used as a study.

We plunged very quickly into explanations. I said that I had come to inquire into the intellectual life of Bonn. C—— said that there was almost no intellectual life left in the whole of Germany, but that nevertheless it was important that I should talk to people and excellent that a writer like myself should understand what was happening in Germany.

Within quite a few minutes and before any of us had mentioned our personal histories during the past five years, we were talking about the war. C—— wanted me to understand that many students from Bonn had gone into the war not wishing to win, but fighting desperately. They fought for their country, but 'they had that monster on their backs—the Nazi Party. They knew that whether Germany won or lost, they themselves were bound to lose.'

C—— said rather aggressively that anyone outside Germany who maintained that it was possible for the German anti-Nazis to prevent war, should make a serious study of the effects of government by terror, propaganda, lies and perverted psychology in modern scientific conditions. 'You seemed to expect us to stand up or go out into the street and say that we opposed the war and the Party. But what effect could that have had except our own destruction? It certainly would not have stopped the war. It was not *we* in Germany but you, the democracies, the English, the French and the Americans, who could have stopped the war at the time of the Occupation of the Rhineland. We were all confidently expecting that you would do so at the time. What were we to think when you let Hitler march in?'

'Don't you think, then, that Germany is responsible for this war?'

'Of course,' C—— replied; 'it is absolutely clear that Hitler started the war. There is no doubt about that at all. It is the first fact that every German must realize. In spite of all Goebbels's propaganda, every German who says otherwise is either an ignoramus or a liar. The trouble with the Germans is that they have no experience of political freedom. Right up to the last century they were governed by ridiculous little princelings. Then they came under the Prussian militarists. They have never freed themselves from servile habits of mind. They have never governed themselves.'

I answered: 'I can quite well understand that the general mass of the people were first deceived and then terrorized by the Nazis. What I can't understand, though, is that no section of educated Germans ever put up any united resistance. For example, how is it that the teaching profession, as a whole, taught all the Nazi lies about race and deliberately set about perverting the minds of the young? I can't believe that this would have happened in England. A majority of English teachers would refuse to teach what they considered to be lies about history and biology. Still less would they teach their pupils to lie. And they would have refused to teach hatred.'

C—— shrugged his shoulders and sighed deeply. 'Although some teachers did in fact resist, right up to the end, nevertheless the profession as a whole was swamped by Nazi ideas. Alas, too many

German teachers are militarist and nationalist in their minds before they are teachers, and they think of nothing but teaching discipline. Unfortunately this is also true to a great extent of the Universities.'

'If you condemn the whole teaching profession of a nation, surely that is very serious? It implies condemning the whole nation?'

'You cut off the head of a king several hundred years ago. The French also rose against their king and their aristocrats. The basis of freedom in the democracies is the idea that it is always possible to revolt against a tyrant. The Germans have never risen against a tyrant. Even today, it isn't the Germans who have risen against Hitler. The Germans always submit.'

BONN

I left the C——s and walked back through Bonn towards the Officers' Transit Mess.

A pleasant road, overshadowed with trees, running parallel to the Rhine leads from the end of the road where they live to the centre of Bonn which, from this end of the town, may be said to begin with the University whose entrance bridges the road. On either side of this broad leafy road there were houses and hotels, many of them destroyed. Heaps of rubble often made it impossible to keep to the pavement.

Beyond the University gate everything, including almost the whole of the main old University buildings, the shopping centre and the market-place is destroyed. Over the gate the wall of the University stood, a yellow colour, surmounted by the gleaming gold statue of St. George against the sky among the high boughs of chestnut trees. But there was nothing except charred emptiness behind this outer wall. Between the centre of the town and the Rhine everything had been smashed by shell fire in the last stages of the fighting. Occasionally I saw written on a wall some surviving Nazi slogan—'VICTORY OR SIBERIA', 'BETTER DEATH THAN SIBERIA', 'WE SHALL WIN—THAT IS CERTAIN', or 'THE DAY OF REVENGE WILL COME'. There was something strangely evangelical about these slogans, and one would not have been surprised to see 'GOD IS LOVE' or 'ABANDON HOPE ALL YE WHO ENTER HERE' among them. Frequently there appeared on the wall a black looming figure with a question mark over his shoulder. At first I thought this might be one of the Nazi leaders, but it turned out to be a warning against spies.

By the banks of the Rhine, the beer gardens, hotels and great houses were all smashed to pieces. In a space amongst the ruins which formed a protected nest, there was a burnt-out German tank. Scattered all round it ammunition lay on the ground—shells the shape of Rhine wine bottles, still partly enclosed in their careful packings of straw and fibre.

The great bridge was down, collapsed into the river. Close to it, by a landing stage, an A.A. gun which had been used as an anti-tank gun, was still pointing with exemplary precision at the end of the bridge on the opposite side of the Rhine.

Bonn stank as much as Cologne or as the towns of the Ruhr. In addition to the persistent smell which never left one alone—like an over-Good Companion—the town was afflicted by a plague of small green midges which bred I suppose in all the rubble and also in rubbish heaps, for no rubbish had been collected for several months and in many streets there were great heaps of waste with grass and even tall potato plants growing out of a mass of grit and stalks and peel.

At night these small flies crowded thick on the walls of the bedrooms. At mealtimes they got into any and every drink. One night I went for a walk along the Rhine. When I returned, the sun had set and the flies lay like a thick bank of London pea-soup fog on either side of the river. They swarmed into my eyes, nostrils and hair, dissolving into a thin green splodge of slime when I tried to brush them off.

* * *

GUILT

One morning I called on C—— again. He was sitting at his table which was piled up with many heaps of books. One of these was *The Ondt and the Gracehopper*, a fragment of *Finnegans Wake*. This contained many marginal notes by C—— explaining the derivations of some of these punning portmanteau inventions of Joyce. The book was inscribed to C—— by James Joyce.

For some time we talked about Joyce. Then he said: 'I want to sell this book, but I don't know how much it is worth'. I said: 'I'll try to find out in London. But in any case you couldn't sell it there now, on account of various Exchange regulations.' 'That does not matter. In a year or eighteen months would do.' 'Why do you want to sell your books? Are you hard up?' 'No I'm not. And in any case there is nothing to buy in Germany. I used to like beautiful books and charming things, but now I want to get rid of them all. I have collected bad editions of all the books which I shall want to read during the rest of my life.' He pointed to some drab rows of books on his shelves. I said: 'I shouldn't sell your books, because in five years' time everything will be different, and then you will probably regret not having beautiful things'. 'No,' he said, 'I know it will be impossible for any German to get out of all this—with any dignity or self-respect—for more than five years. We have made ourselves hated all over the world, and now we are condemned to imprisonment in the ruin which is Germany. In five years' or in ten years' time I shall be an old man. I am already sixty.'

Later I discovered that he certainly had another reason for selling his things. He was afraid that during the coming winter his wife might need a store of cash in order to save them from starvation.

We talked of France. I told him that I had seen Sylvia Beach, who was formerly Joyce's publisher. I said that she had been interned during the Occupation of France. I told him that before the war I remembered seeing in her shop a beautiful girl aged eighteen or so. This girl was Jewish. The Germans had ordered Sylvia to give her notice. Sylvia explained that she was an American and that as a citizen of the United States, she did not recognize the anti-Jewish laws. The Germans then interned Sylvia. The girl was put on a train for Poland. She was never heard of again.

I spoke also of my friend Ghisa Drouin. She also was Jewish and she had, while caring for her family in Paris, been subject to the laws relating to Jews. She had to wear the Star of David, to sit on a special bench in the park, to travel in a special compartment of the Métro, and she was only allowed to shop between certain hours in the morning. In order to keep her family, she had to shop at other hours, knowing all the time that if she was caught she also would be put on a train bound for Poland.

When I was in Paris in May I dined with the Drouins. Ghisa sat at one end of the table, her husband at the other end, and opposite me was their little son, Georges, aged ten. Ghisa started talking about the Germans when they were in Paris. She told how they made a special choice sometimes of deporting the oldest and the youngest member of a family, a grandmother and a grandchild, for example.

At this, Georges, who had been watching us with large eyes said: 'And they took away one of my comrades from school'.

'Yes,' said Ghisa quickly, 'they took away a school friend of his, aged eleven, together with his grandmother, aged seventy-five.'

'And we never heard of him again,' said Georges. On his mouth there was a strange expression, a frozen mouth of a Greek tragedy mask. We changed the subject and talked of other things.

There was a silence. Then C—— touched my arm and said: 'When you spoke of guilt a few nights ago, I wanted to tell you something. It is that the Germans *are* guilty of the most terrible crimes, and that they can build nothing new unless they repent of them.

'After the last war, when I was a young man, I was full of hope that we could build a new Germany. But we failed, and during these years I have felt an increasing and indescribable disgust for this people. I have no faith in them at all. And as for myself, I know that I shall be an old man before we have recovered from this.

'What can we hope of a people who accepted as a slogan Goering's "Guns instead of butter", and who yet at the same time were so incapable of drawing conclusions that right up to the outbreak of war they went round proclaiming "The Führer is so clever, he will never lead us into war"?'

BENEDETTO CROCE

AN INSCRIPTION

(Composed at the request of an American who sought out Croce at Sorrento and expressed to him the wish to erect a memorial stone in the cemetery at Caiazzo.)

Presso Caiazzo
Nel luogo detto San Giovanni e Paolo
alcune famiglie campagnuole
rifugiate in una stessa casa
furono il XIII Ottobre MCMXLIII
fucilate e mitragliate
per ordine di un giovane ufficiale Prussiano
uomini donne infanti
ventitre umili creature
non d'altro colpevoli
che di avere inconscie
alla domanda dove si trovasse il nemico
additato a lui senz'altro la via
verso la quale si erano volti I tedeschi.

Improvvisa uscì dalle loro labbra
la parola di verità
designando non l'umano avversario
nelle umane guerre
ma l'atroce presente nemico
dell'umanità.

William H. Stoneman
giornalista Americano
che vide con orrore e pietà le salme degli uccisi
pone questa memoria.

'In Caiazzo at the place called SS. John and Paul, several families of country-folk taking refuge under the same roof were, on 13 October 1943, shot down with rifles and machine guns by the orders of a young Prussian officer; men, women, children, twenty-three humble creatures, for no other fault than having thoughtlessly, on being asked where the enemy lay, pointed out to him the direction in which the Germans had turned. Unrehearsed came to their lips the word of truth, indicating not the human adversary of human wars but the vile enemy of mankind who stood before their eyes. William H. Stoneman, American journalist, who saw with horror and pity the bodies of those killed, erected this memorial.'

[*Translated by* G. RAYNER HEPPENSTALL]

ROBERT LOWRY

LAW AND ORDER

THERE was a speed limit but they didn't pay any attention, they were in no mood to give a good goddamn about anything and they drove the command car for all it was worth south down the highway toward Rome. They were in terrific spirits after the unbelievable good luck of getting the passes to Rome for New Year's Eve, away from their lousy puptents and the sound of guns and the snow. There'd been no snow since they'd left the mountains fifty miles behind them and now at eight-thirty it was a crisp clear moonless night and it was New Year's Eve in 1944—Rome was ahead of them, Rome, female and civilian, Rome, like a big shiny toy that was theirs to play with, to be bawdy and loud in, to lose themselves and the war in completely.

They were three American Fifth Army infantrymen in a fast command car driving like mad down a highway in Italy toward everything they wanted in this country. In June they'd helped storm Rome, come through it behind the tanks—it had belonged to them then. It would belong to them again, they were burning the miles, putting the war behind them. With the begrudged passes they'd gotten the last minute, and the battered car with the white star on the hood, they were going back—to the fabulous city, to the great day of their lives.

'Gimme that bottle,' Muggleston said. He was a small bulldog-faced taxi driver from the Bronx and he did everything quick, including taking the big drink of cognac. 'And gimme that city.' He gasped with the stiff throatful. 'Here,' he shoved the bottle under the driver's nose, 'drink some of that stuff and see if you can't get Minnie into high gear. What're you crawlin' along like this for? You want us to spend the night on the road?'

Tex Gorman drank with one hand but didn't let his foot up from the accelerator. Always quiet, always aloof, never smiling, he was a skinny red-haired fellow who had the D.S.M. for killing eight Germans at Salerno. Tex Gorman was a corporal and Muggleston and Fat Stuff Banion were P.F.C.s. They were all three crowded into the front seat and feeling good and warm with the cognac.

'Maybe even the war will end tonight,' Fat Stuff said. 'They're in Saarbrucken tonight.'

'They're in Saarbrucken and we're in crap,' Muggleston said, drinking again.

'Wait'll you get some beautiful piece up there in one of them double beds and you'll change your mind,' Fat Stuff laughed. Of the three, only he was easy-going, laughing after everything he said. Muggleston was high-pressured and loud and Tex was aloof, a Texas kid who'd lived all his life on a farm and had somehow come to take everything seriously, even the army.

'I guess you expect the whole town in the street,' Muggleston said.

'Hell yes I do,' Fat Stuff laughed. 'The whole goddamn town. Especially the women.'

'Especially the women!' Muggleston shouted, and took another drink.

'Rome will be a madhouse tonight,' Fat Stuff laughed. 'Rome will be better than in June.'

'Maybe all the whores'll be puttin' out free on New Year's!' Muggleston shouted.

'They'll all be screaming "Hurrah for the Americani! Hurrah for Singer Sewing Machine!"' Fat Stuff laughed.

'Here, have another drink,' said Muggleston, shoving Fat Stuff. 'Hey, driver, let's drive this thing.'

'We're going to Rome on New Year's Eve!' Fat Stuff said, beginning to shout almost as loud as little Muggleston. 'We're going to do it all in one night!'

'We're going to get the syph., the clap, and blueballs, all for free!' Muggleston shouted.

'To the syph. and the clap and the blueballs!' Fat Stuff shouted, and took a big drink. 'All for free!'

'I'm drivin',' Tex said, not feeling that good.

'What town is this?' Fat Stuff asked, quieter now.

They were in the outskirts of Rome. The streets were dark, nobody around.

'*Stars and Stripes* said it'd be all lit up tonight,' Tex said. '*Stars and Stripes* said there wouldn't be any curfew.'

'To hell with *Stars and Stripes*,' Fat Stuff said. 'It tells you you go home after twenty-four months overseas and here I am in number twenty-eight.'

'You go home in a box in twenty-four months,' said Muggleston.

'No, it really did say that,' Tex said. 'And look at it.'

'These are the suburbs,' Muggleston announced authoritatively. 'Everybody's uptown.'

'Hey, let's take off our helmet liners,' Fat Stuff said. 'What the hell are we wearing these helmet liners for? You'd think we was soldiers from up front.'

They all took off their helmet liners.

'The cognac's all gone,' Muggleston said, looking at the empty bottle disappointedly. Fat Stuff took it out of his hand and threw it—they heard the splash of glass behind them.

'First bottle's all gone, but we're heading for bottles two, three and four, fast,' Fat Stuff said.

'And women,' said Muggleston.

'I bet you all the girls will be dancing in the middle of Via Tritone,' Fat Stuff laughed.

Tex looked at him seriously. 'Do you really think so?'

'Yes, I really think everything tonight. We gotta find another bottle quick.'

'Another bottle,' Muggleston said. He was feeling best of all. 'And goodbye to the f—— army.'

The Villa Borghese is an enormous park atop one of Rome's tallest hills. The American Red Cross had taken over the casino there and made of it an enlisted men's club, where cookies and coffee were sold and where ping-pong could be played. Across from the casino was a parking lot reserved for G.I. vehicles.

But when, at nine that night, Fat Stuff and Tex and Muggleston arrived to leave their car at the parking lot they found the casino dark.

'I could use a doughnut,' Fat Stuff said.

'We got more important things to consider,' Muggleston said. 'We'll get some eggs and stuff down in some wop house.'

They came out through the arch in the old Roman wall to a street that went winding down the hill into the heart of the town. But that street was completely dark. They started down. 'Looks like nobody's around,' Tex said. And then they saw a G.I. across the street.

'Hey, where are all the lights?' Muggleston shouted.

The G.I. stopped and looked over at them. 'Yer askin' me,' he said. His voice sounded bitter—the wind carried it away from them, so that it seemed to come from a long way off.

'Why them dirty liars,' Tex said, personally betrayed.

'To hell with lights. Who wants lights?' Muggleston demanded loudly. 'What I want don't need no lights.'

They walked faster, bent forward against the wind, shoved their frozen fingers into their pockets.

'Boy, wait'll you see the swell babes we find around the square down here,' Muggleston said too loudly.

But when they rounded the corner at last and the square came in view—that square, Piazza Barberini, which G.I.s, returning from pass, had described as a kind of paradise, where beautiful women in fur coats mingled by the dozens, waiting for their buyers—they saw a scene of such desolation that their feet almost stopped moving.

'Great God,' Fat Stuff said, 'the whole U.S. and British armies are here.'

In vague scattered groups, some walking, some standing still passing bottles between them and keeping a close eye out for anything in a skirt that might wander along, the soldiers in the square were like restless lost figures out of a nightmare. No bright lights lit up their faces. The cafés and all the business houses were dark. Though they entered the square and stopped, Fat Stuff and Muggleston and Tex did not become part of the soldiers there. Not drunk enough yet, they looked with detachment at what was going on. Two soldiers were crumpled at the curb, puking, and another was surrounded by his buddies as he leaned against a building and shouted vague threats at the world.

'For Christ sake,' Muggleston said, 'where are all the girls?' He turned on a staff-sergeant who was drinking from a bottle. 'Guys who been down here said they was more girls than you ever saw on this street.'

The staff-sergeant finished drinking and wiped his thick lips. 'Don't ask me where they are,' he said. 'Maybe they're all home with their families—plenty of 'em live with their families.' He thought a moment. 'Maybe they're afraid to come out because of all the drunks.'

'But there ain't no curfew!' Tex, who was perhaps most disappointed of all, broke in. 'The lights are all supposed to be on, the way *Stars and Stripes* wrote it.'

'Wasn't it any better than this earlier in the evening?' Fat Stuff asked. 'Wasn't everybody out then celebrating?'

'No,' the staff-sergeant answered. 'It's the worst night I ever seen. It's the most dismal night I ever seen in Rome.'

'It's the worst night I ever seen, too,' said Tex, and with that admission the cold world seemed to close in around them.

'Come on!' shouted Muggleston, undaunted. 'Come on, let's screw out of here and find something. Come on.'

So the three of them screwed out of there down Via Tritone, feeling better now they were moving again.

'There's something in this goddamn city and we'll find it,' Muggleston said, more sober and more ferocious.

'You'd think the celebrations would be right downtown if there was any,' Tex said. '*Stars and Stripes* said there'd be plenty of celebrations.'

'The city looks like something the army dreamed up tonight,' Fat Stuff said. 'Maybe the Red Cross made all the girls get off the street tonight so there'd be more room for us to have a good time.'

'That's why they didn't turn the lights on, too,' said Tex, inspired. 'So we wouldn't know it was Rome and maybe think we was back in the States.'

'Come on, you guys,' Muggleston shouted. 'We'll find something to drink and we'll all feel better.'

'You show us,' Tex said.

'Sure I'll show you.' And he turned abruptly and led them up a pitch-black street, walking a step or two ahead of Tex and Fat Stuff with his newly commissioned leadership.

A flashlight blinded them.

'Turn that off,' Fat Stuff hissed.

'You chaps Americans?' the Limey soldier with the flashlight asked.

'What the hell do you think we are?' Fat Stuff asked. 'Turn that off.'

The flashlight went out. The Limey was walking over to them. 'Few of our chaps have a biddy up the alley here,' the Limey said. 'You boys want a go at it? You're welcome.'

Tex and Fat Stuff didn't answer, but Muggleston said, 'Sure, where is she?'

'Come on, what d'you want to go up there for?' Fat Stuff asked. 'Come on, we'll find something on our own.'

'Come on and get some of this. We can get some more later.'

'You go on,' Fat Stuff said. 'We'll wait here.'

So they leaned against the building while Muggleston went up the alley with the Limey.

'They was about fifteen Limeys up there, all with one girl in a doorway taking cracks at her,' Muggleston said when he came back ten minutes later. 'They was all drunk and I think she was passed out cold.'

'Was she young?' asked Tex.

'I couldn't tell,' Muggleston said, excited. 'But she didn't even grunt, she just laid there. It was too dark. Look what I got!' He pulled out an unopened bottle of cognac. 'It was setting against a building so I grabbed it.'

They opened it with a knife and each took big drinks. It smashed against the bottom of their stomachs and shot out through them in fine flames, making Rome and the New Year's Eve come to life within them.

'Here's to you, you Texas son-of-a-bitch,' Muggleston said, 'even if you are from Texas!' and he took another drink and they all laughed as if it were some great eternal joke that had always been between them: the places, in far-off golden America, they had come from, and the place they were now. The different things they were in America—Texas, Indiana and New York—and the same thing, Government Issue, they had to be tonight.

And they went on up the black street more slowly, each with the cognac in him beginning to believe that after all something good might happen to them, even if the start had been lousy, even if the lights weren't on and *Stars and Stripes* was a liar and Rome was a fable—dead. Even if tomorrow was close by: the mountains, the snow, the danger, the war, the G.I. army and the G.I. law and order.

They were lost now in the black maze of Rome's backstreets, and though the wind lashed them harder they felt cosier, warmer, closer to home and closer to each other. The little triumvirate walked along with their arms around each other, aglow with the cognac, aglow with the New Year that would mean the war's end in Italy. They passed two Welsh soldiers sitting on the curb singing a song in a brogue they couldn't understand, and that made them want to sing.

'Let's sing "When Irish Eyes Are Smilin'",' Muggleston shouted. 'Come on, all together, "When I-rish Eyes Are Smi-lin', all the world——" Come on, come on, all together.'

'Don't know it,' Tex said.

'What do you know?'

'I know "Deep in the Heart of Texas",' Tex said softly.

'All right, all together. I don't know the words but I'll string along.'

And so they went along singing, Muggleston's uncertain high voice, very loud, Fat Stuff's deep growl, and Tex's flat soft melancholy voice. It all ended up in confusion—the three of them laughing and chasing each other up the street.

They came out on to Corso Umberto, clean of civilians like the rest of the town. A weapons-carrier flew by loaded with G.I.s, one of whom shouted, 'Goin' to the rest camp?' back at them.

Was it that contact with other soldiers on their way to bed that changed their mood? Or was it the singing? They were seized with the same melancholy suddenly. It entered each of them at the same moment and each reacted differently. Tex became silent, able to walk along forever in his emptiness, without saying a word. Fat Stuff laughed, a short laugh, and said, 'I think we've had it, men'. Muggleston felt more responsible than ever for finding them something of New Year's Eve here, and said, 'By God, we'll start knocking on doors and telling these damn Guineas to spread their tables and bring out their daughters. Bunch of goddamn Fascists.'

But the bitter wind blew away his words. And the ancient city, unconquerable, aloof to all they needed of the world, drew farther and farther away.

They went past the Victor Emmanuele monument, on up to the pitted terrifying ruins of the Colosseum, back again and up the steps to Via Nazionale, through the great tunnel to Via Tritone. Once they saw a W.A.A.F. with an English lieutenant and the W.A.A.F. shouted 'Happy New Year!' to them in a crisp voice that didn't invite them over. And once two American officers with nurses passed in a command car singing 'Off we go into the wild blue yonder'. But these things gave them nothing, only made them know more acutely that their New Year's was lost—that they'd come all these miles only to get the realization pushed more thoroughly into their brains that they were in the army, apart from personal things. They were lost. They knew their big holiday was lost and yet they kept walking.

At ten-thirty Fat Stuff said, 'What're we going to do?' and they kept on walking.

At eleven Tex said, 'We might as well find a place to sleep,' but they didn't stop.

At eleven-thirty Muggleston growled, 'I'm getting goddamn tired of this crap'. Still their legs moved.

And then they heard the music. American jazz. A great blurr of female laughter. 'Sometimes I won-der why I spend . . .' Good old 'Stardust'. They were back on Via Vittorio Veneto walking up toward the Red Cross.

All three saw at once. A door of one of the officers' rest camp hotels that lined the street was open and they could see into a mammoth ballroom all decorated and smoke-filled, with paper ribbons hanging from the ceiling and Italian girls and American officers dancing and a G.I. band, really good, really in there, playing the great American music that took the three G.I.s out here on the street four thousand miles across blue water into the warm haze that was America in their minds. All there was of America in Rome that night was this one good thing, this music that got inside the three of them and stirred their blood, and they knew this was what they wanted, just to get in there, just to be with it.

'Come on,' Muggleston said.

'Ha,' Fat Stuff said. 'I wanta see you try.'

'We can't get in there,' said Tex the corporal.

As if to emphasize his statement, a tall negro M.P. guard with a white helmet, a white braid around his arm, and a big forty-five on his hip, stepped out of the shadows. He didn't look at them or away from them, but they felt he had moved to show them he was there. He waited impassively.

Muggleston had turned pale, his eyes glistening.

'Come on,' Tex said. 'Don't try anything.'

Muggleston walked toward the door and Tex grabbed his arm.

'Don't try anything,' Tex said.

Muggleston jerked away. He went toward the door.

The M.P. towered over him.

'How 'bout us going in and listening to the music, Mac?' Muggleston said.

'Officers only in this hotel,' the M.P. said in a soft voice, sure of itself.

'We wanta listen to the music,' Muggleston said.

The M.P. looked down at him, his eyes soft, certain with authority.

'Don't start nothin', soldier.'

Muggleston moved to go by him. The M.P. grabbed his arm.

'One more move outa you, soldier,' the M.P. said, 'and you gonna have trouble.'

Tex and Fat Stuff got Muggleston by each arm and pulled him away.

'You dumb son-of-a-bitch,' Fat Stuff said.

'Let go my arms,' Muggleston said, shaking them off. 'I'll kill that nigger bastard.'

But when they let go his arms he didn't move to go back. He was quiet and sullen now, thick with anger and frustration. He moved along small and Irish and terrible, all that was wrong with the world clotted in him and needing action. Now he felt instinctively what it was he needed to celebrate his lousy New Year and his lousy twenty-eight months overseas in the infantry with. He needed fight. Blood, teeth, the soft pulp of a face under his hand. That was all he needed. Let the world have the rest, the soft stuff, the dames and dancing, the music, let them have their lousy liquor and their lousy hotels, all their lousy soft stuff.

'That nigger bastard son-of-a-bitch,' he said again, expressing everything in this small way.

The dry imminent feeling spread to the other two. They had held him back before, sensing the consequences of battering an M.P., but now the consequences seemed nothing compared to what they had out of the world. Nothing. *Niente.*

'Ha,' Fat Stuff laughed, but there was no reason for his laughter.

No reason a-tall.

Niente.

Nothing.

Happy New Year, Rome.

F—— you, Rome.

They came round the corner into Piazza Barberini and only a scattering of G.I.s, all drunk, were left.

'Big fight here,' a little Southerner without a hat told them. 'Looka that blood on the curb. Four Limeys and a whole pack of our guys. Did you ever see so much blood? M.P.s all over the place half an hour ago.'

They saw the blood, the broken glass of bottles, the puke in the gutter, three Americans sleeping like Mexicans against the closed bar, their arms flung out from them as if broken, the wind-swept square, the city of Rome half an hour before midnight.

'Here, have a drink,' the little Southerner said.

They drank. They walked on. Fast and eager. Knowing that something had to happen. Down Via Tritone, their blood singing. Past the *Stars and Stripes* office. Past the big P.X. Their blood pounding high.

They were almost to Umberto when Muggleston happened to turn his head and see him. He grabbed Fat Stuff's arm.

'Look.'

The other two also saw him now, and all three responded to what was in Muggleston's mind. Two hundred yards behind them, on the other side of the street, came a lone white M.P., walking fast and looking scared.

'Come on,' Muggleston said between his teeth.

Through his greater need for action he had become their leader. They followed him across the street.

He went in between the columns of the arcade at Umberto and Tritone.

'Christ, it's dark in here,' Fat Stuff said.

It was dark and big and ominous in there. They stopped.

They heard the M.P.'s footsteps coming closer, walking on his rubber-soled G.I. shoes, walking fast.

'That son-of-a-bitch,' Muggleston said.

They stood behind one of the big columns and waited for him. Their blood leaped when he came around the corner and crossed the street heading for the arcade.

'Let's kill that son-of-a-bitch,' Muggleston breathed.

Their blood pounded in their ears. There was only one pulse between them, what they were going to do was the only thing left for them to do.

Now with the light still on him, just as he was coming up on the curb, they saw the white flash of his pistol braid, the shine on his combat boots, the white helmet with the lean bony face—a hard-boiled big-city face like Muggleston's—under it, innocent.

Muggleston crouched slightly and as the M.P. came by the pillar Muggleston's left came up from the pavement and crashed against his jaw and the other two came battering in on him from the rear and he crumpled without a sound, without putting up his hands, and they were all three on him, battering his face furiously, but he was gone, a piece of limp meat, their blows bruising and breaking his body.

Fat Stuff was up first. 'Get up . . . get out of here——' he whispered, grabbing Muggleston's shoulder. Muggleston had the M.P.'s head by its two ears and was banging it against the stone pavement, the flat sound magnified in the big cavern which was the arcade. Tex Gorman was sitting down beside the M.P., looking very sick and very drunk, his chin resting on his chest.

Fat Stuff dragged Muggleston up with one great heave, but Muggleston clung to the M.P.'s two ears and brought him along—then let go so that the body fell back on the pavement with a thud.

Muggleston was crying and limp with exhaustion. He sobbed in high little squeals that he couldn't stop.

Fat Stuff brought Tex to his feet, too, and with his arms around both of them led them through the arcade to Umberto.

'I think we killed him,' he whispered, breathing hard. 'Let's scram.'

That brought them all to life. They began to run, haphazardly, up the street toward the Victor Emmanuele monument. Their ears were ringing, a strange lightness was in their heads, but they were freed. They were freed of their boredom. All of their nastiness was gone. They had mashed up Law and Order and their New Year's Eve was a big success. They had brought their violence with them on their pass, all the way to the great civilian fiesta city, and it had served them, it had freed them.

They slumped on a bench in the Piazza d'Italia, puffing and breathing hard, not saying a word, their very guts limp.

. . . When *Blooom!* went the first blast, and *Chooom! Chooom! Chooom!* went the second, third and fourth.

'Ack-ack,' Fat Stuff said, sitting up straight. Then he laughed and turned to Muggleston, who had looked up from his bleeding hands, his face strained and old.

'It's New Year's!' Fat Stuff shouted. 'It's twelve o'clock, you guys!'

As if in answer, all the countryside around Rome opened up, all the bored men in the gun emplacements who'd been waiting hours for their moment of celebration poured lead into the sky. From way off came the little *pouff-pouffs* and from nearer the big blasts of heavy guns.

'Happy New Year, you drunken sons-of-bitches!' Fat Stuff laughed, and got off the bench. 'Come on, let's go find ourselves a room. It's New Year now. It's all over. It's 1945. Let's go!'

The other two got up slowly and went along with him.

'I need a drink,' Muggleston mumbled.

'It's a cold damn night,' Tex said.

'We'll find a bottle,' Fat Stuff said. 'And a room. Happy New Year, kamerads!'

The guns were still blasting out as they reached the top of the steps and started up Via Nazionale. Near the Canadian Club they picked up an Italian who said he could fix them with a room and *vino*. They followed along three paces behind him, their hands in their pockets.

EPILOGUE

ROY FULLER

THE DIVIDED LIFE RE-LIVED

Once again the light refracted through the dusty crimson air
Leaves the spaces of the evening blurred and bare.
Bats that flicker round the edges of the square Victorian lawn
Symbolize the bourgeois souls from life withdrawn.

Now the nightingale arouses us upon the withered tree
With its disappointing, moving melody,
And against the chalky purple thrown by distant main-road arcs
Flow the tired suburban leaves like mouldy sparks.

Here the mower furred with grass like filings round a magnet's
  pole,
Teacups left for ants to make our fortunes droll;
While we sit and try to think that everything is not too late—
Sparrows sitting on the sad outfield of fate.

Once and only once we were in touch with brutal, bloody life
When we got in or kept out of global strife;
And in desert or in dockyard met our coarser fellow men,
Wielding friendly gun or scrubber, not our pen.

How we innocently thought that we should be alone no more,
Linked in death or revolution as in war.
How completely we have slipped into the same old world of cod,
Our companions Henry James or cats or God.

Waiting for the evening as the time of passion and of verse,
Vainly hoping that at both we shan't get worse:
While outside the demon scientists and rulers of the land
Pile the bombs like busy crabs pile balls of sand.

And the best that we can wish for is that still the moon will rise
Enigmatic, cracked and yellow to men's eyes,
And illuminate the manuscripts of poems that foretold
All the ruin and survival of the old.

BERTRAND RUSSELL

THE OUTLOOK FOR MANKIND

THE outlook at the present time is one in which there is a possibility of a happy outcome, but also a possibility of graver disaster than has ever yet befallen the human race. If the happy outcome is to be realized, it will only be because all the powerful nations become aware of the risk of universal disaster. At present, nine people out of ten shut their eyes to this risk, because they prefer a short life and a (more or less) merry one to the survival of their children, or rather to admitting that their children are not likely to survive unless something drastic is done.

Let us begin by enumerating the logical possibilities, without regard to the question whether they are probable or desirable.

First: Russia may convert the Capitalist world, and a Communist empire extend over the whole earth.

Second: Russia may revert to Capitalism, and take to willing co-operation with the West.

Third: Each side may concede to the other a definite sphere, and the world may be divided as the medieval world was divided, between Christendom and Islam, perhaps with occasional minor conflicts as inconclusive and peripheral as the Crusades.

These three possibilities do not involve a world war. If there is a world war, there are three further possibilities:

Fourth: America may be victorious and establish an American world empire.

Fifth: Russia may be victorious and establish a Communist world empire.

Sixth: The war may end in a draw, after which, presumably, each side will prepare for the next bout; or, possibly, they may belatedly revert to the third possibility, as was done at the Peace of Westphalia after the Thirty Years' War.

Let us consider each of these six possibilities.

The first, namely, the victory of Russia by political and propagandist methods, falling short of war, seems to most people in the West highly improbable, and in this view I concur. But I think that to the Soviet Government it seems by no means unlikely. Soviet economists hold that America will suffer an appalling depression, and that all the countries which depend economically on America will be plunged into destitution. (The few Russian economists who expressed a different view have been silenced or liquidated.) This destitution, it is held, will convert the populations to Communism. Consequently, everything that hinders economic recovery in the West is to Russia's interest; in particular, pro-Communist feeling in trade unions is very convenient.

I think a great deal of Russian policy is inspired by the hope of achieving 'peaceful' penetration. Already, largely owing to Western mistakes, the policy has succeeded throughout Eastern Europe, and has good chances of success in Italy and Germany. But I think only ignorance, political and economic, enables Soviet rulers to hope for success in America and Great Britain, and the chance of success in France is very much less than it seemed to be some time ago. Nor is America likely to suffer from a severe depression so long as the Marshall Plan and the risk of war keep American production capacity fully occupied.

The importance of our first possibility, therefore, is not in its likelihood, but in the Soviet belief in its likelihood.

The second possibility, the conversion of Russia to Capitalism, is so improbable that I shall waste no time on it.

The third possibility, that of a rigid delimitation of spheres, is the one which would be adopted if all governments were sane. It has, no doubt, grave difficulties. Germany and China and Persia would have to be partitioned. The Russians would have to discourage Communist propaganda in the West. It might be found necessary to prohibit all trade and travel between the Eastern and Western halves of the world. But given sufficient determination, such a policy might preserve world peace for a long time.

Such a policy might have been practicable if the Soviet Government had been in a different mood. But all the evidence seems to show that the Russian rulers do not believe in the possibility of genuine peace between Capitalism and Communism. One of them, they think, must destroy the other, either by war or by propaganda; and Dialectical Materialism has decreed that the victory will rest with Communism. Whatever might have been possible at one time, I do not think anything can now be done to destroy the Soviet belief in inevitable conflict. This belief is derived partly from experience of Capitalist intervention in the early days of the Russian Revolution, partly from Marxian dogma, but partly also from a surviving belief in 'Holy Russia'. I think we are apt to underrate the element of nationalism, as opposed to Marxism, in the Russian attitude. I am afraid, therefore, that, unless the West can acquire a preponderance of power which the Soviet Government finds undeniable, the hope of securing peace by a delimitation of spheres is very slight. It must be admitted, also, that there are almost insoluble diplomatic obstacles: Constantinople and the Straits, the Arab world (including Palestine), the oil of Persia, and the trade of China, are among the most difficult. It is true that these, severally and collectively, are not worth a world war, but I doubt whether governments will think so.

The fourth possibility, that of a war in which America is victorious, is one which, apparently, most Americans have come to think the most probable of the six. Its course will depend upon whether the Russians have atomic bombs or not. In either case, it may be assumed that they will occupy the Continent up to the Straits of Dover within a few weeks of the outbreak of hostilities. Prominent Continental opponents of Communism will be liquidated. Almost the whole middle class will be set to forced labour in Siberia or on the shores of the White Sea. The Americans will be forced to drop atomic bombs, not only on Russia, but on places in Western Europe where they believe that there are concentrations of Russian forces. What has survived from the late war in France, Belgium, Holland, Germany and Italy will be destroyed in the course of American bombardment. And if, in the end, the British and Americans expect to be welcomed as liberators, there will be little except ghosts to welcome them. It may be assumed that our side, if victorious, will insist on a change of regime in Russia, and will try members of the Soviet Government as war criminals. A White Terror will replace the Red Terror, and will probably be at least as terrible. Of those whom war has spared, a large percentage will perish of hunger or disease. Utter ruin will overtake the whole territory from Calais to Vladivostok.

What, meanwhile, will have happened in Great Britain? If the Russians, by that time, have atomic bombs, all our large towns and centres of industry will be practically wiped out, and a considerable fraction of our population will die. Nor is it to be expected that, when our side has achieved victory, Great Britain will recover anything like the position we hold at present. Two victorious wars have brought us to the verge of ruin; a third victory would inevitably precipitate us into the abyss, if it had to be won against atomic bombs. But if Russia does not have atomic bombs, it is possible, though scarcely probable, that we shall not suffer *very* much more in the next war than in the last.

At the end of such a war, the Americans, presumably, would forbid all other nations to possess any of the more destructive weapons. They would establish a military government of the world, which would make peace secure. In the course of a century or so the world would recover from the ravages of war, and mankind might enter upon a period of peaceful prospects, provided the United States used its victory wisely. Beyond a time of appalling disaster there is a hope, on this hypothesis, of a real solution of the world's troubles.

The fifth possibility, that of a Soviet victory, is in one respect like the fourth: it would lead to the establishment of a single military government, which would make great wars impossible. But this would be at the cost of making the world a prison, where the non-Russian population would be engaged in slave labour under conditions of extreme hardship. Every department of art and thought would be minutely regulated by Moscow bureaucrats, to the point where both art and thought would soon stagnate. The only hope for a liberation of the human spirit would be in the gradual growth of laziness and corruption in high places, leading, perhaps, ultimately to a renewed chaos, out of which progress might come as it came after the Dark Ages.

The general behaviour of the Soviet Government since 1945 seems to show that those who inspire its policy believe that they could win a war against the West. I think they are wrong, and it seems a safe assumption that the United States Government thinks they are wrong. Totalitarian regimes are apt to over-estimate their strength, partly from contempt for what seems to them the weakness and slowness of less despotic states. Hitler thought he could win; the Japanese thought they could win. They were mistaken, and I think Stalin is repeating their mistake. But let us try, for a moment, to look at the issue from his point of view.

I think Stalin believes that, both in America and in Britain, munition workers would strike if asked to work for a war against

Russia; that crypto-communists would afford him an admirably efficient secret service; that American and African negroes would rebel against white domination; and that among wage earners even those who were not actively pro-Russian would be very lukewarm in their hostility. I think he has not been told the truth about the efficacy of atomic bombs, because the few Russians who know the truth would risk falling into disfavour if they told it. I think the whole Russian nation, from Stalin downwards, under-estimates the part played by America and the British Commonwealth in the defeat of Germany. And lastly, I think they all believe that God (whom they have renamed 'Dialectical Materialism') is on their side. Those who think such delusions incredible should read the biography of Marx. Throughout his life he thought his Party was on the verge of success. A hundred years ago, in the opening words of the Communist Manifesto, he represented all the governments of Europe as trembling before the Communists, of whom there were at that time seventeen. His disciples, ever since, have faithfully echoed the Founder's optimism.

I come at last to the most dreadful of our six possibilities, namely, that there may be a great war ending in a draw, followed by a feverish effort on both sides to renew the combat on more favourable terms. The next war, assuming that it comes fairly soon, will not, I think, put an end to the human race, nor even to civilization. South America and New Zealand are not likely to suffer catastrophically, and probably the central portions of the United States will emerge more or less intact. If the war ends in a draw, this will also apply to large parts of the U.S.S.R. But with a little more science and a little more preparation, such mild and gentle warfare can soon be superseded by fiercer methods. Not only will atomic bombs be more numerous and more powerful, but bacteriological weapons will probably be made available, and the soil may be rendered incapable of yielding crops. The danger of radio-active clouds is by no means negligible, and they might exterminate all life on the earth, not only human life, but also that of animals and plants. All this is soberly to be expected if the next great war is not the last. And it will not be the last unless one side is completely victorious. Therefore, if war breaks out in some near future, we must not wish to see it ended indecisively, however horrible it may be.

The above review of possibilities has been necessary before considering what we should attempt and what it is permissible to hope. It seems to result from our survey that what would be best would be an agreement to partition the world and not interfere in each other's zones; next to that, a war soon, ending in an American victory; next, a Russian victory; and, worst of all, a draw. I am afraid it is useless to advocate a partition by agreement, because the Russians will not observe agreements. The only possible way, so far as I can see, of avoiding a war between Russia and America, is to make it obvious to the Russian Government that, in a war, America would be victorious. It is obvious that the Marshall Plan, combined with a West-European Union, gives the best hope of this, as well as of bringing victory to the West if there is a war. But for the reasons already given it is very difficult to persuade the Russians that they would not win. I do not myself believe that it is possible to persuade them, and therefore I expect a war. Nevertheless, we should do all in our power to make the Russians afraid of war. Fortunately, the measures necessary to that end are exactly the same as those involved in preparing for war if it should come, namely, to build up the economic and military strength of Western Europe in close alliance with the United States.

There are various things that the Western governments ought to do. The United States Government is doing as much as American public opinion will tolerate towards building up the strength and unity of Western Europe, and making it evident that, for both economic and military reasons, it is to the interest of Western Europe to co-operate closely with America. But I think there is one further step which ought to be taken by the United States and Great Britain jointly, and that is to inform the Soviet Government, as well as the governments of the Balkan States conterminous with Greece, that any further breach of treaty will be considered a *casus belli*, and so will any further *coup* analogous to that in Czechoslovakia. The Communist governments in Eastern Europe have all been established in spite of agreements for the preservation of democracy; no more of this sort of thing should be tolerated. It is too late to save Finland, but not too late to save the other Scandinavian countries, which obviously are next on the list of Russia's victims. We should also be firm about Austria, and should do our utmost to preserve Italy from Communist domination.

One of the worst muddles made by the Western Powers has been in regard to Germany. It has been obvious for at least two years that there was no hope of a single government for Germany short of a war, but our governments have been dilatory from unwillingness to face facts. Given that Germany must be divided, we ought to try to secure the support of Trizonia. Instead of doing so, we have reduced rations to so low a point that Western Germans, in large numbers, have begun to look to Russia for salvation. It is obviously to our interest to see that they are adequately fed, and that the industry of the Ruhr is revived as fully as possible, with proper safeguards to prevent it from being used against us. But so many people are still thinking in terms of the last war rather than the next, that a sensible policy as regards Germany encounters violent opposition, especially in the countries that the Nazis occupied. The widespread reluctance to face the probability of another world war has made it difficult to bring home the necessity of treating Germany, not as our late enemy, but as our potential future ally.

The British Government is to blame for failure to make the British public realize the situation. Even if the Russians do not have atomic bombs, England must suffer appallingly. If the liberation of France, Belgium and Holland had been delayed a little longer, German V.2s would have destroyed most of London. Russian rockets, we must assume, will be at least equally effective after the first few months of the next war. It is therefore clearly the duty of the British Government to concert with the Dominions a large-scale scheme of emigration, especially for mothers and children. If our population were reduced to twenty millions, mostly adult, we could live on home-grown food, and there could be a great deal more dispersal than is possible at present. Not only would innumerable lives be spared to become the next generation, but our defensive strength would be greatly increased. The promotion of large-scale emigration to the Dominions and to British Africa is, to my mind, far more important than a frantic effort to stimulate our exports, and is only prevented by a widespread lack of courage in facing facts. Aircraft construction ought to take place mainly in Canada, since everything in Great Britain will be liable to destruction by bombs.

In France, the strength of the Communists seems to be on the wane, but is still great enough in the trade unions to weaken

France seriously in the event of a war. Every possible effort should be made to diminish the hold of Communism on French wage earners. This is mainly an economic question, and therefore one in which the United States must play the decisive part. I think that a rapidly developing public opinion in America is making it increasingly probable that Congress will sanction what is necessary.

Italy is a more dubious case. What ought to be done on our side is essentially the same as what ought to be done in regard to France, but success is more questionable. It is, however, still probable that, by vigour and courage, Italy can be kept on our side.

The general policy of forming a Western European Union is undoubtedly right, but it should be pursued more quickly and more wholeheartedly. Western Germany should be admitted, not as a dependency, but as an autonomous state, subject to certain safeguards. There should be complete military and economic co-operation among the States of the Union, and a realization that without this there is little hope of escaping from utter devastation.

There are, of course, many aspects of the Russo-American conflict which are not European. China, Persia, and the territory of the Arab League are all involved. In none of these should a policy of appeasement be pursued. For sooner or later, as after Munich, further appeasements will be felt to be intolerable, and then we shall be weakened by previous concessions.

In the policy of the Western Powers, there should be two paramount aims. First, to secure peace if possible; second, if that is not possible, to secure victory. There is only one way in which peace can be preserved, and that is by such a show of strength that Russia will not venture on any further aggression. I doubt whether this is possible, and therefore I fear that we may have to seek victory rather than peace. But as the measures required are exactly the same in either case, the issue can be left to the future. If the preponderant strength of the Western Powers can be made obvious to the Soviet Government, there may be peace; if not, there will be war, probably within a few years.

To sum up, in conclusion, what has been said earlier: if there is war, the destruction, especially in our own country, will probably very greatly exceed what happened in the last war. But I have little doubt that, in the end, the side led by the United States will be victorious. When that happens, it is probable that a single military government will be established over the whole world, and that, therefore, great wars will cease. Provided the necessity for such a single government is adequately realized, mankind may, after the next war, enter upon a period of unexampled peace and prosperity. The future is not all dark: there is a gloomy tunnel to be traversed, but beyond that a gleam of daylight begins to be visible.

II

ENTERTAINMENTS

R. C. TREVELYAN

SIMPLE PLEASURES

BY Simple Pleasures I mean those for whose enjoyment the exercise of the intellect or the imagination is not necessary. Thus I would not include among them pleasures that are mainly artistic and contemplative, such as watching a ballet or a sunset, or listening to music. Also, in order to limit my list, which must be arbitrary and cover but a small part even of my own experience, I shall exclude the more complex social and erotic pleasures, those also of games, of sport, and of the palate. Many that might seem to be childish are really not so, and are enjoyable at any time of life. But purely childish pleasures, such as taking rides on a long stick, or pretending to be a railway train, generally require more imaginative make-believe than an adult is capable of: so these I have excluded.

Most of our simple pleasures consist of immediate and unsophisticated sensuous reactions to common daily objects and processes that make up the world as we know it. They are congenital and sometimes unconscious parts of our mental and emotional life, governing our tastes and desires, and colouring our more conscious and elaborate states of mind. They are the raw material out of which happiness is composed, and the soil into which poetry strikes its roots.

Some classification will be necessary, that my list may not degenerate into a random catalogue. But many pleasures would seem to belong to more than one class, either because they come to us through more than one of our senses at the same time, or else because the emotions they arouse may vary on different occasions.

PLEASURES OF SIGHT

To watch drops coursing down the window-panes of railway carriages or down the sides of a bath, making a favourite in the race now of one drop, now of another.

To see the wind racing in waves of light and shadow across the tall grasses of a hayfield, or through a silver-green field of oats.

An elephant walking.

To watch young rabbits at the edge of a cover, chasing and jumping over one another. To hear the doe, when she is aware of you, thump on the ground a warning to her young with lifted hind legs.

Walking through a wood in May to come upon a brood of fox-cubs sauntering among the bluebells and campions near their earth. If you are on their lee side and move stealthily, you may sometimes come within a few yards of them and watch them unperceived for quite a long time.

To see a fox anywhere and anywhen.

On a station platform or at a level-crossing to stand within a couple of yards of a train passing at full speed.

To watch from a carriage window the engine-smoke drifting, eddying, vanishing over the fields.

To see the waves breaking on a sandy or a shingly shore—the green luminous transparent crystal of its arching back, as each new wave curls over and falls—the difference between the strength and the reach of the successive waves—where the sand is level, the smooth shallow wash, embossed with foam, running in with a hiss, but soon slowing, pausing, turning, then flooding back to meet the oncoming wave. If the beach be shingly, the grand multitudinous noise, like a vast sigh, as the spent wave drags a myriad pebbles back with it a few inches.

As when heav'd anew
Old ocean rolls a lengthened wave to the shore,
Down whose green back the short-liv'd foam, all hoar,
Bursts gradual, with a wayward indolence.

KEATS, *Endymion*, II, 347.

Drifting thistle-down or silvery willow-herb seeds.

To watch the flight of pigeons, rooks, sea-gulls, or dragonflies.

A gull dropping down on to the water with upright wings, then folding them on its back as it settles.

To watch groups and lines of sparks running this way and that in the soot covering the back of a fire-place.

To look down over the bows of a ship in calm weather, and see the prow cutting and cleaving the water.

> The marvellous behaviour of her hair,
> Bending with finer swerve from off her brow
> Than water which relents before a prow.
>
> LASCELLES ABERCROMBIE, *Mary and the Bramble.*

To walk early in May through an oak-wood, where the birch and hazel undergrowth is sparse enough to allow vast carpets of bluebells to stretch away continuously in all directions.

A star gliding down the sky; a single, double, or triple rainbow; the moon rising or setting beyond a high rocky mountain-ridge.

To stand watching the woodman sawing through the heart of a tall oak tree. They pause to knock their wedges deeper into the widening cleft; then saw a little, but soon pause again, and stand peering up and consulting. They slip the saw out of the crack, and hammer in a new wedge. At each stroke the whole tree shudders through all its branches and twigs. Now it is moving. Gently at first it falls, slowly and silently; then with a loud crackling roar smites the earth and lies still.

To watch snow falling; and next day, after a frost, to see the wind send the loose snow scudding over the hard crusted surface of the field, or lift and whirl it away in clouds and eddies.

PLEASURES OF SOUND

The hoot of an owl; the cry of a curlew, a golden plover, or a peewit; the cawing of rooks and jackdaws; the distant croak of a lonely raven; the cooing of doves; the shout of a cuckoo.

When listening to a nightjar churring, as he squats along the dead branch of a pine-tree, to hear him slightly alter the pitch of his churr without bringing it to an end. Then to see him wing silently away into the dusk, yet now and then uttering a strange high-pitched cry, or clapping his wings together loudly above his back.

A donkey's bray from a distance.

Listening to the sound of a hay-cutter, or of a scythe, or to the hum of a threshing-machine.

The sound of unseen horses' hooves; the tap of cricket bat and ball on a summer's day; the rhythmical purring sound of milk spurting down into a pail.

The sound of skates, and the noise of a stone thrown along ice.

To go through a house tapping various hard substances with one's knuckles or finger-tips, and distinguishing the subtler differences of resonance, given out by solid or hollow wood in furniture, panels and doors, by stone or plaster walls, by bronzes and boxes and water-pipes, et cetera.

The confused bleating, and the smell, of a large flock of sheep on the move.

To hear from inside a house the faint sound of rain beginning to fall outside.

When in a wood the summer sun comes out again after having been hidden for a time, to hear a myriad flies suddenly begin buzzing and humming again in the tree-tops.

When lying awake at night to hear the faint sound of trucks being shunted a long way off.

To lie on the beach listening to the indolent waves breaking slowly—'Each ere it breaketh pausing long as it can'.

To sit beside a small brook and listen to the varied sound that comes from its tiny cascades, near and far, as it falls from pool to pool. One may often distinguish a number of quite different sounds, each with its own monotonous pitch and quality, loudness and softness, yet all delicately orchestrated together into one many-toned harmony.

Walking along a country lane, when the wind is too weak to stir the foliage of the trees, to be surprised by a steady murmuring sound overhead, and, looking up, to see that it comes from a great aspen poplar, whose myriad of light-hung leaves are fluttering and rustling against each other incessantly, be the breeze never so light.

On a summer's day to become suddenly aware of the fierce hum of a swarm of bees.

PLEASURES OF TOUCH

The feel, to the touch of one's fingers, of leaves, grasses, cloth, paper, metals, jade, china, wood, et cetera.

The feel of the first drops of rain on one's bare head, face and hands.

Cutting the pages of a book with a long ivory paper-knife. This is a pleasure, even though we know the book to be unreadable. A wooden or metal knife is a poor substitute. Postcards, envelopes or hairpins are ignoble and treacherous tools.

To feel and hear acorns or husks of beech-nuts crunched beneath one's foot, or the crackle of thin white ice covering a puddle.

To walk with one's feet brushing through dry chestnut or beech leaves.

To pick up a mole that has come to the surface, and feel it struggling in one's hands for a short time.

Stroking the soft nostrils of a horse.

Playing with the wax of a lighted candle; breaking off a stick of wax that has run down the side of the candle, and melting it drop by drop in the flame.

PLEASURES OF SMELL

The scent of new-mown hay.

In the streets of a town to come suddenly upon the smell of an unseen brewery, or of coffee-beans roasting.

The smell of wood-smoke, or of a peat fire.

The odour of a new sponge, of resin, of gummy poplar leaves, of the rain-soaked earth after a drought.

The smell of a railway or traction engine, when one is a boy.

The smell of horses and stables, of cow-sheds, farmyards, and manure heaps.

The scent of unsmoked tobacco, of cedar-wood cigar-boxes and spills, of boots and shoes, and of Harris tweed.

PHYSICAL PLEASURES

Stretching, taking deep breaths, yawning, sneezing, scratching.

Running barefoot on smooth grass or sand, or walking barefoot on high fells after rain, through plashy grass and mossy bog.

Rolling naked on the snow before plunging into the sea. The delicious warmth, so it then seems, of the sea-waves.

To bathe in the sea by moonlight, especially when a fresh wind is blowing inshore, driving the waves rapidly before it, while a late-risen, low-hanging moon is lighting up their long round backs, leaving the troughs in shadow, so that nothing of the water is visible except its impetuous silent swiftness, long lines of brightness and darkness sweeping noiselessly past one.

Chewing grasses; unsheathing and eating grains of wheat or oats; sucking honey from clover flowers.

Running down the steep rough side of a hill. One must look, not at one's feet, but a yard or so in front of them, and must know with instinctive certainty where to place one's feet. Also descending a steep gravel slope, or a scree of small stones, at full speed with long strides, throwing one's weight on the heels.

Walking as far as one can without losing one's balance along one of the rails of a railway line.

All the operations of shaving with an old-fashioned Tubalcain[1] razor are pleasurable: first stropping (preferably with a wooden strop); then lathering with a fragrant soap; last shaving with a blade warmed by dipping it in hot water; the firm rhythmical sweep of the razor, the methodical disappearance of the soap, and the final washing of the face with cold water. I do not know whether shaving with a safety razor be a pleasure or a martyrdom, as I have never tried it.

After a hot bath, to let the water run out, and then turn on the cold tap and sponge oneself all over with cold water.

To sit in a small rowing or sailing boat, and hold one's hand over the side in the cool water.

PLEASURES OF INDOLENCE

To lie on one's back in grass or heather looking up into the blue sky.

> Those who at the height of noon
> Loll back on scented heather late in June
> And sound beyond blue, blue and blue beyond.

T. STURGE MOORE, *Danae*.

To lie on a sofa looking at the varied decorations of one's book-shelves. But this may easily become a complex emotion of pleasure or regret; the pleasure and pride of a collector and possessor, or regret at having read so few of the books, or the thought that so many are not worth the trouble of reading.

To sink down, tired, into an armchair, or into one's bed.

Desideratoque acquiescimus lecto. CATULLUS.

To lie back, looking up into the branches of a huge beech-tree, or of a dark yew, studded with scarlet berries.

Lying in bed on a summer morning, to hear big flies or bumble-bees bump from outside against the window-panes from time to time.

[1]Tubalcain, the son of Lamech and Zillah, was 'an instructor of every artificer in brass and iron'. Genesis v. 20.

FEARFUL PLEASURES

Seeing a snake. Even to come upon a harmless grass-snake sleeping in the sun, to touch its tail with one's finger, and watch it start moving, at first sluggishly, then swifter and swifter, till 'with indented glides' it disappears in the grass—even this is to me a somewhat fearful pleasure; though less fearful than nearly treading on a long black snake in the grass of a Ceylon garden. I seem to remember every place where I have ever seen a snake, which is evidence, if not of the pleasure, at least of its fearfulness.

After swimming too far out from the shore, and turning to swim back in fear of currents, to seem at first to be making no progress, but at last to perceive from the position of the rocks that one is a little nearer to the land, and will reach it safely in time.

To stand close up to a cage in a Zoo, in which a lion is roaring his loudest and fiercest. Donald Tovey once told me how his five-year-old brother was seen standing stock-still facing a roaring lion, and was heard muttering to himself: 'Lions are very kind to little boys'.

In the old days of horse-vehicles, to cross a crowded street without waiting for the policeman to hold up the traffic. One should always walk, and only take to running when imminent danger threatens. If two try to cross together, the risk is more than doubled.

Solitary rock-climbing, where I have sometimes found myself in positions in which there seemed to be no way of going up or down without great risk of falling. While the danger lasted, the fear was stronger than the pleasure; but when it was over, the pleasure was intense.

A thunderstorm is a very wonderful pleasure. When I was young I was afraid of the lightning, but not so much as to spoil my delight in the thunder. I have now for many years delighted in the lightning too. No sound moves me so much as thunder, whether crashing overhead or muttering convulsively from afar. No sight is grander than an approaching storm—the lurid light—the torn cloud-masses, rapidly mixing and severing—the veil of rain sweeping nearer, streaked with lightning flashes. I have heard that Beethoven was once discovered on a hill-top conducting a real thunderstorm. Lucretius, however, writes:

> Whose limbs cower not in terror, when beneath
> The appalling stroke of thunder the parched earth
> Shudders, and mutterings run through the vast sky?

Such terror seems to have been common even among Roman matrons, for Cato, the rigid old Censor, let it be known that he never embraced his wife except during a big thunderstorm; so that, as he said, he was a happy man whenever Zeus was thundering. One would like to know whether he observed a similar rule with regard to the slave-girl with whom at one time he cohabited.

TOWN PLEASURES

Some of these town pleasures are now obsolete, for London at least has changed much since I was a young man, and is still changing rapidly. Hansoms, horse-buses, crossing-sweepers and Italian organ-grinders are extinct, and yellow fogs are not what they were.

When crossing the Charing Cross footbridge, to look down on the flow of the river and on the Thames barges, and, if it is low tide, on the lovely smooth shining surface of the mud. Then to look up across the old Waterloo Bridge at St. Paul's and the City churches.

A ride in a hansom cab. This was a fearful pleasure, because, if the horse should fall, one would be thrown forward on to the apron of the cab, and might be seriously hurt.

To sit on the top of a horse-bus, just behind the driver, and watch his skilful driving, and the broad bare backs of his horses.

To give a penny to an old crossing-sweeper, or throw a sixpence out of the window to an Italian organ-grinder, who sings as he grinds, with a monkey on his barrel-organ.

It used to be a great delight to me as a boy to press hard with the end of my stick against a row of iron railings as I walked, and so produce a marvellous *glissando* on a single note.

To stop and watch a Punch and Judy show in a bystreet.

To hear the bell and the street-cry of the muffin and crumpet man approaching and receding.

To grope through a good thick yellow fog listening to the weird sound of unseen feet and horses' hooves.

To get up at dawn and walk across London to Covent Garden, when the streets are empty save for an occasional policeman or coster's donkey-cart. At Covent Garden to watch the old women shelling peas, and expert market-men carrying a tower of a dozen or more round baskets balanced on their heads.

To pick up and pocket a sixpence or shilling from the pavement of a street.

When walking through the crowded streets, to look for a second or so straight into the eyes of someone as he approaches and passes by us. We then have the illusion that by the expression of the eyes—the eyes alone, without the help of the other features—the whole character and temperament of the passer-by is revealed to us—happiness or misery, kindliness or moroseness, humour and intelligence or stupidity.

> The magic streets allure me, faces strange
> Who pass and pass, and haunting human eyes,
> Eyes that I love, and never see again.

LOGAN PEARSALL SMITH, *Sonnets.*

PLEASURES OF WATCHING INSECTS

To come upon a huge ant-hill in a pine-wood. To watch the activities of ants, large or small.

To see a spider weaving her web.

> A noiseless patient spider,
> I mark'd where on a little promontory it stood isolated,
> Mark'd how to explore the vacant vast surrounding,
> It launched forth filament, filament, filament, out of itself,
> Ever unreeling them, ever tirelessly speeding them.

WALT WHITMAN

The sight of hundreds of spider-webs, all their threads sagging with the weight of the morning dew, each web a marvel of bright silver, gleaming against the dark bushes.

To watch closely how a centipede walks.

Teasing a wood-louse till it curls itself into a ball, then watching how within less than a minute it warily unrolls itself and scurries away.

To watch a hover-fly poising motionless, then darting to another spot to poise again, then alighting with outstretched feet on some object. To listen to its two faint notes, when poised in the air, and when resting—so different, yet both such beautiful 'gossamers of sound'.

To watch a humming-bird hawk-moth drinking honey from a flower on hovering wing, with long tongue uncurled and outstretched.

PLEASURES OF DESTRUCTION, OF FIRE, AND OF WATER

Lighting a fire, and watching the flames spread from match to paper, from paper to wood, from wood to coal; feeding the fire with coal or wood, and reviving it when nearly dead, with or without bellows.

Tearing up and burning superannuated letters and papers.

It is to me a great pleasure (though perhaps at the same time a great grief) to watch anything, from a forest or a house or a haystack to a small cardboard box, consumed by flames; and the flames themselves are infinitely various in beauty.

Slashing down nettles or thistles with a walking-stick; cutting out with a knife dandelions and plantains with as much of their roots as possible.

Killing clothes-moths and mosquitoes.

To watch the incoming tide creep up, surround and undermine a child's sand-castle, until gradually it has all slidden down into the wash.

My father used to teach us, when we were children, how to dam up a small stream, till we had formed quite a big pool for paddling in. At last we broke the dam and watched with delight the water sweep down in a magnificent rushing flood. This, though a childish pleasure, my father seemed to enjoy as much as we did.

Where there are pools of standing rain-water in muddy lanes and cart-tracks, it is a great pleasure to open channels through the mud with stick, hands, or boots, so as to invite the water to flow away to some pool or stream on a lower level. Homer shows by one of his similes in the *Iliad* that he, too, before he grew blind, must have loved the pleasures of playing with water.

'And just as when a man, who guides a rill, leads its stream from a dark spring among his plants and garden plots, a mattock in his hands, and flings away obstructions from the channel; and as it flows onward, all the pebbles are swept along, and swiftly it glides murmuring down the steep slope, and outstrips him who is guiding it.'

LOGAN PEARSALL SMITH

'IVANHOE'

Gus Gosling wasn't a young man who talked with ease, and as he motored along the Clapham Road and through Balham with the Beilby-Browns of Leighton Buzzard, he couldn't have put very clearly into words his sense of the mysterious charm of London, with all its unexplored regions and unknown interiors. And if, by some gift of tongues or other miracle, Gus had been able to express; and if the Beilby-Browns had been subtle enough to comprehend the feelings by which his consciousness was coloured, he dumbly felt that the communication of such impressions wouldn't have been received with much enthusiasm by these old Bedfordshire friends. The outcome, they might have regarded them, of experiences and London initiations in which they hadn't participated, and concerning which Sophia Beilby-Brown at least entertained rather serious misgivings.

'How much wiser it would have been for poor Gus,' she had more than once remarked of late to her Percy, 'how much more sensible for him to have stuck to his gardens at Dumplings! About gardening Gus does know something; they say he's an expert really. And if our friends, the Trottons of Trotton Court, haven't called—Lady Trotton you know is one of my father's patients—the society of Leighton Buzzard is quite good enough for him; he's quite a beau at old Buzzard. But in London he's lost, lost, I can tell you. I consider that Charles Street set he hangs on to a lot of trashy people: they're nobodies really. And they take up nincompoops, Lady Lawcourt says—and Gus *is* a nincompoop—and then drop them like hot potatoes. And as for Gus's Lady Blanche, you ought to hear what Sybil Lawcourt has heard about her Ladyship!'

Gus, whom this cultivated daughter of the Leighton Buzzard practitioner would sometimes describe as 'The Shenstone of Bedfordshire' (she had attended a university extension lecture on Eighteenth Century Poets), Gus had done well, she thought, to settle down on the little property—so like Shenstone's Leasowes—he had inherited from his great-uncle, the rich Bedford hatter (who had made a fortune by making into straw-hats the golden straw of the district), and to devote himself to the adornment of that miniature park. What better, indeed, could he have done, when she had let him know that Percy, the ambitious son of the Leighton solicitor, was to be her choice, and had married this young lawyer and had gone with him, and the brilliant career he felt sure lay before him in the legal circles of London.

'But how unwise of poor Gus!' she exclaimed, when on visiting Leighton Buzzard a few years later, she learnt that her former admirer, after making a little show-place of Dumplings, to which even the Trottons would take their guests to see the gardens, the artificial waterfall, and the vistas he had opened with views of the river (again like Shenstone, with his grand Lyttelton neighbours)—that Gus had been carried off by one of the grandest of these guests—in fact by Lady Blanche Tassell, that famous leader of fashionable taste, and had been installed by her in lodgings not far from Charles Street, where she lived and entertained in splendour.

But Sophia was a good-natured creature; her head hadn't been turned by Percy's success (and her own) in legal circles; so that when they got back to their Bedford Square flat, she had sent a note to Gus, inviting him to come and see them. She was genuinely fond of her former suitor; and he would be glad, she felt sure, to meet again his old Buzzard friends. He would be impressed, moreover (for she knew Gus had taste), by the rich mahogany pieces, the etchings and Japanese fans with which she had adorned their flat, and especially by the great shiny Royal Academy picture—their latest purchase—that gave light and glory to it all. But they hadn't changed really: nor, she felt sure, had Gus changed.

Yet, she soon began to wonder, was he really quite the same Gus? In the 'buzz of old Buzzard', as she wittily called the Bedfordshire gossip, he seemed to take no interest. Even of Dumplings and gardening he hardly spoke; and he never mentioned the Trottons; even about Percy and his legal career he made no inquiries; he hardly glanced at their etchings and Japanese fans, and ignored the great picture, 'Love and May Blossom', by Sir Augustus Staircase, R.A. What he talked of mostly was Lady Blanche Tassell, and the way she was now completely redecorating her house in Charles Street.

The clever Sophia soon twigged what had happened; the decorating of houses, Sybil Lawcourt had told her, was now the rage in Mayfair; well, if Gus had been dragged into that sort of thing by those sort of people, let him come down to the villa she and Percy had just taken and furnished at Binstead in Surrey. That would teach him what they knew—and there was nothing Bloomsbury didn't know—about tones and harmonies and period pieces. Would he come the next Saturday? Percy would drive them all down in their new Sunbeam.

Gus accepted the invitation gladly; but having guessed—for he wasn't quite as stupid as he seemed—the attitude of Sophia towards his London friends, he did not mention Charles Street again as they motored through what seemed to him the endless streets of the outer suburbs. And when there flashed on his eyes from the window of a furniture shop in Upper Tooting a gleam of green colour, he restrained his impulse to ask the motor to stop. He half believed that what he had seen was the radiance of green lacquer, the rare, the famous green lacquer of which Charles Street possessed one small specimen. He decided, therefore, to return to Tooting as soon as possible for further investigation. For Gus had a flair, as Lady Blanche sometimes told him; beauty would flash on him in gleams he must follow; doors into Paradise would seem to open; and if he held himself back, what awful remorse would then haunt him! haunt him sometimes for years. And now, if it really was green lacquer he had seen, if it turned out to be a really fine specimen of this rare commodity, what a thing it would be to talk of in Charles Street, where, whatever he might have said in Bedford Square, he was accustomed to sit in silence when questions of taste were under discussion.

Our hero, troubled as he was by the dread of an enlarging person, forced himself, when in London, to take long promenades; and on the first opportunity after his return from his week-end visit, he accomplished a double purpose by traversing, this time on foot, the streets through which he had passed in the Beilby-Browns' Sunbeam. Along the Clapham Road and up and down Balham Hill he followed the gleam, and found its origin at last in Upper Tooting. Nor had his flair deserted him, for in the window of a furniture emporium there shone what he believed was a really fine old specimen of the green lacquer. But a great disappointment now awaited him; the cabinet, he was informed, was probably sold; two ladies had been in that morning and asked to have it sent to their home in Balham; only, however, on approval, so that if the gentleman would call again in a few days, there was still a chance that he might secure it. Gus did call again, after getting his eye in, so to speak, at Charles Street. On this second visit he found that the cabinet was for sale;

the Balham ladies (benighted beings!) had decided not to keep it. The price would be a strain on his modest resources; he gave, however, his name and address and secured its refusal for a few days, meaning in the meanwhile to ask for the expert advice of Charles Street about so important a purchase.

Gus started back, his thoughts full of green glamour; this was his first adventure of this kind, and he was greatly excited by it. It turned out, however, to be a day of exciting adventures, for on his walk back to London his somewhat protuberant eyes were caught by another and even more surprising gleam. This illumination was a white glimpse through a door left open by chance in the wall surrounding a villa residence in Balham. The door had 'Ivanhoe' inscribed on it, and 'Ivanhoe' he saw was a plain house of no architectural pretensions—the kind of stucco villa which can be found in almost any London suburb. The door in the wall, however, revealed a view of the most surprising garden he had ever seen. And there, like a glory in its midst, was the mass of white blossom which had caught his eye in passing. What on earth could it be, he wondered. Could it be the *Tecta Orbis Niveus*, a magnificent, an incredible specimen of that rare Tibetan shrub which Reginald Farrer had discovered, and of which there were supposed to be only three plants in Europe? The splendour of this exotic blossoming reawakened his horticultural passion, and drew him, moth-like, through the door and across the lawn. He quite forgot that he was trespassing, until, as he stood filling his sense with the sight and scent of the flowering marvel, he became aware of the presence of a young woman who was digging in a nearby border. 'I'm sorry!' he cried, 'it's dreadful of me—but the door was open—do tell me, is it *Tecta Orbis Niveus*?' It was, the young woman replied, as she leaned on her spade and gazed at him smiling. She was neither young nor strikingly handsome, but Gus fell for her, as the phrase is, at once; and at once the two of them plunged into horticultural talk. In the general inspection of the garden which followed, Gus felt that he had seen more marvels, and acquired more information than had fallen to his lot in the whole previous course of his experience. It was a miracle of Perfection—there was no other word for it—Perfection, set down in a London suburb, far beyond anything he had achieved in his little Arcadian realm at Dumplings. Rarest of all its wonders was a bush of that most incredible of Reginald Farrer's discoveries, the *Reginalda*

Caerulea, of which he must have sent a slip to Balham himself. It hadn't yet explicated in Europe its great petals of a blue, Farrer had written, beyond even that of the gentian which had ceruleated the gardens of Europe. They hoped, however, Gus was told, that in eighteen months or so they would see it in flower.

When at tea-time his new friend asked him into the house to meet her sister, who was, she told him, the one of them who really knew about gardening, he was met, as they entered the house, by another surprise. For 'Ivanhoe', commonplace as it looked from the outside, was within even more incredible proof of wealth and exquisite taste than the garden. There was not much in the way of furniture in the spare quiet rooms, but each piece, and each picture on the walls, he felt, was a masterpiece, perfect, and beyond price or question. Correggio's 'Agony in the Garden' was as pretty as the garden-fête of Watteau, which hung by it; Crivelli's exquisite 'Circumcision', Fra Angelico's 'The Entombment' and his 'Rape of Europa', the Vermeer of Delft, the Chardin 'Still Life', set the standard of this small collection; while a Berthe Morisot and a small Whistler represented the nineteenth century. As he stood before this blue picture, he was introduced to the older lady, a plain, charming spinster of about thirty-five, he thought. And when, after a pleasant half-hour of conversation, he took his leave, it was with enthusiasm that he accepted the invitation to come to 'Ivanhoe' again some Wednesday afternoon, if he could find the time. Find the time! Could he find time for anything else? he asked himself, as he walked home through a transfigured Balham. He had received, he felt, a baptism of the spirit, an ideal of perfection had been revealed to his eyes, a touchstone placed in his hand which might turn to brass much that he had previously regarded as gold.

But when he reached London, and walked through Charles Street towards his lodgings, the green cabinet, which he had quite forgotten, began to gleam again in his memory. He was dining in Charles Street the next evening; the inhabitants of that region, and perhaps Lady Blanche herself, might be interested in his discovery. And even perhaps the great gardener and picture-collector, Sir Tresham Tresham of Place, whom he was half-promised to have the honour of meeting at last.

This honour was his; he was introduced to that master of appreciations, to whose authority even Lady Blanche herself paid homage.

There were several other guests; Gus talked of the marvellous villa-residence he had found at Balham, contrasting it, boldly, with the villa of the Beilby-Browns at Binstead. Of this abode, and of his friends, its owners, he gave an ironic account (for his eye was an acute organ of observation) that caused laughter in Charles Street. Gus in fact tasted for the first time that cup of magic, the intoxication of wagging his tongue—or at least of thinking he wagged it—in the amusing, malicious talk of the *beau monde*; light, perfidious talk of a kind never heard in the shire of Bedford, nor in Bedford Square either. Yes, Gus was a success that evening; his voice was listened to; so that when he spoke of the green cabinet at Tooting, and asked the advice of these connoisseurs about his project of its purchase, Lady Blanche's thoughtful eye lit up. 'We'll motor out there tomorrow and see it,' she declared decisively, 'and you, Tresham, must come with us.' So the following afternoon Lady Blanche's car carried the three of them to Balham; and at the first glance of the green cabinet, Lady Blanche, after one look at Sir Tresham, took command of the situation. The price? Let it be sent at once to Charles Street, she rapped out.

This prompt appropriation of his prize, with no subsequent explanations, almost took Gus's breath away; and when he found the cabinet established in the most prominent position in Lady Blanche's drawing-room, he was still more amazed to hear her describe it as one of the happiest of her discoveries; for if she did possess any gift, it was the gift, she said, of making lucky finds in the most unlikely places. Against such assurance Gus did not dare to protest. That Sir Tresham, who was also present, seemed by his silence to corroborate this legend, made our hero feel more beyond his depth than ever; and when the bill for the cabinet arrived at the address he had given at Tooting, and it was intimated that the account already sent to Charles Street had received no answer, Gus decided that it would be prudent to settle the matter himself, and say nothing about it.

These were deep, and, he dimly suspected, dangerous waters; and indeed his suspicion was only too soon confirmed, when a maelstrom seemed suddenly to open in Charles Street; when the rains descended and the wind blew on that house, and Gus's help was requisitioned—to a degree beyond his imagination, and indeed, beyond his means—to keep its roof in position. All the more welcome, as a refuge for his troubled spirit, did he find his visits to Balham, whither he would often walk in his oldest clothes, and spend the afternoons in digging. The Miss Runkles (Runkle, he had learned, was their name) were always making changes, and would pitilessly root up and destroy plants which they felt they could replace to advantage. Then Gus would have tea with these charming, quite merciless young women, with whom he would plead, but in vain, for some respectable, long-established, long-domesticated shrub they had decided to get rid of.

Of these afternoons he sometimes felt he boasted too much in Charles Street. Some intuition, some premonition, and indeed the chaff of his listeners about his conquests in the suburbs, warned him that these two phases of his life, its Mayfair and its Balham aspects, should be kept further apart in his conversation.

But Lady Blanche never listened: she said nothing. The preoccupation of this lady was plainly to base her position more firmly than ever on the green cabinet, the fame of which was widely spread through Mayfair, and attracted Royal visitors to Charles Street, and even reached, across the Tottenham Court Road, to the ears of Sophia, who, however, when she questioned Gus about it, received nothing but vague answers. Of the cabinet and of Lady Blanche he never spoke a word to the Miss Runkles, feeling that they took no more interest in Mayfair than Lady Blanche took in Balham. Nor did Sir Tresham either, he thought, till one evening, when they walked away from Charles Street together, the Baronet surprised Gus by casually remarking, 'I'd rather like to have a look at that garden you're always gassing about; perhaps you can take me there one day?'

Gus asked and received permission to bring his friend to Balham, and as they journeyed thither Gus felt that Tresham's attitude was slightly ironic. How, he wondered, the place and people would mirror themselves in the worldly, fastidious eyes of his companion? But soon he became aware that his real anxiety was about a much more important aspect of the situation. The real, the profound question was, he realized, not what Tresham would think of 'Ivanhoe', but what 'Ivanhoe' would think of Sir Tresham. His misgiving lest the distinguished, almost famous, collector might not perhaps pass muster at the Balham villa, brought home to him in startling fashion the respect with which he had come to regard those accomplished, unfathomable young women. But luckily all went well; the Miss Runkles were perfect, as they were always perfect in their fine accomplished ease. Tresham too was perfect; seemed indeed to bud and blossom in that atmosphere, revealing a genial simplicity and urbane sense of kindly fun of which Gus had never seen the slightest sign in Charles Street. They talked, how they all talked, until at last the conversation fell on books, when Gus dropped out; the book-world being for him an unknown region, and its jargon a language of which he didn't understand a word.

Tresham, though from the beginning plainly all eyes, had hitherto looked at everything without a word of comment; but when the Miss Runkles brought out some little, brown old books with almost effaced gilding, he exclaimed, 'I say, I say!' and then, after examining for himself the rows of volumes, he threw himself into an armchair and cried, 'Those first quartos!—where in God's name did you get them? I thought I was a book-collector, but we live and learn.'

At last they took their leave, begging permission to come again. Certainly they must come again—come some Wednesday afternoon. And if the sisters themselves should go to Italy, as they thought of doing, their acquaintances from London mustn't forget to come on the anniversary of this visit, 15 July, wasn't it? at exactly four o'clock, when they might find the *Reginalda Caerulea* in flower.

'Who in Heaven's name are they?' Tresham asked of Gus as they walked back along the Balham Road. 'Who indeed?' Gus echoed. 'All I know is what they have told me, that their father had a draper's shop in Balham. I believe they lived for years in Italy.'

'Who do they know, who are their friends?' Tresham queried further. 'What wealth and what wonderful friends they must have!'

'Wonderful,' Gus agreed, but who they were and what was the social background of the Balham ladies he had no notion; beyond the local vicar he had never heard them mention the names of any other acquaintance. But Reginald Farrer must have been a friend—Gus had seen copies at 'Ivanhoe' of his two famous accounts of his Tibetan expeditions to search for plants; *On the Eaves of the World* and *The Rainbow Bridge*, affectionately inscribed to 'Fortunata and Mary Runkle'. And people were always sending books and plants to 'Ivanhoe', and they went out a lot, Gus was certain.

The two of them agreed to leave it at that. After all, who were the friends of these Balham young women, the means by which they had acquired their sure connoisseurship and priceless pictures? The Museum directors who advised them, the gardens and private collections they frequented, the undreamed of circles, that, in Italy or elsewhere, they illuminated with their presence, were their own affair; it was enough to be allowed on Wednesday afternoons to go to 'Ivanhoe'. Gus and his companion took full advantage of this privilege.

When it became known, as it soon did become known in Charles Street, that Tresham had also begun to frequent Balham, jocular allusions to the subject became more frequent (though Lady Blanche said nothing), and it was taken for granted there that both Gus and the Baronet were about to lead to the altar two long-nosed spinsters from the suburbs. Ah, if these words spoken in jest could only prove true ones! Gus sighed; for himself he did not dare entertain the notion; and although he suspected sometimes that Tresham might be nourishing some such project, he felt that there was an austerity, a kind of Diana-like aloofness in the attitude of the Miss Runkles that must make any such hope a vain one.

Still Lady Blanche said nothing.

Discussions of the Good and the Beautiful were what genuinely interested this earnest thinker (and no one who knew her could doubt that her interest was genuine); badinage, she would frankly admit, rather bored her. Still her silence seemed curious to Gus, till one day she broke that silence by remarking, 'I should like to see that garden at Balham—could you let me motor you there one afternoon?' When the young man hesitated, Lady Blanche added 'Very well then, get them to tea in your rooms and ask me to meet them.' Gus hoped the Miss Runkles would refuse, but his invitation was accepted without comment; and although Tresham, whom he also invited, did not appear, and Gus had not felt it necessary to accept Sophia's kind, if surprising, offer to come and pour out tea for Lady Blanche (for he knew Sophia's opinion of that lady) and suggested also that Percy might look in on the party later, if he could find the time for it; yet the occasion was, Gus thought, a great success. His rooms were pretty, and decorated with the prettiest of flowers, for his flair had not failed him. He had never seen Lady Blanche look more lovely, in her rich costume and great hat; the Miss Runkles were quietly dressed, as indeed they were always. Lady Blanche evidently laid herself out to please them, and although she invited herself to 'Ivanhoe', she did it with such half-shy supplication, that Gus could not imagine that the plain and plainly dressed young women from Balham were anything but flattered by the request of this lady whose golden kindness and gentle, affectionate sweetness had won his most sincere devotion.

When Gus next called at Charles Street, he found the visit had already taken place, and Lady Blanche was full of praise of his dear, quaint, delightful friends and their sweet little garden. She must have them at Charles Street; they would arrange a little dinner. The little dinner, however, never took place and Gus never again saw the Balham sisters. The Miss Runkles were not at home, the maid informed him, the next Wednesday, and on several subsequent Wednesdays, when he rang the door-bell of 'Ivanhoe'. That the same sentence of exclusion had been passed on Sir Tresham too, he learned one evening, when, dining in Charles Street, they met in the drawing-room before their hostess had come down.

'She's done us in!' the Baronet surprisingly exclaimed.

'You mean Lady Blanche? Why should she?'

Tresham gave an odd look at Gus. 'Oh well, it's perhaps because they made her feel dowdy. That no woman ever forgives.'

'Dowdy!' exclaimed Gus, 'but they dress with such plainness!'

'Plainness you call it! The plainness of Paris and Paquin takes some beating.'

'But why is the beating for you and me? And how could she do it?'

'Oh, she told some black, hellish lie, perhaps, she's quite capable of doing it. As you know, and you must know—with all her sweetness and graces, she's a Fiend—no, not a Fiend, but a Vampire. But probably she merely repeated the things people said—the things we let them say. The jokes—they're fastidious, they're ruthless young women.'

'The jokes were beastly,' Gus answered. 'Do you think Lady Blanche heard them? She didn't seem ever to listen.'

'Hear them! Vampires like Blanche hear every word—you can bet on that!'

Gus was silent a moment; then, his slow brain almost exploding with a burst of thought, 'I'm afraid,' he exclaimed, 'it's worse than that. The lie they wouldn't believe, and they might perhaps forgive the jokes—I don't know. But they couldn't forgive Lady Blanche. I mean they saw us through her—she shed a lurid light. As you say, they're horribly fastidious, they're ruthless. They don't care to be mixed up with this sort of thing.'

'You mean?'

'I mean the snobbery, and well, all sorts of second-rateness. The Jezebels of Mayfair and the smell of its gutters—and other things!' The two interlocutors looked hard at each other. How much, each wondered, did the other know?

'You mean her wickedness?' asked Sir Tresham.

'Wickedness?' Gus was astonished.

'Yes, wickedness! you know what the great Oscar said: "Paint me with a background of ruined families". That's the way our Blanche ought to be painted. Ruined families and friendships and broken careers and arches! Well anyhow, she's done for us now.'

'Yes, they've turned us down,' Gus reiterated. 'We're after all not good enough. They've turned us down just as they turned down that cabinet.'

'The green cabinet?' They both moved in front of it.

'Yes, I never told you, but before I—before Lady Blanche—bought it, they had had it at "Ivanhoe" on approval and sent it back. It wasn't good enough—like us, it wasn't quite up to the mark. Damn it!'

'Damn what?' asked Lady Blanche in her sweet, chanting voice. She had come unobserved into the room while her guests were staring blankly at that piece of furniture.

'We were talking of "Ivanhoe",' Gus blurted out, wondering how much Lady Blanche had heard.

'Ah,' chanted Lady Blanche, 'you mustn't damn "Ivanhoe"—those sweet, dear people—we're tremendous friends!'

Gus didn't believe, he couldn't believe this. If Lady Blanche had closed the door of 'Ivanhoe' on them, she had slammed it, he felt sure, even more decisively on her own precious person. But she had done what she wanted. And how she had done it, they would never know. But what did she care?

How much she did care, to what extent she had been damaged by her collision with 'Ivanhoe' and what it stood for, was, however, apparent before long. The first symptom was the disappearance of the green cabinet, and its subsequent appearance for sale at a fabulous price in a Bond Street shop. This was the beginning of a general disintegration and breaking up of things. In the autumn, Lady Blanche, declaring herself dissatisfied with material objects, came to give more and more of her time to the investigation of immaterial apparitions. She soon attained as great a prestige and as exclusive a position in the spiritual world (which had now become fashionable) as the one she had previously achieved in the world of taste. Among the aristocratic soul-searchers who now filled her new house Gus was no longer welcomed, though Tresham, he understood, had been carried up into the higher sphere in the assumption from Charles Street, whence Lady Blanche moved into a big house she built at Hampstead, 'Tabernacle' she called it; it rather overshadowed the Garden Suburb. The Charles Street set dissolved, like one of those floating islands which come together and dissolve on tropical seas; and Gus fluttered back to his old friends, the Beilby-Browns, who received him all the more kindly, since his wings had been singed, as Sophia had often told Percy they would be singed, by his misadventures in Mayfair. However, after the forced sale of 'Dumplings', Percy had procured him a job in the Bedfordshire solicitors' office, and he was quite a beau once more in the best Leighton Buzzard circles. But to London this portly beau (slightly damaged and indeed planet-struck by a remote silvery orb of which Sophia had no notion) would be sent now and then on the firm's errands. As one of these occasions happened to coincide with the date when the *Reginalda Caerulea* was expected to expand its blue flower, Gus went alone for a bus-ride along the Balham Road. As he stared at 'Ivanhoe', in passing, he saw the drive of that residence was full of motors, and there was also a carriage with coachmen and footmen and fine horses.

Strains of music floated on the air: there must be a garden-party, and the Dance of the Happy Spirits in the Elysian Fields was being played by wind and string instruments. By Gluck, wasn't it? Gus's memory for music wasn't a good one, and his thoughts were now distracted by a sight that somewhat perturbed him. Was that Sir Tresham who was just entering the gate of 'Ivanhoe', and the lady in the car with him—was she Lady Blanche? It was neither, he saw to his relief the next moment; for gazing back as the bus jolted on he saw the Baronet himself on the bus gazing back at 'Ivanhoe' before it vanished. He also was regretting, no doubt, the tryst he couldn't keep either. He looked depressed, and rather shabby, Gus thought, and certainly older. Had he, too, been forced to sell Place, Gus wondered, to help raise a Tabernacle at Hampstead? Gus went back on the bus-top and shook the hand and sat down by his former acquaintance. They talked of current events, and the weather, and Gus spoke of Leighton Buzzard, and the prospects of a good crop of Bedfordshire straw in the Luton district where he now lived.

But of 'Ivanhoe' and the Miss Runkles, or of Charles Street and Lady Blanche, they said not a word.

JOHN BETJEMAN

A SUBALTERN'S LOVE-SONG

Miss J. Hunter Dunn, Miss J. Hunter Dunn,
Furnish'd and burnish'd by Aldershot sun,
What strenuous singles we played after tea,
We in the tournament—you against me.

Love-thirty, love-forty, oh! weakness of joy,
The speed of a swallow, the grace of a boy,
With carefullest carelessness, gaily you won,
I am weak from your loveliness, Joan Hunter Dunn.

Miss Joan Hunter Dunn, Miss Joan Hunter Dunn,
How mad I am, sad I am, glad that you won,
The warm handled racket is back in its press,
But my shockheaded victor, she loves me no less.

Her father's euonymus shines as we walk
And swing past the summerhouse, buried in talk,
And cool the verandah that welcomes us in
To the six o'clock news and a lime juice and gin.

The scent of the conifers, south of the bath,
The view from my bedroom of moss dappled path,
As I struggle with double-end evening tie,
For we dance at the Golf Club, my victor and I.

A SUBALTERN'S LOVE-SONG

On the floor of her bedroom lie blazer and shorts,
And the cream-coloured walls are be-trophied with sports,
And westering, questioning settles the sun,
On your low leaded window, Miss Joan Hunter Dunn.

The Hillman is waiting, the light's in the hall,
The pictures of Egypt are bright on the wall,
My sweet, I am standing beside the oak stair,
And there on the landing's the light in your hair.

By roads not adopted, by woodlanded ways,
She drove to the club in the late summer haze,
Into nine o'clock Camberley, heavy with bells
And mushroomy, pinewoody evergreen smells.

Miss Joan Hunter Dunn, Miss Joan Hunter Dunn,
I can hear from the car park the dance has begun.
Oh! full Surrey twilight! importunate band!
Oh! strongly adorable tennis girl's hand.

Around us are Rovers and Austins afar,
Above us, the intimate roof of the car,
And here on my right is the girl of my choice,
With the tilt of her nose and the chime of her voice,

And the scent of her wrap, and the words never said,
And the ominous, ominous dancing ahead.
We sat in the car park till quarter to one
And now *I'm engaged to* MISS JOAN HUNTER DUNN.

MAURICE RICHARDSON

WAY OUT IN THE CONTINUUM

THIS is decapitated head No. 63, Universal Institute of Cerebral Physiology, electrotelepathecasting in all directions in space-time. For the benefit of you earth-dwellers and third dimensionals who think you are living in what you call the past, I will describe my day.

It is hour 1 of day 97 year 3946—by an odd little coincidence just 2,000 years after the outbreak of the First Great Atomic War, but don't let that worry you; it didn't last long and nobody won.

I repeat: it is hour 1 and the artificial blood supply apparatus to which I am attached is standing on its bench in the Lab overlooking The Park of Giant Vegetables. The blood pump has just switched over to 'day'; it's working beautifully smoothly, giving me what they call Mild Euphoria, a rich, vital, but not too stimulating, mixture. The Lab attendant in whose charge I am is filling in my morning reaction chart, and if I roll my eyes I can just catch sight of her profile. She is a pretty little thing, one of the latest products of the Interplanetary-Racial-Cross-Fertilization Institute. On the Earth side her ancestry shows Chinese, West African Negro, Cape Cod and Kentish Weald. The Neptunian comes out strong in her aquamarine skin—I always call her Bluey. From her Venusian mother she inherits the small pomegranate-shaped third breast and from her Uranian grandfather a striking organic feature which I hardly know how to describe to you listeners because it is, quite literally, like nothing on earth. . . .

As soon as Bluey sees I'm awake she gets busy on my breakfast. I'm not fussy like some of these Decaps who are always wanting their schedule changed. I always want the same thing at the same co-ordinate. Maybe it's because I wasn't decapped until I was what you time-slaves would call middle-aged; the Lab Super says I'm a grey head on green-painted shoulders and slaps my pressure gauge in a hideously familiar way; but what can one do? *Il faut souffrir pour être immortel.* Anyhow, my breakfast has been the same now for the last two hundred years by your reckoning: oysters washed down with black velvet, followed by durians.

The oysters come along on a conveyor that passes them one by one under the mechanical fork which is geared to an interrupter mechanism that synchronizes with the liquid-intake pipe so that every few mouthfuls there is a pause for a drink. At any moment, in case of accidents, I can interrupt the whole works by putting out my tongue; this breaks a photo-electric circuit. Some Decaps can't stand the mechanical feeder; they insist on being spoon-fed by their attendants. Poor old 33 choked and spluttered fit to burst the first time they tried it on him. He got in such a state they had to black him out altogether; deep unconscious therapy they call that; we get a good deal of it.

I'm reckoned a fast eater, so Bluey sets the dial at 5 and we're off. The motor starts up with a gentle appetizing purr; the fork pricks into the first Colchester—home grown in the Lab's sea-fruit farm—lifts it and pushes it nice and slowly towards my lips. And for the next three hours there's not a happier Decap on the bench.

When breakfast's over, Bluey detaches the rubber bag into which three gross of Colchesters, two dozen durians and a gallon of black velvet—I've told you I'm a fast eater—have dropped, and empties them down the chute. She makes a point of doing this in front of me so I'll know there's no deception. There's been a regulation about this ever since 33 complained he was being given food he'd already eaten and bit the Lab Super's thumb as a protest.

Then she slips a milligramme or two of pituitrin B into the bloodstream to counteract any cerebrotonic cortical allergy to nicotine and fits a big fat juicy Havana into the pink rubber fingers at the end of the cigar arm.

After that we have our regular morning tiff. Bluey, who's always trying to raise what she calls my 'cultural and political level', plugs in to the Universal Brain Trust programme.

'For Marx's sake turn off that crap and give me my feely set!' I howl.

'Now, 63,' says Bluey, 'you know perfectly well you're not allowed to play with your feely set till after lunch. Lab Super's orders. You wouldn't like to get me into trouble, would you?'

'Yes,' I always come back, 'there's nothing I would like better, and you know it.'

I consider this restriction on the use of feely sets an unwarrantable interference with the liberty of the cerebral hemispheres. If Decaps of pronouncedly thalamotonic type such as 33 and 25 wish to spend eternity in a feely trance, that's their affair. I may attach more importance to consciousness myself, but that doesn't mean I'm not partial to a quarter of an hour's feely-play after breakfast; I find it goes very well with the first cigar of the day. But Lab Super or no Lab Super, I'm not standing for Agit Prop from the Universal Brain Trust. After all, we Decaps have some privileges in exchange for our artificial bloodstreams that are open for any biochemist with a new molecule to meddle about with, to say nothing of the loss of our trunks and limbs. And not the least of those privileges is: no compulsory Agit Prop.

As usual, Bluey and I compromise. No feelies till after lunch, but instead of UBT a game of four-dimensional chess with Decap 81. Bluey wheels me and my blood supply down to 81's end of the bench. I warn her not to leave my apparatus standing too close to 81, while she and 81's attendant are connecting up the model continuum frame and getting out the space-time counters. You see, 81 is a biter. It's an odd contradiction because not only is he senior Decap, but in other respects he's far and away the most cortical type in the Lab; hyper-intellectual, quite rarefied, he looks down his nose at me and calls me the clubman. This snapping must be some sort of nasty little hypothalamic tic, I suppose. One time when something went wrong with the conveyor belt of the skull-scrubbing machine and we all got joggled up much too close together, his teeth met in 33's ear and they had to black him out before they could make him let go. However, nothing can go wrong at four-dimensional chess, unless he spits at me—and that's not so terrible. He can't cheat because the whole thing is electronically controlled.

All is well. We've had a very close game lasting about three weeks by your old earth duration measurements. It's time for preprandial black-out, during which they give our cerebral arteries a high-pressure blow-through with this new peptone-plasma solution the Martian physiologists are so hot on. Then comes lunch.

There's not an awful lot to tell you about lunch except that, as with all our meals, we get the best of everything and as much of it as we like for as long as we like. We Decaps are never bothered by lack of appetite. Our palates, freed from the stomach's and liver's bondage, are ever avid, and we go on champing and swallowing and savouring our favourite dishes for days on end. On special occasions such as Gourmet Club Meets I've known lunch last a month, and it might be going on still if our jaw muscles didn't have to rest. On shellfish day, last Club Meet, I scoffed a hundredweight of assorted Dublin Bay prawns, scampi, langoustes, ecrévisses, durian-fed Venusian landcrabs, and those delicious giant Martian lobsters which you used to get in the Lake of Blood before it was drained by order of the Universal Brain. As for drink, 16, who's of a statistical frame of mind, calculates that at a little six-hour snack affair he drank two dozen bottles of old-fashioned claret, a firkin of Lunar Fungus Vino Fino, and a litre or so of the new Plutonic inorganic liqueur—radio-active but quite harmless. They make it from crystals found in the deposits left by the cosmic ray maelstroms, and it's supposed to stimulate your historical consciousness.

After the usual post-prandial metabolic check-over and a precautionary electroencephalogram to see that no brain storms are on the way, Bluey fixes the cap with the feely electrodes over my skull, inserts the 'smelly' plug up each nostril, and switches on.

This afternoon the Play Time Station is disseminating a life-size electronic model of θ 5466, the young Mercuric musical comedy actress who made such a smash hit in the spectacular feely revue 'In a Rocket to the Moon with Ashtaroth'. Her feely dialogue is specially written for her by Peoples' Playwright No. 1. She's a very popular number with the Decaps, and as I roll an eye sideways along the bench I catch sight of no fewer than seventeen of her. Personally I'm not very keen on these Mercuric females. I may be old fashioned; or perhaps it's because I'm very nearly a pure Earth type, although Engels only knows I'm no snob, I've not a vestige of planet prejudice, but I can't see the point of all these extra limbs and appendages. I like a girl to be a girl—not an octopus. However, I tell Bluey to leave me plugged in.

I must say the kid (after all he's only 300) who wrote that dialogue knew his stuff. Writing feely dialogue is damned difficult. You have to be prepared for all kinds of reaction situations and have standard pattern alternative lines written ready to answer each one according to the electrotelepathic vibrations registered at the central feely station. No wonder the feely technicians are reputed to be such harassed types.

As a matter of fact, we get an example of how things can go wrong this afternoon. Poor old 33, who never can let well alone, says to his electronic model: 'But θ 5466, how can a lovely stream of quicksilver like you possibly love an old billiard ball like me?'

This, of course, is an easy one for the dialogue writer; he's got it all taped and typed long ago—commonest reaction pattern for all numbers over fifty.

The electronic model of θ 5466 passes a score or two of her silver-gilt antennæ lightly over Decap 33's mug and answers pat: 'Because you're wise and chiselled like old ivory, because you're rugged. . . .' But at this moment something goes wrong with the apparatus at the Central Feely Station, the needle sticks in a groove or something, and all poor old 33's electronic model of θ 5466 can say is: 'You're rugged, you're rugged, you're rugged'. And 33 thinks he's being made fun of and tries to savage her. It's a good thing he's only a limbless Decap in the Lab and not an ordinary number in a public feely parlour, otherwise there'd be a scandal and a lot of flashes to the *Universal Times* about what beasts these old numbers are and how life ought to end at 20 for all outside the physiology labs except prime numbers. Meanwhile there's hell and damnation to pay on our bench. All the feely dialogue seems to have got jammed and all seventeen electronic models of θ 5466 are squawking: 'You're rugged, you're rugged, you're rugged'. 33's scalp starts to crackle and they have to black him out. They also have to black out 81, who's managed in the confusion to get quite a bit of his θ 5466 between his teeth. Resident physiologists come rushing in and the feely sets are switched off.

However, as I'm so calm and give so little trouble I'm allowed to tune in my telecast set to the new experimental station under the auspices of the Cosmic Historico-Physical Institute. This aims to reconstruct the so-called past by means of trapping and amplifying the electronic vibration reflection patterns. They say it'll be given a public wavelength soon on account of its high educational value, but I don't know so much. It's another of our Decap privileges to tune in on it pretty regularly, and I can tell you they've been having a lot of trouble.

This afternoon they're in a rare state of excitement; the announcer says they're catching scenes—and picking up the dialogue too—at the court of an ancient British Earth King, Charles II. Well, I'm no great shakes on history, but it all smells faintly phoney to me. First there's a hell of a blur; then we see a redhead in a cartwheel hat upsetting a basket of technicolour oranges which bounce like tennis balls. Whereupon we hear a voice yell: 'Cut', and a notice which says: 'Scene 2, take 96', and it turns out just as I thought all the time, we've got caught up in the twentieth century with a primitive British Earth film outfit making an early squawky about Nell Gwynne, a plucky proletarian girl who, so *we've* always understood, organized the Chelsea Pensioners Union and led them into action at Peterloo.

They've got a long way to go before they perfect this thing. Indeed, from what I've heard I shouldn't be at all surprised if we didn't see some of the research workers of the Cosmic Historico-Physical Institute joining us Decaps on the bench before long. It seems the history they're picking up in space-time doesn't altogether square with the stuff we're taught in poli-class. Take another little episode from Earth history, for instance, the year 1941, in the middle of the second lesser Earth war. Now we've always been taught that it was the German agent Beelzebub Trotsky who piloted Hess's plane on his famous flight to Britain, and they'd have made it, too, if Lord Claude Cockburn, the historian, editor of the famous weekly paper *The Truth*, hadn't taken off in a rickety old helicopter from the roof of the *Worker's Times* and shot them down over Buckingham Palace. Well, from what I've heard, and you'd be surprised how rumours get around, the Institute boys have picked up the death-scene of Trot and it happened over a year before in another part of the world altogether. Seems he was clocked by a loony, one of his own disciples, in Mexico.

But that's not all. I'm told the Universal Brain has been saying that not only can you rewrite history, but in these days you can also re-enact it. And he's planning to send whole armies of electronic agents out into the continuum—or back into the past as you Earth-dwellers would say—to make bloody-well certain once and for all that history ran true to text-book form. So look out for squalls in the continuous present.

I'm not saying any more about this. Judging by the stuff Bluey's just slipped into my bloodstream, I've said too much already. I don't want to forfeit any privileges. A Decap has nothing to complain of. How can he have? He's only to express his lightest whim for it to be gratified instantly. And he's never anxious or depressed for more than a few seconds before they either black him out or pep him up with an extra dose of Euphoria mixture.

It's evening now. I rather think I've been blacked out for a bit. They're closing the gas-tight roof over the Park of Giant Vegetables, preparatory to pumping in the nitrogen mixture. I sometimes wish they wouldn't grow those Vegetables quite so damned big. It's the first evening they've let it get really dark for quite a time; I remember now, the astronomers are a bit worried about a cluster of white dwarfs way out towards the edge of the galactic disc. They're going to knock hell out of their nuclei around midnight. Proton bombardment. Make space a bit less crowded. Ought to be some classy fireworks.

It's Bluey's night off. She's going to some electrical orgy or other on one of Jupiter's satellites, and is looking very taking dressed in nothing but a swarm of fireflies. I tell her to be careful she doesn't lose her body and she laughs and hands me over to the tender mercies of my next-door neighbour 64's attendant, who's got a deal too much Martian in her disposition for my liking. 33, who's already had a brush with her, thinks she's a slapper. He suggests I provoke her so she loses her temper and then we can report her to the Lab Super. But I'm not having any. Me for a quiet time. I shall be quite happy listening in to the latest Universal Sabotage case. A space rocket carrying enough atomic explosive to blow the poor little Earth clean off its orbit, and manned by a crew of Martians disguised as Saturnines was spotted by the Interplanetary Security Police lurking in a crater on the Moon. They were immobilized by general paralytic ray and caught absolutely red handed, just in time. They had Atomic time rockets trained on the Earth and a barrage of leaflets printed in Saturnine to follow. With such strained relations between the Earth and Saturn it would have touched off an interplanetary war for certain. Typical piece of Martian provocation, heavy handed but effective. We're all wondering what's behind it, and I'm very much looking forward to the trial. The preliminary examination showed that all the accused had been heavily inoculated against truth drug, so the Universal Prosecutor's having their skulls lifted off and electrodes inserted straight into the cortex for direct stimulation. They'll talk.

They've just wheeled back 62, my next-door neighbour on the other side. Been out on one of his high-speed jaunts, attached to the head of a light rocket. He says the sensation is quite extraordinary, and I can well believe it. Damned if I'd go near the things. 64 says three new Decaps are coming in tonight—all from the Cosmic Historico-Physical Institute. What did I tell you? I don't suppose they'll be allowed consciousness for a good many years yet. 64 also says the latest Solar System gossip is that the Universal Brain's decided the Earth has got senile and is due to be retired before long. He thinks they'll disintegrate it. I should worry!

Very bad news. If Bluey was in charge she'd fill me up with Euphoria right away, but this Martian oaf is hopeless and an old-fashioned sadist. The Nazis of the Universe, that's what we call the Martians.

After dinner the Lab Super paid his usual visit. I thought he looked a little odd—embarrassed about something. After he'd trolleyed along the line of benches and glanced at the reaction charts he said he had something rather important to tell us. It appears the Universal Brain Trust has just drawn up a new millennial plan. The meaning of the Martian provocational plot has convinced it of the urgent necessity for a new and far more intense drive for increased and ever-increasing co-operation, collectivity and general oneness. In this drive we Decaps are to play an important part, 'a vanguard role' were the exact words. A research programme has already been drawn up and experimental work is to be begun at once with a view to promoting closer and ever closer biochemical physiological and ultimately cerebral relationship between Decaps in organized groups. They will begin by blacking us all out and re-connecting our blood supply to large pumps in groups of six so that every six Decaps will share the same blood supply system.

That's only the beginning. The ultimate aim is total cerebral community. Larger and larger brains, until they get something altogether new. What good that will do, search me; but that won't stop them. They're going to try everything—electrical inter-connection, rays, surgery, cortex grafting, all the isms and asms in the ology. As I told the Lab Super, they might just as well bang our heads together and be done with it. And who do you think they're teaming me up with? 33, who's the most troublesome Decap in the whole

Lab and a sex maniac into the bargain. 81 the notorious biter, 45 and 46 whom we suspect of having once been a squared couple because of the way they nag each other, and a prime number who's volunteering to be decapped so as to give us tone and cosmic consciousness—in other words a ruddy cerebral nark. Some chain gang! And of course the whole thing is an absolutely flagrant breach of our Decaps' contracts. I wish I'd got into my little bit of trouble a millennium or two earlier when they still went in for capital punishment. I wonder what's become of my trunk and limbs? What sort of head have they got on my shoulders now? A prime number's, I'll bet. I thought I recognized one of my hands the other day on a visiting delegate. Hope it gets him into trouble.

Thank the Absolute . . . here comes Bluey, summoned back from her orgy on account of the crisis in the Lab. She looks a bit dishevelled because they had to dematerialize her and send her home on the beam. Rather a lot of the fireflies seem to have gone out. . . . But what's the sense in my making silly cracks like that when in a few days I'm going to be just one great big happy family? This is really ghastly. Still, perhaps the astronomers will go too far, explode the whole cluster of white dwarfs and negate the universe?

I don't know what I've been saying, but you're not to take any notice of it. Bluey has just given me a great big shot of Morpheus Five and I've never felt so good for the last two hundred years. The Lab Super's got a wonderful new experiment planned for us and we're all going to lose our rotten petty little individualities and be all together in a wonderful oneness.

Already I feel wonderfully at one with everyone. Eyes closing now. Good night, Earth dwellers and other poor time slaves. Don't you wish you lived with us in the luminous numinous? Onwards: Forward, Sideways, Backward, Upward, Downward and Outward into the continuum! Progressive March!

PAUL GOODMAN

IDDINGS CLARK

Lo! on every visage a Black Veil!—*Hawthorne.*

I

In the assembly-room of the Northport High School they were celebrating the day before Christmas. All the children were present in the seats and a crowd of parents in the rear, and many graduates—some of whom were parents and some collegians home on vacation. The greatest hilarity and yet decorum prevailed, as always (so that many held that 'the best part of the holiday season is the High School celebration'). This year was given a pageant of the Nativity, but only half-reverent, for at intervals a great burlesque Santa Claus rolled in, did tumblesaults, and so forth, while two end-men bandied jokes. All this was invented and directed by Mr. Iddings Clark, M.A., a teacher of English, a mind so spirited and original, with modern notions of Art (considering the community); and these masques have since been collected and printed. He was also in charge of the singing. To see him high on the platform, waving his arms, lifted everybody to enthusiasm; ordinarily a shy, almost reserved man, on such occasions he was red with pleasure and crowned with joy. Recent students of his, home from college, crowded beneath him to the platform. The song rang through the hall:

'Jingle bells! jingle bells!
Jingle all the way!'

—when suddenly, in the midst of a note, the conductor fainted away, and fell from the platform on his face. A cry of horror rang through the hall. The young men who had been at his feet now bore him up; they laid him on the platform and loosened his collar—he was pale—and dashed a glass of water in his face. His eyes fluttered open and he came to. 'It's nothing,' he said. 'I see you all clearly. I am so happy having around me my friends so bright and close. Everything is exactly as it was.'

The fact is that at the moment he was about to faint—perhaps because the blood rushed from his head, or that the electric light faltered, or for some other reason—at that moment he beheld over everything a cast of darkness. He saw on each face a veil. It was the Black Veil in the harrowing story of Hawthorne (from which I have taken the motto for this story). At one instant all faces were lit up—the lights overhead ablaze and the falling snow outside—and all printed with an indulgent smile at the well-known song; the next instant, though their mouths were open wide, the sinister shadow was everywhere apparent! A teacher of literature, Iddings Clark was only too well acquainted with Hawthorne's unnatural romance; twice a year for eight years he had read through with his classes the tale of *The Minister's Black Veil*. But although each time he came to that awful outburst 'Why do you tremble at me alone? tremble also at each other!' he was so moved that the sweat appeared on his brow, he hardly thought that it would come to this. As if we experience works of art with impunity! The next instant he fainted away.

He sank in the dead faint and the light came and went. Then there was no more light and his soul was profoundly torn—accompanied by violent trembling and shaking in all his limbs, so that the students among whom he had fallen felt the body quiver in their hands. This quietened, he began to rise again through the zones of light, and he had a dream: that he was walking on Hooker Street in the snow and he saw, with a sense of appalling loneliness, that all the passers-by wore half-masks like highwaymen; then he entered the school and stark naked stood before his class. With a cry, he awoke.

II

That night, Christmas Eve, Iddings Clark went to the home of Otto, an instructor in chemistry, to trim the tree for his five-year-old daughter. To spend the night thus had become almost a custom. 'Yet soon,' said Otto, 'she will be beyond the age for Christmas-trees.'

'I am all right,' said the English teacher in a strained voice. 'Anyway there is a compensation for everything! How well Emerson put it!'

He was famous as a decorator of trees! For here also—as in the clever masques he composed—sparkled such fancy and originality, in the dramatic contrast of white lights and the deep boughs, not without a touch of wild wit, such as a jack-in-the-box in the heart of it. People dropped in at the house where he had decorated the tree.

'How strange your tree is tonight, Iddings!' cried the chemist. 'It looks almost sinister; you can't mean to leave it so. All the tinsel, the silver globes, the dolls, candy-canes, and lights are crowded down in one corner, pell-mell, without beauty or order. The rest of the tree is black. Why have you cut out a little recess in the dark boughs, and there put, so lonely, the silver star that is supposed to ride so brightly at the top? And around it four upright candles, one above, one below, on the left, and on the right, so rigidly?'

'We must snatch at least this much order from the riot.'

'But the star itself is not balanced; it leans to one side. . . . Why did you arrange the candles in a cross? It doesn't fit Christmas.'

'They are four soldiers.'

Frau Otto looked attentively at the young man and said, 'You are feverish—I can see by your eyes.'

'Remember this afternoon—,' said Otto.

'I've been neglecting a cold; it's nothing. Perhaps you could give me an aspirin tablet.'

She dosed him with two, and a cup of hot milk to wash them down. 'You can't go out now in a sweat,' she said. 'We must put you up overnight.'

'Oh!'

'We'll sit up just a few minutes.'

At the opportunity to stay and talk the English teacher was overjoyed. He smiled and at once started to talk about himself, saying, 'I remember when I was a boy, I lived in Boston, and at night I used to walk on Washington Avenue, among the bright lights, and look in the faces of all the people! Dr. Otto, did *you* ever do anything like that? I mean, not necessarily in Boston . . . ' He sped on in the same vein. After a few moments, Frau Otto rose and excused herself—though indeed there was nothing scandalous that he had to say; for what could a person so young and sober have to confess?

'You're strange, Iddings!' said Otto, thinking of the uncanny tree, which, he felt, would frighten his child. 'Maybe I ought to call the doctor.'

'A different person exactly!' said Clark. 'I don't apologize for talking about myself because nothing is more important than that we understand one another.'

'I understand you less and less.'

Soon it was past midnight. The chemist began to foresee that the Christmas in his house was ruined; in the morning he would not be up to greet his daughter; and what a rude fright was in store for her when she saw the Christmas tree. He speculated on the possibility of putting his guest to bed and then stealing down to redecorate it. He could not foresee that this tree would be the merriest his daughter ever had; for throughout the morning, her newly-gotten toys—dolls, a house and furniture, a mechanical fire-engine—all lying neglected, she kept climbing a chair to right the lopsided star and then, dancing for joy, knocked it away again with paper balls aimed from across the room.

In the afternoon, several visitors, teachers, dropped in at Dr. Otto's—Messrs. Bell and Flint; Dr. Croydon, the dean; and Miss Cohalan, the registrar. Iddings Clark continued, in the same nervously intimate strain; his sleep had been only moderately feverish, enough to generate almost pleasant dreams—and these he now proceeded to expound in minute detail.

Otto took Dean Croydon aside. 'He's not well. I tried to keep him in bed but he won't stay.'

'What is his temperature?'

'Normal.'

'You see,' cried Clark, 'there is nothing we're not capable of!'

'Nothing is more false!' said the Dean sharply. 'Nothing is falser than when we think ourselves creatures of any chance fancy, not as we really are—just as, brutally frank with rage, we tell our friends what we think of them in a rage, not what we really think.'

The situation rapidly became strained; the social atmosphere spoilt. Each of the friends cast his eyes upon the ground to avoid looking at the others; only Iddings himself eagerly sought them out with his eyes.

'When all know too much, all are ashamed,' thought Otto.

'It's lucky he's taken ill during the holidays; he'll be better by the start of school,' thought Dean Croydon.

III

On New Year's Day, which fell on a Tuesday, Iddings Clark was scheduled to deliver the annual Hooker Lecture on Literature, in the auditorium of the High School. And this year an extraordinary audience had gathered, for not only was Clark always a treat as a lecturer, but everyone remembered the dramatic incident that had befallen him the week before, his dead faint in the midst of the singing. Many children, as well as the grown-ups, came to stare at him in curiosity; the ushers were given orders to shunt those boys not with their parents up into the balcony—and there they sat, staring down, their lips pressed against the shiny rail.

Dean Croydon introduced the speaker as their 'beloved friend who occasioned so much anxiety on the day before Christmas, but who has since quite recovered'. The subject of the lecture was 'The Incentives of Poetry'.

When the English teacher stepped to the front, however, he seemed the opposite of quite recovered—thin, white, with sombre eyes. Everywhere there was a leaning forward to see him better. He said in a strained voice, 'I had intended to speak of poetry as objects and forms, and of the excitement of *inventing* something: for there is a pleasure in creating a new structure, or in elaborating a living plot, as if a man were Prometheus. But instead I shall speak of it as communication, and why it is that one person talks to another.

'But talking to you, as Meyer Liben said,' he cried suddenly, 'is like talking to a wall!'

As he spoke the pink colour mounted in his face, and his dark eyes burned. He made no gestures, but with white-knuckled fingers gripped the edges of the lectern, and his voice came forth over his hands. '*Come alive Galatea!* cried that famous sculptor, *that I may talk to you!* and he kissed a statue not yet free of the formless rock. What a sad pity that the centuries of evolution could not create a human friend for him!'

People looked at each other.

'Very lonely,' said the lecturer. 'Such exact symbols—but only poets pay close attention, and they adopt this language for their very own. The poets speak only to the poets. To talk to you is like talking to a wall!'

'Our friend Iddings,' whispered Miss Cohalan, seated behind the speaker, leaning across to Dean Croydon, 'he seems beyond the bounds of order. His sentences come in gusts.'

'I have not heard more moving eloquence,' said the Dean sharply. (One would not have expected him to say this.)

'The French poet, Charles Baudelaire, wrote:

> Le bourdon se lamente, et la bûche enfumée
> accompagne en fausset la pendule enrhumée,
> cependant qu'en un jeu plein de sales parfums,
> heritage fatale d'une vieille hydropique,
> le beau valet de cœur et la dame de pique
> causent sinistrement de leurs amours défunts—

"in a game full of dirty perfumes, the handsome knave of hearts and the queen of spades, gossip sinisterly of their dead loves." Why did he say *this*?

'And he wrote:

> Et le printemps et la verdure
> ont tant humilié mon cœur
> que j'ai puni sur une fleur
> l'insolence de la nature—

"the springtime and foliage humiliated me so, I took punishment on a flower for the insolence of nature." Why *this*?

'J'ai plus de souvenirs que si j'avais mille ans— "I have more memories than if I were a thousand years old!".'

At this sentence many in the audience started.

In the balcony the children began a whispered debate.

'He says he is a thousand years old!'

'No. He says it was as if he was a thousand years old.'

'Mr. Clark is a *thousand years old*!'

'Quiet! quiet!' said the usher.

The afternoon growing late, the snow outside falling thicker—the hall became dim. Yet all, straining their eyes in the dusk, thought that they saw the speaker clearly.

'This is a common experience,' he said, 'young people in love are unable, no matter how hard they try, to keep from talking about the person.'

'But when they are *out of love*, still wounded, not yet healed, hopelessly hunting around in every direction for sympathy—then they *still* talk (making all ashamed).'

Suddenly—just as he had begun, and as he continued—he stopped. His voice no longer came in separate gusts across his white-knuckled hands. But the faint light that seemed to play on him on the platform persisted.

They began to clap and abruptly found themselves in pitch darkness. The applause grew loud. There was a hubbub of people trying to put on their coats and goloshes in the dark. At last the lights came ablaze. Blinded, the people took this opportunity to add to the infectious applause, but the speaker had slipped away during the darkness.

'Would the young man have us go around confessing each other?'

'No. It is only that we read poetry more sympathetically.'

'Come alive, Galatea! cried that famous sculptor.'

'How pale he looked at the beginning; then how flushed he became.'

'I thought that he was going to keel over again.'

'How was he at the end?'

'You couldn't tell, it was so dark.'

IV

The next day, it was a Wednesday, school reconvened. The snow lay deep on the ground, but the sun shone brightly; it reflected from the snow and sky, and poured into the large-windowed classrooms. At nine o'clock, flushed and damp from a snowfight, the boys and girls came trooping in.

Out of his little cubicle off the English lecture-room, Mr. Clark stepped to face his class: he was stark naked except for his spectacles and a Whittier in his right hand.

With cries of fright the young people fled up the aisle and through the doors they had just entered; before the period-gong had finished sounding, the classroom was emptied—except of one small girl who sat spellbound in the front row, and a boy who stopped near the door on his way out.

'I'll tell Dean Croydon,' he said, and left.

Now Rea, the small girl, and the teacher of English were left alone, facing each other, she seated behind a desk, he standing naked beside his table.

'Why don't you run off with the others, child?' said Iddings.

'I'm hot and tired with playing; I'd rather stay here for the class.'

'They have an unexpected holiday out of me.'

'Won't there be a class, Mr. Clark?'

'The assignment was *Snowbound*, by Whittier.'

'I read it all!' cried the girl.

'It's not a great poem. What the devil prompted him to write it?'

She stared at him closely, from head to foot, and said, 'Is it true, what they say, Mr. Clark, that you are a thousand years old?'

'A thousand years! Heavens no.'

'They say that you said you was a thousand years old, and I see that in some places you're grown all over with hair.'

'I am thirty-one,' he said smiling.

'I'm thirteen, just the opposite,' said Rea. She kept looking up into his face.

'What's your name, girl?' he said sharply, 'my glasses are sweated over and I can't see you clearly.'

'Rea.'

'Rea! that's a strange name. It means the guilty one. Rea. Is there any of the boys you love?'

'Donald Worcester.'

'Come here, child,' he said in a tight voice. 'Have you told him that you love him?'

'I wrote on the school-wall with chalk,' she cried, 'REA LOVES DONALD W. Just as if somebody else wrote it.'

She rose from her bench and came beside the teacher.

'That's *right*!' he said. 'Now he must tell you.'

At this—as if for no reason—she burst into sobs. At the same time the door in the rear opened, and in came the Dean with a posse of instructors summoned from their classes for this extraordinary occasion. With a cry of fright the girl fled across the bars of sunlight out of the room.

'She's crying. What did you do to her?' asked the Dean.

'I did not!'

'Iddings! what's the meaning of this?'

'It's the story of Hawthorne's, *The Minister's Black Veil.*'

'I don't remember. It's many years since most of us read Hawthorne,' said the Dean.

'I at least shan't wear a black veil!' exclaimed Iddings Clark exaltedly, and a wave of colour swept over him, from his feet to his forehead.

The Dean took off his coat and flung it round the shoulders of his trembling friend.

'This is serious; this is awful, Iddings Clark,' he said. 'We won't hear the end of it. Where are your clothes? Get dressed. It's *my* fault; I knew it was coming. At least we'll try to hush the matter up. It won't come before the School Board. But how can I answer for the consequences?'

ANTONIA WHITE

THE MOMENT OF TRUTH

ON the stone floor inlaid with coats of arms, only a few couples were dancing, yet the hall was filled with the lisping of feet. The music was as insistent as the band striking up when a man falls from a trapeze.

'Hardly anyone is dancing,' said Charlotte to the unknown man beside her, 'yet whenever I put out my hand, I touch someone.' But the stranger seemed not to have heard her. All his attention was taken up with the piece of string which he was twisting into elaborate bends. At first she was hurt because he was ignoring her. Then she realized that he was telling her something by means of the string. She tried to read words in the loops and twists. He tied a slip-knot and drew the noose over one finger. 'Is that ——?' she began, and checked herself. For she had made an absurd mistake. The man beside her was not a stranger, but her husband, Richard.

And was she after all at Faringay? There was something not quite right about the hall. Looking up, she read the motto on one of the dark arches, *Ne crede Byron*. The arch: the gilt letters were just as she remembered them, but the words should have been *Labor ipse Voluptas*.

She must keep quiet, ask no questions, draw attention to nothing, least of all to herself. Now the hall was entirely empty of dancers. But though the band brayed like a steam organ, she could still hear the whispering feet. There was no longer anyone near her, but a woman laughed close by her ear and an invisible skirt brushed her knee.

With every second the danger was growing. Looking for a way of escape, Charlotte noticed a door she had never seen before. Printed on it in large Gothic letters was the word MURDER.

Now she knew that she could not be too careful. She must act very quietly, very normally. She walked over towards the buffet, feeling her way through the unseen dancers. They would not make room for her but pressed against her, jostling and holding her back. She dared not wince or cry out though she could feel hands passing up and down her spine, pinching her arms, stroking her throat. An invisible man embraced her, pushing his thighs against hers. A finger was thrust in her eye. A woman's bracelet caught in her hair. But, keeping back her terror, she went on slowly making her way through the crowd of laughing enemies.

By the buffet the space was clear. The man in the white cap carving a ham with a long thin knife raised his head and looked at her with eyes bolting from a doll's face. He leant over the table and ran the knife blade caressingly down her arm. 'I *know*,' he whispered. It had come. She must get out. In a second it would be too late.

'Richard! Richard! Richard!' she screamed from bursting lungs.

* * *

The cry Charlotte heard as she broke through to the safer world was the thinnest wail, less audible than the pounding of her heart. She put out her hand to touch Richard and her knuckles encountered only wood. She seemed to be lying in a coffin that heaved under her with a shuddering creak. Was she awake or had she struggled out of one nightmare into another? She forced her eyes wide open and took deep gasps of breath. The air, smelling of oil and paint, was suffocating but it was the air of the tangible world. Groping along the ledge she found a switch and turned on the dim cabin light.

'Richard,' she said.

There was no answer.

Leaning over the edge of the bunk, she listened for his breathing. She heard nothing but the straining creak of the ship and the crash of the waves against the port-hole. His dressing-gown swung towards her from the opposite wall and stayed suspended at a wide angle till the wall swung forward to meet it. The wall itself swerved from the straight and the dressing-gown lapsed back on to it. She stared at it as it swayed, hung suspended and dropped until she began to feel its sickening rhythm behind her eyes and had to look away.

At last she made herself climb down and peer into the lower bunk. The sheets were folded with the precision of a hospital bed. On the pillow lay nothing but Richard's watch. She picked it up, looked at the time, and crouched back on the bunk, dangling the watch by its strap. It was half-past one; more than two hours since he had kissed her good-night and gone up on deck. Why had he left her for so long?

Ever since she had begun, a few months before, to have oppressive dreams, she counted on finding him near her when she fought out of them, always calling his name. He had learnt to slip an arm round her, even to mutter reassuring words, without waking from his sleep. Now that he was not there when she needed him such bitterness rose up in her that she could feel an acrid taste in her mouth.

The next lurch of the narrow cabin flung his dressing-gown against her knee. Snatching it from the hook, she huddled into it, meaning to go up on deck and find him. But she felt sick. Her knees bent under her and she dropped back, stooping, on the bunk.

The cabin was growing smaller, hotter, more imprisoning every minute. She seemed to have swollen to enormous size. The heavy man's dressing-gown was stifling her but she could not make the effort to take it off. Her skin pricked as if hairs were starting out of it. The bitterness vanished in the beginning of a terror worse than the nightmare, the waking terror from which there was no escape. She could neither bear to be alone in this dim, lurching cupboard nor get up strength to burst open the door. With eyes stiffening in their sockets, she could only crouch there, gripping the watch-strap as if it were a life-line.

Trying to keep the fear from closing in on her, she focused all her mind on the watch. To her it was part of Richard's body. The silver back was stained from four years contact with his flesh. It had marked him too, printing its shape in a white fetter on his wrist. Night after night the beat of its tiny metal pulse had sounded like a second heart, a fraction of him that remained awake while he slept. It had become so intimately his that, fingering it in his absence, she seemed to be touching something to which she had no right.

She had not held it in her hand since she had taken it shining from its case and given it him the night before they were married. The next morning, just as she was leaving her room to go across to the church where his father was waiting to marry them, he had run into her, breathless and laughing.

'My watch, Charlotte! I can't be married without my watch! I've raced back from the altar for it.'

She remembered how he looked, bright-eyed and ruddy from the November wind, his hair sleeked, a flower in his coat—the picture of a bridegroom.

But try as she would to hold the image, the tide of panic went on rising, sweeping her back from the real world. The watch slipped to the floor. She dropped back on the bunk with closed eyes and gasping mouth like a drowning woman beaten off from a lifeboat.

'Charlotte!'

His voice called her back. It sounded in the core of her ear, yet it seemed to come from another dimension like the voice of the nurse to which one wakes after chloroform. She forced up her eyelids and looked at him. He filled the cabin, standing over her in his loose oilskin coat.

'Charlotte, dear, are you awake or asleep?'

With a huge effort she made herself open her mouth and speak, only to say in a dry whisper:

'Your watch. On the floor. Don't tread on it.'

He picked up the watch. His face, as it stooped to the level of hers, still glistened with spray, and his hair was damp and ruffled.

'What is the matter, Charlotte? Are you ill?'

'I had a bad dream,' she said, staring past him.

'And I wasn't there, I'm sorry.'

'What does it matter?'

'Oh, Charlotte, not that voice. And why look at me as if I were an enemy?'

'Not an enemy. A stranger,' she said wearily.

'I shouldn't have stayed away so long.'

There was regret in his tone, not the mechanical gentleness she had lately come to expect. It softened the shell of her hatred. She sat up and let him put his arm round her shoulder. Sitting side by side, their heads leaning together, their foreheads drooped, they seemed to be mourning a common loss.

'What was your dream, Charlotte?'

'I woke before it became too bad. It was about Faringay.'

'You are haunted by that house. Why do you keep dreaming about the past?'

'I can't inhabit the present any more.'

His arm tightened as the ship gave a lurch.

'We shouldn't be talking so late. We may be keeping people awake in the next cabin.'

She drew away from him in anger. Then she laughed.

'You inhabit the present all right.'

'It makes you so angry that I do. Yet one of us must.'

'Perhaps one is enough,' she said almost gaily.

He stood up and tried gently to draw her to her feet. But she shook her head and settled back on the bunk. He loomed above her, balancing on his strong legs, adjusting them to the movement of the ship.

'Don't you ever have dreams, Richard?'

'Mine don't make stories like yours.'

'Do you never have a dream that seems more true than life? That shows you something you never knew before—or were afraid to know?'

He began to wind his watch.

'Sometimes, perhaps.'

'You don't tell me them.'

She glanced up and saw his face set and heavy. In the dim light the shadows under his eyes were dark as bruises. She knew he was tired out but she hardened to him.

'I don't always dream of the past, Richard.'

He went on turning the knob of his watch.

'You'll break the mainspring,' she cried in a burst of rage. Then, bitterly, 'I forgot. You'd never ill-treat a piece of *machinery*, would you?'

He laid the watch down carefully and took her by the wrist, pressing his fingers on it as if feeling her pulse.

'Charlotte!' he said quietly and urgently, 'Charlotte! You must get some sleep now.'

He pulled her up against the dead weight of her resistance.

'I'll help you into your bunk.'

'No. I feel sick.'

'You'll be better lying flat. It's beginning to calm down. Up on deck I could hardly keep my legs.'

'Then why did you stay so long?'

He kissed her forehead.

'Up you go. Carefully.'

As she scrambled up clumsily, a sudden roll shot her forehead against an iron staple and Richard cried out.

'You needn't pity me about physical pain,' she said. 'It's a relief.'

'You don't want that heavy old dressing-gown. You'll be far too hot.'

She took it off and let it fall.

'I don't remember putting it on. I must be a little crazy.'

He smoothed her pillow, pulled the harsh sheets over her and putting back her tangled hair, began to stroke her forehead. For a minute she lay with closed eyes, not resisting him. A tear oozed under her eyelid and crawled down her temple.

'Will you sleep now?' he said softly.

Her eyes sprang open.

'You say I always dream of the past. What about my other dream? The one about your leaving me?'

'You've dreamt that ever since we married, haven't you?' he said in his same soft voice, still stroking her head. She jerked it away from his touch.

'I shall go on dreaming it. Until it comes true.'

'Has it ever been near coming true?'

'How should I know?' She closed her eyes once more. A wave exploded with a gentle crash against the port-hole.

'If only we could open it and get some air,' said Richard.

Though Charlotte had withdrawn too far into herself to care about the heat or the reek of oil, she knew how they must sicken his wind-freshened senses. Yet she beat her fist against the ledge of the bunk, crying:

'You mean I am stifling you. Go on. Say it. Say it.'

'I will say nothing of the kind,' he whispered in patient fury. She bared her teeth and tried to strike him, but he leaned over her pinioning her shoulders like a lover or a murderer. She lay helpless for a moment, gasping with anger. Then suddenly she smiled.

'Why do I have to behave like this? Why can't you stop me?'

He smiled too and shook his head.

'Let me go now,' she said, speaking for the first time in her normal voice. 'You needn't hold me down. I am not dangerous.'

He took his hands from her shoulders and began to stroke her arm as if he were expertly and mechanically stroking an animal.

'I know,' he said.

She lay with closed eyes, quiet but unappeased. There was something she wanted to tell him, something urgent which kept flitting just out of reach of her thought like a forgotten name. He kissed her lightly and began, quietly as a thief, to lower himself into his own bunk. When she remembered what she had been groping for and softly called his name, he did not answer.

* * *

Their bedroom in the Hotel Berrichon was square and low-ceilinged, with a floor of red tiles arranged in a honeycomb pattern. Stiff yellow lace curtains were looped back from the window that looked out over the whole expanse of the Baie de la Fresnaye. Madame Berrichon leered at Richard and Charlotte as she patted the red eiderdown of the enormous bed.

'You will hardly find a bed so comfortable in the whole of Brittany. My neighbours are satisfied with the old-fashioned *lits clos*—mere cupboards. But I am from Paris. I am civilized. I do not look on a bed as something in which one huddles oneself to sleep like an animal. In Paris we say that the bed is the battlefield of love.'

'Indeed,' said Richard, politely. Charlotte turned away with a sigh of exasperation and began to pour water from the tiny cracked pitcher into the basin.

'Madame is annoyed?' said Madame Berrichon, in her hoarse purring contralto. 'One does not say such things to English ladies? Forgive me. I am a person of impulses. I do not weigh my words.'

'Are we the only people staying here?' asked Richard.

'Yes, Monsieur. It is early in the season. And in any case few people care for a place so remote. Only those who wish to be alone with nature—or painters—or ——' she lowered her heavy wrinkled lids, 'lovers.'

'We only found it by accident,' Richard said, with an uneasy glance at Charlotte's back. 'We set out from St. Malo this morning and we've been driving all day. My wife is very tired.'

'Believe me, it was no accident,' said Madame Berrichon. She faced him squarely, a solid shapeless figure in her dark shawl and black calico skirt. A shaft from the setting sun struck her face like limelight, showing up the black down on her upper lip and the open pores of her yellow skin. 'Nothing happens by accident in this life. I had an intuition that you would come—so strong that I sent my husband into Matignon to buy langoustes and other good things. He will tell you my intuitions are always justified.'

'I am sure they are, Madame,' said Richard, meeting her eyes with a stare of polite impertinence.

'You laugh. You think I am a foolish old woman,' she said with dignity. 'It is true I do not concoct verses, only good dishes. But at heart, Monsieur, I am a poet. And whether you believe me or not, I am in touch with the most subtle forces of nature. I know by a certainty I cannot describe—a magnetic current in my blood perhaps—that you were both sent here for a purpose. And if you do not know it, Madame your wife knows it, though she pretends not to listen to me.'

Charlotte did not speak or turn round until Madame Berrichon had glided out of the room, moving heavily yet swiftly over the tiles in her felt slippers.

'She's right. We can't get away even if we want to. She's a spider—a witch.'

'Well, she's got an ideal web or castle. It's an old sea-mill, she told me. Built right out into an arm of the bay. When the tide's up, there's water on three sides of the house.'

'In fact we are really prisoners,' said Charlotte.

'You forget there's a fourth side. Stop thinking about Madame Berrichon and come and look out of the window.'

'I'm frightened of that old woman,' said Charlotte, moving slowly up to where Richard stood by the window.

'You should paint her and get her out of your system. You could do a wonderful portrait of her—a cross between a Balzac concierge and the Delphic sibyl.'

'I shall never paint again,' said Charlotte gloomily. 'I can't see outside things any more. Only beastly things in my own mind.'

He drew her arm through his with a brotherly gesture.

'All the same, come and look out of the window.'

They leant together on the low narrow sill.

'You could dive straight out of the window into the sea,' she said.

'You'd better not try. See those dark patches under the surface? Rocks—jagged rocks too. You wouldn't have a chance.'

'What's happened to the sun? A few minutes ago there was a blazing sunset. Now look.'

The sky was overdrawn with fine cloud like a fog in the upper air. After the windless heat of the day, a breeze sprang up from nowhere, fanning gusts of invisible rain as fine as dust in their parched faces.

'Perhaps the wind and the rain come up with the tide,' said Richard. 'Can't you feel it's only on the surface? Underneath the air is still as hot and solid as ever. You can almost see the rain turning into steam.'

'How deep is the water?'

'Twenty or thirty feet I should say. Probably we're left high and dry when the tide goes out. Just rocks and mud.'

'What are those birds, Richard? The white ones. They're not ordinary gulls.'

Between the grey sky and the olive green sea white birds skimmed to and fro, a few feet above the surface, their black heads bent towards the water. Every now and then they dropped like stones into the sea, then flashed up again in an arrowy curve. Richard waited till one settled on an old boat moored to a ring in the wall.

'Look! do you see his forked tail? They're sea swallows: you can't see the fork when they fly—they move so fast—the feathers all whirl together.'

'Like spun glass: like the birds with spun glass tails we had on the Christmas tree.'

For a moment Charlotte forgot everything in the pleasure of watching the shooting, diving swallows. Then she turned from the window with a sigh.

'I wish I were a bird. Or even a rock or a patch of seaweed. Anything—anything but a human being.'

She went to the basin and began to wash her hands. Richard threw himself on the bed.

'Is that water warm?'

'No. It's icy—like mountain water.'

He yawned. 'Then I can't shave. You'll have to put up with me with a beard.'

'You can't look worse than I do,' said Charlotte, peering at herself in a greenish speckled mirror. Suddenly she turned and faced him.

'Richard, why didn't you tell me?'

'Tell you what?' he said, in a voice lazy, yet guarded.

'That I've suddenly aged ten years.'

'Don't talk nonsense.'

'You're not looking at me.'

'I don't have to. There's nothing the matter with your face. It's that absurd glass.'

'The glass can't give me those lines. Or those shadows under my eyes.'

'Then it's the way the light falls. Stop being morbid.'

Her face was strained and searching.

'Richard! seriously, I *do* look terrible, don't I?'

He smiled at the ceiling.

'Of course you look a little tired. Who wouldn't, after that night on the boat and driving all day in the sun and dust. Two nights' rest and you'll look wonderful.'

She turned her back on him again, fiercely dragging a comb through her soft fair hair that had gone limp from the heat.

'I hate my face,' she muttered: 'hate it! hate it! hate it!'

'Well, I don't,' he said good-humouredly. He swung himself off the bed and stood up, stretching his firm handsome brown arms. 'Come down and have a drink. We both need one.'

The dining-room was large and dim, lit only by three small windows on the landward side. It was paved with the same dull red honeycomb tiles as the bedroom and furnished only with two dark presses and a dozen tables covered with red and white oil-cloth. At the far end, like a huge well-head filled with stones, the shaft which had once held the hoppers of the mill thrust up through the floor. Underneath, though muffled by the stones, the tide could be heard gurgling in the empty shaft.

They sat down at the only table that was laid. Through the window they could see a small, dusty courtyard with a battered table, a few iron chairs, and a fig tree. A yellow mongrel was asleep on one of the chairs; at the table sat Monsieur Berrichon, a wizened little man in a beret and a faded blue blouse, sipping a glass of wine, round which the wasps hovered and buzzed.

Beside Charlotte's plate lay a passion-flower, a star of thick green-white petals with a fringe of blue rays. From the centre of the star four dark stamens stood up, lined with bright yellow pollen and three curious bosses like nail heads. She picked it up and sniffed its strong fleshy scent.

'How did this come here? It couldn't be you, Richard?'

He smiled and shook his head.

Madame Berrichon's felt slippers shuffled on the tiles behind her. Charlotte dropped the flower and turned to find the old woman at her elbow, holding out in both hands an enormous knobbed red sea-spider. The creature's body was larger than a crab; its long spiky arms waved viciously and helplessly trying to clutch the black shawl.

'You see, Madame? I could not resist proving to you that we expected you. Tonight I can only give you a simple meal—but to-morrow, a little feast.'

Charlotte drew back from the waving, clutching tentacles.

'Aha! you are nervous? He is a wicked fellow, no? He would like to crush your hand with those pincers—but we are Christians, are we not? We repay evil with good. I have the water already boiling in my kitchen to give him a nice hot bath.'

'Please take it away,' said Charlotte, shuddering.

'Madame is too sensitive,' said Madame Berrichon, winking at Richard. 'I sympathize. I am sensitive myself—to a degree you would not understand. But one must be a realist too. Providence has arranged that many things should only be good and useful when they are dead.'

She retreated slowly to the kitchen, still talking half-threateningly, half amorously to the sea-spider.

'Do you think it was she who put the passion-flower there?' asked Charlotte, when the kitchen door closed behind Madame Berrichon.

'She's quite capable of it.'

Charlotte pushed the flower away from her.

Louison, Madame's rosy-cheeked, eighteen-year-old niece, in her blue apron and sabots, trotted in with their soup. She glanced at the passion-flower and flushed.

'Madame is offended that I put this flower on the table?'

'Oh, was it you, Louison?' Charlotte drew it back to her. 'No, I love it. I was showing it to my husband.'

She felt herself blushing in her turn.

'But you see, Louison, I can't wear it, I haven't a pin.'

The girl took a pin from her apron and fastened the flower to Charlotte's dress. They both smiled.

'There, Madame. Now you look like a bride.'

Blushing again and glancing at Richard under her fingers, Louison picked up her tray and trotted off again, her sabots pattering like hooves on the tiles.

'There—you see,' said Richard triumphantly. 'It's not all black magic here.'

Charlotte fingered the flower, feeling suddenly old and exhausted. 'She's charming. All the same, it's a little ironical to be treated like a bride.'

As she drooped, Richard seemed to revive. His eyes widened and shone as he filled their glasses with the cheap red wine.

'Drink up,' he said, looking aggressively young and healthy. 'Here's to your getting better.'

Charlotte drank too.

'A thoroughly sensible, practical wish. If Louison heard it, that would be the end of her honeymoon illusions.'

'Charlotte, you know as well as I do that nothing can go right for us till you're cured.'

'Cured of what? There's nothing the matter with me.'

'I wish that were true.'

'Then act as if it were,' she said recklessly. 'You treat me as if I were sick or mad, and I become sick and mad. It's your fault.'

He opened his mouth as if he were going to speak. Instead, he finished his glass and filled it up again.

'Perhaps the only thing that's really wrong with us, Charlotte, is that we don't drink enough.'

'Maybe it's as simple as that. You always used to say you hated drink.'

'I've said a lot of idiotic things.'

Charlotte stared at him. His face, which she was accustomed to seeing gentle, controlled, almost too anxious to please, looked defiant, even a little dissolute.

'Richard, you're different in some way.'

'Well, shouldn't one be different on a holiday? Or perhaps you haven't seen me for so long you've forgotten what I'm like?'

'Nearly six weeks. We've never been apart so long before.'

'No.'

'It's supposed to be a good thing for people who are married, isn't it?'

For no reason—or perhaps because of the wine—she suddenly began to feel confident, almost exultant.

'I'm sure it's an *excellent* thing,' she said emphatically.

'Is it?' He sipped his drink, frowning.

'I've been such a *fool*, Richard.' She took a deep gulp of the harsh wine. 'Working myself up into such a state over nothing. But I can be different, too, you'll see.'

'You couldn't help being ill.'

It was again the voice she dreaded; gentle, reasonable, placating. But she could ignore it.

'I'm not ill, I tell you. I've just been giving way to myself. Illusion, nothing but illusion. But everything's going to be all right now. Don't I look different already?'

She smiled theatrically, feeling the flesh stretched and tingling over her cheekbones.

'You look splendid. All the same, you must take things quietly for a bit.'

She made a face.

'You're worse than the doctors.'

'You always rush things so. I get giddy trying to keep up with you.'

'I'd like to get the car out and drive for miles. Let's get away from the old witch and her mill.'

'Wait until tomorrow. You don't know how tired you are.'

She put down her glass and sighed.

'It's no good. I believe you want to depress me. You want me to be wretched. So that everyone can pity you and say what a wonderful husband you are to that tiresome woman.'

'Don't talk nonsense,' he said, gently.

'We're never in the same mood at the same moment. Why is it? A moment ago, you were gay and I felt flat. Now I'm gay, and you're wilting before my eyes; is it the same with all married people?'

'I don't know: I daresay.' He lit a cigarette. 'Is there anything you'd like to do?'

She smoked for a minute or two, greedily and mechanically, scattering ash on the oil-cloth.

'No, nothing. You make me feel there's no point in doing anything.'

'I'm not much good to you, am I, Charlotte?'

He swept up the ash she had dropped into a neat little heap.

'You're too good, that's just the trouble. Too patient, too considerate. Everything I do irritates you; even the way I smoke a cigarette.'

'Oh, I can put up with that,' he laughed. 'My tidiness is a vice; something you have to put up with.'

'If you only had one grain of viciousness or disorderliness.'

He blew the little heap of ashes on to the floor.

'You know me through and through, don't you? No wonder you find me so dull.'

'I don't know you,' she said thoughtfully. 'I only know what you say and do.'

'Isn't that enough? The trouble is I'm too simple for you.'

'You're not simple; you're not simple at all,' she sighed. 'Or am I the only woman incapable of understanding you?'

'You've such an itch for understanding things, haven't you? Why can't you accept me as I am?'

'I do more than accept you,' she said quietly, 'I love you.'

He looked down, avoiding her eyes, his face heavy and clouded.

'Yes. I suppose you feel that is more.'

Her throat went dry.

'You don't want to love me. Is that it? Does that mean——?'

He would not let her finish. 'Don't let's discuss what words mean. I tell you we won't get anywhere with words.'

'Why not, with the right words?' she insisted obstinately.

He jerked his head like a horse on a too-short rein.

'I tell you I haven't your idolatrous respect for words.'

'Yet you're so careful with them. You never exaggerate as I do. Never say more than you mean.'

He smiled. She noticed again how tight-lipped and secret his mouth was in contrast to the almost aggressive frankness of the eyes. The lips always looked bruised and chafed as if they were made of older, more worn material than the fresh skin of his face.

'I expect it's just part of the tidiness that infuriates you so.'

'At any rate you're honest. I cling to that.'

'Poor Charlotte. It's a negative thing to cling to.'

'It's enough,' she boasted, knowing that she lied.

* * *

Charlotte lay back in the great bed watching Richard moving about the room, unpacking her suitcase and folding her clothes.

'Why don't you let me do anything for myself tonight?' she said.

'You're tired.'

'But it could all wait till tomorrow.'

He smiled and went on inexorably arranging everything in perfect order. When everything was in place, he spread his heavy dressing-gown over her feet.

'You'll be cold in that great icy bed.'

'But aren't you coming to bed yourself?'

'Very soon, I'm going to take a turn outside first.'

Her face stiffened with disappointment as she watched him slipping a jacket over his short-sleeved shirt.

'Just as you like,' she said listlessly.

'Don't be angry, Charlotte. You know what a fool I am about strange places. I can't settle down till I've got my bearings.'

She managed to smile.

'Then of course you must go.'

'You can be an angel when you want to.'

She laughed, pleased at having controlled herself.

'You're thinking, why can't I always be?'

'Yes, why can't you?' he mocked.

'I'll tell you,' she said, sliding her fingers under the cuff of his jacket and stroking his bare wrist. 'It wears one down, being married to a man who always gives such excellent reasons for everything he does.'

He kissed her hand, disengaged himself gently and went out, closing the door stealthily as if she were already asleep.

But she was no longer sleepy. Fighting down an impulse to call him back, she sat up in bed, clenching her hands round her knees and staring in front of her. Because it was not yet quite dark outside, she felt like a child sent to bed for punishment. She got up and padded round the room; the cold slippery tiles were ice to her bare feet. The mantelpiece distracted her for a few minutes with its load of photographs, oleographs of the Sacred Heart and the Little Flower, black-framed memorial cards, and brass vases filled with *immortelles*, all set out with precision like the ornaments of an altar on a starched cloth edged with crochet lace. She examined the photographs with interest, recognizing Madame in a wedding group, Louison in the long white dress and veil of a First Communicant, Monsieur Berrichon, twenty years younger, in an ill-fitting army uniform. But these were quickly exhausted. How was she to kill time till Richard came back? She could not lie in the cold bed staring and thinking. In the last months she had become afraid to think. Her very thoughts were tarnished. They split and unravelled into meaningless ends. Often she believed she was going insane. Something inside her seemed to have died and to be filling her mind, even her body, with corruption. Now it was as if she had accidentally overheard a terrible secret and that everything she did or thought was an attempt to stop her ears and forget. At other times she was like a person who must guess an impossible riddle on pain of death and who has only a few hours left in which to find the answer. Outwardly her life went on as before, except that for some months she had been growing languid, irritable and prone to dreams which oppressed her for days.

She had come away for this holiday determined to shake off the shadow. With all his vigorous sanity, Richard himself had lately begun to look moody and careworn. She guessed it was for his sake as much as hers that he had made her give up work for a time and go away alone to the country. It had been dull misery being away from him, yet now that she saw him again she felt more shut away than ever, as a drowning man feels his isolation more bitterly when he can see people walking on the shore. There were moments when she hated him, but they were nothing to the loathing she felt for herself. Yet even her self-hatred was not pure; it had an element of gloating in it; a strain of vile pleasure, as well as disgust.

Tonight, she told herself, she would not give way to it. Already she could feel herself slipping. When Richard came back there must not be a repetition of the night on the boat. What could she do to pass the time in a sane, normal way until she felt safe enough to put out the light? She remembered that there was a detective story in the pocket of the coat Richard had worn on the journey. She opened the door of the cupboard and saw the coat hanging inside. The green and white cover of the book showed over the top of the pocket. As she pulled it out a letter fell out with it. It was a thick letter in a blue envelope, unopened. She picked it up and stared at it, for she knew the writing. Her immediate thought was 'This is really meant for me'. The conviction was so strong that she was on the point of opening it though it was clearly addressed to 'Richard Crane'. She glared again at the envelope as if by doing so she could change what was written on it. Then she saw it was not addressed to their London house, but to a *poste restante* near Waterloo. The shock was so great that she felt nothing but a mild exhilaration. The exhilaration had nothing to do with her mind, which remained perfectly blank; it was altogether physical, as if she had drunk something warm and stimulating.

There was a knock at the door. Thinking it was Richard, she slipped the letter into the coat pocket and darted back into bed, pulling the sheets up to her chin. She could feel that her eyes were shining and her face set in a mask of bright expectancy as she called out 'Come in'.

It was Madame Berrichon, carrying a steaming glass on a saucer with the air of a priestess carrying a sacred vessel.

'I had a little conversation with Monsieur, your husband,' she said, as she majestically approached the bed. 'It appears you have been indisposed, Madame, and have bad nights. I have taken the liberty of bringing you something to make you sleep.'

A thought flashed up in Charlotte's mind; a thought so fantastic that she did not attempt to brush it away. 'He has sent this woman to poison me.'

Out loud she said politely: 'It is kind of you, Madame, but drugs don't have the effect on me. I sleep better without them.'

'This is no drug, Madame. I myself abominate drugs. It is a tisane made of wholesome natural substances, a distillation of passion-flowers, to be exact.'

She glanced at the passion-flower, wilting in a glass on the chest-of-drawers.

'A charming flower, no? Alive it gives us pleasure; dead it gives us peace.'

'My husband made a mistake, Madame Berrichon. There is nothing the matter with me.'

Madame Berrichon stooped and brought her face close to Charlotte's, fixing her with huge eyes, the colour of black coffee.

'I do not need to be told you are ill,' she said, in her hoarse purr. 'I do not judge as doctors. I judge from deeper sources. And I tell you you are not only ill, but in grave danger.'

'Nonsense,' said Charlotte, wishing she could laugh, yet feeling her throat contract. 'You are trying to frighten me. Why?'

'Certainly not, Madame. I am speaking only for your good. How do I know? Because Providence has given me a nature of extraordinary sensibility. And I pay a price for it. When others suffer, I suffer in every fibre of my being. Tonight you will sleep, but I, I shall not close my eyes.'

'You are too sensitive, Madame,' said Charlotte coldly, remembering the sea-spider.

'Sensitive, Madame, that is too banal a word. Good Catholic as I am, I dare not go to Mass. The chanting disturbs my nerves too much.' She turned up her eyes till only half the iris showed in the blood-shot yellowish whites. 'Believe me, Madame, I have only to see my Piboulette with her ducklings, to think of my dog Nanasse, to weep like a child.'

Madame Berrichon brought her eyes into focus again and thrust the glass into Charlotte's limp hand.

'You must drink, Madame. Before it gets cold.'

Powerless, only wanting to be rid of the woman, Charlotte took a sip of a hot liquid, bitter as alum.

Madame Berrichon watched her greedily, anchoring her hands to her solid hips.

'A trifle bitter? There are many bitter things in life as you, Madame, are still too young to know. But this bitterness brings sweetness. When you have drained every drop—piff, paff—you will be in the arms of Morpheus. So deeply asleep that your charming husband on his return might suppose you dead. So, another little, little sip.'

On a sudden impulsion Charlotte launched the glass through the open window. It fell with a faint splash into the sea.

'Softly, Madame,' said the woman without moving. She gave an imperturbable, pitying leer. 'You see, I am not angry. With hysterics, one must be patient.'

'I am not an hysteric,' Charlotte muttered between her teeth.

'Quite so, quite so, my poor little lady,' the other purred. 'What more natural? So handsome a husband—of course one would not wish him to find one asleep. So very sound asleep too.'

Charlotte felt locked as if in one of her nightmares. She bit her lips so as not to scream for Richard. She looked wildly round the room, staring imploringly at each object he had so carefully arranged, his brushes, a jar of brilliantine, her own powder bowl, as if they could exorcize this presence. But implacably her eyes were drawn back to Madame Berrichon's face.

'He is late, is he not, the charming husband?' said Madame Berrichon, moving away very slowly but still fixing her with the obscene eyes of a witch and a midwife.

She did not speak again until she reached the door.

'Believe me, Madame, I do not hold your ingratitude against you. You are not responsible for your actions. I have done what I could. You prefer to reject it. I hope you will not suffer for it.'

She lingered a moment in the open door, like an actress leaving the stage.

'I too, Madame, have a good husband.'

Then shrugging her black woollen shoulders, she added very softly with a cunning, confederate smile:

'All the same, my little lady, when I look for warmth, for understanding, for fidelity, I turn, not to any human being, but to Nanasse my dog.'

* * *

When Richard came back an hour later, he found Charlotte sitting bolt upright in bed, her hands knotted round her raised knees. She did not turn her head as he came in but glared straight in front of her with round glassy eyes. A bright blue woollen scarf sagging round her shoulders took all the colour from her face. She looked at once like a sick child and an immeasurably old woman.

'Charlotte,' he said, feeling his heart contract with pity and terror. She did not speak or move. He took a step towards her.

'My dear, what is it? Are you ill? Have you had a dream?'

Still not looking at him, she spoke at last in a small, dry, high-pitched voice.

'Curious, aren't you? For such a *very* incurious chap.'

The pert words coming out of the stiff, livid face shocked him as if a corpse had begun to giggle. He sat down on the bed and taking her by both shoulders began to shake her.

'Charlotte, for God's sake.'

Her body rocked to and fro under his hands like a doll's. When he left off shaking her she went on in exactly the same tone.

'You might at least be decently polite to her. After all she is a friend of mine.'

Though he was in the direct line of her stare, he felt she could not see him.

'Charlotte,' he said quietly, 'can you hear me speaking?'

Her expression changed. She turned her head as if she expected to find him at her side.

'Yes,' she answered fretfully, 'of course I can hear you. What are you saying?'

Still quietly he went on.

'Now will you turn your head and look at *me*.'

There was a long pause before her head very slowly came round.

'And now, Charlotte, will you tell me what and who you are talking about?'

Her fine, almost invisible eyebrows went up. The eyes grew rounder still.

'Oh, *that*,' she said, like an impudent child. 'Didn't you know?'

'For Heaven's sake, stop this.' He crouched forward staring back at her like a hypnotist. Her eyes stayed blank and glassy; then a flicker of helpless terror came and went like the dart of a fin under ice.

'My dear, you *must* tell me. What is it I've done? Or that you imagine I've done.'

At last her eyelids relaxed. She tried to speak and could not, until she had passed her tongue two or three times over her dry lips.

'How do I know? I don't read letters.' She closed her eyes and added in a whisper, 'yet'.

He let out the breath he had been holding on a long sigh.

Sitting back on the bed, he took her hands in his. She struggled for a moment to tug them away, then let them lie cold and inert in his grip.

'Listen to me,' he said. 'You are torturing yourself in your imagination. About what?'

'You should know.' Her voice was reasonable but aloof.

'I will tell you what I think. You have found a letter written to me by,' he swallowed, 'by someone we both know.'

'By Rachel Summerhill,' she said loudly.

'Mightn't there be a dozen explanations of that besides the one you're thinking of?'

'Even you can't invent a dozen reasons on the spur of the moment?' she said, glib as an actress. He let go of her hands abruptly.

'All right, if you want a scene, we'll have a scene. God knows I ought to be good at them by now.' He stood up.

She clutched wildly at him.

'No Richard, no Richard': her face crumpled up. 'I'll behave myself. Only don't be angry, don't leave me alone.'

'I'm not going.'

She put her hands on her cheeks as if to hold the skin and muscles in place.

'It's the not knowing I can't stand. I don't care how bad it is. You must tell me.'

'Suppose there's nothing to tell?'

She examined him with an old, searching, impersonal gaze. He gazed back at her unflinchingly.

'Your eyes never tell anything.'

'I'll answer any question you like.'

'Truthfully?'

'Yes. But, Charlotte, for both our sakes, think carefully before you ask.'

Suddenly she sighed, looking at him almost with friendliness.

'I wish I had no memory.'

'So do I.' He risked a faint smile.

She looked not at his face, but at the coat pocket over his heart.

'Rachel Summerhill. Somehow I didn't think she'd be the first. If she is the first.' She was silent for a minute. Then she began to mutter, like a child muttering to itself but meaning to be overheard. 'It doesn't make sense. I used to have to force him to stay in the days she came to see us. He said she was such a bore. What was it he called her? An American college virgin carrying the torch of knowledge on graduation day.'

He put his hand under her chin and lifted her head, gripping her jaw so firmly that she winced.

'Ask your questions. Or keep quiet,' he said roughly.

She wrenched her face away.

'Was it pleasant, making love with her? Who enjoyed it most, you or Rachel?'

In spite of himself, his hands flew up towards her neck. She gave a spurt of excited laughter.

'You don't have to answer now.'

But the words he was trying to keep back burst out, not through his throat, it seemed to him, but through his ribs. Automatically he put both hands on his chest as if to stop a flow of blood as he heard himself say:

'It was the only real thing that ever happened to either of us.'

Even then, Charlotte was so silent that for a whole minute he could believe he had not spoken and was merely watching words, written in smoke, fading on the air. He believed it until he looked at Charlotte's face and saw on it the same fear and exaltation he could feel on his own. For what seemed a long time they confronted each other, each searching the other's face like a mirror, in an intimacy of disaster.

A gust of wind blew out the stiff lace curtains at the window. Charlotte gave a long shuddering sigh like a person waking from an anaesthetic. Her calmed face suddenly decomposed. She flung herself on Richard, tearing at his coat, butting his chest with her head.

He did not resist, but let her hammer him with blind, childish blows. Her whole body shook with dry sobs of anger. Finally, weak and breathless, she stopped battering at him and tried to push him away. He remained immovable, secure in himself and strong enough to pity her.

Charlotte dropped back, exhausted, on the pillows. Then, staring at the ceiling, she began a long monotonous babble like the babble in delirium. At first he tried not to listen. Then in spite of himself he was sucked into these endless coils of words. She raved quietly on and on, not attacking him, but coldly, ferociously accusing herself. For long intervals she would show no consciousness of his being there, then she would implore him to go farther away.

'It's not safe for anyone to come near me. You don't understand. I am poisoned, poisoned right through.'

He did not dare to deny or to interrupt. The terrible words multiplied and multiplied, till he seemed to be watching the multiplication, cell by cell, of a cancer. He clenched his hands till the nails were white. He longed, like a fish gasping for water, not for Rachel herself, but for the thought of Rachel, cool, limited, single. But the thought of her could no more form in his mind than a snowflake could form in a hot room. It seemed to him that for all eternity he would never see anything but the lace curtains, the naked electric light, the photographs, the harsh blue scarf, and Charlotte's distorted face. To shut them out, he hid his face in his hands. But he could not shut out the voice. It went on: a rise and fall of sound in which he no longer distinguished words.

Then abruptly, it stopped. Other different noises followed. They conveyed nothing to him. He did not look up. He could feel Charlotte was no longer there in the bed. But he could not look up. A long time seemed to pass. Then a rasping, metallic noise behind him made him start so violently that he thought he must have fallen asleep. Uncovering his face and jumping up he saw Charlotte at the wide open window, carefully hoisting herself on to the ledge outside. In two steps he was behind her, holding her round the waist. She crouched down on the ledge and turned a blind, set face to him, not struggling, but resigning herself to his hold. They stood for a moment in a grotesque embrace; then, with the force of an uncoiling spring, Charlotte threw herself forward, nearly dragging him with her. Lurching half over the sill he could see far below the dark masses of slippery, jagged rock, half bared by the ebbing tide. He regained his balance and braced his knees, making his thighs and legs heavy. She was struggling now with unbelievable fury like a sail full of wind. His arms turned numb; his feet slithered on the floor but he still did not let go. Suddenly Charlotte seemed to dwindle to half her size. Turning, she slipped through his arms like a fish, and dropped down over the sill. For a second her white face hung suspended in the frame of the open window, then disappeared leaving only the two clinging hands. Richard reeled back, too weak to make any more effort.

The hands were relaxing their grip. They no longer seemed to have any connection with Charlotte. He found himself watching them impersonally, waiting for them to disappear. His head was beginning to clear. He drew a deep breath of the cold, sea air and felt deeply refreshed. Now his head was perfectly clear. It contained a single thought.

'I want her to die,' he said to himself.

In the overwhelming relief of acknowledging it his muscles suddenly asserted themselves and adjusted themselves with extraordinary skill. He made a dive forward from his hips, reached down, caught Charlotte under the armpits and dragged her up through the window. A tremendous wave of exultation in his own strength, in the exquisitely stressed and balanced movement he had just made went over him. The limp dead weight of her body as he pulled her in and held her against him, her feet dangling, seemed no more than the weight of a small animal. He lowered her gently till her feet touched the floor. She leant on him unresisting, her head against his shoulder.

Still with one arm round her he closed the window and pulled the curtains. Then he lifted her up, laid her on the bed, turned out the light and lay down beside her. She was still panting and shivering. He pulled his thick dressing-gown over them both and waited till her breathing was calm before he spoke. He was no longer frightened of anything he might say to her.

'Silly Charlotte. Why did you have to do that?'

She lay against him with an abandonment of trust he had never before felt in her.

'You wanted me dead,' she said peacefully.

He started, but she neither stiffened nor shrank away.

'You said so. Didn't you know?' Her voice was only a sleepy murmur.

He was too drunk with delicious torpor to answer. There was no more need for words; for the first time in their life together they were in complete accord. As they sank into the same profound sleep, they did not press closer, but their breathing gradually timed itself to the same rhythm till, at the vanishing point of consciousness, a single pulse seemed to beat through their two bodies.

JAMES LORD

THE BOY WHO WROTE 'NO'

IN Harkton it would have been quite impossible not to take account of it. Harkton was a small place, which took account of everything. And this seemed so strange.

It was on the side-walk in front of Hovey's Dry Goods Store, just across the square from the city hall. 'NO', written in large white chalk letters on the cement side-walk. There was something disturbing about it, something indefinably and persistently disturbing. Because it had a look of finality and of aggressiveness about it, that word, the way it was written there. It could not possibly have been the work of prankish school-children; they would never have gone to such obvious trouble. The letters were very large, they covered the entire side-walk, stretching vertically from the store front all the way to the curb, a distance of at least six feet; and each letter had been carefully retraced several times, enlarging it. In addition, the writing must have been done at night, after ten o'clock, since surely no one would have attempted such a thing as long as there was a chance that people would be passing through the square.

Someone had sent for the sheriff, and he came across from the city hall in his shirt sleeves. For it was spring, brief as that season always seemed to be in Harkton, though so much the more poignant for its briefness. A fair breeze wafted odours of reviving fertility through the town. The sheriff took a deep breath and yawned. He was a large man, but large without being tall or fat; there was a mass to him, a physical presence that imposed itself. The silver star badge of his office seemed most appropriate pinned on his belt. He walked toward the group of men that stood clustered round in front of Hovey's and he greeted all together with a hearty, 'Good morning, boys'.

Matthew Hovey stepped out to meet him. 'Morning, Ralph,' he said. He was a sharp-eyed, sharp-nosed, thin, sleek man. Matthew Hovey, not more than thirty-five or so. He'd inherited the store from his father, and had made it flourish; some said he was the richest man in town, but that was merely gossip. He took the sheriff by the arm and, in a tone half mocking and half serious, said, 'Now just have a look at this. Make a little room for the sheriff, boys.'

For some moments the sheriff stared pensively down at the enormous 'NO' there on the side-walk. He grunted. 'Well, well,' he said, apparently perplexed. He pinched his lower lip between thumb and forefinger and frowned. 'Well, now I've seen it. Now what? I know just as much about it as you do.'

'Something peculiar about it, it seems to me,' muttered Hovey, almost petulantly. 'It's too big. And why right in front of my store?'

'Oh, it's probably just a gag,' said the sheriff. 'You'll probably find out all about it before the day is over.'

'Yes, it's probably just some sort of a gag,' echoed a number of the others in the group.

'Maybe so,' agreed Matthew Hovey grudgingly.

And there was nothing to be done but erase the letters. Hovey called his errand boy. The curious group withdrew a little distance along the side-walk and the huge 'NO' was promptly obliterated by the errand boy with a mop and pail of water. The damp cement, where the letters had been, dried quickly in the warm spring sun. Now that the word had disappeared, what more was there to be said?

For a few minutes the group of men remained, chatting; then one by one they went off about their business. That day there was some talk and speculation in the town about the appearance of that 'NO' there on the side-walk in front of Hovey's. But it didn't last long. During the afternoon something of greater interest took place. It was said, and the news moved fast, that a little girl had been bitten by a dog, that the dog was rabid, that the dog had gone mad and would have to be tracked down and shot, that the little girl might have to be rushed forty miles to the hospital in Granville, and so on, and so on. In reality the little girl had only been pawed by the dog, an old but still playful collie; it was her obstinate shrieking as her mother carried her home and her screaming insistence that she must have been bitten which initiated the excited and varying reports. By nightfall no one any longer thought of the 'NO' which that morning had seemed so strange.

But the next day people were obliged to think of it again, because there was another. The second 'NO' by itself probably would never have aroused any curiosity at all, it would have been erased and forgotten; but it was immediately linked in the general mind with the first. It was less spectacular, less conspicuous, far less large, apparently scrawled hastily. However, what it may have lacked in presentation it certainly compensated for with an excess of temerity. The first 'NO', after all, though it had indeed seemed to reflect upon Hovey's, had been written on the side-walk, which was public property. But the second was there, for all to behold in consternation, written in white soap across the always-spotless pane of glass set into the wide redoubtable front door of the Harkton Savings Bank. Now the affair could no longer be dismissed as 'probably just a gag'. Matthew Hovey proclaimed in tones of indisputable certitude that there was 'something mighty peculiar about this'. And of course someone was sent to bring the sheriff.

Elias Turner, president of the Bank, refused to be at all concerned with the matter. He remained in his office, munching at a thick cigar; but he sent his son Seth, a lanky taciturn young man who was expected eventually to become president in his turn. Eyed by inquisitive speculators, Seth Turner stood at the top of the Bank's imposing front steps. The Bank was the only building in Harkton, even including the Baptist Church, that had such steps: eight of them, of massive grey granite, with black iron hand-rails at either side. 'A bank's got to have an important look about it,' old Josiah Turner, Seth's grandfather, had said; and he'd ordered the steps built.

When the sheriff arrived, the group of curious men and women crowded forward, anxious to miss no detail. 'There's something mighty peculiar about this, if you ask me,' said Matthew Hovey, who had followed the sheriff up the steps. A number of the others murmured their assent.

'What do you make of it, sheriff?' Seth Turner asked placidly.

This time the sheriff was obviously more than perplexed; he was irritated. 'Well, there's nothing to be gained by standing around staring at it,' he said. 'The only thing to do for the time being is to get it cleaned off there. And, Seth, you can tell your father that I'll see what can be done about this.'

The offending letters were forthwith wiped away, and after a little while the group of curious onlookers dispersed. But they talked, discussed, wondered; the news made a rapid circuit of the town. Nor was there this time any other event to supplant it in the public attention. All eagerly awaited the following morning to see whether there would be another 'NO'. Harkton looked at itself and wondered.

In his office the sheriff paced up and down. His deputy sat with his chair tilted against the wall, and in one hand lazily swung a tattered copy of *True Detective*. It was obvious, the sheriff muttered, that there was only one thing to do: they would both have to sit up that night hoping to surprise the stealthy writer at work. He was thoroughly annoyed. After all, he said, the whole thing was quite silly. Why not simply ignore it? But there was an election now not too far in the future. And besides, who would change the ways of Harkton?

That night there was a brilliant three-quarter moon which threw down its steady beam into all corners of the square. The evening was mild, such a one as rarely came upon the town, filled with a vague and enveloping fragrance. Harkton had gone to bed and now was still. The sheriff's office window looked out upon the square. He and the deputy sat there together, with a pot of strong coffee on a little electric stove between them. They didn't talk. The sheriff irritably drummed the thick square ends of his fingers against the chair arm. It was nearly eleven.

When midnight had finished striking from the belfry of the Baptist Church, the deputy said, 'Maybe he won't be coming'.

'Maybe he won't,' said the sheriff.

'And even if he does write "NO" somewhere, maybe it won't be in the square.'

'Maybe.'

'It's a nuisance, having to sit here waiting like this.'

'Yes.'

They took some coffee, and some time passed while they drank.

Then suddenly in the moonlight they saw him. How confidently he walked out there toward the middle of the square, so serene, even as the surest of wild animals in the depths of its safe jungle is serene. He made not a single furtive motion, and his shadow preceded him with assurance as he went, like a guardian. In the centre of the square he stopped and stood still, looking round.

The deputy got up abruptly. 'Let's go get him,' he whispered.

'No, no, wait, sit down, be quiet,' replied the sheriff impatiently. 'We've got to have some proof that this is really the one. He hasn't done anything yet. There's no law that says a person can't walk around after midnight. We'll have to wait and see what he does.'

They did not have to wait a long time. After one or two minutes of placidly surveying the square, the figure out there stooped and began to make wide swift motions with one arm above the pavement. He was obviously writing now. When the sheriff and the deputy burst out from the city hall and started running toward him, he was up at once with a bound and running away from them. He ran much faster than they, and he might easily have escaped; but he was unlucky. As he reached the corner he dropped something. He turned back to pick it up, and they caught him. Not too gently they dragged him back between them to the centre of the square, to see what he had been doing. And there it was—how quickly he'd written it—a great red 'NO' painted across the pavement; it was red, the colour of blood, and shone with macabre insinuation under the moonlight. A small paint can stood next to it. In one hand the captive held his paint brush, which he had dropped in his haste. He was but a boy.

'It's George Sickles,' said the deputy.

The sheriff grunted. 'So you're the one who's been writing "NO" like this all over the place,' he exclaimed angrily. He shook the boy by the arm, hard. 'Now what's the idea? Do you think this is a joke?'

George Sickles was a tall boy, with quite thin narrow shoulders and wide hips and excessively long arms, with straight red hair, and with a large dark birthmark in the centre of his very very white right cheek. He stood unresisting between the two men, but he didn't reply to the sheriff's questions. He remained impassive.

'And what is your father going to say about this?' demanded the sheriff.

George didn't answer. He didn't appear to be frightened and he didn't act as though he were aware he'd done anything wrong, anything for which he might be punished.

'What are we going to do with you?' said the sheriff, shaking the boy again roughly. 'Eh? What are we going to do with you, do you think?'

'I don't know,' George said. His voice was quite high-pitched for a boy of seventeen or eighteen, but it was steady. He didn't look at either of the men; he just stood there, with the paint brush held tight in one hand.

'All right now,' said the sheriff, 'we'll escort you straight home. And if I know Edwin Sickles, and I certainly do, he'll have something to say about this. Pick up your paint can and come on.'

Submissively George picked up the can of paint. He put the brush into it and held it in front of him away from his clothes. Then the three of them started off, the boy between the two men, leaving the stark crimson 'NO' alone in the centre of the square in the moonlight.

Edwin Sickles was Harkton's dentist, a most respected personage in the community, member of the school board and stern upholder of the Baptist Church, of which his wife Martha was a deaconess. He was not young; indeed he was old enough to have been George's grandfather, and he acted his age. His hair was white, always fastidiously in order, and his face was wrinkled, but not laxly, not in the usual irregular manner of age: every crease, every furrow was set, precise, hard, as though fixed by a will stronger than the flesh. The word most often and most aptly used to describe him was: *spare*. Dr. Sickles was not known to be a mirthful man. He wore a pair of steel-rimmed spectacles. His wife Martha was very much like him, though she spoke less. She wore dresses which even in Harkton were considered, though not disrespectfully, to be old-fashioned. She was bony and flat-chested, her lips were almost as waxen as her cheeks, and she had a slight but distinct moustache. Edwin and Martha Sickles had had two children. The eldest, Edwina, their daughter, was married and had two children herself and had already begun to resemble her mother. George had been the product of his parents' ending middle age, an outcome of the last possible flicker of whatever passion they had known, more or less of an accident, to which the mother and father had reconciled themselves with becoming fortitude. George's childhood and youth had not been merry. In high school he was neither a very good nor a very bad student; he was not particularly companionable.

The Sickleses' doorbell was an old-fashioned manual one, mounted on the inside of the front door, and it rang with an echoing clang clang clang in the silent night as the sheriff tugged on the enamel-knobbed handle. There was a moment's tense expectant wait, then a light went on in the front room upstairs. Dr. Sickles's head appeared in the window; his hair was as neatly combed as ever and he had on his spectacles. 'What is it?' he asked calmly, looking down.

'It's the sheriff, Dr. Sickles. I think you'd better come down. We've got your boy here.'

'I'll be right down,' said the doctor.

Lights flashed on simultaneously in one of the neighbouring houses and in the house directly across the street. Heads appeared at windows.

In his habitual unhurried and meticulous manner, Dr. Sickles unbolted and unlocked the front door. He was dressed in a brown flannel bathrobe and had on carpet slippers. 'Please come in, sheriff,' he said. The two men and the boy entered and the doctor calmly closed the door behind them. 'Now what's the trouble, sheriff?' he asked.

'Well, doctor, it seems your boy's the one who's been writing "NO" around the town, first on the side-walk in front of Hovey's, then on the front door of the Bank, and tonight we caught him after he'd painted "NO" in red paint smack in the middle of the square.' All three men looked at the boy, who still held his paint can in front of him, mutely; he didn't look at them. 'And seeing as how it was your boy, doctor,' the sheriff continued, 'I thought we might as well bring him right along home and let you handle this yourself. After all, there's no question of putting him in jail. He sure didn't mean anything wrong. Everyone knows how kids are sometimes.'

'I appreciate your understanding, sheriff,' said the doctor. 'May I speak to you for a moment outside? George, you will wait here.'

The three men went outside and stood for some moments talking on the doorstep. Then the sheriff and the deputy went away. Dr. Sickles came back inside. His wife, who had been listening unseen at the head of the stairs, now appeared in her long white nightdress, with her hair done up in curlers like little horns all over her head. She stared down at the two below, but did not speak.

The father looked at his son. 'If that paint can came from my cellar,' he said, 'please take it back to its place at once.'

'Yes, father,' replied the boy docilely and he went to do as he had been told.

When he came back, his father said, 'Now you will please explain to me just what this whole business is about.'

'I don't know.'

At the head of the stairs there was a distinct gasp of vexation from Mrs. Sickles.

'Now look here, George,' said the doctor tersely, 'it's getting along to be one o'clock, and I want to hear an explanation of all this directly.'

'I can't explain.'

'You did write the word "NO" as the sheriff said, did you not?'

'Yes.'

'Why?'

'That's what I don't know,' said the boy. He did not appear frightened or troubled. He was placid, and he had an air of being but vaguely aware of the present. 'I really don't know what first made me write "NO". It was late at night, it must have been as late as this, or later maybe. I'd been for a walk, and I . . .'

'You'd been for a *walk*!' repeated his mother from above, incredulous.

'Yes. I went out the back door. I'd been for a walk out beyond the town in the grove where there's a stream running through, where I often go to walk, and I was coming back. It was such a very beautiful night, it was all quiet, and there was a moon.'

'We aren't interested in the moon,' exclaimed the doctor impatiently.

'And I happened to have a piece of chalk in my pocket.'

'How did that happen?' asked Mrs. Sickles.

'I must have gotten it at school.'

'In other words, you'd stolen some chalk from the school,' she said.

'I had the chalk,' George continued. 'And I remember I'd taken it out of my pocket. I had it in my hand as I came into the square, as I was walking along, and it just seemed that it would be a good idea to write something. It was the way I felt then, that's all. And I felt from the first that all I wanted to write was the word "NO", just that and nothing else. That was enough. And so I did write it, there on the side-walk in front of Hovey's.'

'What a shame,' Mrs. Sickles murmured indignantly.

'And how about the second time, on the door of the Bank?' asked the doctor.

'That was about the same, but still more on purpose. I'd taken the piece of soap with me on purpose.'

'And tonight, with the paint it was altogether on purpose.'

'Yes.'

'And why?'

'I don't really know. It was just the way I felt again, about everything. Maybe I didn't like the way they'd so easily erased what I wrote the other times.'

'And you thought the paint wouldn't be so easy to erase.'

'Yes.'

'Well, we'll see.' The doctor pursed his lips and hooked his thumbs on the bathrobe sash. 'In short, as I see it,' he said, 'you were simply defacing public and private property for your own amusement. You were deliberately committing a criminal offence. Now tell me: do you expect to be punished?'

'Yes.'

'What do you expect?'

'The strap.'

'Well, you're mistaken. I've decided to let you punish yourself, tomorrow morning. Fortunately it's a Saturday and you're free from school. And I hope that after this we'll have no more trouble from you. What do you think the people in town are going to say? Perhaps you didn't stop to consider the embarrassment this will cause your mother and me.' He paused, as if to let the weighty purport of his remarks achieve their full effect; but George's expression did not change. 'Well, there's nothing more to be done tonight. In the morning you'll know how I've decided to let you punish yourself. Now you can go up to bed.'

'Good night, father,' the boy said, and he started up the stairs.

As he passed his mother at the top and bade her good night also, she said, 'And before you go to sleep you'd as well pray God to forgive you for being such a troublesome boy'.

'Yes, mother.' He went into his room and softly closed the door.

As the parents returned to their bed, Mrs. Sickles complained, 'He might at least have said he was sorry.'

'There wouldn't be any purpose in him saying something he didn't mean,' replied the doctor. 'I'd know, and he knows I'd know.'

'What is the punishment you've decided on?' whispered the woman as she pulled up the covers around them. 'Tell me.'

The doctor pressed a switch, and the room fled into darkness. 'You'll know tomorrow morning,' he said.

The next morning was summer. The sun came up pale in a haze, dragging after it a static mass of heat. It was Saturday morning, as always the busiest of the week. Already before nine o'clock the square was filled with a coming and a going of people and vehicles. However, in the centre of it there was quite a crowd that stayed still, collected around the crimson 'NO' painted on the pavement. But it was not an astonished crowd, such as on the two previous occasions had collected around the place where 'NO' was written; rather it was a crowd that seemed to be waiting. When nine o'clock tolled in brazen rhythm from the belfry of the Baptist Church, the people turned expectantly.

And there came George Sickles, alone. His father and mother stayed behind him on the side-walk to watch. He was dressed in overalls and he carried with him a quart ginger ale bottle and a handful of rags. As he approached, the crowd drew apart to let him pass, and there were smirks and whispered remarks: 'That's him . . . he's the one who's been writing "NO" all over . . . it's George Sickles . . . he isn't a little loony, is he? . . . fancy anybody thinking of doing things like that . . . and here he is now, right on time, like the sheriff said he'd be . . . poor Doc Sickles must sure have a burden with that boy . . . and what do you think the idea was, writing "NO" all over like that? . . . well, he's a peculiar one all right, and no question about it . . .'

George reached the place where the 'NO' was painted and he kneeled down in front of it. Uncorking his bottle, he poured some turpentine from it on to one of the rags and began rubbing at the base of the first vertical of the letter 'N'. Fortunately the paint was not yet quite dry, and it yielded to George's efforts with rag and turpentine, but slowly. The crowd pressed around to watch, snickering. The boy did not appear at all disconcerted by the audience; he worked stolidly and did not look at anyone.

In the crowd there were numbers of boys and girls from the high school, George's classmates. One of the boys called out, 'Tell us, George, what's this "NO" all about?' George didn't answer. 'What's the matter, George? Won't you talk? Won't Georgie tell us why he writes "NO" on the side-walk?' The girls began to titter encouragingly. 'Georgie, Georgie, don't you know why you write "NO"? Oh, oh, Georgie, don't you know that "NO" is no thing to go around writing?' The crowd now started to laugh outright, approving the youth.

George's face, as the laughs increased, slowly began to change in colour from its natural white to a darker and darker red. He tried to work more rapidly, but in the hot sun the paint became more and more difficult to remove as he progressed. He was panting and the perspiration ran in little trickles around the back of his neck. In his haste he scraped the skin off the knuckles of his right hand against the pavement; some drops of his blood fell, mixing with the paint he worked to obliterate and indistinguishable from it.

Prompted by the laughs of the crowd, the taunting youth continued: 'Oh, Geo, don't be so slow to clean up that "NO". Next time you'll know better. Why don't you say something, Geo? Maybe the only thing that Geo knows is "NO". Speak to me, Georgie, come on. Or maybe you'd rather sing. I know just the song, too. I know your song, Geo.' And he began to sing the refrain of a song which everyone in the crowd surely knew, a song perennially sung. '*No, no, a thousand times no, I'd rather die than say yes! No, no, a thousand times no, I'd rather die than say yes!*' The crowd knew the song indeed and hilariously took it up, singing with amusement and enthusiasm at the humour of the situation. The singing grew louder and louder. All around the square, people leaned out of windows to look on and laugh. Apparently everyone knew very well what was happening. The song continued, '*No, no, a thousand times no, I'd rather die than say yes!*' The uproar of singing and laughter actually echoed between the sober fronts of the buildings. And the breathless heat of the forenoon increased.

The object of all this derision continued steadily at his task, which was now almost done. But he was obviously not unmoved by the hilarity he caused. His face and neck had flushed scarlet, and his ears seemed literally to pulsate with this evidence of shame. On his cheeks there were tears, or perhaps those drops were merely of sweat. Yet he made no voluntary sign of response. And at last the last trace of red paint had been removed from the pavement; there remained only a few fast-drying spots of turpentine and the little pile of crimson-stained rags. The quart ginger ale bottle was empty. George stood up slowly, rubbing his knees with both hands; he took the bottle and the soiled rags and walked away.

The crowd parted to let him go, but it moved along for a little distance after him, as far as the edge of the square, still laughing and singing its ridicule, apparently unwilling to relinquish such a sure source of amusement. At the edge of the square the boy turned for a moment and stood confronting those who mocked him. He didn't say a word or even make a perceptible gesture; he simply stood and looked at the crowd, as though his mere regard were reproach enough. But the crowd, far from being discountenanced, was all the more amused and its mirth swelled to a pitch, the song became a roar: '*NO, NO, A THOUSAND TIMES NO, I'D RATHER DIE THAN SAY YES!*', accompanied by shrieks of delighted laughter.

George turned away. He walked rapidly, and the crowd did not follow him any longer. He reached a corner and turned, and then he was by himself finally. He began to run, as fast as he could, breathing furiously, his head lowered, and he didn't pause until he reached home, where he rushed at once to the cellar and locked himself in.

The general hilarity in the square diminished little by little and, appeased, the crowd slowly dispersed. One after the other the citizens of Harkton went off about their ordinary business. The windows around the square emptied of spectators. And soon the town had resumed its usual air. During the rest of the day people continued to talk of what had happened, but no one imagined that the incident might not be at an end.

And least of all Dr. Sickles. He was very contented with the success of his punishment; indeed he had not dared to expect that it would be so effective. To be sure, George's reaction had been less than he might have hoped, but he knew that the boy was not ordinarily demonstrative. Since it was Saturday, Dr. Sickles spent only half the day in his office; he spent the rest at home, working in the vegetable garden which he set out every year at the back of his house. George helped him, of course. The two did not speak of what had happened that morning. They spoke at all only when it was necessary in the course of their work. One of Dr. Sickles's fast beliefs was that to talk when one had nothing useful to say was a waste; and what was wasteful he could not tolerate.

That evening, before the family went to bed, the doctor locked both front and back doors and took the keys upstairs with him. The father and mother and the son said good night to each other as they always did, dutifully, and retired. The night was warm, clinging; no breeze stirred the air as Harkton relapsed into the silence of its nocturnal torpor.

Always in the morning, on Sunday as well as during the week, Mrs. Sickles rose precisely at a quarter of seven, 'without need of any contraption to warn that it's time', she was fond of proclaiming. She would dress rapidly, then wake her husband, and, as she went downstairs to prepare breakfast, would rap peremptorily on her son's door. The day began with that routine, which was calculated according to her certainties and which never varied.

But on this Sunday morning there was a decided variation. As she came to the bottom of the stairs she stopped, she stared, her two hands involuntarily rose in the air, and she gasped. There, in the centre of the round braided rug that covered the hall floor, the rug which was an heirloom, having been made by her 'poor dear mother with her own hands', there was the word 'NO', written in large letters with white chalk. For the long slow-passing time of an entire minute she stood transfixed, staring, incredulous, as though some optic fault must be deceiving her. But there was no error. She pressed her lips together tight and inhaled slowly through her nose while her nostrils quivered. Without haste she turned and walked determinedly back upstairs, went to her door and threw it open. Dr. Sickles was sitting on the edge of the bed, naked.

Now, in all of the forty-three years that they had been married, the doctor and his wife had never seen each other nude, more or less by tacit agreement. Of the naked body of the other each knew only as much as the sense of touch could convey, and neither apparently had ever desired to know more. But on this morning, startled from her routine by what she had just seen on her rug and returning to the bedroom unexpectedly, Mrs. Sickles for the first time saw a man's complete nakedness. Startled again, precipitated into complete discomposure, she stammered something unintelligible, then turned her face away. The doctor hastily clutched at the bedclothes and pulled them up to cover his nudity. 'What is it?' he asked brusquely. 'What do you want? Why do you come bursting in this way?' He grimaced with displeasure.

'I'm sorry, Edwin,' said the woman. 'But I wanted to tell you that that boy has written "NO" in chalk on the rug at the foot of the stairs.'

For a moment the doctor didn't answer; his grimace became a frown. Then he said, 'If you'll wait outside one minute, I'll put something on. I'll be right there.'

His wife closed the door and waited in the narrow hall. When the doctor came out, he was dressed in his bathrobe and slippers.

Without speaking, he went downstairs and stood looking at the large white 'NO' written there against the darker colours of the rug. He stooped and touched the 'N' with one finger; a tiny cloud of chalk dust arose. 'I'll have the boy clean this off immediately,' he said.

'Oh, I'd rather do it myself,' protested Mrs. Sickles at once. 'He'd be sure to make a mess of it. And besides, the last time you let him off with just cleaning up what he'd done, the lesson didn't have much effect, to judge by this. Maybe this time you'd better think of something a bit more practical, if you know what I mean.' And she went off toward the kitchen.

The doctor frowned more than ever, but he didn't answer. He turned, walked back up the stairs, and entered his son's bedroom without knocking.

George sat fully clothed on the bed in his small unornamented room. His hair was mussed and his face had a pinched and rather feverish look, which might have been the result either of anxiety or sleeplessness. He didn't stand up when his father came in, which was unusual.

'Go fetch the strap,' ordered Dr. Sickles.

The boy stood up then and went to do as he was told. 'The strap' was kept in a small tool-shed behind the house; it was a long heavy black leather thong, which had obviously at one time been part of a horse's harness, studded all along at intervals of a few inches with tiny decorative brass knobs. It was the instrument of physical punishment habitually used upon George, though in the past he had seldom given provocation for its use. And always hitherto the scene of such punishment had been the shed, where he was obliged to bend over an old sawhorse while his father vigorously applied the strap several times to the seat of his trousers. This time, apparently, there was to be a difference.

When he re-entered the room, his father calmly took the strap from him and said, 'Close the window. I don't want the neighbours to hear this,' which was surprising, because it had always before been conspicuous that, when he was beaten, George never made any outcry.

The window was pulled down. 'Now undress,' said Dr. Sickles. For a moment there was no response. The boy stared in silence at the man, as though he had not heard. 'Undress!' Dr. Sickles repeated tersely. George obeyed, and when he stood stripped before his father, the latter said, as he swung the heavy length of the strap tentatively in one hand, 'Now go and stand against the wall, and remember that this is for your own good.'

In the kitchen below, as she went from the cupboard to the table, Mrs. Sickles heard the first blow of leather against flesh, and her whole body replied to the sound with a shiver that transfixed her where she stood, with her fingertips poised tensely against the table. At each successive stroke something shuddered, pulsing, all through her, her whole face twitched, and her breathing became more and more irregular. Suddenly from upstairs came the first trembling shriek of pain, followed by others. With a hoarse gasp Mrs. Sickles relaxed, everything about her abruptly went limp. She sat down and leaned against the table, panting; her mouth hung open loosely and her eye focused upon nothing.

Then the shrieks ceased. It was quiet throughout the house with a strange and consuming quietness.

By the time Dr. Sickles was dressed and shaved and downstairs, his wife was busy at the stove, cooking buckwheat cakes. 'Ah, this smells good,' said the doctor heartily, taking his familiar place at the dining-room table. Before eating he sat for a minute and methodically snapped the joints of the fingers of both hands, as was his habit.

A little while later George came down. In one hand he purposefully carried the strap, which he took back to its customary place in the shed. Then he returned to have his breakfast. He didn't say anything; no one of the three spoke. The boy sat gingerly straight on the very edge of his chair and ate little, and what he ate he ate fast. He was finished well ahead of the other two, who had started before him. 'Excuse me, please,' he said, getting up from the table.

'You'd better go and get yourself ready for church,' said Mrs. Sickles.

'If you don't mind,' George said slowly, 'I'd like to be excused from church today. I don't feel much like it.'

'Nonsense!' exclaimed his mother indignantly. 'Excused indeed! You'll be nothing of the kind. Now go upstairs this minute and get on your black suit. You haven't been to church often enough, that's one thing wrong with you.'

The boy nodded and went out.

Before the family left to go to church, Mrs. Sickles had time to clean the chalk off the rug, which afterwards appeared just as ever.

Nevertheless she proclaimed, 'That rug will never be the same again, because I'll never be able to look at it without thinking of that word there in the middle of it'. So saying, she gave an upward glance of earthly resignation and carefully drew on her black net gloves. And then the father and the mother and the son, all three dressed in black, decorously departed to go to church.

The Baptist Church of Harkton was painted a medium brown on the outside and the interior was all bright amber. The pews and the walls and the Gothic-raftered ceiling were of blond maple, highly varnished and shiny. The six square windows on either side were set with translucent amber glass, which gave the interior an effect of perpetual garish sunlight. The chancel was merely a raised platform with a pulpit and a reading desk and three Gothic chairs upholstered in brilliant purple. To one side was a bench for the choir and a foot-pedal harmonium. Down the centre aisle stretched a vivid scarlet carpet.

The habitual and designated pew of the Sickles family was well toward the front, only three rows behind the pew of Elias Turner. There on this particular Sunday sat Dr. and Mrs. Sickles, their son George, their daughter Edwina, her husband Calvin Sutter, and the two Sutter children, Martha and Calvin, Jr. There they sat in silence waiting for the service to begin. George squirmed uneasily on the straight-backed wooden bench, grimacing his discomfort. His mother nudged him with her sharp bony elbow and frowned reproof. He sighed.

At last the service started, and it was very long. The topic of the sermon was, as it not infrequently happened to be, 'The blessed state of the harmonious community living in the sight of Our Lord'. The Reverend Mr. Willowby spoke crisply, fixing his congregation with an austere regard; his voice rose and sank in calculated emphasis, like a ship in the ocean swell. His thin long forefinger was often raised in admonishment. 'I will mince no words', he declared, 'in my determination to strive ever onward with this flock toward Righteousness. But at least we can be thankful, we can lift up our hearts in thanks that we are on the right road. Though our steps may sometimes err, we know the only way. And it is not the easy way, it is not, oh no, it can never be the way of vain pleasure. We must humbly bow our heads before the suffering which is meted out to us. Those who righteously endure will be thrice blessed. Ah, indeed the peace of the soul is not something easily come by.' He clasped his hands in front of him, looked for a moment toward the rafters and then at the congregation once more, where all attention duly awaited his next utterance.

Or almost all attention. George Sickles seemed not to be able to sit still. He twisted and shifted his position on the bench constantly, and his grimaces and half-repressed sighs suggested not only pain but impatience. Mrs. Sickles nudged him, as she had done already at least a dozen times, and gave him another furious look. Some of the people sitting in nearby pews observed that all was not harmoniousness in the Sickles family, and they glanced briefly at each other with brows knowingly arched.

Finally the sermon reached its end. 'And so may the Lord, in His infinite wisdom and mercy, look down upon our transgressions and find it in His heart to forgive them, as we forgive our transgressors. And in turn may we, His servants, become ever more worthy to glorify His name as we strive onward with certainty toward Righteousness. Amen.' Then, after a time of contemplative silence, there was a prayer, a hymn, there was an announcement of church-sponsored events for the coming week, there was an anthem 'A Beautiful City is Zion' sung by the choir, during which the collection was received, there was a prayer of benediction, and at last there was the recessional hymn, during which the choir got up and slowly filed out.

After the service it was customary for the pastor to greet the members of his congregation in the vestibule as they departed. As the Sickles family passed he remarked, without smiling, 'Seems George was a little restless this morning'.

'He didn't sleep very well,' said Mrs. Sickles hastily. Then, after a moment's hesitation, she added, lowering her voice, 'Perhaps, pastor, you might have a talk with the boy some afternoon if he comes around to the manse.'

'Why, of course,' replied the pastor. 'You know how glad I always am to be of service when I can.'

Then the Sickles family moved along outside and started walking home. It was tradition in the family that Edwina and her husband and children take Sunday dinner with her parents. And there they went, seeming certainly a proper family: the grandfather and grandmother, the son and the daughter, the son-in-law, and the two grandchildren. Martha Sickles Sutter, the granddaughter, was a strong fair-haired young girl, only a year and some months younger than her Uncle George, a fact which she seemed to find ceaselessly amusing. Calvin Cawley Sutter, Jr., the grandson, was eleven, but he had already begun to resemble his father in more than name; he had a round stolid young face, straight sandy hair, and he was plump.

They all walked for a while without speaking in the full heat of the Sunday noon. Then Martha Sutter said, 'Uncle George sure was fidgety in church. Maybe he was just itching to write "NO" again somewhere the way he did in the square. Were you, George?' She giggled maliciously.

'Hush up that talk right now,' said her mother.

'Sure is a fine day today,' remarked Calvin Sutter. 'Summer's getting off to an early start this year. Ought to have good crops if it's not too dry.' Calvin was Harkton's insurance agent.

'Yes, it's a fine day,' affirmed Dr. Sickles, glancing with professional casualness at the cloudless sky. 'We'll have it fine for several days now.'

Sunday dinner at the Sickleses, being a family tradition, was always lengthy. On this particular Sunday, before the dinner was quite ready, George went into the kitchen, which was contrary to all practice.

'Dinner's not ready yet,' announced his mother tartly.

'I know,' said George. He looked uncomfortably at his sister and his niece, who smirked. 'But I was wondering if I could have a little something to eat here in the kitchen instead of sitting at the table.'

Abruptly an appalled and appalling silence emptied the kitchen of its ordinary sounds. The two women and the girl stared at George in paralysed astonishment, almost in alarm. Mrs. Sickles was the first to regain her aplomb. 'And why, may I ask,' she said coldly, 'shouldn't you eat in the dining-room along with everybody else?'

'You know,' George murmured. 'It's just that I don't feel very much like it.'

'The same way you didn't feel like sitting still this morning in church and embarrassed me there in front of everybody,' retorted his mother. 'Ridiculous. You'll not be pampered in this house, and you'd better realize it. Either you eat in the dining-room like everybody else or you don't eat, and we'll have no more talk.'

Edwina Sutter vigorously nodded approval of her mother. Young Martha snickered audibly.

George did not reply at once. He stood still, looking at his mother, while his mouth grew thin and his face gradually suffused with dark red. His hands clenched into fists. He inhaled loudly. At last he blurted, 'All right then. All right, I won't eat at all. I'd rather go hungry. I'd much rather go hungry.' He strode to the kitchen door, wrenched it open violently, and went out, slamming it behind him so hard that it didn't catch properly and jumped open again. He disappeared without a backward look around the corner of the house.

Mrs. Sickles went at once to tell her husband what had happened. 'We're in for a lot of trouble with that boy,' she concluded bleakly.

'Time will tell,' said the doctor. 'At any rate, he'll be sure to come back when he gets hungry. And then we'll see. In the meantime, there's nothing to do but carry on just as usual. Is the dinner ready?'

'It won't be long.'

And, tradition prevailing, the Sickleses' Sunday dinner took place as usual. George's plate was removed, his chair put to one side, and no one spoke of him. The doctor and his son-in-law talked at length of Harkton's future commercial possibilities, the Sutter children chattered pointlessly, surveyed by their mother, and Mrs. Sickles came and went with heaped platters. After dinner the family went and sat in the small parlour until Calvin Sutter, towards three o'clock, said, 'I guess we'd better be getting along'. For, if it was tradition that the Sutters have Sunday dinner with the Sickleses, it was equally tradition that they have Sunday supper with Calvin's father, old Augustus Sutter. And hence they departed.

'I hope everything will be all right with George,' Edwina whispered to her mother at the door.

Mrs. Sickles raised both hands, as in a gesture of disavowal. 'I don't know,' she said. 'It's the boy's responsibility, not mine. It's up to him.'

Left alone, the doctor and his wife had their separate occupations. She busied herself upstairs with her needlework, while he remained alone in the parlour, re-reading his already well-read copy of Benjamin Franklin's *Autobiography*. The afternoon thus gradually waned, in silence. Outside it was sultry. A layer of colourless cloud came up from the south and slowly filled the sky, covering the sun.

When it was time for supper, George had not yet come back. 'I suppose he *will* come, sooner or later,' said Mrs. Sickles.

'Of course,' said the doctor, tucking an end of his napkin into the space between two buttons of his vest. 'Where else do you think he could go?'

Daylight dwindled, little by little. Dark began spreading over upon the heat of the town. In the hush an uneasy wind suddenly started. And afar in the coming night now and then throbbed a sound of thunder.

At nine-thirty George still had not come. 'It's time for bed now,' said Dr. Sickles. He went and locked the front and back doors and one by one turned off the electric lights. 'The boy knows what time we go to bed. Maybe if he has to spend all the night out alone, it will do something to sober him a little.'

'He has his best suit on,' said Mrs. Sickles as they went up the stairs together.

'That can't be helped,' replied the doctor imperturbably, yawning.

During the night the heat did not diminish. It pressed close and heavy about the town, and the distant thunder continued. But it didn't rain. All stayed still, clutched in the exhausting warmth. The blackness was unmitigated.

In the morning it was only a few minutes past six when the doctor and his wife were awakened by a persistent clanging clang clang clang of their front door bell. The doctor went to the window and looked down. Below stood the sheriff. 'I'll be right down,' said Dr. Sickles grimly. In the room, as he put on his slippers and bathrobe, he said to his wife, 'It's the sheriff again. It must be something about George.'

'I told you we were going to have trouble with that boy,' she exclaimed.

The sheriff did not come inside the doorway as the doctor opened for him. 'Awful sorry to have to disturb you again this way, doctor,' he began. 'But I got the call from old Elias Turner himself.'

Dr. Sickles gritted his teeth. 'I suppose it's the boy again,' he said. 'Has he been writing "NO" again? Where this time?'

'It's pretty serious this time,' replied the sheriff. 'It's not only in one place. It's all over the town. He must have used a rock to scratch on the glass with. It's on the front door of the Bank again, and on the plate glass windows of Hovey's, and Miller's Pharmacy, and Anderson's Grocery, and half a dozen other stores. The letters are furrowed right into the glass, so that they'll never come out. And the worst of all is the Church. He must have had a knife with him, because the word "NO" is carved in letters a foot high right on the front door.'

The doctor gasped, closed his eyes a moment, and inhaled very slowly. Then he said, 'The boy isn't here, sheriff. He hasn't been here since yesterday noon. You can come in and look if you want to.'

'No, no, doctor, if you say he isn't here, that's good enough for me. Do you know where he might be? This is a pretty serious thing now. It's not a joke any more, and I'm afraid we're going to have to take some sort of action. Where do you think we might find him?'

'I'm not sure,' replied the doctor. 'But I know that he often goes for walks in a grove out east of town where there's a stream. He might be there. I hope you find him. But if you do, don't bring him here, above all. Take him to the gaol, where he belongs.'

'I'm afraid we'll have to,' said the sheriff. He shook his head. 'It's too bad.'

'It's the boy's own fault,' said the doctor.

Just as his father had suspected, George had taken refuge in that little wood which, for no apparent reason, stretched some distance along a wide shallow stream east of Harkton. He sat on the ground leaning against a tree-trunk by the stream's bank. He sat still there, watching the water as it rushed in numberless tiny cascades over the rocks. His clothes were rumpled, they had lost all shape, one sleeve of the jacket had got torn somehow. His hair hung straight down above his eyes, damp. In his outward appearance everything was certainly hapless and forlorn, yet he seemed to be quite placid nevertheless. An aura of dreamlike tranquillity enveloped him. When the sheriff and his deputy came tramping along irritably through the woods, looking for him, he did not even try to flee. He went with them, and they took him to the gaol in the cellar of the city hall.

There was no one in Harkton to dispute that George Sickles was undoubtedly more than just a public nuisance, though he was perhaps not a serious menace to the community. Some said that he must be insane and 'ought to be sent to the State loony bin', an imputation which Dr. Sickles, when he heard it, angrily and vehemently denied. The whole town talked intensely of what should be done with the prisoner. But the process of municipal law-enforcement, once started, pursued its own preordained course.

Two days after his arrest George was driven by the sheriff to Granville, where he was lodged in a cell of the county gaol. After ten additional days of waiting there was a hearing. It was brief. An uninterested judge posed questions to those concerned, noted the sternness of the boy's parents, noted the apparent general opinion of Harkton's citizens, noted the boy's unwavering calm, and, 'after due consideration, for the boy's own good', sentenced George Sickles to serve eighteen months in the State reform school.

For several weeks thereafter Harkton talked very much of the Sickles affair. Everyone approved when Dr. Sickles paid to have all of the defaced plate-glass replaced and bought a fine new door for the church. But the doctor and his wife, people noticed, had suffered from all that had happened; both looked older and weary. The town, even as it pointed at them and whispered, sympathized. And then, as the weeks became months, other subjects of conversation came to the public attention and the Sickles affair began to be forgotten.

At the State reform school, far far away from Harkton, farther than he had ever been before in his life, George did not seem to be unhappy. He was assigned to work in the institution's laundry, where he worked well and did as he was told. He gave no trouble. The authorities left him alone. During his few periods of free time he read and re-read a book which he had borrowed from the reform school library—*Gulliver's Travels*. Once every two weeks he was allowed to go to the movies which were shown in the dining-hall. He did not make any particular friends among the other boys, either in the dormitory or at the laundry, but he was companionable with them. He received no messages from outside the institution and he sent none.

It was when George had been at the reform school for almost a year that both his parents suddenly died, within nine hours of each other: the doctor from a complicated thrombotic condition, and Mrs. Sickles as the result of a heart attack she suffered while hurrying out of the house to call for help for her husband, who lay in agony upstairs. George was told that he might be granted special permission to attend the funeral, but he declined to go, explaining that for him his parents had been dead a long time. This the authorities considered evidence of a callousness they had not previously observed in the boy.

In time he received two letters, one from his sister, the other from Douglas G. Foss, Harkton's lawyer. His sister wrote not to express an appropriate grief nor to commiserate, but to say how sure she felt that their parents' death had been hastened by the shame George had brought upon them. She added that Calvin Sutter had been offered a more important agency in another part of the State by the insurance company he represented. Thus she and her family would very soon be leaving Harkton, nor need George ever expect, she stated, after he was released from reform school, to receive any sort of support from her or her husband, even if he should find out where they were and follow them. His sister told him that he had been disinherited by his father and mother, and that she considered she no longer had any family obligations toward him. 'In spite of all the difficulty and sorrow you have caused,' the letter concluded, 'I don't let myself feel any ill-will toward you and I hope you may still be able to make a decent respectable life for yourself.' The lawyer's letter was very brief and formal, merely serving to confirm that George had indeed been disinherited and to state that he had no possible claim, present or future, to any portion of his parents' joint estate, which was left entirely to his sister.

He read both the letters twice and then tore them up.

At the time of Dr. and Mrs. Sickles's death and the moving away of the Sutter family, Harkton's attention again for a while dwelt upon memories of the 'affair', but not for very long. There were other things. There was a rather serious drought in the region. It was June, and some of the young people were marrying. There was the high-school graduation. There were all the usual things. Life in the town continued without remarkable events. It was summer and the weeks went by in the heat.

And anon, the summer months one after the other passed. The drought turned out, after all, not to be serious. The intenseness of the heat by degrees abated. Around in the surrounding country there were the annual harvests; the crops were good. School began once more. Imperceptibly the days, each one a little more and a little more, grew shorter. Autumn matured, passed its full moment quickly, and aged toward winter. Frost came. The leaves fell and blew away or were burned in smoky fires at dusk. The town prepared itself, living in expectation of the cold and the ice soon to come. Then there was the first snow; it came drifting gently in late November, swirling across the plains, and tenderly but implacably possessed the town. It was winter now, and Harkton's attention turned upon the winter.

Then something astonishing happened. George Sickles came back. Almost no one in recent months had spoken of him, and those who had had spoken of him as of something past, a matter permanently settled, as they might have spoken of the dead. Perhaps it was even more astonishing than his return in itself that no one should have anticipated it; but such was the fact. Why had he come back here? people asked each other. He simply appeared one day in the square, and the passers stared at him.

But he was not the same George Sickles as before, which was doubtless all the more disturbing. There was a change in him. It was, to be sure, a quite banal change, one to have been expected. George was no longer a boy. He was taller than before, and broader, and he obviously shaved now; and there was a sure new air of strength about him. The citizens of Harkton regarded this change at first with surprise and then with mistrust, because it had come about not only in a foreign place, but in a place and under circumstances which they all united to consider reprobate. No one greeted George back to his native town.

He did not appear at all distressed by this, however. He rented a small drab furnished room, near the old railway station, in a boarding-house frequented principally by truck drivers. And he set out to find some employment, but without success. Everywhere he applied he was brusquely refused. As the days passed and his bill in the boarding-house increased, he still had no work.

Seeing him again, the town naturally remembered what had happened a year and a half before. People talked, and speculated, and wondered how long it would be before he would be making trouble again. Since he could find no work George spent most of the day standing around in the square, though it was very cold. He didn't speak to anyone but he looked at the people one by one as they passed. The people were annoyed by his staring, they didn't know what to make of it, and they complained to each other. They all agreed that no good could possibly come of his return to Harkton. Sooner or later, they said, something unfortunate was bound to happen; and it would probably be sooner than later. And they were right.

It was a chill windy night toward the middle of December. George had been back for a week. Harkton, beneath its layers of snow and ice, lay quiet. From the belfry of the Baptist Church had just sounded ten o'clock, chiming vibrant upon the frigid air. Around the square the street lights made isolated spheres of white still desolation. Nothing moved.

By chance that night it happened that the sheriff was working late in his office, as he often did near the end of the year, bringing up to date his annual record. He finished his work for the evening at a quarter after ten, got into his heavy sheepskin coat, his cap, his boots, and his mittens, and set out for home. But as he crossed the square, to his amazement, he saw someone coming from the other side. It was George Sickles. He had on an old wool mackinaw, but no boots, no gloves, no hat. The sheriff stopped, but George kept on, did not look at the sheriff, and would have passed without speaking.

'Where do you think you're going?' asked the sheriff.

George started. He glanced at the sheriff. 'I've been for a walk,' he answered.

'A walk!' grunted the sheriff dubiously. 'I can imagine you'd be going for a walk this night, dressed like you are. I'll bet you didn't expect to meet me, did you? You wouldn't be up to your old tricks, would you? Do you really expect me to believe you were out for a walk?'

'It doesn't matter whether you believe it or not,' said George, shrugging.

The sheriff stepped forward and put a firm hand on George's shoulder. 'Now look here, son,' he began, 'you . . . '

'Take your hands off me!' George exclaimed, interrupting. He shook away the sheriff's hand and stepped back several paces. 'Leave me alone. I haven't done anything, and I don't like people touching me.'

'Is that so?' retorted the sheriff angrily, moving forward with his hand still outstretched. 'You're getting a little too fresh.'

George backed away again. The sheriff lunged forward, started to run. But George was quicker and more agile, unhampered by a heavy coat or boots. He raced to the other side of the square and along the side-walk toward the corner, with the sheriff pursuing him. He was well ahead and might have gotten away with ease; but again he was unlucky.

It was obvious that the sheriff was being out-distanced and that for him to continue the chase would be futile. Panting, he stopped as he reached the side-walk. He frowned angrily. Putting both hands up to his mouth, he shouted, 'Stop or I'll shoot!'

The fugitive did not stop. He was passing just in front of the Bank. As the sheriff's threat reached him through the freezing air he swerved abruptly to the side. And one of his feet came down on a little stretch of smooth ice. He lost his balance. His arms flew up, but he could not save himself. He fell swiftly backward and to one side and came down with a splitting impact against the Bank's massive granite steps. He uttered one cry; the *o* sound of it pierced the icy quiet for but an instant. Then his body lay still, sprawled there.

Hurrying forward, the sheriff saw that he did not stir, his eyes were shut; but he was breathing. With difficulty he managed to get the inert body to his office. He telephoned to Dr. Carsby to come at once.

Some whiffs of spirits of ammonia sufficed to revive George, yet he still did not move or speak. He lay motionless on the floor and looked at the two men who stood above him. They spoke to him and impatiently told him to get up, but he simply lay there blinking. After a brief examination the doctor decided that the boy must have injured his spine in the fall and be temporarily paralysed. There was nothing to do but get him to the hospital in Granville. After telephoning their respective wives to inform them of the accident and the ensuing necessary trip, the two men got George on to the back seat of the doctor's car and drove to Granville.

At the hospital there the doctor's diagnosis was confirmed. It would be necessary for George to remain for observation. The sheriff and the doctor departed.

Several days later, after numerous X-rays, a complete diagnosis of George's condition was concluded. His injury was not great, yet it was very grave. Recovery *was* possible, but only by means of an operation and subsequent special treatment. However, the operation was so difficult and delicate a one that no local surgeon would ever have dared to attempt it, and the special treatment was so costly that certainly no facilities for it existed any nearer than Chicago. If the operation and treatment were not possible, as indeed the Granville hospital staff expected from the first, then the only recourse would be to a limited and old-fashioned therapy, which, though in time it might effect some improvement, would doubtless leave the patient totally paralysed for life.

Such were the facts which the doctor in charge of George's case wrote to his sister, whose address had been supplied by the sheriff. Edwina Sutter's reply came forthwith: she regretted to learn of her brother's accident, but she was certainly in no position to undertake extravagant expenditures on his behalf.

Consequently, after a delay of a week or more, George was transferred as a charity case to the county home for the destitute, a huge old frame building on the outskirts of Granville. He was then not quite twenty years old.

In Harkton, when they learned what had happened, the people said that it was too bad. But such accidents had a way of happening. And they had all known from the beginning that things were bound to turn out badly for George Sickles. They repeated to each other the facts of the affair as evidence that they had been right. It had been fatal, they said. And no one disputed that indeed things had turned out badly.

At the county home in Granville George was one of thirty men, all of the others aged and feeble, who occupied a long corridor-like bare-walled ward. There the years passed by him. He grew thin, grew gaunt, his hair turned a drab colour and began falling out. He couldn't move or speak; everything had to be done for him. Often the other occupants of the ward, in their senility, made fun of him. He had no visitors. He had no distractions. On fine days occasionally he was rolled in a rickety wheel chair out on to a veranda in the sun. There he would sit, twitching a little, and at times his head would jerk spasmodically from side to side as though in a gesture of indomitable dissent.

ALBERTO MORAVIA

BACK TO THE SEA

THE countryside was flat with great meadows over which the daisies scattered their soft whiteness far and wide. On the horizon the pinewood closed in the meadows with a long unbroken wall of solid and motionless greenery. The car proceeded slowly, and as though unwillingly, jolting over the holes in the unpaved road. Through the glass of the windscreen Lorenzo could see the mass of the pinewood coming to meet him, as if it were moving—melancholy, mysterious, hostile. Lorenzo had planned this outing as a way of sweetening his relationship with his wife. But now, confronted by her solid silence, timidity again overcame him. However, as they approached the pines he said: 'Here is the pinewood.'

His wife didn't answer. He lifted his hand and adjusted the mirror over the windscreen. As they were setting out he had turned it towards her and during the drive he had done nothing but observe her. She had sat firm and erect, her gloved hand on the door, her coat folded on her knees, her white linen shirt open as far as her breast. Her slender neck rose up out of the shirt like a graceful stem. On her sunburnt face and red mouth her freckles and the soft down of her lip set a veil of shadowy sensuality. But her eyes, small and black, gazed ahead obstinately, and the upward sweep of hair over her forehead gave her whole face an aggressive and hard look. She had something simian about her, Lorenzo thought; not so much in her features as in her sad, decrepit and innocent expression, like that of certain small apes. And like an ape she pretended to an attitude of offended dignity which he knew she was entirely incapable of.

The pinewood was near now and appeared less dense than from a distance, with red trunks leaning this way and that as though they were just going to fall against each other. The car left the road and went over a stretch of bare, soft ground over which the wheels bounded gently. The pinewood was deserted; here and there, in the shadow, was an uninhabited chalet, with closed shutters. Then the wood brightened, the air appeared white and trembling; the sea.

Lorenzo would have liked to announce the sea as he had announced the wood; but his wife's silence seemed even more determined, and she wouldn't be able to resist the temptation to snub him—the sight of the sea caused him such genuine delight. So he remained silent and drove over the bare soil. The car stopped and for a moment they sat motionless in the shadow of the lowered hood. They couldn't see the sea in detail yet but they could hear it, now the engine was turned off, with its varied and diffused murmur in which each wave seemed to have a different tone. 'Shall we get out?' he suggested at last.

His wife opened the door and put out her legs, hindered by the narrowness of her skirt. Lorenzo followed and closed the door. Immediately they felt the sea wind which was strong and warm and fierce, lifting clouds of sand and dust from the rough ground.

'Shall we go down to the sea?'

'Yes, of course.'

They set out across the clearing. The bombardments had ruined much of the promenade; there were wide gaps here and there in the cement paving. There were still a few pillars standing; others had been thrown down and were gradually being covered with sand which the wind blew in long tongues as far as the middle of the clearing. As they set their eyes towards the beach they saw that it was criss-crossed in every direction by barbed-wire entanglements. The wind blew under the barbed wire, smoothing out the sand. Far away the thorny threads of steel stretched, wrapped in a white and furious cloud of dust.

They found a way marked out by poles which led through the barbed wire to the sea. Lorenzo let his wife go ahead and followed at some distance behind. He did this so as to look at her with leisure as he had done earlier in the mirror of the car. When he had finished his manœuvre he reflected that perhaps the most unfortunate part of all his misfortunes was his tardy and unforeseen falling in love with his wife. He had not loved her at first, he had married her in a hurry so as to prepare himself for his political career. And now that the empty and noisy luck which had dazzled him for so many years had come to an end, he had fallen in love with her—but she had no use for his love. Or rather, a sort of pungent lust had been kindled in his blood, which was shy and gauche, like a youth's love. As he followed her he watched her with a sad and surly desire that amazed him. She was tall, thin, elegant, boyish; and when her long strong legs, robust in relation to the thinness of her bust, moved clumsily over the uneven sand, they recalled the legs of very young horses still awkward in gait. Lorenzo looked especially at those legs on which innumerable hairs could be seen through the transparence of her stockings; hairs, black and long, which looked as though they had been stuck on to the skin and were supine and lifeless. She didn't have them plucked as many women do. When she put up her hand to arrange her hair, disordered by the wind, he seemed to make out the blackness of her armpit through the linen shirt and he felt deeply uneasy.

They reached the sea. Offshore the wind was pushing up long and sonorous springtime billows, rolling one upon the other; but farther out the sea was almost calm with alternating streaks of turbid green and dark violet. For a while Lorenzo stood beside his wife, looking at the waves. He picked out one as far away as his eyes could see, in fact at its birth, and then followed it as it rose, overturned on the rump of the one ahead of it, and passed on beyond it. As the wave lingered, lost its way in the ebb and died at his feet, his glance leapt back to the sea in search of another. He didn't know why, but he wanted at least one of those innumerable masses of water breaking on the shore to overcome its hindering rivals and the slowing-down impact of the backwash; to hurl itself on to the shore, pass beyond himself and his wife, mount the beach and wreathe in its farthest foam the barbed-wire defences and the clearing. But it was a vain wish and suddenly he understood why he wanted it so much. As a child, on stormy days, he loved to watch the varied impetus of the waves and now and again, when he saw a bigger and stronger one spread quickly up the beach as far as the cabins, he used to think ambitiously: 'I shall be like that wave'. He shook his head vigorously to banish the recollection, and, turning to his wife, he asked her: 'Do you like it?'

'The sea?' she said indifferently. 'It's not the first time I've seen it, you know.'

Lorenzo would have liked to explain his feelings, yes, to tell her about his childish imaginings; but a sort of hopeless timidity prevented him from speaking. He felt a strong impulse to free himself from his preoccupation and at least seem carefree. He bent down and picked up a stone so as to throw it as far as he possibly could. He counted on the violence of the action to cast away his pain together with the stone. But the stone was deceptive. It was as big as his fist but light; it was pumice and porous with holes. It fell near, floated on the crest of a wave and grounded in the sand at his feet.

He experienced a feeling of bitterness as though this was the silent answer given by reality to his aspirations. His suffering, too, was like that pumice-stone and he hadn't the strength to cast it far away; it would always come back with the jetsam and black debris that the rough sea vomited on to the shore.

He came closer to his wife and put his arm round her. He wanted to walk with her along the sea's edge in the health-giving wind that blew against them, in the clamorous solitude of the waves breaking on the shore. But she pushed him away, startled and stubborn. 'What's the matter with you?'

'Don't you want us to go for a walk?'

'It's too windy.'

'I like the wind,' he said. And alone he took a few steps along the shore. He felt he was behaving desperately, outside the calculations of reason, like a madman. And this sense of madness was increased by the crashing of the waves and by the wind blowing into his hair, his eyes. 'I've completely lost my head,' he thought coolly, and he started to go towards a little heap of sand which had been formed round some abandoned and rusty object.

'What are you doing?' he heard his wife ask angrily. 'Where are you going? There are mines about.'

'What do I care about mines,' he answered with a shrug. He would have liked to add, 'or if I'm blown up,' but he was silent out of modesty. He turned to see what his wife was doing. She was still standing facing the sea, looking bored and undecided. Then she said: 'Don't play the hero; you know you want to live,' with a contempt which wounded him and seemed unfair. He turned back with a leap and took her arm. 'You must believe me when I say that now at this moment I don't care a fig about dying; in fact, I'd be glad.' He squeezed her round firm arm tightly and noticed with pain how easily the contact turned his despair into desire and made it insincere in spite of himself. She looked at him and said crossly: 'Leave me alone ... it's your usual tale ... and then ...' Then, after a moment, 'Do what you want, but I won't follow you. I haven't the slightest wish to die myself.'

Lorenzo left her and went purposefully towards the little mound. His feet sank, his shoes filled with sand. The mound was no more than fifty yards away; he reached it and discovered it was an old petrol tin. The sea had corroded and rusted it and the wind had three-quarters filled it with sand. Beyond, the beach stretched on as far as the eye could see, swept by the grazing wind, traversed by fine black barbed-wire entanglements which looked like closed up scars in the soft whiteness of the sand. He stopped a moment, undecided, dazzled by the reflection of the cloudy sky, and then turned back.

His wife was no longer there. Lorenzo picked his way through a narrow passage between the barbed wire towards the clearing. His wife was standing by the car, one hand on the door, the other on her forehead so as to set her hair. 'And now what are we going to do?' she asked.

'Shall we eat?' he replied in a cheerful voice, though really he felt hardly capable of speaking let alone being cheerful.

'Where?'

'We can go into the pinewood.' Without waiting for a reply he took the basket of provisions from the back of the car and set out in the direction of the pines. His wife followed him.

They crossed the clearing towards the remains of what had once been the local restaurant. In the white dusty light the half-buried ruins rose from the convulsed ground with upright stumps—pale outside and coloured within like decayed teeth. The cement stairway leading to the main hall in which people used to eat overlooking the sea mounted one or two steps and then suddenly stopped above a hollowed-out chaos of pieces of ceiling, twisted and rusting iron and blocks of mortar and bricks. The other rooms inside the crumbled walls were recognizable from similar ruins agglomerated in one single dusty pulp. They walked round the ruins and he said: 'You remember last time we came here?'

'No.'

'Two years ago. Things were already going badly, but I didn't want to face it. You had a wisp of something round your breast and another round your waist which passed between your legs. You were very brown; you had a little turban round your head. Now,' he went on in an unexpectedly strained voice, 'I realize you are very lovely, but then it was as if I didn't see you; I was thinking only about politics, and I let all those idiots who followed us around make love to you.'

'And then?' she said drily.

'Nothing.'

Behind the restaurant was a lawn and the rough and dirty grass was all mixed up with sand. Thick bushes and twisted trees with branches extending like arms grew on the edge of this lawn. The bombardment had thrown a piece of the café piano into the middle of the lawn: the keyboard with a few white notes and a great hunk of splintered wood was exactly like an animal's jawbone with a few putrefying teeth. The grass all around was scattered with felt hammers. Another part of the instrument, the frame, had been hurled into the fork of a tree. The metal strings hung from it and curled like pendant branches of an unusual creeper.

Lorenzo searched for a withdrawn spot with blind and absorbed premeditation as though the issue was not one of love but of crime. His wife followed him some way behind with a look that seemed to him increasingly discontented and jibbing. The pinewood was full of little grassy glades surrounded unevenly by the bushes of the undergrowth. Finally, he thought he had found what he was looking for. 'Let's sit down here,' he said, and slid to the ground.

She remained standing for a moment, looking around. Then, slowly, stiffly and contemptuously, she sank on to her thighs and sat, abruptly pulling her dress over her knees. Lorenzo pretended he wasn't looking at her and began to pull the provisions out of the basket. There were lots of packets, big and small, all wrapped up carefully in white tissue paper, the kind used in fashion shops. And there was a bottle of wine.

'Was it you who packed the basket?'

'No, I got the maid to do it.'

He spread out a napkin on the grass and carefully arranged the eggs, the meat, the cheese, the fruit. Then he uncorked the bottle and put the cork back into it.

'Would you like an egg?'

'No.'

'Meat?'

'Give me a roll with a slice of meat.'

Lorenzo took one of the rolls which had already been divided and buttered, put in two slices of meat, and handed it to her. She took it fastidiously without thanking him and ate it unwillingly. With his head still down and without a glance at her, Lorenzo took a hard-boiled egg and bit at it hungrily, then filled his mouth with buttered bread. He felt a sorry kind of hunger which seemed of the same kind as his desire for his wife. Hunger and lust grew and prospered on his despair, he thought—as though he were no more than a corpse without life and will and his wants had grown on him in the way hairs grow on the beards of the dead. He ate one egg, then another, then a third, hesitated, and then ate the fourth as well. He enjoyed biting into the elastic whites and feeling the soft yolks crumbling under his teeth. He ate with emphasis and now and then put the bottle to his mouth and took long gulps. After the eggs he turned to the meat; there were two kinds, a roast in large red slices, and cutlets fried with breadcrumbs. He didn't look at his wife but ate, and as he ate he felt turgid vitality swelling his veins though his spirit remained sad and empty. This vitality, associated with such despair, made him desolate as though it were a useless and ironical form of wealth. At last he lifted his eyes and offered her the bottle without a word. She still had her roll—she had only eaten half. She shook her head.

'Aren't you eating?'

'I'm not hungry.'

Lorenzo finished eating, then collected the eggshells and other remains, wrapped them in a piece of paper and threw them far away. He put the half-emptied bottle back in the basket. He carried out all these actions with wilful doggedness as though it were a matter of setting his own disturbed mind in order rather than the provisions. His wife, who had now finished her roll, began touching up her face with hand-mirror and puff. 'And now,' she said, 'shall we go?'

'Where?'

'Home.'

'But it's early.'

'You've seen the sea,' she said unkindly, 'you've had lunch. You don't want to sleep here, do you?'

Lorenzo watched her, not knowing whether to be infuriated or humiliated by this obstinate enmity. Then he said in a low voice:

'Listen. I've got to talk to you.'

'Talk to me? We've already talked enough.'

He slid on to the grass with an effort and sat beside her.

'I'd like to know what your grievance is.'

'I haven't one: only I don't see why we must go on living together, that's all.'

'You no longer feel any affection for me?'

'I never felt any, and less now than ever.'

'But there was a time,' Lorenzo insisted, 'when you used to throw your arms round my neck if I gave you a present or some money. You used to hug me, kiss me, and say you loved me.'

'I liked getting presents,' she said, obviously annoyed by this reminder of her childish greed, 'but I didn't love you.'

'You pretended then.'

'No, I didn't pretend exactly.' Lorenzo understood that she was being sincere. In a woman of her kind gratitude for gifts closely resembled love: indeed perhaps it was the only love she was capable of.

'But I', he bowed his head, 'feel for you, since things have been going badly, for the first time in my life, you see. . . . I don't know how to say it.'

'For heaven's sake don't say it,' she exclaimed derisively.

'Well anyway, can't I know what you have against me?'

'Against you?' she replied, growing angry. 'I have the fact that I don't want to be the wife of a jail-bird.'

'I was only in prison a few days, and anyway it was for political reasons.'

'So you say. But others say there was something else, and . . . that you might be locked up again tomorrow.'

Lorenzo noticed a slight uncertainty in her tone, as if she were repeating hearsay instead of thinking things out for herself.

'You're talking about things you don't understand. I bet you haven't even known who I am nor what I've been doing in all these years that we've been together.'

'Don't be absurd,' she said contemptuously.

'Well then, tell me.'

'You were . . .' she hesitated. 'Well, you were one of those who were in control.'

'That's not enough. What was my office?'

'How do I know,' she said scornfully. 'All I know is that everyone referred to you as one of the authorities; but you were always changing, at one time you were one thing, at another time another. I had something else to think about than your jobs.'

'Yes,' said Lorenzo gently, 'you had to think of Rodolfo, Mario, Gianni.'

She pretended not to hear the names of her lovers—all of them as young and silly as herself. Lorenzo went on:

'At least you know what has happened since the time when I was an official? Do you?'

He saw her lift her shoulders impatiently. 'There you are, now you're taking me for a fool; I'm much more intelligent than you think.'

'I don't doubt it in the least, but tell me what has happened.'

'The war came: Fascism came to an end; that's what happened. Are you satisfied?'

'Fine. And why do you think I lost my career?'

'Because,' she said, unsure, 'now the government has been taken over by the enemies of Fascism.'

'And who are the enemies of Fascism?'

This time she lifted her eyes to heaven, tightened her lips, and said nothing. A kind of rage seized hold of Lorenzo. This igorance, he thought, was far worse than any kind of facile condemnation. It made even his mistakes, not to mention his few merits, fall into a void; there remained no more trace of his life than of his footsteps, a little while ago, on the sand along the shore.

'What was Fascism?'

Again the same silence. Abruptly Lorenzo seized her by the arm and shook her. 'Answer, you beast, why don't you answer?'

'Leave me alone,' she said sullenly. 'I don't answer because I know you want to tie me up and make me change what I think. I don't want to stay with you any longer, that's all.'

Lorenzo was no longer listening. The contact of that arm had once again aroused his desire. He looked at her skirt stretching tightly over her thighs as she sat; the softness and warmth and weight of her flesh seemed to communicate themselves to the material. At the sight of this he felt his mind melting away and his breath catching. Nevertheless he said slowly:

'Don't you realize you're leaving me at the very time when another woman would remain faithful, and for motives you don't even see clearly, for some whim or piece of gossip?'

'I realize that many women in society don't invite me to their houses any more, nor greet me in the street. I've already warned mother that I want to go back to her. That's all; I don't want to stay with you any more.' She stood up.

Lorenzo looked her up and down. She stood erect and scornful, her legs in an ungainly attitude because of her skirt which was too tight and her heels which were too high. He realized that it would be easy to fling her to the ground, disarm her contempt. Those legs of hers, hampered by the tightness of her skirt, were like her character which was limited by her silliness. He felt a violent desire to upset her balance. With one thrust of his whole body he threw himself on her legs and toppled her over on to the grass. She fell headlong and, startled into fury, she said: 'Leave me alone. What's the matter with you?'

Lorenzo didn't answer but threw himself on her, crushing her under his body. He said: 'I am what I am', holding his lips against hers as if he wanted to send every word into her mouth. 'But you're not really better than me; you're a silly, empty, corrupt girl; as long as it suited you you stayed with me. Well then, now it doesn't suit you any more you'll stay with me all the same.'

He saw her look of terror and then she said again, almost in supplication: 'Leave me alone'.

'I won't leave you,' said Lorenzo between his teeth. He knew, because he had proved it in the past, that his wife, for all her fury, would give way before his violence in the end. At a given moment she always seemed to be overtaken by a kind of languor or complicity with the force she was being subjected to, and then she yielded and became passively loving as though all the previous repulses had been no more than deliberate coquettishness. This was another characteristic of her silliness—the incapacity to carry any feeling, whether hostile or friendly, to its conclusion. And so, when they began struggling, she defending herself and he trying to overcome her defences, Lorenzo suddenly saw in her little innocent eyes the tempted, passive and languid look he knew so well. At the same time he felt her resistance weaken. Then she said in a low voice: 'Stop, I tell you; someone might see us.' And that was already an invitation to go on.

But he felt a sudden disgust at his victory. After all, nothing would be altered, even if she yielded. He would get up lovelessly from the body he had enjoyed; she, scornful and untidy, would pull down her crumpled skirt; and with the first words uttered their disagreement would begin again, but with the added disgust at the meaningless mechanical coupling. And it wasn't that that he had wanted when he brought her out for the day's trip.

With a brusque movement he left her and drew himself away on the grass. She sat up looking injured and deluded. 'Don't you know that violence gets you nowhere,' she said crossly.

Lorenzo felt like bursting out laughing and answering that on the contrary violence was perhaps the only thing that worked with her. But at the same time he couldn't help recognizing that what she said was true; for what he really needed violence didn't get anywhere.

Despite this he said cruelly: 'That doesn't alter the fact that if I'd gone on a bit longer you'd have opened your legs.'

'How vulgar you are,' she said with sincere disgust. She rose to her feet, clambered through the bushes and set out determinedly for the clearing.

Lorenzo stayed sitting on the ground with his eyes on the grass. When he thought over his wife's replies it seemed as though he too no longer knew what he had done or stood for all those years. 'She's right,' he thought, 'it was all an empty dream, a delirium, and now I've woken up.' As he looked back over those years he realized that he couldn't remember anything except his constant cordiality—cordiality to his inferiors, his superiors, his friends, his enemies, to strangers and to his wife. He reflected that in the end his cordiality must have had a bad effect, for after so much talking and smiling he now felt incapable of either; as if his tongue had dried up and the corners of his mouth become sore. In these conditions even an idiot like his wife found her game easy.

He jumped at the distant throb of a car, and paused a moment listening; then, suddenly suspicious, he leapt to his feet and began to run across the pinewood, leaping over the bushes and the uneven ground towards the clearing. When he arrived there, panting, it was only to find it empty. The air was still full of the dust raised by the car in which his wife had fled.

It seemed a worthy ending to the day and he didn't even feel annoyed. He could probably get a lift back on a military truck. At worst he would have to walk a mile or two to the main road; plenty of cars passed there and he could easily get a lift.

But as he set out along the path through the pinewood he felt the call of the sea, a longing to go back again to the everlasting motion, the everlasting clamour, before returning to the city. And then he wanted to do something he would never have dared to do in front of his wife—take off his shoes, roll up his trousers and walk along the sea's edge in the shallow water of the ebb and flow of the waves.

He was aware, too, that he wanted to walk along by the edge of the sea to prove to himself that he didn't care about his wife's flight. But he knew that that wasn't true, and when he sat in the sand to take off his shoes he noticed that his hands were trembling.

He removed his shoes and socks, folded his trousers up to below the knee, and picked his way through the barbed wire to the water's edge. He set out walking in the ebbing and flowing water, with shoes in hand, his head bowed and eyes lowered.

His attitude was that of thought but he wasn't really thinking. He liked seeing the surf pass beyond his feet, rise along his legs and form a whirl of water round his ankles, then flow back peevishly, carrying away the sand beneath his feet, tickling like something alive. He liked, too, to keep his gaze down and see only water to right and left, turbid, swirling, sprinkled with white rings of foam. The sea near the shore was full of a black sedge which each wave threw on to the sand and then carried away again in the backwash. There were minute sticks like ebony, oval and smooth scales, tiny wood splinters, myriads of little black objects that the movement of the turbid sand-laden water kept in continuous turmoil. The transparent shells of tiny dead crabs, green seaweed and yellow roots put some splash of colour into this carbonized chaff. When the surf ebbed the sedge clung gluttonously to his feet making an arabesque of black on their shining whiteness. Here and there some flotsam of larger bulk floated in between one wave and the next, in the ground-glass turmoil of the foamy water. He saw something not far away of uncertain colour and shape which made him think of an animal; but as he drew near, overcoming the water's pressure, he discovered that it was the wooden hoof of a woman's orthopaedic shoe. Little shells of pallid amethyst had spread thickly over the toe making a kind of dense tuft, while the heel was still covered with red cloth. As he was looking at the remains a high foamless billow passed by, rapidly bathing him as far as the groin. He threw the shoe away and turned nearer to the shore.

He didn't know how long he walked along the strand, his feet in the riotous water, on the soft and fleeting sand. But by dint of looking down at the waves which broke ceaselessly on his legs and passed beyond towards the unseen shore he felt a kind of dizziness.

He lifted his eyes over the sea and for a moment he imagined he saw it tall and upright like a liquid wall. The sky on the horizon was no more than a streak of vapour. There some sea bird was skimming the skin of the water in distant and dangerous flight which revived the thought of the drunken violence of the wind. Dazed, he nearly fell under the weight of a heavier billow. And the clamour of the waves seemed suddenly to become shriller and fiercer as though redoubled by the hope of his collapse.

Almost fearfully he turned towards the beach, thinking to get out of the water and sit down for a moment on the dry sand. He had walked a long way. He had left the clearing and the ruins far behind. Here the sand, mounted in dunes and defences, was criss-crossed by barbed wire and stumps which looked like people holding hands with arms outstretched so as to block the way. His attention was attracted by a thick bank of black and shining seaweed underneath which the waves had hollowed out the sand. He jumped as far as this seaweed and, touching the ground with one hand, he leapt on it.

The torrent of seaweed and sand which soared into the air with a thundering echo darkened his eyes to the sky for a moment as he fell back in the whirlpool of the explosion. He thought he was falling headlong for ever in a perpetual din of cataract. But silence and immobility followed. He lay supine in the water; the noise and movement of the sea were singularly sweet and distant under a sky again visible. The water pulled him under by the hair; head down and feet up, his body moved with the passage of a wave, and he saw a large red stain hastening towards the shore with the rings of foam and the black debris. Then another wave came and pulled him under and he closed his eyes.

[*Translated by* BERNARD WALL]

ANONYMOUS (Eighteenth Century)

MRS. WHITE

DURING the Southern Sung dynasty there lived in Black Pearl Lane, in Hangchow, a man called Hsü Hsüan. He was left an orphan at an early age, and had been put in the charge of his brother-in-law, a certain Li Jên, who was employed at the Governor's office. He lived in Li Jên's house, but during the day he helped in the management of a drugstore kept by his uncle, Merchant Li. He was only about twenty-one, but was generally regarded as thoroughly steady and reliable. The Ch'ing-ming Festival was at hand, and he decided to go to the Pao-t'a Temple and make offerings to his ancestors and burn some prayer-slips. The evening before, he talked the matter over with his sister. Next day he rose early, bought some paper horses, incense sticks, sutra-banners, paper cash, and the like, and as soon as he had breakfasted he changed into new clothes, put on his best socks and shoes, made up his prayer-strips, paper cash and horses into a neat bundle, and went straight to Merchant Li's shop.

'Uncle,' he said, 'I want to go to the Pao-t'a Temple and make offerings to my ancestors. I should be obliged if you would allow me a day's leave.'

'I am glad to see you showing a proper filial spirit,' said Merchant Li. 'By all means go at once, and come back at your own convenience.'

On leaving the shop, he made for the Ch'ien-t'ang Gate, crossed the Stone Coffer Bridge, and went straight up to the temple. Here he at once came upon the priest in charge of offerings, who dispatched his prayer-slips with the correct ritual, burnt his paper offerings, and came with him to the Great Hall. After admiring its beauties, he had some refreshments in the Guest Chamber and parted from the priest who had officiated for him. It seemed a pity not to take advantage of his holiday, and he set out to have a thorough look round. He had just reached the Shrine of the Four Sages when, quite unexpectedly, clouds came up from the north-west, a fog closed in to the south-east, and soon a slight drizzle began to fall. It did not at first look as though it would last very long. But one shower followed another, and soon it became a steady downpour. Seeing that it was getting very wet underfoot, Hsü Hsüan decided that it would be a mistake to wait any longer, and taking off his new shoes and socks he made them into a bundle which he tied to his belt, and went barefoot to the quay at the Hall of the Four Sages to look for a boat. The river seemed at first to be completely deserted, and he was beginning to be afraid that he would not be able to cross, when he suddenly saw an old man sculling a boat close inshore, almost under his very nose, and at the first glance he recognized Chang A-kung, a boatman whom he knew very well indeed. Much relieved, he called out: 'Chang A-kung, take me to the Yung-chin Gate!'

The old man brought the boat alongside, and, seeing that it was Hsü Hsüan, he said: 'You've been caught in the rain, young master! Make haste and come aboard.'

Hsü Hsüan was already in the boat, and the old man had sculled him something like twenty yards from the shore when someone called out from the river bank, 'Take us, too!'

Hsü looked up and saw that the people who wished to become passengers were a lady dressed in white widow's weeds and her girl attendant, who was dressed in green and was carrying a bundle. When the boatman saw them, he paddled the boat back inshore and said:

'I suppose it's the same thing with you—you've been to the tombs and got caught in the rain. Well, look sharp and get on board!'

As soon as the lady and her companion were in the boat, they greeted Hsü very respectfully. He jumped to his feet, returned the salutation, and then stood aside, saying: 'Madam, pray take a seat under the awning'. When she had settled herself under the awning, the lady kept on stealing quick glances at Hsü, her eyes dancing like autumn waves. Steady young man though he was, it could hardly be expected that the sight of this extremely good-looking lady, accompanied by her very elegant maid, should not produce some effect upon him. He was just wondering whether he might venture to start a conversation and had decided not to, when to his surprise she addressed him first, asking him to tell her his name and surname. Then she asked where he lived, and he told her how he lived with his relations and worked in the druggist's shop. Presently, when opportunity offered, he said he would esteem it a great favour if she would confide to him the name of her distinguished family and indicate their place of residence.

'I am the sister,' she said, 'of Captain White and Chamberlain White. I was married to a Mr. Ch'i, but unfortunately he died. He is buried not far from here, and as today is the Ch'ing-ming Festival, I have just been visiting his tomb, to make offerings and clear the ground. I was on my way back when this sudden storm came on, and if I had not been so fortunate as to get a lift in your Worship's boat, I should indeed have been in a quandary.'

This led to further trifling talk, and they were quite surprised suddenly to discover that the boat had reached the Yung-chin Gate. They were about to disembark when a look of embarrassment came into the lady's face.

'We made a very early start,' the maid explained to Hsü, 'and were in such a hurry that we forgot to bring any small change with us. I wonder if you would mind paying the boatman? We will return the money when we get home. You may be sure we shall not fail to pay our debt.'

'Oh pray, ladies, at your convenience,' said Hsü. 'So small a matter is of no consequence at all.' So saying, he paid off the boatman and they all went on shore. It was still raining hard, and as it was getting late they set out at a good pace.

'I live at the end of the Lane of the Two Tea Stores,' the lady said to Hsü. 'If it is not troubling you too much, perhaps you would consent to come home with me and have a cup of tea. Then I could give you the boat money at the same time.'

'I am afraid I must be getting home,' he said. 'It is very late already. But some other time I should be happy to pay my respects.'

At this the lady and her maid immediately left him and set out into the rain. Hsü, keeping as far as possible under the eaves of houses, made his way to the house of some relatives who lived at the Three Bridges, in order to borrow an umbrella. He was just coming out on to the Yang Embankment, under the shelter of the umbrella, when he heard someone call out: 'Mr. Hsü, not so fast!' He glanced hurriedly over his shoulder and saw that it was the lady whom he had taken into his boat. She was standing all alone under the projecting eaves of a tea store.

'How comes it, Madam,' he said, 'that you have got no farther than this?'

'As the rain showed no sign of stopping,' the lady said, 'and my shoes were wet through, I told Little Green to go home and fetch me an umbrella and something fresh to wear on my feet. I don't know what has become of her. Might I walk a few paces with you under your umbrella?'

'I have only a very short way to go,' he said. 'You had better take the umbrella. I will fetch it tomorrow.'

'That is really very kind of you,' she said, 'but I feel I ought not to do that.'

However, he handed her the umbrella and went off, keeping under shelter as far as possible. On reaching home, he had supper and went to bed immediately. Here he lay tossing from side to side. He could not stop thinking about the lady of the boat, with whom he had fallen very much in love, and when at last he managed to snatch a moment's sleep, it was only to dream of her. Things were going very well, and indeed just reaching a climax, when he woke with a start, to hear 'the golden cock thrice crow'.

When it was light he got up and went to the shop. He made a pretence of attending to business; but it was as though his mind and soul were all the while elsewhere and nothing he did went right. The moment he had eaten his dinner, he said something about having to go on an errand in the town, and rushed out. He made straight for the end of the Lane of the Two Tea Stores, and began to inquire for Mrs. White. No one had ever heard of her. He was wandering vaguely about, when Little Green came running towards him from the east.

'Sister,' he said, 'where is it that you live? I have come to fetch my umbrella.'

'Follow me, Sir,' she said. She took him with her and they had not walked far when she said, 'It's just in here'. Hsü looked about to get his bearings and saw that it was a high building, opposite the wall of Prince Hsiu's residence.

'Please come inside and take a seat,' said Little Green when they had passed through the gate. He followed her into the central hall. In a low voice, going towards the inner room, she said, 'Madame, Mr. Hsü is here'. She answered from within, 'Ask him to come in and have a cup of tea'.

Hsü hesitated for a while, very uncertain whether it was proper for him to accept such an invitation. But Little Green kept on urging him to consent. 'What's the objection?' she said. 'Go right in.'

He went into the inner room which on each side had four blind windows of lattice-work, while in the middle there hung a curtain of green cloth. He pushed back the curtain and found behind it an alcove with a table on which was a vase of Tiger Beard Irises, four very good pictures on the walls, between which there hung right in the centre a painting of some deity. On the incense-stand were ranged some old copper incense-burners and flower vases.

Mrs. White met him with the warmest greetings. 'It was entirely owing to you that I came to no harm when I got caught in the rain yesterday,' she said. 'I cannot thank you enough.'

'Please say no more about it,' said Hsü. 'Such a trifling matter is really not worth mentioning.'

When tea had been served, he rose to go; but at that moment Little Green came in with wine, fish, fruit and so on. He hastened to excuse himself, saying, 'Thank you very much indeed, Madam, for this kind thought, but I really ought not to put you to so much trouble'. He drank a cup or two of wine and then rose saying, 'It is getting very late. I must be going.'

'I know that this meagre repast is a poor inducement to stay, and I am only venturing to detain you', she said, 'because last night I was obliged to lend your umbrella to a relative. I must beg you to stay and drink a few more cups of wine while the umbrella is being fetched.'

'I am afraid I cannot wait,' he said. 'It is very late.'

'I am sorry you cannot wait for the umbrella,' the lady said. 'All I can do is to suggest that you should come and get it tomorrow.'

'By all means,' he said, 'by all means!' And with that he thanked her and went away.

Next day he again made a feeble pretence of attending to business, but his impatience soon became more than he could endure and, inventing a story about some business that he must attend to, he stole off to Mrs. White's house to fetch the umbrella. Noting how early he had come, she again had wine served and begged him to stay and drink a cup or two.

'I don't like to see you putting yourself out so much,' said Hsü, 'just because I lent you a tattered umbrella.'

'I am only asking you to have a friendly drink,' she said. 'It has nothing to do with the umbrella. Just drink one cup; there is something I want to discuss with you.'

He drank several cups and then said, 'What is it, Madam, that you want to discuss with me?'

Thus questioned, Mrs. White poured out another cup, set it in front of Hsü with her own hand and said, 'You may be sure that in your honoured presence and with the eyes of that holy image upon me' (and here she pointed to the picture on the wall) 'I should not dare to speak anything but the truth. Since my husband died, I have been quite alone in the world. It seems that Fate was reserving me for you. Why else should we at the very first glance in the boat two days ago have felt so deep an attraction for one another? If I am not wrong in thinking that you love me distractedly, why do you not find a good match-maker and arrange for a lifetime of wedded bliss?'

Hsü, when he heard this, was overwhelmed with joy; but on reflection he saw that, working as he did in Merchant Li's shop and having no proper home of his own, he was really in no position to set up as a married man. Seeing him ponder deeply and make no reply, she said, 'I entreat you to say frankly whatever is in your mind. What is it that makes you hesitate to reply?'

'Madam,' he said, 'that you should honour me with your affection cannot fail to move me deeply. But I am only an employee in very straitened and humble circumstances, and on thinking over the matter carefully, I do not see how I can accept this proposal.'

'Well, if you don't want to marry me,' said Mrs. White, 'there is no use in your trying to force yourself into it. But if what you have just mentioned is the only difficulty, I have ample means, and you have no need to worry on that score. Bring me some money,' she called out to Little Green, who went into an inner room and brought back with her a packet which she handed to her mistress. Mrs. White, without looking at it, passed it straight on to Hsü, saying as she did so, 'Take this to meet your expenses for the moment. If you find you want more, you have only to come and ask for it.'

He received the packet respectfully, in both hands, opened it and saw at the first glance that it contained a fifty-tael silver ingot. At the sight of it his whole face lit up with pleasure. He put it carefully in his sleeve, saying, 'As soon as I have made all the necessary arrangements, I will come back and inform you'. Then he rose and took his leave. Just as he was going Little Green appeared with the umbrella.

He went straight home and put the money in a safe place. Then he brought back the umbrella to the people he had borrowed it from and afterwards went straight to bed. Next day he got up early and taking some small silver change of his own he bought some chicken, goose, fish, meat and so on, as well as various kinds of fruit and a jar of good wine, and invited his brother-in-law and sister to dine with him. The invitation came as a great surprise to Secretary Li.

'What has suddenly made you decide to throw away your money like this?' he inquired.

'There is a matter about which I want you both to give me your help,' Hsü replied.

'In that case,' said Li, 'you had better tell us all about it at once.'

'Let's drink a cup or two first,' said Hsü.

When they had all taken their seats in due order of precedence and had a drink, Li began to question him again.

'I cannot thank you and my sister enough for taking charge of me and bringing me up,' said Hsü in reply. 'I am now thinking of getting married. The match is from my point of view a very suitable one, the lady has indicated that my chances are good and it should be possible to arrange the affair without much effort. But my parents are dead, and I shall have to ask you and my sister to sponsor me in this matter.'

The first thing that Secretary Li and his wife thought of when they heard this was that they would certainly have to pay the expenses of the wedding, and they answered coldly:

'A marriage is a big matter. We should prefer to discuss your plan together quietly before giving you an answer. For the moment let us go on with the wine.'

They finished the wine and the party broke up without any further allusion to Hsü's proposal.

Some days later, as nothing more had transpired, he said to his sister, 'Have you and your husband discussed that affair yet?'

'No, it has not been mentioned at all,' she said.

'Why hasn't it been discussed?' he asked.

'He's been so harassed by business ever since,' she said, 'that I haven't liked to raise the question.'

'I quite understand why it is that you are not in a hurry to talk about it,' said Hsü. 'You are afraid that I shall ask you to pay.'

So saying, he fished out the silver ingot from his sleeve and handed it to her, saying: 'I can deal with the expenses. All I ask is that you should act as my sponsors.'

'Well,' she said, laughing, 'if you can do yourself as well as that out of the proceeds of our uncle's shop, no wonder you are thinking of making a stylish marriage. I'll keep the money here and talk to your brother-in-law when he comes in. I am sure it will be all right.'

Not long afterwards Secretary Li came home, and she showed him the money, saying, 'He's got the money for his wedding. He only wants us to sponsor it. I don't see why we shouldn't do that at once.'

Secretary Li took the ingot, turned it over and over, carefully examined the lettering with which it was inscribed, and cried out all of a sudden: 'The worst has happened! This ingot may well bring ruin upon our whole family.'

'I never heard such nonsense,' said his wife. 'How can a single piece of silver do all that harm?'

'You don't understand,' said Secretary Li. 'Fifty silver ingots have just disappeared from Commander Shao's strong-room without the seals or locks being so much as touched. The prefect of Lin-an has been made responsible for the arrest of the thief and there is a tremendous hue and cry. So far, the prefect has not found any clue, and he has put up a notice authorizing the arrest at sight of anyone found in possession of this money. The list gives particulars of the marks and numbers of the ingots. A reward of fifty taels will be given for the arrest of the thief. Anyone withholding information or giving shelter to the criminal will be sent with his whole family to do military service on the frontiers. This ingot you have shown me has the markings described in the notice. If we hide it away and do not report to the prefecture, sooner or later someone will denounce us and we shall get into trouble.'

When the wife heard this, she was so scared that she shook till her bones rattled. 'We can't be sure,' she said, 'whether he really stole it or only got it from someone else. What ought we to do about it?'

'It's no business of ours whether he stole it or borrowed it,' said Li. 'It's he who must take the consequences of his own actions. There's no reason why the whole family should be ruined.' So saying, he took the ingot to the prefecture and denounced Hsü Hsüan. The Governor of Lin-an, having verified that this was indeed one of the missing ingots, at once sent his men to arrest the criminal. Soon afterwards Hsü arrived, under arrest, at the Governor's Court. Governor Han addressed him in a loud voice:

'Fifty ingots have disappeared from Commander Shao's strong-room without disturbance either of seals or locks. A denunciation has been made by Secretary Li, and I have one of the ingots here in Court. It appears that it was found in your possession. That being so, where are the remaining forty-nine? As the theft was committed without disturbance of seal or lock, this is a case not only of theft, but also of sorcery. Your best course will be to make a straightforward confession.'

So saying, he ordered his men to get ready the screw and rack and other instruments of torture.

On discovering for the first time why he had been arrested, Hsü hastened to explain matters. 'I am not a sorcerer,' he said. 'Let me tell you exactly what happened.' And he told the whole story of his meeting with Mrs. White in the boat, how she had borrowed his umbrella and he had gone to reclaim it, and how she had invited him to drink with her, proposed marriage and lent him the money.

'Who is this Mrs. White?' the Governor asked, 'and where is she to be found?'

'She told me,' said Hsü, 'that she is the sister of Captain White and Chamberlain White. She is living at the entry to the Lane of the Two Tea Stores, in a high, black-painted house standing well above the highway, opposite the wall of Prince Hsiu's residence.'

Governor Han then instructed his constable Ho Li to take Hsü Hsüan to the Lane of the Two Tea Stores, arrest 'the female delinquent, White,' and bring her into Court for interrogation. Ho, accompanied by a workman, then conducted Hsü to the tall, black-painted house that had been described. It was obvious at the first glance that it was uninhabited and had been so for some time. He detained and questioned the local beadle and the near neighbours of the house. They all told the same story: Deputy Magistrate Mao had once lived there, but about six years ago he and his whole family died of the plague and since then, as a ghost had frequently been seen going in and out of the house with a shopping basket, no one had dared to live there. As for a Mrs. White—there was no one in the district of that name.

'It's clear she doesn't live here,' said Ho Li. 'Are you sure you haven't made a mistake?'

'I am quite certain this is the house,' said Hsü, who was utterly bewildered by the sight before him. 'What I cannot understand is how the house has come to look so derelict in the space of only three or four days.'

'Well,' said Ho Li, 'if you are sure this is the right place, the only thing we can do is to force the gate and go in.'

So saying, he told the beadle to get to work. The gate was forced and they all pressed in. The interior was dark and cold; not a soul was to be seen. They broke into one room after another on every floor; nowhere was the slightest trace of anyone having set foot there. At last, when they opened the door of a room at the very top of the house, they saw at the far end of the room the figure of a strikingly handsome woman dressed all in white, sitting on a low couch. Uncertain whether it was a live person or a ghost, they all stood rooted to the spot. Only Ho Li, mindful of his mission, found strength to cry in a loud voice: 'Mrs. White, I presume! I have here a warrant signed by his Excellency Governor Han authorizing me to bring you for interrogation about an affair of money, in which the man Hsü Hsüan is also involved.'

The lady neither stirred nor uttered a word of reply.

The constable saw nothing for it but to pluck up his courage and herd the whole crowd into the room. They were all pressing forward when there was a sudden crash, like a thunder-clap out of the blue. They were so startled that the whole crowd fell over one another in a heap. But nothing more occurred and when they had recovered from their fright they began again to edge forward towards the couch. As they approached, a dazzling shimmer met their eyes. Piled up high on the couch was a great heap of silver; the lady was nowhere to be seen. They counted it and found that there were exactly forty-nine ingots. Ho Li then told the people to divide the bars between them, carry them into the court-room and hand them in one by one. When he had made a detailed report of all that had occurred, Governor Han at once discharged the beadle and neighbours.

'It is evident,' he said, 'from what I have just heard that this is a case of sorcery, in which none of these witnesses are involved.'

Hsü Hsüan, however, was found guilty of handling stolen goods and was sentenced to confinement in the Penal Camp at Soochow. The missing money was duly returned in full to Commander Shao, who handed over the promised reward of fifty taels to Secretary Li. The case was then closed, but Secretary Li, having got fifty taels by denouncing Hsü Hsüan and seeing that his denunciation had landed Hsü in the Penal Camp, did not feel quite easy in his mind and gave the whole reward to Hsü for his travelling expenses. He also got Merchant Li to give Hsü letters to two acquaintances in Soochow, one of them a magistrate's clerk called Director Fan, and the other a Mr. Wang, who kept an inn near the Chi-li Bridge.

Weeping bitterly, Hsü parted from his sister and brother-in-law and in company with his police-escort took boat to Soochow and arrived at the Penal Camp. He soon managed to get his two letters delivered to Director Fan and Mr. Wang. They both exerted themselves on his behalf and, by laying out a certain amount of money in high places and low, they procured a certificate that he had been duly incarcerated and gave it to the escort, who went away satisfied. Hsü, without having had to suffer the least hardship or discomfort, settled in at Mr. Wang's. Here he sat alone all day, very disconsolate.

He had been at Soochow for half a year and was getting very tired of his solitary existence, when suddenly one day Mr. Wang, the innkeeper, came to him and said: 'There is a carrying-chair outside, with a young lady in it, attended by her maid. They are asking for you.'

Hsü was astonished. He could not imagine who would be likely to call upon him. He hurried to the gate and found to his surprise that it was Mrs. White and Little Green. The mere sight of them put him into such a rage that he could hardly stand upon his feet.

'Tormentress!' he cried, 'you have done me deadly injury. By stealing public money for me, you got me into a desperate plight and brought upon me all the rigours of the law. And now you follow me to Soochow! What brings you here, I should like to ask?'

'Dear one,' she said, 'it is all a mistake. You must not be angry with me. I have come on purpose to explain it all to you.'

At this point, Mr. Wang, who was afraid people would be shocked if they saw the two of them having out their say in this public way, outside the inn gate, came out and said to Mrs. White: 'If you have come on purpose to see Mr. Hsü about something, wouldn't you rather come inside and have a talk?'

Mrs. White at once made as though to walk straight in, but Hsü barred her path, saying: 'No, no, she is an evil spirit, not a woman. You must not let her in.'

The innkeeper turned an astonished gaze upon Mrs. White, examined her attentively from head to foot and then burst out laughing. 'Oh, come!' he said, 'Where in the world was there ever an evil spirit that looked in the least like this? You have no right to say such things about people. It's quite all right, Madam, please come straight in.'

Mrs. White walked boldly in, was presented to the innkeeper's wife, and then said to Hsü: 'From the moment I yielded myself to you, you became my husband and master. How could I possibly have intended to bring harm upon you? If I gave you money, it was because I loved you. How could I know that it would get you into trouble? If there is anything wrong about where the money came from, that is my late husband's fault; for I got it from him. It is not a woman's business to know anything about such things. Yes, a woman, not an evil spirit! That is an absurd delusion that has come into your head because you have a grudge against me. It is to clear all this up that I came here today. I am quite prepared to go away. . . .'

'Enough of this!' cried Hsü. 'When the constable came to arrest you, I distinctly saw you sitting on the couch. Then there was a loud crash, and when I looked again you had disappeared. Human beings cannot vanish in that way. You are certainly an evil spirit.'

At this she laughed. 'The bang you heard,' she said, 'was Little Green knocking the big bamboo pole against the panelling, to bring the dust down. But it gave the people such a fright—I suppose they thought the place was haunted, for they all seemed scared out of their wits—that after a while I retired behind the curtains at the back of the couch, just to give them a chance to recover from their fright. However, they were much too afraid to look for me, and as soon as they caught sight of the money, they could think of nothing else. When they went away, I thought I had better go into hiding for a while, and I went to my mother's sister, who lives opposite the Flower Treasure Temple. In the end I heard quite by chance that you had been sent here. So I put together a few things and came to see you and to ask what is going to happen about our wedding. However, as you have got it into your head that I am an evil spirit, the sooner I go away the better.' So saying, she rose, and made towards the door.

But the innkeeper and his wife would not hear of her going. 'What, go straight back, after coming all this way!' they exclaimed. 'You'll surely stay with us just for a night or two?'

Mrs. White was beginning to explain that it was out of the question when Little Green broke in:

'I am sure it is very kind of our host to be so pressing. Don't you think, Madam, we might stay just a night or two, so as to have time to talk things over. You mustn't forget that some time ago you *did* agree to marry Mr. Hsü, and it's rather difficult for you now to take up such a stiff attitude towards him.'

'Mercy on me, or I'll die of shame,' rejoined Mrs. White. 'How can I, a lone female, possibly think of remaining under this roof?'

'If you really did once agree to marry him,' said the innkeeper's wife, 'I am sure you wouldn't want to go back on your word. You couldn't do better than look at the calendar to see which would be a lucky day, and have your wedding here.'

Hsü had been absolutely convinced that she was an evil spirit. But she completely cleared up every suspicious point in so convincing a way that in the end he could only suppose he had done her an injustice. Moreover, her great beauty could not fail to have some effect upon him. It was not long before he yielded to the persuasion of the innkeeper and his wife and agreed to the marriage. Mrs. White's purse seemed well supplied and they were both able to have a very good time. After their marriage her subtle and bewitching ways cast such a spell upon him that he was completely bemused. She seemed to him like an enchanted being from a happier world, and he only regretted that their marriage had so long been delayed.

Time passed quickly; they had been married for six months when one day in the middle of the second month Hsü went with some friends to look at the image of Buddha's Nirvana in the Nirvana Temple. At the gate of the temple he saw a Taoist selling herbs and distributing charms. For no particular reason Hsü went and watched him at his work. On catching sight of Hsü, the Taoist at once exclaimed in great consternation: 'Sir, there is a dark exhalation rising from the top of your head. It is certain that you are in the toils of an evil spirit, who has already done you great injury. You had better take care.'

All Hsü's former suspicions were at once revived. He fell upon his knees and begged the priest to save him. The Taoist then gave him two charms, telling him to burn one at the third watch and keep the other hidden in his hair. As soon as he reached home Hsü secretly hid the first charm in his hair and kept the other ready to burn when the third watch sounded. He was waiting for the hour to come, when Mrs. White suddenly heaved a deep sigh:

'To think that though we have lived together as man and wife all these months,' she said, 'you should have no trust in me at all, but only believe the evils that others say of me! At midnight, at the third watch, you mean to burn a charm and bedevil me. Well, burn your charm, and we shall see!'

Thus exposed, Hsü did not for the moment feel at all like carrying out his intention. But Mrs. White snatched the charm from him and taking it to the lamp she burnt it herself. The burning of the charm did not produce the slightest effect upon her, and she said, laughing: 'What about that? If I were a spirit, it would surely have made me appear in my true form?'

'It was not my idea,' said Hsü. 'At the temple I met an itinerant Taoist, who assured me that you were an evil spirit.'

'Very well then,' said Mrs. White. 'If he says I'm an evil spirit, let us go to him tomorrow and ask him to change me into my true form. Then you will know where you are.'

Next day they left Little Green in charge of their things and went off together to the temple. When they got there, the Taoist was in the act of handing round his charms, and he was surrounded by a great throng. Mrs. White stepped up confidently to the fringe of the crowd and called out in a loud voice: 'You ignorant low mountebank, what do you understand about it! How dare you come here with your devil pictures and demon spells, deceiving all the people with your gibberish?'

The Taoist was very much taken aback by this sudden assault. At the first glance he saw that there was a strange look in the lady's face, and knew that she was not what she appeared. 'I must warn you,' he said, 'that the art I practice is the magic of the Five Thunders and the Heavenly Heart. By its virtue all monsters and evil spirits who swallow my charms at once show themselves in their true form. Being what you are, I hardly imagine you would care to try the experiment?'

'Let these people be witness,' said she, smiling. 'Write out a charm, and you shall see me swallow it.'

He hurriedly wrote a charm and gave it to her. Quite calmly she took it from him, scrunched it into a ball, put it in her mouth and, having been handed a drink of water, she swallowed the charm right down. Then she stood for a while with a smile on her face. Nothing whatever happened to her, and the onlookers with one accord began to hurl abuse at the magician. 'Enough of your nonsense,' they cried. 'How dare you say that a fine, well-bred lady like this is an evil spirit?'

The Taoist, while they heaped abuse upon him, could only blink and gape. He had not a word to say.

'A miserable, strolling imposter like that, trying to take away the good name of a respectable married woman! The depths of Hell would be the proper place for him. But to spare the feelings of all you gentlemen, I will only give him a hanging.'

So saying, she muttered some kind of imprecation in a low voice and the Taoist immediately began to shrink into himself with his hands crossed in front of him, exactly as though he were being bound with a rope. Then he began gradually to leave the ground till he was hanging in mid-air, moaning and screaming all the while.

The astonished spectators acclaimed a miracle, and Hsü was so astounded that his wits almost forsook him.

'That will do for the present,' said Mrs. White. 'If it wasn't for knowing that the constable would butt in, I would gladly have let him stay there for a year.'

So saying, she blew gently in his direction and the Taoist at once sank to earth again. As soon as he recovered his footing he scampered off as fast as his legs would carry him, only wishing, as the saying goes, that his father and mother had not forgotten to provide his heels with wings. Soon he had vanished into the distance like a leaf whirled by the wind.

As for Hsü and Mrs. White, they went quietly home and continued to live much as they had done before this trouble arose between them.

Buddha's Birthday, the eighth day of the fourth month, came round and Hsü thought he would like to go to the Ch'êng-t'ien Temple and see the festival.

'I believe it's a wonderful sight,' said Mrs. White, and when the day came she put out new clothes for him to wear, and produced a gold-painted fan with a coral pendant, saying as she gave it to him, 'Come back in good time, or I shall be worried about you.'

He promised not to be away long, and decked out in all his finery he swaggered off to the temple, eager to join in the fun.

When he got there, he became aware that some exciting piece of news was being passed from mouth to mouth. The gist of this confused babble of talk seemed to be that a certain Pawnbroker Chou, on visiting his strong-room, had found that a considerable quantity of jewelry and clothing was missing, and that a warrant was out for the arrest of the thief. Hsü paid no particular attention to this news and had soon mingled with the crowd of worshippers and pleasure-seekers of both sexes who had come there to make holiday. He little suspected that the eye of the detectives, who had noticed that his clothes and fan corresponded closely to those described on their list, was already upon him. Presently someone stepped up to him and said very politely:

'I wonder if you would mind letting me have a look at that fan?'

Suspecting nothing, Hsü handed him the fan. There was no doubt that it was one of the missing objects described on the official list. The detective at once shouted:

'This is your man! The fan he is carrying is on the list.'

Immediately a number of men sprang forward and bound Hsü fast with rope. He began trying to explain matters, but no one listened. The Governor's court happened to be in session and Hsü was brought for immediate trial.

'You were arrested,' said the Governor, 'wearing clothes and carrying a fan that are described in a list of missing goods. Where are the jewelry and other valuables? A true confession on your part will save you from a thrashing.'

'The things I am wearing and the fan,' said Hsü, 'please your Worship, were given to me by my wife; I did not steal them. I beg your Worship to make a thorough investigation.'

'Nonsense!' said the Governor. 'The things correspond exactly to those described on the list, and it is no use trying to put it on to your wife. And where is your wife at present?'

'At Mr. Wang's inn, Sir,' said Hsü, 'at the Chi-li Bridge.'

The Governor then told his men to take Hsü to the inn, arrest the person whom he identified as his wife and bring her back for interrogation.

'What's all this about?' asked Mr. Wang, astonished to see his inn invaded by this crowd.

'Mrs. White has got me into trouble,' said Hsü, 'and they have come to arrest her.'

'She isn't here,' said the innkeeper. 'When you didn't come back from the temple, she and Little Green went there to look for you and never came home.'

When the police heard that Mrs. White was not there, they put the handcuffs on Mr. Wang instead and brought him back to court.

'A lady looking for her husband is not likely to be anywhere very far away,' said the Governor. 'I shall make Mr. Wang responsible for finding her. The defendant Hsü is to remain in custody till this Mrs. White can be produced. I will then go into the matter again and give judgement.'

Pawnbroker Chou was in court, listening to the proceedings, and suddenly at this moment one of his servants rushed up to him and announced that all the missing objects had been found, in an old, empty box in the gallery of the strong-room. The pawnbroker went home and found that everything was there, except the fan with the coral pendant.

'It's clear it wouldn't be fair to convict him only on the score of the fan,' said the pawnbroker. 'There might be another just like it.'

He went back to the Governor's office and privately informed the official in charge of the matter that a fresh situation had arisen, and asked that Hsü might be released. The case was therefore not proceeded with; but it was decided that Hsü was 'unsuited to the locality' and he was 're-allocated' to Chên-chiang.

It so happened that just when he was about to start, Commander Shao sent Secretary Li to do some business for him at Soochow. Li remembered about Hsü and hurried to Wang's inn to see what had become of him. Hearing that he was being moved to Chên-chiang, he said to Hsü:

'I have an old friend at Chên-chiang, who allows me to call him "uncle". His name is Li K'o-yung and he keeps a drug-store near the Needle Bridge. I'll give you a letter for him. You'd be very well off at his place.'

Hsü took the letter and in a few days arrived with his escort at Chên-chiang. They went straight to Li K'o-yung's house, and he delivered the letter, saying:

'I am the brother-in-law of Secretary Li at Hangchow. I have a letter from him here in which he asks you to do what you can for me.'

Li K'o-yung read the letter and at once asked two of the officials who were in charge of Hsü to come in and have something to eat, while at the same time he asked those who were still on duty to come with him and Hsü to the Governor's office, to clear their papers. Here, by a discreet outlay of money, he obtained permission for Hsü to lodge with him, provided that he stood security, and came home. The escort obtained their certificate, and went away. When Hsü got back, he fell on his knees and heartily thanked K'o-yung. The letter had mentioned that Hsü had worked as overseer in a drug-shop, and K'o-yung asked him to stay and work for a time in his own shop.

After watching him for several days, he saw that he understood the business thoroughly and was quite delighted with him. Hsü was afraid that the other assistants might resent his intrusion, so he invited them all to have a drink in a wine-shop, just to get on friendly terms with them. When the party had broken up and Hsü paid the bill and gone out into the street, he became aware that he was a little unsteady on his legs and, fearing that he might bump into people, he was careful to walk well to the side of the road, right under the eaves of the houses, watching his step all the while. Suddenly an upper window was flung open and someone emptied out some water, which only just missed him. Hsü halted.

'A nice wife you'd be to have about the place!' he shouted. 'Haven't you got any eyes in your head?'

The woman came running downstairs. 'Don't scold me!' she said. 'I didn't do it on purpose.'

He looked up, and who should it be but Mrs. White! Hsü burst into a terrible rage.

'Thief, sorceress,' he screamed, 'how many more times do you intend to be the undoing of me? Already you have put me twice in dock on a criminal charge. So this is where you came to hide when you disappeared from Soochow!' So saying, he rushed forward and seized her, crying: 'This time, believe me, matters are not going to be settled out of court!'

'You know the saying,' she answered smiling, '"one night as man and wife: a hundred nights' pardon". There's no need to be so hasty. Just let me explain matters to you, and if you think I acted wrongly, be as angry as you please! The clothes and fan I gave you that day all belonged to my late husband, and were honestly come by. It was only because I loved you so dearly that I wanted you to wear them. How could I have foreseen that they would be wrongly identified? That was fated in your horoscope; it was no fault of mine.'

'How was it,' asked Hsü, 'that when I came back to look for you at the inn, you were not to be seen, and have now turned up here?'

'When I went to look for you at the temple,' said she, 'I heard that you had been arrested. I felt certain that I should be implicated and, anxious to preserve my good name, I made Little Green hire a small boat and came here to stay with my mother's brother till I got further news of you. That was only my duty. I married you, and "am yours till death and after". Never would I dream of running away from you. And now that we have had the good fortune to meet again, no matter how great the difficulties, I do not mean to send you away.'

She went on coaxing and cajoling him till he was completely won over and the rage that at first had filled his whole heart entirely subsided.

'So you have been looking for me ever since you came to live here?' he said at last.

'Who else should I be looking for?' she said. 'But come upstairs.'

He trailed upstairs after her, in a state of abject collapse.

He spent the night there. They were again on the most affectionate terms; presently he moved his belongings and they lived as man and wife exactly as before. On Li K'o-yung the apothecary's birthday they bought some candles, pastries, handkerchiefs and other small presents and went to his house to congratulate him. They found that he had set out mats and was entertaining his friends and relations with wine.

Now Li K'o-yung was of a very amorous disposition. He noticed at once that Mrs. White was uncommonly good-looking, and he kept on stealing covert glances at her. After a time, Mrs. White wanted to retire for a moment and the children's nurse was told to show her where to go. Li K'o-yung slipped into a corner and, waiting till Mrs. White was in the back yard, he tip-toed after her and peered through a chink in the door. What he saw was very different from what he expected. Here was no lady 'fair as flower or jade', but a huge white snake, stout as a well-bucket, lying coiled upon the privy. Its eyes, like two great lamps, blazed with a golden light. Li K'o-yung was scared to death. He rushed away, and had just turned the corner when his legs gave way beneath him and he lay unconscious on the ground, with green face and purple lips. Here he was found by the nurse, who told Li K'o-yung's old mother. She and the manager of the drug-store administered a dose of life restorer, and he began to come round. The old lady at once asked what had been the cause of the attack. He was, of course, unable to give the real reason, and only said:

'I have been out of sorts for several days and suddenly felt a bit dizzy. But please don't let me spoil the party.'

When the guests had taken their leave, Mrs. White reappeared. Being afraid that when they were together in the shop, Li K'o-yung would tell Hsü what he had seen, she thought out a plan, and in accordance with it she sighed heavily.

'A party of this kind is surely a cheerful occasion,' said Hsü. 'Why are you sighing?'

'I hardly like to tell you,' she said. 'You have always told me that this Li K'o-yung was a nice old man. It's all a pretence on his part. Would you believe it, when he saw me get up to leave the room, he slipped round behind me and tried to seduce me! He tore open my dress, and started fondling me. I began to scream, but then I thought of all those people sitting inside and did not like to put him publicly to shame. So I threw him to the ground and managed to slip away. But I had such a fright, I don't know how I shall ever work it off.'

'Well,' said Hsü, 'he doesn't seem to have done any real harm, and as he is my master, there is nothing we can do except put up with it. But you had better not go there again.'

'I've still got twenty or thirty taels of silver put away,' she said. 'As things are, why don't you part from him, and set up a small drug-shop of your own on the quays? Wouldn't you rather be your own master?'

'All right,' said Hsü, and went off to discuss the matter with Li K'o-yung, who, having had this fright, was not at all anxious to keep him.

The new shop was a great success and business improved every day. The seventh of the seventh month came round, which the people keep as the Dragon King's Birthday. Hsü wanted to go and burn incense, but Mrs. White was very much against it. Seeing that he had quite made up his mind, she said at last:

'Well, if you must go, keep to the big halls in front and at the back of the temple. Whatever you do, don't go into the priest's cells, chatting with those baldheads, or they will be pestering you for alms.'

'I won't if you don't want me to,' he said. 'Just as you please!'

He went to the river, took a boat and made straight for the Temple of the Golden Hill. He went first to the Hall of the Dragon King and burnt incense, and then strolled about, just to have a look round. Without thinking what he was doing, he wandered into the priests' quarters. He saw a number of priests gathered together round someone who was apparently preaching a sermon. He had no sooner set foot there than he remembered his wife's injunction and beat a hasty retreat. But the preacher had already noticed him and, remarking to his hearers, 'There is a very bedevilled look in that man's face,' he asked one of his attendants to tell Hsü that he should like to have a word with him. By the time the attendant reached the doorway, Hsü had already left. Seeing that the visitor was giving them the slip, the preacher picked up his Meditation Staff and himself set out in pursuit. When he reached the terrace in front of the temple he saw that a great crowd of people who wanted to cross the river were standing at the gate, waiting for a heavy gale to subside. Suddenly, in the very heart of the stream, he saw a small boat flying through the waves at a tremendous speed.

'Look at that little boat!' the people cried out in astonishment. 'Fancy it putting out in a storm like this! And what a pace it's going at, too!'

Hsü, who was standing in the middle of the crowd, stretched himself in order to see over the heads of the people. To his surprise he saw that the two figures standing in the prow of the little boat were Mrs. White and Little Green. He was about, in his amazement, to ask them why they had come, when Mrs. White called out to him from afar:

'Husband, there is a high wind, so we thought we had better come to fetch you. Come down to the river and get on board at once!'

For the moment it really seemed the best thing to do, and he was just going down to the boat, which was now nearing the shore, when the preacher caught sight of him from behind and called out to Mrs. White in a loud voice:

'Monster, what brings you to this place?'

So saying, he raised his staff and was just about to strike out at her, when Mrs. White, Little Green and the boat disappeared under the waves.

Hsü was so horrified and amazed that his soul scarcely clove to his body.

'Who is this priest?' he hurriedly asked the people standing by.

'He is the Master of the Ocean of Law,' said someone who knew the priest, 'and he is reckoned as the Living Buddha of the day.'

The man was about to tell more, when the Master sent one of his attendants to bring Hsü Hsüan to speak to him.

'Where did you first meet this monster?' he asked.

Thus questioned, Hsü told him the whole story from the very beginning.

'No doubt this meeting was determined by your *karma*,' said the priest. 'But only an uncommon degree of physical passion could have led you to fall again and again into so blind and senseless an infatuation. Happily, your ordeals are now nearly over. Go back at once to Hangchow and practise constant devotions. If you have any trouble with her again, come and see me at the Temple of Pure Mercy, to the south of the Lake.'

Hsü warmly thanked the priest and hurried home, to find that Mrs. White and Little Green had indeed disappeared. There was, of course, no longer the slightest doubt in his mind that they were both evil spirits.

Early next morning he went to Needle Bridge and told the apothecary Li K'o-yung what had happened.

'As a matter of fact,' said Li, 'I saw her in her true form when she came here on my birthday, and was frightened nearly to death. But I was annoyed at your setting up on your own, so I didn't feel like saying anything about it. But now that the matter has been cleared up, I don't see any objection to your coming back and living here for the present.'

However, a few days later a general amnesty was declared and all offenders, except those guilty of very heinous crimes, were allowed to return to their homes. Hsü was delighted to hear this news, and having thanked Li K'o-yung for all his kindness, he went back to

Hangchow and at once called upon his brother-in-law and sister, before whom he prostrated himself four times. When his prostrations were over, Secretary Li said to him reproachfully:

'On two successive occasions when you got into trouble with the authorities, I took a good deal of trouble to help you, and I think you might at least have sent me a wedding-card just to let me know that you had got married during your absence. It seems to me inexcusable.'

'But I haven't got a wife,' said Hsü, 'and I don't know why you should suppose that I have.'

He had not finished speaking when his sister came out from the back rooms, accompanied by Mrs. White and Little Green!

'I don't know why you shouldn't own up,' said Hsü's sister. 'It's not a crime to get married, and anyhow, here *is* your wife!'

'No, no, Sister,' cried Hsü, utterly dismayed, 'she is an evil spirit. Do not believe a word she says.'

At this point Mrs. White joined in the conversation.

'Since we became man and wife', she said, 'I have never failed in my duty towards you. Why should you listen to what strangers tell you and let them estrange you from me? If you disown me, what is to become of me? As a married woman I have no other home but yours.' So saying, she burst into a frenzy of convulsive sobbing.

Hsü, quite beside himself, dragged his brother-in-law to the door and hastily told him of all that had happened. 'There is not the slightest doubt,' he said, 'that she is a White Snake Spirit. Surely there must be some way of getting rid of her.'

'If she is really a snake,' said Secretary Li, 'there ought not to be any difficulty. There is a snake-charmer called Dr. Tai who lives opposite the White Horse Shrine. He's extremely clever at catching snakes. I'll go with you and arrange for him to come here and catch her. That's the thing to do.'

They found Dr. Tai standing in his doorway. 'What can I do for you two gentlemen?' he asked at once.

'There's a large white snake in my house,' said Secretary Li, 'and we want you to catch it for us. Here is a tael of silver, and you shall have something more for your trouble when the snake is caught.'

Dr. Tai took the money and asked what address he was to come to. 'You gentlemen go home,' he said, 'and I'll follow you presently.'

He hastily prepared a jar of red orpiment and a jar of boiled medicine-water, and went round to Li's house. He was met by Hsü, who directed him to the inner apartments. Dr. Tai found the door that led to the women's quarters locked.

'Is anyone there?' he said, knocking.

'Who are you,' a voice asked, 'and what right have you to be here?'

'A very good right indeed,' said Dr. Tai. 'I was specially asked to come and catch a snake.'

Mrs. White realized at once that Hsü had sent for him to catch her.

'There's a snake here all right,' she said laughing. 'But I doubt if you will be able to catch it.'

'My family has been in this line of business for seven or eight generations,' said Dr. Tai, 'famous snake-catchers, all of them. I should be surprised if this particular job was beyond my powers.'

The door suddenly opened.

'If you are so sure you can catch it, then come in!' she said.

He pushed aside the curtain and was just about to enter the room when there swept past him through the doorway a gust of dank wind, so icy-cold that his hair stood on end and he saw a huge serpent, as big round as a well-bucket and with eyes like great lamps, shooting itself straight at him. This sudden apparition so startled him that he fell over backwards, and his orpiment bowl and medicine jar were smashed to pieces. The snake opened its great blood-red mouth, bared its snow-white fangs and made as though to bite Dr. Tai. In the nick of time he scrambled to his feet and ran for his life back to the reception hall, where he was met by Secretary Li and Hsü Hsüan.

'Well, how did the snake-catching go?' asked Secretary Li.

'You can have your money back,' said Dr. Tai. 'Snakes I can deal with, but not fiends. This job nearly cost me my life.' And without turning his head, he rushed out of the house.

For a moment Hsü and the Secretary stood face to face, utterly nonplussed. Soon, however, they heard the voice of Mrs. White calling to Hsü to come to her.

'What effrontery,' she cried, 'to send for a snake-catcher to catch me! Look here, once and for all! If you treat me properly, I'll do anything in the world for you. But if you don't, I shall bring a hideous end not on you only, but upon this whole city and everyone in it!'

When Hsü heard this, his heart turned cold and his gall quaked. Not daring to say a word in reply, he rushed out into the street and left the town by the Clear Wave Gate. Here he hesitated for a while, not knowing what to do next. Suddenly he remembered the Master of the Ocean of Law, and how he had said to him, 'If you have any more trouble, go to the Temple of Pure Mercy and ask for me'. As his feet had carried him at random as far as this, why not go a little farther and try to get help from the Master? He went on to the Temple of Pure Mercy and asked the superintendent if the Master of the Ocean of Law ever visited the temple.

'No,' said the superintendent, 'he has never been here.'

Deprived of this last hope and not daring to go home, Hsü fled to the Long Bridge and, staring at the blue waters of the Lake, he said to himself, 'Surely it would be better to put an end to all this by my own death, rather than live on only to involve others in my calamity?'

He was just going to jump in, when a voice behind him said, 'Young man, why are you throwing away your life? If you are in trouble, let us talk it over together.'

He turned his head and saw that it was the Master of the Ocean of Law hastening towards him in his cassock, with his alms-bowl slung over his back and his Meditation Staff in his hand.

'Save me from death, oh, save me!' cried Hsü, kneeling in a posture of utter submission.

'Where is the monster now?' asked the Master.

'In my brother-in-law's house,' said Hsü.

'Go quietly home,' said the Master, handing his alms-bowl to Hsü, 'and when your wife is not looking ram this bowl down on to her head. Don't just put it there, but press it down with all the strength in your body. You have nothing to be afraid of. I know what I am about.'

He thanked the Master heartily, and went home, where he found Mrs. White, no longer in serpent form, sitting in the parlour hurling the foulest abuse at everyone, right and left. He slipped up stealthily behind her when she was not looking and rammed the bowl down on her head, using all the strength in his body. He went on pressing and pressing, down and down, till at last the bowl completely covered her and she could not be seen at all. But even then he dared not let go, but went on pressing down the bowl with all his might. Then suddenly a voice spoke from inside the bowl:

'How can you bear to inflict this miserable death upon me after we have lived so many years together as man and wife? Let go for a moment, I entreat you. It is not much to ask.'

He was just wondering what to do next when someone announced that there was a priest waiting outside, who said he had come to exorcize an evil spirit. Hsü at once asked Secretary Li to go and let him in.

'I've got her safe in here,' said Hsü when the Master arrived. 'I must ask your Reverence to dispose of her.'

The Master muttered some unintelligible spell, and then lifted the alms-bowl. There lay Mrs. White, shrunk to only about seven or eight inches long, face downward, looking for all the world like a discarded puppet.

'What cursed monster are you,' roared the priest, 'that you have dared molest a human being? I charge you to confess.'

'I was a white python,' she answered. 'During a great storm I and a green fish came for shelter to the Western Lake. We happened to meet Hsü Hsüan, and I became so enamoured of him that I could not contain myself and broke the laws of Nature. Fortunately, whatever else I have done, I have inflicted mortal injury on no one, and I look to your Reverence to show compassion to me.'

'Sins of the flesh,' said the Master, 'are a very serious matter and cannot be overlooked. But in view of the self-discipline that you exercised for so many hundred years, you shall not be utterly annihilated. Now show yourself in your true form!'

Mrs. White at once turned into a white snake and Little Green into a green fish. The white snake raised its head and looked at Hsü.

The Master put both creatures into his alms-bowl, pulled down a fold of his dress so that it covered the top of the bowl and carried it to the Thunder Peak Temple. Here he put the bowl down and got workmen to bring stone and brick and build a pagoda on top of it. Hsü Hsüan then appealed to the faithful and collected so large a sum that the pagoda was carried to a height of seven storeys, so that the white snake and green fish might never be able to come out again into the world of men. After they were safely pinned down, the Master pronounced the following quatrain:

> Sooner shall the Western Lake run dry
> Than the Thunder Peak Pagoda fall
> Sooner shall the river tide not rise,
> Than the White Snake come back into the world.

When the Master had recited this verse, the people did homage and scattered. But Hsü earnestly desired to take Orders. He took the Master of the Ocean of Law for his teacher and was finally tonsured and ordained standing under the pagoda. He lived piously for many years and then one night died suddenly, without illness. The priests brought a pyx, cremated him and put his ashes under a cairn in front of the pagoda.

Marvels are for the most part not worth relating. But it is a marvel that has made the Thunder Peak famous among the wonders of the Western Lake. So those who admire the Thunder Peak Pagoda will of necessity wish to acquaint themselves with the strange story of its origin.

[*Translated from the Chinese by* ARTHUR WALEY]

HERMANN HESSE

A LIFE IN BRIEF[1]

During the early post-war years I made two attempts to give a kind of summary bird's-eye view of my life for the benefit of my friends, to whom at that time I had become somewhat of a problem; they were written in fairy-tale form and in a semi-humoristic vein. The first of these remained a mere fragment, 'The Magician's Childhood'; the second was a venture, in the manner of Jean Paul, to forecast my future. It was entitled 'A Conjectural Biography' and appeared in the *Neue Rundschau* in Berlin in 1925. In the present story this has been subjected to only a few unimportant corrections—it had been my intention for several years to unite both works in some way, but until now I had been unable to find a suitable means of reconciling the two that are so different in tone and mood.

I WAS born towards the end of the Modern Age—shortly before the world started to slip back into the Middle Ages—under the sign of Sagittarius, with a favourable aspect of Jupiter. My birth took place in the early evening of a warm July day, and the temperature of that hour is something that I have sought and loved unconsciously all my

[1] By permission of Rochefort Productions (Literary Property) Ltd. Copyright by the author.

life, and which when absent I have felt to be painfully lacking. I could never bear living in cold countries, and all my voluntary journeys have been towards the South. I was a child of pious parents whom I loved tenderly, and whom I should have loved even more tenderly had they not made me acquainted too early in life with the Fourth Commandment. Unfortunately commandments have always had a fatal effect upon me, however just and well-meaning they may have been; I who am by nature as docile as a lamb and pliant as a soap-bubble have, even from earliest youth, deliberately set my face against commandments of any kind. I had only to hear the words 'Thou shalt not' for everything that was in me to rise up in revolt, and for me to become stubborn and intractable. It is easy to understand that this peculiarity had a very disadvantageous effect upon my school years. Our masters taught us, in that amusing branch of study which they called World History, that the world had always been ruled, guided and changed by men who had broken with the laws of their ancestors and had made their own laws, and we were told that these men were worthy of reverence. Only this was just as much of a lie as all their remaining teachings, for if one of us, whether with good or evil intent, ventured to show courage and protest against some commandment, foolish custom or convention, he was neither revered nor held up as an example, but was punished, ridiculed and repressed by the cowardly authority of the teacher.

Fortunately I had already learnt the most important and valuable things in life before going to school. I had fine, alert and delicate senses, upon which I could rely and from which I could draw much enjoyment; and even if at a later date I was to fall incurably under the allurement of metaphysics, and may at times have mortified and neglected my senses, it is the atmosphere of a tenderly developed sensuousness in matters of sight and hearing that has remained constant and true to me and plays a living part in the world of my thoughts, even when they appear to be abstract. I had therefore a certain equipment for life, which as I have already mentioned I had acquired before my school years. I was familiar with the ins and outs of our town, the chicken-yard, the woods and the workshops of the craftsmen; I knew the trees, birds and butterflies; I could sing songs and whistle through my teeth, and much beside that makes life worth while. To this, of course, must be added the knowledge obtained at school that came easily to me and amused me: for example, I took a real pleasure in the Latin tongue, and composed Latin as well as German verses at a very early age. For the art of lying and diplomacy I must thank my second year at school, when a tutor and a junior master put me in possession of this faculty after I had brought down upon myself one misfortune after another as a result of my childish frankness and candour. Both these teachers clearly and successfully enlightened me of the fact that honesty and the love of truth were not characteristics that they looked for in their pupils. They blamed me for a misdemeanour—quite a trivial one—that had taken place in the classroom, of which I was completely innocent, and as they could not bring me to admit that I was the culprit a veritable state-trial ensued. They whipped and tortured me; but far from wringing from me the desired confession, they succeeded only in scourging out of me any belief I may have had in the propriety of the teaching profession. In the course of time, thank goodness, I came to know teachers who were just and worthy of respect, but the damage was done: not only my relationship with my schoolmasters but with authority as a whole was falsified and embittered. Generally speaking I was a good scholar during the first seven or eight years of my schooldays—at least I was always among the first pupils in my class. Only when that conflict began—which no one who is destined to be a personality is spared—did I become more and more at odds with the school. Some twenty years later I was to understand the full significance of those struggles, but at the time they were very real and all-embracing, and brought me, much against my desire, the greatest unhappiness.

The fact was that I wanted to be a poet—a poet and nothing else. From my thirteenth year onwards I was quite clear in this conviction. But gradually I became aware of another painful fact: it was possible to become a teacher, a parson, a doctor, a craftsman, tradesman or post office official, also a musician, painter or architect, for towards every vocation in the world there led a path, there were preliminaries, a school, a course of study for the beginner; but for the poet there was nothing. It was permissible and even an honour to be a poet—that is to say a well-known and successful poet, but unfortunately in the majority of cases one was by that time already dead—but to *become* one, that was impossible; to *wish* to become one a farce and a scandal, as I soon learned. I quickly absorbed all there was to know of the situation. A poet was something one must be, not something one should try to become; furthermore, an interest in poetry and individual poetic talent made one suspect to the teachers, and in consequence one was either distrusted, ridiculed or even grossly insulted. The poet, at one with the hero and with all strong, beautiful, courageous and unusual figures and efforts was magnificent in the past, and every schoolbook sings his praises; but in the present and in reality he was hated—and presumably the teachers were appointed and trained expressly to prevent the development of free and complete human beings, and the possibility of great and noble deeds being performed.

I saw nothing but an abyss stretching between myself and my far-off goal, everything became uncertain and devalued and only one fact remained constant: I wished to become a poet whether it were difficult or easy, whether it were laughable or laudable. The external consequences of this decision—in fact this curse—were as follows.

At the age of thirteen, when the struggle had already begun, my conduct left so much to be desired both at home and at school that I was banished to a grammar school in another town. A year later I became a pupil in a theological seminary, where I learned the Hebrew alphabet and came near to grasping the significance of the Dagesch *forte implicitum*; when suddenly the storm broke. It welled up from within and completely engulfed me, leading to my flight from the monastery school, to punishment with rigid detention, and finally to my expulsion from the seminary.

For a while I took pains to advance my studies in a college, but there, too, detention and dismissal were my lot. For three days I became a tradesman's apprentice, ran away once more, and for several days and nights caused my parents great anxiety by my disappearance. For six months I helped my father, and then for a year and a half I was taken on as a probationer in a mechanical workshop and turret-clock factory.

In short, for more than four whole years everything I did that was required of me went awry, no school would keep me, and I could hold no apprenticeship for any length of time. Every attempt to make a useful citizen of me failed, often with shame and scandal, flight or dismissal. And yet it was generally admitted that I was talented and even that my intentions were honest. In addition to this I was always passably diligent—I have always admired the high virtue of idleness with awe, but have never been an adept in the art.

At the age of fifteen, after I had failed at school, I began consciously and energetically to educate myself; it was fortunate, and proved a source of constant joy to me, that there was in my father's house a huge ancestral library, a whole roomful of old books, which contained among other treasures the entire German poetry and philosophy of the eighteenth century. Between my sixteenth and twentieth years, not only did I cover reams of paper with my own poetic efforts, but during those years I read half the classic literature of the world as well as the history of art, and studied languages and philosophy with a tenacity that would have been amply sufficient for a normal school course.

Then I became a bookseller in order at last to be able to earn my own living. In any case, I had much more in common with books than with the vices and cast-iron cog-wheels that had tormented me so much as a mechanic. At first this plunge into the new and newest literature was an almost intoxicating pleasure, but I soon realized that spiritually life in the mere present is insupportable and senseless, and that a spiritual life is made possible only by a steadfast relationship with the past, with history and with the old and age-old. So, after my preliminary pleasure had been exhausted, I felt a need to revert from this spate of modernity to the ancient, and I accomplished this by transferring to an antiquarian bookseller. I remained faithful to this vocation, however, only so long as I needed it to earn my own living. At the age of twenty-six, as a result of my first literary success, I gave this up as well.

And so at last, after many storms and sacrifices, my goal was reached. I had, incredible as it seemed, become a poet, and had apparently won in my long tough struggle with the world. The bitterness of my school and adolescent years, to which I often so nearly succumbed, was now laughed at and forgotten; relations and friends, who had previously despaired of me, now smiled amicably. I had won. Now my stupidest and most worthless actions were found enchanting—and I too was extremely enchanted with myself. I noticed for the first time in what abominable loneliness, asceticism and danger I had lived for so many years; the warm air of recognition did me good, and I began to be a contented man.

For a good while my outward life followed a calm and pleasant course. I had a wife, children, and a house with a garden. I wrote my books and was esteemed as an amiable poet, and I lived at peace with the world. In 1905 I helped to found a periodical which was directed primarily against the personal government of Wilhelm II, without however taking these political aims too seriously. I travelled extensively in Switzerland, Germany, Austria, Italy and India. Everything seemed to be in order.

Then came the summer of 1914, and both internally and externally everything took on a different aspect. It appeared that our former prosperity had been based on unsure foundations, and that now a period of adversity, that great Educator, was beginning. The so-called Heroic Age had dawned, and I cannot say that it struck me as being any better equipped, worthier or more heroic than all the others. The one thing that made me different from most of my fellow men was that I was lacking in that great consolation that so many of them seemed to possess—enthusiasm. I was brought violently back to earth, and found myself once again in conflict with myself and the outside world; I had to return to school for a second time, I had once again to unlearn the contentment I had felt with myself and my fellows, and with this experience cross over the threshold of initiation into life. I have never forgotten a trifling experience that happened to me during the first year of the war: I was on a visit to a large military hospital, where I was trying to enrol as a volunteer and to adapt myself intelligently to this changed world. It then still seemed to me possible. In that hospital for the wounded I met an old spinster who had been in good circumstances before the war, and who was now doing her duty as a nurse. She told me with touching enthusiasm how glad she was that she had been allowed to live through this Heroic Age. I found this comprehensible, because for this lady it had required a war to make her change her lazy and selfish elderly spinsterhood for an active and worthier life. But as she informed me of her good fortune in a corridor full of bandaged and mutilated soldiers, which ran between wards filled to overflowing with the disabled and the dying, my heart turned right over; and yet, although I understood this good woman's enthusiasm so completely, I could neither share it nor approve of it. If ten wounded soldiers were needed to bring happiness to each enthusiastic hospital nurse, then the price was far too high.

No, I could not share in the joy over the Heroic Age. From the very beginning I suffered miserably under the war, and defended myself desperately year after year against a misfortune that seemed to have fallen from outside and from out of a clear sky, while all around me the world behaved as though it were enchanted by this misfortune. And when in the newspapers I read articles by writers who purported to have discovered the blessings of war, the exhortations of the professors, and all the war-poems from the studios of famous poets, I was even more wretched.

One day in 1915 I let slip an admission of this misery in public, and added a word of regret that even the so-called men of the spirit found nothing better to do than to preach hatred, spread falsehoods and hold the great misfortune in high esteem. The result of this modestly outspoken regret was that I was declared a traitor to my country in the newspapers—a new experience for me, for, despite several clashes with the Press, I had never yet been in the position of one who is spat upon by the majority. The article which contained this particular indictment appeared in twenty different papers in Germany, and of all the friends I thought I had among the journalists, only two dared to speak on my behalf. Old friends informed me that they had nursed a viper in their bosoms, and that their hearts no longer beat for me, the degenerate, but for the Kaiser and their Country. Anonymous letters of abuse came in their hundreds, and booksellers let me know that an author with such subversive views no longer interested them. I became acquainted for the first time with a pretty little ornament with which many of these letters were adorned: it was a little round stamp bearing the inscription *Gott strafe England*. One might have thought that I laughed heartily at this lack of understanding on their part, but I could not bring myself to do so. This experience, in itself so unimportant, brought about the second great transformation of my life.

It will be remembered that the first change occurred at the moment when I consciously made the decision to become a poet. The former model pupil Hesse had from then on become a bad scholar, had been punished and thrown out, could do nothing right, and had caused himself and his parents care upon care—and all this only because he could see no possible reconciliation between the world as it was, or seemed to be, and the voice of his own heart. This repeated itself anew during the war years. Once again I saw myself in conflict with the world in which I had hitherto lived in peace. Once again everything failed me, I was alone and wretched, and all that I said and did met with misunderstanding and hostility. Again I saw a hopeless abyss yawning between reality and that which to me seemed desirable, reasonable and good.

But this time I was not spared a heart-searching. It was not long before I found that I would have to look within myself for the source of my suffering and not in the outside world, for I saw clearly that no man or God, let alone I, had the right to accuse the whole world of madness and brutality. There must therefore have been some disorder within myself that had brought me into conflict with the world: and in truth there did exist a great disorder. It was by no means a pleasant task to come to grips with it and try to achieve some reintegration. One thing was quite certain: my former good relations with the world had not only been too dearly bought but had become as hollow as the peace of the outside world. I had thought, by reason of the long and difficult struggles of my youth, to have earned my place in society, and at last to have become a poet, but in the meantime success and prosperity had had their usual influence upon me, and I had become contented and complacent—and when I looked closely, as a writer I was hardly distinguishable from the popular light novelist. I had become too prosperous, and now that adversity, which is always a hard and energetic school, had brought its host of cares, I learnt more and more to let the affairs of the world take their own course and to busy myself with my own part in the chaos and guilt of the whole. I must leave it to my readers to study the effects of this preoccupation in my writings. Yet I always nourished the secret hope that in time my people too—not as a whole, but perhaps large numbers of aware and responsible individuals among them—would undertake a similar scrutiny of themselves, and that instead of laments and abuse against the evil war, the evil enemy and the evil revolution, the questions would be raised in a thousand hearts: how am I personally responsible, and how can I free myself from guilt? For innocence can always be recaptured when one recognizes one's sorrow and guilt, and suffers to the end instead of searching for the guilt in others.

As this new change began to appear in my life and writings, many of my friends shook their heads, many of them also forsook me. But all that belonged to the changed image of my life—just as the loss of my house, my family and other possessions and comforts. This was a period of daily farewells, and every day I was astonished that I could suffer it all and still live, that I could still love anything in this strange life that seemed to bring nothing but pain, disappointment and loss.

However, I must add that even during the war years I had something in the nature of a good star or a guardian angel. Although I felt very much alone in my suffering, and up to the beginning of my transformation found my fate a perpetually unhappy and undesirable one, this very suffering and my distracted state served as a protection and armour against the outside world. I spent the war years in such an abysmal environment of politics, espionage, corruption and opportunism as even in those times it would have been difficult to find in many parts of the world in so concentrated a form. Actually it was in Berne, the centre of German, neutral and enemy diplomacy, a town that overnight had become over-populated with diplomats, political agents, spies, journalists, speculators and profiteers. I lived among diplomats and soldiers, and associated with men of many and often enemy nations, and the air around me was a veritable network of espionage and counter-espionage, informing, intrigues, political and private activities—and of all this during those years I noticed absolutely nothing! I was pumped, informed against and spied upon, was suspected, alternately by the enemy, the neutrals and my own countrymen; and noticed nothing at all. Only long afterwards did I learn some of the details for the first time, and could not understand how I had managed to survive untouched and undamaged in this atmosphere—but it had been so.

With the end of the war my transformation was complete: my ordeal of self-scrutiny had reached its peak. My sufferings had nothing more to do with the war or the fate of the world at large, nor did the thought of Germany's defeat, which we abroad had foreseen for the past two years with certainty, hold any further terrors. I was sunk completely within myself and in my own destiny, but I had the impression at times that I was grappling with the fate of Man as a whole. I found mirrored within myself all war, all the blood lust of the world, all the irresponsibility, coarse sensationalism and cowardice of Man. I had first to lose my self-respect, and then my self-contempt . . . and finally nothing remained but to plumb the depths of Chaos in the hope, alternately rising and falling, of rediscovering nature and innocence once more beyond. Every aware and truly enlightened man—it would be a sheer waste of effort to speak of the others—at one time or another takes this narrow path through the wilderness.

Sometimes when friends abandoned me I felt a certain grief, but never discomfort. I looked upon their estrangement as a substantiation of my chosen path. These former friends were quite right when they affirmed that previously I had been a sympathetic poet and human being, whereas now, in my present problematical phase, I was simply intolerable. On questions of taste and character I had by this time advanced to a point where there was no one among them to whom my language was intelligible. Their reproaches were probably justified when they told me that my writings had lost their beauty and harmony. Such statements only made me laugh, for what is beauty or harmony to a man who is condemned to death, or who is running for his life from beneath collapsing walls? Perhaps, contrary to my lifelong belief, I was not a poet at all, and the whole of my aesthetic activity had been a mistake. Why not indeed? But even that was no longer of any importance.

Most of that in which I had come to believe during my infernal journey had proved worthless and a fraud, including perhaps my frenzied belief in my vocation and talents. Yet how insignificant that was now. What I had once envisaged with conceit and childish joy as my mission in life was no longer there. I saw my task—or rather my way of salvation—no longer in the realms of lyrical poetry or philosophy, or any other similar specialized art form, but only in allowing that little that was truly vital and strong in me to live its life, only in absolute fidelity towards that which I still felt living within me. That was life, that was God. Later, when such times of high and perilous tension are over, everything looks strangely different, because the erstwhile contents and their nomenclature become meaningless, and that which was holy yesterday may sound almost ludicrous today.

As, in the spring of 1919, the war at last came to an end for me too, I retired to a remote corner of Switzerland and became a hermit. Because all my life (and this was a legacy from my parents and grandparents) I had been deeply engrossed in the wisdom of the Indians and the Chinese, and because I partly expressed my new experiences in Oriental metaphor, I was frequently referred to as a 'Buddhist'; but at this I could only laugh, because I knew in my heart that no one could be further removed from that belief than myself. And yet there was a grain of truth in it, as I was to learn later. If it were somehow conceivable that a man might choose his own religion, I know that I personally, due to my innermost yearnings, should have chosen a conservative one—such as Confucianism, Brahmanism, or the Catholic Church. I should have made this choice out of a desire for the antithesis and not because of an innate affinity, for it was only by chance that I was born the son of pious Protestants: I am a Protestant by nature and disposition (hence my great antipathy to modern Protestantism shows no contradiction). The true Protestant defends himself against his own Church and others alike, for his nature accepts more easily the 'becoming' than the 'being'; in this sense Buddha too was a Protestant. My belief in my craft and in the value of my literary work had been uprooted since my transformation, and writing no longer gave me any real pleasure. But a man must have some pleasure, and even in my most miserable periods I made this demand. I could renounce justice, reason, the supposed meaning of life and the world—for I have seen that the world comes through magnificently without the aid of these abstractions—but I could not renounce a little joy; and this longing was now one of those small flames within me in which I still believed, and out of which I thought to build my life anew. I often sought pleasure, dreams and forgetfulness in a flask of wine, which often enough brought me solace, and I was duly grateful. But it was not enough. Then one day I discovered a brand new joy: at the age of forty I began to paint. Not that I presumed to be a painter or wished to become one, but painting is wonderful recreation and makes one happier and more patient. From then on my fingers were not only black from ink, but red and blue. Many of my friends were angered afresh by this new manifestation. In this I am always unlucky; whenever I undertake something essential, happy and beautiful, people invariably become unpleasant. They would like one always to remain the same and never alter one's face; but my face rebels and often wants to change. It is a vital need.

Another reproach they levelled at me I also found to be quite just: they accused me of lacking in a sense of reality. Neither my writings nor my paintings do in actual fact conform to reality, and when I compose I often forget all the things that an educated reader demands of a good book—and above all I am lacking in a true *respect* for reality. I consider it to be something one should trouble least about, for it is ever present and burdensome enough, while there are other more important and beautiful things to call for our care and attention. Reality is something with which no one under any circumstances can ever be content, something which should never be adored and revered, for it is the hazard and refuse of life. And this shabby, constantly disappointing and barren reality is impossible to change except by a denial of it and by showing that we are the stronger.

In my poems, then, the normal respect for reality is often absent, and when I paint, my trees have faces and the houses laugh, dance or weep—and generally it is difficult to recognize the tree for a pear or a chestnut. Yes, I must submit to this reproach. I confess that my own life often appears exactly like a fairy-tale, and I often feel and see the outside world in perfect harmony and accord with my inner feelings—which I can only call magic.

Sometimes I committed stupid blunders. For example, I once made a harmless statement about the famous German writer Schiller, whereupon a number of South German Bowling Clubs declared that I was a profaner of national shrines. But happily for years now I have succeeded in refraining from making any more utterances that are likely to desecrate holy relics and make men scarlet with anger. I see in this some progress. And because so-called reality no longer plays a very great part in my life, because I am often as full of the past as the present, events of today already seem to me endlessly remote, and I can no longer distinguish the future from the past as clearly as most people do. I live a great deal in the future—and so I have no need to bring my biography to a close with the present day, but may safely let it proceed. . . .

I will now relate in short the full span of my life.

During the years up to 1930 I wrote a few more books, finally to turn my back on this profession for ever. The question as to whether I was to be reckoned a poet or not was taken up by two industrious young men and used in their theses for their doctorates. But the question remained unanswered. A careful observation of the newer literature revealed that the stuff that goes to make a poet had, in modern times, shown itself in such an extraordinarily diluted form that the difference between the poet and the literary man could no longer be determined. From this objective analysis the two candidates came to diametrically opposed conclusions. The first, rather more sympathetic, was of the opinion that such ridiculously triturated poetry was not entitled to the name and was valueless as literature; that which was called poetry today might just as well be allowed to die a peaceful death. The other was a confirmed admirer of poetry, even in its most rarefied forms, and considered that it was better to allow, out of caution, a hundred non-poets to be accounted as poets than to be unjust to one who still had perhaps a single drop of true Parnassian blood in his veins.

My chief occupations were my painting and the study of Chinese methods of magic, but during the years that followed I became more and more absorbed in music. It was my ambition in later life to write a kind of opera wherein human life in its so-called reality would be taken far from seriously and even held up to ridicule; it would instead be made to shine out in its eternal value as an image—as the fugitive garment of Divinity. The magical conception of life has always been near to me: I had never become a modern man, and had always found Hoffmann's *Golden Vessel* and even *Henry of Ofterdingen* to be more valuable text-books than all the world's history and natural history books; the latter, whenever I read them, had always seemed to me like so many charming fables. But now I had reached a period of life when it was senseless to build up and elaborate any further an already complete and sufficiently differentiated personality, when my task lay rather in allowing my precious ego to sink once more into the world, and to bring it into line, in the light of the transitory, with the eternal and changeless orders. To express these thoughts or life moods seemed possible only through the medium of the fairy-tale, and I saw in the opera the highest form of the fairy-tale—presumably because I could no longer truly believe in the magic of words in our misused and dying language, whereas music appeared to me as a living tree upon whose branches Hesperidean apples could still grow. I wished to achieve in my opera what I had not entirely succeeded in doing in my poems: to give an exalting and charming sense to human life. I wished to extol the innocence and inexhaustibility of nature, and to depict its course to the point where it would be compelled through inevitable suffering to turn to the spirit, the far-off opposite pole, to portray the oscillation of life between the two poles of nature and the spirit with all the serenity, glitter and perfection of the rainbow's arch.

Unfortunately, I did not succeed in finishing this opera; it suffered much the same fate as my poetry. I had felt obliged to give up writing poetry when I realized that everything which seemed to me important to say had been said already in *The Golden Vessel* and *Henry of Ofterdingen* a thousand times better than I could have said it. And so it went this way with my opera, too. No sooner had I completed my year-long musical studies, written one or two preliminary scores, and tried to visualize as penetratingly as possible the actual sense and content of my work, than I suddenly perceived that my opera was likewise nothing more than a striving to say what had already been said magnificently in *The Magic Flute*.

So I laid this work aside, and turned my full attention to the practice of magic. If my artist's dream had been an illusion, and if I were not capable of producing a *Golden Vessel* or a *Magic Flute*, then I was born to be a magician. I had advanced sufficiently along the Eastern Way of Laotse and in the I Ching to know for certain the hazardous nature and commutability of so-called reality. I now compelled this reality to conform to my conceptions of it through magic—and I must say I was overjoyed at the results. I must also admit that I did not always limit myself to that enchanted garden which is known as White Magic, for from time to time I drew the small living flames within me over towards the Black Art.

When I was well over seventy, and just when I had been awarded the twin distinction of honorary degrees by two Universities, I was brought before the judges on a charge of seducing a young girl through the instrument of magic. In prison I asked permission to busy myself with my paints, and this request was granted. Friends brought me in colours and artist's materials, and I painted a miniature landscape on the walls of my cell. Once again I had turned to art, and all the shipwrecks I had previously experienced as an artist did not prevent me from draining once more this most exquisite beaker, from once again refreshing my heart and building a small but beloved toy world like some child at play, from once again putting aside all wisdom and abstraction in favour of the primitive joy of creation. So I painted again, mixed my colours and dipped my brush, tasting once more the rapture of all this infinite magic: the gay light ring of vermilion, the pure full tone of yellow, the deep emotion of blue, and the harmony of their mixture culminating in the palest of greys. Happy and childlike I indulged in my game of creation and painted a landscape on the cell wall; it contained all that in which I had found pleasure during my life—rivers, mountains, sea and clouds, peasants at harvest time, and a mass of lovely things that I had enjoyed. A miniature railway ran through the centre of the picture; it led up the side of a mountain and the train, whose engine had already disappeared into the mountain-side, looked for all the world like a worm in an apple; it was just entering a small tunnel from whose mouth issued clouds of woolly black smoke.

Never before had a game brought me so much pleasure. I quite forgot, in this return to my art, that I was a prisoner and an accused man—and that there was really little hope of my ending my life anywhere else but in this cell. I even forgot about my magical exercises, for I seemed to be sorcerer enough when I painted dwarf trees or a small bright cloud with my fine brush.

In the meantime so-called reality, with which I was now completely at variance, did its level best to destroy and ridicule my dream. Nearly every day I was led out under guard into the most dismal offices where, amidst a host of papers, sat unsympathetic men who questioned me, were unwilling to believe me, snapped at me and treated me alternately like a three-year-old child and a hardened criminal. You do not necessarily have to be an accused person to become acquainted with this remarkable and truly hellish world of bureaucracy: you need only desire to change your address, to get married, procure an identity card or a passport to be obliged to descend into this hell and waste hours in the musty rooms of this world of papers. Of all the infernos that man in his strangeness has devised for himself this has always appeared to me to be the most diabolical. You will be questioned, barked at by bored, impatient and joyless men who disbelieve your simplest and truest statement, and you will be treated either as a schoolchild or a criminal. But all this is common knowledge. I should long since have been suffocated and have withered right away had not my colours time and again consoled me, and had not my picture—my beautiful miniature landscape—brought me renewed life and a breath of fresh air.

One day I was standing before my picture when the warders appeared with their usual wearisome summons, wishing to tear me away from my pleasant occupation. I felt a sense of fatigue, and almost a revulsion against all this activity—against the whole of this brutal and soulless reality. The time now seemed ripe to make an end of it all: if I were not allowed to play my innocent artist's game in peace, I must resort to that more serious art to which I had devoted so many years of my life. This world was unbearable without magic.

Recalling my Chinese ritual, I stood for a while with my breath held, and slowly released myself from the illusion of reality. I begged the warders in a friendly tone to be patient for a moment while I climbed into my little train in the picture, as there was something there that I had to attend to. They laughed in their usual manner—for they looked upon me as mentally deranged.

I made myself small, climbed into my little train, and drove it deep into the tunnel. For a short while the woolly smoke could be seen pouring from the round hole in the mountain; and then it slowly evaporated and with it the whole picture, myself included.

The warders stared at the blank wall in the utmost embarrassment.

[*Translated by* MERVYN SAVILL]

III

GLIMPSES OF GREATNESS

V. VERESAYEV

A DAY WITH TOLSTOY

Translated from the Russian by V. H. Orfenov

IN 1902 I was deported from St. Petersburg by Sipyagin[1] and returned to my native Tula. A year before, my book, *A Doctor's Journal*, was published, and produced 'a great stir' both in Russia and abroad. In the spring of 1902 I was about to start on a journey when this letter arrived:

From Tatiana Lvovna Sukhotina,
Gaspra (estate of Countess Panina),
Koreiz,
Taurida Government

Dear Sir,

I have decided to ask for your help, which, perhaps, you will be able and willing to give me. You have probably heard of my father's long and serious illness. He is still quite helpless and can hardly turn in his bed without assistance. The condition of his heart makes it essential that he should have constant medical care. We are trying to find a doctor who would live with and look after my father. Do you know of anyone willing to undertake this post? We offer a salary of 100 roubles a month, all found, and the fare to the Crimea. If we are fortunate enough to get my father back to Yasnaya Polyana (and there is every hope now that we shall), the doctor will have to accompany him and live in our house. We shall, of course, pay all travelling expenses. I hardly need mention how important it is for us that the doctor should be a sympathetic and tactful man, as it is difficult enough for my father to accept any service, and he is sure to be worried by the thought of someone living in the house expressly to look after him.

[1] Then Minister of the Interior in Russia.

Please forgive me for not addressing you properly, but I do not know your full name. Should you think of a suitable person, do let me hear at the above address. I may tell you that my father admires your writing very much and thinks you have great talent.

T. SUKHOTINA (*née* Tolstoy)

This letter filled me with happiness, pride and fear. It was clearly a delicate suggestion that I should volunteer for the post. Despite their immense circle of friends, the Tolstoys had approached me, a complete stranger. It was obvious that, as the author of *A Doctor's Journal*, I seemed a suitable person to look after their father. Even if it were not so, I had every right to offer my services, but for a whole week I was torn by doubts. To live in close proximity to Tolstoy, to see him constantly in his intimate surroundings, to have the chance, so rarely granted, of studying a great man in his everyday existence! I could record all that I heard and saw, not on bended knee, like the worshipper of some prophet or genius, but as an impartial observer unafraid of the ugly and the ludicrous. But how rare are such books about men of genius! How dull, pompous and lifelessly-great they appear in their biographies and the reminiscences of disciples and followers!

Such were some of my thoughts when I received the letter, but there were others too of a different kind. I was then only a very young doctor, fresh from the university, lacking in self-confidence and experience. How, under such circumstances, could I take the responsibility for a life so precious? The slightest lapse in vigilance or failure to realize the seriousness of some symptom—and the death of Leo Tolstoy might be for ever on my conscience. My authorship of *A Doctor's Journal* was another complication. Tolstoy's negative attitude to medicine and its attempts to 'resist' and 'correct' nature by inadequate means was well known. This point of view, to a certain extent, was upheld in my *Journal*, and Tolstoy, I knew, had read and approved of my book.

There is a story of two doctor's assistants where one comes to see the other and finds him glum and weary.

'What is the matter with you?'

'I am not well, have a headache and feel shivery.'

The guest with a solemn face tries to take his friend's pulse, but the sick man grins and shakes his head.

'Oh, drop it, don't be a fool, we both know perfectly well that the pulse does not exist.'

Well, if something like this happened to me? If I prescribed for Tolstoy and he said: 'Oh, drop it, you and I know very well that the pulse does not exist. Didn't you explain in your *Journal*?'

At last I put an end to my indecision by going abroad. From Milan I sent a letter to Tatiana Lvovna to say that I did not dare take the responsibility for the life of Tolstoy, so precious to me and to everyone.

During the next year (1902–3) I received several invitations to visit Tolstoy; these messages were sent through a friend of Leo Nikolaevich, L. N. Nikiforov, a charming old man who had to pass through Tula each time he returned from Yasnaya Polyana to Moscow. But I was overwhelmed by fear and could not make up my mind for a long time. At last, in August 1903, I found sufficient courage to go.

I went together with the Liberal member of the Zemstvo,[1] G., and a doctor acquaintance of mine. We left Tula about 11 a.m., travelling by *troika*. The faces of my companions reflected my own feeling, akin to religious excitement, something between dread and joy. The nearer we got to Yasnaya Polyana, the paler grew our faces and the more animated we became. G. told us of his conversations with a peasant from a village close to Tolstoy's estate:

'Do you see Tolstoy?'

'Oh yes, ever so often.'

'Well, what is he like?'

'Not bad, a serious old man. If you meet him on the road he will talk to you; then it's as if he put out his hand to keep you away: "don't get too near, I am a Count".'

We all laughed nervously. Our carriage had now turned off the Kiev high road and was rolling along a country lane. At a distance we saw a man with two children walking across the fields. We entered the gates with two turrets, familiar from photographs, into the Yasnaya Polyana estate, and as we were driving down the long avenue of birches, one of us said: 'What if it happens to us! Don't get too near, I am a count.'

The outlines of the house appeared through the trees; our carriage stopped at the entrance and Sofia Andreevna Tolstoy came out to

[1]The Rural Council.

greet us. Her manner was cordial and gracious, and it was easy to imagine how beautiful she had once been. Afterwards we were taken to the lower veranda, where we had coffee with Tolstoy's daughter, Alexandra, his son Leo, his doctor (whose name was, I think, Nikitin), and a few other persons, including children. The Countess asked if we had not seen Tolstoy, who had gone to walk in our direction, and when we replied that we had passed a man with two children crossing the fields, she said it must have been him with their grandchildren. Later she took us into the garden and spoke of her long novel, just finished. In answer to our questions she smiled: 'How could the wife of Leo Tolstoy have anything published! No, I sent it to the Rumiantsev Museum, let them do what they wish with it after my death.'

We returned to the veranda; somebody said: 'Leo Nikolaevich has come back.' Soon came another report: 'He is resting now.' Over an hour passed when at last we heard: 'He is up and will come down in a moment.' My heart began to beat faster than at the worst of school examinations. Then with light, swift steps, Tolstoy entered through the inner door. I had always imagined him tall and broad-shouldered, and it was a great surprise to see a very thin and rather small old man with drooping shoulders but with remarkably young and quick movements, in spite of his recent illness. He greeted us and sat down. I noticed the rare beauty of his hands. And like an experienced horseman who takes the reins with an assured gesture, he began a conversation, drawing us all in with the greatest ease and simplicity. First he talked to me about my *Journal*, then turned to the Zemstvo doctor:

'You probably disagree with Vikenty Vikentievich on many points?' (How and where did he manage to find out my full name?)

The doctor answered from his corner rather sullenly: 'Yes, I do.'

There was nothing in Tolstoy's manner to suggest a formal audience. He treated us as though we were old acquaintances and, having learned our names, never made a mistake in addressing us. He listened with great attention and we felt that he was genuinely interested in all we had to say. His exquisite breeding blended perfectly with a conscious desire to treat everyone as a friend. But I still think that there was something more in his attitude towards ourselves and that he took a real interest in us. After all, why should Tolstoy, so avid for life in all its manifestations—from a distant star to the smallest insect—not feel an interest in everyone he met? I remember thinking then of what Pascal says: 'The greater the man's intelligence the more interesting people he discovers around him; mediocre persons do not seem to notice the difference between man and man.'

In the midst of our talk Leo Nikolaevich suddenly turned to his doctor and asked whether he was to go on with some drops for his heart. While the doctor felt his pulse, Tolstoy looked at him with docile, childlike animation. 'Yes, go on taking the drops,' the doctor said at last. 'How many? Fifteen or twenty?' Ah well, perhaps it was not quite so difficult to have him for a patient as I had imagined; perhaps the pulse did exist after all.

Dinner was announced and we went up to the first floor. On the stairs Tolstoy said to me:

'Are you married?'

'Yes.'

'Any children?'

'No.'

His face darkened.

'How long have you been married?'

'Six years.'

He grew silent but looked at me severely and I knew at once that his whole attitude had changed. He remained polite and gentle in his manner, but all the former warmth in his eyes had disappeared.

A huge room, shining parquet floor, old portraits on the walls, and in one corner a marble bust of Tolstoy. Sofia Andreevna sat at the head of a long table, Leo Nikolaevich on her right. Men-servants wearing gloves waited at dinner. Special vegetarian dishes were served for Tolstoy. He asked me why I lived at Tula, and when I explained that the Minister of the Interior had deported me from Petersburg, he said with envy in his voice:

'I have never been fortunate enough to be deported or sent to prison.'

After dinner Tolstoy suggested a stroll. It was fine and sunny, but in places there were puddles from yesterday's rain. Leo Nikolaevich walked with his light gait, his long, silvery beard stirring in the breeze. He spoke of the need for moral perfection and of the highest happiness attained by man through love.

I said: 'But what if men do not hold such love in their hearts. They understand that real happiness lies in this love yet they cannot feel it. Is this not the greatest tragedy of man?'

Tolstoy shrugged his shoulders as though bewildered.

'I don't follow you. If it is clear to men that happiness lies in love they *will* live in love. If I stand in a dark room and see light through the door, and if I need light, is it possible for me not to go where I can find it?'

'But, Leo Nikolaevich, the characters of your books prove that this is not so simple. Olenin, Levin, Nekhludov see the light yet have not sufficient strength to go to it.' But Tolstoy only made the same perplexed gesture. Yet he kept asking questions and listened seriously and attentively, anxious to grasp my idea of tragedy; then again:

'Forgive me, I don't understand.'

In my turn I felt bewildered; how could Tolstoy, of all people, fail to see that the sole tragedy of his 'seekers' lay in their inability to 'live in goodness', in spite of their belief that the only approach to happiness is through such a life.

I related the story of a young girl who had ruined her life slowly but irrevocably and sacrificed her delicate health, work and affections to save the life of another girl whose fate was already sealed. In my naïveté I imagined that this story would be particularly near to Tolstoy's heart, since he had taught so persistently that true love is not concerned with the end. I remembered the emotional intensity with which he had told the legend of Buddha offering his body to feed the starving tigress and her young. But when I looked at Tolstoy, his face was puckered with impatience and pain. He shrugged his shoulders and exclaimed in a low voice: 'God, what a story!' I was dumbfounded, but one thing suddenly became clear: had he ever witnessed an epileptic Hindu giving his body to feed a starving tigress, he would have thought it the greatest desecration of life. The very word 'tragedy' seemed to grate on his ears; with a caustic smile he muttered:

'Tragedy! . . . I remember when Turgenev used to come . . . it was also nothing but tragedy, tragic' . . . .

The way he said these words suddenly made me conscious of a deep sense of shame and a strange question flashed through my mind: 'but is there anything truly tragic in life? Is it not all merely pretence?'

Then Tolstoy began to discuss a book sent to him by Mechnikov: *Essai de la Philosophie Optimiste*. He spoke with indignation and scorn of it and about Mechnikov's ignorance.

'Professor Mechnikov wants to correct nature. He knows better than nature what is essential for us and what is not. There is a word in Chinese—"shu". It means respect, not for some particular person or thing, but for everything that exists; for these weeds by the fence because they grow, for this cloud overhead, for this muddy road . . . when shall we learn to have reverence for life.'

As far as I can remember in the translations from Confucius the word 'shu' is generally rendered as 'do not do to your neighbour what you would not have done to you'. It would be interesting to know where Tolstoy got his interpretation. Probably from the Chinese intellectuals who visited him.

When we returned to the drawing-room for tea, we sat at a large round table lit by a lamp with a huge shade—the corner so often drawn by artists. While Sofia Andreevna played Patience my companion, G., went to the hall and brought the complete collection of the journal *Liberation* (at that time edited abroad by P. B. Struve), which he presented to our host. Tolstoy accepted the books, saying 'Thank you, how interesting!' As he turned over the pages, G. began to speak about the aims of the journal. 'Ah, yes, political freedom,' said Tolstoy, waving his hand contemptuously, 'it is neither necessary nor important. What *is* important, is moral perfection and love, these, and not freedom, create kindliness among men.'

G. began to argue rather indulgently: 'But you must agree, Leo Nikolaevich, that freedom is necessary if only for teaching that same love.' G.'s manner was respectful, but he spoke in a condescending tone as if he were addressing a very charming but obtuse child. He preached in truisms on the felicity of political freedom. How stupid it was! Did he really think that Tolstoy had never heard those arguments before and could be convinced by such banalities? And that revolting, self-satisfied, indulgent tone! . . . But suddenly my progressive friend seemed to have disappeared into thin air—Tolstoy simply ceased to notice him and changed the conversation; yet, whatever subject was discussed, he stubbornly returned to the necessity of moral improvement and love for our fellow men. While we talked, Tolstoy's son, Leo, red-haired, with a very small head, sat with outstretched legs in an armchair and played with his fingers.

His bored face reflected but one thought: this is new to you but I am tired of it, so tired!

Tolstoy had grown pale, his lips were parted, he seemed exhausted; we got up and took our leave.

As we drove under the deep blue vault of a starlit August night, my many confused thoughts refused to unite into a single impression. I could not help thinking of the famous portrait by Repin, where Tolstoy stands bare-footed, with his thumb in his belt, a gentle 'non-resisting' expression on his face. I felt that the portrait was false and tendentious. There was nothing in Tolstoy of Christ, St. Francis, Prince Mishkin or the man of the Repin portrait. Those swift, light movements, those small eyes under bushy eyebrows, flaring up with such youthful arrogance and caustic irony! Then I remembered his reaction to my story of the self-sacrificing girl. . . . I thought of *War and Peace*, and Natasha's words about Sonia: 'To him that hath shall be given, and to him that hath not shall be taken even that which he hath'. Sonia is the 'he' that hath not. Perhaps she is without egotism, I don't know, but everything has been taken from her. . . . And then I recalled again the persistence with which Tolstoy turned every conversation into a sermon on moral perfection and our bleak boredom as we listened.

When, on my return, I was asked about Tolstoy, I replied that I might have easily taken him for a rather rigid and dull Tolstoyan, contrary and inconsistent. Whether you talk about astronomy or tomato-growing he returns to his theme of moral perfection and love, somewhat threadbare through incessant repetition.

But strangely enough, as time went on and I re-read Tolstoy's writings and thought of him as he was on the day of our meeting, his creative work began to acquire a new meaning for me, as though my unimportant personal impressions had suddenly revealed some unknown aspect of his genius. It was like a thick mist which descends on a frosty night and in the sunlight of the next morning is transformed into a crystal covering, arraying the garden—so bare the day before—in a new and complete loveliness.

In the spring of 1907, when returning to Russia, I travelled from Warsaw in the same compartment with M. S. Sukhotin.[1] We talked a great deal about Tolstoy (I was then writing my book on him and Dostoievsky), and I told Sukhotin how I understood the

[1] Tolstoy's son-in-law.

epigraph of *Anna Karenina*: 'Vengeance is Mine and I will repay'. I had always felt that in *Anna Karenina* is embodied Tolstoy's deepest spiritual substance, his unshakable faith that life is essentially joyous —not sombre—and should lead man towards happiness and harmony; that it is our own fault if we do not obey its calls. In her marriage with Karenin, Anna was a mother, never a wife. She did not love Karenin, yet gave him what is beautiful when there is love but becomes false and horrible without it. And life would not tolerate it. Anna was conscious of the power beyond her by which she was torn from her ugly existence. Had she honestly surrendered, a new life might have opened before her. But she was overcome by ignoble fear, she dreaded being condemned and outlawed by 'Society'. Her love was sullied by this falsity and lost all meaning except that of a forbidden delight. She had become a mistress and nothing else, just as before she was a mother and nothing else. Vainly she tried to go on with her sterile existence, but again life would not have it. Something in Anna was outraged and killed.

We can only accept in silence the verdict of supreme justice. If man fails to follow the deepest commands of the heart and timidly turns away from the great gifts life has to offer, if thoughtlessly he turns against all that is best in him, who is to blame for his destruction? 'Vengeance is Mine and I will repay.'

Sukhotin seemed interested: 'I wonder what Leo Nikolaevich would think of your interpretation.' 'Do ask him and tell me,' I said, 'I am convinced that he intended to convey something quite different, still it would be very interesting to know.' At first Sukhotin seemed to hesitate and explained how reluctant Tolstoy was to discuss his works of fiction, but in the end he promised to ask him and write to me. In a month came this letter:

Yasnaya Polyana,
23rd May 1907

Dear Vikenti Vikentievich,

Please do not think I had forgotten to ask Leo Nikolaevich about the epigraph, but as I told you before he dislikes discussing his imaginative works, and it was only a few days ago that I found an opportune moment to speak to him about 'Vengeance is Mine'. To my regret he disagreed with your idea. I say, to my regret, because I prefer your interpretation and have a feeling that Tolstoy himself likes it better than his own. When I explained to him why I was anxious to know, he said: 'Ah yes, it is very interesting but I must repeat that I chose the epigraph to show how all the wrong done by man leads in the end to bitterness, the bitterness Anna Karenina tasted, which comes not from man but from God. Yes, I remember quite well. That was what I meant.'

I am very glad to have complied with your wish.

Yours,

M. Sukhotin

HENRY D. DAVRAY

MALLARMÉ AS I KNEW HIM

Every day I have under my eye a portrait of Stéphane Mallarmé. Of all the counterfeit presentments of my contemporaries I have kept by me, it is one of those I prize the most. It is many a long year since I had it framed, and it has borne me company in all my wanderings. Whenever I go into fresh quarters, it is always one of the first pictures I hang up on the wall. It serves me as a twofold remembrancer, calling back as it does to my mind, a vision not only of the poet but of his delineator.

There are not many portraits of Mallarmé extant, but such as there are are highly prized. He was painted by Manet, Renoir and Gauguin, etched by James McNeill Whistler, and drawn by other artists such as Luque, Vallotton and Cazals. Photographs of Mallarmé are rare indeed. The best known, if not the only one, is that which figures as the frontispiece to the collected edition of his *Poésies*. It shows him full face, thrown over his shoulders the travelling rug with the small check pattern which he kept on, even indoors, for fear of catching cold. This photograph is certainly a speaking likeness. There he is, just as I saw him many and many a time, one eye wider open that the other, a tuft of brindled hair to the left of his forehead, a long typically Gallic moustache, a short goatee beard and a wide-flowing tie encircling a tall collar.

The portrait I have of him shows just his face, looking straight at you. It is an excellent likeness, though it is little more than a sketch.

It is the work of the Norwegian artist, Edvard Munch, who drew it in 1892 and exhibited it with a selection of his other work in a Bond Street Gallery, a little before the present war. At the end of the last century, Munch stopped for a time in Paris to put the finishing touches on his artistic education. He was assisted by a subsidy from the Norwegian Government, as were a good many other Scandinavian painters and writers to whom the brilliance of the City of Light was an irresistible attraction.

Munch was a very indifferent linguist, and it was a very considerable time before he could express himself in more or less intelligible French. As, however, he knew a little English, we succeeded, by having recourse to both languages, in arriving at something that bore a tolerable resemblance to conversation. This linguistic experience served as a bond between us and we became close friends. Munch had heard a good deal about Mallarmé from his fellow countrymen, who eagerly joined in the rather fulsome admiration for the poet of 'Hérodiade', which was then professed by the younger generation in France. As soon as he got to know that I had the *entrée* to the poet's Tuesday reception, he begged me to introduce him, and one day, with the consent of the Master, I took him along with me. Munch was vastly impressed by Mallarmé's profoundly expressive countenance and was forthwith seized with the idea of painting his portrait. He implored me to make known his desire. As I knew how almost morbidly sensitive the poet was and how he detested anything even remotely resembling publicity, I thought twice about it and tried to persuade Munch to give up the notion. But Munch refused to be discouraged. The upshot of it was, I got over my qualms, made my request and had it refused. However, Mallarmé had displayed so much grace and charm in signifying his refusal and I had such a poignant consciousness of the effect the refusal would have on my young Scandinavian friend, that I returned to the charge, and to such good effect that Mallarmé, yielding to my representations, agreed to fix a date for the first sitting. That sitting was fated to be the first and the last: it had no sequel. Twenty minutes went by and then Mallarmé, speaking in English, told the dumbfounded artist that he could stand it no longer and asked him to terminate the sitting.

Filled with disappointment, Munch came straight to me and recounted his misadventure. He had brought his drawing with him and I asked him to show it to me, fully expecting to see a mere preliminary note, something quite rough and ready. Judge of my surprise when I found myself contemplating what seemed to be a finished portrait and a perfect likeness. I told Munch what I thought of it. He would not believe me, imagining I was only trying to let him down gently. He protested emphatically that another sitting or two were absolutely necessary if the work was to be anything like finished, adding that, all the same, he realized that his dismissal was final. At my request, Munch left the sketch with me, and in the course of the next few days I got a number of French friends of mine to look at it. They all shared my opinion of the drawing and persuaded Munch not to destroy it, which would have been nothing short of a tragedy.

On the following Tuesday I turned up at Mallarmé's full of contrition at having been the means of inflicting upon him such a disagreeable experience, and had made up my mind to tell him so. He did not give me the time. He explained that, after a quarter of an hour or so, the task of remaining absolutely still became unbearable and that, try as he might, he had had to give it up. With his usual courtesy, he expressed his deep regret and begged me to tell Munch how sorry he was, adding, moreover, that the Norwegian, even in that short time, had managed to produce an excellent portrait and that any attempt to improve it would, he was sure, inevitably have the opposite result.

When I told him what had passed, Munch was both deeply touched and highly gratified. Forgetting his disappointment, he made a point of going and thanking the poet in person. This incident that ended on so happy a note won him an enviable prestige with the Scandinavian artists' colony who were in the habit of foregathering at the Closerie des Lilas, at cocktail-time and after dinner, under the chestnuts in the Place de l'Observatoire. He was the man who had done a portrait of Stéphane Mallarmé!

In those days I was living near the Luxembourg Gardens, on the edge of the Quartier Latin, and visiting Mallarmé meant going from one end of Paris to the other. Means of transport were not so many nor so rapid as they are today, and I am inclined to think that one would have done just as well to go on Shanks's pony. If you wanted to get from the Quartier Latin or Montparnasse to the Batignolles, you could take a horse-bus that would land you at the Gare St.

Lazare. Mallarmé's abode was situated well beyond the outer Boulevard, beyond the tunnel that enclosed the down line. At the point where the up-line leaves the station the permanent way is open to the sky and is flanked on the eastern side by the last few houses that form the rearguard of the Quartier de l'Europe. I remember, as I strode light-heartedly up the Rue de Rome, wondering to myself in which of those houses Zola had lodged the hero of *La Bête Humaine*. I was struck by the contrast between Zola's ruthless, powerful realism and the delicate, subtle turn of mind of the poet to whose discourse I was about to listen.

Such as enjoyed the privilege of hearing Mallarmé's talk, never forgot the experience. His guests were comparatively numerous, and among the few who survive to this day are: Paul Valéry, Edouard Dujardin, Albert Mockel, Paul Claudel, André Fontainas, Camille Mauclair, André Gide; but what a multitude have passed beyond the veil! Teodor de Wyzewa, Jean de Mitty, Pierre Louys, Gustave Kahn, André Lebey, Jean de Tinan, Jules Laforgue, Théodore Duret, Félix Fénéon, René Ghil, Henri de Régnier, Francis Vielé-Griffin, Laurent Tailhade, Bernard Lazare, Charles Morice, Pierre Quillard, Ferdinand Hérold, Stuart Merrill, Marcel Schwob and his friend Charles Whibley, who, in those days, had rooms with amazingly low ceilings, beneath the shadow of St. Sulpice. These were the most fervent worshippers at the shrine, but there were other more casual droppers-in to be seen from time to time, journalists like Jules Huret and Georges Docquois, distinguished foreigners such as George Brandès and Arthur Symons and, on some rare occasions, George Moore, under the wing of Edouard Dujardin.

Whatever the diversity that characterized this motley company of artists, writers and poets, all were united by the same basic intellectual affinity. There were others who came, lured by curiosity, or the desire to be in the swim, but these soon disappeared and were seen no more, probably realizing that the spiritual atmosphere was of too Attic a rarity for them to breathe with comfort.

Mallarmé's house was in no way different from its neighbours; it was just as painfully commonplace as they. It was, in fact, one of those structures, erected during the period immediately following the Franco-Prussian war of 1870–1, for the accommodation of middle-class tenants of restricted means or of persons engaged in one of the so-called learned professions. The rooms were cramped and lacking in even the most elementary comforts. In putting up these houses, landlords and architects alike seem to have been actuated by one single motive, namely to pile as many as possible of those exiguous dwellings one on top of another in order to obtain the maximum of rent from the minimum of space, utterly regardless of the convenience and well-being of the tenants. My youthful imagination would have desired that a man of Mallarmé's distinction should have been housed in a spacious and luxurious abode and have lived and moved and had his being in surroundings befitting the nobility of his mind. He possessed none of those worldly goods which some men inherit from well-to-do parents, nor did his work provide him with the means to secure those material advantages which only money can command. His resources were limited to what he earned as a teacher of English in a Paris *lycée*. It was doubtless in the hope of creating for himself a supplementary source of income that he compiled *Les Mots Anglais*, which a sub-title defines as a 'Petite Philologie à l'usage des Classes et du Monde', a sort of manual for students of English, of which, strolling one day along the quays, I was lucky enough to come across a copy on a second-hand stall, and thus possessed myself of a volume as scarce as it was little sought-for. He could never have made much money from it. What he ought to have done was to have it taken up by the Board of Education and put on the list of text-books to be used in English classes. The little manual would then have been constantly reprinted and its author would have been the recipient of substantial royalties. But in order to get his book thus officially adopted, he would have had to do the sort of scheming and wire-pulling which, to a man of Mallarmé's temperament, would have been in the last degree repugnant. His salary sufficed to procure him his daily bread, and, satisfied with that, he devoted his leisure, in the words of Henri de Régnier, 'to the sole pursuit of Beauty and Truth'. That sort of ambition, adds Henri de Régnier, is not one in which the public is particularly interested. But it interested the little group of faithful followers who gathered round him every Tuesday in the little room which was both his dining-room and drawing-room and in which he was accustomed to receive us with unaffected courtesy. Nevertheless, it was well that his friends and admirers did not all put in an appearance at one and the same time, for there would not have been room for them. When the pressure became too great, the first comers would discreetly withdraw. I was one of the youngest, and times without number I had to remain standing, leaning against the wall under some precious picture, or supporting my elbows on the tall carved oak sideboard with its freight of pewter and pottery.

Once in the poet's presence, you forgot all about the lowliness of the surroundings; your whole attention was centred on the fine, engaging countenance, the light that shone in the depths of the gentle eyes; you heard nothing but the subtly delicate modulations of his voice; you were laid under the spell of his singularly winning personality, you felt that you were in the presence of a being of rare distinction, of a true aristocrat. Mallarmé was assuredly one of the most fascinating of all talkers. His discourse, easy, lucid and familiar, was clearly born of long and patient meditation. Whether his subject was art, or life, or poetry, his dearest theme of all, everything he said was luminous, delicate and to the point. He had original ideas to offer on every subject he touched upon, and they were expressed in phrases of incomparable felicity, phrases of a lucidity astonishing for an author whose writings bore the reputation of being nebulous and esoteric in the last degree. His talk, which he illustrated with anecdotes recounted with exquisite taste and skill, glowed with intelligence, with an understanding of life and man as amazing as it was profound; and it was marked by a complete detachment from material things and the more sordid aspects of human existence.

One of these Tuesdays, I had just arrived, and was slipping in as inconspicuously as possible behind my elders, so as not to interrupt the discussion, when I heard myself being addressed point-blank by the Master. For some time past I had undertaken the task of writing the section denoted 'Lettres Anglaises' in the 'Revue du Mois' (that is to say the periodical stocktaking of outstanding events in the realms of politics, literature, science, art, music, etc.) of the *Mercure de France*. It thus fell to my province to give an account of the various English books which their authors or publishers had sent to the *Mercure* for review. I also had to chronicle events of importance in the literary world and to write the obituaries of any persons of eminence in the Republic of Letters, or rather in the British section of it, who might have departed this life during the period under review. Before long I shall be able to celebrate the fiftieth anniversary of my discharge of this function, which only the occupation of Paris by the insufferable Hun has compelled me to intermit.

A little while before the occasion to which I have just alluded an Australian poet had sent the *Mercure* a slender volume of poems. When I came to examine these effusions I found that the poet had printed them without stops and without capitals! I did my level best to get at the meaning, but at last I had to give it up. Perhaps I threw up the sponge too soon; it is possible, for I freely confess that I have never much cared to cudgel my brains over such verbal intricacies. Be that as it may, these poems, innocent alike of commas and full stops, soon bemused me like a Chinese puzzle, and this was the impression of them I had thought to convey, not without a touch of irony, in my review. Mallarmé animadverted on me with some severity for what I had done, whereat I was not a little abashed. It happened that the Australian poet had also sent a copy of his book to Mallarmé, accompanying it with a long letter in which he declared himself his disciple and expatiated with fulsome eloquence on the admiration with which Mallarmé inspired him.

Before replying to the Australian, Mallarmé had taken immense trouble trying to solve the enigmas, and protested that he had succeeded, the truth of which statement he proceeded to demonstrate by reading one or two brief specimens. I freely admitted that the poems had a meaning, but protested that I could not, for the life of me, see why the poet had deliberately neglected to drive that meaning home by disdaining the customary signs and symbols expressly invented for the purpose, the use of which might have saved his readers an unnecessary headache. Mallarmé then embarked on one of his subtle disquisitions with the purpose of demonstrating that a poet might advantageously discard those lets and hindrances which, according to him, the signs of punctuation really are, and pointed out that, so far as he was concerned, he made the most sparing possible use of them. I had it on the tip of my tongue to rejoin that this did not always tend to facilitate the elucidation of his poems, but deemed it politic thereby to observe that, in conversation, the intonation of the voice, the play of the features, the gesticulations of the speaker, took the place of punctuation, and that he himself employed these means to perfection. At this juncture Paul Valéry broke in with a remark which diverted the conversation into another channel, the art of public speaking, and I was not a little relieved to be released from the pillory. Nevertheless, I had been taught a lesson and, afterwards, when I came to compose my copy, I wrote with circumspection, never failing to bear in mind that I had Mallarmé among my readers and my critics.

In 1892, having been a teacher of English in various provincial colleges and Paris *lycées* for some thirty years, Mallarmé retired on a pension and henceforth spent the greater part of the year in his little house at Valvins. No sooner did the days begin to lengthen than away he hastened thither, nor did Paris see him again till the first chill days of autumn. In those days I spent many summers at Marlotte on the outskirts of the Forest of Fontainebleau, the summer resort of a whole colony of literary folk and artists of every nationality, Americans, Englishmen, Scandinavians, Belgians, Frenchmen. I was an ardent cyclist, and that was in no way singular, for, in those days, when a motor-car was still a primitive thing, a rare phenomenon, every one had his 'bike'. And so, perched up on my two wheels, I ranged at will the splendid forest with its lovely vistas and picturesque demesnes; I went and visited the various friends I had in the peaceful villages that slumbered undisturbed along its edge.

At Bois-le-Roi, there was Pierre Quillard, poet and socialist, champion of the persecuted Armenians, as intrepid in his onslaught on the bloodthirsty Sultan Abdul-Hamid as, later on, with Bernard Lazare and Francis de Pressensé at his side, he showed himself fearless and indomitable in his defence of Captain Dreyfus. At Samois, there was Elémir Bourges, who, 'far from the noise and smoke of town', pursued in peace his solitary meditations. At Grez and at Montigny, on the banks of the Loing, with the Scandinavians Wilhelm Krog, the brothers Krag and the Danish poet Obstfelder, all of them addicted to *piolter*, which they quaffed in brimming bumpers, Runciman, the musical critic of the *Saturday Review* and Charles Conder, who had been a pupil of Cormon before drawing designs for fans which he painted in water-colours on panels of white silk, both used to spend holidays of voluptuous ease, sipping their absinthe at any hour of the day whenever the fancy took them. At Vulaines, Paul and Victor Margueritte continued their fruitful collaboration. At Barbizon, one after another, came the line of painters loyal to the shades of Millet and of Corot. At Avon, Edouard Dujardin had his stately country house standing in the midst of a park adorned with splendid trees, whence on certain days he would go down to Valvins and there converse with Mallarmé.

Thus I had no lack of objectives for my excursions. One day, being bidden to luncheon at Dujardin's, I found there—he had come for the week-end—no less a person than George Moore, with whom my host was on particularly friendly terms, and whom I had already come across in London, where he was, in those days, dramatic critic on one of the principal dailies. After lunch, a victoria came to fetch us and conveyed us to Valvins, where we spent the rest of the afternoon in Mallarmé's little garden, listening to the poet as, for George Moore's benefit, he commented up and explained his 'Phénomène futur', of which Moore published an English version in the *Savoy* for July 1896.

It also happened that I sometimes went alone to Valvins. From the towpath where the Seine takes a gentle curve in the reach between Valvins and Samois, I was to catch a glimpse of his skiff with its white sail in which the poet used to make short tacks across the narrow reach. He would hail me cordially as I hove in sight, and sitting myself on the river's bank, alongside my bike, we would chat awhile together. If, as often happened, I had just got back from England, I would give him the latest news of what was afoot in the world of letters over there, telling him about the younger men, writers and poets, who were beginning to attract attention at the time. He took a particular interest in Arthur Symons, who published a verse translation of 'Hérodiade' in the last number of the short-lived *Savoy*, of which he was the editor. He had a specially warm place in his heart for Ernest Dowson, John Gray and Hubert Crackanthorpe, who had been to visit him in Paris. The youthful pioneers of the Celtic Renascence, and above all W. B. Yeats, struck him as full of promise, while, among the older men, it was George Meredith of whom he thought the most.

He kept himself very much up to date about intellectual activities in England, and, beyond a doubt, his knowledge of this country and its literature must have had its influence on his own line of thought. But, so far as I am aware, no one has hitherto attempted to go into this question, and it is certainly not a task which I myself shall undertake. It has been stated that when, at the age of twenty, he came to London, his purpose was to improve his English in order that he might be the better able to savour the writings of Edgar

Allan Poe. And, in point of fact, the first work he published—it appeared in 1874—was a translation of *The Raven*, accompanied by the original text and embellished with five drawings by Manet. In 1888 he brought out, under the imprint of Deman of Brussels, *Les Poèmes d'Edgar Poe*, with a tailpiece and a portrait by Manet. It appeared as a quarto and only one hundred copies of it were printed. An edition published the same year by Vanier of Paris was disavowed by Mallarmé on the ground that it was not in accordance with the text. In 1876 he published in Paris, from the French original, *L'Histoire du Caliphe Vathek*, by William Beckford, which was reprinted in 1880, and again in 1893. In the year 1888, the book-publishing department of his friend Dujardin's *Revue Independante* published his version of *Mr. Whistler's Ten o'clock*.

These names and titles are not without their significance. It seems beyond question that what Mallarmé sought at all costs was something out of the ordinary, remote from the commonplace, the work of original minds of a similar mould to his own. Such examples of his work as we possess are certainly esoteric and we may well question whether all those who professed the Mallarmean cult were quite the adepts they pretended to be, even in regard to such portions of his work in prose or verse as were generally reputed the least recondite. For example, on 1 March 1894, at the invitation of Frederick York Powell, his *ami de trois jours et toujours*, he delivered a lecture before the Taylorian Association at Oxford. He had chosen as his subject 'Music and Letters', and so elaborate were the arabesques of style and expression with which he festooned his discourse that I do not think it would be rash to affirm that, of all his audience, however complete and accurate their knowledge of French, only a handful had the vaguest idea of what the lecturer was driving at. York Powell may have been one of the exceptions, one of the rare *illuminati*—York Powell, that intellectual acrobat, that curious explorer of the *arcana* of abstruse languages who, while occupying the chair of Modern History at Oxford, found time to give lessons in Law, Early English, French and German, compiled an *Icelandic Prose Reader*, a *Corpus Poeticum Boreale*, translated the Faereyinga Saga, the authentic quatrains of Omar Khayyám, and presided over the deliberations of the Irish Text Society. The following day, thanks to Charles Whibley's brother, Mallarmé gave the same lecture, the same but 'with a difference', as he put it, at Pembroke College, Cambridge, where listeners who understood him could hardly have been more numerous. Be that as it may, this visit of his to the two ancient universities caused him a lively satisfaction. He told us all about it a few days after his return. The grave, urbane decorum of it all, the deference paid to him in these antique homes of study and learning and meditation, were well calculated to give him pleasure. York Powell's original and arresting figure had greatly struck him, and he was vastly entertained by various little personal details I was able to give him about that versatile professor.

Some little time afterwards the lecture was published in book form. It consisted of scarcely more than three thousand words occupying thirty-eight of the eighty pages of thick paper which made up this slender volume, the rest being taken up with an introductory dissertation and notes, which were supposed to assist the reader to understand the text. It is stiff reading, all of it. Mallarmé expresses ideas which he had, no doubt, long been excogitating; since the time, in fact, when, of a Sunday, he might have been seen at the Colonne Concerts, seated on a form in the promenade and anon pulling out a sheaf of papers from his pocket, and scribbling down, from time to time, notes doubtless suggested by the music to which he had been listening.

Together with a host of others, these notes were intended to be used in connection with the definitive work he had in contemplation but which he never managed to complete. What did they contain? We may take it that but few passages had received the final touch. Anyhow, no use has been made of them up to the present. After his demise, they remained in the hands of his widow, and when she died they passed to Mademoiselle Mallarmé. She left them unconditionally to her husband, Dr. Bonniot, whom she married pretty late in life, for, contrary to a report as false as it is persistent, she was never the wife of Paul Valéry. Dr. Bonniot, who was a medical practitioner, was also deeply versed in literature and professed an unbounded admiration for Mallarmé. He came near to thinking that he was the only living being possessed of a thorough comprehension of his work. Some people considered this pretension as a little overweening and were rather perturbed at the thought of the use so fanatical a disciple might make of the papers over which he had the fullest control. But, so far, he has suffered them to remain a dead-letter; and furthermore he stoutly declines to show them to anyone, which, perhaps, is the best that could happen.

Mallarmé died after only three days' illness, on 8 September 1898. The news of his sudden departure filled us with consternation. I was confined to my bed at Marlotte when the news reached me, and so I was not among the little group who followed Stéphane Mallarmé to his final resting place. He is buried on the hillside which looks across to the waving forest, in sight of the tranquil river where the white sail of his skiff had so often been the virgin sheet on which, in dreams, he had traced so many of his wondrous 'divagations'.

Some days later, being on my feet again, I made a pilgrimage to Valvins, and, as we were mounting up the hill, Victor Margueritte, in a voice faltering with emotion, told me about the little silent group of mourners who, a few days earlier, had made their way along the dusty road, beneath the autumn sun, sorrowfully following the lowly village hearse as it bore to the grave all that was mortal of one whose like we shall not look upon again, whose spirit will not die.

AUGUSTUS JOHN

WILDE AND CONDER

THESE were the days of the New English Art Club, the *Yellow Book* and the *Saturday Review*. A strong Gallic cultural infusion was noticeable in the more active artistic and literary circles of London. Will Rothenstein spoke familiarly of names which were already almost legendary. He seemed to have met all the outstanding figures in Paris and drawn them too. His lively intelligence and wit, associated with an insistent and vigorous personality had a compelling quality impossible to withstand. His introduction of the then little known personality of Goya in a book he published at this time opened up a new, wonderful and not too distant world where the artist lived dangerously and with the athleticism of a bull-fighter coquetted with death under the affrighted eyes of his favourite *Maja* to an accompaniment of the fatal music of guitars.

Will Rothenstein, Robert Ross, More Adey and Arthur Clifton opened the Carfax Galleries in St. James's and I held my first show there. It was not unsuccessful, and with £30 in my pocket I proceeded to France where, with Rothenstein, Conder and Orpen and two or three ladies, we passed a summer at *Vattetot-sur-Mer*, a village near Étretat in Normandy. According to Rothenstein, I was to expect on meeting Charles Conder, to find a kind of bull-necked athlete before me. I was surprised therefore and somewhat relieved too when he turned out to be the charming but not physically formidable type I was to know so well. Though he may have formerly been the husky fellow described by Will, he appeared, when I met him, to be singularly out of training. He wore his blond hair rather long and a pendant lock always fell over one malicious blue eye. His exhausted and muffled voice was sometimes almost inaudible, making his conversation a little difficult to follow. Perhaps he counted on leaving his audience to some extent in a state of doubt as to his meaning. His gait was inclined to shuffle, for he was, as he admitted, somewhat gone at the knees. However, he was still capable of great endurance, and walking from Vattetot to Vaucotte out-distanced everybody, and was always first in at the Casino. Conder, with a bottle of Pernod at his elbow, painted fans, filling the silken fabric with personages out of the *Commedia dell' Arte*; but these, under his hand, had by a process of exquisite contamination, acquired a dreamy and erotic refinement caught from Watteau and Saint-Aubin, and still further aggravated by contact with the nostalgic imagery of Paul Verlaine. Balzac, too, provided numerous motives for his weak but sympathetic pencil, and the actors of the *Comédie Humaine* are presented by him, through the medium of lithography, in an envelopment of warm and over-scented luxury.

At the conclusion of this *villégiature*, Rothenstein, his wife, Conder and I repaired to Paris and spent a week or so lunching and dining in the company of Oscar Wilde, now released from prison and inhabiting a modest hotel on the left bank. I was curious to see this monstrously celebrated person of whom one had heard so much and certainly, when I did, it was reassuring to find his behaviour, as far as I was concerned, to be perfectly correct, friendly and even paternal. Not having been to Oxford, I was unable to speak the peculiar sub-dialect fashionable among his contemporaries, and I could only sit silently and marvel at this genial, sentimental, urbane, but rather portentous personage. After a series of Maraschinos he would be in good form and hold the floor in masterly fashion. It is true his audience was always sufficiently subservient and deferential and responded to his sallies with the dutiful appreciation of a hired *claque*. Conder, alone, behaved at times like a naughty boy, and when he would pour his wine into his soup, drew from the Master the rebuke that 'Vine leaves in the hair was all very well and indeed beautiful, but such childish folly was both tiresome and undecorative'. When Alice Rothenstein, fearful for my reputation, persuaded me to have my hair cut, Oscar, the next day, was very grave and reproachful, and said I might at least have consulted him before taking so important a step. I myself was disappointed to find that he wore his own hair short. Tugging at his dewlap he would discourse wittily after his manner and, with mild and affectionate regret, recount his recollections of the boyish misadventures of his sons. On the whole I was glad when I could escape from the overcharged ambience of this de-caged and now maneless lion, and with Conder seek greater ease and comfort in less august company.

I have never been a great Oscar fan though I loved his jokes. I found *De Profundis* sentimental and false, the Ballad second-rate, but *The Importance of Being Earnest* perfect. *The Picture of Dorian Gray* made a strong but unpleasant impression on me when I read it as a youth; later I re-read it and found it a thoroughly amusing thriller. Wilde was a big and good-natured fellow with an enormous sense of fun, impeccable bad taste, and a deeply religious apprehension of the Devil. A great man of inaction, he showed sound judgement when, rather than face freedom on a yacht in the company of Frank Harris, he preferred to sit where he was and await the arrival of the police.

One evening at the old Café Procope, long since demolished, a somewhat dramatic confrontation took place. Oscar, Conder, I and a strange being known as Bibi La Purée had met at this pre-Revolution establishment. Bibi had been the devoted friend and factotum of Verlaine. Will Rothenstein told me that Bibi, on Verlaine's death, followed the funeral *cortège* of his master, weeping copiously, but consumed by his irresistible passion for umbrellas, returned from the melancholy ceremony, bearing a sheaf of these commodities as his day's pickings. A nocturnal bird, he had the appearance of an undernourished and fugitive Voltaire. I found him greatly to my taste. Enters Robert Sherard, a superb specimen of blond manhood and a walking testimonial to the virtues of Dr. Tibble's Vi-Cocoa—his favourite restorative. Oscar at once rises and leaves the building. (Evidently he didn't fancy a scene.) Robert Sherard then sits down and treats me to a long diatribe on O.W., whom he had befriended loyally during his trouble and since, only to be rewarded with indifference and even ingratitude. Oscar had said: 'Robert Sherard is wonderful, he defends me at the risk of my life!' R.S. offered to present me with the complete works of his former hero, duly inscribed: 'There's not one of them worth a damn.' (He seemed thoroughly disillusioned.) Unwilling to encumber myself with a parcel of rubbish, I did not avail myself of his generosity. We passed an interesting night visiting a series of *boîtes de nuit*, till I and my fair companion took leave of Sherard, Conder and Bibi at the first pale gleams of a typical Parisian dawn.

Paris then was still French and its manners had not been entirely vitiated by the transatlantic interpenetration. Frenchmen were still virile, and the bistro the resort of honest men.

With Conder and Sherard I once visited Ernest Dowson at Catford, a suburb of London where Sherard's wife kept a bricklayers' lodging house, and had offered asylum to the sick poet. The poor fellow was very dejected indeed and wasn't particularly pleased to see his friends, but I found him *sympatique*. Conder and I decided to stay at Swanage, where a lady, Mrs. Everett, kept a convenient boarding-house. Here Conder did a good deal of his best work, painting out of doors. Being at the seaside it was inevitable that a love-affair should ensue. A charming and talented Irish art-student provided Conder with the requisite opportunity and an engagement followed. When Conder interviewed the young lady's mother to declare his intentions formally, he was met with the objection of a certain disparity of age between the parties concerned, 'In any case,' he was told, 'there need be no hurry! You remember that Jacob waited seven years for Rachel.' 'Yes,' replied Conder, 'but you remember too that Jacob lived to the age of 376!' The marriage never took place. At the same time I myself felt the compulsion of the sea air, for a handsome young Viennese, who in strict incognito served at table, now captured my affections, diverting them for a time from an earlier and what proved to be a more permanent allegiance. Anna Carolina's defences, though aided by a perverse and exasperating tactic, proved in the end to be not insurmountable, and when I left she promised to rejoin me in France, where I had arranged to go with my friend Michel Salaman. My letters, however, were intercepted by Mrs. Everett, who, much to my annoyance, dissuaded the Viennese from carrying out the plan. Perhaps after all she never took me very seriously. Salaman and I spent some months at Le Puy-en-Velay and were joined by the Rothensteins for a while. Will made numerous drawings of the old portions of the town. Pushing south as far as Notre-Dame-des-Neiges we spent the night at the Trappist Monastery, being each accommodated in a cell, and next morning given wine and cheese for breakfast. Rothenstein seemed to think that Huysmans might be there, but we could obtain no information about him. The silent and bearded monks went about their labours in the fields; a lay but uncommunicative brother attended to our needs.

MEMOIRS OF THE LATE PRINCESSE EDMOND DE POLIGNAC

BEFORE the Franco-German War of 1870 my parents lived in Paris, on the Boulevard Malesherbes, in a large apartment near the Parc Monceau, and there my sister and three of my brothers were born. During the war, at the time when the Commune was impending, my father was advised to leave France, and so came to England with my mother and six children.

He bought a house in Grosvenor Gardens, No. 32, which I remember vaguely, but after spending a year in London he found the winter climate rather severe, and being unable to go to the South of France, went to a most beautiful part of England—South Devon. I still think that there are few spots lovelier than Torbay, with the coloured, rolling countryside that leads up to Dartmoor as far as Tavistock; the surrounding counties seem grey compared to the rich red of the Devon rocks and fields, against which the ilex trees, with their dark green foliage, make even in winter so rich a contrast.

My father decided to settle in Paignton, where he built a house that is now the Torbay Country Club. He died while I was still a child, and it was only when my mother remarried, about 1878, that we returned to live in Paris, where she bought a large house near the Bois de Boulogne—27 Avenue Kléber, which had been built by a Mr. and Mrs. Phalen, Americans who had come to live in Paris many years earlier.

Like most such houses at that time, this contained a great many large reception rooms, some furnished in the Louis Seize or Empire styles then fashionable, and others in the Sarah Bernhardt manner. The principal and largest room—my mother's *Grand Salon*—soon became a centre for musical and artistic gatherings, and I can never forget that in it I first responded to great classical music. A week seldom passed without the performance of some Quartet, played by the finest performers in Paris on instruments which were then unique and are now, I suppose, unobtainable—for they were all from a double quartet of Stradivarius instruments that my mother had collected after much research.

Thus from my earliest youth I constantly heard all the great works of Beethoven, Mozart or Schubert, including the last Quartets of Beethoven, Nos. 10 to 17, which were then considered almost incomprehensible. The Fourteenth Quartet impressed me particularly, and I remember that on my fourteenth birthday, although I was offered a little watch from Boucheron's or a fan painted by Chaplin, the famous portrait painter, I chose as a present or 'birthday surprise' a performance of my favourite work by Beethoven—the Fourteenth Quartet.

As was usual in large families, the parents decided very early which child should become a musician, a painter, an architect, or a diplomat; and it was decided that I was not to study music but to learn painting at an *atelier* in the Rue de Bruxelles, conducted by a Monsieur Félix Barrias.

Although I secretly loved music most, painting attracted me almost equally, and I spent all the time possible at the Musée du Louvre, without understanding much of what I saw there, but forming the strongest likes and dislikes, some of which have since been modified by time.

Of course, whilst in Devonshire I had seen practically no painting at all, but at the annual Exhibitions of Modern French Painting in

Paris—the then famous *salons* at the Palais de l'Industrie, somewhat similar to the Royal Academy Exhibitions—I disliked the conventional *pompier* paintings then in vogue, which seemed to me then as dull and depressing as they do now.

Besides these annual *salons*, it was customary to put up wooden buildings near the Palais de l'Industrie in the Champs Élysées, and the Exhibitions held there were frequented as a curiosity by visitors who went into roars of laughter at the products of *L'École du Plein Air*, and were specially indignant at *les ombres violettes* in the landscape paintings, accustomed as they were to the bituminous and ochre tints of the accepted academic masters. There was a small but determined group of ardent admirers of the new School, and strangely enough I was at once attracted by works which were not only condemned by critics and connoisseurs, but which were always refused admission to the neighbouring Palais de l'Industrie. The works of the Impressionists, such as Edouard Manet, Claude Monet, Sisley or Boudin carried me away. I was thrilled by the beauty of this art which seemed to give me a new insight and throw a fresh light and meaning on all that surrounded me in the visual world. My family did not approve of this new School, and my enthusiasm was at once put down as eccentric, promoted by a wish to excite attention, and deserving only of discouragement. But nothing was ever more spontaneous or sincere, and I was always anxious to learn anything I could about Edouard Manet and his first steps in painting.

Among the frequent visitors at my mother's house was the American painter, Edward May; he was my godfather, a very good-looking and talented artist, who had lived in Paris since his childhood. He had been a pupil of Thomas Couture, whose enormous picture, '*Les Romains de la Decadence*', is still in the Louvre. Need I say that Edward May criticized very bitterly my admiration for Manet who had studied painting at the same time as himself; he often spoke of him as a 'crank' who had been the laughing stock of all his fellow-pupils, known to the entire painting class as *Le Michelange du mauvais*. I took no notice. At the painting class I attended every day my admiration of Manet was a standing joke, most of the pupils having decided that he did not know how to draw, that his colours were ridiculous and his subjects beneath contempt.

Manet died while I was in my early teens; I was heartbroken, though I had never met him. Summoning up my courage I had gone once to his studio, 77 Rue d'Amsterdam, to ask his *concierge* to give me the visiting card which was nailed to the master's door; and this I treasured for many years.

A few months later, Monsieur Barrias moved the whole of his *atelier* to 77 Rue d'Amsterdam, Manet's studio, which was larger than the room in the Rue de Bruxelles, and in this studio I worked for many years. Thus I soon struck up a friendship with the *concierge*, questioning him on all sorts of subjects connected with the master. One day he showed me a fine pencil drawing of Manet, by Fantin-Latour—the first sketch of his well-known portrait—and consented to sell it.

The *concierge's* name was Aristide; he was an Indian, and I was much amused when he told me that he occasionally acted at the Théâtre des Arts, Boulevard des Batignolles, specializing in the role of *un traître orientale*.

My ambition was to buy a picture by Manet as soon as I was able to do so. Some time later Ernest Duez (himself an excellent painter) spoke to me of Manet's work 'The Woman in White', which is the portrait of his sister-in-law, Madame Manet, *née* Morisot, and which he had seen in Madame Edouard Manet's house when he had called there with John Sargent after the great painter's death. I still have the note I received from Duez, telling me that Madame Manet wished to sell the portrait, at a price which now seems incredibly low. No one, of course, at that time thought of buying such a picture.

My instant and spontaneous admiration for the early Impressionists has never changed or wavered. I felt from the first that they were right, and even in the tradition of the great Masters; but the feeling against them was very strong, not only among the profession and popular artists who taught painting in the Atelier Julien and such classes, but in most families; it was considered eccentric and revolutionary to care for anything outside the Academic painting that held its sway in the annual *salon*. Baudelaire understood the importance of Manet at once—he was a prophet in every art—but few critics had a good word for the Impressionists' school, and when Manet died in 1882, the most dreaded and the most read art-critic of the day, the great Albert Wolff of the *Figaro*, whose judgement was supposed to be 'final', wrote an article which, while allowing that Manet paintings were sometimes of interest, ended by these ominous words, 'but what will remain of all his work ten years hence?'

Well, ten years, twenty years, sixty years, have passed, and now Manet's pictures are in every National Museum, in Europe and America, and nothing has tarnished their freshness and vitality, and what remains now of Albert Wolff's opinions or of the works he extolled in his anxiously awaited articles?

Degas was painting the portrait of one of my fellow pupils in Barrias's studio. (This was then in the Rue de Bruxelles, and he lived quite near in the Rue de Turin.)

With a beating heart I climbed up the dark steep staircase that led to his *atelier*, for I admired his works more than I can say, including his wonderful copies of some pictures in the Louvre, and other early Renaissance pictures by Gentile Bellini and Mantegna.

Degas was painting the portrait of the beautiful Madeleine Fleury and I sat in a corner. At that time my great admiration for Claude Monet and the Impressionists made me feel certain that only painting from nature was admissible, so it was a shock to see that Degas was painting from drawings and that the whole colour scheme of his portrait was chosen from the Persian rug that was near at hand, from which he had composed a palette.

I remember that in speaking of some landscapes that Madeleine Fleury was then painting, he said, to my great surprise: 'To paint a landscape of the sort you describe, the best way would be to take a *toile de vingt paysage*, to paint the sky emerald green, and then put the canvas in a corner, *faire un bon déjeuner* (he was a great gourmet of the old French school), and leave the picture alone for several days.'

Before my dazzled eyes, he brought out over a hundred pictures, sketches, and sepia drawings and I was overwhelmed with admiration, and of course much too terrified to say a word: when the seance was over, and we parted, I went downstairs first, and Degas (as I afterwards heard) said to my friend: 'Who was that half-wit you brought with you? She never said a word about my pictures, nor about any of my drawings', and I understood from that moment that, however humble one may be, any great artist expects some praise when showing his work even to the most ignorant visitor.

Sargent was a pupil of Carolus Duran. His early exhibits at the annual *salon* caused a great sensation. Tall, very distinguished and extremely good-looking, he at once became a conspicuous figure in Paris society. An excellent musician, he was the friend of the young composers, a frequenter of all the concerts, and nearly as much devoted to music as to painting. His first pictures were greatly appreciated, but when he painted the wonderful picture of a celebrated beauty, Mme Gauthareau, it was very bitterly criticized, so that he took a dislike to Paris and went to London for some months, where he soon decided to stay permanently. The picture was considered indecent because of the simplicity and extreme *décolletage* of Mme Gauthareau's black evening dress—for this was the time of puff sleeves and endless tulles. Now the dress looks quite modern and causes no surprise to the visitors to the Metropolitan Museum in New York.

Sargent lived in London in Tite Street for many happy years, surrounded by a circle of admirers and friends. Here he painted his decorative work for the Boston Library and all the great portraits that now hang in the National Gallery or the Tate. Few artists have been more widely and warmly admired, and I have always considered his life a remarkably happy one; and so was his death, for he died in bed in his sleep, his spectacles pushed up over his forehead and in his hands a volume of Voltaire that he had just been reading.

L'école du plein air was superseded by painters who had *Les lanternes tournées en dedans*: to quote Jules Laforgue's admirable expression. They created the *surréaliste* and subconscious school, pursuing other objects and aims also, doubtless contained in some of the paintings of the Old Masters. I have never understood why people should be dogmatic about Works of Art, for if the aims of their creators are different surely they are free to choose any mode of expression they like, and there can be no question of dogma outside of which there is *point de salut* where beauty is concerned, and their work will be appreciated by those who feel as they feel, and see as they see.

But I think that originality differs entirely from eccentricity, and I could never see any novelty in works that combine the dullest and most antiquated technique, reminding one of every Academy, or of the Boecklin school, simply because there is something unexpected in the composition of the picture—such as three eyes in a portrait, a snail or a lobster or chest of drawers in the middle of a human face, or some other eccentricity that really doesn't matter much; still, as the effect of a work of art depends not only on the work of art but on ourselves . . . even psychologically and physiologically, it is quite reasonable to suppose that these works appeal to many others—and so much the better, for, thank God, there is no hard and fast rule about the beauty of a Work of Art; some great masterpieces have for centuries been admired by those we consider the greatest and best judges, but others, many others, in fact whole schools, have been admired sometimes more or less, at different periods, according to the environments and circumstances that, according to Taine, play such an important part in general taste.

Among those who were always seen at these informal gatherings was Jean-Louis Forain, whose caustic wit was the amusement and terror of Paris at this time. He and his wife had a delightful and very modern house in the rue Spontini, near the Bois de Boulogne, built for them by Grand'Pierre, a young and already much admired architect who afterwards built a house for Jean de Reszke and rebuilt one for me in the Avenue Henri Martin.

We often dined with Monsieur and Madame Forain. The top floor of the house was entirely devoted to a large studio in which Jean-Louis often let me sit, and sometimes work, while he drew or sketched, or prepared some of his wonderful lithographs.

Not only was his conversation brilliant, but he had known intimately nearly every great artist of his day, and I eagerly listened to his stories of his life with Verlaine and Rimbaud. They had been great friends of his, and he had for some time shared rooms with them. He had been present at many scenes between them, but in no way confirmed the general view of the friendship that bound these two great men.

Forain had been very poor and had known the hardest times in his early youth. At that time he had struck up a great friendship with Villiers de l'Isle Adam, the author of the wonderful *Contes Cruels*.

Among the gatherings at the Forains, I remember one on the day that Zola's *J'accuse* appeared, and I am bound to say that Jean-Louis Forain, who afterwards showed himself such an ardent anti-Dreyfusard, was greatly impressed by the article, which he read out to me with admiration for the author and indignation at the story he told. Forain was, and always had been, a devout Roman Catholic and one of the few men I knew who believed implicitly in the personality of the devil. Everyone now knows how the *Affaire Dreyfus* grew into something which developed hatred of every kind in Paris; families were split up, husbands and wives parted, and it was not unusual at a dinner to see guests leave the room if anyone appeared of an opposite opinion from their own. That first night Forain was sincerely moved by Zola's arguments, although during the evening he said to me, laughingly: 'I have drawn so many comic figures of Jews and it will be so easy for me to continue to do so, that I cannot change my line now; I have no choice but to become an "anti-Dreyfusard".' I am quite convinced that, as time went on, Forain's opinion of the case became really sincere, especially as his nationalist principles grew more and more marked; in his work, as in his thoughts and behaviour, he became increasingly religious and he never failed to take Communion and to observe very strictly the commands of the Church.

When I used to sit in his studio while he did his drawings or lithographs, which were generally on sacred subjects, he would often talk to me about the restoration of famous pictures, deploring that such work should be undertaken by those who had no idea of the technique in which the pictures had been painted. Forain frequently took me to the Louvre, to examine various pictures by the Old Masters, in which one could trace the first *preparation*: usually in *grisaille*: and he thought that those who restored the paintings would inevitably remove the *glacis* with which the original artists had finished their works—after a most careful preparation.

* * *

Gabriel Fauré is so mingled with all my memories of music in Paris that it is difficult for me to know how to begin to speak of him.

I first met him in a very lovely corner on the coast of Normandy, Villerville, near Trouville, a little fishing village close to Pennepie, and the Château de Blosseville where I spent many summers in my early youth. Here a little colony of painters and musicians usually collected to spend the summer months. I constantly met Gabriel Fauré at the comfortable and cheerful house of that excellent painter Ernest Duez, a great friend of Edouard Manet, or in the studio of Roger Jourdain, or of Erraguris, the Chilean painter, and his lovely wife.

Gabriel Fauré was about twenty-eight when I first knew him, and he had already written a number of beautiful songs, nocturnes, impromptus and other piano compositions that he often played to us, and from the first I was enthusiastic about them, for they seemed to me—as they do now, half a century later—worthy to rank with those of Chopin or Schumann. Sargent's drawing of Fauré is well known. It was done several years later, but Fauré had changed very little and with his dark complexion, wavy steel-grey hair and wonderful deepset eyes, he had a very powerful expression, and his charm of manner made him instantly sympathetic.

He had already written two quartets, piano and strings, which are both perfect in their way, and are today in the repertory of nearly all the leading quartet ensembles in the world, and there are surely no more lovely works for strings and piano than these. What can be more spontaneous than the First Quartet and the slow movement of the Second—this has always seemed to me one of the most beautiful and original of inspirations.

Gabriel Fauré was born in 1845 at Pamiers in the south-west of France, and studied harmony and counterpoint with Niedermeyer, whose school for organ and composition was considered less severely academic than the Conservatoire, and more respectful of the pupils' natural tendencies. Certainly from his earliest works up to his last, there is a remarkable continuity in Fauré's leading characteristics—the same well defined and infinitely expressive phrases that have remained as pure and melodic as the day they were written. His subtle harmonic treatment of these inspirations has made them invulnerable to time—for, as he sometimes said, '*J'ai reculé les limites de la délicatesse*'.

Some years after I met Fauré he married Mademoiselle Fremiet, daughter of the well-known sculptor, whose equestrian statue of Joan of Arc stands in the Rue de Rivoli near the Louvre. Her two sons were very delicate children—her whole life was devoted to dragging them through various illnesses—but they grew up and one became a great biologist, now a professor at the Collège de France, the other a popular writer and lecturer.

In later years Fauré became organist at the Madeleine, later again professor at the Conservatoire, and then Director of the Conservatoire, all after having been supposed for so many years to represent the anti-Conservatoire spirit. One of his most gifted pupils was Maurice Ravel.

Gabriel Fauré wrote very slowly, constantly aiming at making his work perfect in form, without losing the spontaneity of the original thought, and I always found him attracted by expressive music and easily bored by works of a too classical spirit. I have often heard Fauré, although an ardent admirer of Bach, speak of some Fugues as utterly boring. But Schumann he particularly loved, and he played most of the piano works better than I have ever heard them played by the greatest pianists. On the other hand he cared little for Brahms—excepting a few songs—and could not bear most of his Symphonies. He first came to London with me in 1896 to give a concert in Frank Schuster's new music room in Old Queen Street, which was to be inaugurated by an orchestral and vocal concert entirely devoted to Fauré's music. It was an unforgettable evening, for the music had been well rehearsed and the greatest artists had gathered together to sing or play. Among other works the exquisite Four-part Madrigal and the Pavane were most beautifully sung and enthusiastically received. Fauré's music had an immediate and very great success; he was surrounded by a group of friends including Sargent, Henry James, Lady Randolph Churchill and her sister Lady Leslie.

Fauré returned to London several times, among others when Forbes Robertson and Mrs. Pat Campbell performed Maeterlinck's *Pelléas and Melisande*, for which he wrote the incidental music, as he had already done for *The Merchant of Venice* at the Odeon.

In 1891 Gabriel Fauré came to stay with me in Venice, where for some months I had taken a small Palazzino at San Gregorio, a lovely little fifteenth-century house that belonged to a Russian, M. Wolkoff, a very old resident in Venice, a friend of Richard Wagner's who often came to see him.

I carefully prepared a quiet room with a piano as a study for Fauré to work in, but I had forgotten how fond he was of cafés; and I am obliged to say that he wrote his five *Mélodies de Venise* at a little marble table at the Café Florian on the Piazza, in the midst of the noise and turmoil of a busy Venetian crowd, rather than in the peaceful room I had arranged for him.

Several Parisian friends were staying with me at the same time as Gabriel Fauré; one of them, Madame Ernest Duez, having a lovely voice, we were in the habit of going out on the lagoon after dinner in a *Peata* (or large fishing boat) and we had got together a little orchestra of five or six musicians. When Fauré brought back nearly every day one of his lovely songs, Madame Duez and the little orchestra rehearsed them on the lagoon, Fauré playing a little portable yacht piano that one of my brothers had given me. And thus I heard for the first time *Mandoline*, *En Sourdine*, and the three other songs that he dedicated to me, and they form the five *Mélodies de Venise* that are so beautiful.

I have always thought that no one admired and understood Verlaine better than Gabriel Fauré, for who could translate into music better the wonderful lines of *Mandoline* or *Clair de Lune*? Soon after his visit to Venice, it struck me that I might ask Verlaine to write a libretto in the manner of *Les Uns et les Autres*, for which Fauré would write the music.

I suggested this to Gabriel Fauré, and he gladly promised to collaborate; and, as he knew Verlaine very well, he promised to write to him and to make him understand that of course I would remunerate him for his work. Verlaine replied that he could not consent to be paid, but that he would like me to open a credit for him at his tailors, his bootmakers or some other of his tradesmen. This was, of course, eagerly agreed to, but some time having passed before I heard anything more of Verlaine, I asked Fauré to write to him again, and Verlaine replied that he had not forgotten our agreement and had now chosen the subject that he was to submit to Fauré.

The subject chosen was the end of the *Comédie Italienne* and the scene was a ward in a hospital in which from one bed to another Pierrot, Columbine, Harlequin and others discoursed on the various aspects of life and love. Verlaine's letter to Fauré, which I have kept, seemed to me promising, and I am sure his libretto would have been wonderful, but I am sorry to say that Fauré refused to write the music, although it would have been a delightful theme that he could have treated marvellously.

Gabriel Fauré appeared at a moment when France was producing a galaxy of brilliant composers such as Emmanuel Chabrier (whose influence became very great after 1918), Saint-Saëns, Duparc, Chausson, Messager, Lalo, Vincent d'Indy, who all were fervent admirers of Richard Wagner, though some became less enthusiastic as time went on. Fauré on several occasions came to stay with me in Bayreuth, and I remember that he deeply admired many pages of the *Walküre* and the *Meistersinger*. How often he spoke to me with warmth of the last scene in the *Meistersinger*, when after Walther's *Preislied* the people turn to Hans Sachs, the Poet, and sing the glory of his art, and their love and gratitude. I remember how much he was moved by this, and years after, at the close of his life, when he was at the height of his fame, Fauré, now bowed down with age and nearly stone deaf, was present at a concert in his honour in the great hall of the Sorbonne. At the end of the concert all those present turned spontaneously towards him with overflowing hearts, and many with tears in their eyes; he could neither hear the music nor the loud applause, but he stood there in the balcony looking down with an unutterably melancholy smile on his handsome face. It was the last time I saw him, and I remembered how moved he had been at Bayreuth when we had heard the great scene together at the end of *Meistersinger*.

He had a keen sense of humour and was intensely alive to the absurdity of the pretentious; but although he was sensitive and sentimental, he was easily carried away by new affections, and was not always a faithful and perfect friend, being too much interested in new ties to trouble much about his old ones. No one could resist his charm of manner, his gaiety, his tenderness, above all his utter sincerity when a new fancy took his heart and mind, as it too often did.

In his last years, Fauré's songs and chamber music became more and more subtle and melancholy. With a few exceptions some of his earlier works like *The Requiem*, *Theme and Variations*, the *Nocturnes*, the *Bonne Chanson* and songs like *Parfum Impérissable* and *Soir*, besides those I have already mentioned, remain to my mind the most flawless examples of his genius.

Emmanuel Chabrier, whom I knew about the same time, was very different. Short, rather stout, but very active, and in fact never still, he was a typical Méridional. He had spent most of his life as an official in the Ministère de l'Intérieur, and began to compose only when he was past fifty. Anyone who has heard *Les gros Dindons* or *Les Cochons Roses* will know that his music is full of colour and vitality; and this was at once recognized in his early irresistibly sparkling composition *España*: which enjoyed a popular triumph. He had already written a certain number of songs, an operette in one act called *L'Étoile*, now often performed at the Opéra Comique in Paris—extremely comic, and originally written to be performed by students in the studio of one of his friends. Chabrier was a great admirer of Richard Wagner—and a great friend (among other artists) of Van Dyck the great Belgian tenor, then principal tenor in Bayreuth. He had long been a great favourite of the Parisian public at the Pasdeloup, and other Sunday concerts, in which works by Wagner were often played.

A few years ago a book was published containing Chabrier's letters, many of them addressed to Ernest Van Dyck, and nothing can give a better idea of musical life in Paris about 1885 than these witty letters. He speaks in them of a musical evening at my house, in which a great many parts of his new opera *Gwendoline* were given for the first time in Paris—though the very enterprising Théâtre de la Monnaie in Brussels had already performed *Gwendoline* some months before.

When I suggested giving a concert in Paris in which the principal parts of *Gwendoline* would be heard, with a reduced orchestra and chorus, Chabrier could not believe his ears, and at once asked most of his musical friends such as Vincent d'Indy, Gabriel Fauré, and Ernest Chausson to take part in it, and in a letter to Van Dyck he speaks of this performance in which he played the piano, Gabriel Fauré the harmonium, and Vincent d'Indy the *timbales* or timpani.

It was a great success, although the public naturally thought the music extraordinarily modern and advanced. It was for this concert that Gabriel Fauré orchestrated his beautiful *Clair de Lune*; and other works by d'Indy and Chausson, now well known, were heard then for the first time. Emmanuel Chabrier was a remarkable pianist. He was most enthusiastic and energetic, and very often after playing the whole act of an opera before dinner, he had hardly swallowed the last mouthful and smoked a cigarette, when he would suddenly remark '*Il y a longtemps qu'on n'a fait de la musique*', would fly to the piano and play again for an hour or two, singing every part of the score: tenor, bass or soprano, at the top of his voice, and rendering on the piano the sonority and tone of a full orchestra. In any discussion, especially on a musical subject, he became extremely violent, most enthusiastic about what he admired, and beside himself with anger at anything he disapproved. He would tear them to pieces with a rich flow of language, full of fantasy and wit, and pour forth torrents of abuse often irresistibly comic. He would end by saying that there were two sorts of music in his opinion, or as he expressed it, '*Il y a la musique: puis la musique que . . . c'est pas la peine*'.

He could never keep still and was very fond of dancing. Often in the middle of an argument he would break off and seizing some female member of the party, dash off in a waltz or polka.

Although he was such an admirer of Richard Wagner I remember that when he joined me one year at Bayreuth he could not bear the religious side of *Parsifal* and predicted that it would be the first of Wagner's operas to grow old. But most of the *Ring* delighted him beyond measure, and even in *Parsifal* there were parts that he greatly admired. In particular he had a great admiration for the Prelude, and I remember that at a certain moment he exclaimed during the performance. 'Ah! I have longed to hear that A flat for the violoncellos for more than ten years, and now I hear it at last'—but he had never been able to come to Bayreuth before, and of course *Parsifal* was never performed anywhere else at that time.

His deep delight at hearing that A flat—and all the enchantment and even amusement he derived from this week in Bayreuth—made me more convinced than ever that the appetite for life, great works, beauty of art or nature, cannot be bought at any price, and that the Cook's Tourist highbrow millionaires who thronged to Bayreuth in later years, if they didn't lack Chabrier's appetite for things, certainly missed all his enjoyment and fun. The picture gallery of the great millionaire may contain many Botticellis whose meaning and beauty remain invisible to the vision, but will he understand beauty felt by the woman who sweeps the carpet?

Chabrier's music has had an immense influence on all French composers, especially in the period between 1910 and 1940, and all his operas: *L'Étoile*, *Gwendoline*, *Le Roi malgré Lui* and his posthumous work *Briséis*, have been revived at the Opéra or the Opéra Comique, and the beauty of his *Ode à la Musique* and of his piano works and songs is more and more apparent as time goes on.

After Debussy's death in 1917 there was a marked reaction from his refined and impressionist style, and the coming age clamoured for more rhythmical and spiritual music. Jean Cocteau's book *Le Coq et L'Harlequin* had a great influence, and a group of six composers was founded under Cocteau's direction. Poulenc, Darius Milhaud, Auric, Durey, Germaine Tailleferre and Honegger formed the group, and their first concert was given in 1919 at the Théâtre des Vieux Colombier—a concert that caused an immense sensation and called forth much criticism and the same sarcastic remarks that had in 1885 been applied to Chabrier and Fauré's music—in fact the same things that have always been expressed whenever anything new appears in any art.

There are no longer literary or political *salons* in Paris such as there were in the second half of the nineteenth century. Towards 1880–90 one of the most celebrated was that of the Baronne de Poilly. Her good-looking son, Gaston de Brigode, had married a sister of the Duc de Gramont (Agénor), and the beautiful Corisande helped the Baronne to receive her guests at the weekly literary dinners at which Émile Augier the doctor, Professor Robin, and Professor Dieulafoy were frequent guests. There was also the young and much sought-after Paul Bourget, whose recent novel, *Cruel Enigme*, had startled and captivated Paris. Léo Delibes, the author of several delightful ballets, was also to be seen, and the philosopher Professor Caro, of the French Academy, was nearly always present. He held a very conspicuous place in Parisian society and had great influence, though his philosophy was often laughed at by the younger and more independent philosophers of the day. It was easy to recognize him as the hero in the brilliant play *Le Monde où l'on s'ennuie*, that was then being played at the Comédie-Française.

Barbey d'Aurévilly was constantly to be seen at these dinners and his remarks on various subjects, or even on his fellow guests, were the amusement of Paris. At one of the dinners Professor Robin came in rather late and announced very gravely that a great Academician, Émile Augier, had died that day. There was general consternation, and the usual expressions of regret, ending by '*C'est une perte irréparable!*'—to which Barbey d'Aurévilly remarked '*En effet c'est une perte irréparable pour le ridicule français—car il était puissamment organisé pour la bêtise*'. Barbey d'Aurévilly wore most unusual clothes, though they probably did not look quite so eccentric in those days as they would now. He affected to wear a lace jabot and very complicated waistcoats of silk, with some old Louis XVth design, with buttons made of amethysts or rhinestones. Paul Bourget told me that when Barbey appeared at one of these dinners in a particularly striking costume, he made some admiring remark: '*Que vous êtes beau ce soir: Monsieur d'Aurévilly:*' and got only this reply: '*Je suis simplement poli*'.

The *salons* of Madame de Poilly were second only to those of Madame Oubornon, but here only one guest at a time was allowed to speak, the hostess having a small hand bell which she rang if anyone tried to interrupt a story. It got about in Paris that on one occasion a young soldier suddenly tried to interrupt another guest who was speaking, but was sternly silenced by Madame Oubornon. When the orator had finished his story, Madame Oubornon turned to the guest who had so rashly intervened and said: 'Now, Monsieur, it is your turn to say what you wanted to say just now'. To which he simply replied, 'It doesn't really matter, dear Madame, it is now too late. I wanted to ask if I might have a few more peas—they were particularly good this evening.'

In these days, when women wear short hair and need a hairdresser only to do an occasional 'Permanent' or setting, it is hard to believe that in 1897 the 'Marcel Wave' caused a great sensation in Paris; very long hair being the fashion, it was a tedious obligation to have it waved by Marcel himself (though he was so sought after this was nearly beyond all hope!) or by Loisel, who besides being a very fashionable hairdresser, was also hairdresser at the Opéra and at the Comédie-Française. As the process of hairdressing lasted a very long time, I always asked Loisel for news of the next productions at the big Theatres, and on one occasion I inquired what he thought of Wagner's *Meistersinger*, to be produced at the Opéra within a few days. I have always liked the *spécialiste*, who sees things and events from the point of his particular *spécialité*.

Loisel replied: '*Eh bien: Princesse: je vais vous dire: Les Maîtres-chanteurs: c'est vraiment bien peu de chose—une malheureuse coiffure au troisième Acte: pas plus. Parlez-moi de la pièce du Châtelet—il y a pour quatre-vingt mille francs de cheveux dans cette pièce-là!*'

He then went on to tell me that his dream was to exhibit an 'Ophelia' at the next Exposition Universelle—Ophelia in wax would be lying on a dark blue velvet background, her long hair streaming behind her, with an incomparable Marcel wave, and ornamented with poppies and cornflowers, and perhaps a few ears of wheat, to denote her madness.

One of the most interesting *salons* I ever knew in Paris was that of the sculptor, René de St. Marceaux and his wife. They lived in the Boulevard Malesherbes, and every Friday there used to be an informal reception, after an excellent dinner. Nobody who had not exhibited a piece of sculpture or a picture, or who was not a composer, a scientist or an inventor would ever be invited to these gatherings, to which no simple *mondain* or mere social star was admitted.

I could fill pages with the names of all the remarkable people I met in this *salon*. It was there that I first saw Maurice Ravel and Claude Debussy; the latter had just sent from the Villa Medici in Rome the beautiful music he had composed for Rossetti's *Blessed Damozel*. He had been awarded the Prix de Rome some years before, and I had always been surprised that he had obtained this academic distinction discerned by the *Institut*. I was interested to learn later that Charles Gounod had been very influential with the jury and had ardently pleaded the cause of the young and totally unknown composer.

When he first frequented the St. Marceaux *salon*, Debussy's appearance was most striking; his short nose and deepset eyes, his fawnlike features and rather curly black hair and slight beard gave the impression of an Italian model, especially as his complexion was very dark and he sometimes wore small plain gold hooped earrings.

At that time Bayreuth attracted all composers, who were greatly impressed and influenced by the wonderful music of Richard Wagner, and it was therefore a great surprise to me to hear Claude Debussy and Maurice Ravel declare that this music did not stir them in the least, and that they much preferred the clearer, more delicate and simple form of Russian compositions, of which they gave us then and there many examples.

Claude Debussy and André Messager used to play *à quatre mains* many scores that delighted us; Messager, the author of *Véronique* and a number of other charming works, was an excellent pianist, and so was Debussy. We never tired of hearing them play.

Among those who crowded round the piano were Gabriel Fauré, Chabrier, Vincent d'Indy, Colotte (who was then thin and frail and newly married to Gauthier-Villars—'Willy'—whose criticisms of the Sunday concerts, signed *Lettres de l'Ouvreuse*, were feared by all the young composers), Jean-Louis Forain, Pierre Louys, Chausson and sometimes Sargent and Claude Monet. Music, books and pictures were discussed among them all, until the night was almost spent.

Sometimes the evening was devoted to a Bach cantata, the soloist as well as the choir being found among the guests.

Maurice Ravel wrote shortly afterwards the music of *Ma Mère l'Oie* for the Théâtre des Arts, and about the same time composed the beautiful *Pavane pour une Infante Défunte*, which he dedicated to me. I was much surprised and deeply touched that he should have attached my name to these lovely pages.

Maurice Ravel had always preferred to keep away from Parisian life, and lived in a Louis Philippe cottage at Montfort l'Amaury some miles from Paris, where I sometimes went to see him. He always avoided any official honour. He refused to be a member of the *Institut* or a Knight of the Legion of Honour. We always remained the greatest of friends, although he rarely came to Paris.

A few years ago, when a concert was organized by my professional musical friends at the Salle Pleyel, and the programme comprised only works that had been written for or dedicated to me, Maurice Ravel was kind enough to conduct the orchestra when it played this Pavane. After the concert, a few friends joined me and the Princesse Ilinsky, who, I imagine, had never heard of him before, as she was not very interested in music. At one moment they seemed to be in very deep conversation, and when I asked, with some surprise, what could be the subject of their serious talk, Ravel turned and said 'Oh! we are talking about death'—an answer that surprised me, especially as they seemed in the highest spirits when they finished their discussion. Some months later I was deeply moved to hear that Ravel had shown symptoms of the terrible illness that ultimately put an end to his life—an abscess on the brain—and for over a year he was slowly losing his memory; he knew too that he could never recover, and I often thought what a great mark of friendship he had given me, and also of the strange subject of his conversation at that supper party—the last time that I ever saw him.

As time went on, Debussy's works were greeted with increasing admiration; he revolutionized music in Paris and the group of his disciples and admirers grew continuously. But when *Pelléas et Melisande* was produced at the Opéra Comique in 1901, sung by the unforgettable Mary Garden with Jean Pellier and Vieulle, it was very badly received by both public and critics. Even the most 'up-to-date' writers laughed at it. Perhaps owing to Maeterlinck's words, many parts were received with peals of mirth. Its passionate sincerity, undeniable beauty and dignity made it invulnerable, and it was given over and over again before a more and more determined and fanatic audience. Time has since made this opera seem even more wonderful, more human and more poetic.

I remember that Gabriel Fauré did not like *Pelléas et Melisande*: and remarked to me after the first performance, '*Si c'est là la musique: je n'ai jamais compris ce qu'était la musique*', but I suspect that he was partly influenced by the fact that Debussy had married Madame Sigismond Bardac, to whom Fauré had dedicated *La Bonne Chanson*, and to whom he had been deeply attached.

Debussy was still young when he was stricken by a severe illness, which obliged him to give up work in Paris. He spent his last summer at St. Jean de Luz in a charming cottage built by an English family, a cottage in which I myself afterwards spent many happy months. I saw a letter written by Debussy to a friend, in which, speaking of the English atmosphere surrounding him, he says, '*Je crois toujours rencontrer Monsieur Pickwick dans l'escalier*'.

Because his death took place during some of the darkest days of the war of 1914–18, it passed almost unnoticed, and only a few attended the funeral of this man who had so enriched the world of music and to whom we owe so much.

During a brief holiday in Italy with my painting master and his wife, Monsieur and Madame Felix Barrias, I had paid a flying visit to Venice, and was so thrilled with the beauty and peace of that wonderful city that my one idea was to return there. When, therefore, my youngest brother married a charming American in the following year, I at once suggested that we should take a house in Venice together for a few months, and spoke to him of a lovely little Palazzo on the Grand Canal, at the Traghetto San Gregorio—the Casa Wolkoff; for, like the Casa Dario next door, it was not really an entire Palazzo, but half only, and so simply called a *Casa*.

The Casa Wolkoff belonged to an eminent Russian writer and photographer, Count Wolkoff, a great friend of Richard Wagner, who had been a constant visitor there during the long years he spent at the Palazzo Vendramin, where he died in 1882.

We spent about four months in this delightful residence, where we were soon joined by many Parisian friends—including Gabriel Fauré and the gifted artists, Duez and Georges Clarin. I spent my time painting on the lagoon, copying in the neighbouring Museum the Accademia—or in the big studio that formed the top floor of the house, with an extensive view not only of the Grand Canal but also of the Giudecca. This attractive Casa was afterwards inhabited by the great Duse, in the days of her romantic attachment to Gabriele d'Annunzio—days of which he wrote later in *Il Fuoco*.

I did not return to Venice for many long years, and when I did so it was with Edmond de Polignac, who was at once fascinated, as I had been, by the radiant beauty of the city. One day after we had lunched with Mr. and Mrs. Curtis at the Palazzo Barbaro on the Grand Canal, he pointed out the enchanting façade of the Palazzo

Manzoni, which was opposite, and exclaimed: 'Ah! that is the place to live in, and we must manage to get it in one way or another!'

The next morning I went to see an agent, who told me that there could be no question of our buying the Palazzo, which was inhabited by a rich South American who was living there very happily with a great friend. But the course of true love rarely runs smooth, and a few months later the same agent came to see me in Paris and revealed that as the result of a quarrel the South American was leaving Venice, and the sale of the Palazzo was not impossible.

For more than forty years I spent several months each summer within the old walls of the Palazzo Manzoni, which had become the Palazzo Polignac.

Before the hideous Hôtel Excelsior was built on the Lido and a long stretch of sandy beach had been reserved for its clientele, before the 'invasion' of fashionable visitors from every continent during the bathing season, Venice was a quiet restful city, especially in the warm weather, when the old Hôtel des Bains attracted only a few amateurs of sunbathing and a few families with numerous children. In those days the Venetian 'palaces' were not expensive, excellent servants were easily obtained, and life was very comfortable even for people with small incomes. In consequence many artists, composers and writers lived on or around the Grand Canal, in more or less luxurious surroundings.

Robert Browning lived in the magnificent Palazzo Rezzonico, and died there. The Spanish painter, Fortuny, Horatio Brown—who lived on the Giudecca, Sickert, whose studio was on the Calle dei Preti, were among those who spent many months in Venice; and among others who lived in larger apartments, or who occupied entire palaces, were Lady Layard, the Countess of Radnor, the Countess de la Baume and the lovely Lady Helen Vincent, whose Palazzo Giustiniani was perhaps the most beautiful in all Venice. Mr. and Mrs. Curtis lived in the Palazzo Barbaro, near the Grand Canal, while Mr. and Mrs. Bayard and the beautiful Miss Muriel Wilson were at the other end, near the station.

Among the visitors during the season were many composers and writers of the day—French, Spanish, English and Italian. The evenings were spent at one or other of these charming houses, and it was no rare thing to hear a Mozart Quartet or a great pianist or singer at some small informal gathering in one of the fine *salas*.

Life in Venice was then absolutely delightful. The Countess de la Baume lived in the lovely Casa Dario, next to the Giardino Barbier, which was at the back of a marble palace that had been begun in the seventeenth century and left incomplete, so that only the ground floor was finished and the large terrace overlooking the Grand Canal. On this terrace we often dined or had coffee in the afternoons.

The Countess de la Baume had made the Casa Dario a marvel of comfort and good taste and had filled it with the finest pictures and the most precious books and musical instruments, and here congregated the *fine fleur* of Parisian art-lovers. I sometimes met at the Casa Dario the Comtesse de Noailles, and her wonderful and gifted sister the Princess Alexandre de Caraman-Chimay, for whom the then youthful Marcel Proust had written a long dedication and preface in his recently published translation of Ruskin's *La Bible d'Amiens*. Léon Daudet, then very young and one of the most brilliant and cultured men I have ever known, was a constant visitor, as was also Henri Gonse the collector, and the great poet Henri de Régnier and his talented wife, the daughter of the famous Heredia and herself a celebrated poet. They spent many months at a time at the Palazzo Barbier, where a few rooms had been repaired and made comfortable for the guests of the Countess de la Baume. After her death, the Marchesa Casati took the Palazzo Barbier—or, rather, the ground floor of this unfinished palace—and there gave a series of fancy dress balls that are now legendary. At one of these balls, held at the time the Russian Ballet was at the height of its glory, she appeared at the top of the steps leading to the garden, in a wonderful costume designed by Bakst, with a tiger stretched out at her feet. The tiger had been drugged, but it was nevertheless extremely frightening, as one came up from a peaceful gondola, to find it lying on the steps of the palace. At the end of the party some of the guests took the tiger on to the Piazza, where quiet citizens who were leaving the theatres were terrified at its appearance. This incident provoked general censure.

But Venice was no longer the quiet city I had previously known. It had become the scene of many noisy parties given by excitable millionaires who seemed to have no respect for the homeland of Monteverdi, Marco Polo, the great Morosini, Goldoni and the endless list of wonderful painters, composers, travellers and writers who have made the glory of this lovely place. The Venetians themselves began to feel that their city was being treated as a sort of Casino—not of the elegant sort we are accustomed to see in Venetian pictures, but a casino like that of Deauville or Monte Carlo.

One year, in memory of my husband, who had known Richard Wagner, I thought of asking the Duke della Grazia, the owner of the Palazzo Vendramin, if he would allow me to have the Funeral March from *Siegfried* played in the courtyard under the windows of the room in which the great composer had died. The Duke consented, and was gracious enough to give a very large afternoon reception, to hear the Banda Municipale play the Funeral March from *Siegfried* in the Cortile of his Palace.

It was a bright, sunny day in the early part of the year, and the Grand Canal looked its best; all the neighbouring houses had decked their balconies and windows with the brilliant hangings which were usually brought out on great occasions, and many of the best-turned-out gondolas in Venice (belonging to the great patrician families of Venice)—at least a hundred—guided beautiful ladies to the steps of the Vendramin Palace. The Banda Municipale played the Funeral March very creditably, the guests crowding round the windows that looked on to the Cortile, and after the concert there was a buffet in the big central room or *sala*. I thanked the Duke profusely for all the trouble he had taken to have my wish carried out, and asked him how many years Liszt and Wagner had been his tenants. He replied: 'Oh, quite a long time—for seven years, at least, off and on; they spent many months here.' 'And did you often see them?' I asked. 'Oh, yes, they frequently came up to have coffee with us after dinner.' I was much impressed, and added: 'And what did they do, and what did they say?' 'They sometimes talked about music, or played the piano.' 'Oh, how marvellous to have known these great men. What a wonderful experience!' The Duke replied, casually, '*Oui, c'étaient deux originaux*'.

I thought of Browning's words:

> Ah, did you once see Shelley plain?
> And did he stop and speak to you?
> And did you speak to him again?
> How strange it seems and new!

It is difficult now to imagine the surprise and enchantment of the Parisian public when Diaghilev first produced his Russian Ballet.

For a year or two I had met this wonderful man at the Grand Duke Paul's. The Grand Duke Paul of Russia and his charming wife Princess Paley had a lovely house in Boulogne, at the very gates of the Bois. I often dined there; everything was perfect: their cuisine was celebrated. The guests were always sympathetic, and conversation was often varied by delightful music, quartettes or songs, and singing by Reynaldo Hahn or Jean de Reszke. Among the guests I often met a tall, energetic-looking young man with a white lock in the midst of his thick black hair, who was no other than the great Serge Diaghilev, to whose marvellous will-power, energy and utter disinterestedness we owe the revelation of Russian theatrical art.

He had opened an exhibition of modern painting in St. Petersburg, and one year he gave a concert of Russian music in Paris and a lecture on Russian Art. But it was only some time later that he brought the whole of his unsurpassable Ballet to Paris, with such stars as Nijinsky, Pavlova, Karsavina, and the beautiful Ida Rubinstein.

For many years Diaghilev came to Paris, sometimes producing an opera like *Boris Goudonov* or *Ivan le Terrible* with Chaliapin, and sometimes a new ballet by some young and much-discussed author; among these was Igor Stravinsky.

From the first it seemed to me impossible not to recognize the importance of this new genius, and I still think he dominates all others who have appeared for more than a quarter of a century. No one has escaped his influence, though, as usual, his imitators are often most obnoxious. No one who was present at the first performance of *Le Sacre du Printemps* can ever forget that evening, for there was a real battle in the Théâtre des Champs Élysées. The howls of some, the applause of others, went on for an hour—the orchestra reduced to silence. Here and there someone would rise and shout out his views at the top of his voice, each party abusing and insulting the other in the most violent way.

I was present each time a ballet was given, and until the end of the Season the same riotous scenes took place, sometimes lasting for more than an hour, the orchestra being reduced to silence. Still the army of admirers grew stronger and stronger, and Stravinsky was overwhelmed with applause when the curtain finally went down.

When the war of 1914 began I happened to be in England, staying with friends in Surrey. Soon I returned to Paris, where I was lucky enough to be able to help the great Madame Curie in some of the most interesting work that she had undertaken. But in the midst of all these tragic circumstances I had not forgotten my musical friends, and in the winter of 1915–16, knowing that Stravinsky was in Switzerland, I wrote asking him to see me when he returned to Paris. He had settled with his family at Morges, being a charming peaceful little town between Lausanne and Geneva, where I had often been to visit Paderewski who had a beautiful house there for many years.

My intention at that time was to ask different composers to write short works for me for a small orchestra of about twenty performers. I had the impression that, after Richard Wagner and Richard Strauss, the days of big orchestras were over and that it would be delightful to return to a small orchestra of well chosen players and instruments. Stravinsky agreed, and suggested setting at once to work on *Renard* —the plot being by a Swiss poet for whom he had a great admiration—Ramuz.

During the coldest months I went to Lausanne to see many friends of various nationalities; the shores of the Lake of Geneva were then, as they are now, haunted by refugees, neutrals and 'observers'.

I often saw Stravinsky, who had taken a house at Morges, where he lived with his wife and family and numerous pale, fair-haired young children. One night he asked me to dine, and came to fetch me, as it was half an hour's journey by train from Lausanne to Morges. Everything was covered with snow and so quiet in the clear moonlight night, so still, that it was not very cold. I shall always remember the happy impression I had as Stravinsky took me into his house, for it looked to me like a Christmas tree, all brilliantly lit up and decorated in the warm colours that the Russian Ballet had brought to Paris.

Madame Stravinsky was a striking figure: pale, thin, full of dignity and grace, she at once gave me the impression of nobility of race and grace that was confirmed by all she did in the following years. In the warmth of her charming house she looked like a princess in a Russian fairy-tale; surrounded by her delicate children, then, of course, very young. But although everything was so friendly and kind, there was an atmosphere of tragedy about the family which turned out to be only too justified, for all were more or less inclined to suffer from lung trouble, which ended pitifully for Madame Stravinsky and one of her daughters quite recently.

I can never forget the delight of that evening at Morges: the table brilliantly lit with coloured candles, and covered with fruit, flowers and desserts of every hue. The supper was a wonderful example of Russian cuisine, carefully prepared by Madame Stravinsky and composed of every form of zakousky, then bortsch, tender sterlets covered with delicious transparent jelly and served with a perfect sauce, various dishes of fowls and every sort of sweet, making it a feast to be always remembered.

I spent the last years of the 1914 war at St. Jean de Luz in an exquisite little house on the top of a hill, in which Claude Debussy had lived the year before. In front there was a cloister with a wonderful view reaching away to the plains and mountains. The house was built in the Basque style and contained a large music-room in which that perfect pianist, Ricardo Vinez, would play to me all the most wonderful pages of Debussy, Albeniz or Ravel—he had worshipped these composers long before they became well known to music lovers. Earlier he had done much to make Fauré and Chabrier known to the public. He devoted himself to this duty just as Jeanne Bathori had dedicated herself to the propagation of their music for the voice in earlier years. Modern French music of the beginning of the century owes much to Ricardo Vinez and Jeanne Bathori. It was through Ricardo Vinez that I got in touch with Manuel de Falla, for whose work I had the greatest admiration. I wrote to him in Spain and asked him if he would consent to write a work for small orchestra and voices that I could produce in my house in Paris.

Directly travelling became possible again I went to see him in Spain and spent many happy hours in his little house in Granada, where, in his simple room containing a table, a few chairs and a small piano, he composed those torrents of poetical and voluptuous music that moved us so deeply. This seemed to contain the very essence of Mauresque Spain, and especially of Granada and the Alhambra he loved so much, with its strange mysterious glades and the haunting sound of its ever-gurgling waters.

Falla lived with an old unmarried sister. They led a truly monastic life. He was very religious; he held strong political views, conservative and royalist; his hatred and indignation when any modern or democratic opinion was expressed amused me very much. He was well below medium height, thin like many Spaniards, and, with his hard, emaciated features and dark complexion, he always seemed to me like a figure carved out of walnut or a medieval saint in discoloured stone.

While I was in Granada I spent an evening with him in the garden of the Alhambra where he took me one night with Segovia, the finest of Spain's guitarists. The garden was empty, and it was a beautiful moonlight night. Falla chose a place where we sat for hours listening to the strange old Spanish music that Segovia played on his guitar as Falla asked—and I can never forget the incomparable beauty of those gardens steeped in music and moonlight.

The work he was writing for me was called *Retablo*. I often saw him in Paris, where he came from time to time. In 1923 he came to conduct the first performance of the *Retablo* in my concert room, where a little stage had been built and the scenery painted by a pupil of Picasso. Besides the principal singers, the part of the Reciter was sung by a young Spanish boy from the Spanish Church in the Avenue Hoche, and the beautiful music for harpsichord was played by Wanda Landowska, for whom Falla had also written the poetic and wonderful Concerto for Harpsichord that she played so often in Paris.

The audience consisted of composers, critics and the usual first-night Parisians, and a box on one side of the room was filled by Spanish friends who had all donned seventeenth-century Spanish costume. The orchestra was conducted by Falla himself, and the *Retablo* had a well-deserved and triumphant reception. He often told me that he composed mostly on his long walks round Granada—these long walks were the preparation for work in the little room—he often said to me: '*Je compose en marchant*'.

Once he came to Venice for a Musical Festival and again conducted the *Retablo* and kindly allowed me to be present at most of the rehearsals; at the last rehearsal I was surprised to see him appear at the conductor's desk his dark face covered with a number of small tufts of cotton wool, but it turned out that he had been badly stung by mosquitoes during the night and had carefully covered each sting on his face with a small wad of cotton wool dipped in ammonia, and had either not troubled or forgotten to remove them before the rehearsal.

What I knew of Erik Satie was that he was born at Honfleur in Calvados, and that in the early nineties he was considered to be a curious, rather humorous figure connected with Sar Peladan who had formed a Rosicrucian Order, the Knights of the Rouge Croix. This strange man was often to be seen at concerts and exhibitions, attracting much notice with his pale emaciated face and long Assyrian black beard, usually clad in a Persian costume. He was held in high esteem and extolled as one of the greatest writers of his day, his novels being written in the noblest language and the most perfect French prose. He at once chose Satie as the official composer of the Rosicrucian Order, and it was during this time that Satie wrote many pages of wonderful music for the various functions and festivities of the Knights.

At the same time he wrote other things that caused endless amusement because of their odd titles—*Morceaux en forme de Poire* or *Musique d'ameublement*. His indications of expression or tempo were still more curious—*Sans exaltation sacrilège* or *Comme une bête*.

Nothing could be more simple and poetical than the Greek dances *Gymnopédies* or the *Noisetier* and many of the beautiful piano duets in *Morceaux en forme de Poire*.

I was very anxious to know Satie, and I intended to ask him to write music for the Death of Socrates in Plato's *Phaedo*. I asked Jeanne Bathori to bring him to dinner one evening. He was then a man of about fifty-two, neither tall nor short, very thin, with a short beard. He invariably wore pince-nez, through which one saw his kindly but rather mischievous pale blue eyes, always ready to twinkle as some humorous thought crossed his mind. I remember that the dinner included roast tongue, which he found particularly good, and when I asked him if he would have another slice, he at once answered, '*Oui, oui, avec plaisir mais . . . pas la tête, je vous en prie, car je pourris la tête de veau*'.

Satie had spent most of his life at Arceuil, quite near Paris, and for over thirty years had never allowed anyone to enter his room. When, after his death, Sauguet, his pupil, and another friend at last entered it, they told me that the dust, books, music, and accumulation of every sort of thing was incredible. At one time of his life Satie had worked under Vincent d'Indy at the Schola Cantorum in the Rue St. Jacques, to learn the rules of fugal composition, and here he often surprised his fellow pupils with the liberties he took with the rules of counterpoint. He told me that they constantly said, 'This is all very well, but you will see what it leads to when you are older—*vous verrez*'; to which Satie added, '*Mais aujourd'hui j'ai cinquante-deux ans, je ne vois encore rien*'.

At the time when I met Satie I had been learning a little Greek and was becoming more and more enthusiastic as I managed to read the tragedies of Euripides or the Dialogues of Plato in the original text. Satie was equally enthusiastic, so he decided to write music for the *Death of Socrates*, and after much thought suggested that the scene should be set in a small *salon* in the Empire Style in which, in arm-chairs, Madame de Wendel and Argyropoulo who knew Greek perfectly, and I myself, would read in turns the glorious words of Plato. At first this seemed an excellent idea, and we spent many evenings talking it over, but in the end Satie decided to give up the idea of the Empire *salon* and to have no scenery at all, and he wrote an oratorio for a woman's voice and a small orchestra. There is no doubt that this is his masterpiece, and nothing could be more moving than this music written for the beautiful words of Plato. When he had finished it he sent me the score, which is now in Paris in my collection of musical manuscripts. Jeanne Bathori sang *Socrates* for the first time in my music-room accompanied by the ethereal music of Satie. Soon after that Satie fell very ill, and we sent him to a nursing home where I saw him for the last time in 1929. He was the gentlest and kindliest of men, and was adored by his friends and by the little pupils who surrounded him at Arceuil and formed the *École d'Arceuil*, in which Sauguet was the most prominent figure.

One of his great friends was the poet Léon-Paul Fargue who was, in his way, a modern François Villon, the most eloquent, truculent and original poet of the animated group connected with the Académie Goncourt. He and Carco were the poets of Montmartre and sang the glories of *La Vie de Bohème*, mixing the language of Villon with that of Aristide Bruant of the *Cabaret du Chat Noir*. Fargue was one of the leading contributors to *Commerce*: that invaluable publication which presented new works by the most brilliant young authors of the day.

Once I had taken a yacht to go from Marseilles to Venice, and I had asked Fargue to join me and some members of my family on this short cruise along the South Coast of France to the heel of Italy. He was delighted to come, and was not deterred by my telling him at once that strict punctuality was to be observed by all on board as we had very little time for our journey, and every day I used to say, 'Tomorrow morning we shall be off Nervi: the launch will be ready at 9.30 to take us ashore, and we start back early in the afternoon'. Invariably as the launch glided away with the rest of the party soon after breakfast, we would see Fargue, dishevelled, rushing up on deck waving his arms frantically, having just awakened after a night spent on deck looking at the stars in the summer sky and drinking endless whiskies and sodas. I am sure Fargue saw nothing between Marseilles and Venice except in his imagination, which apparently was quite sufficient, for he wrote a most wonderful description of his cruise in the *Zara*.

At one time he had quarrelled with the Count de X, who had given a marvellous party at his house in Paris, at which some of Fargue's poems were recited. I forget exactly what caused the trouble, but it became so embittered that it was decided a duel must be fought. Count de X was an excellent host, and his parties were the best in Paris, but he was not a great scholar, and his spelling was often at fault. When he challenged Fargue, Fargue replied that he was quite willing to fight a duel, but that as the offended party he had the right to choose the weapons, and he added, '*J'ai la choix des armes et je choisis l'orthographie—vous êtes mort*'.

The last time I saw Fargue, he told me that he had left his old house far away on the Canal St. Martin and that he had taken a new apartment in the Montparnasse quarter where he very kindly invited me to dinner, for, he said, 'I now have a cook *à faire loucher les dieux*', but of course I knew Fargue well enough to understand that both the apartment and the cook were purely figments of his imagination, and in fact he had taken a small room in an hotel in the Boulevard St. Germain, where I hope he has remained.

I first knew Reynaldo Hahn in the early nineties, while he was doing his *service militaire* at Versailles, for he used to come to the delightful parties in Madeleine Lemerre's[1] studio, to which she invited not only *toute la société Parisienne*, but also all the artistic world of musicians, painters and writers.

Reynaldo Hahn and that excellent pianist Edouard Risler were both doing their *service militaire* and used to appear at these parties in uniform, and play and sing until any hour of the morning: as both were wonderfully gifted, it was a joy to hear them perform all sorts

[1] A flower-painter, very fashionable in her time, who illustrated Proust's first book, *Les Plaisirs et les jours.*

of music, for they were ardent admirers of the classics and all the more modern music we cared for in those days.

Reynaldo not only had an exquisite voice, but sang in the perfect way composers have, which seems quite natural or untaught. No one ever thought, 'How did he take that note—was it from the throat or from the diaphragm?' or 'Was that trick taught by Jean de Reszke or by Madame Marchesi or some other great teacher?' It did not matter at all how the note was taken, for it was always exactly as one imagined the song should be sung, and I do not think I have ever heard anyone except Reynaldo and Dame Ethel Smyth sing in this way: a way that no one can ever forget who has heard them perform.

Later on our acquaintance developed into a real friendship, and I constantly saw Reynaldo Hahn, whose early works delighted me, especially the *Études Latines*, the *Bal chez Béatrice d'Este* and many settings of words of Verlaine and *Le Ruban Dénoué*.

He was a great admirer of Gabriel Fauré, of Gounod and Bizet, whose *Adieux de l'Hôtesse Arabe* he sang in the most moving and unforgettable way. In Paris and in Venice we spent innumerable evenings together performing every sort of music—French, German, Italian or English. I remember him, for instance, singing Gounod's beautiful setting of Byron's *Maid of Athens*. Reynaldo also sang the music he himself had written for poems of Robert Louis Stevenson.

Year after year in Paris I constantly gave concerts in my music-room, and, although music by Bach or Schubert or Mozart was nearly always included in the programme, new works by young composers were very often heard, some of which must have sounded very strange to the patient audience, though many have now become well known and familiar. At some of these concerts Reynaldo's name appears on the programme coupled with his new Concerto for Piano or some other composition—but whether because he was no longer very young, or because the new generation had musical aims which he did not like, he developed a certain aversion from the most advanced young composers and for many years hardly ever came to my concerts.

Some years ago I met him and reproached him laughingly for this. He frowned, and in a half-laughing way replied, 'Until my dying day I shall always hate everything you like in music', to which I said that one cannot hate Mozart, Bach or Schubert, and that their music was always played at my concerts. 'Yes, possibly,' he answered, 'but you are too fond of the *va de l'avant*, and I absolutely cannot stand their ideas.' Upon which we decided to lunch together and talk over our differences of opinion. I remain very grateful to Reynaldo. I treasure his friendship, and I admire his wit.

DOROTHY BUSSY

SOME RECOLLECTIONS OF PAUL VALÉRY

THESE few recollections of Paul Valéry will perhaps seem unsuited to the personage of such a profound thinker as Valéry undoubtedly was, but they may give an aspect of him which, however slight and superficial, may yet show some of his fundamental characteristics and deepest convictions.

He was at ease with us (probably with everyone), generally gay, always spontaneous and natural, never caring to hide his humours, giving way unaffectedly to his fancies and absurdities. If one asked him a question, he answered readily, and one felt he answered the truth without disguise and with no other motive than sheer love of truth—swayed neither by self-interest nor self-respect, nor indeed by any sort of respect, whether for persons or opinions, impelled by his whole nature, in small things and great, to look truth unflinchingly in the face, to follow it wherever it might lead, with a courage that to most men seems almost superhuman.

In his talks with us he touched superficially on things he discussed more profoundly in his writings. But he adapted himself to his listeners and the subject he returned to most willingly (in spite of his laughing declaration that he never thought of poetry) was, if not poetry, then language.

His constant dwelling on the *technical* side of poetry, on the details of *métier*, on the importance of composition, all form part of the great theory that lay at the bottom of his teaching: The *method* that gives a man the power to produce a work is what matters and not the work itself.

I first met Paul Valéry a great many years ago (I forget the exact date) at Madame Muhlfeldt's, where he was in the habit of looking in about six o'clock in the evening when his work with M. Lebey of the Agence Havas was over. It was André Gide who introduced me to this very select Parisian *salon*. On that day there were only four or five *habitués* present—all men of distinction (among them were M. Louis Artus and young M. François Mauriac, then at the beginning of his career). I was the only woman and the only undistinguished person there. Mme Muhlfeldt received her guests lying, like a beautiful sea-lion, on her couch. Valéry was the last to come in. To the general public he was then little more than a name, round which a mysterious legend was accruing of the extraordinary esteem in which he was held by a few of his most important contemporaries.

Two little works of his—*Introduction à la Méthode de Léonard de Vinci* and *Une soirée avec M. Teste*—had, it is true, appeared some twenty years earlier, but they were very short and very abstruse, and when the publication of *Charmes* and *La Jeune Parque* achieved for him the reputation that enabled him to stand for the French Academy, many of the immortal forty had scarcely heard the new candidate's name and still less read his works.

That evening I had my first impression of Valéry—not a conspicuous figure, but unostentatiously elegant, with a perfectly natural ease, distinction and grace. He began to talk as soon as he came into the room and everyone listened. There was nothing dictatorial about his talk. I remember he described a lecture he had attended at Montpellier University. The lecturer—a doctor—was speaking of some obscure and mortal disease. Beside him, on the platform, as a living illustration, there stood, stripped to the waist, a poor man suffering from this complaint. No one who heard Valéry describe the look of the doomed man listening to his symptoms being pointed out to the public, and the callousness of the professor, could ever accuse him of being inhuman.

It happened that I was living at that time in the South of France, almost next door to one of those immortal forty who knew very little about this particular candidate when he came to pay him his first regulation Academic visit. The visit, however, was often repeated; Valéry stayed many times in the villa across the way and very often escaped from his more important hosts to spend a less official afternoon or evening with us. Once, indeed, it was with us he stayed a whole week rather than across the way, but the time when we most enjoyed his conversation was during the four or five days that he sat to my husband for his portrait. It was this that gave me the idea and the opportunity of taking a few notes of his talk. I set them down here just as I noted them at the time, disjointed and incomplete as they are.

* * *

Valéry sits in an armchair facing the painter, beside whom I am placed so that the sitter may be kept animated by having someone to talk to. My task is not difficult. The slightest interjection—a simple show of interest which, indeed, isn't show, sets him going. He doesn't attempt to *pose*. Simon is doing him *au vol*. He rolls and smokes endless cigarettes. He doesn't exactly fidget, isn't exactly restless, but mobile, '*d'une extrême mobilité*', says Simon. His face is almost liquid, the expressions flow over it so quickly and smoothly. He rambles on in a kind of disconnected monologue; laughs low; blinks; suddenly opens his eyes very wide and *drinks* the light; shuts them both; shuts only one. His great, dark blue eyes are not piercing (like Gide's) but absorbing. They rarely see outside objects, unless he deliberately looks at them; it is his own thought he is gazing at. He very often makes a contemptuous 'pooh' with his mouth. 'Et puis je m'en f—s!' is his favourite interjection.

Janie sits on the table just behind him. I have begged her to take notes as he talks, but she is afraid of being caught. Every now and then he quotes a few lines of poetry and sometimes turns round and appeals to her to supply a word or a line, which she very often can. 'C'est épatant d'avoir son livre comme cela derrière soi!' Sometimes he tries to catch her out.

'Le sujet de la *Jeune Parque*?' he said one day. 'C'est la physiologie et la psychologie d'une jeune fille—comme Janie, par exemple.'

Today, *à-propos* of I don't know what, it was of Victor Hugo he talked. 'Victor Hugo, c'est l'homme qui a fait les plus beaux vers. Rien n'est plus beau, rien n'est plus fort que lui par moments. Il a une virtuosité incomparable.' He then recited the last lines of the great poem on Théophile Gautier's death in *Toute la Lyre*.

His articulation which, as a rule, is so bad (he talks as if his mouth were full of potatoes) that one has the greatest difficulty in following him, becomes perfectly clear when he reads or recites. His voice is deep, sonorous, rolling, but he speaks low, uses very little emphasis, doesn't like readers 'qui cherchent l'effet'.

When he had finished the passage he commented on it and pointed out a few special lines:

. . . et ce grand siècle avec tous ses rayons,
Entre en cette ombre immense où, pâles, nous fuyons.

This line, he said, produces its effect of shade and terror, not so much by the meaning of the words themselves, as by the audacious use of its alliterative vowels, stretching out to an interminable length and the strange huddle of the final hemistich. And in the next two lines with their abrupt and almost cacophonous consonants:

Oh! quel farouche bruit font dans le crépuscule
Les chênes qu'on abat pour le bûcher d'Hercule! . . .

he made us hear the rhythmic strokes of a ferocious axe. And then he went on:

Le dur faucheur avec sa large lame avance
Pensif et pas à pas vers le reste du blé . . .

With barely an epithet, by sheer force of sound and rhythm, the slow, heavy, inexorable tread of the reaper advances towards us. Valéry's reading was an incomparable lesson in elocution and the inexhaustible capabilities of the French alexandrine.

'Ah! C'est beau cela! C'est absurde de dire le contraire; c'est un très grand bonhomme. Mais l'époque l'a gâté. S'il était venu 40 ans plus tard—1860 mettons—il aurait été bien meilleur; il aurait évité ce romantisme, cette rhétorique; il aurait donné plus à la musique et moins à l'expression oratoire. C'est amusant le mot de Cocteau: "Victor Hugo est un fou qui s'est cru Victor Hugo", mais Victor Hugo n'était pas bête comme le disent les imbéciles. Il a quelquefois *fait* la bête mais il ne l'était pas.' He gave a sketch of the subject of *Le Mot* and said: 'Ce n'est pas de la poésie évidemment mais c'est d'une virtuosité prodigieuse, fabuleuse. Ah! Quelle force dans le métier!' He quoted another line of Hugo's (I can't remember it) and pointed out the accumulation of *a*'s. And then he quoted two lines from Mallarmé's *Les Fenêtres*:

Ivre, il vit, oubliant l'horreur des saintes huiles,
Les tisanes, l'horloge et le lit infligé . . .

'Qui d'i's!' he exclaimed, 'Ah! il y a longtemps que je n'ai tant dit de poésie. Je n'y pense jamais à la poésie—jamais.'

I asked him, I don't know why, whether he had ever read *Paradise Lost*. 'Non. C'est très difficile, n'est-ce pas? Je suis très paresseux. Et puis j'ai très peu lu. Je n'oserais jamais avouer les livres que je n'ai pas lus.' Then, laughing heartily, 'En général je ne lis que les livres dont je fais les préfaces! Figurez-vous que je n'ai découvert Racine qu'en 1910. Je dois dire que j'ai trouvé ça *assez fort*. Sans images! Faire de l'effet sans effet, c'est ce qu'il y a de plus difficile. Mais Corneille! Voilà un écrivain magnifique! Et Bossuet! p—p—p! C'est le plus grand écrivain français, sans aucun doute, le plus grand.' He repeated this constantly and with great fervour. 'D'autre part, j'ai lu des livres que personne n'a lus. Des livres de technologie. C'est ça qui m'intéresse. Je ne lis pas pour apprendre les sentiments du monsieur qui écrit les livres. Je me fiche des sentiments du voisin. J'ai les miens! Ce que je lui demande ce sont des *moyens*.'

'La richesse c'est la possibilité. Un homme riche dit: "Si je veux faire cela, je le *peux*!" Il n'y a que cela qui soit intéressant—non pas de *faire* les choses mais de *pouvoir* les faire. Le *pouvoir*!'

'La théorie de l'art—il n'y a que cela qui m'intéresse. Quant aux œuvres—je m'en fous!'

He talked much during one of his visits of a subject which he discusses lengthily in some of his writings—the difference between music and poetry, between the poet and the musician:

'La musique est faite tandis que la poésie n'existe pas. Le musicien a ses notes, ses timbres etc. Il n'a plus qu'à s'occuper de la partie supérieure de son art—la combinaison. Le poète n'a que le langage, les mots. Mais le langage est une chose qui sert, qui est pratique, donc anti-poétique. Le musicien est soutenu par son art; le poète doit lutter tout le temps contre son instrument.

'Je voulais autrefois faire un ouvrage sur le langage, mais c'est terriblement difficile et j'ai échoué. Je ne sais pas qui pourrait faire cela. Il faudrait peut-être un mathématicien, mais d'habitude les mathématiciens n'ont pas le sens du langage. C'est un cerveau comme Laplace qu'il faudrait. Moi, j'ai essayé, mais je ne suis pas assez fort. Je me suis dit, "Ceci, n'est pas pour toi".

'Il y a beaucoup de livres sur le langage et il y en a d'excellents, mais il y a un tas de choses dont ils ne traitent pas. Les Grecs avaient très bien divisé le langage en deux parties—la logique formelle—ils n'en connaissaient pas d'autre—et la rhétorique (le mot est impropre), c'est-à-dire ce qui est figures, métaphores, la partie pour le tout, etc.; mais tout cela est bien insuffisant. Ils ont indiqué le chemin pourtant.

'Oui, c'est par rapport au cerveau que cela m'intéresse. Tout cela est intimement lié aux fonctions du cerveau. Mais il fallait commencer par inventer un langage—des symboles pour ainsi dire, mathématiques. J'y ai travaillé longtemps; j'ai des tas et des tas de notes à ce sujet.

'Mais il y a une partie de la littérature dont on ne s'est presque pas occupé et qui certainement pourrait donner quelque chose si l'on avait la force de s'y mettre—c'est la composition. On n'a jamais fait une pièce *composée*—un peu longue évidemment—oh, une centaine de vers. Je ne parle pas des crescendos, des montées, des descentes etc. —tout cela est élémentaire . . .'

'Comme une fugue, par exemple?'

'Oui, justement. La composition des parties. Personne ne fait cela. Ni pour la prose du reste. Il faudrait y réfléchir, l'étudier énormément, pendant longtemps. Mais toujours dans toute chose la préparation devrait être très longue et l'éxécution très rapide.'

One day he pulled out the support of the desk of my bureau—a thin, narrow, straight piece of wood. 'Ha! Ha!' he laughed, 'cela, c'est très voluptueux.' Then, with great care, he balanced a china cup on it, which he had been using as an ashtray (une 'cinéraire amphore', he said, and quoted almost the whole of Mallarmé's sonnet).

'Oh!' he said, 'n'ayez pas peur, je ne la casserai pas. Mais je peux vous dire que ma spécialité c'est de racommoder les choses qui sont cassées. Je suis très fort pour cela. C'est un travail très amusant et très philosophique. C'est la transmutation de ce que nous avons cassé en ce que nous aimerions que nous n'eussions pas cassé.'

He never missed an opportunity of a dig at philosophy, psychology, etc. Talking about his volume of essays *Variété*, which had recently come out, he said that he would probably bring out several more volumes of *Variété* with slightly different trends. For instance, the next *Variété* would be 'plus ou moins philosophique—si l'on peut employer ce mot *obscène*'.

He described the poet Emmanuel Signoret, who, towards the end of his career used to become extremely muddled (he drank himself to death—unfortunately, for he had unquestionable gifts). One day someone mentioned psychology in front of Signoret who, being half-seas over, had not quite grasped what had been said: 'Oh, tout ça, tout ça, vous savez—la psychologie, la photographie, la théologie —', he had exclaimed angrily. This, said Valéry, was the correct attitude towards these subjects.

'Est-ce que le livre de Thibaudet sur Mallarmé est bien?' we asked him. 'Bien et mal,' he answered. 'Il y mêle un tas de choses. Bergson, etc.' Then, chuckling a good deal, 'Thibaudet, c'est le Professeur Ivre—ivre de livres. C'est comme le *Bateau Ivre*:

Comme je descendais des livres impassibles
Je ne me sentis plus guidé par les bouquins.

Son livre sur moi? C'est effrayant. Il veut à tout prix faire de moi une espèce de second Bergson. J'estime beaucoup Bergson. Je m'entends très bien avec lui, nous avons beaucoup de points de contact, mais ma pensée est tout-à-fait différente de la sienne. Je ne donne pas du tout à l'instinct l'importance qu'il lui donne. L'élan vital etc. c'est un mot, ça ne veut rien dire. Et Thibaudet a fait ce livre sur moi à cause d'*un mot* dans la *Jeune Parque*.' He then quoted a line of the passage which describes the act of going to sleep:

. . . la devineresse
Intérieure s'use et se désintéresse.

'Il dit que j'ai employé le mot "se désintéresse" dans un sens bergsonien, tandis que c'est un mot extrêmement simple que j'ai employé dans le sens ordinaire.'

He spoke of the importance his imaginary reader has for the writer. 'Il est évident que l'on écrit pour que quelqu'un vous lise. Le public? Oui. Mais quel public? Un public de choix. En y réfléchissant, ce public se réduit de plus en plus jusqu'à ce qu'il vous semble qu'il ne reste plus qu'une seule personne qui puisse vous comprendre. Alors c'est une lettre qu'on écrit. C'est pour cela que les lettres sont souvent d'une importance capitale dans l'œuvre d'un auteur. Et puis il vous arrive de croire qu'il n'y a que vous-même qui puissiez comprendre votre pensée. Alors à quoi bon l'écrire?'

'Il y a deux espèces de lecteurs—le lecteur passif et le lecteur actif. Le lecteur passif subit. Le lecteur actif s'arrête à chaque phrase et fait des objections. Il cherche à se rendre compte comment l'auteur a été amené à mettre *telle* chose dans son livre. L'auteur doit prévenir toutes les objections qu'on peut faire. Et puis dans un livre vous n'agissez plus. C'est un duel dont vous êtes absent.'

'J'étais un très mauvais élève—oui, à Montpellier. Je n'ai jamais pu apprendre le grec. C'était un camarade qui me faisait toujours mes versions grecques. J'étais toujours en punition. Le professeur de rhétorique était un imbécile. Un professeur du lycée m'a écrit dernièrement pour me dire qu'il avait mis ma photographie dans l'étude. "Mais monsieur," lui ai-je écrit en réponse, "qu'est-ce qui vous prend? Vous êtes fou. J'étais un très mauvais élève et je m'en flatte."'

It was in the spring of 1925 that he said to me, 'Je suis un éternel fatigué. Mon hiver a été affreux. J'ai eu tous les embêtements possibles et de tous les genres. Ah! que je suis mal fichu—au moral et au physique!

'Je n'ai eu le temps de rien faire. Tout mon temps est pris par des imbécilités—faire partie de Comités qui décernent des Prix Littéraires! C'est idiot! Du reste je juge très mal la littérature. Comment pourrais-je en juger? *Je n'y crois pas*. Quand on lit des romans, on se dit à chaque phrase, "Cela pourrait être autrement. Il n'y a pas de raison pour que cela ne soit pas autrement." Alors comment voulez-vous qu'on s'y intéresse?'

'But', I interposed, thinking of *Werther*, *La Nouvelle Héloïse*, and so many 'epoch-making' works, 'les romans *agissent*, il faut y croire.' Valéry's thought, however, was fixed on the credibility of the work itself. 'Il faut y croire!' he laughed, 'p—p—c'est comme ça qu'on justifie toutes les religions!'

'Barrès? Non, je n'aime pas beaucoup cela' (and one felt that this was an understatement, pushed to an extreme for the sake of politeness). 'Il appartient à la race des grands charlatans. Lui, Madame de Noailles, Rostand, d'Annunzio—il y en a eu quatre ou cinq comme cela de nos temps. Cela joue avec des choses comme la mort, la volupté, Jeanne d'Arc, Jésus Christ, p—, p—, p—. Ça n'est pas très décent.'

'Claudel? Oui, c'est un grand poète—un grand poète . . . Mais il n'a ni élégance ni économie—Il se sert d'une grue pour soulever une cigarette.' He said this as he was rolling his cigarette with a single elegant gesture.

Shortly before one of his visits, I had been discussing with an English poet *Le Cimetière Marin* and I told Valéry that B.T. had particularly objected to three lines in it:

Comme le fruit se fond en jouissance,
Comme en délice il change son absence
Dans une bouche où sa forme se meurt . . .

'Ah! Ce sont les seuls bons vers du *Cimetière Marin*. Oui, vraiment ils ne sont pas trop mauvais ceux-là. Ah! si j'avais toujours écrit comme cela, j'aurais fait quelque chose de pas trop mal. Tout le reste de mon œuvre, je m'en fous, mais ces trois vers, j'en suis assez content. Alors, s'il n'a pas aimé ces vers, il n'a pas dû aimer non plus,

Le changement des rives en rumeur.'

'Justement, il m'a fait une scène à propos de ces vers.'

'Oui, c'est assez difficile. C'est très elliptique. Ça veut dire tout simplement que les vagues font du bruit dans l'air. J'ai écrit le *Cimetière Marin* parce que je voulais faire des vers de dix syllabes. C'est une forme qu'on a très peu employée en français. Ça devient vite vulgaire, surtout quand le vers est divisé en 5—5. Les vers du *Cimetière* sont de 6—4 ou de 4—6. Il y en a un de 5—5. La Fontaine en a fait de très mauvais en 5—5. Victor Hugo en a très peu fait. Baudelaire en a fait. *La Mort des Amants*, par exemple:

Nous aurons des lits pleins d'odeurs légères . . .

Ça ne donne pas de très bons résultats. Au fond le *Cimetière Marin* c'est le vers du Dante:

Per me si va nella città dolente . . .
Ce toit tranquille où marchent des colombes . . .

'Je me suis amusé à mettre le *Cimetière Marin* en alexandrins, en ajoutant deux syllabes à chaque vers:

Ce toit tranquille et pur où marchent des colombes . . .

Puis je lui ai coupé les cheveux.'

'But at any rate,' he said, 'je peux me flatter d'avoir donné le coup de grâce au vers libre.'

He once complained that it was said of him that he spent too much time at tea-parties and with society ladies. He declared that he certainly preferred the company of a pleasant woman of the world to that of a third-rate intellectual.

There had recently been a controversy between Gide and certain Roman Catholics on religious matters. The thing was a misunderstanding, said Valéry. 'Pour Gide, le royaume des cieux est en nous,' whereas for the Catholics, 'it's somewhere over there', pointing with his stick to the sky. 'On s'est trompé de royaume!' he said with huge chucklings.

Was the story he told us about a visit he once paid to London an imaginary fable? Was it a mere illustration of an attack of ennui? It seems impossible to believe it literally. He was staying in a London boarding house, he said. It was Sunday and there was a fog. He decided to commit suicide, and chose hanging as his method. But a cord must be found. He set about looking for one, but in the course of his search, he came upon a book, which of course he opened. It was a collection of funny stories by Alphonse Allais (how did it get there, one wonders?); they amused him so much that he went on reading and by the time he got to the end, his desire to find a cord had left him.

In the evenings, as we were sitting over the fire, he used often to read aloud poetry to us and talk about what he read. One evening it was Villon's *Prayer to the Virgin* that he read, beginning

Dame des cieux, régente terrienne . . .

He said that Villon was one of the greatest of French poets, and that much as he admired Ronsard and the Pléiade, it was perhaps a pity that they had inclined the course of French poetry so definitely towards the ornate, decorative, Italian style and away from the more specifically French manner of Villon. Not till Verlaine had that note been struck again.

We asked him to read us something out of *Charmes*. He chose *La Pythie*. In some book, discussing, I think, inspiration, in which he didn't believe, he dwells on what he told us briefly that evening. 'God sometimes gives a poet a single line—he must find the others himself. I wrote *La Pythie* round a single line which God gave me:

. . . Pâle, profondément mordue . . .

One evening he talked of the great difficulty of introducing a *period* into a poem—a passage, that is, of some ten or twelve lines without a break.

'How rare it is to find such a passage! What skill, what power is needed for such an achievement!' Then he pulled down from the little book-case over the mantelpiece, a volume of Racine. 'But here is one!' he said. 'A superb accomplishment!' He opened the book at the scene where Esther, having dismissed her chorus of young girls, kneels down alone on the stage and sends up the prayer to God which begins:

. . . O mon souverain Roi,
Me voici donc tremblante et seule devant toi,

and contains the great period of ten lines which he read aloud to us:

Pour moi que tu retiens parmi ces infidèles,
Tu sais combien je hais leurs fêtes criminelles,
Et que je mets au rang des profanations
Leur table, leur festins et leurs libations;
Que même cette pompe ou je suis condamnée,
Ce bandeau dont il faut que je paraisse ornée
Dans ces jours solennels à l'orgueil dédiés,
Seule et dans le secret je le foule à mes pieds,
Qu'à ces vains ornements je préfère la cendre,
Et n'ai de goût qu'aux pleurs que tu me vois répandre.

It is impossible not to hear an echo of this passage in *la Jeune Parque's* invocation to the stars, in which Valéry himself has attempted and perhaps succeeded in accomplishing what he considered a rare and consummate achievement—a period in verse:

Tout-puissants étrangers, inévitables astres,
Qui daignez faire luire au lointain temporel,
Je ne sais quoi de pur et de surnaturel,
Vous qui dans les mortels plongez jusques aux larmes
Ces souverains éclats, ces invincibles armes
Et les élancements de votre éternité,
Je suis seule avec vous, tremblante, ayant quitté
Ma couche; et sur l'écueil mordu par la merveille,
J'interroge mon cœur quelle douleur l'éveille,

Quel crime par moi-même ou sur moi consummé? . . .
. . . Ou si le mal me suit d'un songe refermé
Quand (au velours du souffle envolé l'or des lampes)
J'ai de mes bras épais environné mes tempes,
Et longtemps de mon âme attendu les éclairs?

Once, when I was welcoming him to our house after a long time had gone by without our seeing him, he took both my hands and kissed them one after the other with a gesture of charming courtesy. 'Alors, vous n'avez pas trop peur du monstre?' he said.

A monster? Yes. But was there ever one so strangely human?

J. P. HODIN

MEMORIES OF KAFKA

I

We are nihilistic ideas born in God's head.—FRANZ KAFKA.

IN ORDER to understand the inquisitorial determinism of Kafka's work, one has to take into account the time in which it came into existence and the ground on which it grew. Of the time it is enough to say it was the pre-war and post-war age. But the ground, Prague, the city where East and West interpenetrate and races mingle, the place where peoples and civilizations have met and influenced each other, centuries of history pervading narrow streets like an intolerable burden, and in the lamp-light by night the Latin thoughts of the Age of Enlightenment fight duels with the sombre world of Dostoievsky's ideas, where religious feuds cast their bloody shadows, and Slavonic melancholy, Jewish Talmudism, Catholic mysticism, Hussite puritanism, carved their runes in the people's faces—only in Prague could fantasies like Kafka's come into existence. Kafka's flight from his parents' house is at the same time a flight from Prague, flight from the weight of tradition, flight from the multitude of tongues into the unequivocal. An analysis of Kafka's work is not complete unless it takes into account the poetic and tormenting influence of Prague.

What follows shows how Kafka's fate and his work are reflected in the mind of an artist who grew up in the same environment as himself.

The painter F. Feigl, now living in England, gave me these reminiscences: 'It was in the year 1894. Kafka and I went to school together. It was the Altstädter Deutsche Gymnasium. He was about ten years old, a thin, frail boy with very big, black eyes, a long skull and pointed ears which gave him a degenerate look. The reason why I remember him so clearly is that his mother always came to fetch him after school, which struck us other children as strange.

'Then I lost sight of him. It was not till 1907 that I heard of him again. In the circle of the group of modern painters known in Prague as "The Eight", Max Brod mentioned during a discussion: "I can tell you the name of a very great artist—Franz Kafka." And he showed us some drawings of his, which evoked the memory of early Paul Klee or Kubin. They were expressionistic. Kafka did not develop his gift for drawing any further. The elocutionist Ludwig Hart told me once: "Do you realize that Franz Kafka is the greatest writer of Prague?" At that time Rilke was no longer in Prague and Werfel had settled down in Vienna. Then we struck up a friendship, Kafka and I. Kafka was associated with a group of writers who used to read their work to each other. I remember hearing Kafka there when he read his sketch "The Scuttle-Rider". The background of this story is the shortage of coal after the First World War. A man rides through the air on a coal-scuttle, to the coal-merchant's. It is like things of E. T. A. Hoffmann's, only less mystical. It made more the impression of something humorous and grotesque. Kafka read it with right feeling for the fine points and in a boyish voice. Boyishness—that is the characteristic that clung to him all his life.

'Later in Berlin he once introduced me to his fiancée. He had an "eternal" fiancée and always said he was not worthy of her. Behind things like these there is hidden a sexual development that is by no means normal. I believe Kafka was afraid of bodily contact. He hated reality. He avenged himself on the causality of the world with a microscopically sharp analytical method. Under the microscope the causality of everyday life becomes a drama. Dimensions lose their sense, because they look quite different under the magnifying-glass from what they are to the naked eye. He makes the events of a story into a novel. His sentences have beauty and order because they are built up on a long-term policy. That was necessary, because his thoughts had a complicated causal nexus. It made him creative in his use of language, just as he was in the analysis of the soul. One could call his writing psycho-analytical, and now it is exploited by people who visualize nothing and so reduce it *ad absurdum*. For it all depends, after all, on what one finds under the microscope.

'Kafka's life was like one of his novels. This lonely man, who had a longing for the romantic—I remember him living for some time in one of the little houses in the Alchimistengasse in Prague—had to work in an insurance company, for a small salary, with slow promotion every five years. He had a tyrannical father, who forced him to lead a dull and sober life, and with whom he had nothing in common. When we met—we used to go for long walks together—he was very eager to get to know something about the other arts. Once we tried to analyse the elements of art. That was about five years before his death. We came to the conclusion that the essential of painting was space, of music time, and of writing causality. That corresponds to the basic elements of sensual perception: spatial, temporal and causal. Then I realized for the first time that his way of writing expressed a new causality, a new causal connection. Kafka did not talk of that again.

'Once I had a discussion about him with Max Brod, who was his squire and herald. For me the interesting question was how far one can go in this displacement of causality. Then I classified Kafka as a romantic. Brod protested against that and said it was a limitation. For me it does not imply a judgement of values.

'To simplify into microscopic or over-life-size terms was typically Continental and basically "baroque". We use a baroque and almost grotesque scale whenever we think of Prague, that fantastic city. Everything fantastic always had a great appeal for the people of Prague. If someone cannot get any coal, it becomes a tragic experience. The "ride" is an idea realized in visual terms.

'I believe I understood Kafka, but he was shy of letting anyone really get to know him. If I recall today the type to which he belonged, picture how he used to move and what he used to do, I understand him better still. Even at that time I assumed that his way of writing was a self-sufficient relief for him. He needed no one else for confirmation. Marriage with a woman, the relationship of of author and public, these are realities. He defended himself against reality, creating for himself a reality of his own, in which he took revenge on the apparent senselessness and injustice of reality by caricaturing it.

'I met Kafka again in Berlin. We often spoke of the same questions. At that time he bought a picture of mine, a Prague study. There was a touch of Munch about it, something uncanny. I once found Prague an uncanny experience, when returning from rationalistic Germany. It was characteristic of him to choose precisely this picture. He seems to have had the typical mixture of hate and love for Prague. He gave the picture to his fiancée.

'Then I suddenly heard that he had died of tuberculosis of the larynx. Fundamentally Kafka remained a boy, to whom it was not granted to grow old. He died in the midst of his youth, while he still faced life with all the curiosity of a child, in spite of the fact that he was over forty.

'Concerning the characteristics of Kafka's work I should like to say that it shows all the signs of a deformed imagination. The deformed comic in a circus, the clown, has a nose that is too long or feet that are too big. All grotesqueness contains the comic element of deformity. Kafka's art was tragic in its deformity, because he put the negative and tormenting aspect of life into the foreground. All his work is like a nightmare; what is typical of it is this dream-like, nightmarish quality.

'Every artist moves between extremes. Yet every liberty has its limits. Cézanne approaches the banal when he paints apples in monumental fashion. Only art-historians and art-dealers, who make a living by it, see things differently. But artists recognize it as the failings of a genius. Even in Prague I felt the torturing quality of Kafka's art. Still more today, when we have to find the decisive ethical standpoint in life. Everything that only underlines egotism, everything merely subjective—the asocial approach gives the impression of genius, but it remains asocial—is of an unhealthy influence. It ran wild in politics, almost like futurism. The whole era was ripe for such ideas, which brought it to the edge of the abyss in politics and in an evolutionary sense to the atomic bomb and to the triumph of analysis. Analysis is a great poison. It is a rhythm of corrosion, a rhythm of the brain.

'True art is always synthesis. Kafka's mind was basically corrosive and analytic. Why is analysis as an end in itself not a mark of genius? Because it has no real content. It has no real meaning. Analysis pretends to be both content and form. Kafka's object was nothing, it was nothingness; he analysed analysis. It was exactly the same in cubism and in surrealism. When they had split up the whole into its elements and finally declared form to be the meaning, these were only human, egocentric delusions. But there one can see how movements come into existence. The surrealists are imitated, Kafka is imitated. Brueghel's picture comes into my mind: the blind men, who are guided by a blind man, all fall into the ditch. The less one can see, the more convulsively one clings to a coat-tail.

'About Kafka I should say that he was honest and did not care about worldly success. He did not want to be praised, and we do not want to find fault with him. What I have said was only to point out his characteristics. The forces of which one gains possession, through analysis, can after all lead to good as well. The artist, too, must be a "critic". The goal appears to me to be a life in which pulses the life-blood of a unified ethical idea. We are still remote from it.'

II

Then I beheld all the work of God, that man cannot find out the work that is done under the sun: because however much a man labour to seek it out, yet he shall not find it; yea moreover, though a wise man think to know it, yet shall he not be able to find it. *Ecclesiastes*

Some deny misery by pointing at the sun; he denies the sun by pointing at misery. FRANZ KAFKA

In July 1923 Kafka left Prague. He settled down in Berlin, determined never to return to his parents' house and to devote himself entirely to writing. It was then that he met the woman with whom he founded a home for the short time that he still had to live.

I have spent many hours with Mrs. Dora Dymant, talking about Kafka and those last months of his life. I am indebted to her for all that she told me so simply, warmly and candidly. Before I begin to quote it, it must first be said, as she herself emphasized: 'I am not objective, I cannot be. It is more than twenty years since Kafka went. But after all, one can only measure time by the importance of one's experiences. Even today it is often difficult for me to talk about

Kafka. Frequently it is not the facts which are decisive, it is a mere matter of atmosphere. What I tell has an inner truth. Subjectivity is part of it.

'I met Kafka for the first time on the Baltic, in the summer of 1923. I was very young then, nineteen, and was working voluntarily in the holiday camp of a Berlin youth hostel, in Müritz, near Stettin. One day on the beach I saw a family playing—parents and two children. I was particularly struck by the man. I could not shake off the impression he made on me. I even followed them into the town, and later met them again. One day it was announced in the hostel that Dr. Franz Kafka was coming to supper. At that time I was in charge of the kitchen. When I looked up from my work—the room had grown dark, someone was standing outside the window—I recognized the man from the beach. Then he came in—I didn't know then that it was Kafka, and the woman with whom he had been on the beach was his sister. He said in a soft voice: "Such tender hands, and such bloody work for them to do!" (Kafka was at that time a vegetarian.) In the evening we were all sitting on benches at long tables; a little boy got up and, as he went away, was so embarrassed that he fell down. Kafka said to him, his eyes shining with admiration: "What a clever way to fall and what a clever way to get up again!" When later I thought of these words again, their central meaning seemed to me to be that everything could be saved—except Kafka. Kafka could not be saved.

'He was tall and slim and dark skinned and had a loping walk that at first made me believe he must be a half-breed Indian and not a European. He swayed a little, but held himself straight. Only he carried his head a little on one side. That was typical of him. It expressed a relationship-symptom. Kafka had the bearing of the lonely man who is always in relation to something outside himself. It was not exactly a kind of listening; there was also something very affectionate about it. I should like to call it the symptom of a need for relations, which expressed something like this: "I on my own am nothing, I am only something when connected with the outer world". Why did Kafka make such a deep impression on me? I came from the East, a dark being full of dreams and premonitions, who might have sprung from a book of Dostoievsky's. I had heard so much of the West—knowledge, clarity, style of living—I came to Germany with a receptive soul, and it gave me much. But over and over again I had the feeling that the people there needed something which I could give them. After the catastrophe of the war everyone expected salvation through the intermediary of the East. But I had run away from the East, because I believed the light was in the West. Later I became less ambitious in my dreams: Europe was not what I had expected it to be, its people had no rest in their innermost being. They lacked something. In the East one knew what man was; perhaps one could not move so freely in society and could not express oneself so easily, but one did know the consciousness of the unity of man and creation. When I saw Kafka for the first time, his image corresponded to my idea of man. But even Kafka turned to me attentively, as though expecting something from me.

'The essential characteristics of his face were the very open, sometimes even wide-open eyes, whether he was talking or listening. They were not staring in horror, as it had been said of him; it was rather more an expression of astonishment. His eyes were brown and shy. When he spoke, they lit up; there was humour in them; but it was not so much irony as mischievousness—as if he knew of something that other people didn't know. But he was entirely without solemnity. Generally he had a very lively way of talking, and he liked talking. His conversational style was full of imagery, like his writing. Sometimes one got the impression of a craftsmanlike satisfaction, when he succeeded in expressing well what he wanted to say. His wrists were very slender, and he had long, ethereal fingers, speaking fingers which took on shape while he was telling a story and accompanied what he said much more than the hands did. Later on we very often amused ourselves making shadows on the wall with our hands. He was extremely clever at it. Kafka was always cheerful. He liked to play; he was the born playmate, always ready for some mischief. I don't think that depressions were a dominant characteristic of his, except before he began to write. They did not appear at regular intervals; usually there was a reason for them which could be traced. For instance, when he came back from town. Then he was often more than depressed; it was almost revolt. It was the time of the inflation. Kafka suffered badly under the conditions. He had a rigorous attitude towards himself. Whatever might happen around him, he had no right to shut himself off from it. So the way to town was always a kind of Golgotha for him. He almost broke down physically under it. He could stand in queues for hours, not only with the intention of buying something, but simply from the feeling: blood was flowing, and so his must flow, too. In this way he experienced communion with an unhappy people in an unhappy time. I can see it clearly as the theme of *The Trial*, where he condemns K., because he tried to shape his life differently from a life of crucifixion. But there is no life except in "crucifixion", and nobody is acquitted by the highest court of all. That is my interpretation. "How can it ever become different?" he said to me at that time. There are Helferich, Hilferding, Rathenau—but no help (Hilfe), no advice (Rat). He felt as if people did not dare to call things by their right names, as if they were trying to hide all tragedy behind fair words.

'We lived in Steglitz, later in Zehlendorf, first in one room, then in two. The first lodgings we left because of the landlady. Kafka described her in *A Small Woman*: "Only out of disgust, out of a never-ceasing disgust that was her perpetual driving-power, did she occupy herself with me"—that was how he put it.

'Kafka had to write; he had to, it was his life-breath. The days on which he wrote were the rhythm of this breath. If it is said of him that he wrote for a fortnight, that means he wrote for fourteen successive evenings or nights. Kafka used to walk around, heavily and uneasily, before he began to write. Then he spoke little, ate without appetite, took no interest in things, and was very sad. He wanted to be alone. In the beginning I didn't understand that; later on I always felt when he was going to begin writing. At other times he showed a great intensity towards even the most ordinary things. But on such days that vanished completely. I can only differentiate between these days, in their various tensions, by comparing them to colours: purple, dark green, or blue days. Later on he liked me to stay in the room while he was writing. Once he started to write after supper. He wrote for a very long time, and I fell asleep on the sofa. The electric light was on. All at once he was sitting at my side: I woke up and looked at him. A palpable change was visible in his face. The traces of the spiritual tension were so obvious that they had changed the face utterly.

'*The Burrow*, one of his last stories, was written in one night. It was in the winter; he began early in the evening and had finished by the morning. Then he worked on it again. He told me about it jokingly and seriously. This story was autobiographical. It must have been the foreboding of the return to his parents' house, the end of freedom, which aroused this panic feeling of fear in him. He pointed out to me that I was the "citadel" in the burrow. He often read to me what he had written. He never analysed, never explained. Sometimes it sounded humorous to me, with a sort of self-mockery. Time and again he said: "Well, I wonder if I've escaped the ghosts?"

'This was the name with which he summarized everything that had tormented him before he came to Berlin. He was as though possessed by this idea; it was a kind of sullen obstinacy. He wanted to burn everything that he had written in order to free his soul from these "ghosts". I respected his wish, and when he lay ill, I burnt things of his before his eyes. What he really wanted to write was to come afterwards, only after he had gained his "liberty". Literature for him was something sacred, absolute, incorruptible, something great and pure. The literature of today is not what Kafka understood by literature. Kafka felt unsure of most things in life and expressed himself very cautiously. But when it was a matter of literature, he was unapproachable and knew no compromise. There he was concerned with the whole. He not only wanted to penetrate to the bottom of things. He was at the bottom. But where the solution of human confusion was in question, he would not have any half measures. He experienced life as a labyrinth; he could not see the solution. He never got further than despair. For him everything was interwoven with cosmic causality, even the most everyday things. One finds this feeling in the East too, a longing for the wholeness of life. In the East there are spiritual matters which have to be fulfilled unconditionally, or else one is unable to live. Kafka felt that. The West has forgotten it. And that is why God has abandoned it. That is why all those things could happen which we have experienced. Therein, so I believe, lies one of the reasons for the interest in Kafka. The consciousness that God has abandoned us.

'I have been reproached for having burnt some of what Kafka wrote. I was so young then, and young people live in the present and perhaps in the future too. After all, for him all that had been nothing but self-liberation! At that time he had no more respect, no more love for his father. He had already recognized him: the man who dominated through possessions and "possesses" even his family. Kafka was very bitter about his father, and time and again, with biting humour, he would tell the story of how he had dedicated a book to him, and when he wanted to present it to him, his father only said coldly: "Put it on the table beside my bed".

'In Berlin Kafka believed that he had liberated himself from the tyranny of his past. But the earlier problems were too tightly bound up with his life. As soon as one touched even a single string of it, all the others vibrated, too. His inner life was of unfathomable depth and unbearable. He did not really hate Prague. He spoke of Prague in the way a European speaks of Europe. What tormented Kafka most was the fear of becoming dependent on his parents. This dependence endangered the "burrow". Hence his thriftiness. He wanted to accustom himself to a spartan life. In Berlin he believed for a time in the possibility of saving his life, in a personal solution for the inner and outer confusion. He wanted to feel like an average human being, with only a few wishes and needs. We made so many plans. Once we talked about opening a small restaurant. He was to be the waiter. That meant seeing everything without being seen, being right in the midst of everyday life. Indeed, he did do it, in his own way.

'He attached great importance to being carefully dressed. He would have regarded it as a lack of courtesy to go somewhere without having his tie perfectly knotted. His suits were made by a first-class tailor and he always took a long time about dressing. It was not vanity. He looked into the mirror without complacency, quite critical and judicial. It was done in order not to offend the world.

'He liked to go shopping; he liked simple people. His appearance with the shopping-basket or the milk-can was a familiar sight in our neighbourhood. In the mornings he often went for a walk alone. His day was strictly planned, all with a view to his writing. On his walks he always took a notebook with him, or if he forgot it, he would buy one on the way. He loved Nature, although I never heard him say the word.

'Among the things of which he was particularly fond was his pocket-watch. When we got into trouble with our landlady about the electric light—for he often wrote all through the nights—I bought a paraffin lamp. He loved its soft, living light and always wanted to fill it up himself; he would play about with the wick and continually found new virtues in it. He did not take a kindly view of the telephone and was distressed when it rang. I always had to answer it. I think he did not feel quite comfortable about machines and mechanical things. He was very fond of my calendar, which had a proverb for every day. Later we had one each and on special occasions Kafka used to "consult the calendar". Once, when I was washing grapes—he was fond of eating grapes and pineapples—I broke the glass. Immediately he appeared in the kitchen, holding the calendar in his hand, and said, wide eyed: "One moment can ruin everything". Then he handed me the page. The truth sounded so trivial. He smiled.

'Although Kafka preferred to remain undisturbed, we often had visitors. I still remember Willi Haas, the editor of *Die Literarische Welt* and Rudolf Kayser of the *Neue Rundschau*. Once Werfel came to read to Kafka from his new book. They were together for a long time. Then I saw Werfel go away, weeping. When I entered the room, Kafka was sitting there completely shattered and he murmured to himself several times: "To think that anything so terrible has to be at all!" He was weeping, too. He had let Werfel go away without having been able to utter a single word about his book. Anyone who put himself into Kafka's hands either had the most encouraging experience or despaired. There was nothing in between He had the same inexorable severity towards his own work. And although he never really believed that he had achieved what he wanted, I believe he never had the feeling that he was a dilettante.

'Kafka never made other people feel uneasy. He attracted everybody, and whoever came to him did so with a kind of solemnity. They walked as though on tip-toe or on soft carpets.

'We were generally alone, and he often used to read aloud to me from Grimms' and Andersen's fairy-tales or from E. T. A. Hoffmann's *Kater Murr*, or from Hebel's *Schatzkästlein*. There was the story of the miner's sweetheart who accompanied her lover to the pit and never saw him alive again. They brought the bodies out into the daylight, but her lover was not among them. Her life passed away; she grew grey and old. Then one day his body was found in a gallery, quite unharmed, preserved by the gases. She came and embraced her lover; she had waited for him all these years and now it was a wedding and a funeral in one. Kafka liked this story for its "wholeness". It was as natural as great things always are. And he loved Kleist. He was capable of reading his *Marquis von O* to me five or six times in succession. He also used to read to me from

Goethe's *Hermann und Dorothea*. He, too, was moved by the love of everyday life that is described there. The chance to live the way he wanted made him enter into a concrete relationship towards home, money and family. In a non-bourgeois sense. I emphasize that because I remember how calmly and objectively Kafka spoke to me about his fiancée. She was an excellent girl, but utterly bourgeois. Kafka felt that marrying her would mean marrying the whole lie that was Europe. And then there was the fear that he would not find time for writing. On the other hand, his engagement was an attempt to acclimatize himself to middle-class life, and at the same time a sort of curiosity. Really he wanted to know everything and to find out about everything. A haemorrhage, connected with his tuberculosis, cleared away all his doubts.'

In young Dora Dymant Kafka experienced that deep-rootedness of the soul of Eastern man. In Western Europe recognition of the tragic situation of the time only rarely goes hand-in-hand with an affirmation of life. Cynicism and pessimism prevail. Martin Buber transmitted to the West the wisdom and cheerfulness of that East where Dora Dymant grew up, and this gift of hers enchanted Kafka. He even wished to return there with her, in order to enter a community and to live a simple life in it. And that was the question to which he devoted himself in *The Castle*. He would have tried it anywhere, but in the West it was probably no longer possible. The problem of having 'no roots' has much deeper causes in Kafka than his biographer assumes.

* * *

Once I directed the conversation towards *The Burrow*, which shows man in his subterranean corridors as a sniffing animal possessed by fear. I pointed to *A Report for an Academy*, in which an ape is forced to become a 'human being'. ('Before that I had so many ways of escape, and now there are none left.') I pointed to the *Investigations of a Dog* and *The Giant Mole*. It is not horror that one experiences in reading them, not the satirical bitterness of Swift, it is not the poetic-moralizing intention one finds in the fables of Æsop or la Fontaine, nor are they socio-political views, as in the *Roman du Renard*, where the author is forced to show humans in animal guise—it is the intention of lowering human existence to the level of animal life, and it contains disgust. Kafka himself must have felt this disgust.

Dora Dymant said quietly: 'I, too, think *The Metamorphosis* is worse than *The Penal Settlement*'. ('Our verdict does not sound harsh. The commandment which the condemned man broke will be written on his body with the harrow.') All the 'animal' aspect is shown against the background of a universal catastrophe, a cosmic misunderstanding, like the one that stares at us with glassy eyes out of *The Imperial Message*: 'The message has been sent out to you. You are there, and the message is there—only the communications are too complicated. There is no chance that the message will ever reach you.' If we compare that with the loving spirit of Saint Francis, who included even the animals in salvation, the deep communion of God, creation, and man that lies in Spinoza's 'Deus sive natura', and his gentle 'Amor Dei intellectu', we shall penetrate deeper into Kafka's way of thinking.

* * *

Kafka's human tragedy soon reached its end. At Christmas 1923 he caught a chill and was in bed for four weeks with pneumonia. At that time he read a great deal, and he was very busy with the proofs of *The Fasting Man*, which had just come.

Kafka did not recover. He knew how ill he was, and he had long wanted to die. An uncle, who was a doctor, came to take him to Prague. This illness was the last and final 'defeat' for Kafka. What went on in his mind then, Frau Dora Dymant has tried to reconstruct from what Kafka once said to her: 'Tearing himself away from Prague, was, even though very late, the great achievement in life without which one has no right to die. The return to his parents' house was the return to dilettantism in life. That particularly tortured Kafka; one could see it in the mental oppression which conquered him.

'I stayed in Berlin. Kafka did not want me to come to Prague, to the house from which all his disasters had come. A part of his total complex was that he hated his father and felt guilty because of it! I assume that he often murdered him in his dreams. At that time I received daily letters from him. They were taken from me by the Gestapo, together with his diaries, and in spite of all attempts no one has succeeded in finding them again. There were about thirty-five letters. In one of them Kafka mentioned "technical errors" in the way man acts towards himself. He was then preoccupied with the question of Tolstoy's fight for his own liberation and discovered some "technical errors" in that. Another time he told me of a dream he had had. Highwaymen had fetched him from his Berlin lodgings, shut him up in a shed in some back yard and gagged him. "I know that I am lost, because you can't find me." And then he suddenly hears that she is still in sight, he tries to tear himself free, thinks he is already free, and has even succeeded in pushing the gag out of his mouth. She only needed to hear his shout—but at this very moment it is discovered by the highwaymen and they gag him again.

'The uncanny thing about Kafka's mortal illness was its outbreak. I felt that he had brought it about by downright force. It was like a deliverance for him; the decision was taken out of his hands. Kafka positively welcomed the illness, even though in the last moments of his life he once more wished to live.

'He left Prague a sick man, but spiritually in good form. It was in a sanatorium in the Vienna Woods, where his sister had taken him, that I met him again. There for the first time tuberculosis of the larynx was diagnosed. Kafka was no longer permitted to speak, and so he wrote everything down: above all, the devastating effect Prague had had on him. He stayed there for three weeks. When the illness became worse, he was taken to a specialist in a hospital in Vienna. There he lay in a room together with many other gravely ill patients. Somebody died every night. He "told" me about it, pointing once to a bed that was empty. Another time he showed me a patient, a jolly man who walked about a lot, enjoyed eating and had a tube in his throat. He had a moustache and shining eyes. Kafka was very pleased that he had such a good appetite. The next day he pointed at his empty bed. Kafka was not shaken, but positively angry, as if he could not grasp that the man who had been so gay had had to die. I shall never forget his malicious, ironical smile.

'From the hospital Kafka was removed to a sanatorium in Klosterneuburg-Kierling, near Vienna. There he lived in a wonderful, permanently sunny room with a balcony! I stayed there with him, and later his friend Dr. Klopstock came. Kafka wrote some letters from this sanatorium: to his parents, to his brothers and sisters, and to Max Brod. The latter came to visit him, after he had given a reading in Vienna, in order not to let Kafka notice in what danger he knew him to be. When he was in the sanatorium, Kafka did no writing, except for the "Conversations" which must be in Dr. Klopstock's possession. He was correcting proofs the evening before he died. At four o'clock in the morning I called Dr. Klopstock, because Kafka had difficulty in breathing. Dr. Klopstock immediately recognized the crisis and wakened the doctor, who put ice-bags on his throat. About noon the next day, Kafka died. It was the third of June, 1924.

* * *

'Years later I often read Kafka's books, always with the memory of how he read aloud from them himself. Then I felt that the German language was a hindrance to me. German is too modern a language, too much of the present day. Kafka's whole world longs for an older language. It was an ancient consciousness in him, ancient things and ancient fear. His brain knew finer nuances than the modern brain is capable of grasping. He is as little the expression of an age as the expression of the fate of a race. Nor is it everyday life that his realism represents: it is an absolute, compressed logic, in which one can live for short moments only.'

* * *

With these words Mrs. Dora Dymant closed her story. From the mantelpiece over the open fireplace, in a grey London house, Kafka's eyes looked searchingly into the darkening room out of the last photograph that he had had taken in Berlin, for his passport. They were the eyes of a man who saw the world as split by incurable schizophrenia, the opposing interests of God and man—reflecting in this way his own schizoid mentality. His negative *Weltanschauung* fed on an affirmation of life that could not be fulfilled; his personal dualism drove him into the blind alley of the despairing dualistic theology of this present time. The future belongs to a life-affirming monism, in whose rays man and creation will be reunited and an all-embracing ethos of reverence for life will ripen, like a sweet fruit out of the smoking blood of the generations.

JANKEL ADLER

MEMORIES OF PAUL KLEE

(Born December 1879, died 29 June 1940)

IN THE year 1931 Klee and I were often together. We had studios on the same floor in the old academy at Düsseldorf. We agreed about a certain knock on his door, one rap with the single knuckle and one flat-hand blow. Too many visitors disturbed him. For years he had been interested in my technical experiments. He himself took days to prepare small canvasses. Later he glued them to pieces of plywood or cardboard in the same way as the old painters of Sienna. The picture began with the start of the preparation of the canvas and finished with the completion of the frame. So that it is not 'of art' but a complete object, an object which makes you richer.

He used to gaze for a long time at his prepared canvas before he began the drawing. The canvas resembled an old piece of Coptic cloth. The warp and the woof acquired an importance of design which the weaver had never imagined. The canvas being thicker or more open in its weaving was of essential significance to his life. It became of great importance to his aims. To the weaver it was dead. Klee would listen to the speaking of this dead thing. He was able to catch a new language with his eyes in this way. Many years after its weaving the canvas was brought alive.

I have never seen a man who had such creative quiet. It radiated from him as from the sun. His face was that of a man who knows about day and night, sky and sea and air. He did not speak about these things. He had no tongue to tell of them. Our language is too little to say these things. And so he had to find a sign, a colour, or a form.

Klee's studio was a spacious room, Spartan and simple. But I do not say empty. Often, when I went in, I did not say 'Good morning', and I was greeted by the smell of cooking celery. He was making soup on a spirit stove. One whole wall was a window. From the window you could see the Academy gardens. There was a gnarled and dusty criss-cross of branches, of crippled grey boughs which took away the view from the outside. Between the branches there were little spaces through which we could see the elevated street going up to the Rhine bridge towards Obercassel. On the other side straight across the street could be seen a little hill which the people called Napoleonsberg. There were strange trees taken from foreign countries which had grown up and closed the horizon.

I have often seen Klee's window from the street, with his pale oval face, like a large egg, and his open eyes pressed to the window-pane. From the street he looked like a spirit. Perhaps he was trying to decipher the language of the branches across his windows.

Much sculpture and drawings of the Aztecs has disappeared, destroyed by the Spanish Jesuits; on Easter Island there are knots on strings made in a language; the great figures there have about them a timeless atmosphere. That is a beginning. Sometimes I think that Klee in his pictures comes near an unravelling, an explanation of such things. For Klee's voice has not so much to do with the service of island faiths or with visions guided by the climate of those places. His concern is more with the human soul. It is more real for him to be near the first word, the element of making known. And to be the after-word of the people who follow in the future.

Klee, when beginning a picture, had the excitement of a Columbus moving to the discovery of a new continent. He had a frightened presentiment, just a vague sense of the right course. But when the picture was fixed and still he saw that he had come the true way, he was happy. Klee, too, set out to discover a new land.

In his Munich days, at the end of summer, Klee used to sit in the late afternoon in his studio with the graphic artist Kubin. In the window the sky was a soft violet. On a table near the window there was a pot with water, which Klee used for his water-colours. He watched the water's reflection of the sky in the pot. To do this he lay on the table, which began to shudder under his nervous weight. Kubin was watching Klee the whole time. After a while he came over near to him. He put his arms round him. Klee said, 'I am not very comfortable—I am not like this—I have nothing to do with this'. Kubin leaned over with his mouth to Klee's ear, and whispered very tenderly, 'swindler'. 'Today I laugh about it,' said Klee, 'but that day I did not laugh.' For me this resembles the revolt of the sailors on Columbus's voyage of discovery.

Klee has the courage to walk this clean-swept platform of the twentieth century and not to continue in the shades of Renaissance standards. He did not try to make a new shadow. He made a survey of this place for others who will come.

Now is the time for statement, to make that which is not a slave to optical comparison, which is no more a fragment. We must make a picture which is a complete manifestation of being.

Picasso, the great innovator of the twentieth century, has knocked on the door of every painter's studio in the world. The richness of his form gives a totality from which to build the scaffolding of new painting.

Klee made the background which reflects the intricate moving of our different lives. Here in the quivering of a leaf he experiences the violence of a thunderstorm. Sometimes it would seem that his pictures extend to the other side of the canvas. We connect with his pictures not only with our eyes, but our whole skin becomes a sensitive surface of eyes. We become the awareness of the barometer. Our sensibilities have been buried by the waste products of this life. Klee takes those crippled senses back to the air and the light.

The functional idea in architecture must come from the new building. But alone there is no movement to progress. The road finishes. For its realization it is necessary for architecture to go coupled with the painting and plastic of today.

Malewicz in Russia, Mondrian in Holland, and Nicholson in England have preached balance in painting. This has a didactic value. But it is more the scholastic of painting than the expressed value. They are not yet pictures but necessary scholastic examples.

Of all the countries at this time perhaps in Britain there is a chance of retaining the spiritual power of this heritage from Klee and Picasso. This realization has to do with this country's future for living and seems the only reason for its secure and continuing peace.

C. GIEDION-WELCKER

JAMES JOYCE IN ZÜRICH

JAMES JOYCE stood in a personal and direct relationship to the structure and the myth of cities. They seemed to him like a collective individual, a story in space-dimension, a great coalescence of life. He embraced them from their past to their present as growing organisms, edifices of history built brick by brick. Even when on a temporary visit, he sought to penetrate into the nature and laws of a city's complex substance, and to listen to its eternal rhythms. To be lord of a city, to hold the threads of its being in his hands, seemed to him direct vitality, and he considered it 'more organic' to be mayor of a town than king of a nation. Just as he could master countless tongues and dialects of the world, so he also knew its wines, dishes and sweetmeats. His interest ranged down to the special cakes of a provincial town, which he carefully fitted, as a regional characteristic apparently due to chance, into the general and coherent unity of landscape and history.

Dublin, Paris, Trieste and Zürich were the cities which played a fateful part in his life. The role of Zürich in this series is no insignificant one. In 1904, when twenty-two years old, he came for the first time to the Swiss town, on his wedding-trip with a handsome wife from Galway. For three weeks he explored, to no avail, the possibility of giving English lessons. A hotel porter, whose power of persuasion was still vivid to Joyce after many years, directed the pair to a hotel (Speer) in the Lagerstrasse (No. 16), whose proprietor later—a special joke for Joyce—bore the name of Dubliner. Eleven years later Italy's entry in the war led the family, now four members strong, back the same way from Trieste. There followed a four years' sojourn, decisive for the development of the author. Joyce, the teacher of English and the author of *Ulysses*, wandered through Zürich: on the one hand a man tied down and struggling to make a living for his family, and already suffering from his eyes; and on the other a free Greco-Celtic philosopher and 'Phantasus', who out of the continuum of Europe created from the Homeric myth his complex epic of the twentieth century. From the primitive germ-cell of Greece—already in early times linked with his Irish home—arose the modern Europe. The Town became a vessel containing all events since the world began.

The Joyce family occupied several houses during its four-year stay in Zürich, in the Kreuzstrasse, Seefeldstrasse (73) and Universitätsstrasse (38) and (29). To his more intimate circle of Zürich friends belonged Philippe Jarnach, deputy orchestra conductor for Busoni, and the soprano Charlotte Sauermann, with whom the flat in Seefeldstrasse was shared. In addition there were pupils: Edmund Brauchbar, a model segment of the many-sided Leopold Bloom as regards his vitality and feeling for reality and wit, Georges Borach,[1] the devoted 'Eckermann', Paul Suter and Paul Ruggiero. The

[1] See G. Borach: 'Talks with James Joyce'. *Neue Zürcher Zeitung*, 3 May 1931.

English painter and writer Frank Budgen,[1] then active at the British Legation, and the actor Claud Sykes and his wife were also there, as well as a number of young Greeks—Greeks were always regarded by Joyce as bringers of good luck and belonged at that time to the atmosphere of *Ulysses*—who lent to the group a national and lingual colour. Here was the variety which had always seemed to him particularly attractive in Switzerland. The constant meeting place during the First World War was the restaurant Pfauen. Later the 'Kronenhalle' became the regular rendezvous, where the Sion Fendant wine, which Joyce christened *Erzherzogin* (archduchess) because of its *Erzgeschmack* (brassy taste); or the Yvorner wine, gradually converted the mood from one of quiet conversation to a plane of joking and phantasy. Joyce's saying: 'Red wine is like beef-steak, white wine like electricity' was analogically applied to his estimation of the human voice, the tenor seeming to him a 'gift of God' a 'supernatural tongue', whilst the bass remained fettered by its healthy stability and the baritone by its beautiful naturalness. He praised the white wine of Switzerland on all occasions (often to the sorrow of his French friends) as the wine *par excellence*, as a 'hovering summer night's dream'. It was only when the sun had utterly gone down that the spirit of the earth of Switzerland rose for him.

All of the then extant prose works of the poet appeared in the *Rheinverlag* (Basel) between 1926–8, translated into German: *Dubliners*, *The Portrait of the Artist* and *Ulysses*. Switzerland again became the starting-point of his poetic expansion. His only play, *Exiles*, had been published in German by Rascher, Zürich, as early as 1919, a year after the English edition. Spurred by his work on this piece, Joyce had undertaken in 1918 in Zürich to introduce the Swiss public to English drama. Under his direction the 'English Players' was founded. In the Kaufleuten, the Pfauen Theatre and the Lucerne City Theatre, works of Oscar Wilde, Shaw and Synge were performed. *Exiles*, modestly placed last in the Irish series, was never produced, due to an internal dispute between actors and manager. In the Circe chapter of *Ulysses* the battles of this Zürich theatre period received their poetic transformation; and it was in front of the Zürich district court that they came to their real conclusion, and that in favour of James Joyce.

[1] Frank Budgen, *James Joyce and the Making of Ulysses*. London, Grayson & Grayson, 1934.

Dublin, the *cité suprème*, eternally metamorphic and beautiful, often must have appeared before the voluntary exile in his wanderings by the lake of Zürich; just as to Victor Hugo, the French exile on the sands of Guernsey, Paris arose out of the sea, the distant, beloved town, *inoubliable*. Apart from this, however, it was true to Joyce's way of thinking and feeling to always discover new similarities in men, history and landscapes, in spite of his already complete grasp of their individuality. The twelve o'clock Bahnhofstrasse, with the living, singular phenomena of the present, was synthesized with his native Dublin. The camera of his mind was always taking double exposures. Thus the fusion became the presentation of midday city life in that master-chapter of his Odyssey.

'What a city!' he would exclaim. 'A lake, a mountain and two rivers.' In this phrase he concentrated the characteristics, richness and universality of Zürich. It is said of Ireland, 'Two voices are there, one of the sea and one of the mountains': he often stood contemplating as an event the meeting of the Limmat and the Sihl on his walks by the rivers. The wide lake was for him a mighty, self-evident Being. It lured him, especially in latter years, to frequent water excursions. That he was on these occasions concerned not with nature but above all with art was a fact that one was only later to learn. They were aquatic word-expeditions undertaken in motor-boats. The smell of fish, blue-green colour, misty haze, a bouquet of associations, must be resolved into one word. It was a question of finding this many-headed word, in order to reveal the genius of the place and hour. Whether the poet finally fished this pearl once and for all out of the Zürich lake must be determined from *Finnegans Wake*, of which he was then working out the last paragraphs; at the time, at any rate, he said nothing about it.

He had already woven various word-jokes about Zürich into the section concerning 'Anna Livia Plurabelle'. 'Well, that's the Limmat' (for limit) . . . 'You don't say the silly-post?' (for Sihlpost) . . . and 'legging a jig or so on the sihl . . . There's the Belle for Sexaloitez . . .' betrays the presence of this atmosphere and its witty transformation and translation into a new speech-dimension.

Mumming and folk-plays, all historical cults, were to Joyce in their penetration of past and present an expression of historical vitality. The *Sechseläuten* (spring festival: literally 'Ringing of six o'clock') was always visited, as he usually stayed in Zürich at this time of the year, and he seismographically registered all of its phases. The watchmen with their wolf-hounds, who attended the last moments of the burning mystic *Bögg* (winter-demon), seemed to him in their sober reality woven into the fantastic symbolism as a special joke.

Once, in a Fendant-mood, he wanted to provide a new stage-setting for the last act of Rossini's *Tell* opera: an apotheosis of Switzerland, represented by countless hotel porters, was to round off the happy ending. Above all the Swiss hotel porter! For Joyce, he was a living information bureau of events of life and of the city, like a daily newspaper; a revelation and source of wit.

As a contrast to the wise and witty side of him, however, there was still a hidden core of primitive nature: the paradox. During thunder storms, richly bestowed by the Zürich summer, he was seized by an elementary mountain-fear, and crept into his hotel in the Bahnhofstrasse 'like the Pope into the Vatican'.[1] The Zürich mountain became a *mont noir* to him when the heavens discharged electricity and, 'like a drunken sailor, indiscriminately hurled down dynamite'.

Days—starting from his religious youth coloured by the changing symbols of the saints—and numbers had a manifold significance and life for him: legendary, historical, magic. All the dates of the calendar were observed according to their content, and the special ones were joyously celebrated. On Fridays a reluctance for travel or any other undertakings reigned. That James Joyce should have been taken ill on a Friday and should have died on the thirteenth of the month, touched all those who knew his attitude.

Joyce had waited impatiently in France to begin his last journey to Switzerland—'that nature preserve-park of the free spirit' as Hugo Ball called it in 1917—after being for many weeks the bewildered witness of a confused and wandering stream of humanity from all lands. 'Here we still know where we stand,' he said, looking around him in a panelled Swiss inn a short time after his arrival. Here he died. On his desk lay two books marked with fresh notes: an Irish one by the Irish doctor Oliver St. John Gogarty (Buck Mulligan), *I follow St. Patrick*; and a Greek lexicon. Ireland, Greece, Zürich . . .

[1] His attitude during the bombing dangers of the war in France was quite other and totally different.

[*This article is reprinted from the* Weltwoche, *Zürich, 18 April 1941*]

T. S. ELIOT

A MESSAGE TO THE FISH

ON 14 January, having read the obituary notice of James Joyce which had appeared in *The Times* of that morning, I addressed to the Editor of that paper the following letter:

SIR,

I hope that you will permit me to submit one or two cautious qualifications to your interesting obituary notice of my friend Mr. James Joyce. That Joyce failed to appreciate 'the eternal and serene beauty of nature' can, I think, be disputed by reference to several passages in *A Portrait of the Artist as a Young Man*, *Ulysses* and *Finnegans Wake*: but being separated from my books, I cannot quote chapter and verse. As for his inability to appreciate 'the higher sides of human character', this stricture would, perhaps, be more applicable to Jonathan Swift, and I should ask the reader, before accepting such a judgement, to consider 'The Dead', in *Dubliners*—one of the finest short stories in the language.

What I chiefly question, however, is the importance at this date of the opinions of men older than Joyce, holding the views of an older literary generation, such as Edmund Gosse, Arnold Bennett, or Æ. To some of Joyce's younger contemporaries, like myself, *Ulysses* still seems the most considerable work of imagination in English in our time, comparable in importance (though in little else) with the work of Marcel Proust. I do not believe that posterity will be able to controvert this judgement, though it may be able to demonstrate the relative insignificance of the literary achievement of the whole period.

Your obedient servant, etc.

As this letter was not published, I wrote a fortnight later to say that I presumed myself free to publish it elsewhere, and received a polite note from the Obituaries Department returning the letter, and expressing regret that restrictions of space had made publication impossible.

It was not a well-written letter, partly because I was ill with influenza when I wrote it. But its oddity is rather more due to the fact that I wished to write something that *The Times* would print, and I entertained the hope that it might get by as an 'Appreciation'. Had I not been hampered by illness and a sense (however imperfect) of the possible, I might have written in somewhat the following vein:

SIR,

I have read with stupefaction your obituary notice on the greatest man of letters of my generation. It is usual, I believe, for editors of newspapers to have ready obituary notices of all notable men and women. This practice is wholly to be commended; but the notices should be written by the right persons in the beginning, and should then be kept up to date. The impression given by your notice of Mr. Joyce is that it was written by someone considerably older than he—someone who by now must be well over fifty-nine. That it was in some sense brought up to date I must believe, since, being an obituary, it mentions the date and place of Joyce's death; but this does not cover the requirements. I am not alluding to oversights such as the failure to mention that 'Work in Progress' was eventually completed and published under the title of *Finnegans Wake*: I refer to the inclusion of trivialities about the man, and the failure to show any understanding of the significance of his work in its time.

I am quite aware that at the present time considerations of space are of first importance. For this reason I venture to point out how you might have saved space. Whatever the various distinction of Sir Edmund Gosse, Arnold Bennett and Æ in other fields, none of them could lay claim to any authority as a critic; and phrases taken from what they said about Joyce many years ago could well have been spared. So could the estimate of your obituary writer. The first business of an obituary writer is to give the important facts about the life of the deceased, and to give some notion of the position which he enjoyed. He is not called upon to pronounce summary judgement (especially when his notice is unsigned), though it is part of his proper function, when his subject is a writer, to give some notion of what was thought of him by the best qualified critics of his time. I suggest also in view of your limitations of space, that to mention that Joyce was one of a 'large and poor family' was unnecessary; and that a silly remark of his when a young man may give the reader the mistaken impression that vanity was the most conspicuous trait of his character, and the equally mistaken impression that we have the authority of Yeats for permission to ignore Joyce's work. And, as you did not have space to mention that *Ulysses* was eventually published in both England and America, it would perhaps have been better to omit mention of its previous suppression.

I must try to make quite clear that the issue which I raise has nothing to do with the difference between my valuation of Joyce's work and that of your writer. I am not concerned with matters of opinion, but with matters of fact; and were my opinion of Joyce still lower than that of your biographer, my condemnation of your notice would be the same. My motives in writing this letter extend much further than loyalty to a friend or desire to see justice done to a particular author. The name and fame of Joyce were known throughout the world: *The Times* has an equally wide reputation. I do not believe that your notice will much affect the world's opinion of Joyce; but I fear lest it may be used as evidence by those who choose to believe that England has lost respect for that one of the arts for which it has been chiefly renowned.

I am, your, etc.,

T. S. ELIOT.

DUNCAN GRANT

VIRGINIA WOOLF

I FIRST knew Virginia Stephen when she and her brother Adrian took No. 29 Fitzroy Square, soon after her sister Vanessa married Clive Bell. It was a house on the south-west corner of the square with a view of the two fine Adams' façades. It was a derelict square. The houses of the great had gradually decayed and were taken as offices, lodgings, nursing homes and small artisans' workshops.

I had taken for a studio two rooms on the second floor of a house on the same side of the square. There was certainly not much gentility left in the district; the only relic of grandeur was a beadle to march round the square and keep order among the children, in a top-hat and a tail-coat piped with red and brass buttons. The Stephens were the only people I remember who had a complete house there; complete with their cook Sophie Farrell, their maid Maud, a front-door bell and a dog, Hans. A close friendship sprang up between Adrian Stephen and myself, and I had only to tap at the window of the ground-floor room to be let in. 'That Mr. Grant gets in everywhere,' Maud once remarked to Virginia. But irregular as my visits were, in a sense they soon became frequent enough to escape notice.

The house was conveniently divided to suit the inhabitants. On the ground floor was Adrian's study lined with books. Behind was the dining-room. The first floor was entirely a drawing-room—the room least used in the house. It was a pleasantly proportioned room, with long windows overlooking the square. It had a green carpet, red brocade curtains; a Dutch portrait of a Lady and Watts's portrait of Sir Leslie Stephen were the only pictures on the walls. In the back part of the room there was an instrument called a Pianola, into which one put rolls of paper punctured by small holes. You bellowed with your feet and Beethoven or Wagner would appear.

Anyone coming into the room might have thought that Adrian was a Paderewski—the effort on the bellows gave him a swaying movement very like that of a great performer, and his hands were hidden.

I do not remember that Virginia ever performed on this instrument, but it must have played a part in her life, for Adrian on coming home from work would play in the empty room by the hour. Entirely empty it nearly always was and kept spotlessly clean.

It was here that Virginia sometimes saw her less intimate friends and it was here that the dog Hans made a mess on the hearthrug when Lady Strachey was paying her first visit, and no mention was made of the fact by either lady.

The more lively rooms were Virginia's own workroom above this, and Adrian's downstairs. Her room was full of books untidily arranged and a high table at which she would write standing. The windows on this floor were double. She was very sensitive to sound, and the noise from the mews and street was severe. The time she gave to her writing was two and a half hours in the morning. She never, I believe, wrote for more than this time, but very regularly.

The study on the ground floor had the air of being much lived in. It was to this room that their friends came on Thursday evenings—a continuation of those evenings which began in Gordon Square before Thoby Stephen died and before Vanessa married. It was there that what has since been called 'Bloomsbury' for good or ill came into being.

About ten o'clock in the evening people used to appear and continue to come at intervals till twelve o'clock at night, and it was seldom that the last guest left before two or three in the morning. Whisky, buns and cocoa were the diet, and people talked to each other. If someone had lit a pipe he would sometimes hold out the lighted match to Hans the dog, who would snap at it and put it out. Conversation; that was all. Yet many people made a habit of coming, and few who did so will forget those evenings.

Among those who constantly came in early days were Charles Sanger, Theodore Llewelyn Davies, Desmond Macarthy, Charles Tennyson, Hilton Young (now Lord Kennet), Lytton Strachey.

It was certainly not a 'salon'. Virginia Stephen in those days was not at all the sort of hostess required for such a thing. She appeared very shy and probably was so, and never addressed the company. She would listen to general arguments and occasionally speak, but her conversation was mainly directed to someone next to her. Her brother's Cambridge friends she knew well by this time, but I think there was always something a little aloof and even a little fierce in her manner to most men at the time I am speaking of. To her women friends, especially older women like Miss Pater and Miss Janet Case, who had taught her Greek, she was more open and less reserved. They were alive to her, by remembrance as well as presence, and had already their place in her imagination as belonging to the world she knew and had left—that life with her parents and her half-brothers at Hyde Park Gate. Henceforward she and her brother and sister had tacitly agreed to face life on their own terms.

I do not think that her new existence had 'become alive' to Virginia's imagination in those first years. She gave the impression of being so intensely receptive to any experience new to her, and so intensely interested in facts that she had not come across before, that time was necessary to give it a meaning as a whole. It took the years to complete her vision of it.

It is very difficult for one who is no writer to attempt to describe so subtle a thing as the 'feeling' of long ago. But I must make the attempt to explain why it was that the effect of these young people on a contemporary was so remarkable. To begin with they were not Bohemians. The people I had come across before who had cut themselves off from respectable existence had been mainly painters and Bohemians. If the Stephens defied the conventions of their particular class, it was from being intellectually honest.

They had suffered much, had struggled and finally arrived at an attitude of mind which I think had a great influence on their friends. If it was an influence Virginia Stephen and her sister were unconscious of the fact.

The impression generally given must have been that these two young women were absorbing the ideas of their new Cambridge friends. And of course this was true up to a point. Saxon Sydney Turner, Clive Bell, Lytton Strachey, Maynard Keynes, were willing to discuss anything and everything with them or before them. It was a gain all round. What the Cambridge of that time needed was a little feminine society. It was a little arid, and if it took almost everything seriously it had mostly left the Arts out of account. It took some things religiously. 'This is my Bible' was said by one, pointing to the *Principia Ethica*, by G. Moore. This eminent philosopher was certainly the overwhelming influence on these young men. Conversations on the 'Good' and the value of certain states of mind were a frequent subject of discussion; and these Apostolic young men found to their amazement that they could be shocked by the boldness and scepticism of two young women.

To be intimate with Virginia Stephen in those days was not to be on easy terms. Indeed the greater the intimacy the greater the danger—the danger of sudden outbursts of scathing criticism. I have the impression that no one had much encouragement for anything they produced. Nor was it looked for. Nothing was expected save complete frankness (of criticism) and a mutual respect for the point of view of each. To work for immediate success never entered anyone's head, perhaps partly because it seemed out of the question. Virginia Stephen was working on her first novel, *The Voyage Out*. It took seven years to finish. But I do not remember that this was thought to be an out of the way length of time in which to produce a novel.

The inner fierceness of her attitude to which I have already alluded is worth remembering, and will possibly surprise those who only knew her in later life when it seemed to have entirely disappeared or to have found expression in quite other ways.

It then expressed itself sometimes, as I have said, by an appearance of acute shyness. Upon an unforeseen introduction, for instance, there was an expression of blazing defiance, a few carefully chosen banalities, and a feeling of awkwardness. It came from a sort of variant of Cézanne's *grapin dessous*, which made her literally turn tail from misadventure. As when she saw Mrs. Humphry Ward advancing along a narrow passage in the Louvre and hid herself behind a totally inadequate post.

No one so beautiful and so fierce could give offence except to the very stupid. But she was capable of inspiring feelings of respect in the most philistine.

This shyness or fierceness was a necessary self-defence in her war with the world. The world must, she surmised, accept her on her own terms or not at all.

If these notes have any interest it is because they may to some revive the memory, to others suggest the existence, of that seemingly very different Virginia Woolf known to a variety of people in later years.

Marriage and possibly a growing appreciation of her work had the effect of seeming to make her very much more at ease in the world.

ROSE MACAULAY

VIRGINIA WOOLF

'SHE HAD animation; she had sensibility; she had elegance, beauty and wit.' Thus Jane Austen, doing her descriptive utmost, might have approved Virginia Woolf. And between the animation, the sensibility, the elegance, the beauty and the wit, the essential quality would have slyly slipped, to look out mockingly from the turn of a phrase in talk, a sudden chuckle, a ridiculous question, a flashing piece of analysis or flight.

What made Virginia Woolf the most enchanting company in the world? Animation? There are plenty of animated talkers. Sensibility? There are many sensitive receivers. Zest? Again, plenty of that. Sympathy? Imagination? Wit? Irony? Culture? Brain? One hesitates to say that there are ever plenty of these; but they are not infrequently to be met. Yet they somehow combined in Virginia Woolf to make a person so rare and so delightful that she is not to be met elsewhere at all, so that getting her 'Come and see me' on a postcard was like being sent a free ticket to some stimulating entertainment.

With her, conversation was a flashing, many-faceted stream, now running swiftly, now slowing into still pools that shimmered with a hundred changing lights, shades and reflections, wherein sudden coloured fishes continually darted and stirred, now flowing between deep banks, now chuckling over sharp pebbles. She was sometimes pleased ironically to pose as the recluse who watched life from a quiet, drab corner, inviting her friends to tell her their fine stories of the world, of the rich parties they had doubtless attended, of the whirl of society from which they had just stepped, into which they would, she assured them, step again on leaving her. 'I think of you,' she would tell an unsociable visitor, 'as going from party to party, spinning round in the social whirl, leading a gay, rich, wordly life. Now tell me what is happening in the *beau-monde*.' The visitor, particularly if young or hero-worshipping, had perhaps hoped for a deep, cultured kind of conversation, about books, about art, about life, about Proust. He sometimes, but not always, got it. Had he (or she) written a book, he might, if lucky, get a verbal review of it, an analysis, appreciation and criticism that was worth more than any printed review. All this public reviewing by authors of one another's books, Virginia regarded as a mistake; she thought that little worth saying was said that way; her notion was that newspaper reviews should only be of the dead; living writers, she said, would do better to review each other by word of mouth and to each other's faces, charging (since authors must live) a fee for doing so. (The scheme, I believe, never achieved a financial basis.)

How recapture or convey talk? That throaty, deepish, wholly attractive voice, throwing out some irrelevant and negligent inquiry, starting some hare—'Is this a great age?' or, 'can there be Grand Old Women of literature, or only Grand Old Men? I think I shall prepare to be the Grand Old Woman of English letters. Or would you like to be?' Or, 'All this rubbish about Bloomsbury. . . . I don't feel Bloomsbury; do you feel Marylebone (or Chelsea, Kensington or Hampstead)?' Comments on people—'One of my geese. Geese usually like me; I have quite a flock; there must be something goosey about me, I'm afraid.' Her ironic, amused slant on clever young writers, 'the smarties'; on a vehement, black-browed talker, 'What charcoal fumes he emits!'; on adolescent University Communists, 'they have no culture, only politics. Quite different from us, who had no politics, only culture'. Her interest in scandal: 'Go on; this is enthralling. People keep telling me different bits of this story; I feel as if a buried statue were being dug up piece by piece.' Her appreciation of people, in all their comic and delightful absurdities, their motley coats, the beauty and grace of the young, the learning of the learned, the wit of the brilliant, the simplicities of the simple. Such appreciation, such flattering discernment and interest, were heady fumes to intoxicate newcomers, evoking in them too often more of response, than was convenient or required.

To tell her anything was like launching a ship on the shifting waters of a river, which flashed back a hundred reflections, enlarging, beautifying, animating, rippling about the keel, filling the sails, bobbing the craft up and down on dancing waves, enlarging the small trip into some fantastic Odyssean voyage among islands of exotic flowers and amusing beasts and men.

Did anyone ever have a dull moment in her company? Did she ever have a dull moment herself? Tragic, yes, since she had imagination, sensibility, and fine-drawn nerves: but dull? Improbable, since life gave her what it did, and she gave what she did to life. Her mischievousness, her firm, gay and determined prejudices, her shaping and creating genius, her haunted and haunting imagination, her sensitiveness, her humour, her scholarly love and knowledge of the past, the fastidiously exquisite and many-coloured form in which she clothed her thought, made her mind a rich kingdom to herself, an excitement to her friends, her writing a spell to bind her readers.

Yes, 'she had animation, she had sensibility, she had elegance, beauty and wit'; and behind all these a rare and fine-spun greatness. Her going seems symbolic of the end of an age. Was it, as she inquired, a great age? Possibly not. But it was, anyhow, an age in which such as she could live and breathe; and it may likely enough be the last of these for a long time.

LUIS PORTILLO

UNAMUNO'S LAST LECTURE

'UNAMUNO died suddenly, as one who dies in war. Against whom? Perhaps against himself; and also, although many may not believe it, against the men who sold Spain and betrayed his people. Against the people itself? I have never believed that and never shall believe it.'—Antonio Machado, 'Notas de Actualidad', in the magazine *Madrid*, Valencia, February 1937.

'Some maintained, during those frantic days, their independence of mind. From the human point of view, it is a consolation; from the Spanish point of view, a hope.'—Manuel Azana, Prologue to *La Velada en Benicarlo*, Paris, May 1939.

THE Ceremonial Hall in the University of Salamanca is a spacious chamber, used only on formal occasions, solemn, austere, the walls hung with tapestries. Through the huge windows enters a shimmering flood of iridescent light which deepens the amber glow of the century-old plinth stones.

This was the setting.

The play was enacted on 12 October 1936 when Spanish Fascism was in its first triumphant stage. The morning was half spent. The patriotic festival of the Hispanic Race was being celebrated.

There they were on the presidential dais: the purple calotte, the amethyst ring and the flashing pectoral cross of the Most Illustrious Doctor Plà y Daniel, Bishop of the Diocese; the lack-lustre robes of the Magistrates; the profuse glitter of military gold braid side by side with the crosses and medals exhibited on presumptuously bulging chests; the morning coat, set off by black satin lapels, of His Excellency the Civil Governor of the Province; and all these surrounded —was it to honour or to overwhelm?—the man whose pride in his incorruptible Spanish conscience was steadfast and straight: Miguel de Unamuno y Jugo, the Rector.

From the front wall, the allegorical picture of the Republic had gone, and there shone from under a canopy the Caudillo's effigy in plump insolence. To the left and right, on crimson-covered divans, the silk of the doctors' gowns and their mortar-boards with gay tassels in red, yellow, light blue and dark blue, symbolizing Law, Medicine, Letters and Science.

A few ladies were scattered among the learned men; in a prominent place, Doña Carmen Polo de Franco, the distinguished spouse of the Man of Providence.

From a packed audience which faced the dais of the elect, with its protective balustrade of dark polished wood, there rose the confused murmur of expectancy. At the far end of the long hall glinted the rounded brasses of a military band, ready to play the obligatory hymns.

The ceremony began. Don Miguel opened it with the ritual formula, spoken in that unforgettable voice of his, thin and clear. Then Don Francisco Maldonado stepped on to the platform, short, fat, Professor of Literature and Salamancan landowner. With affected, baroque diction and vast erudition, he delivered a colourless and circumstantial address. At the end, he expressed his hope for a better future, with kindly and sincere emotion. He descended the steps among cheers and applause, bowed to the dais and returned to his seat. He was followed on the speaker's platform by Don José Maria Ramos Loscertales of Saragossa, tall and lean, with fluid gestures, flashing eyes, sober and precise of speech, his sensitive face in perpetual motion, expressing a subtle and enigmatic irony. He spoke of the mortal struggle raging at the time—yet another circumstantial speech. Its thesis: the energies of Spain at white-heat in a crucible of passion—and like gold from the crucible, Spain would emerge in the end, purified and without stain, in her true colours which rejected the taints artificially imposed on her. Clamorous ovation.

And then rose General Millan Astray. With ostentatious humility, he preferred to speak from his own place. His appearance was impressive. The General is thin, of an emaciation which pretends to slimness. He has lost one eye and one arm. His face and his body bear the indelible tattoo of horrible scars. These savage mutilations and gashes evoke a sinister personality; his angry and rancorous bearing kills any compassion his mutilations might have inspired.

He had been the organizer of the *Tercio*, the Spanish Foreign Legion for operations in Africa; he had been the creator of an iron, inexorable discipline to which the reckless fugitives from other social discipline submitted of their own free will. He had gained those wounds which to many seemed glorious, to some ever-exploited, and to all horribly impressive, in those fantastic Moroccan campaigns which had been Spain's bitter nightmare under the regretted aegis of King Alfonso XIII, called 'The African' in his day. Yet the unquestionable nimbus which surrounded the figure of the General was due to the gruesome originality, to the mysterious paradox of his battlecry: '*Viva la Muerte!*'—'Long live Death!'

Barely had Millan Astray risen to his feet when his strident voice rang out, as though bursting from that heroic chest bedizened with a galaxy of crosses, the testimonials and rewards of gallantry.

First of all he said that more than one-half of all Spaniards were criminals, guilty of armed rebellion and high treason. To remove any ambiguity, he went on to explain that by these rebels and traitors he meant the citizens who were loyal to the Government.

In a sudden flash of intuition, a member of the audience was inspired so as to grasp the faultless logic of a slogan which common minds had thought the product of an epileptic brain. With fervour, he shouted:

'*Viva, viva la Muerte!*'—'Long live Death!'

Impervious, the General continued his fiery speech:

'Catalonia and the Basque country—the Basque country and Catalonia—are two cancers in the body of the nation. Fascism, which is Spain's health-bringer, will know how to exterminate them both, cutting into the live, healthy flesh like a resolute surgeon free from false sentimentality. And since the healthy flesh is the soil, the diseased flesh the people who dwell on it, Fascism and the Army will eradicate the people and restore the soil to the sacred national realm . . .'

He made a pause and cast a despotic glance over the audience. And he saw that he held them in thrall, hypnotized to a man. Never had any of his harangues so subjugated the will of his listeners. Obviously, he was in his element . . . He had conquered the University! And carried away himself, he continued, blind to the subtle and withering smile of disdain on the lips of the Rector.

'Every Socialist, every Republican, every one of them without exception—and needless to say every Communist—is a rebel against the National Government which will very soon be recognized by the totalitarian States who are aiding us, in spite of France—democratic France—and perfidious England.

'And then, or even sooner, when Franco wants it, and with the help of the gallant Moors who, though they wrecked my body only yesterday, today deserve the gratitude of my soul, for they are fighting for Spain against the Spaniards . . . I mean, the bad Spaniards . . . because they are giving their lives in defence of Spain's sacred religion, as is proved by their attending field mass, escorting the Caudillo and pinning holy medallions and Sacred Hearts to their burnous . . .'

The General lost himself in the maze of his own vehement outburst. He hesitated, irritated and defiant at the same time. In these straits, an enthusiastic Fascist came to his rescue and shouted:

'*Arriba España!*'

The crowd bowed their heads in resignation. The man went on, undaunted:

'Spain!'[1]

Mechanically, the crowd responded: 'One!'

'Spain!' he repeated.

'Great!' chorused the obedient public.

'Spain!' the Blue Shirt insisted, implacably.

'Free!' they all replied, cowed.

There was an obvious lack of warmth and listlessness in these artificially produced responses. Several Blue Shirts rose to their feet as though pushed by invisible springs, and raised their right arms stiffly in the Roman salute. And they hailed the sepia-coloured photograph on the front wall:

'Franco!'

The public rose reluctantly and chanted parrot-like:

'Franco! Franco! Franco!'

But Franco's image did not stir. Neither did the Rector.

Don Miguel did not rise to his feet. And the public fell silent and sat down again.

All eyes were fastened in tense anxiety on the noble head, on the pale, serene brow framed by snow-white hair. The uncertain expression of his eyes was hidden by the glitter of his spectacles.

Between the fine curve of his nose and the silver of his Quixote-like beard, his mouth was twisted in a bitter grimace of undisguised contempt. People began to grow uneasy. A few suddenly felt a recrudescence of their old rancorous abhorrence. Some admired

[1] *España Una, Grande y Libre*—'Spain One, Great and Free'—is the obligatory Falangist slogan which is converted on all solemn occasions into chorused responses to a leading voice, as in the following scene.

the serene fearlessness of the Master and feared for his safety. The majority were gripped by the voluptuous thrill of imminent tragedy.

At last, Don Miguel rose slowly. The silence was an enormous void. Into this void, Don Miguel began to pour the stream of his speech, as though savouring each measured word. This is the essence of what he said:

'All of you are hanging on my words. You all know me, and are aware that I am unable to remain silent. I have not learnt to do so in seventy-three years of my life. And now I do not wish to learn it any more. At times, to be silent is to lie. For silence can be interpreted as acquiescence. I could not survive a divorce between my conscience and my word, always well-mated partners.

'I will be brief. Truth is most true when naked, free of embellishments and verbiage.

'I want to comment on the speech—to give it that name—of General Millan Astray who is here among us.'

The General stiffened provocatively.

'Let us waive the personal affront implied in the sudden outburst of vituperation against Basques and Catalans in general. I was born in Bilbao, in the midst of the bombardments of the Second Carlist War. Later, I wedded myself to this city of Salamanca which I love deeply, yet never forgetting my native town. The Bishop, whether he likes it or not, is a Catalan from Barcelona.'

He made a pause. Faces had grown pale. The short silence was tense and dramatic. Expectation neared its peak.

'Just now, I heard a necrophilous and senseless cry: "Long live Death!" To me it sounds the equivalent of "*Muera la Vida!*"—"To Death with Life!" And I, who have spent my life shaping paradoxes which aroused the uncomprehending anger of the others, I must tell you, as an expert authority, that this outlandish paradox is repellent to me. Since it was proclaimed in homage to the last speaker, I can only explain it to myself by supposing that it was addressed to him, though in an excessively strange and tortuous form, as a testimonial to his being himself a symbol of death.

'And now, another matter. General Millan Astray is a cripple. Let it be said without any slighting undertone. He is a war invalid. So was Cervantes. But extremes do not make the rule: they escape it. Unfortunately, there are all too many cripples in Spain now. And soon, there will be even more of them if God does not come to our aid. It pains me to think that General Millan Astray should dictate the pattern of mass-psychology.

'That would be appalling. A cripple who lacks the spiritual greatness of a Cervantes—a man, not a superman, virile and complete, in spite of his mutilations—a cripple, I said, who lacks that loftiness of mind, is wont to seek ominous relief in seeing mutilation around him.'

His words rang out crystal clear. The heavy silence gave them resonance.

'General Millan Astray is not one of the select minds, even though he is unpopular, or rather, for that very reason. Because he *is* unpopular. General Millan Astray would like to create Spain anew—a negative creation—in his own image and likeness. And for that reason he wishes to see Spain crippled, as he unwittingly made clear.'

At this point General Millan Astray could stand it no longer and shouted wildly:

'*Muera la Inteligencia!*'—'To death with Intelligence!'

'No, long live intelligence! To death with bad intellectuals!' corrected Don José Maria Pemán, a journalist from Cadiz. A few voices seconded him, many hands were clenched to check an imprudent impulse to applaud the aged Rector. The Blue Shirts felt tempted to become violent, true to totalitarian procedure. But a most unusual realization of their numerical inferiority strangled this impulse at birth. Arguments flared up round the names of academicians who had disappeared or been shot. Irritated 'sh's' came from various sides. Some gowned figures had gathered round Don Miguel, some Blue Shirts round their vilified hero.

At last the clamour died down like the sound of surf on the beach, and the groups dispersed. Don Miguel again became visible to the assembly, very erect, his arms folded and his gaze fixed straight ahead, like the statue of a stoic. Once more his word dominated the hall.

'This is the temple of intellect. And I am its high priest. It is you who are profaning its sacred precincts.

'I have always, whatever the proverb may say, been a prophet in my own land. You will win, but you will not convince. You will win, because you possess more than enough brute force, but you will not convince, because to convince means to persuade. And in order to persuade you would need what you lack—reason and right in the struggle. I consider it futile to exhort you to think of Spain. I have finished.'

The controversies flamed up again, interrupted by sudden waves of unanimous silence.

Then Don Esteban Madruga, Professor of Common Law, a straightforward and truly good man, took Don Miguel by the arm, offered his other arm to Doña Carmen Polo de Franco, and led them out of the room. Unamuno walked with perfect dignity, pale and calm. Franco's wife was so stunned that she walked like an automaton.

The Junta in Burgos was consulted. Franco's orders came: they were inexorable. If the offence was considered grave enough, the Rector of Salamanca was to be executed without delay. The offence was indeed considered to be so, but somebody who was better advised realized that such an act would fatally injure the prestige of the nascent 'Movement of Salvation'. It was therefore never carried out.

Don Miguel retired to his home. His house was kept surrounded by the police.

And shortly afterwards, thus guarded, Miguel de Unamuno died suddenly on the last day of 1936, the victim of a stroke of the brain, achieving lasting peace.

DENTON WELCH

A VISIT TO SICKERT AT ST. PETER'S

I HAD been in Broadstairs for months, trying to recover some sort of health after a serious road accident.

My doctor, knowing that I was an art student, tried to persuade Sickert to come and see me, but he wouldn't. I was told that he stormed off down the street saying: 'I have no time for district visiting!'

That was while I was still in bed. When at last I got up, someone engineered an invitation to tea on Saturday afternoon. So he did not escape me after all.

Just as I was about to leave the nursing home for St. Peter's, Sister sailed into my room closely followed by Gerald, an art school friend. He had evidently come all the way from London to see me.

I controlled my face as best I could and said:

'I'm going to tea with Sickert. What are you going to do? Can you wait here till I get back?'

He gave me one rapid glance and then said firmly:

'I'll come too.'

I was horrified. 'But you haven't been asked!' I burst out.

'That doesn't matter. One more won't make any difference.'

Feeling powerless in my convalescent state against his strength of will, I let him climb up beside me in the aged taxi which bore us swayingly to 'Hauteville'.

Sickert had not lived long in the house and it was still being altered. One entered through what at one time had been the 'cloak-room'. I remember with vividness the slight shock I received on being confronted with a glistening white 'w.c.' as soon as the door was opened.

Mrs. Sickert stood beside it, welcoming us charmingly, with great quietness. She led us into what must have been the original hall. It was now a sort of dining-room, furnished with a strange mixture of interesting and commonplace things. An early Georgian mirror with flat bevelling and worn gilt frame hung over the Art Nouveau grate. Seen thus together, each looked somehow startling and new.

We left our coats and passed on into the much loftier and larger drawing-room. The first thing I noticed was that the floor was quite bare, with that stained 'surround' which makes the white boards in the middle look so naked. By the sofa stood a stringy man who was about to go bald. The pale gold hair was still there, but one could tell how thin the crop would be next year. He looked at us with piercing eyes and fidgeted with his teaspoon. Mrs. Sickert only had time to tell us that her husband was still resting but that he would be down soon, before this man engaged her again in earnest conversation. She could only show us attention by pouring out cups of tea. My cup was of that white china which is decorated with a gold trefoil in the centre of each piece. Gerald's was quite different. It was acid-blue, I think, with an unpleasant black handle and stripe; but I noted that both our spoons were flimsy and old. I turned mine over and saw, amongst the other hall-marks, the little head of George III winking up at me.

I looked at the other things on the table, at the brown enamel teapot, the familiar red and blue Huntley and Palmer's tin, and at the strange loaf which seemed neither bread nor cake. In spite of myself, I felt that at last I was seeing Bohemian life.

I was glad that the man was keeping Mrs. Sickert so busy, for it gave me time to stare at everything in the room. I saw that along most of the walls ran narrow panels, almost in monochrome. They looked like bas-reliefs flattened by a steam-roller. They were most decorative. Mixed with these, but standing on easels or resting on the floor, were some of Sickert's own paintings. Gwen Ffrangçon-Davies dressed in Elizabethan farthingale and ruff, with harsh white light on her face, looked out from a picture mostly green and red.

Toylike, bustled ladies and Derby-hatted men, all in soft greys and pinks, skated on a country pond. Pinned to the canvas was the original *Punch* drawing from which the composition had been taken.

Near the fireplace stood the long, brown haggard picture of the miner with his swinging lamp, just come up from the pit, grasping his wife fiercely and kissing her mouth.

As I was looking at this last picture Sickert appeared in the door. My first sight of him was rather overwhelming. Huge and bearded, he was dressed in rough clothes and from his toes to his thighs reached what I can only describe as sewer-boots.

He had seen me staring at the picture and now said directly to me: 'That picture gives you the right feeling, doesn't it? You'd kiss your wife like that if you'd just come up from the pit, wouldn't you?'

I was appalled by the dreadful heartiness of the question. I found myself blushing, and hated him for making me do so.

Sickert came right up to me and looked me all over.

'Well, you don't look very ill,' he said. 'I thought you'd be a terrible mess. Didn't you fracture your spine or something?'

I nodded my head.

He made an amusing, whining baby's face.

'Look here, I'm very sorry I didn't come and see you, but I can't go round visiting.' He waved his hand round the room. 'You see I have to keep painting all these pictures because I'm so poor.'

He took up a position with his back to the fireplace. Mrs. Sickert got up and carried a cup of tea to her husband. The stringy man also rose and floated to the door. He was still talking to Mrs. Sickert over his shoulder, and the last words I heard as he left the room were: '. . . couldn't pass water for six days!'

This sounded so surprising that for one moment I forgot Sickert. Then I remembered him with a jolt, for he had begun to dance on the hearth in his great sewer-boots. He lifted his cup and, waving it to and fro, burst into a German drinking-song. There was an amazingly theatrical and roguish look on his broad face.

I could not believe that he always drank his tea in this way, and I felt flattered, because he seemed to be doing it especially for us.

I don't know how long the dance or the song would have lasted if the front-door bell had not rung. Sickert suddenly broke off and waited, while Mrs. Sickert hurried out of the room.

She returned with a Mr. Raven whom I had met once before. After giving him a cup of tea, she left him standing on the hearth beside Sickert. He sipped his tea in silence for a few moments; then he began to feel in his breast-pocket. At last he brought out a rather crumpled, shiny object, and I saw that it was a photograph.

'This is my mother,' he said, pushing it under Sickert's nose.

Sickert drew back perceptibly, and gave a grunt which might have meant anything.

Mr. Raven continued unruffled. 'Interesting face, isn't it? If you'd like to do a painting of it, I'd be very pleased to lend you the photograph for as long as you liked.'

There was another grunt from Sickert.

When Mr. Raven realized that this was the only answer he was going to get, he turned very red and hurriedly thrust the portrait of his mother back into his breast-pocket. He looked just as if he had been caught in the act of displaying an indecent postcard.

Gerald and I exchanged glances. I think we were both sorry for Mr. Raven, and yet glad that his efforts towards cheap immortality for his mother had been frustrated.

Sickert, evidently prompted by Mr. Raven's action, opened a drawer in a cabinet and also produced a photograph.

'Isn't she lovely?' he said, holding it out to me.

I took the yellowing little *carte-de-visite* between my fingers and saw that it was of some young woman of the eighties. She had her back to the camera, so that her face was seen in profile, resting on one shoulder. She appeared to me quite hideous with a costive, pouchy look about the eyes and mouth.

I wondered who she could be. Perhaps she was someone famous; or perhaps she was one of Sickert's past wives or mistresses.

I felt in a very difficult position. Thinking as I did, I hated to be sycophantic and say, 'Yes, she's beautiful'. So I compromised very clumsily by answering:

'The photograph is so tiny that I can't see very much of her; but I love the clothes of that period, don't you?'

Sickert snatched the photograph from me.

'Tiny! What do you mean by tiny?' he roared.

He held the picture up and pointed to it, as if he were demonstrating something on a blackboard; then he shouted out in ringing tones for the whole room to hear:

'Do you realize that I could paint a picture as big as this' (he stretched out his arms like an angler in a comic paper) 'from this "tiny" photograph as you call it?'

Horribly embarrassed and overcome by this outburst, I smiled weakly and cast my eyes down so that they rested on his enormous boots.

I was not thinking of his boots. I was thinking of nothing but the redness of my face. But Sickert evidently thought that I was curious, for the next moment he had opened another attack with:

'Ah, I see that you're staring at my boots! Do you know why I wear them? Well, I'll tell you. Lord Beaverbrook asked me to a party and I was late, so I jumped into a taxi and said: "Drive as fast as you can!" Of course, we had an accident and I was thrown on to my knees and my legs were badly knocked about; so now I wear these as a protection.'

In a dazed way, I wondered if he meant that he wore the boots to protect the still bruised legs, or if he meant that he intended to wear them as a permanent safeguard, in case he should ever again have an accident as he hurried to a party of Lord Beaverbrook's. I thought of the sensation they would create amongst the patent-leather shoes.

By this time I was so exhausted that I was pleased when Sickert turned his attention to Gerald. He started to talk about politicians, and I thought it was clever of him to guess that Gerald had an enormous appetite for tit-bits about the famous.

As I sank down on the sofa beside Mrs. Sickert, I heard them begin on Anthony Eden. Sickert was describing his good looks. He must have sensed that I was still listening, for he suddenly turned his face on me, and his eyes were twinkling with fun and malice.

'Ugly ones like us haven't a chance when there's someone like Eden about, have we?' he called out across the room.

I was so surprised at being lumped together with Sickert in ugliness, as opposed to the handsomeness of Anthony Eden (who had never struck me as anything but middle-aged), that I took him quite seriously and could answer nothing.

I hurriedly tried to compensate myself for the humiliation by telling myself that, although it might not be saying very much, I was undoubtedly by far and away the best-looking person in the room, and this in spite of my long illness.

Mrs. Sickert saw that I was ruffled and very kindly started to talk about my career. She asked me if I intended to go back to an art school when I was well enough. We discussed the various objects in the room. She told me that the two glittering monstrances had come from a Russian church. We went up to them and I took one of the sparkling things in my hands. The blue and white paste lustres were backed with tinsel. They were fascinatingly gaudy and I coveted them.

We sat talking together on the sofa for a little longer. Through our words I caught snatches of what Sickert was saying. Gerald evidently had got him on to Degas and anecdotes were streaming out. Gerald was drinking them up thirstily, while Mr. Raven hovered rather uncomfortably at the edge of the conversation.

At last he decided to go. Coming forward, he coughed slightly and held out his hand to Mrs. Sickert. Then, as he passed Sickert on his way to the door, he felt in his pocket and with almost incredible courage brought out the crumpled little photograph again.

Putting it down on the table, he said simply:

'I'll leave this just in case. . . .'

His voice tailed off as he saw the completely blank look on Sickert's face. I knew exactly what was coming and waited for it.

Sickert gave the same enigmatic grunt. It was somehow quite baffling and insulting.

Mr. Raven crept unhappily to the door and Mrs. Sickert followed swiftly to put salve on his wounds.

Immediately Raven was out of the room Sickert became boisterous. He started to dance again, thumping his great boots on the floor. Gerald and I caught some of his gaiety. We did not mention Raven, but I knew that we were all celebrating his defeat. It was pleasant to feel that Sickert treated us as fellow-artists. I wondered how many people each year asked him to paint pictures for love.

As Mrs. Sickert did not return, we went into the hall where Sickert dragged on our coats as if he were dressing sacks of turnips. Then dancing and singing in front of us, he led the way through the 'cloak-room' to the front door. I half expected some remark about the shining flush-closet, but none came.

It was dark outside. We walked over the greasy cobbles. Sickert was still leading us. He threw open the creaking stable-yard door and stood there with his hand on the latch. He looked gigantic.

We passed through and started to walk down the road.

'Good-bye, good-bye!' he shouted after us in great good humour. 'Come again when you can't stop quite so long!'

And at these words a strange pang went through me, for it was what my father had always said as he closed the book, when I had finished my bread and butter and milk, and it was time for me to go to bed.

IV

PERSONAL ANTHOLOGY

W. H. AUDEN

LAMENT FOR A LAWGIVER

Sob, heavy world,
Sob as you spin
Mantled in mist, remote from the happy:
The washerwomen have wailed all night,
The disconsolate clocks are crying together,
And the bells toll and toll
For tall Agrippa who touched the sky:
Shut is that shining eye
Which enlightened the lampless and lifted up
The flat and foundering, reformed the weeds
Into civil cereals and sobered the bulls;
Away the cylinder seal,
The didactic digit and dreaded voice
Which imposed peace on the pullulating
Primordial mess. Mourn for him now,
Our lost dad,
Our colossal father.
For seven cycles
For seven years
Past vice and virtue, surviving both,
Through pluvial periods, paroxysms
Of wind and wet, through whirlpools of heat,
And comas of deadly cold,
On an old white horse, an ugly nag,
In his faithful youth he followed
The black ball as it bowled downhill
On the spotted spirit's spiral journey,

Its purgative path to that point of rest
  Where longing leaves it, and saw
Shimmering in the shade the shrine of gold,
The magical marvel no man dare touch,
Between the towers the tree of life
  And the well of wishes
  The waters of joy.

  Then he harrowed hell,
  Healed the abyss
Of torpid instinct and trifling flux,
Laundered it, lighted it, made it lovable with
Cathedrals and theories; thanks to him
  Brisker smells abet us,
Cleaner clouds accost our vision
  And honest sounds our ears.
For he ignored the Nightmares and annexed their
    ranges,
Put the clawing Chimaeras in cold storage,
Berated the Riddle till it roared and fled,
  Won the Battle of Whispers,
Stopped the Stupids, stormed into
The Fumblers' Forts, confined the Sulky
To their drab ditches and drove the Crashing
  Bores to their bogs,
  Their beastly moor.
  In the high heavens,
  The ageless places,
The gods are wringing their great worn hands
For their watchman is away, their world-engine
Creaking and cracking. Conjured no more
  By his master music to wed
Their truths to times, the Eternal Objects
  Drift about in a daze:
O the lepers are loose in Lombard Street,
The rents are rising in the river basins,
The insects are angry. Who will dust
  The cobwebbed kingdoms now?

For our lawgiver lies below his people,
Bigger bones of a better kind,
Unwarped by their weight, as white limestone
  Under green grass,
  The grass that fades.

W. H. AUDEN

SONG

Deftly, admiral, cast your fly
  Into the slow deep hover,
Till the wise old trout mistake and die;
  Salt are the deeps that cover
  The glittering fleets you led,
    White is your head.

Read on, ambassador, engrossed
  In your favourite Stendhal;
The Outer Provinces are lost,
  Unshaven horsemen swill
  The great wines of the châteaux
    Where you danced long ago.

Do not turn, do not lift, your eyes
  Toward the still pair standing
On the bridge outside your memories,
  Indifferent to your minding:
  In its glory and its power
    This is their hour.

Nothing your strength, your skill, could do
  Can alter their embrace
Or dispersuade the Furies who
  At the appointed place
  With claw and dreadful brow
    Wait for them now.

GEORGE BARKER

SCEPTRE-STRUCK, SPELLBOUND, BELOVED

Turn on your side and bear the day to me
Beloved, sceptre-struck, immured
In the glass wall of sleep. Slowly
Uncloud the borealis of your eye
And show your iceberg secrets, your midnight prizes
To the green-eyed world and to me. Sins
Coil upward into thin air when you awaken
And again morning announces amnesty over
The serpent-kingdomed bed. Your mother
Watched with as dove an eye the unforgivable night
Sigh backward into innocence when you
Set a bright monument in her amorous sea.
Look down, Undine, on the trident that struck
Sons from the rocks of vanity. Turn in the world,
Sceptre-struck, spellbound, beloved,
Turn in the world and bear the day to me.

JOHN BETJEMAN

THE OLD LIBERALS

Pale green of the *English Hymnal*! Yattendon hymns
  Played on the *hautbois* by a lady dress'd in blue
  Her white-haired father accompanying her thereto
On *Serpent* or *bass-recorder*. Daylight swims
On sectional bookcase, delicate cup and plate
  And William de Morgan tiles around the grate
And many the silver birches the pearly light shines through.

* * *

I think such a running together of woodwind sound
  Such painstaking piping high on a Berkshire hill
  Is sad as an English autumn heavy and still,
Sad as a country silence, tractor-drowned.
For deep in the hearts of the man and the woman playing
  The rose of a world that was not has withered away:
Where are the wains with garlanded swathes a-swaying?
Where are the swains to wend through the lanes a-maying?
  Where are the blithe and jocund to ted the hay?
  Where are the free folk of England? Where are they?

* * *

Ask of the Abingdon bus with full load creeping
  Down into denser suburbs. The birch lets go
  But one brown leaf upon browner bracken below.
Ask of the cinema manager. Night airs die
To still, ripe scent of the fungus and wet woods weeping.
  Ask at the fish and chips in the Market Square.
  Here in the firs and a final sunset flare,
Serpent and *hautbois* only moan at a mouldering sky.

E. E. CUMMINGS

POEM

what if a much of a which of a wind
gives the truth to summer's lie;
bloodies with dizzying leaves the sun
and yanks immortal stars awry?
Blow king to beggar and queen to seem
(blow friend to fiend: blow space to time)
—when skies are hanged and oceans drowned,
the single secret will still be man

what if a keen of a lean wind flays
screaming hills with sleet and snow:
strangles valleys by ropes of thing
and stifles forests in white ago?
Blow hope to terror; blow seeing to blind
(blow pity to envy and soul to mind)
—whose hearts are mountains, roots are trees,
it's they shall cry hello to the spring

what if a dawn of a doom of a dream
bites this universe in two,
peels forever out of his grave
and sprinkles nowhere with me and you?
Blow soon to never and never to twice
(blow life to isn't: blow death to was)
—all nothing's only our hugest home;
the most who die, the more we live

E. E. CUMMINGS

POEM

jake hates
       all the girls(the
shy ones,the bold
ones;the meek
proud sloppy sleek)
all except the cold
             ones

paul scorns all
         the girls(the
bright ones,the dim
ones;the slim
plump tiny tall)
all except the
          dull ones

gus loves all the
          girls(the
warped ones,the lamed
ones;the mad
moronic maimed)
all except
       the dead ones

mike likes all the girls
             (the
fat ones,the lean
ones;the mean
kind dirty clean)
all
  except the green ones

WILLIAM EMPSON

SUCCESS

I have mislaid the torment and the fear.
You should be praised for taking them away.
Those who doubt drugs, let them doubt which was here.

Well are they doubted for they turn out dear.
I feed on flatness and am last to leave.
Verse likes despair. Blame it upon the beer.
I have mislaid the torment and the fear.

All losses haunt us. It was a reprieve
Made Dostoevsky speak out queer and clear.

Those stay most haunting that most soon deceive.

And turn out no loss of the various zoo
The public spirits or the private play.
Praised once for having taken these away
What is it else then such a thing can do?

Lose is Find with great marsh lights like you.
Those who doubt drugs, let them doubt which was here
When this leaves the green afterlight of day.
Nor they nor I know what we shall believe.
You should be praised for taking them away.

LOUIS KENT

I. SCRIVNER

Here he lies strawless in bed,
Unbudding and sapless,
SAMUEL GARDNER.

Sure with a wheel on a shaft
BEN WHEELWRIGHT was hapless:
His own stopped dead.

Gardner's Maria was daft
Over Wheelwright's John.
Under the rose she bore—
God pardon her!—
Truelove, his son.

Truelove sailed on the water
And drank on shore.
He shipped WILL DYER'S daughter,
Keeping her pure of all stain
But a sailor's son.

The boy had an eye for a stone
To weather the wind and rain,
Carving them all but his own:

BEN WHEELRIGHT
SAM GARDNER
his daughter MARIA
T. JONSON called
SAYLOR
and his wife
JOAN DIER.

I might have cut stone like my Dad,
Or the sea like Grandfather,
But I am no hand for a tool
Or a trade:
I would rather
Write tales, like a fool,
Since I do nothing well
But spell:

Here
ICHABOD SCRIVNER
Lies cold:
Straighter than any,
Shorter than many
He told.

LAURIE LEE

EQUINOX

Now tilts the sun his monument,
now sags his raw unwritten stone
deep in October's diamond clay.

And oozy sloes like flies are hung
malignant on the shrivelled stem,
too late to ripen, or to grow.

Now is the time the wasp forsakes
the rose born like a weakly child
of earth-bed's pallor, death-bed's flush.

Time when the gourd upon the ground
cracks open kernel or decay
indifferent to man or worm.

Time of no violence, when at last
the shocked eye clears the battlefield
and burns down black the roots of grass,

And finds the prize of all its pain,
bedded in smoke, on leaves of blood—
love's charcoal cross, unlost, unwon.

LAURIE LEE

DAY OF THESE DAYS

Such a morning it is when love
leans through geranium windows
and calls with a cockerel's tongue.

When red-haired girls scamper like roses
over the rain-green grass;
and the sun drips honey.

When hedgerows grow venerable,
berries dry black as blood,
and holes suck in their bees.

Such a morning it is when mice
run whispering from the church,
dragging dropped ears of harvest.

When the partridge draws back his spring
and shoots like a buzzing arrow
over grained and mahogany fields.

When no table is bare,
and no breast dry,
and the tramp feeds on ribs of rabbit.

Such a day it is when time
piles up the hills like pumpkins,
and the streams run golden.

When all men smell good,
and the cheeks of girls
are as baked bread to the mouth.

As bread and beanflowers
the touch of their lips,
and their white teeth sweeter than cucumbers.

LOUIS MACNEICE

THE LIBERTINE

In the old days with married women's stockings
Twisted round his bedpost he felt himself a gay
Dog but now his liver has begun to groan,
Now that pick-ups are the order of the day:
O leave me easy, leave me alone.

Voluptuary in his teens and cynic in his twenties
He ran through women like a child through growing hay
Looking for a lost toy whose capture might atone
For his own guilt and the cosmic disarray:
O leave me easy, leave me alone.

He never found the toy and has forgotten the faces,
Only remembers the props . . . a scent-spray
Beside the bed or a milk-white telephone
Or through the triple ninon the acrid trickle of day:
O leave me easy, leave me alone.

Long fingers over the gunwale, hair in a hair-net,
Furs in January, cartwheel hats in May,
And after the event the wish to be alone—
Angels, goddesses, bitches, all have edged away:
O leave me easy, leave me alone.

So now, in middle age, his erotic programme
Torn in two, if after such a delay
An accident should offer him his own
Fulfilment in a woman, still he would say
O leave me easy, leave me alone.

MARIANNE MOORE

A FACE

'I am not treacherous, callous, jealous, superstitious,
supercilious, venomous, or absolutely hideous':
    studying and studying its expression,
    exasperated desperation
        though at no real impasse,
        would gladly break the glass;

when love of order, ardour, uncircuitous simplicity,
with an expression of inquiry, are all one needs to be!
    Certain faces, a few, one or two—or one
    face photographed by recollection—
        to my mind, to my sight,
        must remain a delight.

S. QUASIMODO

MAN OF MY TIME

Sei ancora quello della pietra e della fionda;
uomo del mio tempo. Eri nella carlinga,
con le ali maligne, le meridiane di morte,
—t'ho visto—dentro il carro di fuoco, alle forche,
alle ruote di tortura. T'ho visto; eri tu,
con la tua scienza esatta persuasa allo sterminio,
senza amore, senza Cristo. Hai ucciso ancora,
come sempre, come uccisero i padri, come uccisero
gli animali che li videro per la prima volta.
E questo sangue odora come nel giorno
quando il fratello disse all'altro fratello:
'Andiamo ai campi.' E quell'eco fredda, tenace,
è giunta fino a te, dentro la tua giornata.
Dimenticate, o figli, le nuvole di sangue
salite dalla terra, dimenticate i padri:
le loro tombe affondano nella cenere,
gli uccelli neri, il vento, coprono il loro cuore.

You are still he of the stone and of the sling,
Man of my time. You were in the cockpit,
With the malignant wings, with the meridians of death,
—I have seen you—inside the wagon of flame, at the
  pitch-forks,
At the wheel of torture. I have seen you; it was you,
With your exact science, persuaded to destruction,
Without love, without Christ. You have killed again,
As always, as your fathers killed, as they killed
The animals who saw them for the first time.
And the smell of this blood is as on the day
When the brother said to the other brother:
'Let us go to the fields.' And that echo, cold, clinging,
Is fastened to you, within your day.
O sons, forget the clouds of blood
Risen from the earth, forget your fathers:
Their tombs sink in the ashes,
The black birds, the wind, cover their heart.

[*Translated by* SIR MAURICE BOWRA]

OCTAVIO PAZ

THREE POEMS

POET'S EPITAPH

He sang until his death
singing to close his eyes
to his true life, his real life of lies;
and to remember till he died
how it had lied, his unreal life of truth.

EPITAFIO PARA UN POETA

Quiso cantar, cantar
para olvidar
su vida verdadera de mentiras
y recordar
su mentirosa vida de verdades.

TWO BODIES

Two bodies face to face
are at times two waves
and night is an ocean.

Two bodies face to face
are at times two stones
and night is a desert.

Two bodies face to face
are at times two roots
and night is the earth.

Two bodies face to face
are at times two knives
and night strikes sparks.

Two bodies face to face
are two stars falling down
in an empty sky.

DOS CUERPOS

Dos cuerpos frente a frente
son a veces dos olas
y la noche es océano.

Dos cuerpos frente a frente
son a veces dos piedras
y la noche desierto.

Dos cuerpos frente a frente
son a veces raíces
en la noche enlazadas.

Dos cuerpos frente a frente
son a veces navajas
y la noche relámpago.

Dos cuerpos frente a frente
son dos astros que caen
en un cielo vacío.

THE STREET

Here is a long and silent street.
I walk in blackness and I stumble and fall
and rise, and I walk, my blind feet
trampling the silent stones and the dry leaves.
Someone behind me also tramples, stones, leaves:
if I slow down, he slows;
if I run, he runs. I turn: nobody,
Everything dark and doorless,
only my steps aware of me,
turning and turning among these corners
which lead forever to the street
where nobody waits for, nobody follows me,
where I pursue a man who stumbles
and rises and says when he sees me: nobody.

LA CALLE

Es una calle larga y silenciosa.
Ando en tinieblas y tropiezo y caigo
y me levanto y piso con pies ciegos
las piedras mudas y las hojas secas
y alguien detrás de mí también las pisa:
si me detengo, se detiene,
si corro, corre. Vuelvo el rostro: nadie.
Todo está oscuro y sin salida,
sólo mis pasos me acompañan
y doy vueltas y vueltas en esquinas
que dan siempre a la calle
donde nadie me espera ni me sigue,
donde yo sigo a un hombre que tropieza
y se levanta y dice al verme: nadie.

[*Translated by* MURIEL RUKEYSER]

BRIAN READE

GIRL DOZING

By the hair she danced him
unmercifully guessed, so fast
that he fell, and she enclosed
him smaller than he ever was
for her or for his mother.

I'm a mouth to kiss your skin,
or a scissor, she was saying,
for your stem. I am.
I wish I were your shadow too
but I would cool you then.

Oh dear. A name to call him
nearer than the smallest name.
There wasn't one, Dear me.
Your balcony I could be
she said, or summer house, or let me
be the room you sleep in.

KENNETH REXROTH

FROM 'ANOTHER SPRING'

I am a man with no ambitions
And few friends, wholly incapable
Of making a living, growing no
Younger, fugitive from some just doom.
Lonely, ill-clothed, what does it matter?
At midnight I make myself a jug
Of hot white wine and cardamom seeds.
In a torn grey robe and old beret,
I sit in the cold writing poems,
Drawing nudes on the crooked margins,
Copulating with sixteen-year-old
Nymphomaniacs of my imagination.

The seasons revolve and the years change
With no assistance or supervision.
The moon, without taking thought,
Moves in its cycle, full, crescent, and full.

The white moon enters the heart of the river;
The air is drugged with azalea blossoms;
Deep in the night a pine cone falls;
Our campfire dies out in the empty mountains.

The sharp stars flicker in the tremulous branches;
The lake is black, bottomless in the crystalline night;
High in the sky the Northern Crown
Is cut in half by the dim summit of a snow peak.

O heart, heart, so singularly
Intransigent and corruptible,
Here we lie entranced by the starlit water,
And moments that should each last forever

Slide unconsciously by us like water.

EDITH SITWELL

EURYDICE

For John Lehmann

Fires on the hearth! Fires in the heavens! Fires in the hearts of Men,
I who was welded into bright gold in the earth by Death
Salute you! All the weight of Death in all the world
Yet does not equal Love—the great compassion
For the fallen dust and all fallen creatures, quickening
As is the Sun in the void firmament.
It shines like fire. O bright gold of the heat of the Sun
Of Love across dark fields—burning away rough husks of Death
Till all is fire, and bringing all to harvest!

See then! I stand in the centre of my earth
That was my Death, under the zenith of my Sun
Bringing a word from Darkness
That Death too has compassion for all fallen Nature.
For as the Sun buries his hot days and rays
To ripen, so the great rays of the heart
Are ripened to wisdom by Death, and great is our forgiveness.

When through the darkness Orpheus came with his Sun-like singing
Like the movements in the heavens that, in our blindness
Could we but emulate, would set right our lives—
I came to the mouth of the Tomb . . . I did not know our meeting
would be this:
—Only like the return at evening
Of the weary worker in the holy field—
The cry of welcome, the remembered kiss!

In the lateness of the season, I with the golden feet
That had walked in the fields of Death, now walk again
The dark fields where the sowers scatter grain
Like tears, or the constellations that weep for the lateness of the
season—
Where the women walk like mourners, like the Afternoon ripened,
with their bent heads;
Their golden eyelids like the drifts of the narcissus
In spring, are wet with their tears. They mourn for a young wife
who had walked these fields,
—So young, not yet had Proserpina tied up her golden hair
In a knot like the branchèd corn . . . So good was she
With a voice like the sweet swallow. She lies in the silent Tomb

And they walk in the fields alone. Then one of the Dead who lay
Beneath the earth, like the water-dark, the water-thin
Effigy of Osiris, with a face green as a moon,
—He who was lying in darkness with the wheat
Like a flame springing from his heart, or a gold sound,
Said to me 'We have been blind and stripped God naked of things
To see the light which shines in the dark, and we have learned
That the gold flame of the wheat may spring from a barren heart.'

When I came down from the Metropolis of the Corn
Then said the ferine dust that reared about me
'I have the famine of the lion, all things devour,
Or make them mine . . . Venus was powerful as me—
Now is she but a handful of dry amber dust;
And my tooth cracked the husk, the dry amber wall
That held the fire of the wheat. That fire is gone!
And remember this, that Love, or I, have ground
Your heart between the stones of the years, like wheat.'

But as I left the mouth of the Tomb, far off, like the noise of the dark wild bees,
I heard the sounds arise from the dwellings of Men, and I thought of their building,
Their wars, their money-making, and of the gold roofs built against Darkness.

And I had learned beneath the earth that all gold nature
Changes to wheat or gold in the sweet darkness.
Why do they weep for those in the silent Tomb,
Dropping their tears like grain? 'Her heart, that honeycomb,
Thick Darkness like a bear devours . . . See, all the gold is gone!
The cell of the honey-comb is six-sided . . . But there, in the five cells of the senses
Are stored all their gold . . . Where is it now? Only the wind of the Tomb can know.'
But I feared not that stilled and chilling breath
Among the dust . . . Love is not changed by Death,
And nothing is lost and all in the end is harvest.

As the earth is heavy with the lion-strong Sun
When he has fallen, with his hot days and rays,
We are heavy with Death, as a woman is heavy with child.
As the corn-husks hold its ripeness, the gold comb
Its weight of summer. . . . But as if a lump of gold had changed to corn,
So did my Life rise from my Death. I cast the grandeur of Death away
And homeward came to the small things of Love, the building of the hearth, the kneading of daily bread,

The cries of birth, and all the weight of light
Shaping our bodies and our souls. . . . Came home to youth,
And the noise of summer growing in the veins,
And to old age, a serene afternoon.
An element beyond time, or a new climate.

I with the other young who were born from darkness,
Returning to darkness, stood at the mouth of the Tomb
With one who had come glittering like the wind
To meet me—Orpheus with the golden mouth,
You—like Adonis born from the young myrrh-tree, you, the
vine-branch
Broken by the wind of love . . . I turned to greet you—
And when I touched your mouth, it was the Sun.

Notes

Verse IV. Lines 9, 10, 11, 12.

'. . . A most sweet wife, a young wife, *Nondum sustulerat flavum Proserpina crinem* (not yet had Proserpina tied up her golden hair), such a wife as no man ever had, so good a wife, but she is now dead and gone, *Lethaeoque jacet condita sarcophago* (she lies buried in the silent tomb).'

ROBERT BURTON: *The Anatomy of Melancholy*

Verse V. Lines 6 and 7.

'The light which God is shines in darkness, God is the true light: to see it one has to be blind and strip God naked of things.'

MEISTER ECKHART: *Sermons and Collations XIX*

Verse IX. Line 3.

'And her deadness
Was filling her with fullness
Full as a fruit with sweetness and darkness
Was she with her great death.'

J. M. RILKE, translated by J. B. Leishman

EDITH SITWELL

A SIMPLETON

To David Horner

In the autumn the season of ripeness when final redness
Comes to the ore and the earth is with child by the sun,
Like the bright gold spangles fall'n from the light of Nature
Flying over the happy fields, the Simpleton
Feeling the warm gold ripen, sat by the wayside
—His broad face having an animal nature (the beast of burden
Who has turned prophet—the beast in our earth unconscious)—
A simple creature, happy as butterflies,
Or as the dancing star that has risen from Chaos.
And the world hangs like a ripe apple—the great gold planets
Lying with Evil and Good in the ripened core.
. . . The old men Abraham-bearded like the auburn
Sun of harvest walk in the holy fields
Where the Sun forgives and remakes the shape of Evil
And, laughing, forgives lean Virtue . . . Gravity yields
The gold that was hidden deep in its earth, in the map-like
Lines of a smile made holy by Light, and the Sun
With his gold mouth kisses the skin that shines like red fire,
And shouts to the lowly, the dust that is his lover,
'See how of my love and my shining I never tire,
But rule over thunders and Chaos: the lore of the bee and the
    great lion's raging
To me are equal in grandeur—the hump of the cripple
And the mountain that hides the veins of brute gold are as one—
And to me the jarring atoms are parted lovers!'
. . . And this is the lore the Simpleton learns from his nature—
Lifting his face in blindness and happiness up to the Sun.

STEPHEN SPENDER

O NIGHT O TREMBLING NIGHT

O night O trembling night O night of sighs
O night when my body was a rod O night
When my mouth was a vague animal cry
Pasturing on her flesh O night
When the close darkness was a nest
Made of her hair and filled with my eyes

(O stars impenetrable above
The fragile tent poled with our thighs
Among the petals fading fields of time
O night revolving all our dark away)

O day O gradual day O sheeted light
Covering her body as with dews
Until I brushed her sealing sleep away
To read once more in the uncurtained day
Her naked love, my great good news.

DYLAN THOMAS

FERN HILL

Now as I was young and easy under the apple boughs
About the lilting house and happy as the grass was green,
The night above the dingle starry,
Time let me hail and climb
Golden in the heydays of his eyes,
And honoured among wagons I was prince of the apple towns
And once below a time I lordly had the trees and leaves
Trail with daisies and barley
Down the rivers of the windfall light.

And as I was green and carefree, famous among the barns
About the happy yard and singing as the farm was home,
In the sun that is young once only,
Time let me play and be
Golden in the mercy of his means,
And green and golden I was huntsman and herdsman, the calves
Sang to my horn, the foxes on the hills barked clear and cold,
And the sabbath rang slowly
In the pebbles of the holy streams.

All the sun long it was running, it was lovely, the hay-
Fields high as the house, the tunes from the chimneys, it was air
And playing, lovely and watery
And fire green as grass.
And nightly under the simple stars
As I rode to sleep the owls were bearing the farm away,
All the moon long I heard, blessed among stables, the nightjars
Flying with the ricks, and the horses
Flashing into the dark.

And then to awake, and the farm, like a wanderer white
With the dew, come back, the cock on his shoulder: it was all
Shining, it was Adam and maiden,
The sky gathered again
And the sun grew round that very day.
So it must have been after the birth of the simple light
In the first, spinning place, the spellbound horses walking warm
Out of the whinnying green stable
On to the fields of praise.

And honoured among foxes and pheasants by the gay house
Under the new made clouds and happy as the heart was long,
In the sun born over and over,
I ran my heedless ways,
My wishes raced through the house-high hay
And nothing I cared, at my sky blue trades, that time allows
In all his tuneful turning so few and such morning songs
Before the children green and golden
Follow him out of grace.

Nothing I cared, in the lamb white days, that time would take me
Up to the swallow thronged loft by the shadow of my hand,
In the moon that is always rising,
Nor that riding to sleep
I should hear him fly with the high fields
And wake to the farm forever fled from the childless land.
Oh as I was young and easy in the mercy of his means,
Time held me green and dying
Though I sang in my chains like the sea.

DYLAN THOMAS

A REFUSAL TO MOURN THE DEATH, BY FIRE, OF A CHILD IN LONDON

Never until the mankind making
Bird beast and flower
Fathering and all humbling darkness
Tells with silence the last light breaking
And the still hour
Is come of the sea tumbling in harness

And I must enter again the round
Zion of the water bead
And the synagogue of the ear of corn
Shall I let pray the shadow of a sound
Or sow my salt seed
In the least valley of sackcloth to mourn

The majesty and burning of the child's death.
I shall not murder
The mankind of her going with a grave truth
Nor blaspheme down the stations of the breath
With any further
Elegy of innocence and youth.

Deep with the first dead lies London's daughter,
Robed in the long friends,
The grains beyond age, the dark veins of her mother,
Secret by the unmourning water
Of the riding Thames.
After the first death, there is no other.

TWO POEMS OF HOELDERLIN

Translated by VERNON WATKINS

HYPERIONS SCHICKSALSLIED

Ihr wandelt droben im Licht
Auf weichem Boden, selige Genien!
Glänzende Götterlüfte
Rühren euch leicht,
Wie die Finger der Künstlerin
Heilige Saiten.

Schicksallos, wie der schlafende
Säugling, atmen die Himmlischen;
Keusch bewahrt
In bescheidener Knospe,
Blühet ewig
Ihnen der Geist,
Und die seligen Augen
Blicken in stiller
Ewiger Klarheit.

Doch uns ist gegeben,
Auf keiner Stätte zu ruhn,
Es schwinden, es fallen
Die leidenden Menschen
Blindlings von einer
Stunde zur andern,
Wie Wasser von Klippe
Zu Klippe geworfen,
Jahrlang ins Ungewisse hinab.

HYPERION'S FATE-SONG

You walk up there in the light
On gentle underfoot, holy Genii!
Winds of the gods glittering
Lightly touch you,
Like the fingers of the harpist her
Sacred strings.

Fateless, like the sleeping
Suckling, they breathe, the heavenly ones;
Chastely kept
In the shy bud, spirit
Blooms everlastingly
New in them,
And the holy eyes
Look, in still,
Eternal clearness.

But to us is given
Never on a crevice to rest.
Still vanish, still fall
Men ever suffering
Blindly from one lost
Hour to another,
Like water from rockhead
To rockhead rebounding,
Year-long into the uncertain thrown back.

HÄLFTE DES LEBENS

Mit gelben Birnen hänget
Und voll mit wilden Rosen
Das Land in den See,
Ihr holden Schwäne,
Und trunken von Küssen
Tunkt ihr das Haupt
Ins heilignüchterne Wasser.

Weh mir, wo nehm' ich, wenn
Es Winter ist, die Blumen, und wo
Den Sonnenschein
Und Schatten der Erde?
Die Mauern stehn
Sprachlos und kalt, im Winde
Klirren die Fahnen.

HALF OF LIFE

With yellow pears the land
And thick with wild roses
Hangs in the lake,
You friendly swans,
And drunken with kisses
Dip your heads
In the pious, sobering water.

Ah, grief, where do I take, when
Winter comes, the flowers, and where
The sunshine
And shadows of the Earth?
The walls stand
Speechless and cold, in the wind
Clatter the storm-vanes.

V

A PROSPECT OF LITERATURE

C. M. BOWRA

THE ODES OF HORACE

It is the fate of Horace's Odes that anyone who knows them at all usually knows them so well that he hardly treats them as poetry. A familiarity inculcated at school does not actually kill our appreciation of them but makes us like them more for their secondary than for their primary qualities. They are indeed rich in the accidental qualities of poetry. Their abundance of quotable lines, their wise observations on many aspects of life, their closeness to much that the ordinary man knows and loves, even their wonderful technical accomplishment, all conspire to hide the fact that they were intended to be poetry and should make their first appeal as poetry. Unlike the work of Catullus or Lucretius, they do not overwhelm the young by an irresistible onslaught on the sensibility, but appeal in a quieter, less exciting way which is not quite what youth expects. This habit, formed early in life, may persist into middle age. We accept Horace; we admire, we like him. But he has not that special, sacred place which we accord to those whose inspiration sweeps in irresistible flight and carries all before it. In the end we may perhaps dismiss him and say that, compared with Catullus, he lacks the authentic divine fire. Or, conversely, we may admire him for just this reason and find his mastery of technique so satisfying that we ask for nothing more. But both positions are based on false assumptions. Horace is indeed a great poet, and great not merely for his apt choice of words but for a strange and special power in them.

The usual approach to the Odes is partly due to the comparisons which we inevitably make between Horace and Catullus or Sappho or Anacreon. For such comparisons he must bear the responsibility. These poets were in some ways his models. He adopted some of their metres and themes and phrases. At the end of Book III he claims proudly that he has been the first to adapt Aeolian song to

Italian verse. Naturally we compare him with his masters and find that he lacks their essential qualities, their speed and directness, their uncomplicated and unconcealed emotions, their divine simplicity, their irresistible, pure song. Whether he writes about the gods or love or war or wine, we feel that something is missing which his models have in abundance, not merely a simple, unsophisticated approach to experience but a fire and a magic which survive in them, as Horace himself saw when he said of Sappho:

vivuntque commissi calores
Aeoliae fidibus puellae.[1]

So long as we compare Horace with Sappho or Catullus and judge his work by theirs, we find him wanting. Yet though he began the comparison himself, it is not in any resemblance to them that his strength lies. He lived in a different age and possessed different qualities. To understand him and to appreciate his achievement we must look not to his models but to his own gifts and to the age which formed his tastes and ideas. We shall then see how remarkable his work is and how worthy of the name of poetry.

Poets may be roughly divided into two classes. In the first, when creative inspiration comes, it has such a force that a poem is written in a single, uninterrupted fit and finished almost without the poet knowing what has happened. Such fits may be separated by long periods of frustration and inactivity, but these are redeemed by the unaccountable moments of creation when all is easy and straightforward and the poet's powers are so controlled by his genius that his words have the peculiar, enchanting and unanalysable power which Paul Valéry ascribes to *le vers donné*, to the magical verse which somehow seems to come to the poet from an outside power. The second class works in a different way. A 'given' line may come to a poet and provide him with his subject, his tone and his metre, but though the inspiration may last through one or two verses, it then flags and fades and leaves him with the difficult task of completing the poem by what is almost an act of will. He must try many experiments or wait in patience until inspiration returns or refashion what ideas he has until they fit into his ideal plan and conform to its inspired start. This process has been described by A. E. Housman

[1] IV 9, 11–12. 'Still live the passions that the Aeolian maiden confided to her lyre.'

and is familiar to many poets. And in practice we are surely not wrong to think that we can recognize its fruits and distinguish between those lines which come to a poet and those which he makes, between *le vers donné* and *le vers calculé*. Valéry quotes as an example the poem of Baudelaire which begins with what is obviously a 'given' line:

> La servante au grand cœur dont vous étiez jalouse,

and proceeds with what is no less obviously a 'calculated' line:

> Et qui dort son sommeil sous un humble pelouse.

Something of the same kind can be seen in other poets. No poet, for instance, has more startling and more inspired beginnings than Donne, but the poems which open with such lines as

> I long to talk with some old lover's ghost
> Who died before the god of Love was born,

or

> When by thy scorn, O murd'ress, I am dead,

do not proceed in the same direct way. They develop complications and complexities; their movement becomes slower and more intellectual; they create in the end an impression different from that suggested at the beginning. Now this is not to say that a poet who works in this way is inferior to one who is carried through a whole poem on a single waft of inspiration. He may have his own successes and his own rewards which are denied to those who rely on the inconstant visitations of inspiration, and his work cannot be judged in the same way or by the same standards as theirs.

To this second class Horace almost certainly belongs. His own statements show that his composition was partly the result of sudden inspiration, partly of laborious toil. He certainly knew the fine frenzy of creation; for in his introductory poem he speaks of the Nymphs and Satyrs who draw him away from other men and in another poem he finds in Bacchus his symbol for inspiration, telling how he sees him on the hills and hears his call to song.[1] On the other hand he believed that a poem demands long labour, and he was not joking when he said that it should be kept for nine years.[2] He compared himself to the bee which flits from flower to flower gathering honey and said that his songs were *operosa*, 'laborious'.[3] He was not

[1] II, 19. [2] *Ars Poetica* 388. [3] IV, 2, 27–32.

a singer who relied mainly on inspiration like Sappho or Catullus; he had his own way of working, and it was more like that of Baudelaire or Donne. At times wonderful lines came to him, and he saw how good they were, but he had to supplement them with other lines less easily found. Indeed there are some poems of Horace in which we can almost distinguish the 'given' from the 'calculated' lines. He will start a poem with an overwhelming dash and brilliance, then continue in a different spirit to a different effect. The first wild onslaught yields to something more meditated and more complex. Such at least is the impression made by poems with such beginnings as

> O fons Bandusiae, splendidior vitro,[1]

or

> Quid fles, Asterie, quem tibi candidi
> primo restituent vere Favonii . . .[2]

or

> Eheu fugaces, Postume, Postume,
> labuntur anni . . .[3]

or

> Nunc est bibendum, nunc pede libero
> pulsanda tellus.[4]

There is a directness of approach, a violent sweep, in these openings which is not maintained in the verses which follow. The speed becomes slower, the ideas more intricate, the style more elaborate, the unity of impression less complete. Horace seems to have begun some poems in an almost Dionysiac excitement and then found that to complete them he must summon all the resources of patience, hard work and discriminating selection.

Though this manner of composition must in the first place have been dictated by the special nature of Horace's gifts, it was well in accord with theories current at the time. Roman poets and critics like to distinguish between *ingenium*, or natural talent, and *ars*, or technique. Both were equally important, in that the first must be purified and disciplined by the second. That Horace shared these views is clear from the recipe for poetry which he gives in his *Ars Poetica*. The poet must have natural talent but he must also have

[1] III, 13, 1. 'O spring of Bandusia, brighter than crystal.'

[2] III, 7, 1. 'Why, Asterie, do you weep for him whom the white West winds will bring back to you when spring begins?'

[3] II, 14, 1. 'Alas, the fleeing years, Postumus, Postumus, are slipping by.'

[4] I, 37, 1. 'Now must we drink, now beat the earth with free foot.'

enough technique to make proper use of his gifts. For all practical purposes he agreed with the doctrine advanced in the treatise *On the Sublime*, probably a work of the Augustan age, that 'the employment of art is in every way a fitting aid to nature; for it is the conjunction of the two which tends to ensure perfection'.[1] In a world where such ideas were prevalent Horace matured and developed his art. He felt that he had been born a poet and lisped numbers in his cradle, but he also felt that uninstructed and uncontrolled singing was not enough and that he must modify and discipline his natural talent with all the art that he could summon to his command.

Such a conception imposes its own conditions on those who try to put it into effect. In the first place it demands a strict form. The poet who has to fuse 'given' and 'calculated' verses into a harmonious unity gains much from the discipline imposed by a rigid frame. Without it he has no clear field in which to work and no exact standard to follow. Horace was indeed conscious of this when he contrasted his own art with Pindar's. For him Pindar is like a river in spate which carries all before it as it breaks its bounds or like a swan in effortless flight through the air.[2] Horace did not see himself like this, and it is significant that in his estimate of Pindar he misunderstood the formality of Pindaric verse and thought that it had no rules. He himself needed a strict form and found it in certain Greek metres used by Sappho and Alcaeus. He adapted them with great cunning; for the Latin language was not ideally formed to receive them. Heavier than Greek, with a greater proportion of long syllables, it needed considerable skill to make it absorb these measures. Horace's Sapphics and Alcaics and Asclepiads are indeed more weighty than those of Sappho and Alcaeus. In the Sapphic line especially Horace's introduction of an almost compulsory break after the fifth syllable as in

Dulce ridentem Lalagen amabo[3]

gives a less airy music than Sappho's various uses of the same metre, and breaks what was once a unity into two separate parts. Nor was this imposed on Horace merely by the nature of Latin; it suited his kind of composition. The slower movement of the line corresponds to the slower march of his poetical moods. It reflects the strong element of meditation, of experience treasured and assimilated,

[1] *De Subl.* 36, 3. [2] IV, 2, 5 ff. [3] I, 22, 23. 'I shall love sweetly laughing Lalage.'

which has gone to his verse. The regularity of Horace's verse-forms and of the movements inside them belong to his special kind of poetry.

In this kind of composition the poet's first task is to secure a perfect harmony between the 'given' and the 'calculated' elements. He must see that what he himself adds to his inspired lines holds its own with them and is not noticeably different in quality. Both Donne and Baudelaire saw this difficulty and met it in their own way by giving so great a variety of content to a poem that we pass easily from one state of mind to another without feeling any disparity between this and that passage. This is an achievement of style. Both poets manage words so well that the most different kinds of experience are harmonized through the individual tone of the language. The result is a special kind of poetry quite unlike effortless song. The will and intelligence, in alliance with an unerring sensibility, create true poetry, but it is not song. It moves more slowly; its effects are less immediately overwhelming; it is richer, more impressive, and often more various; thought plays a larger part in it; its texture is richer, and its structure more muscular. If it loses in speed and grace, it gains in richness. And this is what Horace's poetry does. It has not the essential fire of Sappho or Catullus, but it has other qualities which they have not, and it gives an entirely different kind of pleasure.

This difference may perhaps be expressed by saying that while effortless song gives the pleasure of perfect melody, that of constructed verse relies less on its tune and on creating a single impression than on a series of small thrills and of individual effects due to the choice and arrangement of words. It reflects not a single, all-absorbing moment but something more complex, and it makes its impression by exploiting not one mood but several. The difference can be illustrated by a comparison between the opening lines of two hymns to Diana, one by Catullus and the other by Horace. Catullus writes with a delightful, straightforward charm:

Dianae sumus in fide
puellae et pueri integri:
Dianam pueri integri
puellaeque canamus.[1]

[1] 34, 1–4. 'We, girls and chaste boys, are Diana's lieges. Let us, chaste boy and girls, sing of Diana.'

This is light and lucid and swift, and it contains a single imaginative experience, the desire of boys and girls to sing of a goddess. Horace opens in quite a different manner:

Dianam tenerae dicite virgines,
intonsum, pueri, dicite Cynthium
Latonamque supremo
dilectam penitus Iovi.[1]

Not only does Horace treat of three gods instead of one, and thereby make his verse less easy to absorb, but he introduces ideas, as Catullus does not, outside the innocent desire to sing. He adds epithets to his deities and makes the attention turn to more than one direction as it follows his movements. The lilt which makes Catullus' poem almost pure song is bound up with the simplicity of his thought; in Horace there is no such lilt because the thought is more elaborate, and the pleasure comes from the richness given to what might otherwise be a simple theme.

Horace's triumph is precisely that he makes his poems rich through countless small touches. While the strict form supplies the music, the words have each a special appeal and charm, a power to startle delight through their apt expressiveness. It may have taken Horace as long as it took Flaubert to find the inevitable word, but he always found it, and when it came, it did much more than carry its burden in its own place. It is thrilling, delightful, uplifting. To secure this result Horace created his own vocabulary, not indeed so refined and delicate as that of Catullus, but closer in some ways to common speech and to that rhetoric into which the Italian falls so naturally when his emotions are aroused. Less adventurous than Virgil, who hardly ever says a plain thing in a plain way, Horace is still adventurous enough in his attempts to give a new life to words by unusual combinations and figures of speech. Above all his words give the impression that they are used for the first time and have not been dulled by habit and repetition. Their almost miraculous aptness catches the attention at once and compels us to see how much they mean. Take, for instance, the opening lines of a poem on the first snow:

Vides ut alta stet nive candidum
Soracte, nec iam sustineant onus

[1] I, 21, 1–4. 'Praise Diana, tender maidens! Boys, praise unshorn Apollo, and Latona deeply loved by highest Jove.'

silvae laborantes, geluque
flumina constiterint acuto.[1]

Each word is not only straight to the point, but lively and vivid. *Stet* calls up the outline of the mountain as it stands solidly against the skyline; the heavy *laborantes*, 'straining', conveys the sense of effort in the woods newly laden with snow; *acuto*, 'piercing', is far more bold and original than its well-worn English counterpart 'piercing'. And though each word has its own precision and distinction and delights us as we come to it, the whole verse gives no impression of being crowded or heavy. We pass lightly from one point to another and see exactly what Horace wishes to convey. This is what he always does. His words, chosen with unfailing care and insight, never fail to be fresh and alluring, and the result is never laborious.

The choice of individual words is matched by Horace's skill in arranging them and building them into a sentence. Latin, of course, with its highly inflected forms, allows a far greater variety of word-order than is possible in English, but Horace's skill lies in exploiting to the utmost the possibilities of this variety. By separating his adjectives from their nouns, by placing the subject of a sentence in an emphatic position not necessarily at the start, by finding an appropriate place for each word according to its importance, Horace gives a new dimension to his poetry. His order is not that of natural speech, but, though in some senses it is artificial, its artificiality makes it the more telling. Nothing is idle in this style, and every word carries not only its own colour and individuality but gains something else through its position. Take, for instance, the closing stanza of Horace's poem on the death of Cleopatra:

Deliberata morte ferocior,
saevis Liburnis scilicet invidens
privata deduci superbo
non humilis mulier triumpho.[2]

[1] I, 9, 1–4. 'Do you see how Soracte stands, white with deep snow, and how the straining woods no longer endure their load, and the rivers are halted by the piercing frost?'

[2] I, 37, 29–32. 'In her determined death more bold, scorning indeed to be led no more a queen on Liburnian galleys, no humble woman she, in a proud triumph.'

The final, splendid stroke comes in the last line with its contrast between the queen, 'no humble woman', and the hideous humiliation of being led in a Roman triumph. So the most important words are kept for this, and what precedes them prepares the way. Yet even in this preparation the word-order is consummately skilful. In the first line Cleopatra's violent and yet determined decision to kill herself appears in the contrast of *deliberata* and *ferocior*. Then the reasons for this decision are unfolded, and we see that the great queen is not prepared to become a private citizen, *privata*, or to yield her pride to the still greater pride of Rome. The result of such an art is that whole paragraphs stand with a special power because they are so closely welded together. The marmoreal Latin words take on a new life through this exploitation of their resources.

In this poetry surprise plays a considerable part. Just as in his choice of words Horace gives a continual delight by some unexpected and yet inevitably right choice, so in the structure of a poem he keeps us intent and awake by the shifts of his moods and the unforeseen character of his development and his close. On the whole his models, Sappho, Alcaeus and Anacreon, do not do this. They usually allow a single mood to dominate and govern a whole poem. And this is indeed the normal practice of lyric poetry. It strikes its note at the start and keeps it to the end. It aims at reflecting a single, harmonious mood and needs no sudden changes or surprises. Horace, with his far less instinctive outlook, does something different. His originating impulses were perhaps not powerful enough to carry him through a whole poem, and he knew that in actual experience, as he felt it, one mood quickly yields to another. His art reflects the wayward movements of a subtle personality which starts with one view of a subject and then changes to another. He turns these vagaries into a remarkable art. For instance, when Virgil went to Greece, Horace wrote a poem wishing him a good voyage.[1] Such poems were common in antiquity, and there were certain rules to which they were expected to conform. They must wish for fine weather, speak of the traveller's virtues, and try to dissuade him from starting. Horace does all these things, but with a special emphasis which gives them a new character. His poem has, as it were, three movements, each of which may be traced to the traditional rules. But in each Horace does something new. He begins

[1] I, 3.

with words of touching affection for his old friend, who is 'half his soul' and asks that he may be safely guided to Greece; then, with a sudden turn, he speaks almost in reprobation of the bold exploits of man and deplores the dangers which they cause; finally he closes not with a denunciation of this bold spirit but with acceptance of it. There is nothing that men will not dare, and he seems to leave it at that. The three movements melt easily into each other, and the poem has a continuous development. It reflects the changing moods of the poet whose emotions are stirred by his friend's departure, Horace often does this kind of thing. It may not be quite what we expect from lyric poetry, but it is entirely consistent with Horace's special art in which variety of mood and the element of surprise play a special part.

By such means Horace gives variety and depth to his poetry, enriching it with many small touches which are outside the scope of unpremeditated song. But this was not his only way of making his poetry rich. He was fully aware of the complexities and mysteries of life and he knew that things are not always what they seem to be. He wished to convey this sense of hidden depths, of unexplored secrets, of unrecognized qualities, and he found to his hand an instrument of the greatest use. In adopting the theology of the Greeks and equating it with their own somewhat shadowy pantheon, the Romans added a great source of riches to their poetry. These gods and goddesses are hardly actual presences as they were to the Greeks; they are symbols of real but indefinable and abstract powers. They can be used to express in concrete form ideas which are otherwise hard to convey because there are no clear words for them. So Horace's Venus is less a goddess than a power of the flesh who unaccountably masters him; his Bacchus is not only the power of wine but the inspiring intoxication which creates poetry; his Hercules is an example of that human spirit, admired by the Stoics, which is lord of itself and therefore of its destiny. So too the great array of Greek stories provided him with many significant examples to illustrate his thought. Instead of having to invent his symbols he found them ready for use, and was able to advance into many new realms with their aid.

By using this material Horace was able to stress the mystery which he found in some of his subjects. Sometimes it has become more mysterious with the years, and we are uncertain to what

Horace refers. But this does not spoil the effect. On the contrary it gives to a single occasion a universal character and raises it from history to poetry. For instance Horace writes an impressive poem on the rape of Helen by Paris and tells of the fearful results which will come from it.[1] His words have an oracular and prophetic dignity, and we can hardly doubt that they were written for some important political crisis, perhaps in the years when it was clear that Antony had finally broken with Octavian and would come to a tragic end. The actual occasion is transcended in the old myth, which is symbolical of all undertakings doomed to disaster because their leaders have in the frenzy of pride violated the laws and consciences of civilized men. The Greek story and its characters are so familiar that the poem lives in its own right and can be brought into connection with any situation which has the same elements of effrontery and defeat. The poetry gains by this release from its original subject and passes beyond the limitations of historical time.

This art of symbolical suggestion can be used for different purposes, and sometimes Horace turns it to quite personal ends. His ode to Pyrrha[2] is, on the face of it, addressed to a beautiful girl whose new lover does not know her wayward character, as Horace does from experience. Horace, after a wonderful opening which calls up her air of artless simplicity, builds his poem on a notable image. Pyrrha is as alluring and as inconstant as the sea. Her lover will weep for her changes of mood and faith, and wonder at the black winds which sweep across her, though now, in his ignorance of the treacherous wind, he thinks that she will always be calm and lovable. The poem closes with Horace's own experience of Pyrrha. He has put votive-offerings in the sea-god's temple in gratitude for his escape. The whole is conceived with a charming imagination, and it gains in strength because Venus is herself a sea-goddess and resembles the element of her birth in her alternations between magical, golden calm and sudden, cruel storms. The Greek idea is made to live again through this symbolical use of it. Horace's Venus is not the Greek Aphrodite, but she is none the less real, and her ways are those of the sea. By such means Horace enriches his poem with hints and echoes and shows how many possibilities lie half-hidden in such a situation.

[1] I, 15. [2] I, 5.

The experience which Horace presents through this accomplished, civilized art is that of a man aware of many sides of life. In him many contradictory elements met, and he was too sincere to try to resolve them into a single, consistent system. He was by birth and tastes a countryman but he spent much of his time in Rome; he was of humble origin but circumstances made him a friend of Augustus and of Rome's new rulers; he fought in Brutus' army at Philippi but later became a pillar of the new system. These contradictions in his circumstances were matched by other contradictions in himself. He was now a Stoic, now an Epicurean; he both detested war, making fun of his own experience of it, and praised in noble words the martial achievements of Rome; he liked hospitality and pleasure but claimed that a simple life was the best; he was at once lax in his views about love and a supporter of Augustus' plans to improve sexual morality. Horace was fundamentally an ordinary man with an ordinary man's waywardness and instability on many important issues. But if he was not consistent, he was scrupulously honest. He believed what he said when he said it, and his poetry reflects not an imaginary self but his real self in all its discords. He understood the different moods of the human spirit so well that he could give to each its own appropriate poetry which rings true in every word. His range is in consequence much wider than that of Catullus. He used the lyric to cover most aspects of the life which he knew and to show what significant or exciting or exalting elements he found in it. Despite his air of a man of the world, his response to any emotional or imaginative challenge was strong and sincere. He absorbed experience not merely with sensitive receptivity but with a response so keen and powerful that it deserves the name of passion.

Horace covered so wide a range that at times he could not help touching on light and even trivial themes. But what matters in poetry is not the nature of a theme considered abstractly but what the poet finds in it, and it is astonishing how much Horace found in some situations which might seem in themselves of little importance. His poems on drinking are much more than tributes to the delights of wine; they belong to his poetry of friendship and are nearly always concerned with the release of the affections which comes with wine. So too, though not all his poems about love are inspired by the flame of pure passion, and some have even a perfunctory air as if Horace claimed to be in love because it was expected of him, they have compensating virtues of charm and gaiety, like the delightful lines to Chloe in which he complains that she flees like a frightened fawn, and protests that he is no tiger in pursuit of her,[1] or the poem to Lydia in which he proclaims his jealousy of her attentions to Telephus and then closes on a more serious note with his vision of what a constant affection ought to be,[2] or his poem to a 'daughter more beautiful than a beautiful mother'[3] in which he playfully points out the error of quarrelling, apologizes for his own harsh words, and asks her to be his friend again. Each situation is real and convincing and has those flashes which turn it into poetry.

The serious and responsible side of Horace's character found its special field of work in Roman political subjects. These poems are usually longer than most of his work, and the presence of six such at the beginning of Book III indicates the emphasis which Horace wished to give to them. In them he exploits his gift for noble aphorism. He is able to present in a few telling words thoughts which lay very deep in the Roman soul. With fine enthusiasm he praised the traditional Roman qualities of simplicity and sacrifice, devotion to duty and love of home. He crystallizes his conclusions into short, pregnant sentences, as when he praises the virtues of Roman breeding:

> fortes creantur fortibus et bonis,[4]

or the honour of dying for one's country:

> dulce et decorum est pro patria mori,[5]

or the prosperity brought to the country by Augustus' rule:

> nutrit rura Ceres almaque Faustitas.[6]

In these short, almost epigrammatic statements experience is refined and reduced to its essential elements, and the monumental words reflect the Roman temper. The poetry is all the stronger because it is constrained in so narrow a form.

There is real emotion in these Roman poems, even if it is wrapped in dignity and majesty. Horace has so fine a sense of occasion that he knows when to reveal his feelings and when to keep them in reserve.

[1] I, 23. [2] I, 13. [3] I, 16.
[4] IV, 4, 29. 'From the strong and noble strong sons are born.'
[5] III, 2, 13, 'It is sweet and fitting to die for fatherland.'
[6] IV, 5, 17. 'Ceres and kindly Plenty nurse the fields.'

There are some topics about which he is not in the least shy, and his treatment of them throws a significant light on the workings of his genius. Some things so disturbed him that he could not but write with something akin to violence about them. If his sense of fitness was wounded, he felt a need to inflict wounds in return on the offender. This accounts for some poems, misjudged by modern taste, in which he attacks elderly women who foolishly labour to look young. Here was something which outraged his deepest feelings, and he replied with what is for him an unusual sharpness, though it is none the less powerful poetry. At one time he mocks Lydia because she lacks the gallants who once used to throng round her and throw stones at her window.[1] At another time he addresses Lyce in words whose fierce exultation betrays some deeper emotion. He begins by rejoicing over her advancing years. It is, it seems, the answer to some prayer of his:

> Audivere, Lyce di mea vota, di
> audivere, Lyce; fis anus, et tamen
> vis formosa videri
> ludisque et bibis impudens.[2]

But he is too honest to keep the whole poem on this note. It is soon clear that his mockery of Lyce rises from the fact that he was once in love with her, and the memory of this prompts him to speak with an uncommon power:

> quo fugit Venus, heu, quove color? decens
> quo motus? quid habes illius, illius,
> quae spirabat amores,
> quae me surpuerat mihi?[3]

What begins with an attack becomes almost a lament, and human feelings of regret and pathos give a new depth.

In these poems we may perhaps detect in Horace a real dislike of finding himself in love. He seems to have felt that it destroyed his

[1] I, 15.

[2] IV, 13, 1–4. 'The gods have heard my prayer, Lyce, the gods have heard, Lyce. You are growing old, and yet you wish to look beautiful, and you play and drink without shame.'

[3] IV, 13, 17–20. 'Where has fled the charm, alas, or where the colour? the comely movement? What have you of her, of her, who breathed love and stole me from myself.'

calm and order and made him the victim of uncontrollable powers. When he felt the approaches of passion, his first reaction seems to have been scepticism and distrust; then his honesty would compel him to admit the truth and he would break into words of deep emotion. Such at least is the impression made by one of his poems to Ligurinus. He starts by saying that he is too old for the onslaughts of Venus, and he tries to laugh her off by telling her to visit one of his friends. Then he takes one of his sudden turns, speaks with absolute candour, and ends his poem with words of astonishing beauty and power:

> sed cur heu, Ligurine, cur
> manat rara meas lacrima per genas?
> cur facunda parum decoro
> inter verba cadit lingua silentio?
>
> nocturnis ego somniis
> iam captum teneo, iam volucrem sequor
> te per gramina Martii
> campi, te per aquas, dure volubiles.[1]

A little later in the same book Horace addresses another poem to Ligurinus and again protests against his cruelty, but by an extraordinary paradox of poetry Horace seems almost to say one thing and mean another. He warns Ligurinus that he will soon lose his beauty and bitterly regret that he has not made full use of his opportunities while he can. But this warning is not cruel or triumphant; it breathes a deep compassion, almost a tragic sense of the brevity of youth and its opportunities. It passes beyond its immediate purpose into the poetry of pathetic lament for lost chances. In it each word falls into the enchanting rhythm and beats with compassion and regret:

> O crudelis adhuc et Veneris muneribus potens,
> insperata tuae cum veniet bruma superbiae,
> et, quae nunc umeris involitant, deciderint comae,
> nunc et qui color est puniceae flore prior rosae,

[1] IV, 1, 33–40. 'But why, Ligurinus, oh why does a tear flow now and then on my cheeks? why does my eloquent tongue fail with unbecoming silence in the middle of my words? In the dream of night I now hold thee captive, now pursue thee as thou fliest over the grassy Field of Mars, now over the rolling waves, O hard hearted!'

mutatus Ligurinum in faciem verterit hispidam,
dices 'heu' quotiens te speculo vederis alterum,
'quae mens est hodie, cur eadem non puero fuit,
vel cur his animis incolumes non redeunt genae?'[1]

Such a situation broke down Horace's defences and made him speak with an unusual force and simplicity.

The theme of death is closely allied to the themes of love and perishing beauty and affected Horace with no less power. It too broke into his ordered scheme of life and left him anxious and uncertain. The reality of death seems to have been brought home to him by the falling bough of an elm-tree which nearly killed him, and though this may not account for everything, there is no doubt about the strength of Horace's feelings. With a remarkably visual imagination he asks what death really means. He looks all round the subject and marks now this aspect of it, now that. He remembers the old Greek myths of Styx and Tartarus, of sinners condemned to eternal punishment, of Cerberus and the Furies. He covers the whole range of thoughts which men have formed about death in the hope of understanding it and knows that it comes alike to rich and poor, that it forbids us to indulge high hopes, that it comes whether we call for it or not, that it means not only the loss of earth and home and wife but even of the trees which we have loved, that not even Orpheus' song can give life to the unsubstantial ghost. Nor is it merely the future which is dark and menacing. The constant menace of death destroys the reality of life and makes nonsense of our fears no less than of our desires, of our escapes no less than of our disasters:

frustra cruento Marte carebimus
fractisque rauci fluctibus Hadriae,
frustra per autumnos nocentem
corporibus metuemus Austrum.[2]

[1]IV, 10. 'O cruel still and lordly with Venus's gifts, when the unexpected winter comes to your pride, and the hair which now floats on your shoulders has fallen, and the bloom that now surpasses the crimson rose has changed and turned into a rough face, then, so often as you look in the mirror at your other self, you will say "Alas! why in boyhood had I not the same purpose as today? Or why to my present spirit do my cheeks not return unspoiled?" '

[2]II, 14, 13–16. 'In vain shall we escape from bloody Mars and the broken waves of the loud Adriatic; in vain shall we fear the South wind that brings our bodies harm.'

Death undermines our confidence in life by showing that in the end everything is equally futile before the final darkness.

Yet though this anxiety is never far from Horace's mind and though it inspired some of his finest verses, it is in most of them no more than a background, if it is even so much as that. Against his doubts and fears he set his positive vision of life, of the joys to be snatched from the fleeting hour, of the friendships and devotions which bring contentment and confidence. He did not ask for too much, and his Epicureanism is always wise and moderate. He knows that quiet pleasures are more satisfying than violent sensations and his special gift is to find poetry in many unrenowned activities. It is perhaps true that a gentle, resigned melancholy released his creative powers in a special degree and that his most characteristic utterance is in such a poem as *Diffugere nives* where the coming of spring turns his thoughts to the cycle of the seasons and the brevity of life. Yet in this there is no real note of complaint; it is true and courageous and has no quarrel with the universe. Horace seems to say that this is what life is and that it is foolish to wish it to be otherwise. This sanity informs Horace's poetry and gives it a peculiar strength. The miracle is that sanity has passed into poetry so fine and so sustained that the four books of the Odes, with their hundred and three short poems, cover a wider range of experience and present it in a more satisfying form than almost any other comparable book written by man.

GERALD BRENAN

A SHORT LIFE OF ST. JOHN OF THE CROSS

St. John of the Cross owes his fame to being one of the greatest and most uncompromising of the Catholic mystics. It is less known that he is also one of the supreme lyric poets of any country or age. It is his poetry that we propose to discuss here. But no poet's work can be properly understood without some reference to his life. This is especially true of St. John of the Cross, whose best poems, though in rather a peculiar sense, are autobiographical. For this reason some preliminary account of it seems necessary.

As it happens, it was a very extraordinary life. Merely as a story it is full of dramatic interest. It takes one into a strange world of ascetics and religious revolutionaries, which turns out to have much the same passions and rages as the world outside. We are shown faked elections and unjust purges and prisons and escapes from prison—all the paraphernalia of the modern Spanish scene—whilst within the microcosm of a convent struggle we get a very real and convincing political issue. How many people, I wonder, know that St. John of the Cross owed his final disgrace to having made himself the champion of the vote by ballot? This makes me think that even those who do not care about Spanish poetry may find something to interest them in his story and be surprised to see how—and from what a strange angle—it throws light upon the situation of the world today.

Juan de Yepes—that was the poet's family name—was born in 1542 at Fontiveros, a village that lies on the borders of Old Castile between Avila and Salamanca. His father was a man of good family who had married below his rank and sunk to the humble position of weaver. A few years after Juan's birth he died, leaving his widow and three sons in great poverty.

Fontiveros is a village of brown sun-dried brick, standing on a wide plain sown with corn. It has no stream to water it, and few trees. In the distance stands a long wall of mountains, covered during the greater part of the year with snow. Here Juan spent his boyhood. To earn a little money he worked for a carpenter, a tailor and a painter, whilst his mother sat at her loom. But trade was bad, the rising cost of living due to the import of Peruvian silver was ruining the wool industry, and when Juan was thirteen or fourteen his mother moved to the neighbouring town of Medina del Campo.

Medina was not then the dusty, decayed place it is today. Its new brick palaces, faced with armorial bearings, its churches and convents and hospitals, and above all its great square, marked the site of one of the largest fairs in Europe. Here, during three months in each year, the streets were thronged with merchants from every part of the world, who came to exchange the goods of Flanders and Germany for those of Spain, and the Indies. Nowhere else in the country, except at Seville, could be seen such movement and animation. And Juan had every opportunity for observing it. Whilst his mother worked at her loom, he was taken on at a hospital that treated syphilitic patients, where his particular job seems to have been to beg for alms in the streets. However, this did not take up all his time. Being a promising boy, he was before long allowed time off to attend first an elementary school and then the grammar school that had just been founded by the Jesuits. Here he remained till he was twenty-one. Since his master, though only four years older than himself, was an enthusiastic Latinist, we may assume that he obtained a fair acquaintance with Ovid, Virgil and Horace.

The profession of priest was the obvious career for this young man of poor family to adopt, and the patron of the hospital, where he had now ceased to work, offered him a chaplaincy if he followed it. But Juan refused. His heart was already set on leaving the world, and he took vows as a Carmelite friar with the name of Juan de San Matías.

His education, however, was not yet complete if he wished for ordination. In the following year, therefore (1564), he went to the University of Salamanca where he remained till 1568, going through the usual triennial course of arts, but giving only a year to theology. Salamanca at this time was a city of churches, colleges, convents and lodging-houses. In spite of its imposing buildings, it was a decaying place, without industry or agriculture: the fine clay loam of its fields had gone out of cultivation and the foreign visitor was struck by a depressing air of poverty and wretchedness, which was not redeemed by the sight of a few richly dressed students.

We know little of Juan's life during his stay here. Did he attend the lectures of the great humanist and poet, Fray Luis de Leon, who a little later was to spend four years in the dungeons of the Inquisition? And what were his theological studies? The teaching of philosophy in Salamanca at this time followed neo-scholastic lines—St. Thomas, with a certain leaning to St. Augustine. As M. Baruzi has pointed out, this would have suited the young friar well. He had not a speculative mind: all he required of theology was a conventional idiom which could be used to frame his experience. Mysticism, on the other hand, was highly suspect. The whole spirit of the university was against it and it was largely through the influence of its professors that a number of Spanish and Flemish mystical works—including such eminent names as Luis de Granada—had been placed on the index. But the teaching of the great Salamancan humanist, Francisco de Vitoria, still had a certain weight, and he had attached the utmost importance to the study of the Bible and of the Early Fathers. This teaching bore fruit, for the Bible was to be Fray Juan's constant companion throughout his life. No Protestant divine ever quoted Scripture more often.

The turning point of the young man's career came in September 1567. Teresa de Jesus, now a woman of past fifty, had arrived at Medina to found a convent of the Reformed Carmelites—that is, of nuns who wished to return to the primitive rule. She wanted also to found a convent or priory (either word can be used) for men and, as luck would have it, discovered that the prior of the Mitigated Carmelite house at Medina was ready to help her. This good man, Antonio de Heredia, was approaching sixty, fond of his dignity and accustomed to certain comforts, so that she had doubts as to his suitability. But he promised to persuade a young, very religious friar of his to join him. This was Juan de San Matías, then on vacation. Dissatisfied with the laxity of his order and with his head full of the feats of the primitive Fathers of the Desert—the adventure literature of young monks—he had been considering joining the Carthusians. But, after listening to Teresa, he agreed to do as she wished, 'provided'—here one sees the young man's impatience—'he did not have to wait long'.

The Reformed Carmelite Movement, of which Teresa de Jesus was the foundress, was a movement whose main—indeed sole—object was prayer and contemplation. Teresa had founded it to teach others to follow the same road towards mystical union on which she had made such progress herself. The friars were to have certain duties of preaching, but the chief part of their life was to be spent in chapel and at solitary devotions. Prolonged fasting, reduced hours of sleep, weekly penances, were required by their rule, but practices of extreme asceticism were not permitted. Instead, there was a certain technique of *recogimiento* or recollection. However, the aim was not simply, as it had been in earlier days, to save their own souls. Prayer was also a weapon. Teresa was deeply conscious of the civil wars and heresies that were tearing Europe to pieces, and hoped by this act of contrition to mitigate them.

Perhaps we shall see these Carmelites best in their historical perspective if we regard them as a new sort of Conquistadors. The age of geographic explorations and adventures had been followed by an age of mental and spiritual ones, represented in France by Montaigne and later by Descartes. Yet it was not a merely intellectual enterprise that these monks and nuns were engaged on: they believed, and in this the authority of the Church supported them, that, if grace were given them, they could carry the whole mind, with its affections as well as its understanding, to union with the source of that mind, which is God. Since love was the motive, Eros the engine in their hull, their course took the form of, and is therefore expressed in, the language of a love affair.[1] It was the extreme of sublimation—the final point, if one likes, of that historic movement of love for the absent, *amor de lonh*, which had inspired the Provençal poets and through them Dante and Petrarch. This was the venture, the *dichosa ventura*, to which Fray Juan de San Matías was now committed. He took vows in November 1568, changing his name to Juan de la Cruz.

There is a charm about the small beginnings of heroic enterprises. The foundation of the first Reformed Carmelite priory recalls in its great hopes and tiny resources the first hermitage by the ruined chapel of the Portiuncula of St. Francis of Assisi. The place chosen was a hamlet, a few miles from Fontiveros, Juan's birthplace, called Duruelo. Today Duruelo is a farmhouse in a shallow valley. A little stream runs between grass fields and thistles: a few willows line it; there are a few evergreen oaks. Beyond the rim of the valley lies the snow-covered Sierra de Gredos, some thirty miles off. Here among tumbled-down buildings and barns—for with the ruin of Castilian agriculture the place was then half depopulated—the four friars founded their first house.

Teresa, who had chosen the site herself, visited Duruelo again that winter. In her *Book of Foundations* she has left us an enthusiastic account of her impressions. Fray Antonio, clad in his white serge cape and brown habit, with a look of gaiety on his face, was sweeping the porch when she came up. 'How is this, Father?' she said to him. 'What has happened to your dignity?' And he replied, smiling, 'I curse the day I ever had any'.

The entrance hall had been converted into the chapel. It was full of crosses and skulls. The attic above formed the choir. At one end

[1] *Aunque es verdad que la gloria consiste en el entendimiento, el fin del alma es amar*. Note in San Juan's handwriting on the margin of the Cántico Espiritual, stanza XXXVIII, *Allí me mostrarías* . . .

of it, close under the eaves, were two little cells or hermitages, giving a view of the altar and so low that one could enter them only on one's hands and knees. Here, with stones for pillows, their feet wrapped in hay, among more crosses and skulls, the friars remained praying from midnight to daybreak whilst the snow drifted on to their clothes through the tiles. They ate from broken crockery and drank from gourds; their only other possessions were a few books, some scourges and bells, and five sand clocks, which the meticulous Fray Antonio had insisted on bringing. Delighted by their enthusiasm, Teresa told them that all the same they must moderate their penances. For example, they must not go about bare-foot.

The foundation of a convent belonging to one of the stricter orders set up an excitement in the sixteenth century that we find it hard to understand today. Four or five nuns, whose faces no one would ever see and whose voices few would hear, had only to barricade themselves in a ruined house for the whole town to be in commotion. For the men of that age believed that spiritual things were not only more important that material ones, but that in a direct and immediate way they controlled them. A convent or monastery, therefore, whose inmates spent their lives in fasting and prayer, was looked on as a sort of power house that radiated benefits upon the whole neighbourhood. Quarrels and dissensions would decrease, the interest on loans would fall, alms-giving would be more abundant, above all, purgatory would be shortened. Thus it was that the little community of Duruelo, as soon as the rumour of its austerities got round, caused a stir in the whole district. Many people came to visit it, including Fray Juan's mother, brother and sister-in-law, who, after the fashion of Spanish families, camped down in the shadow of their successful son. An anecdote tells us how much he disliked these interruptions and how, when out preaching, he would refuse the meal offered by the parish priest and retire to the edge of a field, by the bank of a stream, to eat his bread and cheese alone. But the community prospered, so that eighteen months later it was necessary to move to a larger and a more convenient building in the neighbouring village of Mancera. Duruelo was retained as a retreat or *desierto*.

The Reformed Carmelites grew rapidly during the next few years. More priories were founded. We hear of Juan de la Cruz acting as master of novices at Pastrana, close to Alcalá de Henares, which not long before had been a great centre of *iluminados*, and then teaching at a Carmelite college at Alcalá itself. Here, no doubt, he continued his theological studies. But it is clear that he was something of a disappointment to Teresa owing to his retiring disposition and to his dislike of responsibility. He shrank from the office of prior and from any organizational work, so that the task of drawing up the Constitution was given to Fray Gerónimo Gracián, a man three years younger than he was, but handsome, well born, gifted, and full of charm and eloquence. This Gracián was a great pleaser of women: he made a deep impression on the elderly foundress and soon became her right-hand man and confidant.

The success of Teresa's reform had raised against her many enemies, the most bitter of whom belonged, of course, to the unreformed body of her own order. But there were doubts and suspicions in some of the higher circles of the Church as well. The Conservatives—and Spain was every day becoming a more Conservative country—looked askance at this 'gadabout nun', who travelled all over the country founding convents for contemplatives and having ecstasies and visions. Only the charm of her personality and her skill in using it to win over her enemies prevented her movement from being suppressed. But there were some who, though they admired her reforming zeal, thought it should be turned from the new channels it had taken and given the task of disciplining the unreformed Carmelites whom she had left. She was to be made, not to form a small élite of spiritual Stakhanovites, but to raise the general level of the conventual proletariat. The Apostolic Visitor, who represented the authority of the Nuncio and the King, was one of the people who thought like this, and in 1571 he nominated her prioress for three years of the large unreformed convent of the Encarnación at Avila. So Teresa returned to the rambling building where she had spent more than twenty years of her life and where the majority of the nuns, lax and worldly in their ways, were hostile to her. To assist her in her task she appointed Fray Juan as confessor and spiritual director to the convent (May 1572).

Let us pause for a moment to see if we can form any impression of Juan de la Cruz's character at this time. I think we can best do this if we try to see him through Teresa's eyes. From her first meeting with him she had been a little ironical about this shy, reserved young man—a little Seneca, she called him—who was only five feet two inches tall and half her age. When she mentioned him in her letters it was to say that he was perfect—but she did not mention him often. The fact is that the men who attracted her were men who had lived in the world and had a talent for dealing with it. Provided they were religious, she did not mind if they had failings, but they had to be cheerful and conversable and to have a certain capacity for practical affairs. Now Fray Juan's whole nature was so strongly inclined to contemplation that till he was past forty he was of little use for anything else. 'We friars do not travel in order to see, but in order not to see,' he once said to a monk, who had asked him to admire certain buildings. In other words, he was the perfect Carmelite—the type Teresa was trying to produce, for whom these innumerable new foundations were made—but her nature was curiously divided between action and contemplation, and it was on the active side that she now needed collaborators.

We detect, therefore, a certain tension between Madre Teresa and her young neophyte during the early years of their acquaintance. 'May the Lord', she wrote on one occasion, 'deliver us from people so spiritual that they will admit nothing that falls short of perfect contemplation'! In another letter she speaks of having 'at various times been annoyed with him'. And we may suspect, from anecdotes that have come down to us, a certain resistance on his part to her blandishments. For example, we hear of his mortifying her by giving her an unusually small host at communion when she had just said that she liked large ones. Then there is that story of his setting out from Baeza with a bag of Teresa's letters on his shoulder and scattering them on the way because, as he remarked, 'a friar should not be encumbered with unnecessary possessions'. This was no doubt a very proper sentiment for a Carmelite, yet to anyone else in Teresa's entourage it would have seemed a sacrilege. However, we do find that, from the time of his establishment at Avila, her views towards him changed. She praised warmly the delicacy of his spiritual direction, his perfect understanding of the finer shades of prayer: in other words, the subtlety of his psychological intuitions. And as the troubles in the order mounted, she came to admire his courage and fixity of purpose. Towards the end of her life we find her twice begging Gracián—in vain, for he was jealous—to send Fray Juan back to her in Castile.

Juan de la Cruz spent five years as confessor to the nuns of the Encarnación. We may safely suppose that this period was especially important for his development. Teresa was writing the *Interior Castle* at this time, and they must have had many discussions upon their spiritual experiences. Did she give him to read the mystical works that had most influenced her—Osuna, Laredo, and Luis de Granada? It is possible that he had not read the first two, for his masters were the earlier classics—St. Bernard, St. Thomas, St. Augustine and the pseudo-Dionysius. We can also see signs of his influencing her, for she wrote down her thoughts upon the *Song of Songs*. But did Fray Juan himself write anything? We do not know, for on the night of 3 December 1577, a gang of men broke into the little house at the end of the convent garden, where he was living with another friar, and carried the two of them away prisoner. He had time to swallow some of his papers and to destroy others; the rest were seized by the people who arrested him.

The cause of this violent action lay first of all in the hatred of the unreformed or Mitigated Carmelites for the reformers. But why had they picked on the retiring and inoffensive Fray Juan? This is to be explained by an election that had just taken place in the Convent of the Encarnación. Teresa's term as prioress was over, her successor had come and gone and now a third election had to be made. There were two parties among the nuns—the reforming party, who wanted Teresa back again, and the conservatives, who wanted someone else. The Provincial of the Order himself came down to superintend the affair and, as feeling ran high and he supported the conservative candidate, he began by threatening to excommunicate any nun who should vote for Teresa. But fifty-five, supported by Fray Juan's exhortations, declared in spite of this their intention to vote for her. The scene that followed has been described by Teresa in one of the most brilliant of her letters. The Provincial took his stand by the grille, excommunicating and cursing those nuns who voted contrary to his wishes and crumpling, striking and burning their voting papers. However, even this did not produce the result that he wanted. He therefore gave orders that none of the recalcitrant nuns should attend mass or see their confessors until they had voted as he desired. When they again refused, he declared the election null and void and appointed the nun who had obtained the lesser number of votes to be prioress.

This typical Spanish election had a typical sequel. The secret fomenter of the dissident nuns, Fray Juan de la Cruz, was beaten up and carried off to prison. Yet had this been no more than a quarrel between nuns, the Carmelite Provincial would never have dared to take such an extreme step. The real causes lay deeper. The Carmelite General, Rossi, wished to restrict the Teresan reform to its present limits and had therefore forbidden them under threat of dire penalties to found any houses in Andalusia. This naturally did not please the reformers, who wished to expand, and so they had evaded the General's orders by appealing to another authority, the Apostolic Vicar, who nominally represented the Pope but in fact the centralizing policy of the King. Empowered by him, Gracián had not only spread the Reform to Andalusia, but had interfered in a very imprudent way with the Mitigated houses. These houses had protested and the General and his representatives were furious with what they regarded as the rank disobedience of the reformers.

But Juan de la Cruz had not been concerned in any of these proceedings. His actions, though irritating to the Provincial, had not in any way been censurable. Why then had the blow fallen on him? The most plausible explanation seems to be that behind the scenes there were more powerful forces at work. The Inquisition was at this time conducting an inquiry into the methods of prayer of the Reformed Carmelites, which, in the words of the great conservative theologian, Melchor Cano, 'savoured of the heresy of the Iluminados'. They had in their hands at that moment a copy of Teresa's Autobiography. Her confessor, Fray Juan de la Cruz, had already several times been denounced to them. The person who had ordered his arrest, the Carmelite Vicar General, was one of their Consultors. It seems probable therefore that one of the motives behind his imprisonment was the hope of getting further materials upon the case. Formal proceedings against the Reformed Carmelites were not a thing to be decided on lightly, for Teresa had powerful friends, some of them among the Inquisitors themselves. The arrest and prosecution of the Primate of Spain a few years previously had had unfortunate repercussions.

But where had Fray Juan been taken? The day after his arrest Teresa wrote to Philip II, saying with her customary outspokenness that she preferred to see him in the hands of the Moors than in those of the Mitigated Carmelites—'they at least would have more pity'. But the months passed and nothing was heard of him. In August Teresa was writing: 'I don't know how it is that no one remembers that Saint'. If he was in the hands of the Inquisition, few people would have wished to remember him.

Actually he was in the Carmelite Priory at Toledo. His prison was a sort of cupboard, used at times as a jakes and so dark that one could not see to read in it. Every day he was taken down to the refectory where he had to eat his crusts and water on the floor, after which he was given the worst punishment known to monks—the circular discipline. Whilst he knelt on the ground the friars walked in a circle round him, scourging him on the bare back with leather whips. Later these disciplines were given him only on Fridays, but they were so severe that they damaged his shoulders permanently and he bore the marks of them to the end of his life.

There were other torments too. For eight months he was given no change of clothing and he suffered cruelly from lice. The cold of winter and the heat of summer equally troubled him. He had dysentery and, like Abelard, believed that the monks were trying to poison him. But a new jailer who came in May took pity on him and allowed him to walk about in a neighbouring room whilst the monks were taking their after-lunch siesta. In this way he was able to keep his strength up.

One evening, we are told, he heard a voice singing a *villancico* or love song in the street outside. The words were these:

Muérome de amores,
Carillo, qué haré?
—Que te mueras, alahé!

'I am dying of love. Dearest, what shall I do? —Die.' And at once he was carried away by an ecstasy. The words, or the idea, of a poem came into his head. As we shall see later, his two most important poems, the *Cántico Espiritual* and the *Noche Oscura*, were both begun in prison, whilst another of his more disturbing ones, *Aunque es de noche*, was completed there. He was able to write them down with a pen and paper which the jailer gave him.

Then one August night a new resolution came to him—to escape. It happened in this way. On the eve of the Assumption of the Virgin the Prior of the Convent entered his cell, and after kicking him brutally and rating him for his disobedience, promised to release him if he would abandon the Reform and return to the mitigated rule. Juan replied that he could not break his vows, but asked if he might be allowed to say mass on the following day, as it was the feast of the Virgin. The Prior angrily refused and went out. But that night Our Lady appeared to Juan in a dream. Filling his cell with light, she commanded him to escape, promising her assistance. This dream drew out an early memory. Once as a little boy at Fontiveros he had fallen into a pond. As he struggled in the mud and water he had seen a well-dressed lady on the bank whom he had taken to be the Virgin. He had stretched out his arms to her, but with closed fists because his hands were too dirty to take hers. Then someone else had pulled him out. He now felt assured that, in spite of his weakness, with her help he would be able to escape from prison.

He set about the business methodically. Thanks to his jailer's laxity he was able to reconnoitre the convent whilst the monks were at dinner. It was a large, new, three-storied building, rising immediately above the gorge of the Tagus on the eastern fringe of the city.[1] At the far end of it he found a window looking out on the river which he thought would serve his purpose. But it would be necessary to find a way of opening the door of his cell and of the room adjoining it, which were fastened by padlocks. He set to work to loosen the staples.

The night he had chosen for his attempt—16 August 1578—came round. As it happened, two friars from another convent were lodged that evening in the room next to his. Since it was very hot, they left the door into the corridor open and laid their mattresses across it to get what freshness they could. Then, as they still could not sleep, they lay awake talking so that two had struck before Juan dared to open the door of his cell. The noise of the staple coming out woke them, but they dropped off again. Stepping across their bodies, he reached the corridor and the window.

It was really a little balcony or *miradorcillo*, supported by a joist that rested on the brick wall. Juan had with him the jailer's iron *candil* or oil lamp, to which he had tied a rope made of strips from his blanket and tunic. He hooked this to the joist and lowered himself. Then he dropped and landed unhurt on the top of the city wall, among loose blocks of masonry. It was very dark and he could hear the noise of the river running in its deep trough below.

[1] It was destroyed in the Peninsular War, but the heaps of rubble where it stood can still be seen. In El Greco's Plan of Toledo it is the large building that rises immediately to the right of the bridge.

A dog was nosing among the offal thrown out of the refectory window. To see how it would go, Juan threatened it and it leaped down into a little *corral* or court. He followed and found himself in an enclosure bounded on two sides by the walls of the Carmelite Priory and of a Franciscan convent for nuns, and on the other, facing the river, by the city fortifications. The dog had vanished over another wall or fence, but when Juan tried to follow, he found it too high for him to climb in his feeble state. Calling on the Virgin and going up to it, he found himself all at once, he did not know how, in the street on the other side.

He was now free in a city he did not know at an hour when the life of all cities is mysterious and strange. The lane he was in led him to the Plaza de Zocodover, where he saw the lights of the stalls and the market women busy arranging their wares: as he passed they shouted out ugly words at him. Then he met a woman leaving her house to go to her stall and asked her the way to the Reformed Carmelite Convent. She told him, but since it would be shut till daybreak, offered to let him remain in her house until then. He refused. Then he came to the door of a gentleman's mansion which stood open. The gentleman, with a naked sword in his hand, was searching his *zaguán* or entrance hall, whilst a servant held a torch to light him. Juan asked his permission to sit in his hall till daylight. The gentleman consented, the door was shut and bolted and the household went to bed.

At daybreak the door was again opened and Juan went out. He had no cape and his tunic was torn and dirty, so that the passers-by jeered at him. But as he hurried along, in all the churches and convents of the city the angelus was ringing. On reaching the Carmelite house he found the nuns at matins. A nun, Leonor de Jesus, came to the grille. '*Hija*', he said, '*Fray Juan de la Cruz soy, que me he salido esta noche de la prisión. Dígaselo a la Madre Priora.*' The prioress, Ana de los Angeles, was called and let him into the convent. A sick nun who needed confession was the excuse for this grave breach of the rules.

The sisters, heavily veiled over their long white robes, collected round. Some light refreshment—pears stewed with cinnamon—was set out, and, as he ate, he told his exciting story. They looked at him with pity. So worn and disfigured was he that—as one of them later said—he looked like an image of death. But meanwhile his escape had been discovered and the Carmelites of the Observance were looking for him. Two friars arrived with *alguaziles* or police officers and searched the outer premises, but did not dare to violate the enclosure. When they had gone, the gates were locked and Juan went into the church. Here he dictated some verses he had composed in prison, but had been unable to write down. Then, in the evening, when the spies of the Observants had gone, a canon of the Cathedral who belonged to the great family of the Mendozas, sent his coach for him and took him away to his own rooms and to safety.

The Carmelite Reform was passing through a moment of great danger. In October a chapter met at Almodóvar, where Teresa and Fray Juan saw one another again. A few days later the Papal Nuncio, Sega, issued a decree placing them under the orders of the Unreformed Carmelites. He censured Teresa and degraded the three leading friars of the Reform. Juan de la Cruz was sent to the hermitage or 'desert' house of El Calvario in Andalusia, on the upper waters of the Guadalquivír. Although he was appointed prior, it was a thinly veiled order of banishment.

One reaches El Calvario today by a road that branches off the main Jaen–Albacete highway and drops into the river gorge on its way to an electric power station. The deep green water flows between red rocks, tamarisks and oleander lean over it, while on the opposite bank the mountain rises up, spur above spur, like a crumpled greyish curtain. To reach the hermitage one must take a path up the hill to the left. The path zigzags through broom and lavender and cistus, among which, if it is spring, one will find small irises, jonquils and bee orchids. Then one comes to a piece of flatter ground. There is a barking of dogs, the bushes give way, and one sees before one a a couple of whitewashed buildings, a walnut tree shading a courtyard and some ancient olives. This is El Calvario.

The six months that Juan de la Cruz spent here were among the happiest of his life. He was thirty-seven. He had emerged from the darkness of prison—'that whale' as he called it—into the beauty of an Andalusian spring and to the sort of wild landscape—*montes, valles, riberas*—that he preferred. Here he completed the poems that he had begun and laid the foundations of his prose works; when he left El Calvario, his poetical career was practically finished. But his happiness was not due only to solitude and to scenery. There were some thirty friars in the little farmhouse on the hillside, and some of them were old hermits from the Sierra Morena who had joined the

Reformed Carmelites a few years previously. (The Carmelite Order had a tradition of descent from anchorites in Palestine which made it easier for them to assimilate these people.) Among them we read of Brother Hilarion, an old man of seventy with flowing white beard and hair, who recalled the Fathers of the Desert; or Brother Alonso, the cook, who picked for salad any herb that his mule stopped to eat. The simplicity of these men must have delighted Juan, whose lighter reading since boyhood had been the legends of the primitive monks and hermits. And there were the younger friars too whom he instructed in methods of prayer, sitting out at sunset or by starlight under the pine trees.

But it was not only men whom he taught. A couple of leagues away over the hills lay the little town of Beas de Segura, in a valley planted with olive trees. Here there was a convent of Castilian nuns, founded a few years before by Teresa. Ana de Jesus, the most devoted of her disciples, was Prioress and she had received two letters from the Foundress recommending Fray Juan as a 'divine and celestial man', 'whose like was not to be found in the whole of Castile' and who would help them greatly on the road to perfection. 'You can't believe', she had written, 'how much I miss him!' It became, therefore, one of Juan's duties to walk over on Saturdays and on the eve of feast days to confess and instruct them, returning to his 'desert' on Mondays. Some of these nuns had made great progress in contemplation and he found more scope than he had done at Avila for his gift of spiritual direction. Strongly as he guarded himself against human attachments, which he regarded as distractions, one may see from the fragments of his letters that have come down to us what a deep and tender impression these sisters made on him. To the end of his life he continued to write to them, and even when he was living in Granada he made a point of going every year to visit them. It was from his spiritual direction at Beas that his later prose works sprang.

In June 1579 Juan de la Cruz moved to Baeza, thirty miles lower down the Guadalquivír. Baeza is a small but ancient city built on a long spur of high land; all around it are rolling hollows of chalk down, green with corn in spring and in summer red with poppies. In the distance, a vast circuit of mountains. The reason for his going there was that a group of professors from the then flourishing university wished for instruction in the new methods of prayer and had asked for a Carmelite college to be opened among them. Juan's business was to direct it. But he seems to have been unhappy there; like Teresa, he had no sympathy with the facile Andalusian temperament and looked back with regret on the peaceful days at El Calvario or at Avila. To console himself, he made frequent journeys to visit his spiritual daughters at Beas.

On his way he used to stop at a Trinitarian monastery close to the village of Iznatoraf where the monks had caught the new vogue for contemplation. I visited this place in 1933 and was told an anecdote that has never, I believe, been published. The prior said that a story had been handed down in his community that San Juan, when he stayed with them, used to disappear from sight into a little room in the belfry and to remain there for many hours on end, looking out through a window. However, as no such room existed, he had always supposed it must be a legend. Then, a year or two before my visit, some repairs had been done to the tower and they had come across it. He took me to see it. It was a tiny cavity, little more than a cupboard, a couple of yards square, but through a loophole in the wall one had a view of hills and green fields.

There are other traditions of this sort about Juan de la Cruz, which were collected in 1616 and 1627, during his process of beatification. He liked to sit and contemplate where he could see water, trees or open sky. Thus at El Calvario we hear of his sitting at all hours of the day or night under the trees, with his friars around him, teaching them how to pray in different manners—sometimes to fix their minds on God alone, but at others to call on the sky and hills, the plants and the *hermosura de las cosas* (beauty of created things) to praise Him. At Granada we learn that he liked to pace, as other poets have since done, beside the rivers Genil and Darro. But what is most striking was his predilection for sitting alone in some dark and confined place, looking out on a distant view. At Pastrana there was a cave on a hill top which can still be seen. At Segovia his cell was at first in a cupboard under the stairs. Then he found a grotto on the summit of a hill, so small that one had to crawl into it on hands and knees, but commanding a wide view of city, mountains and fields. Here, at the end of his life, he used to spend many hours by day and night in contemplation. This love of certain aspects of Nature—stars, dawn, trees, hills, water—and, above all, silence, that sonorous insect-humming silence of Southern countries, is everywhere reflected in his poetry.

The struggle in the Carmelite Order was now ended. A period of growth and prosperity had set in for the Reform and in January 1582 Juan de la Cruz became prior of the new house at Granada. Here he remained quietly till 1585. The Convento de los Mártires—all religious houses are *conventos* in Spanish—was built on a spur of the Alhambra hill, just below the present Hotel Washington Irving. The elm woods had not yet been planted and the summit of the hill was bare, but the convent windows looked out over the flat green expanse of the Vega, dotted with white farms and olive trees and bounded on the left by the Sierra Nevada. Here, with one of the most beautiful views in the world before him, he wrote his four prose works in the form of commentaries on his poems. His character seems to have matured and expanded with the responsibilities of office. We hear of him confessing the poor every week and visiting the hospitals. As prior he was an important person in the city and for the first time one gets the impression that he had attracted attention and found admirers. There were, moreover, two things that must have given him pleasure: his brother had come to work at Los Mártires as mason and gardener, and the nuns of Beas had founded a convent in the city. The society of sisters of the same order provides a tender and romantic element in the harsh barrack life of a monk, and Juan, with his natural refinement, appreciated it.

Yet one must doubt whether the nostalgia he had felt at Baeza for his native Castile had altogether left him. Granada was not an attractive city at that time. The Moorish population had been expelled a dozen years previously and a new and uprooted class, with the vices and pretensions of colonials, was moving in from the North. Sullen-looking slaves filled the streets and, whilst the newcomers quarrelled over points of honour and precedence, the fertile countryside was going to ruin. The triumph of the Cross had turned this once-prosperous city into a camp and a brothel. As a point of curiosity we may note that at the Puerta de Elvira there still lived an old Moslem *beata*, a follower of the great Sufi mystic Al Gazzali, who practised the same sort of imageless contemplation that Juan did himself.

Juan's quiet life was brought to an end towards 1585 when, without giving up his priorate, he became Vicar Provincial for Andalusia. This was a post that required frequent journeying all over the south of Spain and sometimes as far as Lisbon and Madrid.

Mounted on an ass—for his strength did not allow him to walk much—with a broad felt sombrero above his white cloak, he travelled the long roads, sleeping in the open air whenever possible, but when it was wet, in the ventas, which were noisier and more crowded than they are today. It was not a life he can have liked, but there were new troubles in his order which he must have found even more disturbing than these journeys.

The Carmelite Reform had emerged triumphant from its struggle with its unreformed brethren, for in 1580, whilst Juan was at Baeza, the Pope had set them up as a separate organization under their own Provincial. Then in 1582 Teresa had died. Her powerful figure gone, dissensions at once broke out among her successors. The Provincial, Gracián, who owed his position to the Foundress's influence (the old woman's love for him is one of the most touching things in her story), was a soft and rather vain man, fond of pleasing others and relying too much upon his powers of fascination. It was the marvellous element that had drawn him to the mystical life and now that this was wearing thin he wished to turn the order towards preaching and missions. This was the more natural since he was an eloquent preacher himself and had had some success in the pulpits of fashionable churches in Seville. But Juan de la Cruz took a different view, though, having once stated it, he withdrew into himself and refused to enter into the struggle for place and influence.

However, a new and much more formidable party was coming to the front under the leadership of Nicolas Doria. Doria was a Genoese banker who had had business dealings with Philip II until, in one of those fits of repentance so common in that age, he became a monk. Partly through the King's influence, and with the backing of all those busy-minded people who had joined the Reformed Carmelites on account of its prestige but with no understanding of its spirit, he was elected Provincial in 1585 in Gracián's place.

Doria was precisely the man whom the authorities and the new spirit of the age needed. The bright extraverted eyes, hooked nose and receding forehead shown by his portrait confirm what we know from other sources about his character. He was a man of action. Narrow, inflexible, despotic, with great business capacity and drive, a rigorous ascetic, he set about organizing the Reformed Carmelite convents (they now numbered nearly a hundred) as though they were a chain store. He had been impressed by the disciplined organization of the Jesuits and by their conception of religion as an affair not so much of the interior life as of obedience and loyalty. He had also—an Italian and a business man—absorbed their ideas on mental reserve, which gave him an advantage over people who, as Spanish monks, had been brought up to say what they thought. No wonder Teresa had not liked him. 'There are some kinds of sanctity I do not understand,' she had written of him in her tart way to Gracián. But it was her fault. The Reform was now paying the price of having expanded too quickly and of having intrigued with the King's party against the General of their order.

Doria's new plan, accepted at a chapter in 1588, was to divide the Reformed Carmelites into six provinces, the heads of which were to be nominated by himself. This committee of seven men, known as the Consulta, would sit in Madrid and from there govern the order autocratically. The old independence of the priors was gone. Worst of all, the nuns would be placed, without representation of any kind, under the friars. New rules were to be given out which would take away their remaining liberties. It was a momentous change to make, for since 1247 the political organization of all Carmelites had been based on a constitution drawn up in imitation of the famous 'democratic' one of St. Dominic. But the friars offered no resistance. Gracián had already been disgraced and his supporters were too cowed to make much protest. Only the nuns showed spirit, and Fray Juan de la Cruz stood by them.

Juan was now Prior of Segovia. He seems to have reached at this time some new peak of his spiritual ascension. We hear of him sitting every night, writing or meditating in his cell, giving only a few hours to sleep and spending long hours in a grotto in the garden. The convent stands outside the city on the banks of the river and on summer nights the valley is loud with the singing of the nightingales. The hill above it, which is enclosed within its grounds, commands a view of the city, the plain and the distant mountains. Here, in a tiny grotto, or stretched out in the form of a cross under an olive tree, he would spend whole nights in contemplation. We have a poem of his, not a good one, which he wrote in a trance or ecstasy.

Then in May 1591 the expected blow fell. A chapter was held in Madrid and he went to attend it. Some dramatic event was expected, for Ana de Jesus, with the help of the aged poet Fray Luis de Leon, who was editing Teresa's works, had secretly obtained a brief from

Rome that gave the nuns the right to govern themselves. 'Who knows,' said a nun to Juan as he was setting out, 'but that Your Reverence may come back Provincial of this province!' 'No, no, daughter,' he replied. 'I shall be thrown into a corner like an old kitchen cloth.'

At the chapter Juan spoke up strongly. 'If at our assemblies men no longer have the courage to say what the laws of justice and charity oblige them to say, from weakness, cowardice or fear of annoying the superior and consequently not obtaining an office, then the order is lost and utterly relaxed.' And he demanded that the voting should be by secret ballot. But the others were overawed and no one supported him. He was removed from his priorate and sent as a simple friar to the 'desert' house of La Peñuela in Andalusia. The King, whose policy Doria was carrying out, refused to accept the Papal brief.

The convent of La Peñuela was an old hermitage that had been taken over some fifteen years earlier, together with its hermits, by the Carmelites. As the place had proved to be unhealthy, the friars had moved soon after to El Calvario. Now it had been resettled. It stood (the exact site is lost today) among evergreen oaks and cistus heath on the slopes of the Sierra Morena, at the foot of the famous pass of Despeñaperros. No doubt the place suited Juan for its great solitude, and we hear of him going out early every morning, before the heat of the day, to kneel by the rushes of a stream or under a tree. Sometimes, as his custom was, he spent whole nights in this manner. But he bore no resentment for his treatment. From Madrid he had written to one of the nuns of Beas:

'*Y adonde no hay amor, ponga amor y sacará amor*.' 'Where there is no love, put love and you will get back love.'

Meanwhile the persecution against him was increasing. Doria's first intention had been to get rid of him honourably by sending him at the head of a mission to Mexico. But when it was seen that the King's support in the matter of the brief could be counted on, it was decided to ruin him completely. He had owed his imprisonment at Toledo to his support of the Carmelite nuns and of their liberty to vote freely according to their conscience; now he would be made to suffer for the nuns again as well as for having demanded a secret ballot.

For this purpose a confidant of Doria, Fray Diego Evangelista, was sent to collect incriminating evidence against him and Gracián in the Andalusian convents. We know something of how he set about this from the sworn depositions made later by various nuns who had been interrogated by him. Diego's method was to question the nuns and, if he could not get what he wanted by threats, to falsify what they said. Some of his questions passed the bounds of decency and a nun at Malaga was made to declare that Fray Juan had kissed her through the grille. We may ask what use it was intended should be made of this document. Gracián was publicly stripped of his habit a few months later and expelled from the country. Ana de Jesus was imprisoned; others of Teresa's followers were exiled to remote convents.[1] But there is reason for thinking that Juan de la Cruz's case was regarded more seriously on account of his great reputation for saintliness and that he would therefore be brought before the only body capable of breaking such reputations —the Inquisition. As the supreme guardian of Spanish religious policy and of its ever-narrowing line of orthodoxy, this body might be expected to act against him. At all events we know that people who had letters or papers of his destroyed them because they feared that it would be dangerous to have anything with his name on it. For example, we read of the large collection at Beas being burned so that the Visitor should not find them 'although the nuns regarded them as the letters of St. Paul'. If it is true that his works were mutilated, it was probably at this time. The last chapters of both the *Noche Oscura* and the *Subida del Monte Carmelo*, in which he had promised to deal with the state of union, are missing. It was a subject on which it had become dangerous to write, even for the most orthodox.

Juan, however, was spared this last indignity. In September he fell ill with fever and ulcers on his leg. To get treatment he was taken to the town of Ubeda, six leagues from La Peñuela and one from Baeza, and placed in the Carmelite house. Yet even here persecutions followed him: we read of the prior coming every day to his cell to

[1] Gracián's later history is curious. He was taken prisoner by Moorish pirates and carried off to Africa. After two years of sufferings there he returned to Rome as a beggar. Clement VIII heard of his case and commanded that he be reinstated in his order. But though Doria was dead, his partisans were still in power and they refused to receive him. He was then—by a supreme irony—taken in by the Unreformed Carmelites. In old age he wrote an account of his life and died in Flanders in 1614. Ana de Jesus lived to carry the Carmelite Reform to France in 1604, dying in 1622, the year in which Santa Teresa was canonized.

reproach and insult him in spite of the great pain he was suffering. Then the ulcers spread to his body: the flesh on his legs rotted. He died at midnight on 14 December 1591, as the monks were ringing for prime. Almost his last act was to ask that some verses of the Song of Songs should be read to him. '*O qué preciosas margaritas!*' he murmured.

Juan de la Cruz's death was followed by some extraordinary scenes which his modern biographers have preferred to pass over in silence. Hardly had his breath ceased than, though it was an hour past midnight, cold and raining hard, crowds assembled in the street and poured into the convent. Pressing into the room where he lay, they knelt to kiss his feet and hands. They cut off pieces from his clothes and bandages and even pulled out the swabs that had been placed on his sores. Others took snippings from his hair and tore off his nails, and would have cut pieces from his flesh had it not been forbidden. At his funeral these scenes were repeated. Forcing their way past the friars who guarded his body, the mob tore off his habit and even took parts of his ulcered flesh.

A contest then began for his body. The patrons of the Priory of Segovia, a noble lady and her brother who had formed part of his circle at Granada, determined to obtain it for their city. After securing a royal warrant, they had it dug up by night in great secrecy. Although nine months had passed since his death, it was found not to have decayed and to give out an aromatic smell. They placed it in a trunk and set off by a roundabout road for Castile.

Here a curious piece of folk lore is reported by San Juan's first biographers. The Guardian Angel of Ubeda wished to defend the body against the Guardian Angel of Segovia. After failing to rouse the monks in time, he appeared by night on a hilltop outside Mártos and called in a loud voice to the bearers to take the body of the saint back to Ubeda. Their hair stood on end. But the Alguazil replied that he was acting on the King's orders and the mysterious apparition then allowed them to pass. We are reminded of the contest between Saguntum and Saragossa in Prudentius' poem on the martyrdom of St. Vincent.

San Juan's body, less a leg left in Ubeda, an arm in Madrid and fingers distributed elsewhere, finally reached Segovia. Dressed and covered with laurel leaves and flowers, it was shown to the city through a *reja*. The face was still recognizable. Other vicissitudes followed, for, after an urgent appeal to Rome, the remaining limbs were cut off and restored to Ubeda. But these, to our modern taste, somewhat ghoulish episodes have an important bearing on our story. Juan de la Cruz, to us who read his writings, is a poet and a mystic. But to his contemporaries he was a saint, with a sanctity doubly proclaimed by his devotion to a holy cause and by the persecutions which this devotion brought on him. The people, with their medieval instinct for such things, recognized this and canonized him in their own way. And it was precisely this overwhelming movement of popular veneration that silenced his enemies and led to the first steps for his beatification being taken twenty years later. In all probability we owe to it the preservation of his poems and prose works.

In appearance Juan de la Cruz was a very small man with dark hair and complexion, a high forehead, arched eyebrows and a slightly aquiline nose. His glance, we are told, was gentle. He went bald early. But of his character there is little to be said. Unlike Teresa, he was singularly devoid of all those picturesque features one calls personality. We see a shy silent man, with downcast eyes, hurrying off to hide himself in his cell, and so absent-minded that, when spoken to, he often did not understand what was said. We note the immense tenacity of purpose that underlay his somewhat feminine sensibility and his entire and whole-hearted disposition to the contemplative life. Perhaps no one ever had a vocation that drew him more irresistibly. We see, too, his great patience—there were the makings of a stoic hidden under his monk's dress—and also a certain psychic force which led to his being greatly in demand for casting out demons—in modern language, curing hysterics. But the thing that strikes us most about him is his wilful and deliberate negativeness. All his contemporaries agree as to his reluctance to speak about himself and his dislike of unnecessary or trivial conversation. His voice was never raised, his face never lost its habitual calm. No one ever saw him lose his composure, or laugh, or show annoyance. Perhaps it was for this reason that his brother priors thought so little of him. And through his books there run like a refrain the words—secret, hidden, forgotten, in disguise, silence, bareness, night. We are left, as he would have wished, with the necessity of describing the character he presented to the world by negations and leaving it to his poetry to display his rich and passionate inner life. As for his prose, though inclined to prolixity, it shows a love for plain and exact statement and a certain gift for psychological analysis. No other writer of his age is so free from rhetoric.

But Juan de la Cruz's life has more in it than the life of a great poet and mystic. It has a historical significance too. The outward tragedy of his last years is also the tragedy of an epoch. Let me try to put this briefly in its proper perspective. The sixteenth century in Spain was a century of religious revolution. This revolution began, as in England and Germany, in an atmosphere of humanism—return to the Bible and the Early Fathers, reform of medieval abuses, a new spirit of seriousness among the laity. Erasmus was the leading figure in this movement and down to 1550 the best of the Spanish clergy and intellectuals were his disciples. Then a sudden change occurred. The rise of Luther had made the Erasmists a centre party and as he grew in strength the situation became polarized into a Reformation and a Counter Reformation. Philip II succeeded Charles V, the policy of reconciliation in Germany failed and the Spanish Inquisition closed down on the Erasmists. But religious feeling in Spain continued to mount and the only outlet left open to it was the ascetic and mystical.

The first signs of this had come some time before from a small group of Franciscans. Influenced by certain Flemish writers, they had described a method of prayer which went beyond the contemplation of Christ's humanity—as taught by à Kempis—and sought union with the divine element. These ideas soon spread beyond the monasteries. All over Castile there sprang up the people known as the Iluminados. They were small groups of pious men and women who had been influenced by Erasmus, but still more by the Franciscan manuals of popular devotion. Being untrained in theology, they fell into various errors, and the Inquisition, which was alarmed by their anti-ceremonial tendencies, suppressed them. But the movement to deepen religious life could not be checked. It broke out in the convents, and, since monks and nuns are subject to strict control and were the declared enemies of the Erasmists, the Inquisition, after a brief period of suppression in 1559, when a large number of mystical works were put on the Index, decided to tolerate it. However it was not a decision that it found easy to make: religion in Spain had always been a conservative or, as Erasmus put it, 'Jewish' thing with little imaginative content. Mysticism was a practice which had come in from abroad. The only Spanish mystic of the Middle Age was Ramon Lull, who had learned what he knew of it from the Moslems. It followed, therefore, that the strong conservative, *cristiano viejo*, element in the country was hostile to it. Their chief representative, the great theologian Melchor Cano, went so far as to declare that the tendency to an interior religion was the heresy of the age, of which Luther was only a branch. In particular he held that the 'taking away of fear and the giving of reassurance' which resulted from mystical practices would undermine the position of the Church. The Inquisition therefore only yielded and tolerated the mystics because it found the impulse in that direction irresistible.

The outstanding movement towards a deeper religious life in Spain was the Carmelite Reform, which gathered together the scattered impulses that had preceded it. It began with St. Teresa's first foundation at Avila in 1562 and, as we have seen, spread rapidly. We may regard it as the spear-head of the second wave of the revolutionary process. Like the French Revolution—like all revolutions—it was a movement in search of liberty, though the liberty it sought was not a political one, but something much more fundamental—an interior one. Freedom for a sixteenth-century monk, though it needed for its exercise what one may call monastic democracy, meant freedom from the human situation of exile from God.

We may say too that, like other revolutions, it had its roots in an economic situation. The discovery of the silver mines in Peru, not long before the Inquisition turned on the Erasmists, had led to a severe and apparently uncontrollable inflation. All through the second half of the sixteenth century cloth factories were closing down, the land was ceasing to be tilled, the Government was sinking into debt. There was a levelling of classes, but the people were ceasing to work and Spain was rapidly becoming a country of impoverished parasites. The reaction to this economic landslide, which would today take a political form, then took a religious one. On the one hand it led—or helped to lead—to a tightening of the censorship and terror wielded by the Inquisition (Conservative Spain lived in mortal dread of Protestant infection), and on the other to a stepping up of the revolutionary enthusiasm. Let us say, if we may strain the analogy so far, to Robespierre and Danton.

Such rapidly developing situations can only end in a crisis. From the immediate point of view one can see that the great increase in the numbers of the Reformed Carmelites was bound to provoke a reaction within the Order, because few people are fitted by disposition for the contemplative life. In the common run of men, mystical practices stimulate the mind to action just as for most young persons of literary bent poetry is a stepping-stone to journalism or politics. But the revolt led by Doria which broke the Carmelite Reform must be seen in a wider aspect, as part of a large general process.

The Order which was to capture Spain in the seventeenth century and resolve the antinomy between the mystics and the Conservatives was the Society of Jesus. Now the fundamental nature of the Jesuit action, as it developed in the course of time, was to damp down and bring to an end the revolutionary religious movement of the sixteenth century and turn its spiritual and intellectual energies into an exterior conformism. The Jesuits were activists. Their conception of religion was political. Loyalty, obedience, discipline were the qualities they sought to inculcate, and in exchange for these they were prepared to relax the demands of the Church on ordinary men and make religion more easy and agreeable. The values of the Renaissance were brought back, though as mere decoration, shorn of their sense of hope and forward movement. An age began that, like our own, was driven back upon its own resources and forced to reflect itself, without stimulus from the past or hope for the future.

But it was a defeated age and it knew it. The convolutions of its Baroque sculpture, the twistings of its poetic idiom, are the marks of a culture that has been turned back and thwarted in its deepest organs of life. The whole tone of seventeenth-century literature in Spain is pessimistic. The men of that time were living in the trough of fatigue and disillusion that follows a great movement that has failed.

Perhaps we can now see that solitary mystic, Fray Juan de la Cruz, as a person in history. St. Teresa came out of the Middle Ages, whereas he belongs, with Luis de Leon and El Greco, to the prime of the Spanish Golden Age. The central activity of that age, the motive force that provided it with its energies, was religion. He was the leading pioneer in that religion, the deepest exponent of its message—what Pascal was to be in a more intellectual land and century. His disgrace and death mark therefore better than anything else the point where the revolutionary movement of the sixteenth century began to ebb and the new forces that were to bind the seventeenth century to take their place. In the absence of any better terminology, we can call this moment a Thermidor.

ALYSE GREGORY

DENIS DIDEROT

WHEN, in the *salon* of Mme Geoffrin at a long anticipated meeting, Diderot was introduced for the first time to Fontenelle, and saw before him a little old shrivelled-up man approaching his hundredth year and dangling an ear trumpet, he burst into a fit of weeping. Fontenelle, who, like the Abbé Galiani, had never been known to shed a single tear, inquired somewhat drily the cause of so spectacular a loss of control. 'It is', Diderot answered, 'that I am impressed with a very singular sentiment.' He could hardly explain to the notoriously unsentimental author of *The Plurality of Worlds* that his clumsy emotion was due to his sudden desolating realization of 'the vanity of literary fame and all human things'. The episode was characteristic of Diderot, of the impressionability of his heart, and of the closeness to experience of his philosophy. It is an index to what made him both so endearing and so eminent a figure of his time. For of all the great Frenchmen of the eighteenth century he alone seems to have received, if not always the whole-hearted approval of commentators and historians, at least their affection. Voltaire has been held up to M. Faguet's inquisitorial disdain, while Rousseau made so many enemies that he could never flee far enough away to escape them all. Diderot made but one, and that one was Rousseau; and it is again characteristic of Diderot that it was through his defence of one friend that he lost the other.

Denis Diderot was born at Langres on 5 October 1713, one year after Rousseau, and nineteen years after Voltaire. His father was an upright and industrious cutler, who regarded this eldest child of his —he had one other son and a daughter—with a combination of pride, apprehension, and benevolent austerity. He allowed him at an early age to attend a Jesuit school in Paris, and Diderot intended to become a priest. This project was soon abandoned, and he studied law with an old friend of his father's, but rapidly lost interest in so dry an employment. When admonished that it was necessary for him to choose a career he replied that it would not be the law, as 'he had no wish to spend all his days in doing other people's business', and it would not be medicine, as 'he had no turn for killing'. On being pressed as to what, then, he did propose to do, he answered:

'But, *ma foi!* nothing at all, nothing at all. I love studies and ask for nothing more.' From this moment he was turned adrift to fend for himself. Certain early years of Diderot's life remain obscure to his biographers. We know that he taught mathematics to a rich man's languid sons, but decided that he would prefer to starve at his pleasure than to stuff himself with the best victuals in Paris and be harnessed to so tedious an engagement. Even as a tiny boy he had said that he would rather be impatient than bored, though no one could be more patient than he if his interest was aroused, and he was very fond of children, having once observed that he loved and respected children and old men because he regarded them 'as singular beings who had suffered a great deal and who had been spared by fate'. He returned from his teaching to a life of semi-vagabondage, picking up odd bits of work, among which was that of composing sermons for a missionary to be distributed in the Portuguese colonies. It was in a café at this epoch that he first came across Rousseau, who had hoped to astonish Paris by his accomplishments as a musician, but, concluding that this was out of the question, had transferred all his ambitions to perfecting himself in the game of chess, at which he aimed to outwit the entire world.

Diderot once likened himself to the weathercock on the church tower of Langres, but it was not an instability of nature that made him thus susceptible; it was his avid intellectual curiosity and his passion for experience that turned him round according to the direction promising him the greatest excitement. '*Vif, ardent, et fou,*' he could be seen at all seasons of the year on the Paris boulevards, dressed in a grey plush suit with torn cuffs, his black woollen stockings darned with white cotton, his head thrust forward in the way that Keats used to carry his head, as if for ever in pursuit of truth, for ever in flight. Even his walking stick he manipulated as if holding it out for the passers-by to see. Diderot always had the air of rushing breathlessly toward life as if he were about to fling himself into the arms of a mistress. He used to frequent a bookshop on the Quai des Augustins, as much because he was attracted by the daughter of the proprietor, Mlle Gabrielle Babuti, as to ferret out answers to the riddle of the universe, answers, indeed, that he never did quite hit upon. This young woman, who later became the wife of Greuze the painter, was not unresponsive to his advances, and it is supposed that they enjoyed moments of pleasure together. At the same time that Diderot discovered Mlle Babuti he discovered Voltaire. He picked up his *Lettres philosophiques* in the shop one day, and, standing with it open before him, continued to turn over the leaves for so many hours that his companion was at last piqued into reminding him that life was not all paper and print. This book had a definite influence on Diderot, for though he kept his head in the air his thoughts were seldom in the clouds. He was neither a visionary nor a man of science. He was an explorer into every crevice of life—sensual, intellectual, and of the market place. He delighted in discussions, he delighted even more in wandering alone by the side of the river, he adored making love, he enjoyed eating enormously, he set great store by his friends, and Nature was ever for him the chief source of man's wisdom and happiness upon earth. It was he who first imbued Rousseau with his ardour in this direction. Diderot peered, probed, and reconnoitred in every direction, opening his heart and his pocket-book to everybody who crossed his path, and observing shrewdly and benevolently the springs of human behaviour.

It was in 1741 that he first met Antoinette Champion, a seamstress, three years his senior, who was living alone with her widowed mother. They were married two years later after she had become his mistress. In matters of marital unhappiness it is usually dangerous to place the blame anywhere but on luck. Diderot's daughter worshipped her father and defended her mother. She said that the souring of her mother's nature was due partly to her father's jealousy, which caused him to keep her away from society in their early life together, partly to their poverty—they had four children of whom only this one daughter survived—but most of all to her father's infidelities. She compared her mother's nature to a piece of rock crystal, noble at the centre but with protruding edges. Unfortunately, in daily life, it is the edges of which we are most constantly aware. It was inevitable that Diderot should become restive with a woman like Mme Diderot, who was a bigoted Catholic, and incapable of understanding either her husband's thoughts or her own. He tried, often with great patience, in their early days together to reconcile their two natures, sometimes beating his head against the wall in desperation. On one occasion, more than ever distraught, he dashed off pell-mell to her priest, who merely looked on at his gesticulations as a frog might stare at a floating leaf in a pond, without a single blink, which set Diderot in a still greater rage, but this time his fury was directed against the Church.

It was when Mme Diderot was away on a visit to his parents at Langres that Diderot formed a relationship with Mme de Puisieux —referred to by Carlyle as 'the scarlet woman'—who was for some years his mistress. She was a writer of even more mediocre talent than Louise Colet, and grasping as well. Fidelity, Diderot once defined, as 'the obstinacy and the punishment of a good man and a good woman'.

The first work of Diderot's which brought upon him the attention of the thinking world was his *Lettre sur les aveugles* (1749) and, as with much of his writing, it is amazingly modern in theory. It had for its essential doctrine that 'all knowledge is relative to our experience, that thought is not the measure of existence, nor the conceivableness of a proposition the test of its truth, and that our experience is not the limit to the possibilities of things'. It was revolutionary enough at the time to land him in prison, fortunately with a volume of Milton's *Paradise Lost* in his pocket, and M. du Châtelet, the husband of Voltaire's Emilie, as his jailer. He devised a method of writing by scraping the slate at the side of his window and grinding it to a fine powder which he mixed with some wine in a broken glass. For pen he used a toothpick. His wife used to visit him at one hour and Mme de Puisieux at another. On one of the occasions of the latter's visits his suspicions were aroused by the fact that she was dressed in an unusually gay manner. She swore, when questioned, that she was attending a fête that evening at Champigny, where no one was to accompany her. Diderot, increasingly suspicious, later scaled the prison walls, went to Champigny, discovered her leaning amorously on the arm of a rival, and at once went off, sleeping the night in the park. In the morning he restored himself to the authorities. He had been permanently cured of his passion for the unfortunate Mme de Puisieux. 'In love I think like a sage and act like a fool,' he once wrote. Diderot's daughter, in her reminiscences of her father, says that his habits were always 'good', that he never liked '*les femmes de spectacle ni les filles publiques*'. She goes on to recount that he was once in love with a dancer at the opera, and persuaded a friend who lived opposite this girl, to allow him to spy on her from one of his windows. One day he saw her attiring herself, and as she pulled on her stockings she rubbed out the spots with a piece of chalk. With every spot that vanished Diderot's passion diminished, and by the time she had disposed of the last one his heart was as whole as her stockings. Diderot has been frequently criticized for talking so freely with this daughter, even as a child; but his indiscretions were always pointed by sober explanations and sound advice. Indeed he treated his little Angélique in an unusually imaginative manner. He always doted on her, and spared neither time nor pains to develop her individual nature, and to counteract the stern disciplines of her mother. When, in the end, he had to give her over to a husband, he experienced a sharp and bewildering access of jealousy which at first caused him chagrin, and then caused him to laugh heartily at himself.

Many people will perhaps have forgotten that the famous eighteenth-century French Encyclopaedia had its inception from *Chambers's English Dictionary*, those quaint volumes, now so outmoded, but still packed with so much pithy and relevant information. Le Breton, a bookseller of Paris, asked Diderot to translate the dictionary into French. In his capacious, excitable, and fecund brain the idea became gradually transformed, and he persuaded Le Breton to allow him to collect from the eminent thinkers of the day articles embodying the new ideas in philosophy, science, and literature, and to incorporate them in a series of volumes (in the end there were thirty-five). The consent of the government was secured, d'Alembert agreed to act as his chief collaborator, and in 1750 the first prospectus was issued. For nearly twenty-five years (1748–72) this stupendous work engaged all Diderot's best energies. He had to meet not only the abuse of his enemies but the desertion of his friends; and what was even worse, the Ecclesiastical Party, seeing the influence of the encyclopaedia spreading and subscribers steadily increasing, managed, in 1759, to have it formally suppressed. To our present-day view the articles appear surprisingly mild. There is no open attack upon religion, or even upon the abuses of the Church. What was alarming to the authorities was the manner in which the contributions took for granted the justice of speculative freedom and religious tolerance. D'Alembert, becoming frightened, resigned his post. The decree did not forbid the continuance of the work and Diderot, excluded both from the Royal Society of London, and from the French Academy, laboured on alone. The crowning stroke came when, just as the enterprise was nearing its completion, he discovered that Le Breton had all the time been deleting without detection, from the corrected proofs, every passage or paragraph which he thought might displease the authorities, while at the same time destroying the original text. Diderot was so struck down by this final betrayal that he burst into a flood of tears, fled from the room, and refused ever again to address another word to Le Breton. The three events of Diderot's life which caused him his greatest anguish were his quarrel with Rousseau, his father's death, and Le Breton's perfidy; and it was the last that pierced deepest into the bone. It was not only the ignorant mangling of his life work that so overwhelmed him, but the responsibility he felt toward his contributors, and his fear that they might think he had deceived them. So undiscerning are even the most intelligent readers, however, that the monstrous liberties taken by this craven type-setter were hardly even remarked upon, and Diderot had, by some chance, kept duplicates of the original articles.

It is satisfactory to know that during the last half of his life Diderot had a friend, incomparably dear to him, to whom he could always turn for refreshment. The exact date of his meeting with Louise-Henriette Volland (it was he who gave her the name of Sophie to symbolize wisdom, saying that she was wiser than Socrates' Aspasia) is not known, but it is supposed to have taken place during Mme Diderot's second visit to Langres in 1756. Diderot was then forty-three and Sophie was nearing her fortieth year. She was living with her mother, a rich widow who had two other daughters, on the rue des Vieux-Augustins, and Diderot spent most of his time between his workroom and their home. He used to visit Sophie by a secret staircase at the back of the house, until one day they were discovered together by her mother. Up to our own century it always remained a hotly contested point as to whether Sophie Volland was, in fact, Diderot's mistress, a matter that absorbed half the pedants of Europe, only pedants having, apparently, the necessary combination of pertinacity, leisure, and frivolity to pursue such evasive points to their last vanishing place. One venerable old canon living in Langres, a celebrated authority on the Diderot family, with a bitter hatred for Diderot, is said to have bounded out of his chair as if he had been stung by a wasp at the mere intimation that their love was a 'blameless' one. On the other hand, M. Michel Corday, who has written a book on 'the love life' of Diderot, was strongly of the opinion that such a relationship was entirely out of the question owing to certain ambiguous and rueful references Diderot made in some of his later letters to Sophie about his *nullité*, M. Corday assuming that no man could write without extreme humiliation about such a matter, and that the last person to whose notice he would ever care to bring it would be to that of his mistress. It is only since a recent edition of Diderot's letters has appeared, published by the Babelon Press (1931), with passages heretofore deleted now copied in from the original text, that the matter has been, to all unprejudiced minds, finally resolved. If the eighteenth century ironically shrugged its shoulders over the *liaison* and the nineteenth century sought to exonerate Sophie from having given herself to Diderot, the twentieth century may, in its turn, exonerate her from having refused herself to him. During ten years of their intimacy she was forced to spend six months of each year at the family château at the Isle-sur-Marne in Champagne; and it is due to these absences of hers that we owe some of the best of Diderot's letters. No exact description of Sophie has come down to us. Diderot used to carry a picture of her in the fly-leaf of his Horace which he had always with him. We know that she wore glasses, that she was slight in build, and that she was universally praised for her *finesse*, her candour, and her brilliant intellect. Grimm refers to her passion for philosophy, another visitor to their house remarks that she has the 'wit of a demon', and M. Tronchin, with a final flourish, tells us that she had 'the soul of an eagle in a frame of gauze'. Diderot himself continually praises her good sense, her sensitive and elevated heart, and her noble intelligence—'*la plus belle âme de femme qu'il ait sous le ciel*'. It is seldom that anyone in any age, or in any country, is fortunate enough to discover someone to whom he can reveal, without regret or apprehension, the multiple sides of his nature. Diderot has frequently been accused of grossness because of certain things that he wrote in his letters to Sophie Volland, but he was no more gross than Flaubert was gross. He was broad spoken in the Rabelaisian sense and he was certainly greedy, but to enjoy good food and to acknowledge it is, surely, to be honest rather than gross. Dr. Johnson once quoted an eminent statesman as saying that most great men died of overeating (a fate he perhaps realized was to be his own).

No one has ever spoken more freshly, more movingly from the heart, than did Diderot in the pages of these letters. It is as if we could hear the very inflexion of his voice, watch the changing expressions of his round, animated, adoring eye. This is the rich mine that every biographer of Diderot has furtively, or boldly quarried. Even Carlyle, with his uncouth sneers about 'an elderly spinster' and 'a virtuous wife', and Morley, the civilized English gentleman, self-consciously embarrassed, have had, perforce, to study with sober zeal these indiscreet and sprightly records. They are a perfect reflection of Diderot's conversation, and he was considered the outstanding talker of his time, though it was a complaint frequently brought against him that he was more given to expounding than to listening. But if he could sometimes exhaust his friends, he seldom bored them and he never alienated them. The monologues of Coleridge, the great talker of *his* day, to whom Diderot has been compared, were like illuminated hoops in the sky, for ever circling round and round with nowhere to jump on and nowhere to jump off, and comprehensible only to himself. Diderot always kept close to actual life. If he was ingenuous he was also sage ('a sage in frenzy'); if he was emphatic he was also *fine*; if he was exuberant he was also weighty; and he was, above all, a Frenchman living in Paris in the eighteenth century who had kept abreast with every new idea, every new discovery, every new metaphysical and theological whimsy. He could shift from subject to subject as easily as a boy leaps over a stream. He could write an advertisement for some hair tonic to help a starving scribbler, or fling himself with a transport of enthusiasm into a study of Hobbes's *Treatise on Human Nature*. He flirted, gossiped, intrigued, analysed, visited peasants and cobblers; went to theatres and concerts and always kept his eyes and ears open to what was going on about him; and all this vast and varied activity was mirrored in these matchless letters. There is no aspect of life that does not receive attention. Anecdotes tragic, comic, equivocal, scandalous, complicated, and pathetic follow one upon the other. An exalted expression of his love is succeeded by an exact enumeration of the delicious dishes he has just injudiciously eaten at the table of the Baron d'Holbach, at whose house on the rue Saint-Thomas, and later, at the rue Royale-Saint Roche, the most distinguished men of the time were royally entertained. 'Imaginez,' he writes of his host, 'un satyre, gai, piquant, indécent et nerveux. . . . Il n'auroit ni offensé, ni embarrassé ma Sophie parce que ma Sophie est homme et femme quand il lui plait.' When Hume visited Paris it was at the Baron d'Holbach's that he stayed most frequently. On one of these occasions he happened to remark that in England there were no atheists, to which his host replied: 'Look about you. You will see seventeen people at this table. Of these fourteen are atheists and the other three have not yet made up their minds.' Horace Walpole wrote back in a letter to Selwyn, 'I sometimes go to Baron d'Holbach's but I have left off his dinners, as there was no bearing the authors and philosophers and savants of which he has a pigeon house full. . . . In short, nonsense for nonsense, I liked the Jesuits better.' Horace Walpole was certainly the great authority of his day on nonsense, but of a somewhat different variety from that to be found in either of the circles he mentioned.

In the spring of 1773 (the year that Johnson travelled to the Hebrides) Diderot paid his famous visit to his great benefactress, Catherine II of Russia. He was inordinately flattered by her reception of him, but he was no courtier—far from it—he was a man who frequently lost his wig (on this occasion he had to return home without it, a fact he sought to conceal from his wife), and who dressed at the gaudy court in the same plain black suit which served him so well when he stole out regularly every Sunday to make love to his Sophie. His irrepressible and irresponsible enthusiasms drove him resistlessly forward, and yet his heart was easily wounded. He had, as he said of himself, no gift for society, being 'either silent or indiscreet', more often the latter. To Bjornsthäl he once remarked that he never found hours pass slowly in the company of a peasant, or a cobbler, or a handicraftsman, but that he had many a time found them pass slowly in the company of courtiers. Catherine treated him with spirit, indulgence, and caution, the kind of caution that prompted her to place a small table between them in their daily talks from three to five (there were sixty in all) to protect her knees, his daughter recounts, from his too vehement gesticulations. He never ceased to praise her wit, her charm, her statesmanship. 'She has the soul of Caesar with the seductions of Cleopatra,' was his observation of her. Of him she remarked that he sometimes looked like a boy of twelve, sometimes like an old man of a hundred. Diderot did indeed have the capacity of changing expression in an astonishing manner. In criticizing a portrait of himself painted by Michel Van Loo he said, 'That dainty coquet is not I. . . . I had in one day a hundred different expressions according to the thing by which I was affected. I was serene, sad, dreamy, tender, violent, passionate, enthusiastic.

. . . I had a big forehead, sparkling eyes, fair-sized features, a head like an ancient orator, a good nature which amounted almost to foolishness, and the rustic manners of old times.' Meister spoke of his profile as being distinguished by a sublime character of male beauty, the habitual expression of his eyes sensitive and gentle, his mouth a mixture of *finesse*, grace, and good nature. But Diderot was by no means a simple character, though he was a transparent one. When he left the court the Empress presented him with a superb fur-lined cloak and a ring with a stone on which was engraved her own portrait, a gift he treasured above all others. It is an irreparable loss to posterity that his undoubtedly voluminous correspondence with Catherine should have been destroyed for reasons of caution at the time of the French Revolution.

As a writer Diderot's gifts were uneven. His articles in the encyclopaedia on the philosophers—Aristotle, Plato, Spinoza, Leibnitz, etc.—still impress us with their originality. His vast reading was always sifted through a sceptical and aroused intelligence. He was a forerunner of Darwin and Lamarck, and in his *Interprétation de La Nature* (1754) he traced in a startling manner the evolutionist theory, a theory that at the time was derided by Voltaire. In his *Rêve de d'Alembert* he propounded the then ingenious supposition, familiar enough to us now, that the human body was but an aggregate of countless living organisms. Diderot's materialism remained always consistently Lucretian, in the sense that it was upheld by imaginative enthusiasm rather than by cold scientific deduction. His fealty to nature was the source of his most intense and his most lucid insights. 'One may compare ideas which have no foundation in nature', he wrote, 'to those forests of the North whose trees have no roots. It needs only a breath of wind, only a small fact, to overturn a whole forest of trees and ideas.' It was this attitude of his which made him attack morality and religion while at the same time defending virtue. Carlyle, who disapproved of Diderot's atheism, refers to his 'dwelling all his life on the thin rind of the conscious', and adds with his usual sententiousness: 'Thus must the sanctuary of man's soul stand perennially shut against this man'—Carlyle, whom Nietzsche, in his turn, described as 'an English atheist who aspired to honour for not being one'.

As a playwright Diderot was never completely successful. What was revolutionary and invigorating in his attitude toward the stage was largely neutralized by the fact that he lacked creative imagination. This also was apparent in his works of fiction. His *Jacques le Fataliste* (admired and translated by Goethe) is witty and brilliant, but it is also monotonous and feeble, like a bird with wings outspread that never quite takes to flight. He had been influenced by Sterne, whom he met in Paris (1762), but he had not Sterne's power of invention nor his capacity to create character. His most outstanding work in this *genre* is his *Neveu de Rameau*, and the secret of its felicity lies largely in the fact that the central figure is an exaggerated portrait of Diderot himself. It is a dialogue full of verve, and on every page there is something that leaps up like a cricket from dry August grass. It was characteristic of him that his famous art criticisms should have had their origin in a desire to gratify his friend Grimm, who, obsequious to pleasure his royal patrons in the North, begged Diderot to jot him down some notes about the *Salon* of 1761. Among all Diderot's staggering activities studying pictures had never for some reason been included, but he at once set off to do as he was asked. His taste could certainly be attacked, and has been by M. Brunetière, to whom Diderot's nature is so secretly disturbing. Sainte-Beuve, on the other hand, hails him as the first true art critic of France, and he was without doubt the first critic who aroused in the public any lively desire to study pictures for the pleasure to be received from them. There were two points, always the same, from which Diderot started out in his appraisal of pictures—the heart and nature. This is why he so often contradicted himself, and did not mind contradicting himself. Are not both the heart and nature given to contradictions? It is also why his criticisms were so vivid, so cogent, so original, so stimulating, and to artists so inspiring; and it is why they were so often beside the mark. Not that he did not require unity in a composition—*la conspiration général des mouvements*—but first of all he must feel behind it some primal freshness and force of intention; or as Cézanne, at so much later a time put it, 'Primary force alone . . . can bring a person to the end he must attain. . . .' '*Les arts de génie naissent et s'éteignent avec les passions*,' Diderot wrote; and '*C'est que le bon stile est dans le cœur*'. But even if his art criticisms, judged purely aesthetically, leave something to be desired, the correspondence that stimulated them, as with his letters to Sophie Volland, remain a matchless record of the literary and artistic life of the epoch. They were not published in book form during his lifetime, but must have been freely circulated as they are mentioned in memoirs of the time.

The relationship existing between Voltaire and Diderot is prolific of interest. They were profoundly different in temperament. Voltaire (who always preferred d'Alembert to Diderot) upheld the monarchy, he was incapable of any complete detachment from mundane values, he was a classicist, an aristocrat in taste, and a Deist without the smallest religious emotion. What he shared in common with Diderot was his rage against cruelty and bigotry, his boundless intellectual curiosities, and his noble tolerance. Voltaire's incomparable literary graces, his limpid, scintillating ironies were outside Diderot's powers altogether. If Swift's wit was 'a razor dipped in oil', Voltaire's was a Toledo blade dipped in a shimmering mountain cascade. Diderot's was neither so deadly as Swift's nor so glancing as Voltaire's, but of the three he was the most truly philosophic, using the word in its widest sense. It was not without reason that he could write to Sophie Volland: 'That I should be acclaimed! That I should be rich! That I should be beneficent yesterday! Tomorrow all may change, and I may remain humble, poor, and useless, without its causing me an instant's chagrin!' It would be impossible to imagine the Dean of St. Patrick's or the sage of Ferney expressing, or even contemplating expressing, a similar sentiment. There is on record but one meeting between Voltaire and Diderot. It was when Voltaire, surfeited with glory, made his last jubilant entry into Paris. Of Diderot he said, 'He lacks one talent, and an essential one—that of dialogue'. Of Voltaire, Diderot remarked that he was 'like one of those old haunted castles, which are falling into ruins in every part: but you can easily perceive that it is inhabited by an ancient sorcerer'.

It was in his affections that Diderot's deepest prides were always finally centred. Even his boastings, and he was not ungiven to boasting, were childishly obvious, as when, wounded by Mme Volland's inscrutable obduracy toward him, he wrote to Sophie: 'Tell her that I am a man of honour, that nothing will make me change. Tell her that the greatest consideration in the memory of men is assured me.' Actually his reputation never seriously occupied him. He scattered his writings about with an extreme of negligence, and though he may have let his eye light now and then on posterity, it was because there was no point at which, sooner or later, it did not light. *Faire le bien et chercher le vrai*, this was the motto he tried to live up to; and the image he created of himself, and to which he remained always loyal, was that of a man of simple virtue and compassionate heart. 'No one steals my life from me,' he said, 'I give it.'

In a brilliant, exhaustive, and sometimes singularly disappointing essay on Diderot, M. Faguet, who is both master and slave of his own classifications, would lead us to discover in him the perfect type of the *petit bourgeois*, an analysis which disregards altogether those sides of Diderot's nature that separate him so entirely from others. If to be audacious in thought, impetuous in action, to spend oneself ceaselessly on vagabonds, thieves, ingrates, and even on adversaries; to eschew all worldly success; and to fall in love at fifty-eight like a boy of eighteen, as Diderot fell in love with Mme de Meaux, while at the same time vowing and believing (and with reason) that his Sophie was the one and only true love of his life, is to be a *petit bourgeois*, then he was one. To be sure, he adored his old father, and treasured his early memories, and never really deserted his wife. He remained at heart a sentimentalist in an age of rationalism, but not with the sentiment of Rousseau, who was really a misanthrope, for Diderot was a sentimentalist living in 'the tumult of his sympathies', while at the same time holding intact the integrity of his perceptions. If he took us down to the dregs of human conduct it was for the sole purpose of raising us up again. He celebrated existence with an unremitting and a cognizant innocence from a heart for ever overflowing, yet for ever attentive to the sufferings about him. Like Benjamin Constant, from whom he differed so essentially in temperament, he thought life could be divided between those who enjoyed and those who suffered, and wherever he came upon the latter he never withheld himself—not from the most humble, not from the most base. The greatest atheist of his age was in this sense the one outstanding Christian. A young man appeared one day at Diderot's door with a manuscript under his arm which he asked him to read. It turned out to be a scathing satire on Diderot himself, who inquired with some surprise why it had been brought to him. 'I am in need of bread', the young man answered, 'and I hoped you would pay me something not to print it.' Diderot, at once, deeply concerned, explained that he was too poor himself to pay anything for it, but that he was sure the brother of the Duke of Orleans, who hated him for his attacks on the Church, would buy it if he would write a dedicatory letter to accompany it. The young man answered that he did not know the Prince and that he could not write the letter. 'I will write it for you,' Diderot said, putting himself immediately to the task. All fell out as had been foreseen, the Prince paid a handsome sum, and the young man dined for once on plenty.

It would be impossible to put Diderot into any final category. He was the first true individualist of France. Comte refers to him as the greatest genius of the eighteenth century. And yet it is not for his philosophy, or for his ideas, original and liberating as they were, that we continue to honour him most, it is because he was above all a man of heart. 'The language of the heart is a thousand times more varied than that of the mind,' he wrote, 'and it is impossible to give the rules of its *dialectique*.' It is these rules that in some indefinable way he communicates to us. If he has left no body of masterpieces, such as Voltaire's, behind him, he has left many lines, and many paragraphs, and even a few pages in which may be discovered writing as noble, and even as exquisite, as any in the French tongue. But above all, he has expressed an attitude toward life which will be always fortifying to dwell upon; for he gives us the courage to enjoy under duress, and the generosity to give without calculation or regret.

Diderot's health never recovered after his return from Russia. He had always suffered from violent attacks of indigestion, and was continually nauseated after eating. In the examination of his body made after his death it was discovered that there were twenty-one stones in his gall-bladder, of which the smallest was as large as a walnut. His heart was enlarged to twice the normal size, and one of his lungs was full of water. Like Balzac, who it was said kept alive on fifty thousand cups of coffee and died of fifty thousand cups of coffee, Diderot had destroyed his frame by constant sedentary labours, often working at his table for fourteen hours at a stretch, without stopping to eat.

On 22 February 1784 Sophie Volland died, and five days later Diderot had an attack of apoplexy. From this he gradually recovered, though he remained very weak. The curé of Saint Sulpice came frequently to visit him during his illness, and they conversed on the most amicable terms. Emboldened by Diderot's apparent complaisance, the curé one day ventured the suggestion that *une petite rétraction* on his part would have a beneficial effect upon the world. Diderot cut him short with the words: 'Admit, Monsieur le

Curé, that I would be acting an impudent lie.' The priest continued to press his point, recalling that he had been obliged to refuse burial to Voltaire, whom Diderot had outlived by six years. To this Diderot's reply was: 'I understand you, Curé. You did not wish to bury Voltaire because he did not believe in the divinity of the Son. Very well, when I am dead, they may bury me where they like, but I declare, I, that I believe neither in the Father, nor in the Holy Spirit, nor in a single member of the entire family.'

At the instigation of Grimm, and after repeated warnings from his doctors that climbing stairs might prove fatal for him, Diderot was reluctantly persuaded to leave his modest rooms on the fourth and fifth floors of the rue Taranne, where he had lived for thirty years, and move into a sumptuous house on the rue Richelieu, provided for him by his faithful patroness Catherine. He made the change in the middle of July 1784. A fortnight later a more comfortable bed was secured for him and he said to the workmen who carried it in: 'You are taking a great deal of trouble for a piece of furniture that will not serve me for four days.' On the following day (July 30) he sat down as usual to his dinner, and at the end of the meal took an apricot. His wife remonstrated with him and he said, '*Mais quel diable de mal veux-tu que cela me fasse?*' and leaning his elbow on the table he reached over for some candied cherries. The silence became unduly prolonged, and Mme Diderot regarding him attentively perceived that he was dead. The priest, on being summoned, arrived with his holy oil, but on discovering that Diderot was no longer alive, he refused to administer it. Mme Diderot, supported by relatives, brought pressure to bear on the curé, promising him benefices for the Church up to eighteen thousand francs if it could be announced abroad that her husband had, before his death, recanted. The curé yielded, absolution was given, and, with solemn, garish pomp, the funeral proceeded. The coffin was lowered under the flags of the Virgin at Saint Roche, and the *affreuse cérémonie*, as his daughter refers to it, was at last accomplished. It was not by the priests, however, that the final trick was to be played; for when, at a later period, the flags were taken up it was discovered that the coffin had completely vanished away, an enigma which to this hour has remained unsolved.

Diderot, who was seventy-one when he died, had outlived Sophie Volland by only three months. In her will she had left him her seven volumes of Montaigne bound in red leather, and a ring that she called her Pauline. His daughter tells us that he had reconciled himself to her death only by the conviction that he would soon follow her. How often had he written to her: *Adieu, mon âme, ma vie, et tout ce qui m'est cher*, looking forward with anguish to their final separation. To her he had expressed the wish that their ashes might be mingled together. 'Everything destroys itself, everything perishes, there is only the world which remains, there is only time which endures.' It was in writing thus that he could bring himself back to a contemplation of existence without fear and without illusion.

BIBLIOGRAPHY

Œuvres complètes de Diderot, publiées par J. Assézat et Maurice Tourneu.

Lettres de Denis Diderot à Sophie Volland, avec une introduction par André Babelon (1930) 3 Vols.

Correspondance Inédite de Denis Diderot, avec une introduction par André Babelon (1931) 2 Vols.

Mémoires de Madame d'Epinay.

Correspondance littéraire, philosophique et critique, par Grimm, Diderot, Raynal, etc.

La Correspondance de Voltaire.

Diderot, par André Billy.

Diderot, par Joseph Reinach.

New Essays Critical and Moral, Thomas Carlyle.

Goethe et Diderot, par Barbey d'Aurévilly (1878).

Dix-huitième siècle, études littéraires, par Emile Faguet.

Sainte-Beuve, *Causeries du Lundi* (Tome troisième).

La Vie amoureuse de Diderot, par Michel Corday.

Un amour inconnu de Diderot, par J. Lortel (*Revue d'histoire littéraire de la France*, 1915).

Nouvelles Études critiques sur l'Histoire de la littérature Française, par Ferdinand Brunetière (Série 2).

Considerations sur les mœurs de ce siècle, par M. Duclos (1751).

L'art au XVIIIème Siècle, par Edmond et Jules de Goncourt.

Mémoires de Mme Roland.

Dialogues of Denis Diderot. Translated with an introduction by Francis Birrell.

In Defence of Shelley, and other Essays, by Herbert Read.

Diderot and the Encyclopædists, by John Morley (3 Vols.).

Jean Jacques Rousseau, by John Morley.

Madame Geoffrin: Her Salon and Her Times, by Janet Aldis.

Diderot, Interpreter of Nature, Selected Writings, with an introduction by Jonathan Kemp.

FOSCARINA ALEXANDER

LEOPARDI

To his contemporaries Giacomo Leopardi appeared as the poet of universal sorrow, and the image which has come to us through the years is of the *sombre amant de la mort* of Musset, the 'Job and Lucretius of Italian letters' of Carducci. Yet ever since De Sanctis wrote his famous essay on Leopardi and Schopenhauer many new aspects of the poet have been studied: the early enthusiastic, adventurous Leopardi of the *Canzone all'Italia*, the lover of Plutarch's heroes, the man who exalted a life of action as opposed to one of study. Even the poems written after 1819, when an affection of the eyes and the breakdown of his health brought about the great crisis of his life, no longer appear as a testament of unrelieved pessimism. In the last few years the poet of universal sorrow has become the poet of universal love, and articles and books have been written on 'Leopardian optimism'.

In an oft-quoted passage of his essay De Sanctis says: 'Leopardi produces the opposite effect to that which he proposes. He does not believe in progress, and he makes you yearn for it: he does not believe in liberty and he makes you love it. Love, virtue, glory he calls illusions and he kindles in your breast an inexhaustible passion for them.' Here we see an analysis of the dualism which leads to such different appreciations of the poet and which, as De Sanctis points out, constitutes the dynamic element of his art. While lamenting his insensibility, he clothes the lament in passionate language; imagination and illusion are for him dead in our modern world, yet imagination, 'the primitive fount of human happiness', and illusion, *le care illusioni* that he thought for ever lost, are for ever reborn. Life is an ebb and flow: now we are as gods, now less than the animals who know the peace and content after which we strive.

Around the central idea of illusion all the themes of Leopardi's thought are built. Illusions are youth and youth is life. Old age brings the loss of illusions—death. But illusions are never totally dead, therefore life subsists, sometimes to a great degree when we are joyous and creative, but for the most part to such a small degree that we are as dead.

Here again we see how two contrary interpretations of Leopardi are possible. If illusion has abandoned us and the world, what is there to live for? Reality is an evil which can only appear good when cloaked by illusion. There is nothing in the world, all is nothingness. Anything we see in it, any joy we may have—illusion. Thus the 'pessimist'. Yet illusion exists, is never completely dead in man's heart, has become such an inextricable part of his nature that he sees all through it; it is the very stuff of our lives. There is nothing in the world, but we are so made that we mask reality and fill the void. Through all Leopardi's poetry this double theme is developed. We never live, for life is always past and always future, memory and hope. We whom imagination and illusion have abandoned are as dead, living corpses; but through imagination and illusion we recapture the past and are again filled with hope.

In Leopardi's poetry the accent is mostly on pain, on the absence of illusion rather than on its vivifying influence, for everywhere he saw decadence: in himself he saw a great soul handicapped by a weak body, in the world around him a generation of lifeless 'reasoners'. For Leopardi, the strong inherit the earth. 'The body is the man', we read in the *Dialogue between Tristan and a friend*, 'because (apart from all else) high-mindedness, courage, the passions, capacity for action and enjoyment, and all that ennobles and vivifies life, depend on the vigour of the body, without which they cannot exist. The weak man is not a man but a child, and less than a child, because it is his fate to stand aside and see others live. All he can do is to chatter. Life is not for him.'

In the paternal library at Recanati, in that 'tomb of his youth' as he afterwards called it, where he acquired his prodigious knowledge and ruined his health, he dreamed of literary glory, a substitute for glorious and patriotic action. Though unable to emulate Plutarch's heroes, he hoped to inflame his contemporaries by word, to be a poet in the true sense. 'Poets,' he says in *Copernicus*, 'by stimulating the imagination, give birth to high-minded and vigorous actions.' The *Canzone all'Italia* and the early patriotic poems are written in this spirit.

Condemned to spend his youth in the death-like atmosphere of Recanati, needing, as he wrote to a friend, 'love, fire, enthusiasm', he lived in the past and in the future, in history and in his dreams of glory. In the ancient Greeks he admired above all their athletic training, their youthful vigour leading to heroic action, their statuesque beauty, all of which he compared with his own sedentary life and subsequent deformity, with his prudent contemporaries. 'I hate the vile prudence which petrifies, fetters and renders us incapable of any great action,' writes this 'Stendhalien'. (It has often been pointed out that his comments on the Rome of his time, that 'necropolis' of philologists and archaeologists, are very similar to those of Stendhal.)

The Greek conception of 'excellence', the 'health and beauty and good habit of the soul' was for Leopardi, as for so many of the romantics, the form in which he clothed his ideal and his dissatisfaction with everyday reality. When confronted with that reality Leopardi rejected it utterly, so greatly did it contrast with his vision. His early years of misery and toil he afterwards described as 'that blessed and beatific age when I still hoped for happiness and in hoping and dreaming of it still enjoyed it', when he *knew* but had not yet *felt* that all is vanity. In youth, he says, ideal and real are one, for we project our vision on the world. When reality and vision fall apart, the dream appears as a mere dream without validity or power to affect the true state of things. The great break in the poet's life, caused by the appearance of truth, is fundamental: it echoes throughout his poetry, it *is* his poetry. The *Canti* are the lament for the loss of illusion, for the unfulfilled promise, for the interruption of life which he likens to early death:

> O natura, O natura,
> Perchè non rendi poi
> Quel che prometti allor? perchè di tanto
> Inganni i figli tuoi?[1]
>
> (*A Silvia*)

The experience which determined his whole attitude to life occurred in 1819 when he was twenty-one years old. His disillusionment had begun two years earlier when, waking after the long night of toil and study which had been his life, he suddenly discovered himself to be a sick, deformed man, doomed to be for ever deprived of love, to 'stand aside and see others live'. In 1819

[1] O Nature! O Nature! Why do you not fulfil what you promised earlier? Why do you so deceive your children?

an affection of the eyes deprived him, for a period, of his sight and of his only distraction, reading. He then experienced a feeling of tedium so intense as to resemble paralysis. 'I felt myself in the midst of nothing,' he writes in his *Zibaldone* or day-book, 'I felt myself suffocated, reflecting and feeling that all is nothing, solid nothing.'

This vivid apprehension of the void provided Leopardi with a central intuition, a 'truth' from which he never departed and from which he drew his philosophy of life. There is little development in Leopardi's thought. It would seem as if, throughout his short life, he continually relearned by experience what his intuition had initially revealed to him. Great truths, he writes in the *Zibaldone*, 'are not discovered gradually but by a sort of enthusiasm of the reason', akin to the frenzy of the poets who 'at a glance, as if situated in a lofty place, take in as much of the domain of human knowledge as requires many centuries before it be discerned by philosophers'. The truth thus revealed to him by his experience was the nothingness underlying appearances. At the same time the theory of illusion was born. For, were all men to realize such a truth, they would, with the loss of hope, lose all incentive to action. In order to inspire man with a will to live, Nature endowed him with illusions, clothed the 'skeleton of things' in bright garments, created phantoms called love, virtue, glory, in which men acquired faith and for which they were ready to lay down their lives. While they believed in phantoms of virtue and happiness they were virtuous and happy. As illusions receded, as the phantoms were unmasked, as virtue appeared a hollow mockery, so men began to lose all incentive to action, became idle; idleness begat crime. The infinite self-love which is man's impelling force and which had until then been employed in outward action for the common good, was turned inward. Man began to desire for himself an infinite happiness unobtainable in a finite world. Instead of rejoicing in the present, he strove after imaginary pleasures, living in a future always out of reach. With the fading of illusions, the free happy state, the *libera nei boschi pura etade*, gave way to an age of idleness, crime and tedium; the age of illusion gave way to the age of reason.

Illusion or imagination is, for Leopardi, the fount of all goodness. Where the imagination reigns, there is beauty, virtue, sensibility. Such an age is the youth of man and of the world, when the laws of nature and heaven are hidden by the veil of myth, when 'happy error' and hope gladden the hearts of men:

alle secrete
Leggi del cielo e di natura indutto
Valse l'ameno error, le fraudi, il molle
Pristino velo; e di sperar contenta
Nostra placida nave in porto ascese.
(*Inno ai Patriarchi*)

The integral world of the Ancients is no more; a break has occurred. Since man no longer projects his image on the world, real and ideal no longer merge but exist side by side. The image, left without a corresponding object, is forced to exist in a void and finally perish through lack of nourishment. The happy bond between man and Nature is no more. Since he abandoned her ways and followed the path of reason, Nature is no longer a mother guiding his footsteps but a stepmother, an indifferent or hostile power. 'Madre è di parto e di voler matrigna.'[1] 'Do you think the world was made for you?' Nature asks the Icelander in the Dialogue. 'It is time you knew that in my designs, operations and decrees I never gave a thought to the happiness or unhappiness of man. If I cause you to suffer I am unaware of the fact; nor do I perceive that I can in any way give you pleasure.' All is equivalent, in a meaningless, drifting world where nothing has value, for all value lay in the discarded illusions. It is against such a world that Leopardi's Brutus, once a believer in the power of virtue, rebels. He commits suicide rather than surrender his individuality to a mechanism, an eternal circle of production and destruction.

In *L'ultimo Canto di Saffo*, the poetess holds out her arms in vain to an unresponsive Nature. Her sensibility is unimpaired, but, reflection having intervened, it finds no correspondence in earthly things, it has lost its vivifying power. The world is dead, birds no longer sing, boughs do not murmur, the water draws away from her foot. Nature, in which she once participated, has become a simple spectacle, an object for study. She cannot, like many more fortunate

[1] Cf. Vigny, *La Maison du Berger:*
On me dit une mère, et je suis une tombe.
Mon hiver prend vos morts comme son hécatombe,
Mon printemps ne sent pas vos adorations.

mortals, restore the contact through the deep and powerful experience of love, for she lacks physical beauty. Sappho too commits suicide, refusing a world where 'only the fair reign over men'. 'The man of imagination, of sentiment, of enthusiasm, deprived of corporeal beauty', we read in the *Zibaldone*, 'is in regard to Nature more or less in the same case as an ardent and sincere lover in regard to a mistress who does not return his love. He rushes forward ardently towards Nature, he feels profoundly all its force, all its enchantment, all its attractions, all its beauty, he loves her with abandonment; but . . . he feels that he has no part in this beauty, so loved and admired. . . . He knows himself to be excluded without hope from and unable to participate in the favours of that divinity which not only is present, but so present, so near to him that he feels her to be within himself and one with himself.'

Thrown back upon himself, the mere spectator of life becomes a victim of tedium, the malady of the clear-sighted, of those in whom reflection has taken the place of action. He can, by dint of distractions, by the cult of ever stronger sensations, by occupying every faculty of the soul attain a certain forgetfulness, an illusion of the infinity to which he aspires. Sappho, in her misery, can still find pleasure in storms and heavy seas. But such palliatives, although recommended by Leopardi (and often mistaken by critics for his final message), are known by him to be a mere sop to an insatiable Cerberus: 'To occupy the soul and not to satisfy desire, which is impossible, but partly to distract it and fill its throat with the cake of insatiable Cerberus: this is the best effect of human pleasure.'

Pleasure is always out of grasp, desire always ahead of realization. When directly opposed desire becomes pain, when simply unsatisfied it is tedium or *noia*. 'Man can never cease to love himself and desire happiness for himself. This desire, when it is not satisfied nor on the other hand directly opposed by that which is contrary to enjoyment, is *noia*. *Noia* is the desire for enjoyment left, so to speak, pure.' Therefore human life is interwoven with pain and *noia*, and one only disappears to give place to the other.

Sensibility forced to operate in a void results in *noia*. The greater the sensibility, the greater the dissatisfaction with the real, the greater will be the resulting *noia* and unhappiness. Who then are the contented, the optimists? The mediocre, the cowardly, those who adopt an ostrich-like attitude towards the evils of life, or the naïve believers in material progress. Theirs is not a true happiness, but a deadening of the sensibility, a comfortable anaesthesia, or an unwarranted pride. Here we have what appears to be a contradiction in Leopardi's thought and which has often been misinterpreted. When in *La Ginestra* he calls upon men to abandon their illusions and face the truth, is he reversing the opinions of a lifetime, as many critics believe? No, for Leopardi often pointed out in his prose writings that the anaesthesia, the deadened sensibility, the pride of the moderns was a very different thing from the vivifying illusions of antiquity: the former are 'errors of the intellect', born of laziness, reason, science and superstition; they are sterile and degrading. The latter are the 'errors of the imagination', productive of all that is good in the world. So clear-sightedness, the malady of the modern age, the father of tedium, becomes a virtue. Only through it can the cobwebs deposited on men's minds by laziness, error and superstition be swept aside. Only the *élite* have the courage to face the truth.

The sensitive man of antiquity, happy because he was sensitive, is no more. The poet, whose sensibility soars above that of other men, once the leader who inspired others to great deeds of valour, is now an exile; his superiority separates him from his fellow-men:

Altri anni ed altro seggio
Conviene agli alti ingegni . . . [1]

(*Ad Angelo Mai*)

Like the *passero solitario*, the solitary sparrow watching sorrowfully the joyous flights of other birds, Leopardi casts longing glances towards his fellow-creatures. He hovers between an ardent desire for life, be it an inferior one, and the proud realization that unhappiness and solitude are the heritage of the great, that his *noia* is sublime.[2] He neither can nor will accept the values of the world, yet his aspiration towards life is too strong for him to rest in a sublime

[1] Great minds require another time and sphere.

[2] 'To be unable to be satisfied by the whole of earthly good, even, so to speak, by the whole world, to accuse things of insufficiency and nothingness, and to suffer from a perpetual lack and sense of emptiness—that seems to me to be the chief sign of greatness and nobility to be found in human nature.'

aloofness. And so we witness the striving towards a reconciliation of the two impulses, towards the creation of a situation in which infinite and finite can meet and, on a different plane, towards a society where the sensitive can live in harmony with their fellow-men. An instance of the union between ideal and real is the ecstasy described in the famous poem *L'Infinito* where, in the words of Professor Bickersteth, 'the man becomes one with his dream, and the world of space and time disappears—*s'annega il pensier mio*—in the Infinite', where there occurs a 'wrecking of the real in the ideal'. The aspiration towards companionship in a society of sensitive beings is expressed in a letter to his friend Jacopssen: 'En vérité, mon cher ami, le monde ne connaît pas ses véritables intérêts. Je conviendrai, si l'on veut, que la vertu, comme tout ce qui est beau et tout ce qui est grand, ne soit qu'une illusion. Mais si cette illusion était commune, si tous les hommes croyaient et voulaient être vertueux; s'ils étaient compatissans, bienfaisans, généreux, magnanimes, pleins d'enthousiasme; en un mot, si tout le monde était sensible (car je ne fais aucune différence de la sensibilité à ce qu'on appelle vertu) n'en serait-on pas plus heureux? Chaque individu n'en trouverait-il pas mille ressources dans la société? Celle-ci ne devrait-elle pas s'appliquer à réaliser les illusions autant qu'il lui serait possible, puisque le bonheur de l'homme ne peut consister dans ce qui est réel?'

But the nineteenth century, *secol superbo e sciocco*,[1] with its faith in material progress and science, is travelling precisely in the opposite direction. Never were the errors of the intellect more prevalent and the errors of the imagination less cultivated. As unity is denied him, the poet can only retire into his own mind and cling to an image divorced from reality, create a 'double' of the real world. 'To the sensitive and imaginative man', he writes in the *Zibaldone*, 'who lives, as I have for long lived, feeling continuously and imagining, the world and its objects are in a sense double. He may see with his eyes a tower, a landscape; hear with his ears the sound of a bell: and at the same time in his imagination he will see another tower, another landscape, he will hear another sound. In this second kind of object is situated all the beauty and pleasure of things. Sad is the life (and such is life usually) which does not see, does not hear other than simple objects, solely the ones which sensation communicates to the eyes and other senses.' 'Could I but preserve the lofty vision,'

[1] Stupid and proud century.

he cries in *Alla sua donna*. For the image suffices in the absence of the real:

E potess'io
Nel secol tetro e in quest'aer nefando
L'alta specie serbar; che dell'imago
Poichè del ver m'è tolto, assai m'appago.

La sua donna, the *cara beltà*, is the ideal woman that cannot be found on earth. And the image, unless it be tied to the earth, is an evanescent thing, soon to be dispersed by the advent of truth:

A noi ti vieta
Il vero appena è giunto
O caro immaginar . . .
(*Ad Angelo Mai*)

But the absolute 'no' to life uttered by Brutus here becomes an 'if'. If the imagination were always operative, if one could substitute the ideal for the real, happiness would be possible. 'Il n'appartient qu'à l'imagination de procurer à l'homme la seule espèce de bonheur positif dont il soit capable,' we read in the letter to Jacopssen. 'C'est la véritable sagesse de chercher le bonheur dans l'idéal comme vous faites. Pour moi, je regrette le temps où il m'était permis de l'y chercher, et je vois avec une sorte d'effroi que mon imagination devient stérile et me refuse tous les secours qu'elle me prêtait autrefois.' Happy is the man, he will write three years later in the *Epistle to Count Carlo Pepoli*, who in old age as in youth can, deep in his thought, make nature beautiful, make death and the desert live:

Ben mille volte
Fortunato colui che la caduca
Virtù del caro immaginar non perde
Per volger d'anni; a cui serbare eterna
La gioventù del cor diedero i fati;
Che nella ferma e nella stanca etade,
Cosí come solea nell'età verde,
In suo chiuso pensier natura abbella,
Morte, deserto avviva.

Given the *caro immaginar*, it is possible for a brief moment to bring back to life the world which died with youth, to portray the beauty which rarely appears in the world, 'Il bel che raro e scarso e fuggitivo appar nel mondo'. If the vivifying spirit is lacking (and this is the conclusion of the poem), then all will be as dead, life a succession of idle pursuits, *noia immortale* the victor in an unequal struggle.

The outcome of the sterility of which Leopardi had complained in 1823 was the *Operette Morali*, a work in prose. When he again wrote in verse in 1826 it was again to stress his sterility and his dedication to that 'bitter truth', *l'acerbo vero*, which he had always combated. 'I seek nothing but the truth which I have so hated and detested,' he wrote to his friend Giordani in 1825. When the spirit is dead, nature becomes a spectacle, an object for study. This state, which had seemed intolerable to his Sappho, Leopardi now accepts with equanimity.

But the truth is that neither at the time of Sappho's lament nor in the 'peace of old age', as he called his present state, had Leopardi ever felt himself completely abandoned by illusion. For that which is such an inextricable part of our nature cannot be entirely effaced. 'Although we are greatly changed', says his Plotinus refuting Porphyrius' arguments in favour of suicide, 'and the power of nature within us is much lessened, we are not so altered but that much of our former self remains, and our primitive nature is not quite stifled within us. . . . And I assure you that neither disgust of life, nor despair, nor the sense of the nullity of things, the vanity of all anxiety and the insignificance of man, nor hatred of the world and oneself are of long duration; although such dispositions of mind are perfectly reasonable and the contrary unreasonable. For our physical condition changes momentarily in more or less degree; and often without any special cause life endears itself to us again, and new hopes give brightness to human things, which once more seem worthy of our care, not indeed to the intellect, but, so to speak, to the sense of spirit.'

The 'truth' revealed by the intellect is for ever denied by the sense of spirit; the imagination will for ever build its own world and a 'double', an 'imago' will exist side by side with the real. The poet, the most sensitive among men, will continue to bring life to 'death and the desert'; by feeling intensely he will make of his very *noia*, which is the negation of life, a thing of life. 'Works of genius', he writes in the *Zibaldone*, 'have this peculiarity that, even when they represent the nothingness of things, even when they clearly demonstrate and make us feel the inevitable unhappiness of life, when they express the most terrible mood of despair, yet to a great mind, even though it may be in a state of extreme depression, disillusionment, blankness, *noia*, and weariness of life, or in the bitterest and most paralysing misfortunes . . . they always serve as a consolation, rekindle enthusiasm; and though they treat and represent no other subject than death, they restore to such a mind, at least momentarily, that life which it had lost. Consequently that which when seen in the reality of things stabs and kills the soul, when seen in imitation or in any other way in works of genius . . . opens the heart and restores it to life. In any case, just as the author, while describing and feeling so strongly the emptiness of illusions, yet retained all the time a great fund of illusion, and clearly proved that he did, by so eagerly describing their emptiness; likewise the reader, however much undeceived both by himself and by what he reads, is yet drawn by the author into that very deceit and illusion latent in the most intimate recesses of the spirit which he was searching. . . . The very contemplation of nothingness is a thing in these works which seems to enlarge the soul of the reader, to exalt it and satisfy it with itself and its own despair. . . . Moreover, the feeling of nothingness is the feeling of a dead and death-inflicting thing. But if this feeling is alive . . . its liveliness prevails in the mind of the reader over the nothingness of the thing which it makes him feel, and the soul receives life, if only for a moment, from the very violence with which it feels the perpetual death of things and its own death.'

As we have seen, Leopardi had long lamented his inability to believe in the old illusions, yet he had noted their persistence against all reason. In spite of disbelief, the old fancies, *gl'inganni aperti e noti*, still retain their power. This is the theme of *Il Risorgimento*, the poem which marked the end of the priod of sterility and was the forerunner of a series of masterpieces. Written at Pisa in April 1828, during an almost happy interlude in a life of bitter struggles against ill-health and financial dependence, it describes the death and resurgence of feeling. It is the illustration of the words of his Plotinus: 'Life endears itself to us again'. Like the exhausted swimmer who once again feels the air fill his lungs, Leopardi exults in feeling itself, in the illusion which, although it knows itself to be a mere illusion, empty of content, can still fill the soul with joy. His *vaghe immagini* do not correspond to the truth, yet he *feels* them within him and it is *as if* they were true. The heart lives:

Da te, mio cor, quest'ultimo
Spirto e l'ardor natio,
Ogni conforto mio
Solo da te mi vien.[1]

But such a state of grace is necessarily short-lived. 'Où trouver un objet qui le satisfasse?' he had written in the already-quoted letter. Where can he find an object to contain this infinite surge of feeling? Not in the finite world, but in his own world of memories, in the infinite world of youth where image and reality were one. Thus, in the second group of Idylls, his greatest poems, Leopardi returns to that 'beatific age' when, living in hope, he was all that his image was, when he could create his own future:

. . . arcani mondi, arcana
Felicità fingendo al viver mio!

Hope created the *arcani mondi*, the 'unknown worlds'; memory can re-create them, for memory is to the past what hope is to the future. The Recanati of the Idylls is an *imago* of his birthplace; Silvia and Nerina an *imago* of the girls he had seen from his window or during his walks, at once the inhabitants and the symbols of that 'beatific' world of youth. Alive and radiant, cut off on the threshold, they represent hope and the blighting of hope. Never has the peculiar quality of adolescence been expressed with such perfection. A time of strife—*di contenti, d'angosce e di desio*—it has a radiance, a life which are never recaptured in later years (when present reality has a hold on us); a double radiance here, illumined as it is by the hope that was its essence and the light shed by memory. Past hopes and present aspirations mingle to form a poetic world with which the real world—the present—is contrasted:

Qui non è cosa
Ch'io vegga o senta, onde un'immagin dentro
Non torni, e un dolce rimembrar non sorga;
Dolce per sé, ma con dolor sottentra
Il pensier del presente, un van desio
Del passato, ancor tristo, e il dire: io fui.[2]

[1] From you, my heart, this last spirit and native ardour and all consolation, from you alone proceed.

[2] In this spot nothing do I see or hear but an image returns to my mind and a sweet memory arises: sweet in itself, but painfully the thought of the present intrudes: a vain desire for the past, however sad; and the voice: I was.

No holiday will follow your Saturday, he tells the peasants in *Il Sabato del Villaggio*, for the holiday exists only in your mind, in your anticipation of it. All the joy of life is in the eve.

The *Canto notturno d'un pastore errante dell'Asia*, perhaps the greatest lyric in the Italian language, is *il pensier del presente*, the clear vision of man's state on earth, the expression of 'nothingness' deeply felt and transmuted into poetry. We might apply to it Leopardi's own words, already quoted: 'The very contemplation of nothingness is a thing in these works which seems to enlarge the soul of the reader, to exalt it and satisfy it with itself and its own despair'. It is the evocation of the void which had always been before him: the immensity of time and space, the passing of all things which had struck him with terror and anguish during the sleepless nights of his youth and which he had described in the first Idylls. Man, represented by a shepherd in a vast lonely desert, addresses the moon, *solinga, eterna peregrina*. Perhaps she, being immortal, knows the answer to man's eternal questions, the aim of a life full of suffering leading to a 'horrid immense abyss', the reason for the apparently aimless movement of the world and the firmament, the reason why the shepherd, unlike his flock which rests contentedly in the shade, can find no solace in nature:

Dimmi, o luna: a che vale
Al pastor la sua vita,
La vostra vita a voi? dimmi: ove tende
Questo vagar mio breve,
Il tuo corso immortale?
. . . .
E tu certo comprendi
Il perchè delle cose, e vedi il frutto
Del mattin, della sera,
Del tacito, infinito andar del tempo.
. . . .
E quando miro in cielo arder le stelle;
Dico fra me pensando:
A che tante facelle?
Che fa l'aria infinita, e quel profondo
Infinito seren? che vuol dir questa
Solitudine immensa? ed io che sono?[1]

[1] See footnote on facing page.

The shepherd receives no answer and the poem ends with a question. For, the poet implies, no answer can come to us from above. Infinity, symbolized by the moon, has no relation to man. Its eternal movement and man's brief course are parallels which never meet. Vast spaces, mystery surround man, a small point in the infinity of space. In moments of ecstasy, such as the one described in *l'Infinito*, he seems to be lifted out of his mortal frame and to partake for an instant of that infinity. Then the immense silence and the trees rustling in the wind, the dead seasons and the sound of the present are not antagonistic but are merged into one; the poet's thought is drowned in the immensity and experiences a 'sweet shipwreck':

Cosi tra questa
Immensità s'annega il pensier mio
E il naufragar m'è dolce in questo mare.

Elevated above himself, illumined by a sort of super-illusion, he is for a moment like a god contemplating the world with new eyes; only to experience a new descent and a new separation.

The opposite mood to that of the shepherd is again expressed in the two poems which follow. *Il Pensiero dominante* and *Amore e Morte* sprang from his passion for Fanny Targioni-Tozzetti, the Aspasia of his later poem; passion which elevated him above the mortal state into a 'new immensity', a 'paradise', where 'wandering under an unaccustomed light', he forgot his earthly condition and lost all trace of reality:

Che mondo mai, che nova
Immensità, che paradiso è quello
Là dove spesso il tuo superbo incanto
Parmi innalzar! Dov'io,
Sott'altra luce che l'usata errando,
Il mio terreno stato
E tutto quanto il ver pongo in oblio.

[1] Tell me, o moon, what avails his life to the shepherd, your life to you? Tell me: where tends my brief wandering, your immortal course?

And you certainly comprehend the wherefore of things and you see the fruit of morning and evening, of the silent, infinite flow of time.

And when I contemplate the stars burning in the sky, I ask myself: why so many sparkling fires? Why the infinite air and that deep, infinite purity? What means this immense solitude? And what am I?

This is the kind of experience of which, in the *History of the Human Race*, he had said: 'When he (Love, son of celestial Venus) comes on earth, he chooses the tender and noble hearts of the most generous and magnanimous persons. Here he remains for a short time, diffusing in them so strange and wondrous a sweetness, and inspiring them with affections so lofty and vigorous, that they then experience what is entirely new to mankind, *the substance rather than the semblance of happiness*.'

We have seen that for Leopardi supreme happiness is given only when the real is viewed with the eyes of the imagination, when feeling transfigures the world. The rarity and briefness of such experiences, the sway that reality has over man, the impossibility of finding on earth the equivalent of the *imago*—this has been his lament throughout the *Canti*. In *Il Risorgimento* he had rejoiced in feeling alone, in the illusion known to be an illusion which, although it finds no corresponding object, yet transfigures all it encounters. In *Il Pensiero dominante* Leopardi is on the verge of a new experience: of the fulfilment which had always eluded him. For, unlike the dream figures he has hitherto worshipped, a real woman fills his imagination, giving and receiving light. For the first time there exists no disparity between his vision and the earthly object; the *angelica beltade* lives not only in his mind but on earth, the *imago* finally held will abide with him eternally:

E tu per certo, o mio pensier, tu solo
Vitale ai giorni miei,
Cagion diletta d'infiniti affanni,
Meco sarai per morte a un tempo spento:
Ch'a vivi segni dentro l'alma io sento
Che in perpetuo signor dato mi sei.[1]

I said Leopardi was *on the verge* of a new experience. For the poem is called *Il Pensiero dominante* and, as has often been pointed out, the poet still addresses his thought rather than the woman. He stands midway between the old world of disunity and a new world of unity in which he cannot fully believe. His experience is now seen

[1] And you, certainly, my thought, you who alone are vital to my days, beloved cause of infinite cares, will remain with me until my death: for in my soul I perceive clear signs that you are to be my perpetual master.

as real, now as a 'dream similar to the dreams of the immortals'. But if it be a dream, the poet says, it is one so powerful, so steadfast against the assaults of reason that it is one with truth, the 'substance' and not the 'semblance'.

In order to experience such a moment of *beatitudine* a lifetime of suffering was well worth while. All past torments come into focus. All opposites are reconciled in this new realization of the meaning of life:

> Pregio non ha, non ha ragion la vita
> Se non per lui, per lui ch'all uomo è tutto;
> Sola discolpa al fato,
> Che noi mortali in terra
> Pose a tanto patir senz'altro frutto.[1]

As life is transfigured by love, so is death. The *abisso orrido immenso* which had appeared to the clear-sighted shepherd, the Nirvana, the state free from pain and tedium for which the poet had longed, become, in *Amore e Morte*, *bella morte pietosa*, the twin of love, the comforter of every noble heart. Made greater by love, the soul is enabled to contemplate existence and death from a new height. Infusing his feeling into the whole of creation, he becomes again, like the Ancients, 'wise in action and not in vain thoughts', he acquires a more than human strength for the battle against fate in which every *nobil natura* must engage. Death, the deliverer from pain, when it comes, will find him 'fully armed and at war with fate':

> Me certo troverai, qual si sia l'ora
> Che tu le penne al mio pregar dispieghi,
> Erta la fronte, armato,
> E renitente al fato.

In these two poems we have an affirmation of life which was implicit in all previous negations. In so far as we love we are masters of the world and of fate.

But what if that strength fails and the illusion, although a 'dream of the immortals', proves to be mortal? Then nothing remains but

[1] No value, no reason has life except by it, for it is all to man; the only justification of fate which placed us mortals on earth to suffer otherwise so fruitlessly.

man alone, disarmed but still defiant, against the 'ugly power which operates against us', and the 'infinite vanity of all things':

> Omai disprezza
> Te, la natura, il brutto
> Poter che, ascoso, a comun danno impera,
> E l'infinita vanità del tutto.

These are the closing lines of *A sè stesso*, the record of a disaster. Nature, no longer merely indifferent, is now identified with Arimane, the Power of Evil, the hostile ruler of mankind. 'Fate gave our species no other gift than death.' Yet it is not to death that he turns, but rather to the stoical defiance of fate which he had voiced in *Amore e Morte* and, years before, in the *Dialogue between Tristan and a friend*. 'To look steadily on the desert of life, to hide no part of our unhappiness. . . . This philosophy . . . gives the courageous man the proud satisfaction of being able to rend asunder the cloak that conceals the hidden and mysterious cruelty of human destiny.'

In order to defy fate 'with head erect and fully armed', a preliminary shedding of all prejudice and error is necessary. In his own case, he must brush aside the error into which he had fallen and which consisted in identifying the real, in the person of Fanny, with the ideal image of his mind. In *Aspasia* he attempts to return to the dualism of *Alla sua donna*, an idealism which denies value to all but the vivifying spirit. A beautiful woman, he says, may so bewitch men that they believe it is she whom they love, but in truth they continue to love their own ideal. 'Not you I loved,' he says, 'but the Goddess who once had life, now a sepulchre in my heart. It was the Goddess I contemplated in your eyes and, having from the beginning seen clearly through your artifice and fraud, for her I bore long and hard slavery.' *Me di me privo* is the way in which he describes his slavery as he struggles to rid himself of his physical love for the very real Aspasia, to transform her into an *imago* and return to the free world of ideas. Life without love is 'a starless night in midwinter', *notte senza stelle a mezzo il verno*; but there is 'proud satisfaction' in freedom from what had been a form of slavery because based on an error, in the return to a clear vision of things.

In *Sopra il ritratto di una bella donna*, the lady, once fair, now turned to mud and bones, a foul and sad sight, reflects the violent changes to which man is subjected and, in particular, his own unhappy experience. 'Thus does fate reduce that which seemed to us the most living image of heaven.' Such is the mortal state. One day inspired by beauty, fount of sublime thoughts and noble feelings which seem to offer a promise of 'superhuman fates, fortunate reigns and golden worlds':

Oggi d'eccelsi, immensi
Pensieri e sensi inenarrabil fonte,
Beltà grandeggia, e pare,
Quale splendor vibrato
Da natura immortal su queste arene,
Di sovrumani fati,
Di fortunati regni e d'aurei mondi
Segno e sicura speme
Dare al mortale stato.

Tomorrow the slightest of causes will destroy that Paradise in an instant and transform the angelic vision into a 'foul sight, abominable, abject'. What then is man? If wholly worthless, mere dust and shade, why such lofty thoughts? he asks, echoing Pascal. If partly noble, why are his worthiest thoughts and feelings aroused and quenched by such ignoble causes?

Natura umana, or come
Se frale in tutto e vile
Se polve ed ombra sei, tant'alto senti?
Se in parte anco gentile,
Come i piu degni tuoi moti e pensieri
Son cosí di leggieri
Da sí basse cagioni e desti e spenti?

Unlike Pascal, Leopardi leaves the question unanswered. It is an 'eternal mystery of our being', *misterio eterno dell'esser nostro*. Life is an eternal and inexplicable ebb and flow. Very early in life Leopardi had rejected the Christian view or indeed any definite view of man's ultimate destiny. Although he belongs to his century and his accent is romantic and religious, he is drawn to the eighteenth-century *Philosophes* whose agnosticism serves to dissipate dogmatism and the 'errors of the intellect'. To the nineteenth, 'proud and stupid century', he opposes the eighteenth, the century of enlightenment.

'Such is life usually,' Leopardi had said of the real, as opposed to the imagined, existence. Yet, in the *notte senza stelle a mezzo il verno* one light remains: the comfort of human companionship and love. Why, he asks in *Sopra un Basso Rilievo antico sepolcrale*, does death, our liberator, come to us in funereal garb? Why do we fear the port more than the storm? Because Nature, who cares not for us, has decreed that our end too must be sad and that, in dying, we must abandon those we love. His Plotinus, when urging Porphyrius to abandon his project of suicide, had said: 'Do not wish to be the cause of such great sorrow to your good friends who love you with all their soul. . . . Let us live, dear Porphyrius, and console each other. Let us not refuse our share of the sufferings of humanity, apportioned to us by destiny. Let us cling to each other with mutual encouragement, and hand in hand strengthen one another better to bear the troubles of life. . . . In the last hour our friends and companions will comfort us, and we shall be gladdened by the thought that after death we shall still live in their memory and be loved by them.'

Thus, after his descent from the great heights of *Il Pensiero dominante*, Leopardi turned again to life, but to life on another plane, to life in what he called the desert. The ideal existence he had, except in rare moments, found impossible of attainment. The other existence—the real—he had at first rejected. But very soon he had come to see in man's awareness, in his acceptance of fate, the greatest proof of his nobility:

> Nobil natura è quella
> Ch'a sollevar s'ardisce
> Gli occhi mortali incontra
> Al comun fato, e che con franca lingua,
> Nulla al ver detraendo,
> Confessa il mal che ci fu dato in sorte.[1]

'Nothing demonstrates more clearly the power and greatness of the human intellect,' he writes in the *Zibaldone*, 'the loftiness and nobility of man, than his power of knowing and entirely comprehending his smallness. When he, considering the plurality of the

[1] Noble spirit is he who dares to confront with mortal eyes our common fate and who, with frank speech, subtracting nothing from the truth, avows the evil which has been given us for our portion.

worlds, feels himself as the infinitesimal part of a globe that is the smallest part of one of the infinite systems that make up the World, and in this consideration he marvels at his smallness . . . is almost one with nothingness and almost loses himself in the incomprehensible vastness of existence; then with this act and with this thought he gives the greatest proof possible of his nobility, of the strength and immense capacity of his mind, which, enclosed in so small and infinitesimal a being, has attained to the comprehension of things so superior to his nature, and can embrace and contain within his thought this same immensity of existence and of things.'

La Ginestra, the long philosophical poem written shortly before his death in 1837, is a breviary of stoicism and love. To the man of his century with his belief in progress, his arrogance and his delusions of self-sufficiency, he opposes the man who comprehends his smallness, the man whom, like Pascal's *faible roseau*, the whole universe conspires to destroy. Only when men realize this fact will they cease to fight amongst themselves and unite in brotherhood against their common enemy, fate. The *ginestra*, the broom, *fior gentile* of the desert, growing in the shadow of Vesuvius where once-prosperous cities lie buried, will one day be obliged to bow its head before the torrent of lava, a head never yet lowered in cowardly supplication nor held erect in frantic pride towards the stars. Among the ruins, as though pitying the sufferings of others, it sends up to heaven a sweet scent that 'consoles the desert':

Or tutto intorno
Una ruina involve,
Dove tu siedi, o fior gentile, e quasi
I danni altrui commiserando, al cielo
Di dolcissimo odor mandi un profumo
Che il deserto consola.

The *odorata ginestra* is Leopardi's last happy symbol, containing in itself a last vision of man and his destiny. Tenacious and sweet-scented, it is the image of the *nobil natura* as he conceived it, stoical and loving. Man has to wage a lifelong battle against fate. Let him then, being fully conscious of its power, accept the challenge, and, by the power of love, comfort and transform the waste land.

RONALD MASON

NOTES FOR AN ESTIMATE OF PEACOCK

THIS opinionated and Epicurean eccentric has found himself a niche. He is appreciated especially by a cultivated, rather restricted set of readers who find an instinctive response in their temperaments to his dogmatic and often arbitrary assertions. Lawyers read him, liberal clergymen, higher civil servants, the professional classes, the older men of letters. The values that he proclaims satisfy their relaxation very well. He is a bit of a curiosity, an isolated specimen, a writer whom it tickles their fancy to read and their vanity to have read. A little nervous about the form society is to take and the place they are going to take in it, they are very much heartened by the gusto with which Peacock's violent common sense reinforces their innermost articles of faith. He pleases this class immensely, in the same way that Trollope pleases them, by his implicit insistence on the foundations on which they themselves are based, and by his bull-like activities in the china-shop of Idiosyncrasy. They sense in idiosyncrasy a threat to stability; and Peacock's invigorating forthright satire smashes to their satisfaction the idiosyncrasy and the threat. Thus he is read by them appreciatively, not critically. Outside this circle he has no very wide public.

Yet it is undoubtedly worth the effort to break through this crust of prejudice to find out what there is in him besides this protective aggressiveness. Nowadays when critics are apt to seize mercilessly upon a writer's confessed or implied ideology before deciding whether his creative work is to be admitted to criticism or not, it is not so easy as it used to be to disinter the secret of the durability of a man like Peacock from the wreckage of his social or political heresies. It is time we were reminded that neither Peacock nor Trollope have lived so long as they have on the strength of comfortable conservatism alone. There was a period of literary criticism —it is all over now—when books and their authors were judged almost solely on their capacity for imparting enjoyment. Of this school of critics Saintsbury was the sanest and most appreciative; and if you want to read a full and fair recital of Peacock's richness, his abiding attraction, you will find Saintsbury's introductions to the novels, reprinted in his *Prefaces and Essays*, unequalled in their own class as a benevolent appreciation of the man and his work. A very important job was done by the appreciative school of critics; they whetted the immediate appetites in a way that no access of sophistication has been able to improve on; and the limitation of that school is not that their criticism lacked acuteness or even profundity, but that the standards they set and the methods they employed could not readily take into account just those factors of historical and social relevance that are essential to the adjustment of the author's literary importance. Had he relevance to his age? If so, how? If his age is in any way related to our own, how may he be helpfully aligned to that relation? And so on. Questions of this sort set a figure more solidly in the round, when adequately answered, than any amount of appreciative quotation can do. The appreciative critics provide a very valuable, but only a partial, answer to the general inquisitiveness which we feel about a good writer. Peacock has been well enough served by them; it is time he was examined in a perspective which they did not afford him; and a recent second reading of the novels has suggested to me that the isolation and comparative obscurity in which he exists today is mainly referable to the lack of any serious attempt to discuss him objectively. He has been left to his circle of willing appreciators, a circle which for social and historical reasons is growing narrower. This is a tentative attempt to break out of it.

A salient characteristic of his work will serve as a sign of its inner nature; an inflexible rigidity of style. He did not develop; it is virtually impossible to guess right at the source of any context selected at random from any of his books, so mature was his style at the beginning of his career and so little had it altered at the end. Somebody said of the younger Pitt, 'He never grew, he was cast'. There is about the temperament and work of Peacock this rigidity, as of cast metal; and the other quality of cast iron, brittleness, is perceptibly, though less strongly, implicit in his style. To remain constant for fifty years shows either superhuman application or incorrigible imperviousness to externals; and considering that he published his first novel, *Headlong Hall*, before Jane Austen died, and his last, *Gryll Grange*, after Bernard Shaw was born, his close adherence to the model he built up for himself can be attributed only to an innate permanent value which change could not affect—unless to a secret obstinacy. (He wrote *Gryll Grange* at 75; and this is at once a wonder and a warning. Sophocles, Shaw, Melville, Landor, Peacock—the list is distinguished but short. Septuagenarians with the *cacoethes scribendi* should study these illustrious examples before going and doing likewise.)

Granted that the stock mould that he kept by him all his life was a formality only, and that we are supposed to be looking beyond formalities—nevertheless we cannot escape the inference that the ideas which were the central dynamic of his creativeness were cast in a stock mould too. Alternatively we could legitimately suspect that there were no ideas, but only a brilliance of original form, many times reproduced. This process has served a good many minor novelists, successful after their kind; did Peacock use spurious methods to kid his way to a reputation which, though not major, is at least illustrious?

It is true enough that what is left of his fame today is not a residue of great creations, separate works of art, but of a personality expressing itself through arbitrary incidental forms. His books are not entities, independent once the navel-string has been severed. We don't say, 'Ah, that reminds me of something in *Nightmare Abbey*', as we might say, 'That reminds me of something in *Esmond*, or *Treasure Island*, or *Moby Dick*, or *Mr. Polly*'. We say instead, 'That reminds me of something in Peacock'. And although that doesn't amount to a final criticism, one way or the other, it cannot help indicating the essential subordination of the work produced to the character of the author producing it. In this way a man may perpetuate character, but not art. And when from this premiss we turn to examine the several novels, it becomes only too evident that the essential individuality, which a single work must have if it is to exist in its own right at all, is present in the temper of his work but absent from the forms in which he expressed that temper. There is none of that dramatic progress from a given point to a given point which is part of the minimum requirement of the novel; and deprived of the *shape* without which separate existence is not possible, these novels remain random lengths of sample Peacock, and do not amount to art.

This does not, of course, invalidate Peacock; it limits our field of search, that is all, since as a pure novelist we can write him off. It becomes clear that his appreciative readers are appreciating him, not the books he has written. But it would also be misleading to suggest, as I may have seemed to be suggesting, that because his novels are shapeless conventionalities it is his thought alone that makes him worth reading. His peculiar liveliness came from other sources as well as from the philosophical ones. Refer back to the class I have indicated as echoing his sentiments. They are generally impatient of novels of ideas. Henry James, for example, E. M. Forster, Edward Upward, Rex Warner, find little response from them. Using these readers as a touchstone, there must be some quality we can find in Peacock which enables him to transmit his own very definite vitality to them other than through the medium of the interplay of ideas. Take away shape from a novel, take away all but the most conventional plot, and what have you left? With Dickens, at any rate, miraculous characters. With Peacock it is not so easy to give an answer. Good satire needs more than naked ideas, and their effectiveness depends a lot on the sort of flesh and blood they are dressed up in.

It is therefore a little disconcerting to find that Peacock does not push his characters much beyond the type stage. These distinctive but obedient puppets do not vary from book to book, any more than the arbitrary antics through which they are put vary either. For the most part the novels are animated *causeries* prinked out with lively comment; the similarity of most of the titles, *Melincourt*, *Headlong Hall*, *Nightmare Abbey*, *Crotchet Castle*, *Gryll Grange*, reflects inevitably the similarity of theme and treatment. Peacock assembles his characters in a convenient collection under one roof, hustles them as quickly and as often as he can into the presence of food and drink, and simply leaves them to talk. The author retires; each protagonist is permitted to speak under the bare signpost of his name in capitals, and in each speech we find displayed in caricature a different humour. All the old tricks of Jonsonian or Restoration comedy are resurrected, and each character is named and invested with the minimum of individuality required for the exercise of the foible he is embodying. Foster, Escot and Jenkison in *Headlong Hall* represent the three standards of optimism, pessimism and the complacent halfway conservatism between the two, and none of the three utters a word throughout to conflict with, or even significantly to amplify, the doctrine which is his only source of existence. Furthermore when Peacock extends his satire to individuals rather than to types, the frequency of his success, as in the delicious Flosky caricature of Coleridge in *Nightmare Abbey*, has rather obscured the essential similarity between his use of 'humours' and his use of individual caricature. Escot is the deteriorationist and nothing else, and nobody gains or loses by his deteriorationism; Flosky is Coleridge and nobody else, and nobody gains or loses by his Estesianism. He is in as complete a vacuum as Escot. He performs for our diversion his ordained and patterned idiosyncrasy, and stops when he is turned off. He is funny in his own vacuum, as Escot, more soberly, is funny in his. The tragedy of Peacock's characters is that not one of them ever hears one word that any other one is saying. They are little isolated bits of Peacock himself, or of Peacock's enemies, and they enunciate their forthright monologues, pause for breath, and resume at the correct interval. Nothing that has passed meanwhile interests or affects them. In this they differ from the protagonists in Restoration drama, who are at least aware of the complex convention in which they are employed, are in fact breathlessly anxious to conform to it, like earnest participants in the lancers; and also from characters in such drama as Shaw's, where 'types' who are introduced do at least play an integral part in the development of the play and often end by being seen in the round, contributing idiosyncrasy to the action and deriving independence from the drama. All this is foreign to Peacock; his art lacks this creative integration. His plots do not affect his characters; his characters do not affect his plots. The characters spin independently, on their own individual axes; the stories, such as they are, proceed unobtrusively without them. The development shown in *Gryll Grange*, where the plot is in part managed by the characters themselves, is noteworthy but elementary; and the story by itself would not arrest attention in a women's magazine.

It would be unsound to deduce from this that his characters are not effective or memorable. Many of them are. Seithenyn, for example, is the only element of life in *The Misfortunes of Elphin* and the only thing apart from *The War Song of Dinas Vawr* that is ultimately worth saving out of that curiously dull book. Magnificently outrageous, he propels himself and the novel he revives into an isolated immortality. He is of Dickensian mould and Peacock either could not or would not duplicate him. He is the only personality Peacock ever invented; for Peacock's other memorable characters startle and please not by their individualities, but by the vigour with which they prosecute their duty, conform to type, vitalize the flat pattern; and, of course, by the volubility of their assertions. Chief among the most successful of the species is the row of eloquent and self-indulgent divines, who have a poor send-off with Dr. Gaster in *Headlong Hall*, but culminate in Folliott and Opimian and are thereby well justified of their preferment. Much of a piece in essentials, they all of them lay down comfortable dogmas, buzz the bottle and quote the late Greek poets; Folliott in *Crotchet Castle* is usually the favourite, but certain pedantries in my constitution have always inclined me to Opimian in *Gryll Grange*. With their Nonnus and their Madeira and their benevolent but implacable Toryism, they form a solid phalanx of pure Peacocks; and delightful as they cannot help being, the value of the creation of such characters is lessened by easy identification with the author.

Peacock was without the enormous vitality that made Dickens's very unevenness memorable, that was able to sustain such comparative failures as Uriah Heep and Mark Tapley into the permanence of household words. Peacock's energy limited itself to wit; and where he managed it best he wrote scenes and paragraphs that Dickens might have signed his name to, like the classic rediscovery of Seithenyn, or a sidelong cynical crack that could have flicked at you out of *Pickwick*:

'. . . an orphan niece, who had made a runaway love-match with an Irish officer. The lady's fortune disappeared in the first year; love, by a natural consequence, disappeared in the second; the Irishman himself, by a still more natural consequence, disappeared in the third.'

Yet he was not cut out like Dickens to sustain creativeness; and his lesser powers have in greater prominence his lesser imperfections.

It is not his characters, then, or even his types, that give Peacock life; they are too occasional and spasmodic for that. His work, if it were sustained by their presence alone, would be much more uneven than it is; in fact, its quality has a consistency about it that would be remarkable if it were not simple to account for it by the salutary rigour that a real knowledge of the classics imparts to self-criticism. The name of A. E. Housman rises spontaneously as a parallel. A true classical scholar turning to creative work will never, assuming him to have genuine talent, write rubbish. Peacock never did, and that helps to preserve safely all that is valuable in his achievement.

There is only one more way to turn now that his characters have failed us, as they do in all but memorable isolated actions, and that is to the ideas embodied in his books. Here we are on rather more rewarding ground, as a personality emerges; a personality whose positive value, once we can gauge it, will help to measure the validity and extent of his position and influence in literature. The prescription is simple: accept the *dicta* of Peacock's favourite characters as corresponding to his own opinions, and for the rest reckon generally that the more far-fetched and ridiculous he makes a set of postulates appear, the more violently he is opposed to them. Flosky's transcendental obscurantism and that of Mr. Mystic in *Melincourt*, also drawn off Coleridge, Cranium's craniology, Seithenyn's *laisser-faire* conservatism, the toadyism of the particular character in nearly every novel who is intended to represent Southey—all these are contrasted understandably with the more acceptable qualities of Peacock's favourite divines, among whom Friar Michael of *Maid Marian* (that neglected but refreshing exercise in satiric romance) occupies a place less pontifical, not to say parasitical, than his black-coated brethren. The distinctions of doctrine are broad enough to enable us to extract from these contrasts a fairly comprehensive set of conclusions on Peacock's general outlook, and if we set him in the context of his age we can better judge whether that outlook had any constructive result when he translated it into words.

You have to remember that this man lived through one of the most turbulent periods in history and chose to write satire as his expression of his considered opinions. He lived as a conscious contemporary of the French Revolution, the Napoleonic Wars, the Romantic Revival, the Corn Laws, the Reform Act, Chartism, the Communist Manifesto, the Great Exhibition, the Crimean War, *The Origin of Species*, the rapid development of the internal combustion engine, the Oxford Movement and the first faint suggestions of Pre-Raphaelitism. Of very few of these things does he appear to be aware. Now Jane Austen, writing in the middle of the Napoleonic Wars, was perfectly justified in sticking to her drawing-room so long as she was consistent about it; but Peacock, swivelling a baleful eye on developments in modern society which happened to displease him, laid about him on a national scale while retaining the prejudices and the predilections of a Regency buck like Creevey. And Peacock, who had ten times the learning and ten times the wit of Creevey, and a capacity for satiric and humorous writing that placed him for short passages in the company of Dickens, lost half his value by this stubborn parochialism. It is not difficult to accuse and convict him of deliberate ignorances.

Yet his awareness shows up startlingly at times, like sudden clear patches in fog. Nothing could be better than the election racket in *Melincourt*, where the gentlemanly orang-outang gets safely returned to Parliament; there is a savour of Gilbert in this, and more than a savour of Dickens again. Eatanswill was not conceived for another twenty years, nor the election in *Middlemarch* (whose more rational realism does not blunt its telling effectiveness) for another fifty or so. Peacock was wide awake to the rotten state of the franchise, and in *Melincourt* he ran the topic neatly in harness with a genial bullyragging of Monboddo's surprisingly perceptive theories on the descent of man and Rousseau's commonly misrepresented conception of the noble savage. Sir Oran Haut-ton is a brilliant idea and a deftly managed character, being in fact the brightest spot in Peacock's most tedious novel; and as there is no reason to suppose that Peacock trusted Darwin any further than he trusted Monboddo, we need not chuckle over Peacock's presumptive loss of countenance on the publication of *The Origin of Species*. Again, there could be no neater summary of articulate Toryism, as lively (or as deadly) in the 1820's as in the 1940's, than in Seithenyn's bibulous defence of the policy of the guardians of the embankment in face of the rising floods:

'The parts that are rotten give elasticity to those that are sound; they give them elasticity, elasticity, elasticity. If it were all sound, it would break by its own obstinate stiffness; the soundness is checked by the rottenness, and the stiffness is balanced by the elasticity. There is nothing so dangerous as innovation. . . . This immortal work has stood for centuries and will stand for centuries more, if we let it alone. It is well; it works well; let well alone. . . . It was half rotten when I was born, and that is a conclusive reason why it should be three parts rotten when I die.'

That is, of course, magnificent; I suppose it has its equal in Falstaff, but not in many other contexts that I can think of. The piercing sanity that could evolve that devastating comment has its obvious application to our far more perilous plight today; and as a parallel piece of clear good sense I would refer you to the doctrines of Mr. Forester in *Melincourt*, who as a character in fiction is an unholy bore, but who seems to represent an earnest and almost crusading seriousness in Peacock that commends him rather to the social reformer than to the lover of satire.

'If in any form of human society any one human being dies of hunger, while another wastes or consumes as much as would have preserved his existence, I hold that second man guilty of the death of the first. . . . What would you think of a family of four persons, two of whom should not be contented with consuming their own share of diurnal provision, but, having adventitiously the pre-eminence of physical power, should either throw the share of the two others into the fire, or stew it down into a condiment for their own?'

Here are the beginnings of a healthy critical disgust with what at that time was only just about to be called capitalism. Forester is an example of the solitary and sincere crusader who, endowed with a little more vision and a little more conscientious indignation than the next man, becomes a burden to his fellows through his martyr-like insistence on carrying through his theories to a practical conclusion. It led him in *Melincourt* to eschew slave-produced sugar and to inaugurate the rather misleadingly named Anti-Saccharine Fête—activities paralleled by the efforts of Brailsford and Nevinson in their persuasive onslaught on the cocoa trade in 1908; it might have led him a century or so later to the uncompromising community-life of the pacifist who weaves his own clothes out of his own sheep's wool rather than align himself with a profit-making and war-waging society. Given the change in contexts, it is not too far-fetched to see in Forester the sign that Peacock had a glimmering of the ghastly alternative facing the modern sensitive mind—kill or die; and in the light of our experience Forester's sugarless tea is as noble and futile as the renunciation of ration-books by his modern successors.

But Peacock did not pursue the transitory gleam; he retired among his favourite wines, weighing his postulates blandly over the beakers and not sparing anyone whose eccentricity jarred upon him. Canning is flagellated, but so is Brougham; the man who wished to return to medievalism gets a gentle beating, but the progress of scientific invention, represented especially by the energies of steam, gets one too, and not so gentle. He wastes on the barren question of paper-money nearly as much paper as was consumed by the misuse he complained of; and anyone who showed himself a connoisseur of claret or the classics was all that Peacock could desire. At times he seems to be using his admirable clarity of expression, his forthright inimitable critical prose, to gratify a splenetic whim engendered by over-indulgence. He hits, and hits hard, not for the reason that the object of his attack has offended against any canon of taste or morals, but because it has happened in the eccentricity of his own mood to annoy him personally. The manifestly unfair attacks on Southey and Wordsworth, and one ill-tempered reference to Burke, are representative examples of this habit. His invective never fails to entertain, but it lapses from the standard of good satire.

For the value of a good satirist is akin to the value of a good critic; it depends on more than his insight or his power of expressing that insight. It varies in the ratio of the consistency of his central critical creed. 'He who frees criticism from the moral duty of placing itself in the service of a general, recognized and pursued life-task is treading the path that leads to nihilism and anarchy.' I feel this to be broadly true, though perhaps a little heavily expressed, and no less true because it happens to be by Hitler and meant in a rather specialized sense in the context in which he used it. Hitler insists on the subordination of critical honesty to a central policy; whereas I am stressing the co-ordination of critical insight with philosophical or moral standards. Criticism without a central set of values is not valuable criticism; it is as worthless as the armament of a battleship without anchor or steering-gear. Peacock wallowed in the heavy seas of the nineteenth century, his magnificent guns superbly manned and mounted. To port lay the fleet of progress, to starboard the fleet of reaction; and so irresponsible was the steering of this formidable vessel that when it let off a broadside it was a toss-up which of the opposing fleets took the weight of it. The models from whom in large part his form and effectiveness were derived, Aristophanes, Lucian, Marmontel and Voltaire, all possessed a central control foreign to Peacock's quicksilver temper, and the damage done by the satire of at least three of these was all the deadlier for the uncompromising consistency of their standards. By their side, and especially by Voltaire's, Peacock is an easy-going old reactionary with a hot temper and a talent for expressing it: he is not favoured by the comparison.

So his ideas do not give him the 'shape' we are looking for, any more than his creation of character or plot did. It is not easy, looking round, to see why he is any more than an attractive story-teller. There is, indeed, a genuine and rather moving consistency and beauty in the expression of his love for the various types of English scenery—the Thames in *Crotchet Castle*, the Lake District in *Melincourt*, the Fens in *Nightmare Abbey*, Wales almost everywhere, the New Forest in *Gryll Grange*; and the bitter note at the beginning of this last book on the subject of enclosures is echoed more than once in other parts of his work not discussed here, and is typical of this real enlightenment in him. There is, of course, one outstanding factor that assists his permanence out of all proportion to his narrative or persuasive ability—his style. It is classic. His immense erudition in Latin and Greek studies had ingrained in him a fastidiousness which was a sure shaper of as clean and clear a prose as his century can offer us. By comparison Macaulay is repetitive and turgid, even Newman frigid and remote; the involved excitabilities of Ruskin and Carlyle are hot air beside him, the classical artificiality of Pater as shallow as the romantic artificiality of Stevenson. His satiric temper, like Voltaire's before him, ground his style to a fine edge. It has orotundities and, as cannot easily be avoided when a classic treats a romantic subject, flatnesses at unexpected places where the emotional intensity required by the context puts too great a strain on the emotional vocabulary at his command—contrast his treatment of wild Nature with his son-in-law Meredith's: the comparison is valuable as it aligns Peacock conspicuously with the eighteenth century, and invests him with a sculptured dignity which gives Meredith with all his red-blooded romanticism the air of an upstart crow, even although he has succeeded where Peacock has failed. And failure and all, Peacock's style is an admirable weapon; and often it is more than a weapon; it is, in the same way as Sterne's, a verbal embodiment of a personality. Firm, trenchant, economical, it accommodates itself to all moods and carries with it into all of them its pervading satiric essence. This gives it an immunity from bathos and bombast alike, and at times an irresistible humour. The strength and precision of his characters' assertions are frequently the chief origins of the characters' life; which is a clear example of how a style formed primarily for criticism can in the process become truly creative. This style has several notable modern descendants; Shaw is not unreminiscent of it even when he is most like Shaw; Belloc at his more pontifical (consciously pontifical, I mean, and hence very slightly self-satirical, as in *The Path to Rome* and *The Four Men*) provides startlingly faithful echoes. A number of our older moderns, revolting in the flush of youth from the crushing incubus of the three-decker, snatched with enthusiasm at Peacock's novel-form and gave it an exhilarating renewal of life. The gap had been partly bridged by Mallock's *New Republic*, but this had been even more of a retreat from the novel than Peacock's; the newer writers sought to manipulate their ideas within the conversation-piece framework and yet to retain the imaginative quality inherent in the novel. Generally they failed; but *South Wind*, *Crome Yellow* and *Those Barren Leaves* were incidental justifications of the attempt.

The style goes for much, then; but it cannot prolong a man's value into succeeding generations with nothing to back it. And it is because I believe Peacock to be of real value, and not so much because I believe him to have gained at the enthusiastic hands of Saintsbury and Priestley more than his due of praise, that I believe it time for a reassessment of him. Entertainment value must not be underrated, and he has that in full enough measure. We shan't come to much harm if we read him simply for fun, although we shall then lay ourselves open to the danger of swallowing him whole, as even Saintsbury did, for the sake of the taste of the jam round the satiric pill. I have sought to show that his abiding value is neither creative nor truly critical, since his characters are not fully formed, his central purpose neither constructive nor consistent, and his satire irregularly aimed; he is Mr. Facing-both-ways, and today when he who is not for us is keenly suspected of being against us, Mr. Facing-both-ways is on unsafe ground. Yet there is one salutary quality in his satire: it is, if absorbed warily, a splendid corrective. Classical to the core, he steered his middle course throughout. Retrogressive reaction he bullied until it was overruled, hot-headed idealism he pricked until it burst. He was a man who hated extremes, and while it is not easy to see in these days whether anything but a considered extremism will ever infuse the necessary recreative faith into a collapsed society, it will be well for the hot-heads to correct themselves in mid-venture with a dose of this thermostatic humour of which Peacock is so efficient and delightful a provider. To regard his aggravating inconsistencies in this light may help us to come to easier terms with this excellent minor novelist. The restricted circle who read him now will, I hope, continue to do so; but I hope, too, that they will be joined by others whose critical discrimination will examine his satire against a wider background and his importance in relation to deeper and more enduring values; and it will be these who will come in time to give him his due.

PETER QUENNELL

THE ROMANTIC CATASTROPHE

BECAUSE Englishmen read the nineteenth-century romantic poets during their most immature, most impressionable and least critical period (when the romantic glorification of youth has a special charm and no real existence can be conceived of beyond the thirties), we have very few of us a clear conception of the romantic achievement and still fewer have attempted to revalue it by adult standards. To make the attempt is both uncomfortable and extremely stimulating. Of the major poetic figures who divide our attention, Coleridge and Wordsworth, Shelley and Keats—Byron for the moment may be excepted, since his chief contribution was personal rather than aesthetic—the latter disappointed us by dying too early, the former by clinging to existence much too long. Just as remarkable as the brilliance of the work they produced was its incompleteness. Youth is the time of unfulfilled aspirations, unkept promises, unachieved desires; and, while trying to analyse the genius of these four very different and all extraordinarily gifted writers, we find that we are perpetually dropping into the conditional tense. Suppose that Shelley had had a worse heart but a better head, and, incidentally, a more sensitive and musical ear . . . suppose that Wordsworth's nature had been more fluid, more resistant to the processes of ossification, and Coleridge's steadier and less diffuse: that Keats had not written with death at his elbow . . . possibility on possibility immediately presents itself. But none of these possibilities was ever realized: over the whole age hangs the shadow of a tremendous *might-have-been*.

We are left face to face with the prospect of what actually was; and that prospect is as strangely irregular as it is full of interest.

By June 1822, when Shelley's featureless and decomposing body was scooped up from the sands of Viareggio—his copy of Keats's poems turned back at *Lamia* in the coat pocket—Keats had been dead for seven months. Coleridge and Wordsworth, however, had respectively twelve and twenty-eight years to live; and the decade that followed, for Coleridge at least, was slow and inglorious. Yet, just as Keats, given different circumstances, might by his sheer poetic gift have bridged the gulf between the augustan and romantic traditions, so Coleridge, had his temperament been more happily constituted and the conflict within himself less acute and prolonged, might have dominated the new literature by force of intellect. For Coleridge had two different faculties not often employed in combination. He was both deeply intellectual and intensely imaginative. His mind was both powerful in scope and adapted to the most delicate minutiae of poetic observation. He could criticize and create with equal mastery. In estimating the poetic works of others, not only could he dive into the resources of a lifetime's erudition—and he had read, as he frequently announced, 'almost everything'—but he could apply the technical knowledge acquired while producing his own.

Yet his failure was crushing and comprehensive. And here, not for the first time, one is confronted by the paradoxical observation that, although men make up an age, the age itself is contributory in making men. A poet may help to shape the future: he is controlled and shaped, nevertheless, by the immediate past and by the influence with which it bears down upon the present, crystallized in the intangible contemporary 'atmosphere'. Coleridge and Wordsworth belonged to the generation that had been excited, almost beyond endurance, by the events of 1789, troubled and horrified by the growth of the Terror and profoundly stirred by the astonishing spectacle of Napoleon's rise. Some had welcomed, some had shuddered at, the Revolution. But, in both instances, the shock went very deep, and the shocks that followed it were demoralizing and, at length, disabling. Thus Wordsworth receded into a graceless conservatism, the youth and strength of his imagination gradually losing ground, enthusiasm giving way to arid prejudice. By 1822, and even earlier, he was regarded, along with Southey, as poetic arch-traitor to the Liberal cause and the hireling representative of a Tory government whose principles and pension he had accepted. In Coleridge's development, the effects of contemporary occurrences are perhaps somewhat less easy to discover; but he, too, after a burst of creation at the turn of the century—practically all the poems that deserve to be remembered were written during 1797 and 1798—experienced a curious falling-off of creative strength, till in 1801 he admitted that the poet was dead in him, while the opium-habit began to claim him more and more definitely, soothing his sense of disappointment and lulling his nerves. Fifteen years later he was an acknowledged addict and had retired to Highgate and the refuge of Gillman's household.

Yet opium was not the sole, nor indeed was it the main, cause of Coleridge's failure. Drug-addiction, like chronic alcoholism, is more often a symptom than the disease itself; though the malady of which in Coleridge's case it may have been symptomatic was of a type that baffles analysis and defies cure. In common with many other writers of the early nineteenth century—De Quincey and Baudelaire are examples that immediately come to mind—he suffered from that odd disease of the volition to which mystics have attached the name of *acedia*, a condition of spiritual despondency and mental paralysis that leaves the sufferer still lucid yet entirely impotent. And then, Coleridge had highly developed moral feelings. It is possible that, had those feelings been less highly developed, and his conscience not so squeamish and not so obstreperous, he might have given them fewer occasions to reproach and torment him. But his sense of duty intensified his sense of failure; and it was his sense of failure that, in spite of every prohibition, human or divine, he was obliged to lull by constant recourse to opium which, temporarily at least, reconciled him to his moral predicament. From a conviction of his own unworthiness he had never been free. At Cambridge it had already begun to haunt him, had ruined his career at the University and driven him first to debauchery, then to enlistment; and, during a much later period, in a letter to Southey, he summed up his tragic obsession once and for all:

'A sense of weakness (he declared), a haunting sense that I was an herbaceous plant, as large as a large tree, with a trunk of the same girth, and branches as large and shadowing, but with pith within the trunk, not heart of wood—that I had power, not strength, an involuntary imposter, that I had no real genius, no depth. This on my honour is as fair a statement of my habitual haunting, as I could give before the tribunal of Heaven. How it arose in me I have but lately discovered; still it works within me, but only as a disease, the cause and meaning of which I know. The whole History of this feeling would form a curious page in a *nosologia spiritualis* . . .'

Disintoxicated, he must justify himself by action. Intoxicated, he found no justification necessary: it was enough that he knew and felt and imagined:

'Laudanum (he told his brother, George Coleridge, in 1798, the year of *Kubla Khan*) gave me repose, not sleep; but you, I believe, know how divine that repose is, what a spot of enchantment, a green spot of fountains and flowers and trees in the very heart of a waste of sands!'

For Coleridge, in fact, as afterwards for Charles Baudelaire, opium provided an intensification, not so much of sensual as of spiritual experience. It procured the key to one of those *paradis artificiels* that are a visionary equivalent of the tree-embowered, rock-walled garden fastnesses, 'enfolding sunny spots of greenery', where the pupils of the Old Man of the Mountain received their training. But he returned to the real world for the most part with empty hands:

'If a man (he wrote, somewhat pathetically, between 1814 and 1818) could pass through Paradise in a dream, and have a flower presented to him as a pledge that his soul had really been there, and if he found that flower in his hand when he awoke—Aye! and what then?'

Alas, of the 'two to three hundred lines' that formed the original *Kubla Khan*, what with the insubstantial nature of such half-fixed reminiscences and the disastrous arrival of the person from Porlock, only an imperfect recollection was ever salvaged; and the fate of *Kubla Khan* was typical of the fate of his other efforts. Remnants, husks, vestiges found their way to the reader; the essential substance remained with Coleridge to furnish his dream-life, just out of reach on the wrong side of the ivory threshold—huge epic poems, gigantic treatises, exhaustive commentaries,[1] all unattempted though in

[1] Besides Coleridge's projected work on the Logos, in five treatises, and his seven Hymns—to Sun, Moon, Earth, Air, Water, Fire and God, 'with a large preface or prose commentary each'—there was his epic on the Destruction of Jerusalem, which was to have occupied him no less than twenty years. 'I should

the mind's eye vivid and definite. Resolutions piled up till their magnitude terrified him. He groaned—moralized—then slipped back into ruinous reverie.

Coleridge's plight has been likened to that of Baudelaire; and, in parenthesis, it is interesting to note that the correspondence between certain passages of *The Friend*, resuscitated in *Biographia Literaria*, and the third section of *Le Peintre de la Vie Moderne*, in *l'Art Romantique*, is very close indeed. 'To carry on the feelings of childhood into the powers of manhood (writes Coleridge); to combine the child's sense of wonder and novelty with the appearances which every day for perhaps forty years had rendered familiar . . . that is the character and privilege of genius, and one of the marks which distinguish genius from talents.' Similarly, Baudelaire, attempting to define the character of genius in the person of Constantin Guys, suggests that we should regard the man of genius as an *homme-enfant*—'a man possessing at every moment of the day the genius of childhood, a man, that is, for whom familiarity has robbed of its brilliance no single aspect of our common life'. For the child (he has already written) everything is *new*: he is always *intoxicated*. Nothing bears a closer affinity to what is called inspiration than the joy with which forms and colours are absorbed by the child. Elsewhere the French poet compares Guys to a man who, spiritually, is always in the condition of a convalescent, reborn after a long illness to the beauty and miraculous strangeness of the world around him. This idea may be paralleled in Coleridge's text, when he declares that it is 'the prime merit of genius and its most unequivocal mode of manifestation, so to represent familiar objects as to awaken in the minds of others . . . that freshness of sensation which is the constant accompaniment of mental, no less than of bodily, convalescence'. Whether Baudelaire was indebted directly to *Biographia Literaria* I have not yet been able to ascertain; but that such a close connection should exist between Coleridge's thought and the thought of one of the

not think (he wrote in 1797) of devoting less than twenty years to an Epic Poem. Ten to collect materials and warm my mind with universal science. I would be a tolerable Mathematician, I would thoroughly know Mechanics, Hydrostatics, Optics, and Astronomy, Botany, Metallurgy, Fossilism, Chemistry, Geology, Anatomy, Medicine—then the *mind of man*—then the *minds of men*—in all Travels, Voyages and Histories. So I would spend ten years—the next five to the composition of the poem—and the five last to the correction of it.'

greatest European poets and most perceptive modern critics shows the boldness and catholicity of his critical insight as it appears again and again in his notebook jottings. But, whereas Baudelaire's critical work at its best is both compact in design and continuous in inspiration, Coleridge's is shapeless and fragmentary. Thus, *Biographia Literaria* is not a complete book so much as a brilliant compilation of paragraphs and chapters. The subtlety of Coleridge's mind involves his method in endless fine entanglements; and (as he himself remarked, in a passage that at once analyses his own weakness and exemplifies the stylistic peculiarities to which that weakness led) 'My illustrations swallow up my thesis. I feel too intensely the omnipresence of all in each, platonically speaking; or, psychologically, my brain-fibres, or the spiritual light which abides in the brain-marrow, as visible light appears to do in sundry rotten mackerel and other *smashy* matters, is of too general an affinity with all things, and though it perceives the *difference* of things, yet is eternally pursuing the likenesses. . . . ' A preoccupation with some particular image or class of images is to be found in the work of most great poets and often serves as a clue to some individual turn of mind; and it is perhaps noteworthy that the pallid unreal glimmer of phosphorescent light, whether in a dead fish, the stagnant ocean that burned round the Ancient Mariner's becalmed vessel, or as he had himself admired it during a Mediterranean voyage,[1] had a particularly moving effect on Coleridge's fancy. The ceaseless agitations of his own mind were as flickering and flamelike, appearing, vanishing, but still renewed. They threw off as much brilliance and as little heat.

He regarded himself as a failure and his contemporaries agreed with him. Shelley had drawn his poetic likeness in 1820:

> You will see Coleridge—he who sits obscure
> In the exceeding lustre and the pure
> Intense irradiation of a mind,
> Which, with its own internal lightning blind,
> Flags wearily through darkness and despair . . .

[1] 'A beautiful white cloud of Foam at momentary intervals coursed by the side of the Vessel with a Roar, and little stars of flame danced and sparkled and went out with it: and every now and then light detachments of this white cloud-like foam dashed off from the vessel's side, each with its own small constellation, over the Sea, and scoured out of sight like a Tartar Troop over a wilderness.'

Yet Coleridge, notwithstanding the tragic diffusion and gradual dispersion of his creative gifts, had the kind of maturity to which Shelley could not aspire and a critical clear-sightedness beyond an enthusiast's scope. The enemies that Coleridge dreaded were those within himself. Shelley's adolescent persecution-mania filled the world with bogeys which assumed now the lineaments of Sir Timothy Shelley, now the pale murderous mask of wicked Lord Castlereagh (that domestic despot but singularly enlightened director of English foreign policy) and now emerged, crudely personified, as Priestcraft and Prejudice. Half the foes he engaged were of his own creation: half the sufferings he endured were self-provoked: and among real opponents he was a desperate but a random hitter. His verse has the same touch of sketchy enthusiasm. The orchestral accompaniment of *Prometheus Unbound* may be supplied by the spheres; but the celestial clockwork is not revolving very smoothly. The voice may be that of an archangel; but, now and then, it cracks on the top register and the result is a singularly appalling dissonance:

The Moon Brother, wheresoe'er thou soarest
I must hurry, whirl and follow
Through the heavens wide and hollow,
Sheltered by the warm embrace
Of thy soul from hungry space,
Drinking from thy sense and sight
Beauty, majesty and might,
As a lover or a chameleon
Grows like what it looks upon,
As a violet's gentle eye
Gazes on the azure sky . . .

The Earth . . . Oh, gentle Moon, the voice of thy delight
Falls on me like thy clear and tender light
Soothing the seaman, borne the summer night,
Through isles for ever calm;
Oh, gentle Moon, thy crystal accents pierce
The caverns of my pride's deep universe,
Charming the tiger joy, whose tramplings fierce
Made wounds which need thy balm.

Many passages even worse than this—more unmusical, more confused and more confusing, more clogged with imagery and muddled in metaphor—might be selected from the products of Shelley's maturity. They are obscure, not as poets of the seventeenth and late nineteenth centuries were often obscure, through undue condensation of meaning, but because the substance of meaning has been beaten out too fine—with no sort of regard for its poetic value—and trembles and shudders ecstatically like a sheet of tin-foil. Shelley confused ecstasy and imagination, just as in the field of politics he confused the hatred of 'tyranny' (which may have a private psychological basis) with a defence of the intellectual principles on which freedom has been established. Indeed, his liberalism never quite emerged from the period when, accompanied by the pretty stupid girl whom he had 'rescued' from her boarding school, he attempted to launch an English revolution with the help of paper boats, handbills scattered fancifully from high windows and messages in bottles committed to the waves. His genius is most apparent when he is least declamatory, when he forgets the helter-skelter rush of rhetorical abstractions that went streaming through his mind, 'Kings of suns and stars, Daemons and Gods, Aetherial Dominations . . . ', gleaming like meteors, blazing like planets, and comes home to the self and the self's perplexities, its loves and its disappointments, the beauty and the misery of a finite universe. Keats's famous reproof was certainly merited. But then, Keats had already arrived at a balance between the imagination and the intellect—or between the creative and critical aspects of an artist's brain—that Shelley's temperament debarred him from ever achieving. It was his business (Keats knew) to create, not legislate. But nothing could be further from the selfish secluded aestheticism in which the deliberately non-political artist (supported by a small private income) is supposed to pass his days than Keats's dedication of all his powers to the intellectual purpose that suited them best and through which they could be exploited to the greatest advantage. It is our misfortune, however, that the *Letters*, which outline his plan of campaign, should show him usually a step ahead of the campaign itself and that even the Odes should strike us, here and there, as an anticlimax.

Yet few poets have accomplished such a remarkable process of self-clarification in so short a space of time.

Sensibly, Keats refused to regret 'the slipshod *Endymion*. That it is so (he told a correspondent only six months after its publication) is no fault of mine. No!—though it may sound a little paradoxical. It is as good as I had power to make it—by myself. Had I been nervous about its being a perfect piece, and with that view asked advice, and trembled over every page, it would not have been written; for it is not in my nature to fumble—I will write independently—I have written independently *without Judgement*. I may write independently, and *with Judgement*, hereafter. The Genius of Poetry must work out its own salvation in a man: It cannot be matured by law and precept, but by sensation and watchfulness . . . That which is creative must create itself.' And *Endymion*, though so evidently the product of an adolescent artist, in love with the idea of writing poetry and somewhat befuddled by an overdose of the Elizabethans, has still movements of astonishing ease and amplitude:

> . . . As when heaved anew
> Old ocean rolls a lengthened wave to the shore,
> Down whose green back the short-lived foam, all hoar,
> Bursts gradual with a wayward indolence.

To re-read Keats's *Letters*, having not looked into them for several years, is an experience at once delightful and disconcerting. So much naïvety coexists with so much maturity, so much vulgarity with so much delicacy of imagination. Here is the suburban poetaster, prolific of schoolboy puns, who collaborated with his friend Brown in painfully facetious letters to Mrs. Dilke and, accompanied by other Cockney sportsmen—we think immediately of a Cruikshank caricature!—scoured Hampstead Heath in pursuit of hedgerow game and went home to tea after bagging a tom-tit; and here, embodied in the same person—unselfconsciously sharing the honours upon almost every page—is a writer of adult seriousness and profound intelligence. His mind was peculiarly honest and utterly disinterested. 'I never wrote one single line of Poetry (he declared in April 1818) with the least shadow of public thought.' The most imperfect and irresponsible artists (he realized) are those afflicted with a strong sense of public responsibility or public self-importance; and, just as the individual must have begun to understand himself and grasp his own limitations before he can hope to interfere beneficially in the existence of others, so the artist must graduate through self-absorption into any extended sympathy with contemporary problems or the world around him. This Keats had deliberately set out to do, holding that the benefits conferred by man on man are 'trifles in comparison to the benefit done by great works to the "Spirit and pulse" of good by their mere passive existence'. It was not that he lacked human interest or human affection. Indeed, contact with other human beings often absorbed him so entirely that 'when I am in a room with people . . . the identity of every one in the room begins to press upon me, so that I am in a very little time annihilated—not only among men; it would be the same in a nursery of children'.

A writer may have too few interests—but also too many. The engine that he employs against the world is necessarily himself; and it is his first duty, therefore, to determine the capacities of that delicate and mysterious apparatus, and by carefully limiting them to define the exact scope of their future activities. Since neither poet consented to undertake this preliminary survey, Shelley's sympathies were as wide, general and ultimately ineffective as the verse that expressed them was often weak and shrill; and Coleridge's speculations were ambitious but futile. Contrast with the achievement and partial failure of his fellow romantic poets, Keats's belief in what he called '*Negative Capability*'—of which Shakespeare, he thought, provided the chief example and the tremendous justification:

'. . . that is, when a man is capable of being in uncertainties, mysteries, doubts, without any irritable reaching after fact and reason. Coleridge, for instance, would let go by a fine isolated verisimilitude caught from the Penetralium of mystery, from being incapable of remaining content with half-knowledge.'

And elsewhere:

'Now it appears to me that almost any Man may, like the spider, spin from his own inwards his own airy Citadel—the points of leaves and twigs on which the spider begins her work are few, and she fills the air with a beautiful circuiting. Man should be content with as few points to tip the fine Web of his Soul, and weave a tapestry empyrean full of symbols for his spiritual eye, of softness for his spiritual touch, of space for his wandering, of distinctness for his luxury. But the Minds of Mortals are so different and bent on such diverse journeys that it may at first appear impossible for any common taste or fellowship to exist between two or three under these suppositions. It is, however, quite the contrary. Minds would leave each other in contrary directions, traverse each other in numberless points, and at last greet each other at the journey's end... Man should not dispute or assert, but whisper results to his neighbour....'

There is a great gulf between the poet who, at the age of twenty-four, had decided that 'the only means of strengthening one's intellect is to make up one's mind about nothing—to let the mind be a thoroughfare for all thoughts, not a select party', and poets who turned their minds into packed committee rooms or, like Coleridge, into debating societies with a single speaker. Keats's nature was entirely innocent of the taint of didacticism; and for that reason alone his conception of poetry seems both more modern than the definitions attempted by many nineteenth-century critics, and also closer to the spirit of the previous age. No augustan poet need have dissented from his view that 'poetry should surprise by a fine excess, and not by singularity; it should strike the reader as a wording of his own highest thoughts, and appear almost a remembrance'. And Johnson himself might certainly have agreed that 'its touches of beauty should never be half-way, thereby making the reader breathless, instead of content. The rise, the progress, the setting of imagery should, like the sun, come natural to him, shine over him, and set soberly, although in magnificence, leaving him in the luxury of twilight'.

What happened to prevent the execution of so bold a design? The student of Keats's *Letters* feels that he is witnessing a tragedy where the enemies of perfection in art and of happiness in life, repulsed along the whole length of a poet's defences, suddenly re-emerge, disguised, behind the ramparts. To begin with, there is talk of the 'sore throat' that followed the Scottish and Irish walking tours of 1818. Then there occurs a casual mention of the daughter of the lady who had moved in next door—her countenance attractive but wanting in 'sentiment', her nostrils 'fine—though a little painful', her mouth 'bad and good', her profile 'better than her full face', her entire personality fascinating but perplexing, 'beautiful and elegant, graceful, silly, fashionable and strange'. Under such travesties may death and love make their first appearance. The 'sore throat' proves impossible to shake off, soon it becomes clear that the disease that had removed Tom Keats is also sapping at the constitution of his elder brother. During the October of that fatal year 1818, the poet had explained to George and Georgiana Keats that he hoped never to marry, that his imagination was strengthening day by day, and that with imaginative strength increased the desire for solitude; but gradually the idea of Fanny Brawne grows more and more powerful. From that moment, death and love work as malicious allies. The earliest letter to Fanny Brawne is dated 8 July 1819; and, as approaching death rapidly speeds up the tempo, the tone adopted mounts in intensity and gains in bitterness. Yet Keats continued to fight a rearguard action. Towards the end of August 1819 he could still write to Taylor, when discussing the financial advantages of a popular success, that he equally disliked 'the favour of the public with the love of a woman', since both were 'a cloying treacle to the wings of Independence': and to his brother, on the 17th of the following month, that nothing struck him 'so forcibly with a sense of the ridiculous as love. A man in love I do think cuts the sorriest figure in the world . . .'

Again and again he affirmed his desire for that condition of moral and spiritual independence in which, he believed, great poetry must find its origin. Deliberately he would deny himself disturbing contacts and hurry through London without a visit to Hampstead, because 'I cannot resolve to mix any pleasure with my days. . . . I am a Coward, I cannot bear the pain of being happy . . .' Very clearly he could see his life as it ought to have been, and only after a prolonged struggle did he abandon himself to his fate as it was. Finally, physical weakness had spoiled his triumph. Death had at once intensified the claims of life and made them impossible either to satisfy in terms of the body or relegate to their proper place in the world of the mind. 'I think (he wrote) if I had a free and healthy and lasting organization of heart, and lungs as strong as an ox's, so as to be able to bear unhurt the shock of extreme thought and sensation without weariness, I could pass my life very nearly alone though it should last eighty years'—But the lungs were riddled with disease and the heart disordered: the fortifications that had guarded his solitude were breaking down: the time had gone when he could postpone voluntarily his chances of happiness. 'I cannot exist without you. I am forgetful of everything but seeing you again—my

Life seems to stop there—I see no further. You have absorb'd me', he told Fanny Brawne on 13 October; '. . . Love is my Religion . . .' The sole reward of that religious cult was a consuming jealousy.

* * *

If Keats was a writer who, although not insensitive to the life of his time, was sufficiently strong to withstand its more malignant influences, Coleridge, Shelley, Wordsworth represent the plight of the intellectual in modern society from three widely separated but complementary points of view. Wordsworth is the type of artist who, after an early expedition into revolutionary experiment, allows himself, for reasons part economic and part personal, to drift back to conservatism once the tide has turned. His was the warm nature easily chilled, the magnanimous spirit strangely susceptible to specious argument, cursed with an instinctive appreciation of the main chance, that in every generation is held up to obloquy. Their former associates may revile such artists: but their pride increases. Too intelligent not to see 'both sides of the question', they lose their youth, their inspiration and at last their integrity in the labyrinth they have created round their own self-love. To the evasions and circumlocutions of middle-age they still bring the obstinacy and the conceit of youth. They are the arch-renegades who remain unconscious of their own apostasy.

Very different was the spiritual doom of Coleridge, whose predicament seems to have reproduced in waking life an experience we have most of us undergone during the course of a nightmare. Then, as the necessity of making some immediate and drastic move becomes more and more apparent, so does the sensation of complete impotence grow more and more powerful. All Coleridge's vices derived from his virtues. It was the fact that he could imagine with such lucidity, and analyse and discuss with such an easy strength, that made it at first difficult, and afterwards quite impossible, to desert the ideal world of reverie and speculation for the disturbing, imperfect world of action. As Shelley said, he had been blinded by an excess of light; as he himself remarked, his illustrations swallowed up his thesis; till every advance in thought became a retreat from reality, and every improvement in the theory of how books should be written a diminution of the ability to set pen to paper. The need—if not the desire—to create had gradually drained away. Between his sensitiveness and a universe which, since the breakdown of his early revolutionary enthusiasm and the collapse of his existence as a husband and father, he had discovered that he could neither like nor understand, he raised the massive barrier of his intellect and his erudition. Raiding parties might break through that Wall of China—he was seldom secure from harassing reminders of the real and actual world; but he could subdue them with the dazzling ray of his superb intelligence, re-cast them in a more agreeable guise, reduce them to abstract terms. It was a system of self-protection that needed constant vigilance. It left little time for the creation of poetic literature.

Shelley no one could have accused of sparing his own sensitiveness; but, because he was enthusiastic rather than critical, and lacked any aptitude for self-discovery, he never succeeded in giving life and literature their respective dues. The connection of Shelley's love for his sister, and consequent hatred of his father, with his detestation of Prejudice, Priestcraft, Tyranny, is so clear as to demand little additional emphasis. A wrong-headed or foolish man may produce magnificent verse; but a poet who is both high-minded and muddle-headed, and feels the impact of emotion without knowing its origin, mistakes excitement for the faculty of inspiration and emphasis for the gift of poetic clarity. Through a contemplation of the careers of such poets as Shelley, and through the services of such biographers as Thomas Jefferson Hogg—anxious to admire but determined to patronize—we have arrived at that identification of Youth and Poetry, according to which every true poet is an adolescent and true poetry is a by-product of immature feeling rather than a considered statement of our adult discoveries. Shelley's revolt against the age he lived in—an age of industrial growth and political retrogression—would have been more effective had its origins been less confused and his view of the poet's functions been less didactic—had he been content (in Keats's phrase) to sit like Jupiter instead of constituting himself a kind of celestial busybody. His liberalism though bold and generous in its expression, rested on a basis that was so insecure as to give a strained uneasy note to his poetic utterance. His choric verse has a breathless speed that is occasionally beautiful: it lacks the 'comprehension and expansion' of the greatest literature.

At last the stage is cleared for the appearance of Byron. Wordsworth, Shelley, Keats, Coleridge were all of them devoted men of letters, unselfishly absorbed in their self-appointed task; Byron represents the intrusion of the brilliant amateur. It was at once the secret of his enormous popular success and the measure of his aesthetic limitations that he should rely so completely on the guidance of instinct. His capacity for deliberate reasoning was not impressive: but, as Goethe once observed, in an often-quoted passage of the *Conversations with Eckermann*, though he understood himself but dimly, he possessed 'a high degree of that daemonic instinct and attraction which influences others independently of reason, effort or affection, which sometimes succeeds in guiding where the understanding fails'. In life and literature he was an unrepentant, indeed an almost unselfconscious egotist; but, whereas Keats might progress through a knowledge of himself to a love and understanding of the world around him, for Byron the self was circumambient—something he could no more escape from than he could escape from his destiny. Both his greatness and his littleness were on the same conspicuous scale; and it is our misfortune that his talents should have been sufficiently dazzling to lend a false dignity to the weaker side of his literary character. His conception of poetry was crude and straightforward. Verse, he said, was the 'lava of the imagination'—its canalization into literature prevented its overflow—and, elsewhere, that it was the 'dream of his sleeping passions', the direct image of some experience he had actually lived through. The poet, in fact, above all other things, must be a Personality!

Few personalities have more than a pathological interest; and it is to Byron's disastrous influence on modern literature that we owe the whole tribe of gifted exhibitionists, ranging in scope from Alfred de Musset to Dowson, who have attempted to 'live' their poems as well as write them. Contrast Byron's deliberate exploitation of the poetic role with Keats's analysis of the artist's character, and once again we return to the regions of *might-have-been*. 'As to the poetical character . . .' (Keats wrote during October 1818) 'it has no self—It is everything and nothing . . . It enjoys light and shade; it lives in gusto, be it foul or fair, rich or poor, mean or elevated.—It has as much delight in conceiving an Iago as an Imogen. What shocks the virtuous philosopher delights the chameleon poet . . . A poet is the most unpoetical of anything in existence, because he has no Identity—he is continually . . . filling some other body. The Sun, the Moon, the Sea, and men and women, who are creatures of impulse, are poetical and have about them an unchangeable attribute; the poet has none, no identity—he is certainly the most unpoetical of all God's creatures . . .'

Had Byron's daemonic example been somewhat less overwhelming, and Keats's lonely voice more sustained and more powerful, how great might have been the benefit to modern poetry and how significant the results that it at length achieved! How different, perhaps, the whole face of contemporary Europe! Nationalism was essentially a romantic movement, and from nationalism springs the half-baked racial theorist with his romantic belief in the superiority of Aryan blood and his romantic distrust of the use of reason. So far-reaching were the effects of the romantic revival that they still persist even in shapes under which they are no longer recognized and among writers who have learned to profess themselves devoutly classicist. For romantic literature appeals to that strain of anarchism which inhabits a dark corner of every human mind and is continually advancing the charms of extinction against the claims of life—the beauty of all that is fragmentary and youthful and half-formed as opposed to the compact achievement of adult genius. The augustan spirit is positive, logical, limited; the romantic mood, masochistic and self-destructive. It was the horrid destiny of the nineteenth-century romantic movement to be born under the twin signs of Youth and Death.

GEOFFREY WAGNER

BEDDOES, CENTENNIAL OF A SUICIDE

It is a hundred years since Beddoes killed himself. Yet, as Horace Gregory has remarked:

> the death which looks gigantically down on the remains of Beddoes, Edgar Poe and Hart Crane, has its reality in a social order that resumed its reckless course after the Napoleonic wars and is now emerging as the threat of world disaster in the terrible guise of Fascism.[1]

[1] Horace Gregory, 'Poet Resurrected', *New Republic*, 29 July 1936, 87, 357–8.

Beddoes's suicide, however, was not the *junger Werther* death of a Kleist (to which he referred in his correspondence[1]), nor is it entirely that 'grimace of cynicism and disillusion'[2] which Dr. Niebuhr tells us underlies all modern life. 'In ages when values crumble and survival has an ever so slight but still perceptible touch of glibness and betrayal, artists are often tempted by suicide, but rarely commit it,'[3] writes Arthur Koestler, and we are reminded of Kit Smart's fear, which he never implemented, that Keats often 'intended' to kill himself, according to Severn and Dr. Clark, and that Schumann, so Wasilewski tells us, longed to commit suicide also. Indeed Dr. Calvin Schmid's researches in Seattle, Washington, which has the highest mean rate of suicide of any town in the U.S.A. (with an incidence of 43·7 per 100,000 of the population of twenty-one years of age and over), reveal that here students have the lowest 'occupational' rate of suicide (8·1) and unskilled manual labourers the highest (277·0). Though this is perhaps a back-handed comment on the direct results of the economy of a country where 22,000 people kill themselves each year (and 100,000 more make efforts of one sort or another and 'fail'), yet Beddoes is more than a mere symptom. Developing his peculiar poetic talents very young, he represents as complete a denial of aesthetic values as we know in literature outside Rimbaud. He published his first poem in *The Morning Post* when he was only sixteen, wrote *The Improvisatore* and *The Bride's Tragedy* as an undergraduate, but after this, despite lavish praise from critics who likened his early brilliance to Keats's,[4] he never published another original work in English for the rest of his life.[5]

But Beddoes's cynicism, his retreat to humour when unable to implement his vision (like Shaw), was really inverted idealism. If

[1] Letter XXXII. 19 July 1830: I have adhered throughout to Gosse's numbering of the letters.

[2] *The Concept of Dread.*

[3] *The Yogi and the Commissar.*

[4] *Blackwood's Edinburgh Magazine*, December 1823; *The Gentleman's Magazine*, October 1823, XCIII, 2, p. 348; John Lacy (pseudonym for George Darley), 'Letters to the Dramatists of the Day', *The London Magazine*, October 1823.

[5] He may have been the author—'B'—of some poems and articles in the *Volksbote* and *Bayerisches Volksblatt*, *c.* 1830–40, but these are mostly political and differ in style and quality from the main bulk of his work.

he was 'the last Elizabethan'[1] he was also the first of the moderns. For he never faded from a brilliant start. By continuing to write in private in a style which alone, by its obsolescence, showed how little he was satisfied by prevailing art standards, Beddoes evinced an heroic irony, a cynicism that was of epic proportions. But by the highest standards his genius was repressed by being expressed almost entirely in terms of revenge. His whole satire is a form of retaliation against a society he so despised. It was a twisted talent, yearning for consummation in the wider social body, retreating frustrated to humour and gall.

* * *

Beddoes believed 'that all autobiographical sketches are the result of mere vanity—not excepting those of St. Augustin and Rousseau'[2] and we would indeed know as little about him as we do of his beloved Webster or Massinger, had it not been for the devotion of Kelsall.

The popular critical trend is to dub Beddoes an 'eccentric',[3] but it is surely his father who deserves this epithet more—that earnest doctor whom Coleridge mentions with such affection in his *Letters* and the unfinished *Hints Towards the Formation of a More Comprehensive Theory of Life*, a physician who once ordered some patients to sleep in his cowshed because he trusted the animal heat of the cows more than any new-fangled man-made heating system.[4] Or perhaps Beddoes's maternal grandfather, Richard Lovell Edgeworth, of whom Virginia Woolf has written so delightfully, was the most 'eccentric' of them all—Edgeworth the inventor who tried to deflect the course of the Rhône, and when that failed, experimented with a carriage to put down its own road surface as it went along. Later, presiding over a household containing twenty-two children of his four marriages, not counting sisters and grandchildren (of

[1] Lytton Strachey, *Books and Characters*, New York: Harcourt Brace, 1922, p. 237.

[2] Letter XLII, 15 May 1837.

[3] cp. Royall Snow, *Thomas Lovell Beddoes: Eccentric and Poet*, New York: Covici-Friede, 1928.

[4] John Edmonds Stock, *Memoirs of the Life of Thomas Beddoes, M.D.*; Atkinson's *Medical Bibliography* is interesting on Beddoes Senior as is, of course, Sir Humphrey Davy in his *Memoirs* (Bristol, 1802).

whom Thomas Lovell was one), Edgeworth invented a variant of the bicycle, the driver walking inside a barrel and thus causing an outer, geared cylinder to rotate at speed; this contraption came to grief in a chalkpit, the 'pedestrian' inside escaping just in time.[1]

For Beddoes's mother was the sister of Maria Edgeworth, whose *Life and Letters* give us useful information on the young poet who was born at Rodney Place, Clifton, on 20 July 1803, in the same year as Emerson. Beddoes was left fatherless at five and used to be taken, with his brother and sister, for holidays to the Edgeworths in Ireland, where Maria read to him.[2] Of this household it was Emmeline Edgeworth who married the Clifton Dr. King and whose daughter, Zoë King, proved such a friend to the poet, not only in his life but after his death. Beddoes attended Bath Grammar School and then entered Charterhouse on 5 June 1807, where Charles Dacre Bevan had the misfortune to be his fag.[3] Beddoes won prizes for Latin and Greek as well as a reputation for rebellion against authority. At the age of fifteen he wrote *Scaroni*, 'a belated specimen of the Maturin and Mrs. Radcliffe School of Terror' Gosse calls it, and then the poem *The Comet*, which was taken by *The Morning Post*. In May 1820 he went up to Pembroke, Oxford, his father's college, where he pursued 'a course of studied impertinence',[4] being dubbed by the dons a 'red radical'[5] and once appearing at a tutorial with a large butcher's knife in order to cut the pages of a dusty volume he had failed to read. In early 1821 he brought out *The Improvisatore* and had by the next year completed and found a publisher for *The Bride's Tragedy*. This work established Beddoes in contemporary letters and it is likely that he started work at once on *The Last Man*, *Love's Arrow Poisoned* and *Torrismond*, as well as many minor lyrics. It was now that Beddoes made the two closest friendships of his life and began the correspondence which gives a unique and vivid picture of his character. At Oxford he met Bryan Waller Procter, author of *The Flood of Thessaly* and *Dramatic Scenes*, and later

[1] The Hon. Emily Lawless, *Maria Edgeworth* (Ch. II), and *Memoirs of Richard Lovell Edgeworth* (London, 1820).

[2] *Life and Letters of Maria Edgeworth*, Vol. I, p. 158.

[3] Bevan's description of the Carthusian Beddoes is appended to Kelsall's *Memoir* in the first collected edition.

[4] Letter from Bevan to Revell Phillips, 26 July 1851.

[5] Douglas Macleane, *A History of Pembroke College, Oxford*, Oxford Historical Society.

made a Metropolitan commissioner of lunacy or, as Beddoes himself put it,

> appointed to a high office in the government of the kingdom of ye moon, upon which, as a retired member of the company of poets, he was, I suppose, accustomed to draw liberally.

In the summer of 1823 he went to cram with a solicitor at Southampton. This was Thomas Forbes Kelsall who preserved Beddoes's manuscripts carefully and published them despite the indifference, and even antagonism, of Beddoes's own family.[1] The fate of the Beddoes manuscripts, their passage to Robert Browning who kept them superstitiously without looking at them for ten years, and their eventual disintegration along with 'Pen' Browning's household at Asolo, is somehow typical of the fragmentary nature of Beddoes's genius, for he would jot down his momentary inspirations on odd, incomprehensibly crowded scraps of paper, the *Early Dramatic Fragment No. X* being written lengthways in the margin of *Alfarabi*.[2] Beddoes had now written *Torrismond* and *The Second Brother*, and was angling for a publisher for a collection of lyrics to be called *Outidana* when his mother died in Italy. He was staying with the Kings at Clifton at this time (1824) and he did not leave Zoë until the last possible moment, arriving in Florence after his mother had died. On returning to England he settled to the life of a leading young intellectual. In his rooms in Devereux Court he met Hogg, Godwin, Peacock and Darley, reminded Mary Shelley of her husband and others of Keats,[3] though Branwhite's portrait, painted at this time, hardly bears out either resemblance. It was now, aged twenty-two, at the beginning of a brilliant career perhaps, lionized by the intelligentzia, that Beddoes made his break. Recognition does not in fact seem to have made him happy: 'I have lived in a deserted state which I could hardly bear much longer', he wrote to Kelsall, 'without sinking into that despondency on the brink of which I have

[1] When Gosse wrote to one of the family for information, he was advised to destroy everything of Beddoes's that existed. Mrs. Andrew Crosse, who later met Beddoes's sister, believed 'that had the MSS. (*Death's Jest-Book*) come into their possession, they would most probably have been consigned to the fire'. (*Temple Bar*, March 1894, Vol. 101, p. 358.)

[2] H. W. Donner, *Thomas Lovell Beddoes;—The Making of a Poet*, Oxford University Press, 1935, and H. W. Donner, *The Browning Box*, Oxford, 1935.

[3] Letter IV, 29 March 1824; later Mrs. Procter told Gosse the same thing.

sate so long'.[1] In mid-July 1825, just after he had written his sympathetic *Introduction* to what he had translated of Schiller's *Philosophic Letters*, he left for Germany where he went at once to Göttingen and matriculated at the University there on the 27th. Except for short visits to England he lived in Germany and Switzerland for the rest of his life, primarily occupied with science. It was a deliberate turn to rational knowledge. He had translated one passage from Schiller as follows:

> My reason is now my all; my only security for divinity, virtue, immortality . . . Reason is a torch in a dungeon. Raphael, I demand my soul from you. I am not happy.

His letters to Kelsall become filled with scorn of poetry, denying himself any poetical call,[2] confessing that

> Shakespeare, Dante, Milton, all who have come next to the human heart, had found no object in life to satiate the restless yearnings of their hearts and appease at the same time the fastidious cravings of their imaginations. Dissatisfaction is the lot of the poet.[3]

Beddoes was not going to be caught the same way. By analogy, dissatisfaction became not only the lot but the impetus of the poet, and the neurotic man, as Nerval believed, became the supremely civilized man, the man of vision. Beddoes's firm sanity would not permit him this view. He kept up his sneer of aesthetic abjuration until, on his death-bed, he wrote: 'I ought to have been amongst other things a good poet'.[4]

For a while Beddoes thought he was happy. Seated on his horsehair sofa, looking across the Elbe with his meerschaum at his side, 'full of Graves and abundantly prosaic'[5] he believed he had found intellectual serenity. From now until 1829 he lived, with breaks for his vacations, at Göttingen studying anatomy under Blumenbach. But his new life did not satisfy him. He discovered that matter is as inscrutable as mind and his letters from 1827 on become heavier, profounder, more unhappy. He began to translate 'the old obscure tedious Nibelungenlied'[6] and had begun what is undoubtedly his masterpiece, *Death's Jest-Book*. In March–April of 1828 he paid a

[1] Ibid. [2] Letters XVIII, XIX, XXII, XXVII and XXX.
[3] Letter XXVII, 21 October 1827. [4] Letter LII, 26 January 1849.
[5] Letter XVII, 19 July 1825. [6] Letter XIV (postmark) 25 March 1825.

brief visit to England to take his M.A., Zoë King claiming his attentions almost exclusively; it was now he wrote in her album the famous autobiographical lines,

Woe again to me!
For now I hear even such an anxious voice
Crying in my soul's solitude, and bewailing
That I had never in my childhood known
The bud of this manifold beauteousness . . .

I might have stood, tho' last, among the friends
Where I am now the last among the strangers,
And have not passed away, as now I must,
Into forgetfulness, into the cold
Of the open, homeless world without a hope,
Unless it be of pardon for these words. . . .

A year later he was to make his first attempt at suicide. Inexplicably, now, Beddoes raced back from 'this dull idle pampered isle'[1] but the same year was back on another short stay, possibly to see about his mother's estates in Shropshire off which he was now living. But though himself an absentee landlord in this way, Beddoes loathed capitalism, which he equated especially with England, probably writing the bitter article 'Zur Zeitgeschichte. England' in the *Bayerisches Volksblatt*[2] and, in 'Lines Written in Switzerland', his most splenetic attack:

Be proud of Manchester,
Pestiferous Liverpool, Ocean-Avernus,
Where bullying blasphemy, like a slimy lie,
Creeps to the highest church's pinnacle,
And glistening infects the light of heaven.
O flattering likeness on a copper coin!
Sit still upon your slave-raised cotton ball,
With upright toasting fork and toothless cat:
The country clown still holds her for a lion.

His 'national anthem', as he called it, went,

Drink, Britannia, Britannia drink your Tea,
For Britons, bores and buttered Toast; they
all begin with B.

[1]Letter XXVIII, 8 April 1828. [2]17 January 1832, No. 7, pp. 62–4.

It is all the more touching when we come across the one sudden piece of home-sickness for his 'deuced dear Island'.[1]

Back in Germany now, Beddoes was indeed actively supporting the German proletariat, the oppressed citizens of Cassel and attacking 'the infamy of the Polish transaction'. He personally entertained many of the leading Polish exiles and was probably writing on their behalf in the *Volksblatt*. On 24 March 1832 he spoke at a banquet in honour of Poland and was arrested after addressing a revolutionary meeting at Gaibach on 27 May. A deportation order was made out for him on 10 July and on the 21st he left for Strasbourg, and later Zürich where he lived until 1840, an exiled exile.

Here he made friends with Johann Schoenlein, whom he rated as great as Boerhaave and Cullen,[2] and with whom he visited England in 1835. It was on his return from this visit that Schoenlein put his name up for a Professorship at the University there, but Beddoes typically refused to comply with the regulation of having to publish and instead lived happily for a time in the town practising as a doctor (he had taken his M.D. on 10 September 1831, but refused to make use of the title[3]) and working on *Death's Jest-Book* about which he was always incorrigibly cynical—it was 'perfectly adapted to remain unread'.[4] But in the Zürich revolt of 1839 Beddoes's friend in the liberal canton administration, Johann Hegetschweiler, was shot in cold blood. Beddoes left Zürich on 9 April 1840, as did also, at this time, the young Gottfried Keller, studying to be a painter, and whom Beddoes joined temporarily in Aargau. He paid another flying visit to London, then returned to Berlin where he first met Dr. Frey whose letters concerning the suicide are so interesting, and from now until 1846 he spent his time mostly between Basle, Zürich, and Baden. In August 1846 he travelled to London for the last time. It is this visit that has always been made so much of in connection with Beddoes's 'eccentricity'. He was drinking heavily, talked continually of skulls and dead men's bones, shut himself up for weeks on end in his bedroom, visited the Beddoeses of Cheney Longville riding on a donkey, and tried to set fire to Drury Lane

[1] Letter XXXIII, 10 January 1831.

[2] Letter XXXVII, 27 February 1834 (Fragmentary).

[3] Letter XXXV, 25 September 1832.

[4] Letter XLII, 25 May 1837.

Theatre with a five pound note. Was he mad?[1] Kelsall does not seem to have thought so when he met him between 6 and 8 June only, writing, however, that: 'He professed an entire alienation from poetry, particularly his own, to which he would not bear an allusion'.[2]

Beddoes returned to Frankfurt at the end of July 1847 and lived there with a nineteen-year-old baker called Degen, 'a nice-looking young man dressed in a blue blouse',[3] so Zoë King timidly described him later. Beddoes lived with Degen for about six months, taught him English and acting, and during this time he cut himself while dissecting a corpse, with the result that he contracted a serious virus infection which laid him up most of the winter. He would give no account of this accident to his friends,[4] saw only Degen, and when he recovered they set out together for Zürich. Here they evidently quarrelled. Degen returned to Frankfurt and Beddoes left for Basle, where 'in a condition of dejected apathy which was pitiful to witness'[5] he took a room in the Cicogne Hotel. 'Il était misérable,' a waiter there later told Zoë King, 'il a voulu se tuer.' The morning after he arrived, Beddoes slit an artery in his left thigh with a razor. He was admitted to the city hospital that day and there attended by Drs. Frey and Ecklin over an illness lasting some months. From the first, Gosse claims, Beddoes was 'grimly determined not to recover'[6] and 'stealthily tore off his bandages'[7] in order to induce gangrene which did, indeed, set in, making it necessary to amputate his leg, an operation Beddoes disguised in a letter to his sister (?) in October.[8] Finally, seeing that he was recovering despite his efforts, Beddoes got leave to hobble out of the hospital on 26 January and, using his authority as a physician, procured some poison (the identity of which is still disputed). At 9.30 that evening Dr. Ecklin found him dead, lying on his back in bed, with a note pinned to his shirt.

This account of Beddoes's end has been challenged by Royall Snow,[9] an American scholar, and still remains an academician's stamping-ground, for the hospital records show Beddoes '*gestorben an Apoplexie*'. But it is now almost certain that the hospital

[1] cf. the writer in *The Athenaeum*, 27 December 1890. [2] *Memoir*.
[3] Gosse, *Introduction*, p. xxx (not, as Snow footnotes it, p. xxxii).
[4] Letter from Zoë King to Kelsall, 29 August 1858, describing her visit to Basle.
[5] Ibid. [6] *Introduction*. [7] Ibid. [8] Letter L, 9 October 1848. [9] Snow, op. cit.

authorities, guilty of lax surveillance of an attempted suicide patient, concealed the true facts.[1]

Beddoes died, as he lived, in a paroxysm of mockery. The last words he wrote in the death-note were: 'Buy for Dr. Ecklin above mentioned, one of Reade's best stomach-pumps'.[2]

* * *

To understand Beddoes fully it is, of course, necessary to study his critical references in Letters II, III, XIV, XVIII, XXIII, XXV, XLVI and LI, but there is only space here to mention his love of the Elizabethans, his contempt for Goethe ('Their follies about his sitting between Shakespeare and Sophocles are laughed at everywhere but in the university'),[3] his great admiration for Tieck and Oehlenschläger, and his interest in the German translations of the social past—Voss's *Homer*, Griess's *Calderon*, Regiss's *Bojardo*, Droyssen's *Aeschylus* and so on.[4] Beddoes was seeking the comprehensive talent; 'Apollo defend us', he wrote in a letter, 'from brewing all our lives at a quintessential pot of the smallest ale Parnassian,'[5] he had but 'a sort of very moderate somewhat contemptuous respect for the profession of a mere poet in our inky age'.[6] It was this lack of the comprehensive vision that sickened Beddoes at his medical researches and laboratory bench at Göttingen, and though he always scoffed at himself ('I would not give a shilling for anything I have written, nor sixpence for anything I am likely to write'[7]), yet he deliberately erected in his plays a fantastic society, beyond bourgeois conventions and customs, an unbridled phantasmagoria which acted for him as did orientalia for Flaubert and Gautier. It was in this world, where bourgeois *mores* did not operate, and where the poet's potentialities could be fully liberated, in subject-matter as in language (for Beddoes believed that the whole of word history should be incarnate in the poet and never shirked archaisms), that we find Beddoes's idealism. For he deliberately attempted to defeat death, creating a fantastic world where humour was equivalent to reason.

The Bride's Tragedy is based on a Richardsonesque Oxford legend of the seduction of a college servant's daughter by a profligate undergraduate. It shows early that blending of the sensuous and

[1] Donner, *The Browning Box*. [2] Letter LII, 26 January 1849.
[3] Letter XVIII, 29 September 1825. [4] Letter LI, 8 November 1848.
[5] Letter XXXII, 19 July 1830. [6] Ibid. [7] Letter XXVII, 21 October 1827.

loathly which was innate in Beddoes's attitude to death, a page out of the Gothic 'romantic agony' which he used so well. The plot, like all of Beddoes's plots, is vague. The characters, judged by the modern fashion of highly specialized characterization, are tenuous and unreal. But they are so on purpose. To say, with Gosse, that Beddoes 'lacked the power to construct a plot and to develop a character'[1] is to forget Isbrand and indeed to miss the point. Beddoes's characters are, as Richard Church has suggested,[2] Flaxmanesque figures of supreme emotion, pity, fear, madness. The hazy, dream-like quality of the characterization was an attempt to synthesize character and plot, for Beddoes sought to avoid the modern tendency to create character at the expense of all other aspects of the art-form, just as he avoided modern diction, debauched as it is of emotional associations and impingements, and went back to the Elizabethans whose vocabulary he found, like Hart Crane (who also used archaisms lavishly), to be the richest.[3] Beddoes's characters have the essential unity of dream characters. Slight, equal, unreal, they yet meet in the dreamer, are emanations of the central idea, and are all equally possessed of it.

This early play is a guilty work. The theme would appear to be the almighty power of love, but as in the Gothic novel the persuasion exercised is just the contrary. The body is the tomb of the flesh and man only lives when he is free of it: we are all, as Chekhov wrote in his *Notebooks*, guilty by the fact that we are alive. So Hesperus, wooing Olivia, tells her that she will not be truly his until they are both dead:

> Though madness rule our thoughts, despair our hearts,
> And misery live with us, and misery talk,
> Our guest all day, our bed-fellow all night;
> No matter, all no matter.
> For when our souls are born then will we wed;[4]

[1] *Introduction.*

[2] Richard Church, 'Beddoes: The Last of the Alchemists', *The Spectator*, 9 February 1929, No. 142, pp. 188–9.

[3] In a letter to Gorham Munson, Crane wrote: 'To get . . . men like Strauss, Ravel, Scriabin, and Bloch into *words* one needs to *ransack* the vocabularies of Shakespeare, Jonson, Webster (for theirs were the richest) and add one scientific, street and counter, and psychological terms, etc.'

[4] *The Bride's Tragedy*, Act II, sc. iii.

Our souls are born when our bodies die. Death is the gateway out of a false, inhibiting existence into the *real*, supernatural 'world o' the dead'.[1] If these should be thought strange terms in which to court a lady, it must be remembered that Hesperus is often Beddoes talking to himself and when Hesperus addresses his own shadow in the dark, tapestried chamber, after having been, as he thinks, deceived by Floribel, he speaks in words that set the whole tenor of Beddoes's life:

I know thee now,
I know the hideous laughter of thy face;

But it is in *Death's Jest-Book* the Beddoesian leitmotiv reaches culmination. Here, then, in a world where skeletons arise and dance gavottes, where dead bones mimic life and a lover dies in agony to the tune of his lady's bridal serenade, we have an unashamed retreat to a completely surreal world, utterly divorced from the economic inhibitions of actual life. The whole work is dominated by Beddoes's finest creation, the court jester Isbrand. He represents the rational man in the play. He is not (as some have seen him) a simple misanthrope, nor is he the stylized buffoon-tragedian, smiling through his tears, like Rigoletto or Canio. Acutely conscious like Beddoes, he wanders through the horror of another dimension, through a world of Elizabethan charnel-houses, a fantasy of Poe or Dürer. He hears the songs that might have been sung by the witches in *Macbeth* and the creatures he meets are the exigencies of this background, mere morality play puppets which put him, Isbrand, in clearer relief. For this play, based as it is on Silesian pseudo-history, Beddoes created his own literature. Episodes were borrowed from Beaumont and Fletcher, Tourneur, Kyd and Schiller. The result is farcically unactable, as Beddoes intended it to be ('No one will ever read it'). But the important aspect of this play is that Isbrand is the only non-melodramatic figure. He is not, however, completely flummoxed by this other world in which he finds himself, as are Celia and Bonario, say, in *Volpone*. Surrounded by a set of puppets, robots in love with death, Hades' bobbins in mummy-cloth, Isbrand is clearly the dramatist's communication with his audience, the rational man, whose reason, here, is humour. And he triumphs.

The backdrop against which Isbrand is set, then, is that of a world, like capitalist society, in love with death, and in this play Beddoes

[1] *Death's Jest-Book*, Act v, sc. iv, l. 357.

revels in voluptuizing death. The grave becomes a bridal bed: the language of lovers, the vocabulary of the courtly love convention, is fused with a death which is life. Sibylla speaks to her ghost lover thus:

O Death! I am thy friend,
I struggle not with thee, I love thy state:
Thou canst be sweet and gentle, be so now;
And let me pass praying away into thee,
As twilight does into starry night.[1]

The body is the tomb, the grave of the flesh. We only live when we die. Here there is affinity with that Catholic metaphysic we find in Donne:

So soul into the soul may flow,
Though it to body first repair.[2]

This is the end of a long movement in literature. It has its origin in courtly love (a psychic need for its age), in the *Roman de la Rose*, which by the end of the sixteenth century becomes that sacramentalizing of the senses we find in Teresa de Jesus and Juan de la Cruz, the *amor de lonh* (later to become Mallarmé's '*l'absence*') that claims the body as but the cumbrous cloth of flesh, 'But yet the body is his book'.[3] It is played out perhaps finally in the sensuous exuberance of an asexual poet like Hopkins side by side with that uterine death-longing of Rilke and the twentieth century. The high, serenely idealized, and feminine sexual love poetry of the masculine feudal age is exploited by the Catholic mystics (especially by Crashaw in England) and finds an acute commentator in Beddoes. What more like Donne's

When bodies to their graves, souls from their graves remove[4]

than Beddoes's

And life is a death,
Where the body's the tomb?[5]

There are many other examples of this in Beddoes's *Outidana*, in poems like the fragmentary 'Death Sweet', 'The Masque of the

[1] *Death's Jest-Book*, Act IV, sc. ii.
[2] John Donne, 'The Ecstasy'. [3] Ibid.
[4] 'The Anniversary.' [5] 'Dirge' from *Outidana*.

Moon' and in *The Bride's Tragedy*, whilst Sibylla laments Wolfram's death to the Duke in *Death's Jest-Book* as follows:

> Aye, say you that he's dead? You mean he is
> No more excepted from Eternity.
> If he were dead I should indeed despair.
> Can a man die? Ay, as the sun doth set:
> It is the earth that falls away from light;
> Fixed in the heavens, although unseen by us,
> The immortal life and light remains triumphant.

She concludes,

> Farewell, my love,—I will not say to thee
> Pale corpse,—we do not part for many days.
> A little sleep, a little waking more,
> And then we are together out of life.[1]

Now it soon becomes clear that Beddoes's interest in the putrefaction of the flesh is not that of Donne (in 'The Comparison'), nor of Baudelaire (in 'La Charogne'), that is, as an assertion of the ultimate truth of man's spiritual life. It is not that of the Carmelites, of the Bürger terror school, of the Elizabethan horror writers, nor of the squeaking skeletons of the De Sade school of *grand guignol*, though there is much of *grand guignol* in Beddoes.

Beddoes speaks of death in the language of a love affair. With him death becomes baroque. It is treated with the heavy physical sensuousness of passionate sexual love. It is the final culmination, maybe the sublimation, of that long trail of love poetry from Petrarch and the Provençal troubadours onwards, that sexual *nostalgie* which now finds expression in our erithistic society in a longing for death, but here, in Beddoes, in a longing for death in entirely physical terms—simply, that is, because death is absent. Thus death is relegated to a frame of reference in life and the death-wish, as Beddoes intended, is conquered. So death becomes comfortable, cloaked in all the associations of sexuality:

> Another hour, another dream:
> A red wound on a snowy breast,
> A rude hand stifling the last scream,
> On rosy lips a death-kiss pressed.

[1] *Death's Jest-Book*, Act II, sc. ii.

Blood on the sheets, blood on the floor,
The murderer stealing through the door.
'Now,' said the voice, with comfort deep,
'She sleeps indeed, and thou may'st sleep.'[1]

The ultimate of sensuous expression is to be found in death. What more repulsive in its *baroquerie*, but what better satire of twentieth-century materialism with its love of luxury than Beddoes's lyric 'Rosily Dying' which concludes,

O pretty rose, hast thou thy flowery passions?
Then put thyself into a scented rage,
And breathe on me some poisonous revenge.
For it was I, thou languid, silken blush,
Who orphaned thy green family of thee,
In thy closed infancy: therefore receive
My life, and spread it on thy shrunken petals,
And give to me thy pink, reclining death.

There is something, too, of the flavour of *The Loved One* about Beddoes's 'Sorrow'. For death, linked to such sensual corruption becomes a critique of man's love of comfort which he tries to perpetuate beyond the grave in elaborate tombstones and effigies. We know that Beddoes saw a 'good collection of Holbeins' at Basle and was enthusiastic about them. Holbein's *Dance of Death*, including the Babies, was added as illustration to Gosse's Fanfrolico edition.[2] The two harmonize because both Holbein and Beddoes were, through the contrast of rich imagery and stark subject, satirizing the philistinism of luxury.

All the characters in *Death's Jest-Book* are, except for Isbrand, automatons in love with death and Beddoes comes forward with some of his finest passages to depict this. A typical example which expresses his gift fairly is in *The Improvisatore*:

Just at his feet a grinning skeleton
Stretched its worm-twined arms of chalky bone,

[1] 'The Boding Dreams.'

[2] The 1890 two-volume edition of Beddoes's works, edited by Edmund Gosse, put out by the Fanfrolico Press, London, on hand-made paper and limited to 750 copies, has been superseded by the definitive edition of Beddoes's works edited by H. W. Donner (Oxford and London, Humphrey Milford, 1935). The best selection is perhaps Ramsay Colles's edition in the Muses' Library series (London, Routledge, and New York, E. P. Dutton, 1907).

And rattled its thin finger in the blast;
Its spiked teeth were dumbly chattering fast,
As if its death-dream were disturbed; by him
Another lay with yawning jawbone grim,
  Through which the cold wind whistled; down its cheek
    Crept death's chill sweat; Rodolph essayes to pass,
  But fear chained down his strength; with struggles weak
    He plunged among the death-cemented mass.[1]

Now there is nothing new simply in this juxtaposition of the physically corrupting and the voluptuous. It is a feature of romantic literature. The convent where De Sade's Justine finds herself has punishment cells where, she is told, *on y place avec vous des rats, des lézards, des crapauds, des serpents*. It is an integral theme in Baudelaire, Borel and the lesser *bousingot*[2] writers, who never tired of describing some fair, fleshly creature, unassailably virtuous as well as beautiful, damned to putrefaction amongst worms and reptiles. In M. G. Lewis's famous *The Monk*, one of the earliest of this genre (1795), the pregnant Agnes is condemned to die in surroundings of which Beddoes would have made the most: she describes them for us with care:

> Sometimes I felt the bloated toad, hideous and pampered with the poisonous vapours of the dungeon, dragging his loathsome length along my bosom. Sometimes the quick cold lizard roused me, leaving his slimy track upon my face, and entangling itself in the tresses of my wild and matted hair. Often have I at waking found my fingers ringed with the long worms which bred in the corrupted flesh of my infant . . .

Luxury and corruption feast on each other. In *King John*, Constance speaks of death Beddoesianly, in words that show us the old bard could overgo them all when he wanted to:

O amiable lovely death!
Thou odoriferous stench! sound rottenness!
Arise forth from the couch of lasting night,
Thou hate and terror to posterity,
And I will kiss thy detestable bones;

[1] Stanza XXV.

[2] I prefer Aristide Marie's spelling of this word to Miss Starkie's.

And put my eyeballs in thy vaulty brows;
And ring these fingers with thy household worms;
And stop this gap of breath with fulsome dust;
And be a carrion monster like thyself:
Come, grin on me: and I will think thou smilest,
And buss thee as thy wife! Misery's love,
O, come to me![1]

With Beddoes, then, tears, bosoms, roses, red blood, all the props of courtly love, are juxtaposed with worms, tombs, skulls, bones. Even in the early *Scaroni* death takes the physical form of a veiled woman, whilst Wolfram's ghost haunts the Duke and advises him that

'Tis better too
To die, as thou art, young, in the first grace
And full of beauty.[2]

'The Phantom-Wooer', 'that loved a lady fair', courts her in these terms:

Young soul put off your flesh, and come
With me into the quiet tomb,
Our bed is lovely, dark and sweet;
The earth will swing us as she goes,
Beneath our coverlid of snows,
And the warm leaden sheet.

But there is something more besides this rather artificial tension in Beddoes. This is not the mere death-wish, nor the model spooking of Donne's 'The Apparition'. Beddoes's ghosts rise and beckon humans to the tomb, but they are surprisingly robust, cadavers of this world rather than of another. This is the point. They are people of this world who are yet not condemned to obey the laws of this world: one feels the whole force of Beddoes's sympathy behind them *as a collective group*, rather than as individuals. Death is therefore reduced to terms of life. The phantoms are really afraid of the worm, sickeningly mortal still. Their honey-sweet syllables, a sort of verbal gangrene, only suggest the more potently their horror at their own decay. It is *grand guignol* cynicism which triumphs, through Isbrand, over the bourgeois society of luxury lovers, on the one level, and over the escape world, the world o' the dead, over death

[1] Act III, sc. iv. [2] *Death's Jest-Book*, Act IV, sc. iii.

itself, therefore, on the other. We know that such was Beddoes's conscious intention from 'Hard Dying' (a poem in *The Last Man*), and especially in a verse-letter to Procter, in which he discusses the growth of his new work, where death is to be 'the fool o' the feast':

> Who's he? I've dug him up and decked him trim
> And made a mock, a fool, a slave of him
> Who was the planet's tyrant: dotard Death:[1]

And so on. Humour, symbolized by Isbrand, was the supreme rational force in Beddoes's universe, what alone distinguished man from the higher mammals. But since Isbrand communicates, is affective, we do not stare at the work as an object, in amazed fascination, as we do with the totally introspective Donne, for we ourselves are involved in the affective representation. To this extent it is romantic and solipsistically idealist. Yet the interesting thing is—and it remains to my mind the ultimate criticism of *Death's Jest-Book*—that Isbrand is an 'individual' in the old-world, bourgeois sense. If this is thought to be reading an economic interpretation into the play, we must remember that Beddoes clearly asked for such. Humour is sanity, he says, and yet he affixes it to an 'individual' (just such as he was in his own life). But humour, above all gifts, is the result of social organization, the product of men *in company*. Even Koestler's theory of humour as the intersection of *associative* trains of words in one bisociative junctional word[2] bears this out, whilst Kant's 'incongruity', Bergson's arrest of the *élan vital* of life, and Nicole's postulation of the moral basis of laughter, all tend to show that a man is not funny unless other men think he is funny. He cannot be funny 'individually'. The first thing we notice in a mental home (and to some extent in modern psychiatric practice) is the absence of a sense of humour. *Death's Jest-Book* satirizes a baroque world, a world fetid with the bourgeois illusion, disgraced by capitalist luxury. This world yields to the world o' the dead, to a society where bourgeois conventions do not operate. But individual man is still rational, he need not lust after the mummy country, as Isbrand puts it. He has his humour. Thus it is extremely significant that Isbrand (like his creator) is alone in this bizarre anticipation of Marxian society. He is an 'individual' in both worlds, for he does

[1] Letter XXI, postmarks 7 March and 13 March 1826.
[2] *Insight and Outlook.*

not share that prophetic longing for death of the (bourgeois) society which is dying, and he sees the absurdity of the robot-like puppets of the other, rising (communist) world o' the dead. He exactly epitomizes Beddoes's own solitude. For, mocking a society, Beddoes had to mock himself. The result is that *Death's Jest-Book* is autobiographical and therefore represents, as did the author's own life, the tragic squandering of a talent. Swinburne and Tennyson thought Beddoes brilliant, Landor (whom he met in Florence) praised him extravagantly, and more recently Emile Legouis has classed him with Shelley and Keats.[1] There is no doubt of Beddoes's greatness but there is no doubt also that he could have been far greater. It is an indictment of modern society that it lamed his expression. It did more, it threw him overboard, like its 'surplus' foodstuffs, and it is pathetic, rather than tragic, that this great figure should have spent a lifetime in trying to make the macabre grotesque, to make laughable Western man's deepest fear, the dread of something after death, the undiscovered country. Beddoes's solution was no solution and this is proved by the increasing madness of our society (I mean literal madness. It is now computed that a conservative estimate of mentally defectives in America puts them at one per hundred of the whole population, and that one out of every ten Americans will spend some of his life in a mental home.[2]) Humour is collective, not individual, but whether collection rather than individuality is what distinguishes man from beast is outside the scope of this essay. But it is a depressing conclusion to centuries of endeavour to think we are only better than apes because we can laugh. For this is what Isbrand says:

> O cap and bells, ye eternal emblems, hieroglyphics of man's supreme right in nature; O ye, that only fall on the deserving, while oak, palm, laurel, and bay rankle on *their* foreheads, whose deserts are oft more payable at the other extremity: who shall be honoured with you? Come, candidates, the cap and bells are empty.

[1] *Short History of English Literature* (1934).

[2] Albert Deutsch, *The Mentally Ill in America*, New York, Doubleday Doran, 1937.

RENÉ DUMESNIL

THE INEVITABILITY OF FLAUBERT

FLAUBERT, states Mr. Aldous Huxley in his essay, *Vulgarity in Literature*, wished his work to have no ornament other than its own essential beauty, without exterior decoration, however beautiful this might be in itself. And he adds that the saint's asceticism was duly rewarded, since there is nothing even remotely resembling a vulgarity in any of Flaubert's writings. Neither is there any pandering to the taste of the day, nor sacrifice to mere fashion. It is, of course, unquestionable that *Madame Bovary*—and probably still more *An Education in Love*—have given rise to a great number of novels whose authors have done their best to follow the precepts of the master of Croisset; but it is equally true that his ideas, his aesthetic theory, and his method of composition, were entirely his own. Flaubert created a literary school, he did not follow one.

The strict self-discipline which has gained Flaubert the title of ascetic is probably the reason why the young writers of today have turned away from so austere a master—and one, moreover, who had already scolded Zola for pandering to the taste of a public greedy for the frivolous and the morbid. When J.-K. Huysmans sent him *Les Sœurs Vatard*, Flaubert acknowledged it in a letter which could be read with advantage by many novelists of today: 'The basis of your style is firm enough, but you seem to me too modest to rely on it. Why try to bolster it up with violent and vulgar phraseology? When it is you who is speaking, why express yourself like your characters? Don't you see that this is the best way of weakening their idiom? That I should not understand some slang expression used by a Parisian footpad makes no matter. If you consider that expression characteristic and therefore indispensable, I bow to your judgement and deplore only my own ignorance of these things. But when a writer, in expressing his own views, employs a mass of words unknown to any dictionary, then I have a right to object. For what you are doing offends me and spoils my pleasure . . . A whole aesthetic is contained in this remark (p. 152): "The sadness of wallflowers withering in a vase seemed more *interesting* to him than the sunlit smile of roses". Why? Neither wallflowers nor roses are interesting in themselves. The only interesting thing about them is the way you describe them. The Ganges is no more poetic than the Bièvre,[1] and vice versa. *If we are not careful we shall relapse, as in the days of classical tragedy, into a class system of subjects and a precious vocabulary. People will come to think that vulgarisms enliven a literary style, just as formerly they petrified it with affected terminology. The rhetoric will be inside out, but it will still be rhetoric.* It hurts me to see so original a man as yourself spoiling his work through childishness. Have more faith in yourself—and don't trust receipts.'

Baudelaire once said that the intoxicating thing about bad taste was the aristocratic pleasure in displeasing. Nowadays, it is only too obvious that many writers, far from wishing to displease, are but trying to flatter the bad taste of a public which longs to be shocked. The rhetoric is turned inside out, but it is still rhetoric. I am less sure that it is employed in the interests of sincerity.

It is difficult to realize that in 1856 *Madame Bovary* should have caused Flaubert to be arraigned before a criminal court for offence to public morals, or that the same judges, less indulgent to Baudelaire than they had been, six months before, to Flaubert, should have ordered the excision from *Les Fleurs du Mal* of ten or so poems which are now to be found in all the anthologies, because they are in fact among the most perfect. Admittedly Baudelaire, when he wrote them, enjoyed the aristocratic pleasure in displeasing, just as Flaubert did when he drew the portraits of Monsieur Homais, of the Abbé Bournisien, of Bouvard and Pécuchet and the inhabitants of Chavignolles. But in attacking the bourgeoisie (I call bourgeois, he said, anyone who is low-minded) he obeyed a high-minded impulse. He was 'getting his own back', as he puts it in his letters; he was avenging the life of the spirit—taking Ariel's side against Caliban. And in fact there is something chivalrous about this gesture of rebellion in face of the prevailing mediocrity. In his *Letter to the Municipality of Rouen*, which had just refused to accept the results of a subscription raised in favour of a monument to the poet Louis Bouilhet, Flaubert breaks out into cries of violent indignation which contrast strangely with the impassivity characteristic of a novelist

[1] The Bièvre is a stream which flows through the dyers' and tanners' quarter at Gobelins; its polluted waters meander between the crumbling walls of the tanneries. Flaubert's letter seems prophetic, for Huysmans afterwards wrote a book about the Bièvre, whose 'ailing aspect charmed him'.

who always effaced himself from his own works and took the greatest care not to display his own thoughts or feelings in them: 'Conservatives with nothing to preserve, it is time you got out of your rut—and since regeneration and decentralization are the pass-words of the moment, get yourselves some fresh ideas! Have a little initiative for a change! The French nobility went down because for two centuries it entertained the same ideas as its domestic servants. Now the bourgeoisie is going the same way because it entertains those of the plebs. I can't see that it reads different newspapers, enjoys different music, or indulges in more dignified pleasures. In both classes I find the same love of money, the same respect for the *fait accompli*, the same iconoclasm, the same hatred of genuine superiority, the same love of disparagement, the same gross ignorance . . . Before you send the proletariat to school, go there yourselves!

'You have the cheek to call yourselves the enlightened classes, but what you need is light on your own minds! Because you despise the intellect you think you're sensible, positive and practical; but only those are really practical who are something else as well. You would not now be enjoying the advantages of industrial progress if your ancestors in the eighteenth century had thought only of im-mediate material utility. . . . All your mental activity consists in worrying about the future. It's time you worried about something else—and you'll have to hurry up or France will fall lower and lower between the twin stools of a purblind bourgeoisie and a monstrous proletarian tyranny.'

It is a good thing that somebody should let fly like this at times. Just because they mostly keep silence, such voices, when they do raise themselves, seem to possess all the weight and authority neces-sary to denounce the least excusable of crimes—those which are directed against the human spirit.

During the Commune, at a time when Paris was distracted by riots which (it should not be forgotten) were originally a protest against the capitulation to the Germans, Flaubert wrote thus to George Sand: 'This is a pretty kettle of fish! Ah well! Never mind, at least I know where I am—no longer in the fearful state of mind under which I have been groaning for six months past. Unlike most people, I can think of nothing worse than the Prussian invasion. The annihilation of Paris by the Commune would cause me less grief than the burning of a single village by "those charming gentlemen".

Ugh! These men of letters who give themselves over to a job like that and grovel to such a tyranny—this is both new and *inexcusable*.'

That cry of rebellion lies at the root of *Bouvard and Pécuchet* and it explains much in that unfinished book, the exact aim of which remains difficult to discern. Alone at Croisset, Flaubert had meditated on the war of 1870, and during its first days he wrote these prophetic lines: 'The nationalist wars may well be beginning again. Before another century is out we shall witness the massacre of several million men in a single battle. The whole of the East against Europe, the old world in arms against the new. Why not? Big collective enterprises like the Suez Canal may well be a kind of rehearsal or prelude to conflicts so appalling that we cannot even imagine them.'

He was one of the first men with foresight enough to realize that material progress is a chimera. Searching about for the causes which were leading his contemporaries so grievously astray, he found them and pointed them out in the afore-mentioned men of letters, 'more barbarous than Attila's Huns', in the dangers of pseudo-science and of that half-knowledge which is but a caricature of real science. He tried to show that the god of these 'scientists' was just an empty simulacrum. Everyone was saying that the Prussians owed their victory to their scholars. Miserable learning, wretched scholars! Such is the fundamental idea of *Bouvard and Pécuchet*, and one which would no doubt have become obvious if death had not interrupted the author in the middle of his work. For the bitter irony of the book, the imperfections and the ambiguities which are the result of its fragmentary state, should not prevent us from recognizing its power and the magnanimity of the vision which inspired it. *Bouvard and Pécuchet* is a warning that was bound to be misunderstood by the majority, who were aware only of the farcical surface and could not perceive the harsh precision of the symbolism. For stupidity means believing in the innate *benevolence* of science; means thinking of it as a kind of universal panacea, a tame divinity; above all it consists in taking science out of its own sphere, confusing *why* with *how*, mistaking mere hypotheses for demonstrated truths, believing that we know what in fact we do not know, and intoxicating ourselves with hollow phrases. Yet *Bouvard and Pécuchet* is not, as some have lightly supposed, an attack on science: Flaubert's intention was to bring to the bar, not his two goodfellows, but the Coulons, the

Marescots, the Foureaus and all the other fools who surrounded them in their village, dragging them down (as they dragged Flaubert himself down) with 'the mass of a Himalaya, the sheer weight of a world's folly'.

Before starting on this novel, and while preparing the third version of *The Temptation of St. Antony*, Flaubert read a quantity of philosophical works, in particular those of Herbert Spencer. This produced an attempt to reconcile Spencer's conception of the Unknowable with Flaubert's own Spinozist views. He did not consider Science and Religion as enemies one of which was fated to be destroyed by the other, but he did believe them to represent the opposite poles of the mind, between which no common standard was possible. So that, while *The Temptation* was a catalogue of fallacies in the negative realm of religion, *Bouvard and Pécuchet* became a review (this time in comic vein) of the errors that result from the lack of a proper scientific method. The book is a legal investigation of the pseudo-religion of science. It is as dangerous to believe that science is necessarily beneficent as it is to assume that the Unknowable can be rationally explained. Although the limits of the Unknowable may seem to recede as Science extends its dominion, there is in reality no contact between the two. 'I am not so much surprised', writes Flaubert to his friend Mme Roger des Genettes, 'by those who try to explain the inexplicable, as by those who think they have succeeded and have put God—or Nothingness—into their pocket. Any kind of dogmatism maddens me!' A wise attitude indeed, but one that exposes him who adopts it to the attacks of all sectarians whether of the right or of the left. To those who cannot bear uncertainty, a belief in the possibility of certainty is some consolation . . .

* * *

To read Flaubert is worth while not merely because he stimulates thought, but because his letters contain instruction of which the applicability remains undimmed. These letters are among the most curious documents which the nineteenth century has left to us. For Flaubert took an active part in the intellectual movements of his time; far from being a mere passive witness, observing, reflecting, noting, he was a leader of his generation and of the following one. At an age when others are still at the early apprentice stage, he already gave the impression of a master. Although he himself had not yet published anything, we find him writing of Maxime du Camp's *Posthumous Book*, which had just come out: 'I seem to hear throughout the book a dim echo of *November*. A kind of Flaubertian fog lies like a blanket over it all. And Du Camp will not be the only one upon whom I shall have left my mark.' This was written in December 1852, four years before the appearance of *Madame Bovary*; but it was true: Flaubert *had* already left his mark on several young writers. He was to influence many more, by publishing books which became the literary gospel of an entire period. His letters alone explain the mysterious authority, the power to fascinate and carry others with him, the far-reaching influence exerted by a man who lived the life of a hermit, away from society, disdainful of success and deaf to the flattery of his admirers.

A yet more general and more profound lesson may be learnt from these letters. To begin with, Flaubert was a model of artistic integrity, of conscientious everyday toil, of craftsmanship (taking the word in its highest sense): virtues which were the direct result of constant self-abnegation, of laborious concentration and extreme self-sacrifice. The man himself passed through days of discouragement when it seemed to him that his task was too heavy and must end by crushing him altogether. The further he advanced, the more his goal appeared to recede. Weariness overcame him sometimes and he would wonder if he had the courage to persevere. But he did persevere, taking up the overwhelming burden and even finding patience to go back in his tracks—to destroy what on a more careful examination he saw to be imperfect—to rewrite all over again, twice and even three or four times, something which had already cost him so much trouble. His own most merciless critic, he allowed himself no moments of weakness or complacency. Having adopted this severe regime once and for all, he never once went back on it. As he wrote to Maxime Du Camp, at the outset of his career: 'I am not primarily concerned with becoming well known, since I believe that fame is completely satisfying only to the vanity of mediocre people. My own aim is a better one: to satisfy myself . . . Success appears to me a result, not a goal . . . I have a dim idea in my head of the elegance of diction and style that I mean to achieve. Until I succeed in this my chief care is to avoid diddling the public! I can quite understand that people who want to become manufacturers should be in a hurry to set up their factories. But if a work of art is good, if it is *genuine*, then what does it matter whether it makes its name in six months, or six years—or even after one is dead?'

These precepts, of a deep and disinterested wisdom, never cease to be valid, whatever may be the password of the latest school or the fashion of the moment. One may like or dislike Flaubert's novels; one may disapprove his art and reject his theories; one may even loathe his style and the view of life upon which his novels are founded. But no one can ignore his precepts without lowering his own intellectual status. Those rules were in no way meant for publicity, they are the expression of intimate belief, a private confession of faith; but their intrinsic nobility confers on them a universal validity: they stand good not only for writers and intellectuals, but for everyone who undertakes any creative work whatsoever.

Patience, dignity, professional integrity: such are the doctrines to be learnt from a first reading of Flaubert's letters. And these doctrines are reinforced by the spectacle of the writer's own life. Of course, the man had his weaknesses; but even when he is in the wrong his obvious distinction of character protects him from meanness or intransigence. One has only to read his letters to Louise Colet to be fully aware of this. When she tries to push him in a direction he doesn't want to go, or requires him to join her in abuse of Alfred de Musset, he tells her straight out that to be someone's rival in love does not affect his moral worth; and he told her this in terms which took her aback. In doing so he showed the same directness, firmness and precision as in dealing with himself. Never for a moment did he entertain the idea of personal profit or of any material advantage, and in this he resembled his own creation, the Dr. Larivière of *Madame Bovary*: 'fanatically attached to his art, practising it with wisdom and a rapturous concentration, contemptuous of honours, titles and degrees, open-handed, open-minded, generous and kindly to the poor, virtuous yet never priggish, he might have been thought a saint were it not that his intellect had a superstitious horror of such things . . . ' Yet people did not fear him, they loved him.

Flaubert worked himself into a condition where ecstasy and pain became one; and he attached value to the exertions which so tortured him. Those pains and those ecstasies produced pages like this: 'I have never swerved from my path since the time when I used to ask my nurse for the letters with which to spell the sentences that came into my head, until this evening when the ink is still wet on the page of erasures which lies before me. I have steered a course as straight and taut as a bowstring, which went on and on. I have watched my goal recede gradually, year after year, as fast as I went. How often have I fallen flat on my stomach just at the moment when I was hoping to reach the end! All the same, I have a feeling that I am not destined to die without hearing at least a distant roar, somewhere or other, of the style I have always had at the back of my head. It ought to make itself heard above the parrots and the crickets.'

The single-mindedness of Flaubert's life is indeed astonishing. It would not be easy to find another example of so constant a will-power, of an energy so unflagging. The last letter I quoted dates from 1852, when Flaubert was in process of writing *Madame Bovary*; and he was to 'fall flat on his stomach' many times before finishing the book and reaching his goal. Those tortures at an end, *Salammbô* was to cause him still worse. And so, with every one of his books, the same troubles and anxieties were to be renewed; for all his life long he remained suspicious of work that came easily and he was as hard as ever on himself. On the final evening of his life, when death surprised him at the grinding task of bringing *Bouvard and Pécuchet* to perfection, he wrote again those words: 'I have steered a straight course, on and on . . . ' And, as in 1852, he might have added: 'The self-doubts which trouble us when we are unknown, remain with us when we become famous. Some of the strongest of us continue to be fretted by them to their dying day.' He himself was eaten alive by those self-same doubts.

But though merciless to himself he never became hard on others. On the contrary, he remained as simple and kind-hearted in life as he was conscientious and undeviating in the exercise of his craft. Always faithful and obliging to his friends, he continued to work for them when they were dead, with no thought but for their own interest and reputation. The best illustration of this is his championship of Bouilhet, when he fought the combined forces of politics and stupidity, and won a victory over the Municipality of Rouen. He published his old friend's *Last Songs* at his own expense, and even here he had a battle to fight. He spared neither time, trouble, nor money, and was indeed—as he loved to style himself—the last of the troubadours.

His letters too contain some very pretty lessons in the art of friendship. Here, too, he proved himself a master. The letters to George Sand are full of tenderness and an almost filial affection; even when he crosses swords with her on aesthetic grounds he does not become disagreeable. She never succeeded in making him give up his 'detachment', but it was for her that he wrote *The Pure in Heart*, perhaps the most deeply felt of all his stories. Yet George Sand was never to read it, for she died on 18 June 1876, before Flaubert had finished the tale invented to please her. The 'dear friend of God' deserved that he should say of her, on returning from her funeral: 'It seemed as though I were burying my mother all over again'. And he, too, deserved that gracious friendship.

* * *

Considering that Flaubert made objectivity the indefeasible rule of his art, and that, throughout his career, he never stopped asserting that only an artist's work, and not his private life, belongs to the public, it may seem paradoxical to claim that his letters constitute his masterpiece. But in the end it is what he tells us about his inner self that we prefer even to those works which caused him the most trouble and suffering; it is the letters he wrote day by day that mean even more to us than the books he accomplished at the cost of so much labour. This is because, familiar and even trivial as they often are, they are so spontaneous, so vivid and idiosyncratic in style, that they are at once an encyclopaedia of literary method and an invaluable guide to living.

Such, it seems to me, are the reasons why we should turn our eyes once more towards the great man of Croisset. It may be that the young are somewhat contemptuous of him. It is true that he has taken his place among the classic writers of all time. Yet he is one of those great masters who remain alive by virtue of the advice he can still dispense. And it is certain that that advice is worth following.

[*Translated by* EDWARD SACKVILLE-WEST]

MERVYN JONES-EVANS

HENRY JAMES'S YEAR IN FRANCE

IN the autumn of 1875 Henry James, aged thirty-two, arrived in Paris. It was by no means his first visit to Europe, for several years of his childhood and adolescence had been spent outside America, but this was his first visit as a writer. It was to be an important event in his life and he had already a premonition of its value. On previous visits he had only too readily laid himself open to absorb European traditions and culture, so his feeling for the past was well developed. In America there was nothing to assuage his thirst and he hankered after the Europe which he was convinced had more to offer him than Boston or New York. What is more, he had come to the turning point of his life: a decision had to be made and it was one that he could make easily. He knew that there was no alternative, that it was only in literature that he could find any sense of fulfilment, and so, looking for a spring-board from which to take the plunge, he turned towards Europe.

Europe was the centre of intellectual and literary activity, and therefore it was inevitable that sooner or later James must migrate there to free himself from the deadening, cloying, sterile puritanism of New English life. After an uneventful year at Cambridge, Massachusetts, he set out in search of the congenial surroundings he needed and the intellectual company he so ardently desired. He arrived as a self-styled apprentice to sit at the feet of his chosen French masters and to learn from them the true meaning of art and the intrinsic value of the written word. He wanted to see at first hand how their minds worked and in what direction they were tending. Above all, he wanted to become part of that splendid circle of writers who represented for him the only live force in contemporary literature and the only movement with which he felt any affinity. He was the right age; for ten years already his life had been devoted to the profession of literature and he had to his credit a number of reviews and critical articles, several stories, and one novel, *Roderick Hudson*, which, at the time of his arrival, was being serialized in *The Atlantic Monthly*.

James took rooms at 29 rue de Luxembourg, intending that Paris should become his home. He found his way easily into society for he possessed breeding, culture and a certain amount of wealth. In addition, he spoke impeccable if somewhat old-fashioned French and, most useful of all, he was an American. It was far easier for an American to pass through the barred doors of London or Paris society than it was for a young Englishman or Frenchman. Henry James knew this and took full advantage of his opportunities to gain *entrée* to literary and artistic *salons* such as those run by Madame Viardot and Madame de Blocqueville. It was through these evenings, and some readily accepted invitations to dinner parties, that he managed to meet his literary idols, and came to know Gustave Flaubert, Alphonse Daudet, Maupassant, Zola, Edmond de Goncourt and, for James the most important, Ivan Turgenev. He wrote from Paris: 'I have been seeing something of Daudet, Goncourt, Zola; and there is nothing more interesting to me now than the effort and the experiment of their little group, with its truly infernal intelligence of art, form, manner—its intense artistic life. They do the only kind of work, today, that I respect; and in spite of their handling of unclean things, they are at least serious and honest. The floods of tepid soap and water which under the name of novels are being vomited forth in England, seem to me, by contrast, to do little honour to our race.'

In April of the following year he wrote to his father: 'You crave chiefly news, I suppose, about Ivan Sergeitch [Turgenev], whom I have lately seen several times. I spent a couple of hours with him at his room, some time since, and I have seen him otherwise at Mme Viardot's. The latter invited me to her musical parties (Thursdays) and to her Sundays *en famille*. I have been to a couple of the former and (as yet) only one of the latter . . . Her Sundays seem rather dingy and calculated to remind one of Concord "historical games", etc. But it was both strange and sweet to see poor Turgenev acting charades of the most extravagant description, dressed out in old shawls and masks, etc.' And further on he wrote the often-quoted extract: 'I had the other day a very pleasant call upon Flaubert, whom I like personally more and more each time I see him. But I think I easily—more than easily—see all around him intellectually. There is something wonderfully simple, honest, kindly, and touchingly inarticulate about him.'

Half a year had already passed when he wrote that letter, and there is already, to the observant eye, a shade of doubt. To obtain a word or two from Turgenev meant long and boring evening recitals at Madame Viardot's. Flaubert was difficult to see owing to his monastic way of life—his 'Benedictine existence' James called it—and although he was on terms of amity with Daudet and Edmond de Goncourt, there was no feeling of friendship or warmth with any of them. He found them all members of a closed circle, not open to outside opinions and influences, and, least of all, prepared to accept an unknown, reserved, perhaps rather pompous, American. So, more often than not, he was thrown back with undoubted chagrin and disappointment upon the not altogether pleasing company of his own compatriots in Paris. Whether they filled the gap satisfactorily we cannot tell; certainly he made full use of them in later years.

It is difficult to discover what really happened during that experimental year, for his own letters say little and his name is absent from the French writers' letters, journals and memoirs. Turgenev, however, did write to W. R. S. Ralston telling him to make a friend of Henry James and describing him as 'a very amiable, sensible, and gifted man, with a tendency towards *tristesse* which will not frighten you'. Turgenev paid more attention to the young Henry James than any of the others, and in return he received all James's affection and admiration. Perhaps James found the circle too close; perhaps he was snubbed or received some rebuff; whatever may have occurred James battled on in Paris, filling his brain with literature and painting, with every detail of the city, of the people, and of Parisian society, all of which he was to use later on. He wrote Parisian letters for the New York Journals and reviews and gave himself up to everything that France and her Capital had to offer him. That he was proud is obvious, and even if his reception was less enthusiastic than he had hoped and anticipated, he was determined to make up for it in other ways. At least those in America who were not altogether sympathetic to expatriate tendencies must not be allowed to suspect his failure. In May 1876 he wrote to W. D. Howells (another New England novelist, but one who never left America and who, in later years, was somewhat critical of James's preference for living in Europe) that he was 'turning into an old, and very contented Parisian: I feel as if I had struck roots in the Parisian soil, and were likely to let them grow tangled and tenacious there'. But later in the same letter some of the truth began to emerge, for he admits: 'I have seen a certain number of people all winter who have helped me to pass the time, but I have formed but one or two relations of permanent value, and which I desire to perpetuate. I have seen almost nothing of the literary fraternity, and there are fifty reasons why I should not become intimate with them. I don't like their wares, and they don't like any others; and besides they are not *accueillants*. Turgenev is worth the whole heap of them, and yet he himself swallows them down in a manner which excites my extreme wonder.' Yet he goes on to say: 'I interrupted this a couple of hours since to go out and pay a visit to Gustave Flaubert, it being his time of receiving, and his last Sunday in Paris, and I owe him a farewell. *He* is a very nice old fellow, and the most interesting man and the strongest artist in his circle. I had him for an hour alone, and then came in his "following", talking much of Zola's 'catastrophe'—Zola having just had a serial novel [*L'Assommoir*] interrupted on account of protests from provincial subscribers against its indecency. The opinion apparently was that it was a bore, and that it could only do the book good on its appearance as a volume . . . On my way down I met poor Zola climbing the staircase, looking very pale and sombre, and I saluted him with a flourish natural to a contributor who has just been invited to make his novel last longer yet . . . '

No doubt part of the trouble was that although he had a considerable admiration for their fearless innovations and experiments, their respect for language and form, and their passion for style—characteristics common to all the Realist writers—he was revolted by their subjects. One of the reasons why he left America, and New England in particular, was the inhibiting and stifling atmosphere of puritanism. But in Paris he discovered the horrible truth: that he himself was equally puritanical and had just as pronounced a sense of morality. Again and again the reader of his reviews and critical essays will find him protesting against what he considers to be indecency. Another distressing factor was that he was unable to persuade the French writers either to read or to listen to him enthusing over George Eliot, who occupied second place in James's estimation of the greatest contemporary novelists—the first being Ivan Turgenev. He found the parochialism of the French writers exasperating and never failed to say so in his reports to America. In every respect it seems that their circle was a closed one.

In July he wrote to his brother from Étretat, where he had spent the summer months, ' . . . my last layers of resistance to a long encroaching weariness and satiety with the French mind and its utterances have fallen from me like a garment. I have done with 'em, for ever, and am turning English all over. I desire only to feed on English minds—I wish greatly I knew some. Easy and smooth-flowing as life is in Paris, I would throw it over tomorrow for an even small chance to plant myself for a while in England.' The inevitable disappointment had to be admitted. His disillusionment was complete, and it was plain to him that his experiment was a failure: indeed it would be to most young men at that particular stage of development. But, little as we know of the actual happenings of that year in Paris, it was clearly an invaluable experience. Even if he had been shocked by Flaubert's opening his door to him clad only in his dressing gown, he was compensated by an occasional hour in Turgenev's 'little green sitting-room' at Madame Viardot's.

Some of his disappointment can be read in the collection of essays which appeared in 1879 under the title *French Poets and Novelists*. These include, amongst others, critical comments on Musset, Gautier, Baudelaire, Balzac, George Sand, and a joint essay on Charles de Bernard and Flaubert, since Henry James did not deem Flaubert worthy of an article devoted entirely to himself. It is only fair to explain that these essays are not so much literary criticism as a list of James's likes and dislikes; for James (to invert his oft-repeated complaint against the French novelists) was not so much interested in the truth about life as in the truth about art. And therefore the reader should not consider this book as a particular example of Henry James's criticism but simply as another sidelight on the development of his mind and thought.

In *French Poets and Novelists* it is Flaubert who suffers most. For James has singled him out as the one most affected by what he considers their greatest literary weakness—indecency. As he wrote from Paris, 'novel and drama alike portray an incredibly superficial perception of the moral side of life. It is not only that adultery is their theme, but that the treatment of it is so monstrously vicious and arid!' This was, of course, a reference to *Madame Bovary* (the novel which pained him most) and to Edmond de Goncourt's *La Fille Elisa*. Again and again he emphasizes this point. 'Everything ran to form, and the successful books were apt to resemble little vases, skilfully moulded and chiselled, into which unclean things had been dropped.' And then: 'French literature abounds in books which have been pushed to the lengths which only a sort of artistic conspiracy of many minds could have reached . . .' Zola too came in for censure: 'Zola is the most thorough-going of the little band of out-and-out realists. Unfortunately the real for him means exclusively the unclean.' This attitude is perhaps a little surprising when one remembers that Henry James himself, in a very different way (perhaps unintentional) is not altogether free of suggestive writing. As Mr. Edmund Wilson has pointed out, *The Turn of the Screw* is filled with submerged sexual symbolism.

Everything was wrong with *Madame Bovary*. It lacked delicacy, charm and 'good taste', qualities which he particularly admired in the early novels of George Sand and (despite a certain vulgarity) in Pierre Loti's *Pêcheurs d'Islande*. Worse still, it lacked reserve, a quality which he especially understood and enjoyed in both Balzac and Turgenev and which was very much to his nineteenth-century New English taste. This feeling for the delicate handling of moral questions had also aroused his admiration for George Eliot (whom he was to meet the following year in London), and it was a quality which he ardently cultivated in his own writing. James preferred respectability to bohemianism and had a very definite code as to what was and what was not permissible in art, life and literature. Flaubert had observed none of the fundamentals of this code. Of *Madame Bovary* James wrote: 'The accumulation of detail is so immense, the vividness of portraiture of people, of places, of time and hours, is so poignant and convincing, that one is dragged into the very current and tissue of the story; the reader himself seems to have lived in it all, more than any other novel he can recall. At the end the intensity of illusion becomes horrible; overwhelmed with disgust and pity he closes the book.' Yet *Madame Bovary* appealed to him more than the other novels of Flaubert, which he felt to be cold, hard, steely, uninspired and calculated literary exercises. As he wrote in the second of his three essays on Flaubert, '*Salammbô*, in which we breathe the air of pure aesthetics, is as hard as stone; *L'Education*, for the same reason, is as cold as death; *Saint-Antoine* is a medley of wonderful bristling metals and polished agates, and the drollery of *Bouvard et Pécuchet* (a work as sad as something perverse and puerile done for a wager) about as contagious as the smile of a keeper showing you through the ward of a madhouse'. At least *Madame Bovary* was coloured by a warmth of emotion, which took off the icy chill and made it more palatable. James felt that Flaubert had sacrificed his imagination, his emotions and even his life to his almost fruitless search for the perfect form, and that in the end it was only an 'immense ado about nothing'. In later years his criticism was less harsh and he even modified his opinion of *Madame Bovary*. Yet he always spoke of 'poor Flaubert', and described him as a great failure in art. For, despite his more lenient opinion, *Madame Bovary* always remained the beautifully worked out but indecent book which had won notoriety through the publicity of a court-room.

Baudelaire he found even less attractive, for the reason that he never really understood him. He completely misconstrued the title *Les Fleurs du Mal*, and talked of the poems as being full of 'rags and bad smells, lurid landscape and unclean furniture'. Although he admitted that Baudelaire possessed a certain talent and some vein of genius he dismissed him as 'childish'. After all, hadn't Hawthorne done it better?

So it was with most of the nineteenth-century French authors whom he read and met. Even his 'adored' Balzac did not escape unscathed, for James was horrified by his preoccupation with money and a little amazed by his obsession with the aristocracy. In spite of his respect and adoration he strongly criticized what he termed Balzac's 'arrant charlatanism' and went on to say that, 'It is probable that no equally vigorous mind was ever at pains to concoct such elaborate messes of folly. They spread themselves over page after page, in a close, dense, verbal tissue, which the reader scans in vain for some little flower of available truth.'

However, no matter what charges he laid at their door, the French novelists were closer than any others to his own particular conception of what contemporary literature should be. And while his personal relations with them were unsuccessful he had at least been able to see and talk to them. He could still respect their craftsmanship, their technical achievements and their pursuit of perfection. He could still, even if his experiment at living a literary life in Paris had also failed, benefit from their consciousness, their awareness and their very definite sense of vitality.

Henry James was not altogether to blame for his lack of success. Even had he been able to reconcile himself to the French way of thinking it is far from certain that he would have been accepted by the French writers, as is proved by the almost parallel experience of George Moore. Moore's acquaintanceship with Zola—no matter how it may have appeared to him in retrospect—was clearly slight. But whereas James kept silent about his failure, George Moore deliberately tried to obfuscate the facts. Yet in some respects he fared better than James, for he did meet Hugo, Mallarmé (he was invited to the Tuesday evenings), and the Impressionist painters, Manet, Degas, Renoir, and others. But he knew them no better than James knew Flaubert or Turgenev.

Before his year's stay was up James knew that it would be impossible for him to go on living in Paris and he began to consider a move to London. He excluded America as an alternative. London would, and did, prove more fruitful. Whatever the real reason for his decision, he had no intention of renouncing his meagre connections with France or French literature. His interest in all its latest developments was paramount, and even as an old man his curiosity was just as keen, for in 1914 he wrote to Edith Wharton asking her to send him Marcel Proust's *Du Côté de Chez Swann*. Perhaps he actually read the early volumes of *A la Recherche du Temps Perdu*; his opinion would have been unusually interesting, for stylistically he had much in common with Proust. Two-thirds of his literary criticism was devoted to French literature, and although he had but little appreciation of poetry (he had a predilection for the works of Browning) it is significant that the only poetry he wrote about was that of Musset, Gautier and Baudelaire.

All through his life he made repeated visits to Paris and there were always friends with whom he kept in contact: One such was Alphonse Daudet, whose *Port Tarascon* he translated and published in 1903, another was Jacques-Emile Blanche. To the very end he had a lively, and not altogether typically American, interest in the latest manifestations of French culture. One visit to Touraine and Provence produced the travel book *A Little Tour in France*, and France provided the setting for several of his novels, among them *The Ambassadors*, *The American*, and the first part of *The Tragic Muse*.

But what he particularly derived from his sojourn in Paris was a sense of analysis. This essentially French faculty, which played such an important role throughout his work, enabled him to lead the novel into a channel hitherto completely unknown and to produce those fascinating prefaces to the collected edition of his works which are something unique in Anglo-Saxon literature. No matter what his feelings may have suffered during that year, it is quite obvious that it was in Paris in 1875 and 1876 that James learnt the craftsmanship of writing and the fundamentals of his art; it was there indeed that he discovered 'the figure in the carpet'. It is also obvious that had he not gone to Paris he would have missed an invaluable experience which greatly contributed to his own genius.

EDOUARD RODITI

ITALO SVEVO

ITALO SVEVO's real name was Ettore Schmitz. He was born in Trieste on 19 December 1861. His mother was Italian, his father was German-Austrian, and there was also a Jewish strain in the family. From 1873 to 1878, Svevo studied in Germany, where he attended a business-school; when he returned to his native seaport, he devoted another couple of years to commercial studies at the Rivoltella School, then was employed, until 1897, in a bank where he observed the background of his first novel, *Una Vita*, published in 1893 and written while he was still a bank-clerk. In 1897 Svevo became partner in a business and, in 1898, published his second novel, *Senilità*: during the remaining years of his life, he seems to have devoted most of his time and energies to various successful commercial activities, often travelling to Venice or Vienna and sometimes farther, to France, England, Germany and Ireland. In 1923 he published his longest and most famous novel, *La conscienza di Zeno*; he also published a few stories, some short, others almost long enough to be novels, which all belong to the later period of his writing and appeared mostly in periodicals after the great success of *Zeno*: *La madre* (1910), *Una burla riuscita* (1926), *Vino generoso* (1926), *La novella del buon vecchio e della bella fanciulla* (1926). *Dalle memorie di un cane*, a short piece, is not included in the posthumous volume of Svevo's collected stories which, however, contains the beginning of *Il vecchione*, another long novel that he had just begun writing when he was killed, in a motor accident near Trieste, in September 1928.

Critics and journalists of many nations have already discussed Svevo in hundreds of articles; interpretatively and disconnectedly, they have tended to appreciate details of his fiction without elucidating their structural significance in the whole work, or have enthusiastically protested that Svevo is far greater than other writers to whom other critics have compared him. Federico Sternberg, in *L'Opera di Italo Svevo*, a pamphlet published in Trieste in 1928, thus insists that his dead friend was a greater writer than Proust; Benjamin Crémieux, a French critic, had dared to recommend *Zeno* to French readers by suggesting that they would discover, in the Italian novel, qualities that they already admired in *A la recherche du temps perdu*. But few of these articles and essays are now worth reading; a careful study of Svevo's fiction teaches us more about his qualities, faults or peculiarities, and about his life and beliefs. In January 1929, *Il convegno*, a Milan periodical, devoted a special issue to Svevo, with a useful bibliography and one excellent essay, *Svevo e Schmitz* (*Svevo, Schmitz e Zeno* would have been a better title), by Giacomo De Benedetti, who investigates the novelist's plural personality, as businessman, citizen of Trieste, novelist and hero of his own stories.

Svevo's works are indeed difficult to place accurately in the complex and conflicting traditions of the Italian novel. The society that he describes is not typically Italian; his characters illustrate many qualities and faults of the Austrian bourgeoisie; his language, far from being the literary Tuscan of classical idealists or the colourful dialect of the realists or *Veristi*, is rather the sophisticated and nerveless jargon of the educated Triestine bourgeoisie that spoke Italian neither as a literary nor as a national language, but as a convenient and easy affectation of local patriotism. Svevo was an Austrian citizen until the end of the First World War, when two of his novels had already been published; all his fiction is clearly set in pre-war Trieste, except the very last part of *Zeno* (the war in and around Trieste), *La novella del buon vecchio* (war-time Trieste), *Una burla riuscita* (post-war inflation in Trieste) and *Il vecchione* (Italian Trieste after the war). Svevo's characters are mostly of the Italian-speaking bourgeoisie, though their names are often Croat or German and many of them speak German; characters picked from the people are described as speaking Triestine or Friulian dialect, mixtures of Italian and Croatian, and the *buon vecchio* does not wish to teach the *bella fanciulla* correct Italian, when he decides to educate her, but German.

Many Italian critics have mistakenly placed Svevo's work in the tradition of late Italian *Verismo*, as another example of that late nineteenth-century regional realism, which, with Verga, put Sicily back on the literary map and, in D'Annunzio's early stories, revealed the primitive Abruzzi; Svevo would thus be the *verista* chronicler of Triestine characters and streets, manners and modes. Most foreign critics, especially Crémieux and the French have vaguely placed Svevo in the general trend of international 'advanced' literature of the post-war, with Marcel Proust and James Joyce, because of his strange use of psychology; a few have more wisely derived Svevo's psychology from Flaubert's realist novels, *Madame Bovary*, *L'éducation sentimentale*, *Un cœur simple*, and *Bouvard et Pécuchet*. It might, however, prove more profitable and conclusive to place Svevo in a context of Austrian literature and compare him to those Austrian novelists whose culture was not strictly German and who often wrote in one or the other of the many languages spoken within the polyglot empire. Svevo shares many characteristics with such writers as Schnitzler, Robert Musil, Broch and Franz Kafka, who wrote in German, and with some Czech and Hungarian novelists. It seems as if the empire, though not always strong enough to impose one language on all its subjects, yet diffused a common Austrian culture among the various peoples within its boundaries.

Attilio Momigliano's *Storia della letterature italiana* discusses several of the later *veristi* and concludes that Grazia Deledda, Tozzi and Svevo are 'anti-literary', but that Svevo is often just 'prosy'. This prosy tone was also observed by De Benedetti: 'His Italian is fortuitous and casual, a language like Italian because it is composed of Italian words, but not according to Italian patterns, Italian by analogy, and organized nomenclature, not an organic language'. De Benedetti objects, as French stylists have in their criticisms of Balzac, to the many technical terms that Svevo borrowed from trades and commerce and used, without any 'polishing', for lyrical or descriptive purposes: 'Portava una barba piena lunghetta, *condizionata in quanto a colore* come la capigliatura'. Svevo says this, in *Una Vita*, of old Lanucci, who was in the habit of dyeing his beard; *condizionata* is the term used by tradesmen, cleaners and dyers, and *in quanto a colore* is one of those pompous pseudo-literary syntagms, 'as far as colour was concerned', that appear in business-letters and in the speech of semi-educated tradesmen such as Bouvard and Pécuchet or Homais. But this is the jargon of a settled or declining bourgeoisie that has established a language of its own, modelled on the elegant forms of the classically minded aristocracy that preceded it and often unconsciously creating a parody of the earlier style; and it seems to have been peculiarly typical of the last liberal decades of the Austrian empire. One finds it throughout the articles and stories of the *Wiener Journal*, in Schnitzler's 'frenchified' prose and especially in the monologue of *Leutnant Gustl*; and it is one of the chief qualities of Franz Kafka, to whose fantasies and allegories this matter-of-fact style adds a real weight, rooting the impossible in the probability of daily experience. Who, reading casually one of K.'s conversations, would at first think that *The Castle* is an elaborate allegory of power, divine and human, of God and monarchy which rule the anonymous citizen's destiny and never give him a chance to understand what he is about and whither he is being led?

Svevo's heroes all seem to be tormented with an intense lust for self-improvement, spiritual or social, for education, wisdom or learning that will better them or their positions; however old, they still think themselves unprepared for the serious business of living. Zeno thus always hopes to cure himself of his vice of smoking, long hesitates between law and chemistry as professions, then does nothing till circumstances force him into business where, much to his own surprise, he is successful. The heroes of *Una Vita*, *Senilità* and *The Hoax* are not content with their petty clerical jobs, consider these far beneath their intelligence and culture, and hope or intend, some day, to devote all their time and talents to writing. The heroes of *Senilità* and *The Hoax*, though they may each have published a novel some years earlier, and both still enjoy, in provincial society, considerable reputations as local intellectuals, are yet both unable now to write anything new. The hero of *The Hoax*, for his own amusement or to compensate his inferiority complex, does indeed compose some animal fables that are included in the narrative, but Zeno also effortlessly composes two such fables and Svevo himself, in his years of literary sterility, wrote *La Madre*, another such animal fable to which he attached very little importance. The heroes of *Una Vita* and *La novella del buon vecchio* both try to compose philosophic treatises, become hopelessly involved and make no real progress in clarifying their thoughts or consigning them to paper in an ordered form. In a bourgeois society of culture-snobs, illusions of intellectual grandeur thus compensate for social or emotional maladjustment; but these illusions no longer need produce any material results, though they may have in the past, and Zeno himself manages to write his autobiography only because this is part of the discipline of his psycho-analysis, whereas Svevo's other heroes dream of writing something only in the vague future or are unable to express themselves.

Such 'hopeless' characters appear in many Austrian novels; the Viennese *Erziehungsroman* had slipped from the lofty level of *Wilhelm Meister* to that, so much more ineffectual, of the higher or lower urban bourgeoisie. In Robert Musil's *Der Mann ohne Eigenschaften*, Ulrich thus leaves the army to become a mathematician, never studies very seriously and is easily distracted from mathematics when he discovers that he is gifted for music; he then becomes involved in politics, later in psychiatry, and finally is interested almost exclusively in a moronic Jack-the-Ripper, whose name fills all the headlines and whom he even visits in prison. And Schnitzler's *Leutnant Gustl*, in his doubts and hesitations about the duel, is even more closely related to a Svevo character, to the hero of *Una Vita* who finally evades a duel by committing suicide.

Momigliano notes, too, that Svevo has also been compared to Otto Weininger, Proust, Joyce and Freud. Neglecting the others, he concludes that Svevo's arid psychology alone should distinguish him from Proust, so much more lyrical; Svevo is more interested in intelligence than in fantasy, his psychology astonishes and convinces in its details but seems uncertain and diffuse in the 'whole', his characters offer too many possibilities and follow patterns that are too synthetic. True, Svevo is more interested in the causality of action than, as Proust, in emotion and memory; but Proust never read Svevo and Svevo can have read Proust only after he himself had written at least two of his three great novels, probably three. Joyce indeed knew whole passages of Svevo's *Senilità* by heart; in 1906, Svevo and Joyce had met in Trieste and Joyce had given English lessons to Svevo. They remained great friends and, after 1923, Joyce recommended *Zeno* to his Parisian friends and admirers, so that Crémieux and Valéry Larbaud translated it and successfully launched it, in 1927, as they had already launched Joyce. But there ends the analogy, one of coincidences, not of reciprocal influences, though both Svevo and Joyce had been strongly influenced by Flaubert before they met in Trieste.

De Benedetti also compares Svevo's characters to Weininger's portrait of the ideal Jew (in *Geschlecht und Character*): 'Hereditarily deprived of every happy instinct of life, lacking all ability ever to relax, gifted with an unstable multiplicity of moral background which allows every shock to shape, influence or deform him'. Weininger, an anti-semitic Austrian Jew, a Wagnerian woman-hater who committed suicide, described all Jews and perhaps himself in these terms; and De Benedetti concludes that Svevo too, 'when he felt the torturing leaven of his own life fermenting beneath the surface of his characters so that the obscure depths of autobiography rise through the mask of fiction, thus obeyed, as a Jew, the suggestions and imperatives of his race'.

Svevo had indeed read Weininger. Zeno's brother-in-law, Guido Speier, 'had adopted the genial theories' of the woman-hater and Macario, in *Una Vita*, seems to have shared them too. But nothing is easier or more misleading than to explain an author's peculiarities by pointing out that he is a Jew. The multiplicity of Svevo's characters, their disquieting instability, anxiety, torturing self-analysis and hesitation, their endless preoccupation with reason and causality, like that of ancient cabbalists trying to explain the cosmogony in terms of rational philosophy, all these are characteristic of Weininger's logical Jew, an 'evil' rationalist in a 'good' irrational world; and they have all been attributed generally, by other anti-semitic critics, to other Jewish or partly Jewish artists, to Heine, Proust, Marcel Schwob, Kafka or Moravia. Musil, in *Der Mann ohne Eigenschaften*, also draws interesting portraits of two different types of Jew: Leo Fischl, a small Viennese businessman, is a Jewish Homais who believes in progress and democracy, in science and realism, while Arnheim, a great Prussian Jew, is a caricature of Walther Rathenau, idealist of genius, great thinker and great statesman, gifted with a multiplicity of talents that assure him success in many fields. But Arnheim's restlessness somehow undermines everything and arouses the suspicions and antipathy of Ulrich; and beneath his apparent ease, Arnheim is perhaps as nervous and unsure of himself as Fischl, whose faith in progress and democracy are always being so grotesquely disappointed. However, if we attribute all these symptoms of a disease common among Jews, Jewish authors and Jewish characters, to the fact that nearly all of the patients are Jews, we are making the same mistake as a physician who, observing that a disease attacks only human beings, confuses this symptom with its cause and declares that the patients are ill because they are all human. The Jew whom Weininger describes consciously and Svevo perhaps unconsciously is indeed a victim of a psychological disease; living in a society that considers him different and often treats him differently, like the Armenian in Turkey or the negro in America, he either tends to imagine himself more different than he really is, so that he lives up to the character attributed to him, or tries to 'cross the line', to ignore the difference in treatment and pretend that he is not a Jew. Both pseudo-assimilation and Zionism, and the ambivalence of the individual hesitating between these extremes, are thus determined by the society's evaluation of the Jew rather than by his being Jewish. And if Svevo reveals Jewish traits in his style or his characters, he is illustrating the environmental influence of Austrian society which achieved the same results in other Jewish writers, Kafka or Schnitzler, or in the Jewish characters of 'aryan' writers such as Robert Musil, rather than the influence of any Jewish heredity.

The influence of Freud, in Svevo's later work, is certainly important. Zeno consults a psycho-analyst, discovers that he has an Oedipus complex, and the whole novel illustrates Freudian theory as clearly as a case-history, though *A Sentimental Journey*, *Adolphe* and *La Nouvelle Heloïse*, written long before Freud's theories were formulated, also make excellent case-histories today. But Eugenio Montale, a few days after Svevo's death, wrote that *La coscienza di Zeno* is 'tortured with the trick of *bovarysme*', thus using a term invented by Jules de Gaultier to designate a peculiarity of Flaubert's characters, in his realistic novels, who all have what Paul Bourget called 'le mal d'avoir connu l'image de la realité avant la realité' and what Gaultier describes as 'le pouvoir départi à l'homme de se concevoir autre qu'il n'est'. Indeed, instead of having only one wrong idea about themselves (Homais thought himself a positivist and scientist, Madame Bovary thought herself a great romantic heroine born to brilliant and spectacular loves, Bouvard and Pécuchet thought they could acquire all knowledge by reading cheap magazines of pseudo-scientific vulgarization), Svevo's *bovaryste* heroes tend to have several wrong ideas about themselves, to change shiftlessly from one wrong ambition or interpretation to another, one unsuccessful venture to another. And thus they achieve the too many possibilities which Momigliano criticized and which relate them so closely to Musil's *Mann ohne Eigenschaften*, another *bovaryste*. The French critic, Benjamin Crémieux is therefore right when he finds *Una Vita* 'strongly influenced by Flaubert'. But the nature of this influence and its exact significance cannot be found in Svevo's style and subject-matter; it is to be found, as indeed in Musil too, in Svevo's approach to the subject and the way he handles it.

In Svevo's first novel, *Una Vita*, the hero Alfonso Nitti is a country lad who, in Trieste, becomes an unimportant employee of the busy Maller Bank; though conscious, at times, of some moral or cultural superiority, he yet feels incompetent and lost in this prosperous and enterprising world. In a moment of weakness or ambition, he becomes the lover of Annie Maller, his rich employer's daughter, a vain and spoilt culture-snob. Nitti's passion is far more insincere and conscious of its insincerity than Madame Bovary's love for Léon. Annie is also insincere, amused and frightened by her daring; and one gradually realizes the inevitability of their parting. Nitti is reduced, by the insincerity of his love and by the very real misery of such unreal happiness, to a passive listlessness which ends in suicide. This is not, however, the romantic escape of a Werther or a Jacopo Ortis, or of the Romantic poets and heroes of the Milanese *Scapigliatura*. In the age of neo-classical tragedy, the stoical hero had preferred death to slavery or disgrace; later, Werther and the early romantics, aristocratic idealists in an age of bourgeois opportunism, had preferred death, in an act of proud defiance, to the disappointments of an inglorious life; the later Romantics and decadents had sometimes advocated suicide as the *poète maudit's* final affirmation of individuality in a hostile world. All these still were, or tried to be, masters of their own destinies. But Alfonso Nitti's despair goes even further than the confused defeatism of the decadent *fin de siècle*; weaker and even more completely defeated by reality and his surroundings, he is led to suicide without any will to resist or defy fate, or affirm himself even self-destructively. Life and reality are his enemies; he remains innocent of his own death. In a more consciously modern novel, as in Svevo's later *Zeno*, the suicide of a Guido Speier is but a manifestation of a neurotic drive or of economic pressure, no longer at all of individual reason or will.

The end of *Una Vita* was death; that of Svevo's next novel, *Senilità*, is hallucination, when the hero finds courage and a strange balance while the author gradually develops a new stoicism. *Senilità* reveals another aspect of *bovarysme*: a false literary idealism which, applied to love, makes Emilio Brentani, a weak character afflicted with literary ambitions, believe that Angiolina, a commonplace provincial demi-mondaine, is a veritable Beatrice. Brentani adorns her with all the qualities of the great heroines of literature; but she is gradually dragging him down, as Odette dragged Swann, to her own shoddy level. With the illness and death of Emilio's sister Amalia, a mouse-like spinster whom he neglects but who heroically conceals until her delirium her unrequited love for his best friend, Emilio discovers how shabby his own jealous love has been. He then abandons Angiolina and returns to his futile life of dreams and vague ambitions; in his mind, he blends Angiolina and Amalia, all the austere qualities of the spinster and the beauty of the whore, and now lives in the imaginary company of a fantastic compound of irreconcilable personalities, real enough to him.

Senilità was published in 1898, five years after *Una Vita*. Critics and readers paid even less attention to it than to Svevo's first novel, though Momigliano, Joyce and others, many years later, declared that *Senilità* was Svevo's best, most subtle and most poetic creation. *La coscienza di Zeno* was published twenty-five years later, in 1923. Did Svevo devote all the intervening years to the creation of his masterpiece? In the preface to the later second edition of *Senilità*, he suggests that he was discouraged by the unsuccess of his second novel and abandoned writing for a long while; and his business, in the difficult years before, during and after the war, certainly claimed much of his time. With *La coscienza di Zeno*, Svevo entered a second period of literary production, in its beginning scarcely more successful than the first. Though Trieste was now Italian, Italian readers were nearly as inaccessible to the Triestine author, whose style was not Tuscan nor regionalistic, as when he had been Austrian. Thanks to Joyce, however, a fragment of the new novel appeared in French, in *Le navire d'argent*, early in 1926; the complete translation was then published by the *Nouvelle revue française* in 1927. Its success, in Paris, was immediate and at once brought Svevo fame even in Italy. In 1926 alone, over fifty articles praised Svevo's work in Italian newspapers and periodicals, more than twice as many as had yet been devoted to him in his whole literary life. During the remaining two years of his life, Svevo was perhaps one of the most discussed and fêted writers in Europe; since his death, his fame has somewhat diminished, though he still influences the style of a few much younger men, such as Alberto Moravia whose *Gli indifferenti* is, in many ways, similar to *Una Vita*, though it may have been influenced only by the same sources, such as Flaubert and the Viennese psychologists.

The work of Svevo's second period, *Zeno* and the stories, distinguishes itself from the earlier work by a greater subjectivity in the treatment of the hero, who tells his story in the first person both in *Zeno* and in the unfinished *Il vecchione*, and by a greater objectivity in the treatment of detail, incident, setting and reality. The characters are thus better integrated and their doubts and hesitations seem more justified, more clearly motivated by their experiences; and their misfortunes, though no less poignant, seem less tragic or even frankly humorous, according to the mood of the reader of these tragic comedies. Though still maladjusted, Svevo's later heroes are eternally and innocently hopeful in their misfortunes, and Zeno even wonders how man ever wandered into this world where he is so obviously a stranger.

Zeno Cosini is a sub-human type, the very antithesis of the Wagnerian or Nietzschean supermen whom D'Annunzio and other Italian novelists tried to portray. Yet Zeno finds, in his own degradation, helplessness and clumsiness, a real greatness and triumph, far more human than the arrogance of the heroes of D'Annunzio's *Il Fuoco* or *Il Piacere*. Zeno is indeed, as Crémieux aptly remarked, of all Svevo's characters, a sort of Triestine brother of Charlie Chaplin; and this little sub-man becomes a real superman through his stoical consciousness of his weaknesses which allows him to overcome them. This consciousness is the only greatness that man, through humility, can ever hope to attain; without it, the superman is a fool or a phoney, wrestling blindly with fate and both preparing and hastening the fall which his arrogance deserves. Federico Sternberg defines the fragile happiness of Zeno as 'the balance of the unbalanced'. Momigliano compares Svevo's world to that of G. A. Borgese's *Rubé*, 'His characters are intelligent but disoriented . . . and thus unadapted to social living'. This congenital inability to keep in step with the surrounding world (and what intelligent or good man, intent upon eternity, can feel at home in our evil and foolish age?), is the cause of all the unhappiness of Svevo's heroes and precludes the success of all conscious action in their lives; it makes them bungle everything that they ever attempt and leaves them pleasantly surprised when chance or unconscious action suddenly produces success. They are relegated to the margin of social and economic activity where, instead of acting, they generally dream, analyse and comment the action of others or the workings of chance. And this detachment is a characteristic, too, of many Austrian heroes, such as Musil's *Mann ohne Eigenschaften*, or Schnitzler's *Leutnant Gustl*, Rilke's *Malte Laurids Brigge* and K. the anonymous hero of Kafka's *The Castle* and *The Trial*; it is also found in some characters of Luigi Pirandello, whose *Il fu Mattia Pascal* is made unfit for human intercourse, much like Adalbert von Chamisso's *Peter Schlemihl*, but arbitrarily and by accident, through no fault or choice of his own, by the mere news of his own death, whereby he officially ceases to exist. Svevo's characters, however, were born unfit for life; their misfortunes are not caused by chance, nor by will.

The structure of *Zeno* illustrates a new departure in the technique of novel-writing. With no true continuity of time and narrative, the book unfolds as a series of detached episodes or essays which all, except for the preface, are written by Zeno in the first person. The preface is added by the psycho-analyst who has been treating Zeno and who first introduces him to the reader: 'I had hoped that the autobiography would be a good prelude to his analysis'; but Zeno had then refused to continue the treatment and, if only to annoy the former patient, the analyst is now publishing the autobiography in spite of its uncomplimentary allusions to himself and his science.

Svevo's style too has changed since his earlier works: it seems even more prosy, its tone almost conversational. But this is a subtle stylization, such as that which Archibald MacLeish has called 'an inversion of naturalness which uses natural utterance for satiric and subjective ends'. Choosing his words objectively from the speech of his contemporaries, Svevo uses them, as do Auden and Kafka, so that their meaning no longer tends only outward, as in ordinary discourse, but inward too, towards the subjective worlds and the private configurations of emotion and meaning in the minds of the writer and his readers. It is perhaps significant that both Svevo and Auden studied modern Austrian psychology and that Auden, at one time, was very much interested in the theories of *Gestalt* which may have influenced also the work of Svevo and Kafka.

Many critics have indicated the influence of Freud on Svevo; but Zeno's analysis is not strictly Freudian, though its method, that of writing an autobiography for the analyst, may have been determined by the fictional or formal considerations rather than by psycho-analytic theory. Each chapter of *Zeno* presents a group of memories and experiences which seem to crystallize around one central episode, such as the father's death or Zeno's marriage, which also determines its title; and although these episodes, together with the memories and considerations that they occasion, are presented with an appearance of chronological order, the story yet tends to disregard time and to adopt a form of circular expansion, reaching out in all directions, past, present and future, from each central episode, instead of following the simple line of traditional narrative. The order of Svevo's minor episodes is often determined by their psychological significance, or their emotional relationship to other episodes. Proust, at the Guermantes ball in *Le temps retrouvé*, lost all sense of time and confused grown daughters with their mothers whom he had known years earlier; in *Il vecchione*, Svevo's aged hero mistakes a girl whom he sees in the present for one whom he knew in the distant past, now a woman as old as himself, and remarks: 'I am not able to find my way very surely in time'.

Zeno experiences this same uncertainty in time, when he tries, in the *Preamble*, to write his autobiography. He had read a psycho-analytic text-book, followed its instructions, prepared paper and pencil. But his experiment fails. In a sleepy chaos of boredom and doubt, the promised resurrection of the past refuses to materialize; finally Zeno abandons his pursuit of the past, since he is now so far from the images which should precede sleep, and decides to repeat the experiment on the morrow.

The second episode, *Smoking*, describes Zeno's success: the past is recaptured, through no conscious effort, but by a natural weakness which leads Zeno, as so often before, to ponder the problem of his dreadful addiction to tobacco. The whole past suddenly unfolds from the memory of an old-fashioned cigarette-package, bearing the Austrian crest of the double-headed eagle, of a type that is no longer sold in Trieste. Proust remembered the whole past of Combray when he tasted a *madeleine*, dipped in tea, like those that he used to eat when he visited his old aunt in her house there; Zeno's memories, in the same manner, now follow this memory of his first cigarettes. He had intended to write his autobiography, following the laws of factual causality, *ab ovo*; now he discovers that his whole life, all his emotional development and unhappiness, seem to have been determined by his smoking. Oscar Wilde once said that he could resist everything except temptation; and Zeno tells us how, unable to cure himself of smoking by merely refusing to smoke, he was forced to adopt the more drastic course of having himself interned in a nursing-home, which involved him in bribing and seducing the nurse to procure himself some cigarettes, then in suspecting his wife of betraying him with the doctor and finally in escaping, by night, like a criminal from a prison or a lunatic from an asylum.

Zeno's resurrection of the past seems almost necromantic: he identifies his own birth with that of the vice which, he thinks, has wrecked his life. He thus establishes some sympathetic connection between the beginnings of consciousness and those of guilt. Until this moment, when all became clear and logical, his vague memories refused to crystallize: Proust was likewise unable to remember anything significant until he tasted his *madeleine*. As in Paul Valéry's verse, '*Entre le vide et l'évènement pur*', between the empty or impotent will to remember and the actual birth of memories, there is an unexplainable blank that even Proust and Svevo were unable to explain logically. This is the 'Let there be light', the cabbalist's mystery of the original gesture of Genesis, the eternally missing link in the chain of rational causality. And just as these two great artists, Proust and Svevo, were both forced to rely on chance to provide them with a beginning, so were they also both unable to find, in the material that they handled, any satisfactory end. For the novel which pretends to be an imitation of its hero's whole conscious life cannot hope to begin at his birth and record everything logically until his death; birth and death are the two points where the artist must rely on chance in plot or on some arbitrary formal device of art. Proust thus makes his novel end circularly where he begins to write the autobiography which becomes his novel; and Zeno's autobiography ends with the psycho-analytic treatment which forced him to write it.

My father's death, the next episode of *Zeno*, is a macabre mixture of tragedy and farce: in an over-eager effort to follow the physician' instructions, Zeno was perhaps responsible for his father's death, though his death was already inevitable. The doctor had said that the dying man must keep absolutely still; but the father is restless in his bed and Zeno tries to keep him still by force. In an angry attempt to strike his son, the old man dies. Zeno had always quarrelled with his father and caused him much worry; he is now overcome by guilt-feelings and, acutely conscious of how disappointing he has always been as a son, even accuses himself of having killed his father.

The story of my marriage then tells how Zeno, unable to extricate himself from a misunderstanding or a deliberately planned trap, is forced to marry, without loving her, the second and ugly Malfenti daughter, a girl who really loves him, after he had been refused by the eldest and the third, both of whom he loved; and then, in this woman who was not even of his own choice, Zeno finds the ideal wife.

The reader thus gradually realizes Zeno's weakness and incapacity. Zeno's natural enemies are all healthier and more successful people; even his wife's little sister, a healthy child, persecutes him by whispering into his ear that he is insane. Guido Speier, at first Zeno's rival and then his brother-in-law, represents the opposite type of the more virile 'extrovert' who takes his successes for granted and, at first, seems to achieve them with ease; the hero of *Senilità*, Emilio Brentani, had found just such a contrary in Balli, 'uomo nel vero senso della parola, il Balli . . . quando si trovava accanto il Brentani, poteva avere il sentimento di essere accompagnato da una delle tante femmine a lui soggette'. In Svevo's earlier novels, the introvert hero remains unsuccessful; in *Una Vita*, Nitti is finally defeated by his rival when Annie Maller jilts him to marry Macario; in *Senilità*, there is no competition, but Brentani is forced to observe Balli's more successful adjustment. In the later novels, the introvert is successful: the hero of *The Hoax* makes a fortune out of the trick whose victim he was supposed to be and Guido Speier, in *Wife and Mistress*, the next chapter of *Zeno*, gets involved in a series of foolhardy adventures which, in *A Business Partnership*, lead him to bankruptcy and suicide. Thus Zeno, though convinced of his own clumsiness and impotence, yet manages to betray his wife and to have a mistress, without experiencing any trouble, whereas his brother-in-law Guido, with his amorous intrigues, stands endless jealousies and complications.

When he wrote *Zeno* and the other works of his second period, Svevo had, it seems, become reconciled to his own helplessness and to the inevitable duality of intention and achievement, character and surroundings, ambition and real life; his heroes are much happier than in his earlier works and, though no better fitted for life than Alfonso Nitti or Emilio Brentani, are treated less hard by fate, causality and their surroundings; they even sometimes achieve success, though much to their surprise and rarely as a result of planned effort. In *Una Vita*, it is Nitti, the hero, who commits suicide; in *A Business Partnership*, the next chapter of *Zeno*, the hero, so convinced of his own inefficiency, yet never loses his head, whereas Guido, the 'virile extrovert', becomes hysterical and commits suicide like any disappointed seamstress; and it is the introvert who then saves the widow's fortune. In *The Hoax*, probably written not much later, Svevo tells how an elderly bank-clerk with literary ambitions is misled, by a practical joker, into accepting a phoney contract for the German translation of his early novel; he then sells the royalties 'forward' and, owing to the inflation of the Austrian currency, finds that, thanks to this valueless contract, he had made a small fortune in Italian currency, like any 'bear' in the foreign exchange market, though he would never have dared to gamble in this manner without the contract. In *Wife and Mistress*, Zeno had similarly earned his father-in-law's admiration by forgetting to sell some shares whose value was rapidly falling, then selling them at a profit months later, when their value had risen again and Malfenti had already sustained a considerable loss by selling 'at the right moment'.

In the last chapter, *Psycho-analysis*, Zeno describes how, pursued throughout life by a feeling of maladjustment, disease or madness, he finally consults a psycho-analyst and finds him far more mad than himself. Nor is this a factual criticism of psycho-analysis or of analysts in general; it is rather a necessary element of Svevo's dialectical plot. The analyst tells Zeno to write an autobiography; the order in which the memories return to the patient and the configurations which they form in his mind may reveal their significance and the source of his neurosis. When the analyst finally tells Zeno that he is cured but must continue his treatment for 're-education', Zeno protests that he is not cured, refuses to continue his treatment and stops writing his autobiography; but at this point the war separates Zeno from his family, analyst and business-manager, all of whom have fled Trieste. And he now finds himself perfectly adjusted and cured, even successful as a business man in very hard times. From Switzerland, the analyst then writes to Zeno that he is not cured and asks for the remaining sections of the autobiography, which Zeno hastens to write and send. . . .

Zeno concludes that all humanity is evil and foolish. He then describes, in a fable to end all fables, what will be the end of our world. But his Day of Jehoshaphat is no longer Dante's: 'When all the poison gases (of the war) are exhausted, a man, made like all other men of flesh and blood, will, in the quiet of a room, invent an explosive of such potency that all the explosives in existence will seem like harmless toys beside it. And another man, made in his image and in the image of all the rest, but a little weaker than them, will steal that explosive and crawl to the centre of the earth with it, and place it just where he calculates it would have the maximum effect. There will be a tremendous explosion, but none will hear it and the earth will return to its nebulous state and go wandering through the sky, free at last from parasites and disease.'

In the difficult decline of the Roman Empire, when civilization, as now, seemed to be menaced from within by itself as much as from without by barbarians, educated Romans began to believe that the end of the world was near; some turned to the pessimistic doctrines of Augustinian Christianity, which affirmed that man was foolish and evil, others to the pagan doctrines of Zeno the Stoic, who explained that the world, every few thousand years, sinks into chaos and flames to rise again, purified and new, as a phoenix from its own ashes. Svevo was perhaps thinking of the Stoic when he chose Zeno as a name for his hero; and Zeno Cosini is certainly far more stoical, in his misfortunes, than Svevo's earlier heroes. In *Il vecchione*, the hero is a very old man, stoically at peace with the world. Had Svevo, an old man, finished his last novel, it would have contrasted clearly with *Senilità*, his youthful anticipation of old age. All passion spent, Svevo found peace, wisdom, mature strength, objectivity, not in hallucination but in reality.

Svevo's plots indeed follow rigidly dialectical schemes which resolve contraries in a steady progression through endless dilemmas, reversals and other devices, from the unhappiness of *Una Vita* or of the beginning of *Zeno* to the happiness of the end of *Zeno* or of *Il vecchione*, from confusion to order, strife to peace. Time thus ɔmes functional in the narrative, no longer what E. M. Forster, ı *Aspects of the Novel*, calls 'and then . . . and then', but a real because'. Plot-devices and humour also acquire a structural value and slapstick misunderstandings generate plot rather than adorn it. Few contemporary novelists have handled plot in this 'tragic' and unrealistic manner with the two-edged ironies of Jewish jokes; and the styles and plots of those who have, Proust, Kafka, Thomas Mann or Musil, are not always as humorous or as imitative of real life as Svevo's. In Svevo's novels, the strong man, a Guido Speier, turns out to be weak; the weak fool Zeno, or the hero of *The Hoax*, turns out to be strong and wise; the lunatic reveals himself sane; the sane man commits suicide. Such novels acquire what Dante called literal, moral, allegorical and anagogical meaning; and it seems as if the novel has thus at last achieved an art-form which allows its action, without extraneous commentary, to illustrate deep philosophic thought and conviction.[1]

[1] This essay was written and first published during the war-years. The invention of the atom-bomb had not yet added further verisimilitude to the ironic predictions of Zeno; and the recent publication, in post-war Italy, of a vast mass of critical and biographical material concerning Svevo, including a posthumous volume of his stories and a pamphlet of memoirs written by his widow, had not yet corroborated much that I already suspected.

ENVOI

Translated from the Anglo-Saxon by

EDWIN MORGAN

Wonder holds these walls. Under destiny destruction
Castles has split apart; gigantic battlements are crumbling,
Roofs sunk in ruin, riven towers fallen,
Gates and turrets lost, hoarfrost for mortar,
Rain-bastions beaten, cleft, pierced, perished,
Eaten away by time. Earth's fist and grasp
Holds mason and man, all decayed, departed;
The soil grips hard; there a hundred generations
Of the people have dwindled and gone. This wall bore well,
Moss-grey and reddened, the revolutions of kingdoms,
Stoutly withstood tempests. That great gate fell . . .
Magnificent rose the fortresses, the lavish swimming halls,
The profuse and lofty glory of spires, the clangour of armies,
The drinking-halls crammed with every man's delight,
Till that was overturned by steadfast fate.
The broad walls were sundered; the plague-days came:
The brave men were rapt away by the bereaver,
Their war-ramparts razed to desolate foundations,
Their cities crumbled down. The restorers lie asleep,
Armies of men in the earth. And so those halls are wastes,
The once purple gates, and the bricks and wood are lying
Scattered with the smashed roofs. Death crushed that place,
Struck it flat to the hill, where once many a man
Brilliant with gold and adazzle with costliest war-trappings,
Happy, proud, and wine-flushed, glittered there in his battle-armour,
Gazed over his treasures, on the silver and the curious stones,
On the rich goods and possessions, on the preciously cut jewels,
And on this splendid city of the far-spread kingdom. . . .